Shane Brown was born in 1974, and lives in Norfolk, UK. He has a PhD in Film, Television and Media Studies from the University of East Anglia. He released his first novel, *Breaking Point*, in 2013 and has since published two more: *The Lookout* and *Ghost of a Chance*. He is also the author of *Queer Sexualities in Early Film: Cinema and Male-Male Intimacy* and *Elvis Presley: A Listener's Guide*. Shane has published articles on Boris Karloff and Bela Lugosi (with Mark Jancovich); silent film star Jack Pickford; the first African-American film director, Oscar Micheaux; the teen sci-fi TV series *Kyle XY*; and portrayals of mental health in North American TV dramas.

Follow the author on twitter: @shanebrown74

Copyright © 2019, by Shane Brown

Photo Credits:

Front cover: © Everett Collection Inc/Alamy Stock Photo

pp. 13, 23, 32, 34, 40, 45, 46, 76, 97, 103, 223, 246, 259, 284, 305, 313, 332, 340, 357 from the collection of Susan Johnson Côté

pp. 27, 28, 33, 53, 57, 72, 101, 111, 118, 120, 135, 142, 143, 155, 168, 177, 190, 200, 202, 204, 222, 226, 252, 256, 263, 268, 277, 279, 281, 292, 298, 301, 306, 337, 348 from the collection of L. Vergara Herrero

p. 35 © CEA/Cache Agency

pp. 60, 98 © ImageCollect.com/Bob Claxton/Globe Photos Inc.

pp. 67, 75, 81, 93, 114, 122, 127, 139, 141, 159, 186, 231, 234, 266, 296, 307, 309, 319, 322, 329, 345 © ImageCollect.com/Globe Photos Inc.

p. 78. © ImageCollect.com/Bernard Wagner/Globe Photos Inc.

p. 90 © ImageCollect.com/Smp/Globe Photos Inc.

p.107 © ImageCollect.com/Nat Dallinger/Globe Photos Inc.

p.132 © ImageCollect.com/Bernard-Globe Photos Inc.

pp. 165, 179, 198 © ImageCollect.com/Bill Kobrin/Globe Photos Inc.

pp. 219, 229 from the collection of George Carpinone

p. 285 © ImageCollect.com/NBC-Globe Photos Inc.

All others from the collection of the author.

BOBBY DARIN: DIRECTIONS
A LISTENER'S GUIDE

SHANE BROWN

ACKNOWLEDGEMENTS

I'd like to start by thanking wholeheartedly a small group of people who have gone out of their way on numerous occasions to help me when I have been picking their brains for facts, figures, general information, articles, and so on. Without their help, encouragement and support, this book may well have ended up as a half-finished manuscript sitting in the bottom of a chest of drawers. So, thank you to:

Susan Johnson Côté,
Matt Forbes

C Ying Ho (何诗莹)
Maura McNamara Pape
Pam Speers
L. Vergara Herrero

Susan Johnson Côté, L. Vergara Herrero, and George Carpinone have all given me access to their collections of photographs, lobby cards and record sleeves for use within the following pages, and I would particularly like to thank them for that. Full photo credits can be found on the copyright page of this book.

I would also like to thank the following people, many of whom are members of Facebook groups dedicated to Bobby Darin. These people have engaged in conversations and discussions with me in those groups, sometimes contributing information and sometimes giving opinions on particular songs or albums or on something I have written elsewhere. If I have missed anyone, then I can only apologise – the writing of this book has taken place over a period of five years, and sometimes it is difficult to keep tabs!

Thank you to:

Dave Adams, Tom Alicandri, Wendy Barton, Susan Bittar, Lyall Blanco, Andrea Braid, Debbie Cantrell, Jill Hoffman Caplan, George Carpinone, Mary Claire Cellamare, Kathleen Cerone, Max Allan Collins Jr., Melissa Comber, Michael J Contos, Bill Coppola, Jack Dagnall, Derek Davis, Kevin Deevey, Gisele Dubson, Donald Mitchell Erwin, William Frost, Ralph Galati, Ron Gartner, Karin Grevelund, Bryan Hank Gowans, Donna Jones, Hannu Juurinen, Kenneth Kelly Jr., Holly Killian, Diane Kogok, Vana Maffia, Beth McAvoy, Shane McCormack, Francis E McNamara, Judith McRae, Carla Mohor, Kondja Negongo Jamie Ney, Judy Pace, Jo Quante, John Michael Raia, Rich Ross, Joel Rothberg, Susan Chartier Schooley, Sharyn Scott, Martha Seeger, Martin Skovhus, David E. Sotheran, Brenda Stone, Sam Tallerico, Ester Toribio, Justin Trent, Leonor Luevano Villa, Gary Walden, Netty White, Cathleen Wiles, Jeff Wolfe.

More than anything I have written before, this book has benefitted from the generosity of others in their sharing of knowledge, enthusiasm, advice, and collections of memorabilia.

I dedicate this lengthy tome to everyone who has helped make this book possible.

CONTENTS

A Note from the Author	11
Introduction	15
Chapter One. Rock Island Line: 1956	25
Chapter Two. Making a Splash: 1957-1958	37
Chapter Three. This is Darin: 1959	69
Chapter Four. I Found a New Baby: 1960	89
Chapter Five. Irresistible You: 1961	129
Chapter Six. Oh! Look at Me Now: 1962	157
Chapter Seven. The Sweetest Sounds: 1963	181
Chapter Eight. Lonely Road: 1964-1965	221
Chapter Nine. Feeling Good: 1965-1966	243
Chapter Ten. Beautiful Things: 1966-1967	261
Chapter Eleven. Questions: 1968-1970	287
Chapter Twelve. I Used To Think It Was Easy: 1970-1973	311
Coda. Here I'll Stay: 1974-2019	347
Appendix A: Fifty Key Albums	359
Appendix B: Lifetime Discography	373

Appendix C: Selected Posthumous Discography	381
Appendix D: Television Appearances	387
Appendix E: Darin Compositions Recorded by Others	405
Appendix F: Filmography	411
Appendix G: Unreleased Recordings	413
Bibliography	417
Index	435

A NOTE FROM THE AUTHOR

The wonderful thing about publishing a book without going through the usual channels is that you are free to do what you want, when you want.

No-one is telling you how long or how short you book needs to be. There is no editor breathing down your neck, telling you when your latest tome needs to be finished. The decision on whether to include images alongside the text is entirely up to the author (and his or her purse-strings), and there are no arguments with a publisher about the design of the front cover. Something which is both a positive and a negative is that an author can go back and revisit their book as and when they want or feel the need to. On the one hand, that can result in endless minor (maybe even mindless) tinkering with no obvious benefit, but, on the other, it allows us to go back to a piece of work and revise it when there is good reason.

The reason for this second edition is mostly due to the amount of archival material that has become available since the first edition was written in 2015. The first edition quoted from, or referenced, around 220 articles that had first been published between 1956 and 1973, but this new version uses close to 600. On an almost monthly basis, more and more newspaper, magazine and trade publication archives appear. This kind of material is, perhaps, what I enjoy working with most, not least because it gives us the chance to go back within our cultural history. In this case, it allows us to see just what people were saying about Bobby (and what he was saying about himself and the world around him) during the time his career was taking place. There is also the possibility of questioning some of the myths and established stories about his career. Certainly, within the pages that follow, a number of well-known "facts" about Bobby and his career are not only questioned but, sometimes, shattered.

Beyond this, around three dozen previous unreleased performances have been issued since 2015, two thirds of which are from Bobby's time with Motown at the end of his career. Thankfully, I have had to "correct" only a few minor issues from the first edition, with the exception of the final chapter, where our understanding of these years has been drastically altered by this new material and the accompanying information issued with it.

I confess that one of my pet hates is when an album is re-released with one or two previously unreleased bonus tracks tacked on the end, forcing anyone who wants them to buy the whole thing again, and I didn't want the equivalent of that to happen with this book. In other words, if I was going to publish a second edition, then it needed a substantial amount of new material included. Approximately 45,000 words have been added to the text, making it around 40% longer than the first edition. Added to this is the inclusion of numerous images. Please note that a few of these have not made it through six decades unscathed, but have been included because of their rarity and/or historical importance.

Each and every section has been revised and/or expanded to some degree, and many new sections have been added. If this is your first purchase of the book, then I thank you. If this second edition has resulted in you "double-dipping" and buying the book for a second time, then I sincerely hope you feel that the new material is worthwhile. I can at least promise you that there will not be a third edition.

Best wishes

Shane Brown

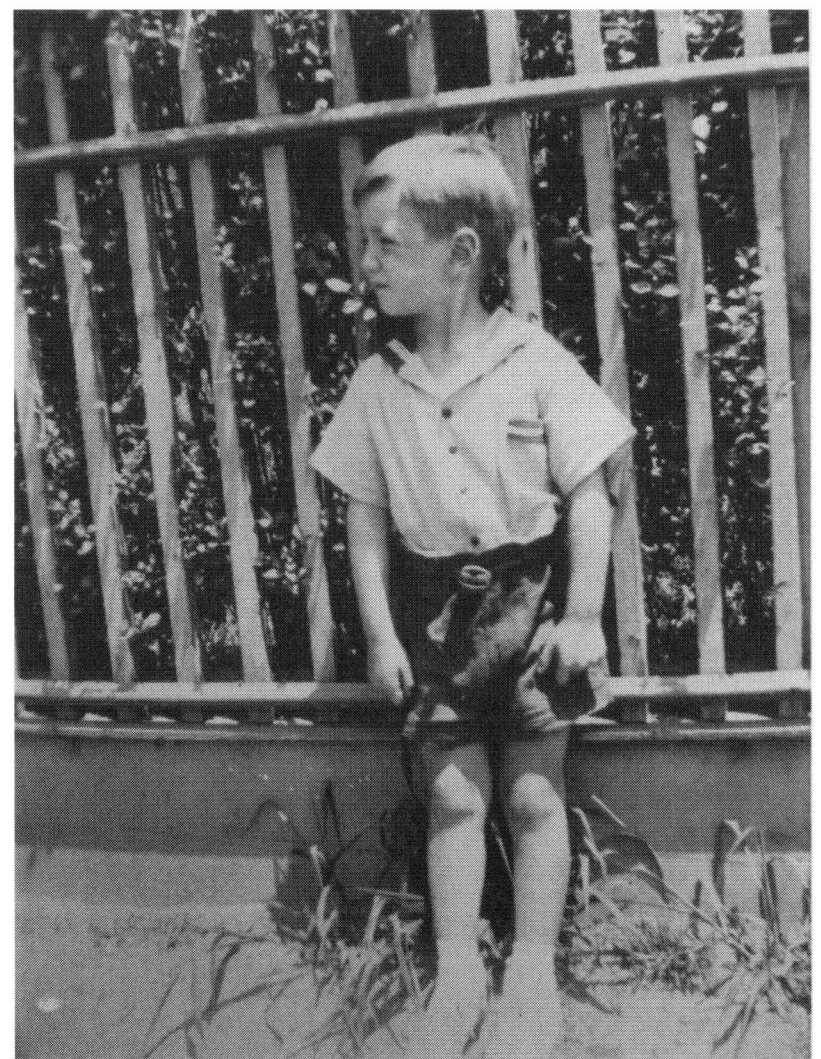

Bobby as a child

INTRODUCTION

My introduction to Bobby Darin came through what might be termed "unconventional means." In the UK in the 1990s, there was a television show called *Stars in their Eyes*, a talent show in which members of the public would be given a makeover to look like the star of their choice and then sing in the style of that person. The idea was that the winner would be the contestant who was the closest sound-alike to their chosen singing star. Despite (or because of) its kitschness and campness, *Stars in their Eyes* was must-see television on a Saturday night during its heyday. In 1995, a man by the name of Lee Griffith won both his heat and the series final performing as, yes, Bobby Darin.

Darin's was a name I knew, but was someone whose work I was largely unfamiliar with. I had become a fan of Frank Sinatra a year or two earlier, and had started exploring his work and that of those he had collaborated with such as Ella Fitzgerald, Count Basie and Duke Ellington. I knew Sinatra's *Mack the Knife*, in which he name-checks Bobby Darin, and so was interested in hearing the original arrangement. I made my way to the local music stores and was amazed to find very little of Bobby Darin on the shelves. I was, if I remember correctly, faced with the stark choice of just two discs. One of them was *Splish Splash: The Best of Bobby Darin, Volume One*, a compilation of the ATCO rock 'n' roll hits, and the other was a compilation of Capitol big band sides, *Spotlight on Bobby Darin*. I went for the latter.

When I got home, I discovered that around half of the disc was made up of songs from the *Oh! Look at Me Now* album, together with six unreleased songs, and four more from other sessions. I listened to the CD and read the liner notes while I did so. They were my first exposure to the Bobby Darin story, and I found myself most interested by the few lines about Darin's time in Big Sur in the late 1960s and his move into social commentary songs during that period. I was a somewhat confused and lost twenty-year-old at that point, trying to figure out who I was and where I fit into the

BOBBY DARIN: DIRECTIONS

"Spotlight on Bobby Darin" CD, 1995

world. Somehow, and for some reason, Bobby's story struck a chord with me. It is hard to explain how or why, but of all my musical heroes (Elvis Presley, Frank Sinatra, Duke Ellington, Johnny Cash) Bobby is the only one who I have constantly found fascinating *beyond* his music-making.

The following year, after a series of temporary jobs, I got my first full-time position at around the same time that I heard about the four-CD *As Long as I'm Singing* retrospective that had been put out by Rhino. This set, and most Bobby CDs at this point, were American releases and could only be found in the bigger stores in the UK, mostly in London, or ordered in especially. I was determined to get the Rhino set, and ordered it through my local HMV, with the set costing me half of my first week's wages.

After a year of waiting, I could finally hear the other sides of Bobby Darin. There were the single sides that I had never heard before; the blues numbers from the mid-60s that were being released for the first time; a big ballad like *Sail Away*, which still remains a favourite; and there was that glorious final disc of Bobby's folk material. Hearing *Work Song*, *Long Time Movin'*, *Long Line Rider*, *In Memoriam*, and *Simple Song of Freedom* was like hearing a different singer.

If I was curious and interested in Darin before, I was totally hooked now. I searched record fairs and second-hand shops trying to find vinyl issues of those albums not available on CD. I managed to find copies of LPs such as *Love Swings*, *Things and other Things*, *Bobby Darin sings Doctor Dolittle*, and then, finally, the holy grail (for me, at least): *Bobby Darin born Walden Robert Cassotto*. I had been looking for a copy for a few years by this point, and this was before the days of relying on eBay, where you can find any album you want at the touch of a button, no matter how rare (and, oh, how

INTRODUCTION

that has taken some of the joy out of collecting records!). When I got home, I realised that my precious copy of the LP was a little more battered than I first thought, and so had to weigh the arm of the turntable down with a penny in order for it to play. But it didn't matter. I was mesmerised by the music coming out of the speakers, and every pop and crackle just seemed to add to it.

Now, in 2019, some twenty years later, things have changed. All of Bobby's original domestic albums have been released on CD at some point. What's more, we have been treated to over three dozen unreleased studio masters from the Capitol years, a live album from 1963, unreleased songs and live cuts from the Direction years, two dozen previously unissued studio recordings from Motown, and the chance to own some of Bobby's TV appearances on DVD. To anyone who wants to go hunting, it wouldn't take long via Amazon, Amazon Marketplace and eBay to collect the complete recorded works of Bobby Darin, and for that we must be grateful.

But what are we to make of the legacy that Bobby Darin left behind? It is one that includes rock 'n' roll, country, swing, jazz, show tunes, folk, easy listening, spirituals, ballads, protest songs, blues, and even film scores. During his lifetime he was accused of switching styles because he wanted to jump on bandwagons, whereas in recent years he has been viewed as more of a musical chameleon.

The bandwagon-jumping accusation isn't *altogether* untrue. After all, it is difficult to imagine Bobby writing and recording the song *You're the Reason I'm Living* in the way he did had Ray Charles not recently had huge success with his *Modern Sounds in Country and Western* LP. But bandwagon-jumping suggests the recording was made simply for financial gain, whereas, considering Bobby's love of Charles, it was just as likely to have been done to emulate, and pay tribute to, his idol. In reality, it appears that if Bobby heard something and liked it, he wanted to try it for himself. But it was always done *Darin's* way, and was never a straight copy of a style or a sound, and that sets him apart.

I have never been happy with people calling Bobby Darin a "musical chameleon." For me, this has a negative connotation – albeit perhaps an unintended one. I'm no expert on chameleons but, while they can change their colour for any number of reasons, we generally associate it with a kind of camouflage, an attempt to fit in to its surroundings so as not to be noticed or found out. When we transfer this idea on to Darin, it then makes him out to be someone who was just changing his style and genre in order to fit in to (or cash in on) the current music scene – which brings us back to the whole idea of jumping on a bandwagon.

We first come across this idea when he recorded the *That's All* album back in late 1958, with the suggestion that he was somehow trying to be Frank Sinatra. And yet, anyone who knows the music of both men will know that there are actually huge stylistic differences between their arrangements and vocal styles within the big band genre. I don't know of a single Sinatra arrangement that has the same sound and feel as *Mack the Knife* or *Clementine*. Sinatra's orchestrations swing in a very different way entirely. In fact, perhaps the nearest Sinatra got to that sound was his version of *Old MacDonald* – recorded after the aforementioned tracks were released, not before – and even then it's not the exactly the same, despite the slow build-up in sound and the modulations in key with each verse. And it wasn't often that Sinatra was as downright brash as the arrangements used for *Softly as in a Morning Sunrise* or *Some of these Days*. Maybe on *I'm Gonna Live Till I Die* – but this was the exception, not the rule. Darin's vocal approach was far different too – he didn't sing from a jazz background as Sinatra did, but he brought rock 'n' roll vocal stylings to the big band sound. I'm not saying this to knock Sinatra in any way – I adore his music – but my point is just that Darin wasn't somehow imitating Sinatra, he was doing it *his way*.

If anything, Darin's swing sound was more like Sammy Davis Jr's than Sinatra's. Check out Davis's version of *There Is a Tavern in a Town*, for example, and you will see what I mean. He got much of his material from the same place as Davis too: the current Broadway scene. Whereas Sinatra was normally reaching back to shows of the 1930s and 1940s, Darin and Davis were often culling material from Broadway in the 1960s and, with Darin, the current Hollywood scene too. Hence the albums *From Hello Dolly to Goodbye Charlie*, *In a Broadway Bag*, *Bobby Darin sings the Shadow of your Smile* and individual tracks such as *What Kind of Fool am I* and *If I Ruled the World*. Despite these connections with Davis, Darin wasn't imitating him either, although both crossed over into rock 'n' roll material and rhythm 'n' blues.

Darin's last album to be recorded for ATCO was his tribute to Ray Charles, and it is true to say it retains much of the Ray Charles sound. However, even this wasn't a straightforward album. Bobby was taking risks here. What other pop singer of the time would spend over six minutes on *I Got a Woman* (and, in a late-60s TV appearance, over seven minutes on *Drown in My Own Tears*)? Most pop singers of the early 1960s were rarely recording songs over two and a half minutes. Darin's *I Got a Woman* doesn't actually work – it goes on for far too long – but at least he was willing to take risks or, to be less kind in this instance, be self-indulgent. Darin was always his own man and recorded what he wanted. Elvis Presley's manager, Colonel Parker, would have run a mile from such an artist. What this ultimately meant was that Bobby was often the only one responsible for the success or failure of an album.

Bobby is again accused of jumping onto bandwagons when he released his folk album, *Earthy!*. And yet, once more, an actual examination of the LP finds that this wasn't any normal folk album but an ambitious, daring (from a commercial point of view) collection of folk songs from around the world. What's more, it is also one of his best albums. In this case, the risk, ambition, and vision paid off artistically. While Peter, Paul and Mary (who he is often accused of copying) were recording songs by Pete Seeger and Bob Dylan, Darin was adapting folk music from across the globe along with a handful of new(ish) compositions in the same style. The musicianship here is

INTRODUCTION

"Earthy" LP, 1963

incredible, and yet the album did very little business commercially.

Darin's next folk album, *Golden Folk Hits*, was a simple attempt to hone in on the Peter, Paul and Mary sound, but he had gone down the artistic route before turning to the commercial one.

Then there have been the comparisons with Bob Dylan when we come to the late 1960s and Bobby's creation of his own label to record his own songs of social commentary. And yet, once again, there is no foundation in these comparisons, as what Bobby was writing and recording often had very little to do with what other protest singers were doing at the time.

They may have been largely ignored on release but, like *Earthy!*, the Direction albums have now gained cult status, particularly in the UK and Europe. The first, *Bobby Darin born Walden Robert Cassotto*, contained songs that were musically simplistic, but the lyrics were what mattered. There is some wonderful wordplay in *The Proper Gander*, while *Sunday* lures the listener in before issuing a damning indictment on organised religion. *Commitment*, the second album, is more interesting musically, and is clearly a more varied selection of songs, and Bobby manages to tie together a beautiful melody with a powerful political comment as in *Sausalito*. Elsewhere he isn't protesting at all, but there is great wordplay and musicality in *Water Color Canvas*, and a dry self-deprecating humour in *Distractions (Part 1)*.

His Motown years were largely disappointing, and yet the 1971 album recorded in Las Vegas (released in 1987) is probably the best live album of his career. Yes, he is relying largely on contemporary covers, but look at what he does with them! People say that Las Vegas saps a singer's artistic vision – but not Darin's. While Elvis's idea of a Beatles medley was a bland re-tread of *Yesterday* with the refrain of *Hey Jude* tagged on the end, Darin came up with a multi-song, almost rhapsodic, masterpiece. And, once again, ambition shone through, as in the extended version of James Taylor's *Fire and Rain*.

There wasn't much musical ambition in the Motown studio recordings, with Bobby trying to adhere to the Motown sound to start with before ultimately turning into a bland balladeer with orchestrations that often should have been torn up and thrown out long before they reached the studio. And there wasn't much ambition on his disappointing TV series either – and yet Darin was still doing what *he* wanted when he could. What other variety show gave over a few minutes each week to a chess game? Again, this was Darin being self-indulgent and ambitious and this time it didn't work – but he hadn't given up despite seemingly losing his way musically in his final years (although appearances on *The David Frost Show* and *Midnight Special* showed exactly what he was capable of when he put his mind to it – as did the concert-style final show of his TV series).

No artist leaves a perfect musical legacy. Bobby Darin took risks, and sometimes they didn't work or he over-estimated his audience. And yet the quality of his recordings is far more consistent than Elvis, Sammy Davis Jr, or even (arguably) Sinatra, who went through several periods of artistic doldrums within his studio work in the late 1960s through to the late 1970s. But one thing I am sure of is that Bobby Darin had no interest in being a chameleon, and changing his genre and style just to fit in or, worse, cash-in. If he changed his style, it was always because he thought he could bring something different to it, that he could add something, that he could move it forward, that he could push the boundaries.

Of course, this discussion is leaving out one important factor: Bobby's health. Having gone through repeated attacks of rheumatic fever as a child, Bobby wasn't expected (or expecting) to live long into adulthood. It was this more than anything that spurred Bobby Darin on to do what he wanted as quickly as he could while he still had the chance, and this, no doubt, was why he was always eager to try new styles and genres and never make the same album twice. As he told *Modern Screen* in 1960, "I've got this feeling I'm gonna die young…so what I've gotta do I've gotta do fast."[1]

It is not an exaggeration to say that he never made the same album twice. For example, Bobby made numerous albums of standards, or songs in that style, and yet no two of them have exactly the same feel or draw their repertoire from the same place. *This is Darin* has less rock 'n' roll phrasing and edge than *That's All*. *Love Swings* tells the story of a love affair, whereas *Two of a Kind* is a duets album using mostly novelty songs as the basis for its repertoire. *Winners* is a wonderful album using just a jazz combo, but *Oh! Look at Me Now* sees Bobby singing a dozen of the most popular and often-sung standards for the first time in a big band setting. And so it goes on.

This isn't to say, of course, that everything Bobby Darin attempted was an artistic success, and most certainly not everything was a commercial success. While Darin made no out-and-out *bad* albums, there are some distinctly average affairs such as *18 Yellow Roses and 11 Other Hits* or the rather drab 1972 *Bobby Darin* LP for Motown, and there are certainly a number of single sides that are hardly awe-inspiring. However, as with anyone who touched as many bases as Bobby did, there were always going to be some curveballs – and for someone as artistically ambitious as he was, there were

---

[1] "I've Got This Feeling I'm Gonna Die Young … So What I've Gotta Do I've Gotta Do Fast," *Modern Screen*, November 1960, 32.

INTRODUCTION

always going to be some projects that didn't hit the mark or were, perhaps, simply *too* ambitious or esoteric for his audience to appreciate.

Darin was also remarkably prolific, recording more material for both ATCO and Capitol than could have possibly been released at the time. ATCO would keep releasing "new" material until several years after he left the label, while Capitol have repeatedly raided their vaults over the last two decades, releasing enough forgotten studio masters to fill more than three LPs as well as a live album. During his career, Darin recorded over 500 songs and it is this music that this book is concerned with.

Bobby Darin: Directions, named after the Direction label Bobby founded in 1968, is not a straightforward biography, and is largely not interested in retelling Bobby Darin's life story. For any reader wanting that, there are fine biographies by David Evanier, Al DiOrio, and Bobby's son, Dodd Darin (among others). These all tell their stories in different ways and with a different emphasis, and all are recommended. There is also the book *That's All: Bobby Darin on Record, Stage and Screen* by Jeff Bleiel, which is a highly informative and remarkably readable biography of Darin as told through his career rather than his personal life.

The book you are currently holding, either in physical format or via a Kindle, is interested in Darin the artist. Session by session, song by song, each and every officially-released studio recording and live performance (plus a few more besides) is discussed, resulting in a highly detailed overview of the remarkable legacy that Bobby Darin left behind. The story is told chronologically by session, although several separate dates are sometimes pulled together under one section when multiple sessions were used with the aim of producing a single album (as in the case of *Oh! Look at Me Now*, for example). Attention is also drawn to Bobby's films and key TV appearances, from his memorable guest slots on programmes such as *The Dinah Shore Show* and *The Judy Garland Show* to his own TV series from 1972-3.

It is worth mentioning here that no official sessionographies of Bobby Darin have been published. This is a very different situation to the one I encountered when writing about the music of Elvis Presley, for whom all the session dates and musicians used are well documented. The recording dates within these pages are drawn from two online sessionographies put together by enthusiasts, as well as from liner notes and biographies. Without the availability of those online sessionographies, this book would not have been possible (at least in this form), and so all credit to the work of Jan-Jaap Been[2] and Michel Ruppli, Dik deHeer, Praguefrank and Michal Gololobov.[3] There are occasions when various sources offer up different dates for the same session(s), and I have tried to reflect that in the headings throughout the book.

---

[2] http://members.home.nl/jaap62/

[3] http://countrydiscography.blogspot.co.uk/2009/12/bobby-darin_10.html

Alongside my own commentary on the music runs the parallel story of how Bobby's music, personality and career were discussed, reviewed and reported in the newspapers, magazines and trade journals of the day. In this new edition, there are excerpts and comments from over 550 different reviews and articles, ranging from trade publications such as *Variety* to major newspapers such as the *New York Times* to movie and music fan magazines – even *Woman's Weekly*! They give us a fascinating picture of Bobby's career as it happened, from how his music was received to how his comments were skewed and misquoted and dogged him in the media for months and years afterwards.

After the main text are several appendices, ranging from the standard list of singles and albums released by Bobby to a list of around 200 television appearances from America, Canada, the UK and Australia, many of which have gone undocumented in books on Darin until now.

I have tried to produce a book that works in two ways: to be read from cover to cover *or* to be dipped in and out of. It is not always possible for this to be totally successful, but my hope is the book is both readable and usable as a kind of reference work.

The ultimate aim here, of course, is to bring the focus back to Bobby Darin's huge musical legacy. By offering a new commentary on the recordings themselves, and by telling the story of Darin's reception in the media, I hope that I have created a book that is of interest and use both to the long-time fan *and* those who are only just beginning to investigate the wonderful work that Bobby Darin left behind. If reading the following pages makes you want to go and listen again (or for the first time) to the albums or songs being discussed (if only to make sure you *do* disagree with me as much as you think you do), then this book has achieved its aim.

Now, make yourself comfortable and let's travel back to 1956 where a teenaged Bobby Darin is waiting to tell us the story of the *Rock Island Line*…

Written by Bobby on the back of the photo:
"December 18th 1952 - Senior Day. Sid Kramer in back, Manny Wolf at piano and me at trumpet (realistic isn't it?)"

CHAPTER ONE
ROCK ISLAND LINE: 1956

Relatively little is known about Bobby's first year or so as a professional recording artist. He was writing songs from around 1955 with Don Kirshner, a graduate from the Bronx High School of Science, which Bobby had also attended. Their first success came through the writing of jingles for radio advertisements, and copyright records from early 1956 show entries for *The Rogers Cha-Cha* (written for a furniture company) and *Wilco Jingle*. The pair also copyrighted their first pop song, *Bubble Gum Pop*, although it is unclear if it was ever recorded commercially.

Also in early 1956, Bobby and Don went to see George Scheck, the manager of a number of young up-and-coming singers. It is at this point, however, that the waters become somewhat muddy. There is little doubt that Scheck managed to get Bobby and Don's songs recorded by other artists prior to Darin himself getting a record deal, but those songs have been listed in various biographies as The Jaye Sisters' *Real Love* and *School's Out*, LaVern Baker's *Love Me Right*, Bobby Short's *Delia* and David Hill's *By My Side*.[4] However, none of these were released before Bobby had a recording contract, with them all hitting record stores in 1957 or 1958, and the two songs by the Jaye Sisters were not even by Darin and Kirshner but by Darin and Woody Harris.

What we *do* know is that Connie Francis, also managed by Scheck and with whom Bobby would have a serious relationship, recorded Bobby and Don's *My First Real Love*,[5]

---

[4] David Hill (also Davy Hill) was a stage name for David Hess, who also recorded the original version of the Elvis Presley hit *All Shook Up*. He was also a songwriter, and his credits include the Elvis hit *I Got Stung*, as well as *Speedy Gonzales* (under the name David Dante). Under his own name of David Hess, he would go on to star in the infamous Wes Craven horror movie *Last House on the Left* in 1972.

[5] Some biographies and internet sites refer to a song from this period entitled *My Teenage Love*. This appears to be a mis-titling of the Connie Francis song written by Darin and Kirshner which has been repeated on a number of occasions.

released in the spring of 1956, and that the novelty number *I Want to Spend Christmas With Elvis* was recorded by Marlene Paula, The Holly Twins, and Little "Lambsie" Penn, with the three versions vying for chart success when released in late 1956, although none of them made an impact.[6]

One day, probably in February 1956, Bobby and Don Kirshner were asked by George Scheck to make a demo of one of their songs (which was probably *My First Real Love*). Darin sang on the demo himself, Scheck was impressed, and soon he had Bobby signed to the Decca label. Biographies have stated in the past that it was at this point that Bobby chose his stage name of "Bobby Darin," encouraged by Scheck as he sought out a recording contract. However, records show that Bobby was using "Darin" to copyright his songs in early January 1956, several weeks before these events occurred.[7]

Probably March 6, 1956: Studio Session

Some singers find their voice the very first time they set foot inside a recording studio, and record some of their greatest work during their early years. Elvis Presley is probably the best example of this, recording the classic *That's All Right* at his very first professional recording session. This was not the case for Bobby Darin, however. In fact, it was over two years after he entered a studio before he recorded his breakthrough single, *Splish Splash*. Prior to that, he seemed to be constantly in search of his own sound, with many of his early records adopting the styles and mannerisms of other singers of the period. He needed something to make him stand out from the rest of the would-be pop stars trying to carve themselves a career in the mid-1950s, and that something was his own identity. Nowhere is this more noticeable than during the sides he recorded during his short tenure with Decca.

The first session for Decca, thought to have been on March 6, 1956, produced two singles: *Rock Island Line/ Timber* and *Silly Willy/ Blue Eyed Mermaid*.[8] A month later,

---

[6] Each of these recordings of the song used a slightly different title. The Holly Twins' recording was called *I Want Elvis for Christmas*. Eddie Cochran played guitar and provided the Elvis imitation backing vocals for this recording, and the song has been reissued on some of the more comprehensive Eddie Cochran CD compilations. The version by Little "Lambsie" Penn was issued under the title *I Wanna Spend Xmas with Elvis*. The Marlene Paula recording used the original title of *I Want to Spend Christmas with Elvis* for the most part, although some pressings were printed as *I Wanna Spend Christmas with Elvis*. This performance was reissued in the 1980s with the artist listed as Debbie Dabney – the reason for the name change is unknown, although it may have been due to the fact that the singer by this point had an established career as a jazz/big band singer under the name of Marlene VerPlanck.

[7] Bobby seemingly wasn't sure of what name to use at this point. He copyrighted songs and jingles in 1956 under the names Bobby Darin, Bob Darin (which he would revert to briefly in the late 1960s), and Bob Cassotto.

[8] Some commentators believe these recordings might have taken place as early as the end of February.

Cash Box featured a picture of Bobby from the recording date, together with A&R director Milt Gabler and musical director Jack Pleis.[9] Given Bobby's future musical direction, Pleis should have been a good match for him, but sadly he didn't get the chance to draw on his jazz background due to the nature of the songs chosen.

Bobby's arrangement of *Rock Island Line* seems somewhat inspired by the types of recordings that Johnny Cash was making at the time at Sun Records (Cash would record his own version of the song in 1957). The structure and instrumentation of Darin's performance is close to that used in Lonnie Donegan's version, which hit the US charts just a couple of weeks after Bobby recorded his own, but had been a hit in the UK earlier in the year. The recording is hardly essential Darin, and today is really just of historical importance. Bobby sounds inexperienced and unconvincing and, perhaps more importantly, the performance doesn't sound authentic. It is as if he is trying to be something or someone he isn't, which is, in many ways, exactly what is happening. This wasn't Darin's natural milieu, and this is a fatal error within folk music, a genre that relies on authenticity. Despite this, there are no signs of nerves from the young teenager whose vocal is somewhat exposed, being backed by just an acoustic guitar and drums.

U.S issue of Bobby's first single, 1956

The B-side of this first single finds Darin turning from a cross between folk and country to a full-on Frankie Laine impression. *Timber* is a faux-work song written by Bobby with Don Kirshner and "George M. Shaw," which was the pseudonym of George Scheck, although it is difficult to ascertain if he had any actual input into the writing of the song, or whether the credit was purely for the purpose of obtaining royalties. *Timber* was firmly in the Laine mould and finds Darin accompanied by backing vocals and percussion-heavy instrumentation. It is a better performance than *Rock Island Line*, and the arrangement cleverly uses a series of fake-endings before the actual conclusion of the song. It sees Bobby for the first time approaching the type of material that would be the basis of his masterful *Earthy!* LP six years later, and the song wouldn't have been out of place on that record had he chosen to re-record it.

Just over a week after the session, the single was released and *Billboard* magazine

---

[9] "Decca Debut," *Cash Box*, April 7, 1956, 26

included a short review of the two sides. Bobby would no doubt have been extremely happy when he read that the "new artist shows solid promise," and that his performance of *Timber* had "spirit and song savvy in evidence."[10] Interestingly, *Billboard* compared the song to *Ghost Riders in the Sky*, and the review in *Variety* also picked up on the fact that Darin had yet to find his own sound, writing that his version of *Rock Island Line* "is compelling, even if Darin sounds as if he's been listening to Harry Belafonte a shade too much for his own good."[11] *Cash Box* was probably the most enthusiastic, saying that *Rock Island Line* is "an exciting folk type song that looks like an all out hit, [and] is treated to a colourful reading by Bobby Darin."[12] *Timber* was described as "another beaty song *(sic)* with an exciting folk flavor [that] is dramatically executed here by the talented youngster. Lad has a fascinating sound and comes over zestfully."[13] Darin was also getting noticed outside of the usual trade magazines, with one writer in a local newspaper stating that "Decca is proud as punch of two new additions: vocalist Roberta Sherwood and teenager Bobby Darin. Both look like hot stuff."[14]

Also recorded at the same session was a song that saw Bobby turning his attention to the novelty rock 'n' roll material with which he would eventually find stardom. *Silly Willy* might have been a step in the right direction, but it was no *Splish Splash*. Much of the problem with the song is the awkward transitions between the two different tempi and rhythms that the song employs, although one has to admire

Japanese single, 1962

---

[10] "Reviews of New Pop Records," *Billboard*, March 31, 1956, 56.
[11] Herm Schoenfeld, "Jocks, Jukes and Disks," *Variety*, March 14, 1956, 50.
[12] "Record Reviews," *Cash Box*, March 31, 1956, 8.
[13] Ibid.
[14] George Laine, "Wax Museum," *Pasadena Independent*, April 20, 1960, 12.

the ambition in trying something beyond a straightforward rock 'n' roll number. It is a shame it doesn't totally work, for there is much to enjoy in Darin's performance, but the various elements simply do not gel together in the way that they should.

Silly Willy is interesting, however, in that it provides us with our first audible indication that Bobby wanted to be more than just a pop singer. While the number is credited to the same writing team as *Timber*, it has its roots in a 1920s risqué jazz number about a drug-addicted chimney sweeper called *Willie the Weeper* which, in turn, later provided the inspiration for *Minnie the Moocher*, a song that Darin would record a few years later. The lyrics of the first verse of *Silly Willy* and *Willie the Weeper* are so similar that it is clear that Bobby knew the more obscure song and was drawing from that rather than the better-known *Minnie the Moocher*. The first verse of *Willie the Weeper* reads:

> Have you heard the story, folks, of Willie the Weeper?
> Willie's occupation was a chimney sweeper,
> He had a dreamin' habit, he had it kind of bad,
> Listen, let me tell you 'bout the dream he had.

Silly Willy barely changes the lyrics at all:

> Listen to the story about Willy the Weeper.
> Willy the Weeper was a long time sleeper.
> He went to sleep one night and dreamed so bad,
> Now let me tell you about the dream that little Willy had.

What is remarkable here is not the fact that Bobby "borrowed" lyrics from an older song (this was not a rare occurrence in pop music at the time), but that he knew the lyrics to *Willie the Weeper* at all. Most of the better-known recordings, such as those by Louis Armstrong and George Lewis, were instrumentals – possibly with good reason due to the song's repeated references to "dope" and taking pills – and so one has to wonder where Bobby heard the lyrics in the first place. If nothing else, it shows just how wide his knowledge of popular music was even at the tender age of nineteen.

The B-side of *Silly Willy* was *Blue-Eyed Mermaid*. If *Timber* saw the singer performing in the Frankie Laine style, then this number sees a move towards Guy Mitchell in a song that has a kind of faux sea-shanty feel. A line or two of the verses steal the melody of *Ghost Riders in the Sky*, although this time this was no fault of Bobby himself as he was not the writer of the song. The ethereal female voices in the backing give the recording some distinction, but anyone hearing this without prior knowledge of the singer's identity would find it difficult to name Darin as the performer. Partly due to the nature of the song, and partly due to inexperience, he sounds quite different here compared even to the other recordings he made for Decca. As with its predecessor, the single failed to make the charts. *Billboard* wrote of *Silly Willy* that the "young singer comes up with a fast and furious bit of nonsense about *Silly Willy* and his dream…Excitement could kick off juke spins."[15] It was not unnoticed that *Blue-Eyed Mermaid* stole part of its melody from *Ghost Riders in the Sky*, but it was still said that "the side is right in the groove with current favour and will bear watching."[16] What is notable is that the single appears to have had less promotion from Decca, and substantially less attention from the trade press, than its predecessor.

Another song, *Rock Pile*, written by Darin in collaboration with Kirshner and Shaw/Scheck, is also listed as having been recorded at these sessions. It has never been released, and it is unclear whether the song was merely attempted and then aborted or if a master take was completed.

On March 10, 1956, Bobby made his national TV debut on *Stage Show*, a programme hosted by bandleaders Tommy and Jimmy Dorsey which had helped to bring Elvis Presley to national attention during his first four appearances on the show.[17] Darin sang *Rock Island Line*, and it didn't go well. Bobby told the story in 1972 on an episode of *The David Frost Show*:

> What happened was that I had forgotten all the lyrics. I covered Lonnie Donegan's record of *Rock Island Line*. I was with Decca at the time. They said, "We have a record here and it's going to be a smash, we'll get a cover record." In those days, you did that. […] I learned it on a Monday, recorded it on a Tuesday evening, and then did *The Jackie Gleason Show* on a Saturday evening.[18] I really wasn't sure of the lyrics, and they weren't about to serve my myopic condition and so therefore they couldn't give me cue cards. So I devised my own which was on the palm of my hand. […] At the end of the show everyone knew what I was doing, of course, except my sweet Mama who said, "You were wonderful, I never saw anyone use his hands like that."

Cash Box noted a fortnight later that "reaction to Darin's appearance on the TVer is

---

[15] "Reviews of New Pop Records," *Billboard*, May 26, 1956, 50.
[16] Ibid.
[17] Elvis would appear twice more on the show on the two programmes immediately following Bobby's appearance.
[18] *Stage Show* was part of *The Jackie Gleason Show*.

1956

reported to have already resulted in heavy advance orders on his platter" of *Rock Island Line*.[19]

After the *Stage Show* appearance, Bobby didn't appear on television again for over a year. He did, however start making live appearances to promote his recordings. He was involved in rock 'n' roll revues such as the one at the University of Detroit on April 15 (above right), where he appeared alongside The Four Aces and The Four Coins, among others. In May 1956, he appeared in a club setting at The Purple Onion, Guilford, Indiana, as the headliner, giving three shows nightly for a week (above left). On May 8, three days after finishing at the Purple Onion, he was performing at the annual concert of the Music Operators of America (MOA) convention, a four-hour show which also featured Nat 'King' Cole, Teresa Brewer, Mahalia Jackson and Pat Boone – and one can only assume how proud Bobby would have been to be sharing the stage with them.

July 11, 1956: Studio Session

When Bobby Darin went back into the studio in July 1956, he didn't try to improve or build upon what he had attempted at his previous session but, instead, tried something completely different in his search for a record that would resonate with the public.

The first release from this session coupled *The Greatest Builder* with *Hear Them Bells*.

---

[19] "Decca Releases First Roberta Sherwood Disk," *Cash Box*, March 24, 1956, 18.

Badly damaged candid, c.1956.

Both songs are semi-religious efforts, and neither are particularly good or original compositions. *The Greatest Builder* is a ballad sung with what comes across as fake sincerity, and the result is almost nauseating. The arrangement is sedate and uses full orchestra and chorus, and has little in common with what most teenagers would have been buying or listening to at the time. Oddly, the arrangement and the material were more in line with what British stars were scoring hits with in the UK charts at the time. For example, Malcolm Vaughan had a number 3 hit in the UK with *St. Theresa of the Roses* a couple of months after the release of *The Greatest Builder*, and there is not a vast chasm between the styles of the two songs. The difference, though, is that Vaughan seemed comfortable singing these types of rather square ballads, and managed to do so with integrity and sincerity, but Bobby manages neither.

Hear Them Bells is better, and finds Bobby singing in a style and arrangement which, as with *Blue Eyed Mermaid*, is most associated with Guy Mitchell. This song is again accompanied by an orchestra and chorus, and has a sound that is close to that used in Mitchell's hits *My Truly Truly Fair* and *Cloud Lucky Seven*, despite the semi-gospel nature of the lyrics. The lyrics are trite, but Bobby manages to give a better performance here, giving a bouncy, lively vocal over a fun, if dated, arrangement.

The problem is that the listener doesn't believe that *Darin* believes what he's singing about, or that this is the style he wants to be singing. Perhaps this is partly to do with the issue of hindsight – after all, in 1968 Bobby released a song, *Sunday*, which attacks organised religion and what he views as its hypocrisy, and here we have songs telling us about the wonders of *The Greatest Builder* and going to church on a Sunday.

Billboard were hardly ecstatic about the single either (and they were usually very easily pleased), stating that *The Greatest Builder* was "not great material of its type" and that *Hear Them Bells* wasn't "hefty on message, but can help carry the better side."[20]

---

[20] "Reviews of New Pop Records," *Billboard*, September 29, 1956, 64.

Variety were more impressed, saying that Bobby gave an "all-out reading" of the ballad and that *Hear Them Bells* is "an uptempo religioso in a get-happy tempo and Darin also belts this one neatly."[21] *Cash Box* referred to Bobby as a "talented songster," and said of *The Greatest Builder* that "Bobby Darin hands in a potent deck as he introduces a dramatic inspirational ballad…Could catch on."[22] It didn't.

Oddly, at the height of Bobby Darin's fame at the end of 1959, Decca decided to re-release this single. As *Billboard* pointed out at the time, the single "bears little resemblance to the present Darin vocal sound. It's a happy sound but fans will find little that's familiar."[23] *Cash Box* were polite in referring to the recordings as "joyful" and "tenderly fashioned," but hardly enthusiastic.[24]

Dealer In Dreams, the A-side of the fourth and final Decca single, is a Darin-Kirshner song which would have worked quite well for Elvis Presley, being similar in style and structure to *Don't Leave Me Now*, which Presley would record twice during 1957 and include in *Jailhouse Rock* (Richard Thorpe, 1957). Bobby's recording misses the mark, however, because it is over-arranged; he is singing a rock 'n' roll ballad with a full orchestral arrangement. With a less square arrangement and a more nuanced vocal, this could have worked well. Despite this, the recording is still arguably the best of the Decca sides, and the song itself is solid and could have been a hit in the right hands.

New Zealand EP, 1960

Help Me was written by Cy Coben, co-writer of *The Greatest Builder*, and again finds Bobby in a strange, alien environment more in line with the British charts than the American ones. This type of big ballad never became Bobby's forte, as he didn't have a voice that really suited it, and here he is once again bogged down with an uninspired orchestral arrangement that only results in Darin sounding far older than twenty.

In their review of the single, *Billboard* picked up again on the idea that Bobby Darin hadn't yet worked out who he was within the recording studio. Whereas *Variety* had

---

[21] Herm Schoenfeld, "Jocks, Jukes and Disks," *Variety*, October 8, 1956, 62.
[22] "Record Reviews," *Cash Box*, September, 29, 1956, 10.
[23] "Reviews of New Pop Records," *Billboard*, December 28, 1959, 27.
[24] "Record Reviews," *Cash Box*, January 2, 1960, 20

compared him to Harry Belafonte on his first single, *Billboard* suggested that *Dealer in Dreams* was "reminiscent of Johnnie Ray" before admitting that it "deserves exposure."[25] Of *Help Me*, they wrote that the recording was "a big, fancy piping of a pleading ballad of genuine appeal." The record-buying public didn't agree, and neither did most of the critics, with this pair of tunes getting the least attention of the four Decca singles.

Other than the release of the singles during the remainder of 1956 and early 1957, Bobby Darin appears to have fallen out of the public eye during this period. We can only presume that he was performing during this time, but unlike the spring of 1956, there appears to be no trace of his activities in newspapers (national or local) or trade magazines. Presumably, this was because he was not the named performer, although this doesn't explain him vanishing from print entirely.

In the end, Darin's short tenure at Decca must have been as frustrating for him as it was for the few people that bought his records. He had recorded eight sides, none of which had attracted much attention from the public or the press, and he was seemingly no closer to finding his own voice than he had been when he first stepped into the Decca recording studios a few months earlier. What is perhaps most interesting about these two early sessions is the number of different genres attempted, from folk through to a rock 'n' roll novelty number, and on to big ballads and semi-religious offerings. It was an early indication of the twists and turns that Bobby's career would take over the next seventeen years.

Rare audience photo of an early live performance.

It would be nearly a year before he returned to the recording studio, and when that finally occurred, it would be with a much more confident sound, and with Bobby positioning himself firmly as a rock 'n' roll singer. For now.

---

[25] "Reviews of New Pop Records," *Billboard*, February 23, 1957, 63.

Publicity Shot

CHAPTER TWO
MAKING A SPLASH: 1957-1958

Bobby Darin might have disappeared from newspapers and trade magazines for reasons unknown in June 1956, but he reappeared in April 1957 with much more positive press than he had been receiving a year earlier. For example, on April 12, the *Cullum Democrat* wrote:

> Bobby Darin is appearing in Birmingham this week at Mike's South Pacific [Club]. Darin has a record out that's doing well around these parts entitled *Dealer in Dreams*. If we just give this fellow a chance he may in just a few years have as high a rating, worldwide, as did Eddie Fisher, two years ago.[26]

Bobby was also making his first appearances at the Paramount Theater in Montgomery, Alabama, in a revue entitled *Teen Time*. In an article in *The Montgomery Advertiser*, it is suggested that the release of *Dealer in Dreams* had created more of an interest in the singer, something which may have well been true (if only on a regional basis) given that it is mentioned in several articles and advertisements in local newspapers of the time. Bobby told the newspaper that he had "just caught on within the past month – and man, is it ever hectic."[27] In the same article, he said that he was planning to change labels "in a few days." That interview had taken place on April 13, 1957, more than six weeks before any deal with a new label was actually made.

In reality, Bobby hadn't recorded anything for Decca since June 1956, and had been dropped by the label by early 1957. In mid-to-late April 1957, Bobby was in

---

[26] "Your's Very Musically *(sic)*," *Cullum Democrat*, April 12, 1957, 5.
[27] "Teen Timers Greet Darin With Cheers," *Montgomery Advertiser*, April 14, 1957, 8.

Birmingham, Alabama performing three shows a night at Mike South's Pacific Club, and he somehow pulled enough money together to book a recording studio and musicians in order to put down four songs that he planned to use to help get himself a new record deal. That session took place in Nashville on May 6, and the recordings he made impressed Ahmet Ertegun of Atlantic Records, and it was soon announced that Darin was signed to their subsidiary label, ATCO, who also acquired the masters for release.

May 6, 1957: Studio Session

When Bobby cut the four demo sides in Nashville, it had been ten months since his second and final session for Decca. The sound he created in these new recordings was very different to those he had used previously, with it being much more stripped back – there is no big orchestra here (possibly because it would cost too much as Darin was funding this himself) – and Bobby using some of the best musicians around, including Hank Garland on guitar and The Jordanaires and Millie Kirkham on vocals. Elvis had been using The Jordanaires on his recordings for nearly a year, and Kirkham would be added to the Elvis sound during the sessions in September 1957 for *Elvis' Christmas Album*. Hank Garland would also play for Elvis between 1958 and 1961, but was already regarded as one of the best guitar players in Nashville by the time he recorded with Bobby on this session. Garland was involved in a car accident in 1961 and, despite recovering, was never able to return to the recording studio. The line-up of top talent on these recordings suggests that Bobby was pulling out all the stops. He had tasted fame having been on national TV, and on a bill that also featured Mahalia Jackson and Nat 'King' Cole, and he wasn't planning to let it slip away without a fight.

Bobby was now placing himself firmly in the sphere of rock 'n' roll, and his first release for ATCO reflected this. *I Found a Million Dollar Baby* is interesting as it was another sign that Darin had interests beyond modern pop. Here, he took an old standard and gave it a rock 'n' roll makeover. The results are enjoyable enough, and certainly more commercial than anything he had achieved the previous year, helped by the musicians he was working with. However, despite the recording being more in line with the chart music of the day, it still wasn't hit material. Interestingly, though, it would be the formula of giving old songs a makeover that would give Bobby some of his biggest successes.

The flip side, *Talk to Me Something*, was a Darin-Kirshner composition and considerably better material than the originals he had recorded during his time at Decca. The performance is hardly a masterpiece (and Bobby can't quite work out whether he is Elvis or Jim Reeves), but there are some nice moments, particularly during the swell in emotion and volume during the third line of each verse when Darin and the backing vocalists sing together.

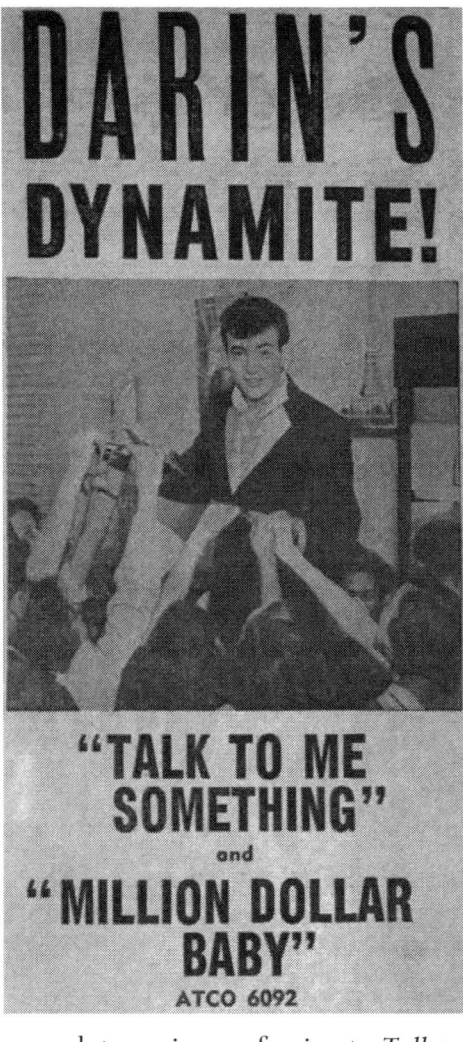

While the first ATCO single is generally listed with *I Found a Million Dollar Baby* as the A-side, an advertisement in *Billboard* for the single lists *Talk to Me Something* first, as does the *Cash Box* review. ATCO were doing something that Decca never seemed to do, which was to promote Bobby's singles. The advertisement in *Billboard* (left) has the headline "Darin's Dynamite!" with a picture of the singer underneath and the titles of both sides of the single.[28]

The single became one of *Cash Box*'s "Sleepers of the Week," with the reviewer saying that *Talk to Me Something* was "a melancholy romancer sentimentally set to a slow blues beat and chanted with great heart by the polished songster."[29] Meanwhile, *I Found a Million Dollar Baby* was a "top-drawer oldie" given a "tremendous revival treatment in today's rock and roll technique." Overall, the disc promised "to be a stepping stone to a promising future." *Variety* thought that the single "should make some headway in the jock and juke fields."[30] Meanwhile, the *Philadelphia Inquirer* thought that the single was important enough to review, referring to *Talk to Me Something* as a "slow and dreamy rock 'n' roll ballad, and the way young Bobby plays with it, should make plays a plenty on the juke boxes."[31]

The *Billboard* review was also favourable, with *Million Dollar Baby* being referred to as a "hefty, rocking, commercial reading of a great standard."[32] Despite being a "commercial reading," however, the single performed disappointingly and failed to chart. However, this was not the story that Bobby would tell *Modern Screen* magazine in an article published in May 1959. Here he is quoted as saying that the song climbed "the sales charts to top twenty tunes. But I was such a novice in the business I didn't

---

[28] "Darin's Dynamite!" *Billboard*, July 1, 1957, 13.
[29] "Record Reviews," *Cash Box*, June 22, 1957, 16.
[30] Mike Gross, "Jocks, Jukes and Disks," *Variety*, June 12, 1957, 60.
[31] Phil Sheridan, "Record Review," *Philadelphia Inquirer*, June 21, 1957, 30.
[32] "Review Spotlight On…" *Billboard*, July 1, 1957, 53.

know how to follow it up. One hit record doesn't make a singer."[33] Neither does a make-believe hit, Bobby!

The other two sides recorded at the session would be held back from release. *Just in Case You Change Your Mind* was another attempt at a rock 'n' roll ballad which was not far removed in style or execution from *Talk to Me Something*, but the performance didn't manage to rise above the ordinary. It was all just a little too similar to other songs in the charts over the previous couple of years, and Bobby's rather polite performance was in need of some "edge." The song itself was not a new one, though, and is an early example of Bobby talking an obscure number and giving it something of a makeover. The song dates back to 1945, when it was recorded by Deek Watson and the Brown Dots (Watson was also co-writer of the song), and the group also sang it in the 1947 film *Boy! What a Girl!* (directed by Arthur H. Leonard). Interestingly, the number had also been recorded in 1946 by Bull Moose Jackson, whose name, it has been suggested, may have been the inspiration for *Bullmoose*, which Bobby wrote and recorded in 1959. Perhaps it was Jackson's recording that brought the song to Darin's attention.

Just In Case You Change Your Mind would be released as a single in January 1958, but it found its real home as filler on Bobby's first album, released in July of the same year. Once again, though, the single was prominently advertised by ATCO within *Billboard*,[34] and *Cash Box* were enthusiastic, saying that "Bobby Darin, a youngster destined to become a name performer, hands in a smooth R & R ballad reading of a

Rare candid of Bobby and friends, c. 1957

---

[33] George Christy, "So You Want to Be a Singer!" *Modern Screen*, August 1959, 53.
[34] "At ATCO a Whole Lotta Shakin' Goin' On," *Billboard*, February 10, 1958, 43.

wonderful oldie. Side has a good blues feeling."[35]

Wear My Ring, probably the first song recorded at the session, didn't receive a single release but instead appeared on the *Bobby Darin* LP. It is no better or worse than *Just in Case You Change Your Mind*, although it has marginally more interest being another Darin-Kirshner original. A month after Bobby cut his version, Gene Vincent recorded the song, and released it as the B-side to *Lotta Lovin'*, a song that reached #13 in the US charts. Vincent's version manages to make the most of the song's potential, taking it at a faster pace, giving it a slight novelty value with the falsetto "Won't you" at the beginning of each verse, and providing an edgier vocal and a fine guitar solo.

August 21, 1957: Studio Session

The four songs recorded in May had resulted in Darin signing with ATCO, and the single release of *Talk to Me Something* and *I Found a Million Dollar Baby* had attracted an encouraging amount of attention, even if it hadn't been a hit record. On August 21, Bobby returned to the studio for his first official session with ATCO, and it is clear from the songs attempted that the intention was to build upon the success of the previous session. Bobby stuck with the rock 'n' roll genre here, and, once again, the results were varied.

The first single to come out of the session coupled *Don't Call My Name* with *Pretty Betty*, both of which were originals by Darin and Don Kirshner. *Don't Call My Name* was by the far the best cut of the session, and certainly the most commercial. However, as with some of the recordings from May, there was still a sense that Bobby was somehow holding back, and the result is ultimately unsatisfying, polite rock 'n' roll which appears to be influenced by Fats Domino, but lacking the vibrancy of his recordings.

Pretty Betty, the flip-side of *Don't Call My Name*, is a step forward in this direction. Bobby's vocal is more exciting, and the guitar solo is competent and energetic. The problem here is the material, with the number being derivative of many other rock 'n' roll songs from the period, most notably the vogue at the time for songs to be based around girls names (*Good Golly Miss Molly*, *Peggy Sue*, *Lucille* etc). Neither song was distinctive enough to stand out from the crowd, and the pairing performed badly.

The single was released in October 1957, and *Billboard* picked up on the influence of Fats Domino on *Don't Call My Name*, as well as stating that the saxophone "comes in midway to good effect. A chorus adds a big sound."[36] Of *Pretty Betty* they wrote that "Darin rocks right along with this one."[37] Elsewhere, reviews seemed more

---

[35] "Record Review," *Cash Box*, February 15, 1958, 10.
[36] "Reviews of New Pop Records," *Billboard*, November 18, 1957, 52.
[37] Ibid

enthusiastic, with Al Wolfe writing that "here is tempo *(sic)* designed for teen-agers and young Darin sets his sights on that particular contingent as he belts out *Pretty Betty*, a genuine house rocker that has shades of *Tutti Frutti*. He furthers his attraction of the young set with another jammer, *Don't Call*, although he slackens the pace on this one."[38] What is clear is that the single had garnered less attention than its predecessor, both from the critics and ATCO itself, which seemed to reign in on the advertising within trade magazines.

Also from this session, *So Mean* suffers from many of the same problems. This ballad is competent enough, and Darin puts in a fine performance, but it is also similar to many other rock 'n' roll ballads of the period, with the main point of interest being that it was another Darin and Kirshner original. Paired with *Just in Case You Change Your Mind* from the May session, it also failed to dent the charts, despite the ATCO advert for the single declaring that the sound of the song was just "'the hippest' to teenage ears."[39]

The remaining song, *(Since You're Gone) I Can't Go On*, is an unremarkable rock 'n' roll ballad with country overtones that has a slightly awkward feel to it, and was held back until it appeared on Bobby's first LP. This was the first song recorded by Bobby that was written by the hit songwriting team of Doc Pomus and Mort Shuman, who would also write *Plain Jane*, which would be a top forty hit for Darin in 1959.

Bobby did not record again until early the following year, but he kept busy with live performances and what are thought to be his first television appearances since *Stage Show* over a year earlier. In July 1957, around a month after the release of the *Talk to Me Something* single, Bobby appeared on *The Big Beat* TV show singing the song, and then in December he was seen on *American Bandstand* for the first time, performing *Don't Call My Name*. It is likely that, in between those two dates, Bobby appeared on local TV shows to promote his live performances and/or his singles. Sadly, however, no documentation has been found to confirm this.

Following the release of *Talk To Me Something*, Bobby's star was on the rise, albeit temporarily and only in certain regions of the United States. He made his third *Teen Time* revue appearance in Montgomery, Alabama in September, and had become popular enough for lunch with him to become part of the prize for those lucky enough to be crowned "Mr and Miss Teen Time." The *Montgomery Advertiser* raved: "In case you squares don't dig this Darin cat, he's just the coolest. Why man, Darin has waxed *Dealer in Dreams* and *Talk to Me Something* and is a top star for the ATCO label."[40] A few days later, it was reported that Collins (Boogie) Walker and Sara Ann Sansom

---

[38] Al Wolfe, "Record Review," *Tyrone Daily Herald*, December 27, 1957, 6.
[39] "At ATCO a Whole Lotta Shakin' Goin' On," *Billboard*, February 10, 1958, 43.
[40] "Teen-Agers to Elect *Teen Time* Winners," *Montgomery Advertiser*, September 1, 1957, E3.

were the winners of the lunch date, with Walker also winning a nine-year-old car as part of his prize.[41] As with the article a couple of days earlier, there were some slight exaggerations within the text, with *Dealer in Dreams* being called a "big hit," and the writer telling readers that thirty of Bobby's songs had been recorded by other singers, which seems an unlikely number at this point.

At the same time as performing at record hops and revues aimed at teenagers, Bobby was also singing in clubs and hotels, with the autumn of 1957 taking him to clubs in Birmingham, Miami, Detroit, and Atlanta. He continued making a name for himself through his live performances. *Cash Box* states that when he appeared in New York at a rock 'n' roll revue in November, "he was booked so late he wasn't even mentioned in the ads or on the marquee. However, after the first performance, when he really rocked the house, his name was quickly added to the billing."[42]

The following month, he was back in Montgomery for another *Teen Time* appearance, with Bill O'Brien, organiser of the event, telling a newspaper that "of all the entertainers I have met, including Eddie Fisher, Bobby is the most talented, most sincere and just the greatest and as long as he makes records, whether they are hits or not, I will still play them."[43] The same newspaper article also states that "he was so popular he was engaged at the Copa Cabana *(sic)* in New York only a few weeks ago." If this were true, then it must have been as a support act, and some three years prior to the autumn of 1960, which has hitherto been thought of as his debut. Sadly, at the time of writing I have been unable to confirm the appearance in 1957.

Bobby ended the year by performing at the Community War Memorial in New York on New Year's Eve, on a bill that was topped by Bill Haley and the Comets (see

---

[41] Stuart Culpepper, "2 Local Youngsters, Bobby Darin Cheered by 1,800 At City's Biggest *Teen-Time* Show," *Montgomery Advertiser*, September 8, 1957, B4.
[42] "R & B Ramblings," *Cash Box*, November 2, 1957, 42.
[43] "Bobby Darin Fan Club is Formed Here," *Montgomery Advertiser*, December 15, 1957, Teen Topic section, 8.

previous page). Despite the illustrious company, a review of the performance the following day singled Darin out for praise, stating that the "chief vocal pyrotechnics came from Bobby Darin, who specialized in hand-clapping and toe-tapping accompaniment to his own singing."[44]

Slowly but surely, Bobby was making a name for himself.

January 24, 1958: Studio Session

Much attention has been paid over the years to the session in April 1958 which produced *Splish Splash* and *Queen of the Hop*, Bobby Darin's breakthrough records. However, this session from three months earlier is just as important in that it shows a significant improvement over what had gone before, with Bobby sounding far more assured and confident and finding his "own voice" for probably the first time. None of the songs were released as singles, with two appearing on the *Bobby Darin* album later in the year, and the other two held back until the *For Teenagers Only* LP in 1960. However, that is relatively unimportant, for this is the session that gave Bobby the springboard to create *Splish Splash*.

Brand New House was a Bobby Darin-Woody Harris original, and the change in the arrangements and vocal quality since the previous session is startling. The sound has morphed slightly into a cross between rock 'n' roll and Ray Charles's brand of rhythm 'n' blues. The beat is more prominent, the brass adds a depth and fullness to the sound, and Bobby's voice is rawer than before. Some of the mannerisms heard on *Splish Splash* are here for the first time, too. This is no masterpiece, and there are times when it is quite clear that Darin is struggling to complete phrases in one breath (which may have been lack of preparation or due to health problems), but this is so much more vibrant than anything he had recorded before. It sounds like a different singer entirely. For a completely different take on the same song, take a listen to Otis Spann's version, featuring Muddy Waters on guitar.

You Never Called also shows significant signs of improvement, this time in Darin's ballad singing. This rock 'n' roll ballad again finds his voice stronger and more assured than on previous songs of this type, and it also finds him more at home in this style. In his earlier rock 'n' roll ballads, Bobby was holding on to the last note of each line, but here that doesn't happen. Instead, he cuts the note off quickly (though not too quickly), giving the number more energy.

All the Way Home, co-written by Otis Blackwell who had penned both *All Shook Up* and *Don't Be Cruel*, finds Bobby back in upbeat territory in a number that mixes an Elvis-like song with a Ray Charles-like arrangement. Darin seemed to be gaining more

---

[44] Brian Sullivan, "Teen-Agers Rock Into '58," *Democrat and Chronicle*, January 1, 1958, 44.

Rare candid of Bobby with a friend or fan, c.1957 or early 1958.

and more in confidence as the session progressed, and he yelps and growls and groans his way through the song. Finally, in his fifth recording session, this is recognisably Bobby Darin.

The last song, *Actions Speak Louder than Words*, is another mid-tempo ballad, and deserves to be better known. This is far better than some of the rock 'n' roll songs recorded immediately <u>after</u> *Splish Splash*, and should have had a single release, backed with either *Brand New House* or *All the Way Home*. Like some of the other songs from this session, the material was better than Bobby was used to, with the number co-written by Berry Gordy Jr., who would go on to become the founder of Motown records, the label that Bobby would join in 1970.

Quite why none of these songs were released as a single is something of a mystery, as the public would have noticed a vast improvement on the singer's previous efforts, and it is quite possible that any single would have at least made a dent in the charts. As it is, these songs remain relatively unknown to this day, and that is a shame as there is much to enjoy in these four sides that give us the first opportunity to hear the *real* Bobby Darin. After recording twenty songs over a period of nearly two years, Bobby had finally found his own identity.

Much of the renewed confidence in the studio may well have been down to the amount of live performances that Bobby had been giving over the previous six months or so. However, the amount of live performances temporarily slowed down at the beginning of 1958, and little information seems to exist about Darin's activities at this time other than that he was part of a rock 'n' roll revue in February 1958, performing on the same bill as Danny & The Juniors and Screamin' Jay Hawkins. There are also no known TV performances during the first months of 1958. The reason for this apparent slow-down in live work is unknown.

April 10, 1958: Studio Session

This April 10, 1958 session basically saved Darin's career. Despite the improvements he had made, there had still not been a hit record, and not even one single released from the previous session. Bobby was given one last chance, and to make sure he could make the most of that chance, Ahmet Ertegun, who had brought Bobby to ATCO in the first place, decided to produce the session himself – one that was split between him and jazz singer Morgana King.

Rare photo by an audience member of Bobby performing for a (mostly) teenage audience, October 1958.

Splish Splash would turn out to be the hit that Bobby had been waiting for. As a piece of material, the song is probably no better than some of the songs that he had recorded a few months earlier at the previous session. Darin employs the same rather aggressive vocal tones in the song as in *Actions Speak Louder than Words* and *Brand New House*, but perhaps the song benefits most from the searing saxophone solo during the instrumental break and the water effect at the opening and closing of the track. This may sound cynical, for it is a great performance, and a song that has stood the test of time and been covered numerous times, but the one thing it has over the efforts of the previous session is the novelty hook. With Jesse Powell's sax solo, the novelty subject matter, and sound effects, it stood out from the crowd and made audiences take notice. It was exactly what Darin was yearning for, and what his career needed: to be noticed by the record-buying public.

The flip of the single was *Judy, Don't Be Moody*, although any of the songs from the previous session would have made for a stronger B-side. That's not to say there is anything inherently bad about the recording, but it is a relatively bland effort that has little of the energy of, say, *Brand New House* or *All the Way Home*, and it follows in the footsteps of *Pretty Betty* in that it is built around a girl's name.

The single received good reviews in trade magazines such as *Billboard* and *Variety*, with the latter referring to *Splish Splash* "an amusing rhythm novelty with an offbeat idea [and] colourfully projected by Bobby Darin."[45]   However, the lack of originality in *Judy, Don't Be Moody* was also picked up on, with the same publication referring to it as "an okay rocker with the by-now over-worked name peg." *Billboard* were hardly ecstatic about the song either, referring to it as having a "listenable chorus."[46] But they were in little doubt about the strength of *Splish Splash*, stating that it was "a blues with a novelty lyric that is belted in a bright rock and roll tempo."[47] *Cash Box* went further, saying that it "looks real good from this end. Darin has a souped up quick beat with a humorous lyric and a top-notch reading. The kids should cuddle real close to this offering 'cause Darin is giving his all. The talented chanter rides hard with an effervescence that captures the listener."[48]

There was also attention in the regular press. Jack Curtis wrote that the song was "an all expense *(sic)* paid trip to Hitsville. Darin takes a blues tune, adds a novelty lyric and belts it out in a bright, fast-moving tempo. The water sound-effect on the opening and close gives the side some distinction, and makes for a talking point, which is always good for sales."[49] He was less enthusiastic about *Judy, Don't Be Moody*, saying it was "not in contention." The pedestrian flip-side of the single turned out to be unimportant, however, as *Splish Splash* made its way to #3 in the U.S. charts and broke the top 20 in the UK.

The same session also produced another hit single, *Queen of the Hop*. Again, the instrumentation was borrowed from Ray Charles, while the subject matter was the same as many other hit singles of the time. The track is brilliantly recorded, making it appear to rock with much more abandon than it actually does. With Darin set back in the mix, we get the effect that his singing is much rawer. The driving beat is front and centre in the mix and, together with another great saxophone solo, the effect is complete. There is also the chance to hear how the song took shape during the session, thanks to a bootleg CD called *Rare, Rockin' & Unreleased* which contains a number of outtakes. It is interesting to hear how the early takes featured a bass singer singing "Queen of the Hop" in reply to Darin during the choruses, before the idea was finally dropped. The song would become Bobby's second top ten single.

Interestingly, the vast majority of the reviews of the time listed *Queen of the Hop* as the B-side of the single, and *Lost Love* (recorded in July 1958) as the A-side. In the charts, those roles would be reversed. *Picturegoer* in the UK referred to *Queen of the Hop* as "rip-roaring excitement,"[50] while *Cash Box* said the song had Darin "rockin' thru

---

[45] Herm Schoenfeld, "Jocks, Jukes and Disks," *Variety*, May 28, 1958, 54.
[46] "Review Spotlight On…," *Billboard*, June 2, 1958, 42.
[47] Ibid.
[48] "R & B Reviews," *Cash Box*, May 31, 1958, 48.
[49] Jack Curtis, "Winter Makes Disk Debut," *Arizona Republic*, June 8, 1958, section 3, 11.
[50] "Cha-Cha is saving the Bands," *Picturegoer*, November 29, 1958, 15

a terrific dance item."[51] *Queen of the Hop* reached #9 in the US Charts, and #24 in the UK.

April 24, 1958: Single Session

After the *Splish Splash* session, Bobby was unconvinced that ATCO would renew his contract. In order to give himself some insurance, he went back into the studio under his own steam, and recorded some more songs including *Early in the Morning* that got sold to Brunswick. The Brunswick label released the song under the pseudonym "The Ding-Dongs" shortly after ATCO issued *Splish Splash*, although with the writers listed as Darin and Woody Harris, it is hard to imagine that many were fooled by the artist credit. With Bobby's contract renewed at ATCO, the song was bought back and released by them under another pseudonym: this time, "The Rinky-Dinks" (presumably the head of the "pseudonym-choosing department" at both Brunswick and ATCO was on holiday at the time). In early July, however, the pseudonyms became pointless, as *Cash Box* takes up the story:

> This past Saturday (19), however, it became nationally known. Darin starred on the Dick Clark Saturday night show via the ABC-TV network emanating from Miami. Bobby sang *Splish Splash*, and Dick presented him with a gold record to celebrate the shipment of the 1,000,000[th] record of the smash. Then Clark announced that Bobby would sing his own brand new follow-up hit to *Splish Splash*, a tune called *Early in the Morning*.[52]

Following the TV appearance, the record was referred to as "Bobby Darin and the Rinky-Dinks." The convoluted history of the recording, and the fact that Brunswick released a cover version by Buddy Holly at the same time probably accounted for it only reaching #24 in the U.S. charts.

Early in the Morning is certainly the best recording that Bobby made during this session, and one of the best over the course of the next three sessions as well. Despite having some limited chart success with this song and *Plain Jane*, recorded some eight months later, Bobby clearly was having problems replicating the success of *Splish Splash* and *Queen of the Hop*, as well as the quality of the recordings that had taken place in January. *Early in the Morning* didn't seem to have a completely natural feel either, but it was considerably better than the three other tunes Bobby recorded on April 28. While the story behind the release of the song resulted in column inches in the trade

---

[51] "Record Reviews," *Cash Box*, September 20, 1958, 16.
[52] "Darin Gets Billing On Rinky Dinks' Record," *Cash Box*, July 26, 1958, 49.

press, the song itself did not. *Cash Box* were most enthusiastic, saying that "the vocal crew comes up with an exciting spiritual-like item that could well be bound for future chart recognition. All concerned, lead voice, the remaining vocalists, and instrumentalists take the opus in terrific rock 'n' roll stride. A socko session worth careful watching."[53]

Early in the Morning was coupled on single by *Now We're One*, which has a half-hearted feel to it, and none of the energy of what had come directly before, although it might have been better with less obtrusive backing vocals. There is also something rather awkward about the end of the bridge in which Bobby sings "la la la la la la" in order to link bank into the next verse. He sounds almost embarrassed to be doing so, and it is one of his most unconvincing rock 'n' roll numbers.

Mighty Mighty Man, isn't a great deal better, sounding like a parody of an Elvis recording such as *Got a Lot of Livin' to Do*, with Darin adopting some of Elvis's mannerisms and making light of them. The flip-side, *You're Mine*, finds Bobby back using the vocal tone that can be heard throughout the 1957 sessions, which is much lighter than he had utilised since then. Inoffensive they may have been, but these two sides were steps *backwards*, not forward, artistically and the single failed to chart, despite a rather delightful advertisement in *Billboard* with the *Mighty Mighty Man* of the title depicted as a caveman (above right). The magazine referred to the song as a "catchy side with a danceable beat."[54] *Variety* also easily managed to contain their excitement by referring to it as "the kind of noise that the kids usually go for," although they seemed to like *You're Mine* better, stating that it had "all the rocking ballad ingredients that the juke set turn into a quick click."[55] There was still some confusion over who the Rinky Dinks were when this single was released in the autumn of 1958, with *Cash Box* telling readers:

> With the Rinky Dinks, [Darin] clicked singing *Early in the Morning*.

---

[53] "Record Reviews," *Cash Box*, June 14, 1958, 12

[54] "The Billboard Spotlight Winners of the Week," *Billboard*, October 6, 1958, 51.

[55] Mike Gross, "Jocks, Jukes and Disks," *Variety*, October 8, 1958, 52.

> Now again with the Rinky Dinks, Darin hands in two smash sides. He has a powerful rocker in *Mighty Might Man (sic)*, a Presleyesque effort that drives. *You're Mine* is a pretty rock-a-ballad loaded with potential. Both could make it big.[56]

*

Just after this recording session, Bobby began performing on television with much greater regularity. In fact, the sheer volume of his appearances over the next fifteen years is staggering. Bobby is known to have performed on around 200 different TV episodes during this period, *not* counting his own TV series in 1972 and 1973, but the actual number could be higher given that we have little record of local television appearance during the late 1950s.

On May 31, 1958 he appeared for the first time on *The Dick Clark Saturday Night Beechnut Show*, and went back on the show a further eight times (nine times if you include the archive footage of his performances used in the final episode in 1960). *Billboard* wrote of his first performance on the Dick Clark show that "Bobby Darin, a poised chanter with a definite charm, [...] socked over *Splish Splash*. [...] Best bets for in-person futures: Darin and the Coasters."[57]

In July, Bobby appeared on *The Buddy Deane Show* in Baltimore – the TV show which was the inspiration for the film and musical *Hairspray* after it was taken off air in 1964 by the broadcaster which refused to integrate black and white dancers. In August, Darin was a guest on *The Bob Crosby Show*. Bobby would soon become one of the most dependable guests on American variety, music, and game shows.

Darin was also fast becoming a must-see live performer and was quickly being noticed not just for his singing but also for his songwriting abilities. Reporting that he had been signed up to appear at the Bridgeport Festival Ballyhoo Show, a local newspaper reminded readers that "several of his songs performed by other artists are making their appearances on current best seller lists. One of these songs, *School is Over*, has been recorded by the Jaye Sisters and at least three other recording groups."[58]

July 1958 saw the release of Bobby Darin's first LP, imaginatively titled *Bobby Darin*. The album contained a mix of previously-released single sides and material from the vaults dating back nearly a year. The record was a distinctly average effort, not least because some inferior tracks were included such as *Pretty Betty*, while the likes of *All the Way Home* were left to gather dust. Even so, the reviews were largely positive. *Variety* suggested that the album was "a natural for the juve buyer. [Darin's] got a rhythm drive that is right in the current market groove and he knows how to give

---

[56] "Record Reviews," *Cash Box*, October 11, 1958, 10.
[57] Bernstein, "Reviewed in Brief," *Billboard*, June 9, 1958, 7.
[58] "Rock 'n' Roll Acts are signed for Festival Ballyhoo Show, *Bridgeport Post*, June 20, 1958, 12.

the oldies a twist that will appeal to his teenage fans."[59] *Cash Box* were similarly enthusiastic, stating that "whether making a soft-beat (*Wear My Ring*) or rhythmic (*Pretty Betty*) vocal case, Darin is there with utmost rock 'n' roll authority."[60]

July 16, 1958: Studio Session

The release of Bobby's first album meant that more recordings were now needed for future single release, but, as it happened, only one song from this session ended up on a single.

I Want You With Me had all the right ingredients to be a hit, tuning in to the rock 'n' roll records of the day without sounding as if it was simply copying them, and featuring a raucous, high-energy vocal from Bobby himself. However, it falls down thanks to its arrangement, with the number never quite taking off. The backing vocals are intrusive and clumsy with their "Bu-zack dum" phrase at the beginning of each line of the verses, and the beat of the song seems lumbering. It would take Elvis Presley to realise the song's full potential, giving a blistering, stripped-down performance on his *Something for Everybody* album in 1961.

Lost Love is something else entirely, and became the flip-side to *Queen of the Hop*, although, as mentioned earlier, it was originally regarded as the A-side. If the previous song sounded cluttered, here Bobby takes away all instrumentation except for the bare essentials and gives a lovely, subtle performance of this unusual ballad that, in many ways, pre-empts the type of singing that can be heard on a song like *Fay-O* from the *Earthy!* album, recorded in 1962. The result is quite beautiful, and was another early hint to listeners that there was more to Bobby Darin than just rock 'n' roll.

The song also attracted much attention in the trade press. In their "Ramblings" column, *Cash Box* referred to the song as "a wow!...*Lost Love* is a gentle folk type lovely the deejays will devour."[61] The song was singled out for praise in the publication's review, calling it a "fragile, touching folk-flavored ballad that's just beautiful."[62] *Variety* viewed it as a "pretty ballad [that] gets a sensitive folk-styled rendition by this talented young singer-cleffer."[63] In the UK, *Picturegoer* declared *Lost Love* to be both "reflective" and "charming."[64] Perhaps it was inevitable that the more commercial *Queen of the Hop* would be the side that DJs and the public picked up on, but *Lost Love* remains a hidden treasure in the Darin legacy that deserves to be much better known.

---

[59] "Album Reviews," *Variety*, August 13, 1958, 46.
[60] "Album Reviews," *Cash Box*, August 9, 1958, 34.
[61] "Ramblings," *Cash Box*, September 20, 1958, 50.
[62] "Record Reviews," *Cash Box*, September 20, 1957, 16.
[63] Herm Schoenfeld, "Jocks, Jukes and Disks," *Variety*, September 17, 1958, 66.
[64] "Cha-Cha is Saving the Bands," *Picturegoer*, September 29, 1958, 15.

Sadly, the remaining two songs of the session were not up to the same standard. *Pity Miss Kitty*, by Woody Harris (who also wrote *I Want You With Me*), is yet another song based around a girl's name – by the end of the year Darin would also have told the world that he wasn't sharin' Sharon and all about *Plain Jane*. *Pity Miss Kitty* is about as original as it sounds, even referring to, among other things, *Johnny B. Goode*, just as *Splish Splash* referred to other songs from the period. The recording doesn't help much, having a peculiar, rasping sound to it, and the song ended up as filler on an album of leftovers, *For Teenagers Only*, released in 1960.

Keep a Walkin' should have been much better, especially when one realises that it came from the writing team of Neil Sedaka and Howard Greenfield. Jeff Bleiel wrote in his 1993 book about Darin that the "track rocked far harder than the duo's songs recorded by Sedaka himself."[65] I'm not sure that is true, especially if you compare it to Sedaka's Jerry Lee Lewis-like romp through *I Go Ape*, with part of the problem being, once again, the muddy sound quality, the fussy arrangement, and the song not being up to the standard to which Sedaka and Greenfield normally wrote even at this relatively early stage in their career.

During August of 1958, Bobby played a series of record hops and shows aimed at teenage audiences, before joining the "fall edition" of *The Biggest Show of Stars of '58* in October of the same year. This was a touring rock 'n' roll show which saw him performing on the same bill as Buddy Holly, The Coasters, Clyde McPhatter, Frankie Avalon, Dion and the Belmonts, and Little Anthony and the Imperials. On most posters for the tour, Bobby's name was prominent, and in fourth or fifth billing thanks to the sizeable success of *Splish Splash* a few months earlier.

The tour was a series of one-nighters, with two shows a night in most cities, and Bobby's time on the tour saw him cover seventeen cities in seventeen days.[66] He must have been exhilarated at being part of such a package of talent, especially as just six months earlier he was facing the prospect of being dropped by his record label, but such a schedule must have been exhausting to someone with his health problems. Reviews of the tour are not plentiful, but *Variety* commented that the package "did okay" when it visited Pittsburgh on October 21st, noting that the first show was filled to "almost capacity," but that the second was only half full.[67]

---

[65] Jeff Bleiel, *That's All: Bobby Darin on Record, Stage & Screen*, (Ann Arbor: Popular Culture, Ink, 1993), 17.

[66] The exact itinerary is not known, but Darin certainly appeared from October 3rd to 19th without a night off, and he is also known to have performed with the package on October 21st. Whether he stayed with the tour beyond this date is unknown at this time.

[67] "R&B Show 14G in Pitt," *Variety*, October 22, 1958, 62.

This French EP from 1961 featured songs from January and October 1958.

October 29 or 30, 1958: Studio Session

This session from the end of October 1958 is particularly interesting not so much because of the results, but because of the songs Bobby chose to record and the arrangements that were used. Gone was the rock 'n' roll sound of the previous few sessions, replaced with sweeping orchestral arrangements, complete with a chorus. Three of the four songs were not rock 'n' roll songs either, but standards, including one, *Here I'll Stay*, co-written by Kurt Weill, composer of *Mack the Knife*. If the previous two sessions had seen him treading water artistically, here Bobby was trying something new which was clearly a precursor to the *That's All* album which he would start recording less than two months later.

Here I'll Stay is a big ballad from the now-forgotten musical *Love Life*, co-written by Alan Jay Lerner and Kurt Weill. The song is important not only because it finds Darin singing a song from the composer of *Mack the Knife* but also because it finds him making his first foray into singing show tunes in the studio (he may have already been doing so on stage), a source of material which would play a prominent part during the rest of his career. Despite the big arrangement with full orchestra, there is still a prominent beat here, meaning that the track doesn't quite veer out of pop/rock 'n' roll territory. However, Bobby's vocal is rather different, with the aggressive sound of the rock 'n' roll recordings completely eschewed in favour of a much more controlled and mature delivery and a voice considerably stronger than had been heard before on a Darin record. The result is not wholly successful, with Bobby getting somewhat lost in the arrangement, but that does not mean it is not pleasurable. What is key here is that, as in the pre-*Splish Splash* recordings, something new is being tried out and Bobby is seeking to find his way to the sound he is ultimately looking for.

A fascinating alternate take (in stereo) of *Here I'll Stay* can be found on the 2009 Collector's Choice label reissue of the *For Teenagers Only* album. While the mix leaves something to be desired, with Bobby's vocals set far back, the performance he gives on this alternate is rather different to the well-known take. If the master sees him sitting somewhere between rock 'n' roll and pop, here he is firmly in the territory of the ballads of the *That's All* album – in fact, one could be forgiven for thinking this take was recorded during the sessions for Bobby's sophomore LP. It is intriguing how he could sound so different within two takes of the same song recorded on the same day.

That Lucky Old Sun was a 1949 psuedo-spiritual/work song that had already been recorded by singers as diverse as Frank Sinatra, Frankie Laine and Louis Armstrong. Darin's arrangement is very much along the same lines as the previous song. Once again, his voice is not yet quite strong enough to pull it off with such a big arrangement, but he gives it his best shot and the recording deserves to be better known than it is. Sadly, however, the performance appears to contain a rather clumsy splice after the first run-through of the bridge section, with Bobby's final note seemingly cut off before it reaches its natural conclusion.

Also recorded at this session was a version of *Some of these Days*, which remains unreleased. This would be a fascinating recording to hear considering a different arrangement of the song would make it to Bobby's first album of standards just a matter of weeks later.

The final song, *A Picture No Artist Could Paint* isn't a standard and certainly has more of a contemporary feel than the other two songs released from this session. The song is written by Aaron Schroeder, who wrote *Good Luck Charm* and *It's Now or Never* for Elvis, but once again Bobby sings this in a more controlled, subtle way than before. It is the least memorable of these recordings, and has something of an under-developed feel to it, being a big ballad running just a shade over two minutes.

December 5, 1958: Studio Session

This session was the last before Bobby started work on the *That's All* album, and there is a feeling here that he is often just going through the motions and simply fulfilling contractual obligations rather than really wanting to be recording this kind of material.

Plain Jane became a modest hit, just breaking in to the top 40 in the U.S., but once again there is a second-hand feel to it. It is yet another song, this time by Doc Pomus and Mort Shuman, built around a girl's name and the lyrics are a slightly more demeaning rock 'n' roll take on *My Funny Valentine*. Whereas the girl in that song has a "figure less than Greek" and a "mouth a little weak," Jane's mouth is "a little too wide," her nose "a wee bit long," and her "shape seems all wrong." The fact that she if referred to as a "plain Jane" instead of a "funny Valentine" also adds to the feeling that the number sits rather awkwardly within today's politically correct society. What elevates the recording is the cracking arrangement, the fact that Bobby seems to be having a ball, and a brilliant saxophone solo by Jesse Powell. In February 1959, *Cash Box* reported that *Plain Jane* would be released in stereo on single as well as in mono, a first for ATCO.[68]

The other songs from the session were not nearly as good. *While I'm Gone*, a Darin original, is a bland and undistinguished ballad that can't make up its mind whether it is a country or rock 'n' roll number. Bobby tries his best to inject some form of class into it, but doesn't quite manage it and the number is over just as it is about to get going. It is unsurprising that ATCO passed over the song when putting together the various LPs aimed at Bobby's younger fans over the next few years.

Hush, Somebody's Calling My Name is loosely based on a spiritual but it is by-the-numbers rock 'n' roll, and both the arrangement and performance seem uninspired and unconvincing.

I Ain't Sharin' Sharon has a better arrangement with Bobby trading phrases with Jesse Powell on saxophone, but the song itself is below par. Even so, ATCO used the song on two different albums within a space of fifteen months (*For Teenagers Only* and *Twist with Bobby Darin*).

One more song was recorded or, at least, attempted. A complete take of *Didn't it Feel Good* has never been released, and all we have are four incomplete takes that appeared on a grey market release. Once again, Bobby seems to have trouble getting the number to take off, and ends the fourth take by declaring "balls!," giving more than a hint that his patience was wearing thin and that he really had little interest in recording the song in the first place.

Bobby had toured with rock 'n' roll packages during 1958 but, by the end of the year, he was beginning to get noticed on the night-club circuit as well. December 1958 saw positive reviews for his performances at Town and Country in Brooklyn. *Variety* declared that "he seems to know where he's heading, has the ability to roll with particular tastes as well as particular audiences, and has an ingratiating manner."[69] They go on to describe Bobby as a "singer with considerable savvy, [who] also indicates that he knows the score musically."

The *Billboard* review gives us an insight into the range of material he was including in his act even at this early stage: *Splish Splash, There's a Rainbow 'Round My Shoulder*,

---

[68] "Atco Stereo Singles," *Cash Box*, February 28, 1959, 46.
[69] Jose, "New Acts," *Variety*, December 10, 1958, 67.

Some of these Days, Mack the Knife, One for my Baby and *Swing Low Sweet Chariot*.[70] Al DiOrio adds *Queen of the Hop, Blue Monday, Hallelujah I Love Her So* and *Where is the One* to this list.[71] In later years, Bobby would use *One for my Baby* as the number around which he built his impersonations act, but there is no mention here of him doing the same, so he may well have been singing it "straight" at this point.

Bobby wanted to widen his repertoire in the recording studio as well, and had already made a tentative stab during the October 30, 1958, recording session. He was pressing ATCO to let him make a complete album of standards with full big-band and orchestral arrangements. Eventually they gave in, and over the course of three sessions in December 1958, he got his own way. In an edition published two days before the first session, *Variety* had stated that whether Darin could "repeat the consistent success of that other youngster, Paul Anka, is still to be proved."[72] In the dozen numbers he cut for the *That's All* LP over the next few days, he proved it beyond doubt.

It was also in December 1958 that Darin started using his fame as a way of voicing his own views about politics and society. It would be another few years before he got heavily involved in political causes, but that didn't stop Bobby from telling an interviewer that:

> the kids of today…are the result of the war years, and that's when the split family came into being. Before the war, America was a country of families. But today, mothers are working, fathers are working – and the children are misunderstood. The movies and TV make us out to be either switch-blade guys or else we're riding around in hot rods cut down from Jaguars.[73]

December 19, 22 and 24, 1958: Studio Sessions
That's All LP

The *That's All* album was recorded over three sessions during December 1958. While it might not be Bobby's very best album vocally, it remains the one that most defines him as a singer and was undoubtedly the record that made the establishment sit up and take notice. It remains a classic.

The album opens with the now instantly-familiar vamp to *Mack the Knife*, the number which would, within a matter of months, become Bobby's signature song and

---

[70] Paul Ackerman, "Darin Packs Rep Savvy on Floor," *Billboard*, December 1, 1958, 10.

[71] Al DiOrio, *Bobby Darin. The Incredible Story of an Amazing Life*, (Philadelphia: Running Press, 2004), 62.

[72] Herm Schoenfeld, "1958: Look Back in Hunger," *Variety*, December 17, 1958, 53.

[73] Dick Kleiner, "One Name, Two Girls: Quandry," *Kokomo Tribune*, December 28, 1958, 15.

Japanese single of "Mack the Knife."

remain so until the end of his life. The song had been written for *The Threepenny Opera*, a German musical drama by Kurt Weill and Bertolt Brecht which premiered in Berlin in 1928 and catapulted Lotte Lenya to stardom. The English lyrics were by Marc Blitzstein and were a loose adaptation of the German, and Louis Armstrong namechecked Lenya in the verse containing the list of Mack's victims during his 1956 studio recording (a rather dubious honour for her, one could argue), and she has remained there in most recordings since, including Bobby's. The song wasn't new to Darin when he entered the studio to record it, as he had been singing it as part of his act for at least a number of months by this point, and maybe longer. Part of the key to the track's longevity is the arrangement by Richard Wess, starting off quietly and building with each successive verse until Bobby warns us to "look out old Mackie is back" at the very end.

This was the first time that Bobby confronted the subject of death in the studio. Recurring bouts of rheumatic fever as a child had left him with a weakened heart, and Darin was well aware that he hadn't been expected to live beyond his teenage years. Artistically, this ticking time bomb was part of what drove him to try and accomplish everything so quickly, and to try so many different genres of music and conquer them within a couple of albums before moving on to do something else. He knew deep down that he didn't have time to structure his career in any other way if he was to accomplish everything he wanted.

While Bobby may have often come across to some as care-free, brash and cocky as a performer, there was also this inescapable motif of death running through a number of his recordings and, in many of these, Bobby appeared to be laughing in the face of it. *Mack the Knife* was the first example, but it would be followed by *Clementine*, the story of an over-weight young girl who falls into the river and can't be saved from drowning. Then there was *Artificial Flowers* about a child who freezes to death after her parents die. It is a tragic story, but not in the hands of Bobby who takes the solemn ballad from the musical *Tenderloin* and turns it into a swing classic. *Goodbye Charlie* is a light-hearted romp concerned with a murder. *Gyp the Cat* is a pastiche of *Mack the Knife* about another murdering criminal.

There were also more serious efforts on the subject. *When Their Mama is Gone* from *Earthy!* is a beautifully sung folk song about the death of a child's mother. From his late 1960s "protest" phase, *Long Line Rider* details the true story of a series of murders on a prison farm, while *In Memoriam* is about the death and funeral of Robert Kennedy. On his TV series in 1973, Bobby covered Gilbert O'Sullivan's *Alone Again Naturally*, in which the singer is contemplating suicide and talks of the death of his parents. These are the key examples, but there are casual references in other numbers too, such as *Minnie the Moocher* who is "pushing up daisies," and *Hard Hearted Hannah* pouring "water on a drownin' man." The list goes on.

With *Mack the Knife* came the inevitable comparisons to Sinatra, and they remain to this day, but they are unfounded, not least because the arrangement of *Mack* and the rest of the album is quite unlike anything Sinatra ever recorded. Darin might have been using a big band sound, and he might have been singing standards, but the styles of the two singers in these surroundings are very different to each other.

Sinatra infused his swing records with a jazz element, and was also a master of conveying the deepest, often darkest, elements of the lyric. His breath control, and how he used it, is legendary. Bobby Darin didn't approach this music in the same way. The orchestration might have had the big band sound, but his vocal often brought *rock 'n' roll* phrasing, not jazz, to the music. Here we don't find the technical brilliance of Sinatra, but something else entirely. The singing is less precise, and the lines of the lyrics are broken up (and Darin's diction is not anywhere near as clear as Sinatra's). Bobby was creating something all his own, not copying Sinatra. As Darin told *Down Beat* in May 1960, "It is Sinatra as a person more than Sinatra as a singer that has influenced me. His outlook on the business and his attitude to performance are the important things. My approach to singing is not the same. Sinatra has a clipped speech. I'm a slurrer."[74] The differences between the two singers are illuminated not just within *Mack the Knife*, but through the whole of the *That's All* album.

---

[74] Gene Lees, "Bobby Darin and the Turn from Junk Music," *Down Beat*, May 12, 1960, 20.

Beyond the Sea would become another classic, and while *Mack the Knife* conjures up images of crime, murder and death, *Beyond the Sea* has become synonymous with romance – and this despite the raucous drum solos that punctuate the instrumental section. Once again, this was a perfect fusion of arrangement, lyrics and vocal that should never have worked, so disparate are these various elements, and yet everything comes together beautifully. Darin would continue to sing the song in concert on TV through the 1970s, even performing an extended version during the taping of the final episode of his 1973 TV series.[75]

That's All is an album programmed as if it were a night-club performance, with a couple of upbeat rhythm numbers at the start and then alternating between ballads and fast numbers throughout the rest of the album until we come to the frantic finale of *That's All* itself, which Bobby would use as a closing number in his live appearances.

Bearing this in mind, *Through a Long and Sleepless Night*, the third track, is perfectly placed. The song comes from a 1949 film entitled *Come to the Stable* (dir. Henry Koster) which starred Loretta Young and Celeste Holm and which garnered seven Oscar nominations, but today is almost forgotten. The arrangement here is completely different to the brash big band sounds of the previous two numbers, and Bobby puts in a performance that utilises the softer, more controlled, part of his range. Perhaps it is a little sentimental, and perhaps the vocal is somewhat affected, but perhaps that is also what makes this album so striking: it *isn't* perfect, and it *isn't* produced with clinical precision in a way a Sinatra recording might be. There is a rawness here, both within the singing itself and the feeling that what we are hearing is untrained, raw talent. Even the sound quality isn't clean and crisp.

Softly as in a Morning Sunrise is taken from a 1920s operetta called *The New Moon*. The treatment it receives here is raucous and brash, both in the arrangement and the singing, and it is clear that the whole point is that it is going against how the song was originally conceived and normally performed (particularly within a vocal arrangement).

There is a possibility that Bobby got this idea from the 1954 Hollywood biopic of the song's composer, Sigmund Romberg. In *Deep in my Heart* (dir. Stanley Donen), Romberg, played by José Ferrer, attends a show in which the song is being performed and is mortified at the up-tempo, crass arrangement of his beloved composition. There is more than just this casual link between the two performances. For example, towards the end of the song, Bobby changes the lyrics in exactly the same way as they are in the film sequence by repeating words: "Softly, softly, as in an evening sunset, sunset." But he goes yet further, breaking the "fourth wall" and talking to arranger/conductor Richard Wess, telling him "the title of this tune is *Softly*, so can we do it that way please?" He then proceeds to sing it louder than ever. It is a brash and cocky move,

---

[75] The song was edited out of that final episode, but edited down and inserted into an the episode three weeks earlier.

totally breaking with convention, and yet it is another thing which separates him from Sinatra, who would never do such a thing.

Sinatra *did* come close, however, on the rarely heard song *Ya Better Stop*, recorded in 1954, in which he shouts as the song starts to fade: "Oh here now, this ain't gonna be another of those fade-away records. Get your grimy hand off that dial, man!" The chief difference here is that Sinatra waits until the song is over before his interjection, whereas Darin is making out that he has almost no regard for the song itself in the way it was originally intended. That, no doubt, was not the case, but Romberg was probably turning in his grave despite the fact that Bobby had just exposed his relatively obscure song to a new generation. *Ya Better Stop* remained unreleased until 1978, nearly twenty years after Bobby's recording of *Softly as in a Morning Sunrise*. Bobby would return to the score of *The New Moon* in 1965, when he recorded *Lover, Come Back to Me*.

She Needs Me finds Bobby back in the same territory as *Through a Long and Sleepless Night*. Here, though, the performance seems more natural and the arrangement has a *film noir* feel about it, and with good reason, coming from a 1955 film, *Pete Kelly's Blues* (dir. Jack Webb), in which it was sung by Peggy Lee under the title *He Needs Me*. As with the rest of the ballads on the album, though, it's not a highlight nor one of the songs that is most remembered after the record has ended.

It Ain't Necessarily So, which closes out the first side of the LP, has quite a different

Bobby in the studio with Ahmet Ertegun, photographed by William Claxton.

feel again. Bobby takes the song from *Porgy and Bess*, edits out some of the less-commercial elements, and transforms it into a number with a smoky, night-club vibe to it. The instrumentation is stripped down, almost bare, compared to the rest of the album, although the arrangement grows with each verse. As with *Mack the Knife*, there are also a number of key changes, but there is no big finish here and the song never really moves away from the night-club atmosphere.

The second side of the album open with *I'll Remember April* and, once again, Bobby seemed to be going out of his way to record a song in a way that it had not been tackled before. This song, introduced in (of all things) a 1942 Abbott and Costello film, *Ride 'em Cowboy* (dir. Arthur Lubin), was normally sung as a ballad, but Darin gives it an aggressive, swinging workout. It doesn't quite come off on this occasion. *I'll Remember April* had been recorded in upbeat versions before, most notably by jazz trumpeter Chet Baker in 1955, but a "West Coast" instrumental jazz quartet is a very different beast to this big band arrangement by Richard Wess, and the melody is just a little too fragile to cope with the onslaught.

The next song proved that Bobby's songwriting abilities went far beyond novelty rock 'n' roll. In fact, many would never have assumed that *That's the Way Love Is* was an original as it fits right in with the established standards on the album. It is also worth noting that no co-writer is credited with this song, unlike the previous self-penned efforts that Bobby had recorded. The number is a brilliant vehicle for Darin's vocal style as well, allowing for rock 'n' roll phrasing once again within a big band setting. Even allowing for the fact it appears to take its cue from the Sinatra song *The Tender Trap*, it is a classy track and one of the best of Bobby's compositions.

The next song, *Was There a Call For Me*, was also an original, this time written by Marty Holmes and Bobby's sometimes-collaborator Woody Harris. This returns us to the sound of *film noir*, but ultimately isn't such an accomplished song or performance as the previous number, although the string-heavy arrangement and Darin's vocal work well.

Some of these Days is a *tour-de-force*, with Bobby resurrecting a song written back in 1910 and most associated with Sophie Tucker. This orchestration became a template that Darin would use again through the years, perhaps most notably for *Lazy River*. It is a perfect vehicle for his talents, gaining more and more momentum as the song progresses, and ending with a bluesy, almost bump-and-grind finish. Bobby would include the song in his 1960 live album, *Darin at the Copa*, as well as on several TV appearances.

Where is the One is the only song on the album that Sinatra had got to first, having recorded the number twice by the time Bobby recorded it. However, the fact that only one of the dozen tracks here had been recorded by Sinatra suggests that Bobby was going out of his way to avoid comparisons before they even began. As with the other ballads, this is less memorable then the upbeat tracks. In fact, it would take

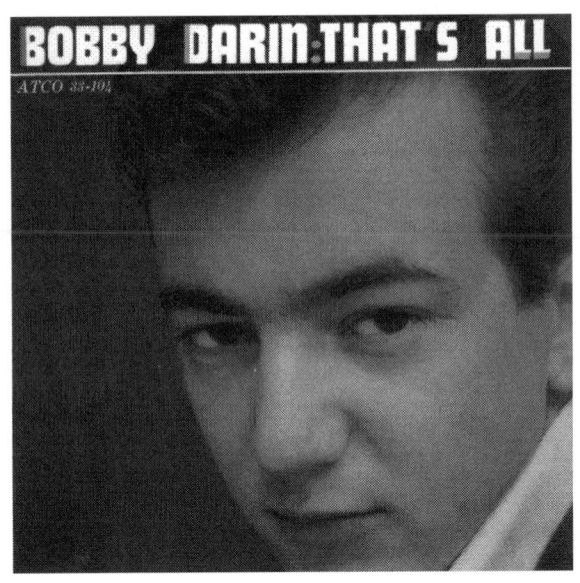

U. S. album cover

Bobby a couple more albums of standards before he mastered the art of ballad singing in this style.

As mentioned earlier, the album is programmed so as to reflect a night-club performance, and ends with the appropriately-titled *That's All*. Once again, Bobby takes a ballad and performs it as an upbeat number, this time taking the song at a frantic pace and featuring an expanded percussion section within the orchestra. It is a masterful ending to the album, and the arrangement is in a style most associated with Sammy Davis Jr, with obvious comparisons to Davis's version of *That Old Black Magic*. Bobby would end his stage performances with the song on many occasions through the years.

That's All was an album that came out of nowhere, but perhaps ATCO were aware that they had something special on their hands, hosting an event at the Plaza Hotel in New York to launch the album.[76] When it was released in March 1959, the reviews were almost uniformly good. *Billboard* told readers that "with this package young Darin proves himself to be one of the brightest talents in a long while."[77] *TV Radio Mirror* declared that "Bobby Darin proves his versatility" in the album, and that "he's headed in the direction of Sinatra."[78] *Cash Box* told readers that Darin is "given a legit singing opportunity and he comes through in pro style."[79] *Variety* remarked that the album shows "up his vocal versatility and should do a lot in helping his career."[80]

---

[76] "Bobby Darin: That's All," *Cash Box*, March 21, 1959, 43.
[77] "The Billboard Spotlight Winners of the Week," *Billboard*, March 16, 1959, 31.
[78] "And all that Jazz," *TV Radio Mirror*, May 1959, 10.
[79] "Album Reviews," *Cash Box*, March 21, 1959, 50
[80] "Album Reviews," *Variety*, March 25, 1959, 56.

Eventually, the decision was made to release *Mack the Knife* as a single and this, once again, brought Darin much attention. *Billboard* underestimated the impact of the track when they simply said that it was "sung smartly."[81] Meanwhile, in an extraordinary article by Joe Csida in *Sponsor* magazine, the writer waxed lyrical about Bobby and his achievements, describing him as "vastly talented," and, on *Mack the Knife*, commented that "Sinatra would have been proud to have recorded this one."[82] *Cash Box* said that the single showed that Darin was a talent that "had arrived," and that he does a "slick and distinctive swing job" on the song.[83] Two months later, the front cover of the publication was given over to Bobby, using the photograph that would soon grace the *This is Darin* album. In the UK, the *Daily Express* announced that "there is no denying the hit-parade-type brilliance in the music. Darin puts it over with a swinging shades-of-Sinatra style. Watch it climb."[84]

A few months later, Bobby walked away with two Grammy awards for his efforts.

The album didn't just bring praise for Darin himself, but also for arranger Richard Wess who, after the release of the album, had become "in demand by a number of diskeries," according to *Cash Box*.[85] It is worth taking a little time out here to take a look at the career of Wess, who, aside from his work on *That's All* and *This is Darin*, is largely a forgotten figure among the fine arrangers of the 1950s and 1960s, and sadly very little is known about him.

Most of what we know about Wess comes from a handful of short articles from newspapers and trade magazines. For example, an obituary in *Cash Box* tells us that he was born in New York "and graduated from the Greenwich School of Music. He studied under Elmer Bernstein and was considered an accomplished musician in his craft."[86] Such key arrangements as *Mack the Knife* for Bobby Darin and *I've Gotta Be Me* for Sammy Davis Jr are highlighted in the article, as are his composing duties for TV series such as *Bewitched*, *Hazel*, and *Farmer's Daughter*, and orchestrations for films such as *The Appaloosa* starring Marlon Brando.

In 1957, over a year before he helped catapult Bobby's version of *Mack the Knife* into the charts, he recorded an album under his own name which attempted to frame him as a jazz pianist, having made his debut as a pianist at Town Hall at the age of twelve.[87] *Billboard* described him as a "smart, tho somewhat restrained pianist," while

---

[81] "Spotlight Winners of the Week," *Billboard*, August 10, 1959, 41,
[82] Joe Csida, "Sponsor Backstage," *Sponsor*, September 5, 1959, 13.
[83] "Record Review," *Cash Box*, August 22, 1959, 8.
[84] Peter Evans, "Disc Verdicts," *Daily Express*, September 18. 1959. 16.
[85] "Wess Arrangements Bring Trade Laudits," *Cash Box*, October 10, 1959.
[86] "Richard Wess Dies at 43," *Cash Box*, March 31, 1973, 128.
[87] Ted Green, "Main Street," *Radio-Television Daily*, October 19, 1964, 4.

highlighting some of the better-known names playing on the album, such as Al Cohn, Mundell Lowe, Tony Mottola and Johnny Smith.[88]

We don't know exactly when Richard Wess and Bobby Darin first met, but the instant connection between the two men is palpable throughout the *That's All* and *This is Darin* LPs. What seems odd is that Darin didn't use Wess again for a studio album until 1964's *From Hello Dolly to Goodbye Charlie*, although he was utilised in sessions for single sides such as *I'll Be There*, *Moment of Love*, and *You Know How*.

There is a hint of a rift between Darin and Wess in 1961, following a substantial article in the *Saturday Evening Post* which centred on an interview with Bobby in which it was implied that Bobby himself had written the arrangements that Wess was actually responsible for. "I listen to classical music," Bobby is quoted as saying. "What I did was to take [*Mack the Knife*] out of Dixieland by changing key six times. The arrangement is *my* arrangement. Ella Fitzgerald does *my* arrangement."[89] The comments, if accurate, were hardly Bobby's finest hour. He may well have been referring to "my arrangements" as ones that he was *using* rather than ones he had *written*, but writer Edward Linn cemented the notion of Darin-as-arranger, stating that "his arrangements, like his songwriting, are done mentally for, like so many popular composers, he neither reads nor writes music. His songs are recorded on tape or acetate, and his arrangements are done in collaboration with trained musicians." No mention was made of Richard Wess or any other arranger. According to an article the following week, Wess was "furious" over the Darin article and was "upset at being 'fluffed off completely' in the article, because he claims he did 57 of the arrangements that made Bobby a star."[90]

During his period of separation from Darin (for whatever reason, and we obviously should not take a gossip column at its word), Richard Wess remained in demand as an arranger for the likes of Ruth Brown, Chris Connor, Caterina Valente and Aretha Franklin. In 1962, he cut another album under his own name, *Mack the Knife and Other Big Band Hits*. The following year, he became the resident conductor on TV's *The Jerry Lester Show*.

In 1964, he and Darin reunited for the *From Hello Dolly to Goodbye Charlie* album but, as good as it was, Wess's arrangements didn't have the same raw energy as their first recordings together. Many tracks on the album sounded as much like Billy May as Richard Wess. Both Bobby and Wess had become more professional, more refined, by this point and the playfulness of something like *Softly as in a Morning Sunrise* is missing, and the same can be said for the arrangements Wess contributed to *The Shadow of Your Smile* and *Venice Blue* LPs. Darin and Wess seemed to be happy working together again, though, and Bobby signed him up in an exclusive contract as composer, arranger

---

[88] "Reviews and Ratings of New Jazz Albums," *Billboard*, April 6, 1957, 27.
[89] Edward Linn, "Little Singer With a Big Ego," *Saturday Evening Post*, May 6, 1961, 59.
[90] Dorothy Kilgallen, "Wess Is Riled," *The Ottawa Journal*, May 21, 1961, 55.

and artist with his own T. M. Music in October 1964. The pair wrote the score for the film *That Funny Feeling* together. It appears that Bobby and Richard Wess didn't work together again after the *Shadow of Your Smile* LP, released in 1966, although a number of recordings with Wess arrangements from the period remain unreleased, and are rumoured to be lost.

Over the next couple of years, Wess appears to have lowered his workload, and has less credits than up to this point. He re-emerged in 1968, with a number of arrangements for Sammy Davis Jr, spread over a couple of albums and singles. In 1969, it was reported that he was "redirecting his time from arranging music for other people to finding new talent and arranging and recording them. He is also looking to break into motion picture scoring."[91] The following year, he produced, composed and arranged an album entitled *Percussion Ltd*, which featured four percussionists on thirty-eight instruments. In 1971, Wess wrote and arranged the music for the film *The Ballad of Billy Blue*.

At this point, the Richard Wess trail stops until his death in 1973 aged 43, less than a year before Bobby Darin. He was unmarried and survived by his parents and a brother. When the great arrangers of the Great American Songbook are discussed, we generally think of Nelson Riddle, Gordon Jenkins, Alex Stordahl, and Billy May, perhaps because of their association with Frank Sinatra and the likes of Nat 'King' Cole and Dean Martin. But Wess deserves a mention, too. His work might not have been as consistent or as prolific, but his best arrangements easily stand alongside anything written by the other gentlemen on that list.

Through the years, it has been reported that there was a surprise at Bobby's move into an album of standards. However, it might not have been as surprising as we have been led to believe, as there was a trend around this time for young rock 'n' roll and pop singers to either include songs from the Great American Songbook on their albums or to create entire albums built around that repertoire. For example, Pat Boone released an album of songs by Irving Berlin in orchestral arrangements in 1957. Meanwhile, Paul Anka released *My Heart Sings* as a single in January 1958 and released an album of the same name later in the year that contained a number of standards, although not necessarily in big band/orchestral arrangements. Just a few months after *That's All*, Frankie Avalon released his *Swingin' on a Rainbow* LP. Interestingly, in all of these cases, the album in question was their sophomore effort – just as it was with Bobby. Meanwhile, Ricky Nelson often included rock 'n' roll-lite versions of standards in his albums from 1960 onwards, and Neil Sedaka released an album of big band and orchestral arrangements of standards, *Circulate*, in 1961 (again, this was his second

---

[91] "Arranger Wess Arranging Own Production Firm," *Billboard*, April 26, 1969, 3.

album). The main differences between Bobby's album and those of most (but not all) of his contemporaries were that *That's All* wasn't just a one-off dalliance with the style and, more importantly, it was a very good, authentic-sounding album – which can't be said for some of those I have just mentioned.

That's All was the turning point in Bobby's career. In the months after *Splish Splash*, he had struggled to come up with another hit record and material of the same quality. After *That's All*, that was not the case. It was the first in a remarkable succession of albums that continued until almost the end of his career. They might not have always set the charts alight, but they were nearly always artistically successful or, at the very least, artistically interesting. From this point on, Bobby would rarely try to repeat previous successes. His albums of standards were always different from each other either in repertoire, instrumentation or concept. Likewise, his albums of folk, country, pop or social commentary material would never cover exactly the same territory as each other.   There would be commercial and artistic failures as well as successes, but the failures came about through a constant ambition and drive to try new things, and rarely through a lack of commitment or interest on Darin's part. *That's All* might be Bobby's best-remembered album, but it was only the beginning.

Signing autographs for fans

CHAPTER THREE
THIS IS DARIN: 1959

By the beginning of 1959, Bobby Darin's career momentum was steadily building - and *That's All* was still to be released. *TV Radio Mirror* ran a four-page story on "The Splish Splash Boy" in its January 1959 issue. "I would make any personal sacrifice to make good," he is quoted as saying in the magazine. "I don't say I think I will or I've got to. I *will*. I want the Academy Award and the Tony and the Emmy. I will be a singer, actor, musical-comedy writer and a serious composer. It's my ambition to succeed at whatever I choose."[92]

In the same article, Bobby talks about the importance of his mother. "Mom has been both father and mother to me," he said. "She is gifted with one of the greatest virtues in the world, understanding. [...] Mom would let me go ahead with anything I wanted to try, and she's been there when I was knocked down. But that's all. I always picked myself up."[93]

Just a few weeks after the publication of the interview, Polly, Bobby's mother, died of a stroke. The various biographies of Darin have different stories of how he found out the news. *Dream Lovers*, written by Bobby's son, Dodd Darin, states that he received the news of the stroke while in the recording studio.[94] Al DiOrio goes one step further and tells us that Bobby was recording *Through a Long and Sleepless Night* at the time.[95] However, that recording had taken place on December 22, 1958 and not February 10, 1959. David Evanier, meanwhile, tells us that Bobby was in Los Angeles

---

[92] Gregory Merwin, "The Splish Splash Boy," *TV Radio Mirror*, 75.
[93] Ibid.
[94] Dodd Darin, *Dream Lovers: The Magnificent Shattered Lives of Bobby Darin and Sandra Dee*, (New York: Warner, 1994), 114.
[95] Al DiOrio, *Bobby Darin*, 70.

watching Jerry Lewis perform, which seems more likely as there is no record of a February 1959 recording session.[96] However, where Bobby was and what he was doing at the time is relatively unimportant. He had lost one of the true constants in his life. Nearly ten years later, Bobby's life would again be shattered when he discovered that Polly, who he believed to have been his mother, was actually his grandmother, and that the woman he believed to have been his sister, Nina, was his real mother.

Aside from personal tragedy, the first half of 1959 saw Bobby's career really take off. In a single week in January he appeared on TV on both Dick Clark's show and a new programme hosted by arranger and composer Buddy Bregman called *Buddy Bregman's Music Shop*. The series was a flop, but Bobby's appearance was not, with him being viewed as "strong support" by *Billboard*.[97]

January 31, 1959: Live Recordings

In late January 1959, Bobby made a rare trip to Australia as part of a rock 'n' roll package. His set in Newcastle, Australia (or, at least, part of it) appeared in 1992 on a "grey market" CD (that's "bootleg" to you and me) called *From Sea to Sea*. It gives us a rare chance to hear him perform on stage in rock 'n' roll mode, before songs such as *Mack the Knife* became a constant in his act whether he was working in nightclubs or as part of a show aimed at teenagers such as this one.

When Bobby takes to the stage, he comments on the heat: "Did anyone take advantage of the 105 degrees today?" he asks the audience. "Did you? Then you know how my back feels!" His delivery is droll, and the jokes don't go down a storm, but once he starts singing he sounds like a different person.

Splish Splash is given a blistering rendition that is only really let down by a rather messy saxophone solo in the first instrumental break. *Early in the Morning* is introduced as having

"From Sea to Sea," the bootleg album that contained the 1959 Australia recordings.

---

[96] David Evanier, *Roman Candle: The Life of Bobby Darin*, (Emmaus: Rodale, 2004), 75.
[97] June Bundy, "Bregman Needs Poise and Polish," *Billboard*, January 19, 1958, 22.

been a bigger hit in Australia than in the U.S. However, the live version doesn't really work particularly well, mostly because Bobby seems to be trying to include some of his night-club patter and asides in a performance not aimed at that audience. The same is true of the dialogue spoken between the songs, which receives very little reaction. *Queen of the Hop* finds Darin back on firmer territory, and while it doesn't match the studio rendition, the performance is still solid. *Plain Jane* is arguably better than its studio counterpart, despite another wayward saxophone solo. Here the night-club spiel comes in for better use, with him getting the audience to sing the chorus with him, even going through the old "girls only" and then "boys only" routine. Such stuff was old hat even in 1959, and yet Bobby makes it sound fresh and fun.

These live recordings are in surprisingly good sound considering their source and unofficial nature, and the rest of the CD is filled with the soundtrack of Bobby's 1967 BBC TV special (recorded in November 1966). The Australian recording isn't exactly classic Darin, but it is interesting to hear, and quite unique given that it is the only recording we have of Bobby's part in a touring package such as this.

March 5, 1959: Studio Session

Less than a month after the tragic events outlined at the beginning of this chapter, Bobby was back in the studio to record one of his best and most fondly-remembered singles.

It would not be an exaggeration to suggest that *Dream Lover* is the best rock 'n' roll love song ever recorded. It is a Darin original that has become a classic, and within it Bobby managed to create a recording that would appeal to both teenagers and his newly-found adult audience. A few weeks earlier, he had recorded a bare bones demo of the song which was first released in 1995. However, for the commercial recording, Bobby changed things a great deal. Not only did he have the rock 'n' roll rhythm section, but he also added strings to it as well as a backing chorus. The arrangement is flawless, as is the vocal. *Billboard*'s rather bland review simply told readers that the song was "a medium rhythm side that is chanted strongly over fine ork support."[98] *Cash Box* didn't seem to know quite what to make of the crossover appeal of the song, stating that it "is an enticing middle-beat ballad stint with a contagious guitar sound."[99] The song became Bobby's biggest single to date, and climbed all the way to #2 in the charts. In the UK, the song was #1 for four weeks in the summer of 1959.

The flip-side of *Dream Lover* was just as good. *Bullmoose* is described by Jeff Bleiel as "perhaps the greatest rock 'n' roll record Darin ever made."[100] Few would argue

---

[98] "The Billboard Spotlight Winners of the Week," *Billboard*, April 6, 1959, 78.
[99] "Record Reviews," *Cash Box*, April 11, 1959, 10.
[100] Bleiel, *That's All*, 23.

Japanese reissue of "Dream Lover" from 1968.

with that summation, other than the use of the word "perhaps." Bobby never sounded better singing straight-ahead rock 'n' roll. *Splish Splash* might be the rocker that he is remembered for, but *Bullmoose* blows it out of the water (excuse the pun). This is a frantic rock 'n' roll party number, helped along by Neil Sedaka's wonderful piano playing and Bobby's playful vocal. *Cash Box* picked up on this, calling the song a "zany romper about an exciting rock 'n' roller and features a great honky-tonk keyboard bit."[101] The main downside was that this was not held back to be used as the next A-side, as it was wasted as the flip to *Dream Lover,* which would have performed just as well with a lesser reverse side, especially as interest in the single was helped along by the release of *That's All* the month before.

May 19-21 and September 3, 1959: Studio Sessions
This is Darin **LP**

After *That's All* had been in record stores for around six weeks, Bobby and arranger Richard Wess went back into the studio to record a follow-up. This timing suggests that Bobby was planning the second album of standards even before the first was released.

As with *That's All*, twelve songs were recorded over three nights to complete the album. However, something clearly didn't quite go according to plan. Four songs from these sessions went unissued and did not appear on the album in any form. In

---

[101] "Record Reviews," *Cash Box*, April 11, 1959, 10.

1976, one of them, *A Sunday Kind of Love* was released on an obscure compilation of Bobby's ATCO sides, but has never appeared on another release since. The three other titles (*The Breeze and I*, *Since My Love Has Gone*, and *The Lamp is Low*) have never seen the light of day, and the tapes may well have been destroyed in a fire in 1978. Quite why they were not used on the LP is unknown, although it was not unusual for Bobby to plan an album, record it, and then return with different songs or arrangements to get it how he wanted it. Whatever the reason, four months later, Bobby went back in the studio to record four different tunes in order to complete the album.

The album opens with *Clementine*, a song credited to Woody Harris but which is actually based on an old folk song. This is essentially a musical sequel to *Mack the Knife*, with the same type of beat underpinning the song which again modulates with each verse. Also present are the hups, eeks and other noises that were present on the earlier recording. However, there are some differences here, and they continue throughout the album. Most noticeable is the cleaner and crisper sound quality compared to that heard on *That's All*. Whether this was intentional or not is unclear, but it results in an album that is not quite as raw as its predecessor. Bobby's vocal is also more controlled. Anyone listening to this song as the LP begins would be forgiven for thinking this was simply *That's All Part Two*, but it is actually a far more sophisticated, polished and refined record.

An alternate take of the song can be found on the 1961 compilation album *The Bobby Darin Story*. This earlier take, presumably issued by accident, features a vocal which contains less mannerisms than the final version – there are far less "eeks" and yelps here. Also, the lyrics are a little more "refined," with Clementine being "sweet" in the first verse instead of "chubby." Some of the live performances from the period also use a slightly different arrangement.

In 2018, *Clementine* is a rather problematic recording – a fine arrangement and performance, but one which is less than politically correct to say the least, as Bobby sings with glee about the titular character being so large that she breaks a footbridge and drowns. "Hey, I'm no swimmer," Bobby sings, "but were she slimmer, I might have saved that Clementine." Despite this, it is still often found on compilations of Bobby's hits, although less often on multi-artist discs of swing or big band recordings.

As with *Mack the Knife*, the single release of *Clementine* occurred a couple of months after the release of the LP itself. *Variety* stated that the song "gets the drive and excitement that'll bring this folk classic to the top of the spinning heap."[102] *Billboard* declared that "Darin swings thru another fine rendition of an oldie that should mean another click. He shows a fine performance, and the side should take off quickly."[103] *Cash Box* were also enthusiastic, talking of how "the tantalizing story 'bout chubby

---

[102] Mike Gross, "Jocks, Jukes and Disks," *Variety*, March 16, 1960, 54.
[103] "Spotlight Winners of the Week," *Billboard*, March 14, 1960, 37.

Clementine has already been burning up the deejay turntables…It also spotlights another great assist from the ork conducted by Richard Wess."[104]

As with *That's All*, Darin seems to purposefully avoid songs associated with Sinatra, and some of the material chosen for *This is Darin* is downright obscure. *Have You Got Any Castles Baby* is a case in point. It was written by Richard A. Whiting and Johnny Mercer for the 1937 film *Varsity Show* (dir. William Keighley), a "let's put on a show" musical starring Dick Powell that is now almost forgotten. Bobby starts the number by singing the verse at a slow tempo with just piano accompaniment. He then moves into the chorus, sung as a mid-tempo swinger. This is where the album starts to deviate from the *That's All* formula. The arrangements and Bobby's vocals are far more "polite." This is not to say this is a lesser album, simply that it is different.

Don't Dream of Anybody but Me is a version of the 1957 Count Basie classic instrumental *Li'l Darlin'* with words added by Bart Howard. Oddly, the vocal version hasn't been recorded very often through the years, with the most notable renditions (beside Darin's) being Mel Tormé's 1959 recording and Ella Fitzgerald's performance that was released on her second and final album for the Reprise label, released in 1971. Bobby's version features an arrangement that has more than a hint of the Basie orchestra about it without obviously trying to mimic that sound. This is a good example of how Darin's performances improved very quickly. The ballads on *That's All* were the least convincing tracks on the album. Here, just six months later, he is handling the slower material with an ease and confidence that he had not shown before, and this slow swing number is one of the highlights of *This is Darin*.

My Gal Sal sees Bobby reaching back even further than usual within popular music history with a song written by Paul Dresser back in the early 1890s. Darin's performance is very much one of two halves, with the first run-through of the song rather weak and not really taking off. The repeat finds Bobby using his higher register and belting out the song with a vocal control not prevalent in his earlier recordings. It is not a highlight of the LP due to the weaker first half, but the second section is show-stopping stuff.

On *That's All*, Darin took the *Porgy and Bess* classic *It Ain't Necessarily So* and turned it into sultry late-night jazz. Here he gives a similar feel to *Black Coffee*, a song most associated with Peggy Lee. It is a good performance, but Bobby had yet to master the art of the torch song, and the song may well have been better recorded with just a small combo such as the one he would utilise for the album recorded in 1960 and released a few years later under the title *Winners*.

Darin's take on Duke Ellington's *Caravan* is much better, with a vocal that is remarkably playful with timing and phrasing. Sometimes there is a linking together of a relatively long phrase with one breath and, another time, lyrics are chopped up into

---

[104] "Record Reviews," *Cash Box*, March 19, 1960, 8.

just single words. Elsewhere, Darin can be found holding words back and delivering them later than the listener anticipates. It is great fun and, once again, Bobby's voice sounds stronger here than in previous sessions, particularly at the climax of the song.

The second side of the album opens with Bobby's version of the title song from *Guys and Dolls*. Here he delivers one of his most Sinatra-like performances, although it is worth remembering that it would be three years before Sinatra got a proper bite at the song himself as part of the Reprise Repertory Theater albums.[105] Darin's version is relaxed, slick, and yet masculine, and his rendition on his 1960 British TV special was one of the highlights of the show.

Down with Love continues with the straight-ahead swinging style but is less effective due to the relatively mundane arrangement that simply isn't exciting enough, particularly from the instrumental onwards. The listener expects it to move up a gear at this point, but it never happens, and Darin's version pales in comparison to exuberant renditions by the likes of Judy Garland and Barbra Streisand.

Pete Kelly's Blues is the title song of a 1955 film that had a cast which included Peggy Lee and Ella Fitzgerald in supporting roles. Bobby had already recorded *She Needs Me* from the film for *That's All*, which had also contained some songs which had a *film noir* feel about them, and this is an extension of that, with much the same kind of arrangement but a more controlled and restrained vocal from Darin himself.

Bobby with Dick Clark and Fabian

---

[105] Sinatra had also appeared in the 1955 film version of the musical, but got to sing very little, including only a few lines in the title number.

The third track of the album, *Don't Dream of Anybody but Me*, was based on a Count Basie number, and Darin channels Basie once again with *All Nite Long*. Here he sings the kind of song that Basie's vocalist of the period, Joe Williams, was famous for, and he's backed by an arrangement that swings in a Basie-like fashion as well. The orchestration for this number was by Buddy Bregman (one of two he wrote for the album). Bregman often wrote rather "square," by-the-book arrangements, but this is one of his best, and is genuinely exciting and this, combined with Bobby's great vocal (which channels more of his rock 'n' roll voice than the other numbers here), makes this a highlight of the LP that, perhaps, would have been best positioned as its finale.

The Gal that Got Away is another example of Bobby attempting a torch song and not quite hitting the mark, with him not plumbing the required depths of despair. This was, and has always remained, a song associated with Judy Garland, and both Sinatra and Sammy Davis Jr attempted versions of the number in the 1950s but neither were any more accomplished than Bobby's. Sinatra hit the mark finally in the late 1970s when he turned the number into an epic torch song medley, pairing it with Rodgers and Hart's *It Never Entered My Mind*. He recorded the medley in 1981 for his great, dark album of torch songs, *She Shot Me Down*.

I Can't Give You Anything But Love ends the album and is the second song arranged by Buddy Bregman. Here, Darin reverts to the type of vocal he used during the *That's All* album, with a slightly more aggressive sound than on the rest of *This is Darin*, with the possible exception of the wonderful *Caravan*.

Sixteen years after the release of the album, one of the discarded songs finally appeared on an obscure 3LP set called *The Original Bobby Darin*. *A Sunday Kind of Love* is a charming performance that is every bit as good as the best cuts on *This is Darin*, and why it was rejected is something of a mystery. *A Sunday Kind of Love* has never been reissued on any official Bobby Darin release, meaning it is one of the few tracks from Bobby's career to remain unavailable throughout the CD era.

That's All had been Bobby's first foray into big band swing, and had been a huge success. It was an album characterised by big, brash (often downright loud) arrangements of a dozen standards. *This is Darin*, on the other hand, was a different LP altogether, despite the two records often being spoken about as if they are very similar. *This is Darin* never hits the dizzy heights of the best tracks on

Rare photo by an audience member, March 1959

That's All, but it is a much more mature and sophisticated effort and, in many ways, the better album. On the face of it, there's not so many chances being taken here – no asides to the arranger, for example, and far less vocal mannerisms – but actually the chances are with the sometimes-obscure song choices and the risk of whether the teenaged fan base would go this one step further into maturity with him. The risks paid off, with the album reaching #6 in the album charts, and staying on the Billboard charts for 50 weeks.

In the *New York Times*, John S. Wilson raved about both Darin and the album:

> Any doubts that Mr. Darin can stand up on his own are dissipated by *This is Darin,* an excellently programmed set on which Mr. Darin's musical personality comes across in electrifying fashion. The flip, casual finger-snapping brashness which gave his *Mack the Knife* much of its vitality is present once again in the out-and-out rhythm numbers, but this time without obvious borrowings. And Mr. Darin has the ability to adapt his personality to the material, subduing the flipness when it would be out of place without sacrificing any of the strong presence that keeps his faster numbers bubbling. He has obviously learned a lot from Mr. Sinatra but the thing that distinguishes him from others who have gone to the same school is the magnetic personality he has built on this solid foundation. This is a disk that belongs with the best work of such masters of the genre as Bing Crosby and Mr. Sinatra.[106]

Cash Box, meanwhile, commented that "Darin comes up with another exciting album,"[107] while *Billboard* stated that "Dick Wess' exciting swinging backgrounds again showcase Darin's artful, stimulating vocal style on a group of nostalgic standards."[108]

By the spring of 1959, Bobby Darin was becoming hot news and the subject of various gossip columns. In *Modern Screen*, a lengthy article appeared purporting to tell of an incident that occurred when Bobby was starting out on his career. The article is introduced by saying "Bobby was getting the works! Glamour…the big time…hot music and a woman, a real woman in love with him…he thought! This was a boy's dream…A Man's Nightmare."[109] The introduction promises much, the article delivers little!

---

[106] John S. Wilson, "Showmanship in Some Pop Singers," *New York Times*, February 21, 1960, X13.
[107] "Album Reviews," *Cash Box*, February 6, 1960, 38.
[108] "Spotlight Winners of the Week," *Billboard*, February 1, 1960, 35.
[109] Paul Denis, "A Boy's Dream…A Man's Nightmare," *Modern Screen*, March 1959, 46.

Meanwhile, Bobby was everywhere. On stage, he was appearing in a range of guises – appealing to teenagers at a series of record hops and rock 'n' roll revues in March, headlining his own shows in April and July, and appearing with George Burns in Lake Tahoe and Las Vegas in May and June respectively. The reviewer for *Variety* was impressed with Bobby's turn in the Burns' show, stating that "Darin makes the stageside stroll with mike in hand for effective interpretations of *Some of These Days*, *Mack the Knife*, and his rocking *Splish Splash*. He's a personable pro at 22, and his presentation and ease are infectious."[110] The performances cemented a life-long father-son relationship between the pair.

Bobby on stage with George Burns in the background

Alongside the concert commitments, Bobby almost bombarded television with his presence, appearing on a series of local television shows during the spring and summer of 1959, mostly aimed at the teenage audience. He returned to *The Buddy Deane Show*, as well as appearing on at least two incarnations of *Juke Box Jury* for different local stations, and several "record hop" and "dance party" type of shows. In late August, he appeared on stage at the Steel Pier Music Hall in Atlantic City, with two of his performances broadcast live on the local WRCV television station. It is thought that most, if not all, of these local TV appearances are lost.

Turning to national TV shows, Bobby appeared on *The Perry Como Show* on April 18th, *Dick Clark's Saturday Night Beechnut Show* on May 2nd and August 22nd, and on May 31st, he appeared for the first time on *The Ed Sullivan Show*, returning on September 6th. In total, Bobby appeared on local or national television at least seventeen times between April and September 1959 – not bad considering he was also appearing nightly for two weeks in Lake Tahoe and four weeks in Vegas during the same period![111]

At the same time, Bobby was branching out beyond purely performing and recording. *Variety* told its readers that he was "launching a new record firm to be

---

[110] Long, "Harrah's, Lake Tahoe," *Variety*, May 13, 1959, 69.
[111] This is only including the appearances we have evidence of through local newspaper articles and TV listings. The likelihood is that the real figure is more than this.

known as Addison Records. He'll be in partnership with Joe Csida and Ed Burton, who run the Csida-Burton management firm and Trinity Music, and attorney Frank Barone."[112] It was reported in *Billboard* less than a week later that ABC-Paramount Records would act as distributor.[113] The venture saw Bobby acting as producer for young singer Jamie Coe, but the label issued only around half a dozen releases, with Darin no doubt too busy with his own commitments once *Mack the Knife* started storming up the charts.

July 22, 1959: Studio Session

This studio session took place between the initial *This is Darin* dates and the make-up session in September 1959. All four songs were written by Bobby, and find him trying to appeal to his younger, teenaged audience, with the intention, no doubt, to try to come up with a follow-up to *Dream Lover*. However, in the end, each of the four songs recorded would be released as single B-sides.

Somebody to Love is probably the best performance here, with Bobby reverting to his rock 'n' roll voice with ease. This is a fine, commercial piece of pop that is well-arranged and sung with zest by Darin. Its release as the B-side of the swing number *Artificial Flowers* is something of a mystery as the two songs are hardly a match for each other, unless Bobby was trying to appeal to both his teenage and adult audiences. *Cash Box* remarked that the song was "a rockin' teen-styled thumper with the chorus adding a gospel feel,"[114] *Variety* noted it had "the familiar Darin drive,"[115] and *Billboard* said that the song "returns artist to his old rock and roll groove on a catchy rocker."[116]

I'll Be There is one of Bobby's best compositions, and is very much in the same vein as the earlier *Dream Lover*. Despite this, the finished recording simply isn't a match for the earlier hit. Part of the blame here lies in Darin's vocal which is just a little *too* earnest in its delivery. The orchestration is also somewhat heavy-handed. As with *Somebody to Love*, the track would end up being released as a B-side, this time to *Won't You Come Home Bill Bailey*, a jazz number. A release strategy pairing two disparate items on a single made little sense. *Cash Box* viewed the song as a "pretty affectionate with a Latinish backdrop *(sic)*."[117] *I'll Be There* would still become a substantial hit, however, but it would happen six years later in the hands of British band Gerry and the

---

[112] "Bobby Darin Organizes Diskery But Continues To Cut For Atco Label," *Variety*, June 17, 1959, 39.
[113] "ABC-Par Gets Darin Label," *Billboard*, June 22, 1959, 3.
[114] "Record Reviews," *Cash Box*, September 17, 1960, 8.
[115] Mike Gross, "Jocks, Jukes and Disks," *Variety*, September 21, 1960, 34.
[116] "Reviews of the Week's Singles," *Billboard*, September 12, 1960, 39.
[117] "Record Reviews," *Cash Box*, May 21, 1960, 12.

Pacemakers. Their single reached #15 in the UK, #14 in the USA, #9 in Australia, and #1 in Canada. In 1969, during his famous sessions at American Studios in Memphis, Elvis Presley also recorded a fine version of the song which ended up being wasted on a budget LP the following year.

Moment of Love is a strange amalgam of styles, which finds Darin trying to merge rock 'n' roll with Ray Charles-style rhythm 'n' blues and the kind of orchestrated big ballads he had tried much earlier in his career. There is a good song here trying to get out, but the arrangement holds it back, particularly the rather prominent female backing vocals.

Finally, we have *You Know How* which, again, has more than a hint of Ray Charles about it. This time, however, the material itself wasn't as good, and the track was held back for two years before it appeared as the flip-side of *Baby Face*.

Bobby Darin spent the rest of 1959 either on stage or on TV. He appeared on TV as the host of *The Big Beat* just over a week before the above sessions, and then appeared on *The Ed Sullivan Show* for the second time in September, with his numbers including a medley of gospel songs made up of *Swing Low Sweet Chariot*, *Lonesome Road* and *When the Saints Go Marchin' In*. By this point, critics and writers were finding it difficult to pigeonhole Darin. One article promoting his appearance on *The Ed Sullivan Show* referred to the twenty-three-year-old as an "adult teenager because he sings in nightclubs as well as for the rock 'n' roll set."[118] Just prior to his September *Ed Sullivan Show* appearance, Bobby gave an interview stating that "I'll always be grateful to Mr. Sullivan because he allowed me to do *Mack the Knife* instead of a rock 'n' roll number. Permitting me to reach the adult audience, just as I do in night clubs, which is very important to me."[119] Bobby went on to say that "television is the great common denominator...Many rock and roll singers who rely on electronic gimmicks to sell their records are lost on television where movement, personality and stage presence are as important as the 'sound.'"

A couple of weeks later, he was a guest on *An Evening with Jimmy Durante*, although the show was hardly a critical success, with Jack Gould of the *New York Times* noting that "it is always nice to have Mr. Durante around, but his show reflected a puzzling trait of vaudeville specials. So much talent on hand but so little thought on how to use it."[120] *Variety* were not much more enthusiastic, referring to it as "an hour of mixed blessings."[121] By the end of the year, Bobby had also appeared on a Louis Jourdan special, a George Burns special, and had been the subject of *This is Your Life*. Perhaps

---

[118] "Bobby Darin – Adult Teenager," *San Antonio Light*, September 6, 1959, 4E.
[119] "Sullivan gave Bobby Darin Chance to 'Reach Adults,'" *Galveston Daily News*, August 30, 1959, 18.
[120] Jack Gould, "TV: Hour with Durante," *New York Times*, September 26, 1959, 47.
[121] Rose, "An Evening with Jimmy Durante," *Variety*, September 30, 1959, 27.

Left to Right: Pete Rugulo, Jimmy McHugh, Louella Parsons, Jackie Cooper, Bobby, Judi Meredith

most notably, he had also made his acting debut in an episode of *Hennessey*.

Meanwhile, Bobby's nightclub performances continued to draw considerable attention. *Variety* wrote of his performances at The Cloister in Hollywood in August 1959 that "Darin's vocalizing lives up to his sound on wax, and his presentations on mike have a surety that belies the performer's youth."[122] Songs performed included *Mack the Knife, She Needs Me, It Ain't Necessarily So, Pete Kelly's Blues*, and *Splish Splash*. Bobby's time at The Cloister also prompted ATCO to host a party for him in order to raise his profile with west coast DJs, and an interview was taped with Johnny Magnus for use on his show.[123] In the same month, however, Bobby had to cancel his appearance at the Playboy Jazz Festival, citing a bad throat.

At the beginning of September, Bobby appeared at the Hollywood Bowl alongside Vic Damone and Anna Marie Alberghetti in a tribute to songwriter Jimmy McHugh, with the music arranged and conducted by Buddy Bregman. Bobby's solo number were *I Feel a Song Coming On, On The Sunny Side of the Street, Exactly Like You, Let's Get*

---

[122] Kafa, "The Cloister," *Variety*, August 3, 1959, 6.
[123] "Darin Opens at Cloister; Atco Fetes Trade," *Cash Box*, August 15, 1959, 35.

Lost, I Can't Give You Anything But Love, I Couldn't Sleep a Wink Last Night, and *Can't Get Out of This Mood.*[124] He also contributed to a number of duets and trios. *Variety* reported the following year that "Buddy Bregman has acquired the right to *Jimmy McHugh Night* at the Hollywood Bowl. LP features Bregman's big band, Vic Damone, Anna Marie Alberghetti, Bobby Darin."[125] Sadly, nearly sixty years later, the recordings remain unreleased. This is a shame considering how few of the songs performed here were recorded professionally by Darin.

In October 1959, Bobby was headlining the Copa room at The Sands in Las Vegas. *Billboard* wrote that he "scored a solid hit with the adult crowd, via a neatly paced package of nostalgic standards, ballads, blues and rhythm tunes. He displayed a tender, expressive way with a ballad, but his most effective moments – and by far the most original style-wise – were his swinging, hard driving, rhythm numbers."[126] In November, his return to The Cloister was covered by Louella Parsons for *Modern Screen* magazine.[127]

When performing at Sciolla's Club in Philadelphia, he broke "all existing records of the 26 year old club."[128] In December, Bobby was performing at Chez Paris in Chicago, with *Variety* commenting that "if Darin has one solid thing going for him, it's his beat. His feeling for it, no matter the tune, is the key excitement, his weapon of authority."[129]

In between club dates, Bobby was also performing for the teenage crowd, such as with his October 1959 appearance at the Brock Campus Deb Jamboree. An article promoting his appearance talked of how he had "displayed amazing polish as a performer before the television cameras, on club floors, and in theaters," before listing a series of songs he had written that had been hits for other performers.[130]

Bobby was also apparently headhunted as the possible star of a new Broadway musical. In July 1959, it was reported that "Jule Styne would like both Bobby Darin and Tommy Sands for his new musical *Saturday Night*, indicating it'll be a teenage crowdpleaser."[131] Whether Bobby would have taken on such a role given his health issues is not known, but the show never came to fruition anyway. Styne would have been performing the role of producer on this occasion, but the composer, a young Stephen Sondheim no less, pulled the show before production even got underway, and the musical would not get a complete performance until 1999.[132]

---

[124] "Hollywood Bowl Program Tonight," *Los Angeles Times*, September 5, 1959, Part III, 8.
[125] "On the Upbeat," *Variety*, August 17, 1960, 45.
[126] June Bundy, "Darin Packs Real Nitery Punch," *Billboard*, October 12, 1959, 11.
[127] Louella Parsons, "Bobby Darin's Opening," *Modern Screen*, November 1959, 21.
[128] "Darin Sets Sciolla Record," *Cash Box*, December 12, 1959, 63.
[129] Pit, "Chez Paris, Chi," *Variety*, December 9, 1959, 66.
[130] "Bobby Darin at Campus Deb Jamboree," *Bakersfield Californian*, October 1, 1959, 31.
[131] Dorothy Killgallen, "The Voice of Broadway…" *Dunkirk Evening Observer*, July 18, 1959, 6.
[132] Steve Suskin, *Broadway Yearbook 1999-2000: A Relevant and Irreverent Record*, (New York: Oxford

However, there was also a negative to all the television and stage appearances, and that was over-exposure. Hal Humphrey wrote a mean-spirited column at the end of the year, stating that "all I want for Christmas is a whole month of television without Bobby Darin…Despite all the exposure, Darin's voice has not grown on me one bit…I say, let's put young Darin on the shelf for a while. He's young and shouldn't be pushed too fast."[133] Sadly, Mr. Humphrey was unaware that Bobby Darin didn't have time to sit on a shelf.

In November 1959, Bobby came away from the Grammy awards ceremony with two gongs, and also gained two more at the Billboard Annual Record Artists Popularity Poll.[134] An edited version of the Grammy show aired on NBC, and Bobby's performance of *Mack the Knife* was declared "outstanding" by *Billboard*.[135] They went on to say it was "the highlight of the evening, and the special effects (comprising characters from *The Threepenny Opera*) that went on while Darin was singing, were superb."

Such critical as well as commercial success resulted in a number of lengthy articles about Darin appearing in magazines in January 1960. In *Screenland*, Bobby told Lee Dumont about his "escape from poverty."[136] The article is intriguing, although, as with all so-called interviews with stars appearing in vintage magazines of this type, one cannot always take for granted that the words printed are exactly the ones that came out of the interviewees mouth. Talking of his youth, Bobby says "what I wanted most of all while I was growing up in poverty [...] was – to get out of it."[137] It doesn't sound much like a Darin line although, later in the interview, he says "I'd like to see everybody experience poverty at some time or other. But I wouldn't want anyone to *stay* in it."[138] Perhaps this was another early hint of Bobby's political motivations.

Elsewhere, he appears to come out with other seemingly deep comments that sound better when first heard than when they are dissected. "I like knowing I'm a success but I don't ever want to 'feel successful,'" he says at another point.[139] It's like a quip from Oscar Wilde. Perhaps Darin is at his most sincere when he discusses his career and how he plans to keep changing styles. "It's hard to tell just what this business of being me amounts to because I keep changing all the time. [...] I'd hate to think of

---

University Press, 2001), 153.

[133] Hal Humphrey, "Bobby Darin Takes It On His Braided Cuff," *Minneapolis Star Tribune*, December 14, 1959, 43.

[134] June Bundy, "Sinatra Topper on Billboard D.J. Poll," *Billboard*, December 14, 1959, 1.

[135] "Real Highspots Mark Grammy Awards," *Billboard*, December 7, 1959, 14.

[136] Lee Dumont, "Bobby Darin's Escape from Poverty," *Screenland*, January 1960, 47.

[137] Ibid.

[138] Ibid, 48.

[139] Ibid, 59.

myself as going on being exactly the same year after year for the rest of my life.[140]

A more bemusing article from the same month can be found in *Australian's Women's Weekly* in which we're told that Bobby wrote the song *That's All* (I wonder what Alan Brandt and Bob Haymes thought of that) and, apparently, he "received immediate offers of further television work" after his appearance singing *Rock Island Line* on *Stage Show* in 1956.[141] At least fiction writers were finding employment in Australia in 1960!

While Bobby's two Grammys were certainly part of the reason for the interest in him in magazines during this period, it was also partly due to what he might or might not have said on Grammy night. The infamous quote "I hope to surpass Frank in everything he's done," supposedly said to Vernon Scott of United Press, was one from which Bobby never fully escaped, despite the fact that he repeatedly said he was misquoted.

All smiles. Left to Right: Fabian, Bobby, Keely Smith, Frankie Avalon

In the months and years to come there were reports of a feud between Sinatra and Darin, but the likelihood is that the feud was as fictitious as the quote. Darin was friends with a number of Sinatra's inner circle, including Nancy Sinatra and Sammy Davis Jr, and he appeared on *The Dean Martin Show* as well. It certainly does *not* appear that he was *person non grata*.

Sinatra paid tribute to Darin in 1984 and again in 1986 when he recorded his own versions of *Mack the Knife*, including Bobby's name in a set of special lyrics that were not only sung in the studio, but also each and every time the song was performed live for the next ten years.

Steve Blauner, Bobby's manager, told biographer David Evanier that he had arranged a meeting between the two men in the early 1960s "and they met and talked. And everything was fine."[142] This meeting may well have been as early as 1960. In an interview with Earl Wilson, Bobby says:

> It's an insult to Frank to compare him with a 24-year-old punk like

---

[140] Ibid, 59.
[141] "Bob's a Boomer," *Australian Women's Weekly*, January 20, 1960, 44.
[142] Evanier, *Roman Candle*, 89.

me. The knockers, the non-rooters, come to see me and say 'He's no Sinatra.' Thank God. I'm not old enough. Frank's been doing this work as long as I'm on this earth…I got to be an idiot not to know Frank's a genius. We even got together and he gave me some pointers. But I never saw him work but once.[143]

It is worth noting that Bobby Darin got to see him work a second time when he was at Sinatra's opening night at the Sands in Las Vegas on February 1, 1961, another suggestion that any animosity between the two men had been resolved by that point, if it ever existed in the first place.[144]

More recently, new evidence has come to light. In 2018, a set of three Frank Sinatra concerts were released under the title *Standing Room Only*. In the one from Las Vegas in 1966, Sinatra praises Darin's talent during a monologue and encourages members of the audience to catch his show while they were in town. Heard now, and with the benefit of hindsight, it is an oddly touching moment to hear Sinatra talk to positively and genuinely about Bobby's talents.

Also, a 1975 newspaper interview with Tina Sinatra finds her talking about a Bobby Darin tribute concert she was planning alongside Nancy Sinatra and Jack Haley Jr. She is quoted as saying, "nobody ever said 'goodbye Bobby,' and we knew him so well…So far my father and Milton Berle has promised to appear, and we figure we'll get the people who were produced by Bobby or discovered by Bobby."[145] This is more evidence that suggests that any feud or animosity was more fiction than fact. Unfortunately for Bobby, many of his quotes and mis-quotes came back to bite him throughout his career. Whether or not there was ever actual animosity between Darin and Sinatra is almost unimportant, as the story will always be told that there was, despite what the evidence shows – even that which literally comes from Sinatra's mouth.

Whatever the truth behind the "feud," Sinatra is a spectre-like figure, haunting the pages of *Life* magazine's January 1960 article on Darin. It was to Shana Alexander that Bobby made another of his most-repeated quotes: "I want to make it faster than anyone has ever made it before. I'd like to be the biggest thing in show business by the time I'm 25 years old."[146] The interesting thing about this article is that *Life* wouldn't have been interested at all in Bobby, except to knock him, if he had remained a mere rock 'n' roll singer. While the *Life* article gave another sign that Darin was climbing the rungs of the show business ladder, he may well have not been happy about author Shana Alexander's disdain of the music that made him famous. Talking of the period when

---

[143] Earl Wilson, "Earl Wilson's TV People," *Des Moines Register*, August 21, 1960, 3TV
[144] Army Archerd, "Just for Variety," *Variety*, February 6, 1961, 2.
[145] Nancy Anderson, "Tribute Planned to Bobby Darin," *Camden Courier-Post*, June 14, 1975, 18.
[146] Shana Alexander, "I Want To Be a Legend by 25," *Life*, January 11, 1960, 49.

Splish Splash was released, she writes that "most of show business was then under the domination of the rock 'n' rollers. Darin was able to make this deplorable situation work to his advantage. A rock 'n' roll hit could be created with such primitive musical tools as the nasal twang and jungle beat, and one hit record could make a singer famous overnight."[147]

Still, each new article on Bobby seemed to reveal just a little bit more of who he was as a person and what drove him. He is quoted here as saying:

> At the bottom of Bobby Darin, is a bewildered, confused, soul-searching, grasping artist who is desirous of truth in art – sickening as it may sound. Now you gently simmer and you lay over this bottom stratum a little bit of human being who craves social acceptance. Sprinkle with a few years of childhood environment. Add years of plain poverty and simmer some more. Add the ability to think as an individual, bake for 19 years, top it off with a very bad experience emotionally, place in oven for three and a half years more, and you've got me.[148]

From 1960 onwards, Bobby was treated differently by much of the media. He had, intentionally or not, made (or was said to have made) comments that some did not like (such as those about Sinatra, or how adults were misunderstanding teenagers), and others that could be twisted in such a way to portray him as big-headed, brash and cocky (such as wanting to be the biggest thing in showbusiness by the time he was twenty-five). To add to this, with nearly thirty known television appearances in 1959, it was likely that some of the more bitter and cynical columnists thought that he had outstayed his welcome and needed to be brought down to earth. Over the next couple of years, and on until his passing and beyond, they would do their best to make sure that happened.

---

[147] Alexander, "I Want To Be a Legend by 25," 50
[148] Ibid, 52.

Bobby in the studio, photographed by William Claxton

CHAPTER FOUR
I FOUND A NEW BABY: 1960

During the course of 1960, Bobby Darin recorded five albums as well around a dozen more tracks intended for single release. Despite his popularity, it was clear that some projects would have to remain in the vaults for the foreseeable future, and ATCO understandably chose what it thought were the more commercial albums for release. That meant that *It's You or No One* and *Winners*, recorded in January and February 1960 respectively, would not see the light of day for several years.

January 25-27, 1960: Studio Sessions
It's You or No One **LP**

It's You or No One was a move away from the template of swinging albums of standards that Bobby had created for his previous two LPs. In fact, all of his remaining albums of standards for ATCO would have a theme or a concept. *Winners* was an album backed by a small jazz combo, *Two of a Kind* was an LP of duets with Johnny Mercer, and *Love Swings* attempted to tell the story of a love affair through a dozen songs.

It's You or No One was more ambitious than all of them. Bobby came up with the concept from the choice of songs to the art work which reflected the very different moods of the two sides of the album. The first side consisted of upbeat numbers arranged by Torrie Zito, whereas the second side was a collection of morose lost-love songs arranged by Bobby Scott. Just as unusual as the concept were the orchestrations, with the swinging side making little use of the brass section, and the ballad side having more of a chamber orchestra feel, and no percussion at all. It is no surprise that, faced with a deluge of Bobby's recordings, ATCO thought that this album was uncommercial

Bobby started the year with a return to "The Ed Sullivan Show." With Connie Francis and Ed Sullivan.

– and, as brilliantly realised and performed as the LP is, they were right in seeing its limitations at retail level. Darin had been accepted as an adult swinger, but this was as much esoteric as it was adult. What's more, despite a number of great performances on individual songs, the album itself simply doesn't work.

It opens with the title song, *It's You or No One*, a song written for the movie *Romance on the High Seas* (dir. Michael Curtiz) in 1948, and first performed by Doris Day. As before, Bobby is digging deeper than the predictable titles within the Great American Songbook. The number opens with the verse to the song, in an arrangement that resembles the work of Gordon Jenkins. By this time in his career, Bobby's voice no longer bore much resemblance to that which he utilised on *That's All* just fourteen months earlier. There is a polish here, and most of the rough edges to his voice have gone. The arrangement basically uses a jazz combo with strings to augment the sound. It's a great performance, with Darin showing his growing maturity. There's none of the mannerisms we're used to; this is straight-ahead jazz singing.

The same sound continues into *I Hadn't Anyone Till You*. By the time of this album's release, Sinatra had recorded and released the definitive version of the song for his album of ballads arranged by Don Costa, *Sinatra & Strings*. Bobby's version is fine enough, but adds nothing new, and the arrangement and orchestration does little to help (especially the prominent vibraphone). The song doesn't swing with the abandon of the previous two albums, and just comes over as nothing more than bright and breezy.

Not Mine was from another film, this time *The Fleet's In* (dir. Victor Schertzinger, 1942). By this point in the album, a problem starts to arise. Each of the six songs on side one have roughly the same tempo, roughly the same orchestration, and roughly the same style of vocal. Each song is well-performed and arranged, but neither side of the LP has highs or lows, just song after song, with them becoming indistinguishable from each other. Despite the amount of planning that must have gone into the album, there is no shape to it.

I Can't Believe That You're in Love With Me manages to break the monotony a little, with a feistier arrangement that benefits from a bigger use of brass, including a fine trumpet break in the instrumental. This is much more like the arrangements and feel that buyers of Bobby's first two albums of standards had come to expect. This 1926 opus is one of the real highlights here.

I've Never Been in Love Before sees Bobby raiding the score of *Guys and Dolls* and, as with the title number on his *This is Darin* LP, he puts in a superlative performance. Again, though, this is the same tempo as what has come immediately before. Bobby's more mature vocal is the distinguishing feature here, but it's all over and done within two minutes.

All or Nothing at All, which ends the first side of the album, is also problematic, with the arrangement marred again by a prominent, and rather jarring, vibraphone part. Here, for the first time in all of his recordings of standards, he was tackling one of Sinatra's signature numbers and his performance fails to measure up. Once again, Bobby was unfortunate to have Sinatra re-recording and releasing the song between the date of this session and the time the album finally appeared.

The second side of the album suffers from many of the same problems as the first. These songs have a slower tempo, and are much moodier – a kind of mini-torch album in fact – but it just doesn't work. Instead of plumbing the depths of the soul, the results are worthy but, ultimately, dull (not a word often used to describe a Bobby Darin album). Darin's vocal performances of these ballads are better than similar material on the previous two albums, but it is the arrangements, and ultimately the concept of the record, that is the drawback here.

The obscure *Only One Little Item* isn't exactly the most melodious of songs with which to start this second side, and far outstays its welcome. Sinatra might have been able to make something out of the material with the help of a classy Nelson Riddle or Gordon Jenkins arrangement, but Bobby doesn't have the benefit of utilising the work of either of those men, and nor does he, at this stage in his career, have the experience with this kind of song to make it memorable.

Don't Get Around Much Anymore should have been a Darin classic, and probably would have been had it appeared on any other album with any other arrangement. However, it comes across here as little more than a dirge. One can only imagine this Ellington masterpiece with a swinging Billy May arrangement on an album such as *Oh!*

Look at Me Now that he would record in 1962. It is not just that the type of arrangement being employed here in general is problematic, but the songs that he has picked for the album seem incongruous as well.

Somewhat better is *How About Me*, which doesn't get bogged down so much in the rhythm-less arrangement. This is certainly the highlight of the second half of the album, with Darin putting his more "pleading" voice to good use here. There are better recordings out there (check out the one on Judy Garland's masterful *Alone* album), but on its own terms, *How About Me* is one of the more successful tracks here.

By the halfway point of the slow side of *It's You or No One*, the music becomes aural wallpaper, and each funereal number just merges into the next. *I'll Be Around*, for example, is a great song, but by this point the listener may well have drifted off, thinking about what to have for supper or the filing that they will need to catch up on when they go to work the next day.

All I Do is Cry bucks this trend somewhat, helped along by the prominent piano part, with the song sounding like a rhapsodic film theme from the 1940s. It is a beautiful number, and Bobby shows off his full vocal range. This is the second of three songs on this side of the album written by Libby Holden, about whom sadly almost nothing seems to be known beyond these three songs and her writing credits on a couple of single sides for other artists.

I Guess I'm Good for Nothing but the Blues, also by Holden, wraps up this strangest of albums. Again, a fine performance but by this point it hardly matters because, as with the first side, the songs have run in together like one long morose medley.

Each individual song here is arranged beautifully and sung with great style and vocal prowess by Darin, but it is the sequencing of the album that is the problem. ATCO, when they became intent on releasing this material, might have done better to chop it up and spread it out over a number of albums. That may sound like sacrilege considering the work that had clearly gone into structuring it and putting it together, but at least that way these performances would have been noticed. As it was, the album sank without trace, with barely even a review from the period to be found. *Cash Box* were one of the few publications to give it some attention. They talk of the album's "first-rate backing" and that it was a "sure-fire smash sales item" – comments which suggest that the album hadn't made it to the turntable in the *Cash Box* offices.[149]

There is some wonderful work here, some of Bobby's best in fact, but these songs are best heard as part of compilations rather than in the album format that Bobby envisaged. However, these issues are part of what makes Darin such an interesting artist: he was willing to take chances and try new things, even if they didn't entirely come off.

---

[149] "Album Reviews," *Cash Box*, June 13, 1963, 22.

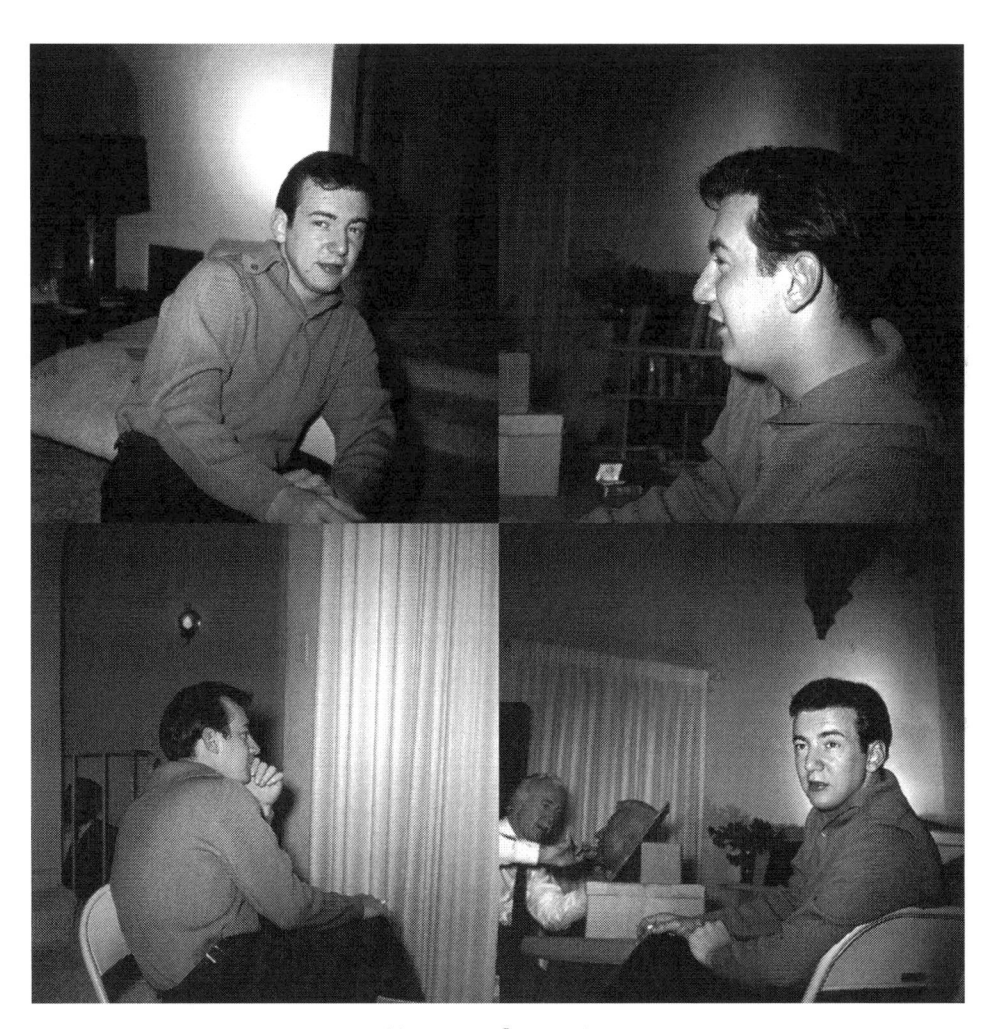

Bobby sitting for a sculpture

February 1-2, 1960: Studio Session
Winners LP

Just a few days after finishing the *It's You or No One* LP, Bobby was back in the studio to record a very different album. In just two days, Bobby recorded fifteen songs, this time backed by a small jazz combo headed by Bobby Scott. Once again, this may well have been an instance of Darin trying to distance himself from Sinatra. In 1959 and 1962, Sinatra performed concerts using just a jazz sextet as backing, but he never recorded an album in the studio with that kind of setting (which is a great loss, it should be added). Here, Bobby records what is, pure and simple, a jazz vocal album. The results are much looser than on any of his other albums of standards and, while Bobby Scott is credited as arranger, it sounds much more as if he put together some basic ideas and the musicians simply took it from there. This group of songs (released on an album and three singles) shows Darin in fine form and demonstrating his versatility in a way that *It's You or No One* ultimately failed to do.

Before discussing the recordings themselves, it is worth talking about how they were released. *Won't You Come Home Bill Bailey* was released as a single backed with *I'll Be There* in June 1960, reaching #19 in the U.S. charts. In November 1962, *I've Found a New Baby* was released as a single side. Then, in June 1964, nine more songs (plus *I've Found a New Baby*) appeared on an album called *Winners*, which was released with relatively little notice. The remainder of the album was filled by both sides of the *Milord/Golden Earrings* single which had been unearthed from the vaults two months earlier and reached #45 in the charts. The problem here is that the sound and orchestration of the single sides (recorded in June 1960 and March 1961) had nothing to do with the distinctive jazz sound of the rest of the album. Two months after the release of *Winners*, ATCO released yet another track from these February 1960 sessions, this time pairing *Swing Low Sweet Chariot* with *Similau*, an odd little number recorded in December 1960. Finally, one more track from the sessions, *Minnie the Moocher*, was paired up with *Hard Hearted Hannah* (already released on the *Winners* album) as a single in February 1965, more than five years after they were recorded. And that's not all! *A Game of Poker* and *I Got a Woman* have never been released at all. The reason for the latter may have been because the song had been released in different arrangements on two other albums by 1964, but why *A Game of Poker* never appeared is unknown.

Such a release strategy is mystifying. When *Bill Bailey* became a hit in 1960, one would think that the obvious thing to have done would have been to place it as the lead track on an album containing the other songs from the same session. For some reason, that didn't happen and, to date, these wonderful tracks have never appeared all together in one place – and yet they are a collection of songs just waiting to be rediscovered.

With its stripped-down arrangement, *Won't You Come Home, Bill Bailey* was an unlikely single release. While Darin had taken old songs and had hits with them in the past, they had always been in big, swinging arrangements, but this was something different. Still, the song manages to draw in the listener from the very beginning, with Bobby's spoken lines before the song starts proper, and that seemed to be enough for it to catch on. As with some of the other songs from the sessions, Darin interacts with the group, spurring them on as he yells "yeah, I like it like that" during the instrumental. Not only is Bobby showing off his vocal abilities here, but also his showmanship. It's a stunning record, and while it wasn't the biggest hit that Darin ever had, the fact that a pure jazz number broke into the top twenty shows just how good it is. *Billboard* magazine referred to the song as "another winning side for Bobby Darin, featuring a great vocal by the lad over smart backing by the Bobby Scott Trio."[150] *Cash Box* stated that "*Bill Bailey* is another oldie Darin makes his own."[151]

The first day of recording had begun with the aforementioned, unreleased *A Game of Poker*, a song by Harold Arlen and Johnny Mercer from their flop 1959 musical *Saratoga*, which was based on the novel *Saratoga Trunk* by Edna Ferber. The stage show starred Howard Keel and Carol Lawrence, who also feature on the original cast recording, one of the few places to find any recordings of songs from the musical. It is difficult on hearing the Howard Keel rendition just how it would have worked in a jazz setting, and the sad news is that we shall probably never find out.

The session then continued with a straightforward rendition of the Gershwin's *They All Laughed*. Despite the relatively mundane arrangement, there is some great interplay between Bobby and the musicians, with each giving the other room to breathe. There is no instrumental section, but enough space at the end of each vocal line for an instrumental fill, normally on vibraphone. The "laughs" on the record are provided by Darin's friend and father-figure George Burns.[152]

Hard Hearted Hannah, a song dating back to 1924, is even better and, as with some of the other songs here, Bobby sings the verse as well as the more familiar chorus. Once again, we can hear just how much Darin is enjoying himself here. Listen closely and you'll hear him singing off-mic during the instrumental. He revived the song a few years later with a full big-band arrangement, performing it on TV on one of his appearances on *The Andy Williams Show*. It works extremely well in this incarnation as well, and it is a shame he didn't record this arrangement at a later date.

There are few disappointing numbers here, but *Anything Goes* certainly fits into that category, despite some tasty piano licks during the first half. The song, written by Cole Porter for his 1934 musical of the same name, is just too slow, and never gets going. It's clearly an attempt at doing something different with the number, but it just

---

[150] "Spotlight Winners of the Week," *Billboard*, May 16, 1960, 41.
[151] "Record Reviews," *Cash Box*, May 21, 1960, 12.
[152] Bleiel, *That's All*, 55.

doesn't work.

What Can I Say After I Say I'm Sorry finds things moving along at a much better tempo, and Bobby gives a gently swinging performance that adds nothing new to the song, but is pleasant enough. As with *Hard Hearted Hannah*, this was a song included in the 1955 film *Pete Kelly's Blues,* bringing the number of songs from the film that Darin covered in the space of just over a year up to four, with *She Needs Me* appearing on *That's All*, and the title song recorded for *This is Darin*.

Between the Devil and the Deep Blue Sea is given a kind of Latin American rhythm before switching to a standard swing feel during the bridge section.

Perhaps the best upbeat track of the whole session is the masterful *I've Found a New Baby*, which begins with Darin's finger-snapping before the various instruments slowly join in. There is a wonderful late-night jazz feel to the whole number, and Bobby Short's piano solo is stunning, while Darin tells him to "growl on it." There is more variation in Bobby's vocal here too. He never sings at full volume and yet still manages to switch between a silky-smooth tone and one that has the rawer sound heard on the *That's All* LP.

Bobby's take on Duke Ellington's *Do Nothin' Till You Hear from Me* is at a slower tempo than usual, and also contains a mistake in the vocal – something very rare for a Darin track. On the line "If you should take the word of others you've heard," you hear that he starts to sing "anyone's dream" instead of "others you've heard," and tries to correct himself, but it is just a little too late. It is surprising he didn't decide to do another take (unless the wrong take was issued by ATCO), or maybe Bobby felt the take had the feel he was after and that won out over redoing it because of the error. Like *Anything Goes*, the song doesn't entirely work at this speed (Ella Fitzgerald also tried it at this tempo with similar results), and it would have been better to hear Bobby belting this out in a full big band arrangement.

Minnie the Moocher gets given a wonderful treatment, with Bobby in full show-stopping form. He makes the lyrics a little more palatable for early 1960s conservative audiences by removing the references to drugs, but it takes nothing away from the authenticity of the performance which comes complete with a rare example of Darin scat-singing, which he does much better here than on the later *Two of a Kind* album. By recording the song with just a jazz combo to back him, he removes the opportunity for anyone to compare it with the well-known Cab Calloway rendition, and Darin's take is a classic in its own right.[153]

Two of the ballads here are among the best vocals that Bobby ever recorded. *What a Difference a Day Made* and *Easy Living* are wonderful examples of just how much his ballad singing had progressed in the year or so that he had been recording standards in the studio. Written for a 1937 screwball comedy, *Easy Living* in particular is truly

---

[153] For the links between *Minnie the Moocher* and *Silly Willy*, see chapter one.

Publicity photo

marvellous and the smoky jazz-club-style playing behind him is a perfect framing for a perfect vocal. *What a Difference a Day Made* finds Bobby taking on a song that, the year before, had won a Grammy award for Dinah Washington. Ironically, Bobby's version of the song is more jazz-oriented than Washington's. *When Day is Done* is another ballad in the same style and with a similar vocal, but it is not quite up the standard of the aforementioned titles, with the vocal just a little too subdued. The song itself is more obscure, being of German origin with lyricist Buddy DeSylva writing English words for it during the 1920s.

The final song of the session is also the hardest to find. Bobby had been singing *Swing Low Sweet Chariot* on stage for a while in medley with *Lonesome Road* in a big band arrangement. However, here it gets a jazz workout by itself in an arrangement that is a cross between *Bill Bailey* and some of the songs he recorded for the folk album *Earthy!* He growls and rasps his way through the spiritual, and the performance is both a bizarre and masterful mixture of styles and genres. The fact that this song has seemingly not re-appeared on CD or LP since its original single release back in 1964 is a great shame, for this is a fine, intriguing recording that deserves to be much better known than it is.

Unlike *It's You or No One*, *Winners* did at least get some recognition when released, helped along by the inclusion of *Milord*, which had been a recent single release. *Billboard*, however, were rather non-committal in their review, referring to the album simply as "romantic and sentimental ballads and up-tempo swingers aimed at the sophisticated set."[154] *Cash Box* weren't excited either, stating the album was a group of "Darin-fashioned ballads and uptempo pleasers."[155] Both publications clearly missed the fact that this is one of the most essential albums that Darin ever made.

February 5, 1960: Studio Session

This session of four (maybe five) songs is something of an oddity. In a series of sessions over a ten-day period, Bobby had recorded two complete albums and a couple of songs to spare. Now, three days later, he was back in the studio again.

Tall Story has been one of the most difficult Bobby Darin songs to find during the CD age. Indeed, it is only in the last few years that it has appeared on CD at all, and only then in Europe thanks to the public domain laws. Originally released as the flip-side to *Clementine*, this jazzy swinger was recorded as the theme tune to the film of the same name, directed by Joshua Logan and starring Jane Fonda and Anthony Perkins. The song comes from quite a pedigree including jazz and classical pianist, composer and conductor Andre Previn, his wife Dory Langdon Previn, and jazz drummer Shelly Manne. Despite the fine pedigree, the song lacks a strong hook, something which draws the listener in. There is no chorus to speak of, and while the arrangement is reminiscent of Marty Paich's work with Sammy Davis Jr, it was actually by Torrie Zito.

I am also going to discuss at this point a song for which the recording date is unknown beyond the fact it was at some point in 1960. I tie *That's How It Went Alright* in here because it is composed by the same writing team as *Tall Story*, was also written for a film (in this case Darin's film debut, *Pepe*), and the arrangement is not dissimilar to the previous title. This is not to say that there is any proof it was recorded at the same session, but it is probably the best guess that we have at this stage. The *New York Times* reported that shooting for the film was underway during March 1960, and so the timing of this session would also be feasible.[156]

Pepe, directed by George Sidney, may have provided Darin with his first big screen appearance, but it was literally a five-minute sequence in a film longer than some Wagner operas – and duller than some Wagner operas. Bobby's move into films had

---

[154] "Album Reviews," *Billboard*, July 25, 1964, 50.
[155] "Album Reviews," *Cash Box*, July 25, 1964, 22.
[156] Murray Schumach, "Film Work Grinds to a Halt; Industry Gloomy as Actor Ready Walkout Tomorrow – No Contract Talks Set," *New York Times*, March 6, 1960, 79.

been announced as early as mid-1959, at which point *Billboard* had stated that he "had been signed by Paramount to a six-year pact which calls for a minimum of one picture a year."[157] *Variety* expanded on this by saying that the contract was non-exclusive, and that the "picture business' renewed interested in diskers was spotlighted earlier this year when 20th Fox grabbed Chancellor's disker, the mono-tagged Fabian."[158] *Cash Box* informed readers that Bobby's deal was "reportedly involving at least a million dollars."[159]

In *Pepe*, Darin plays himself in a nightclub scene, performing *That's How It Went All Right*, yet another song in which he sings about death/murder. Despite the macabre lyrical content, this is a better number than *Tall Story*, even if takes a while to get going. Darin's vocal is more aggressive than it had been on this type of material for some time and the performance is a showstopper. The problem was that very few people heard it. The song was released as a single, with director George Sidney narrating events on the set of the film as the flip-side. The film flopped as badly as the single, and the soundtrack album did little better, although it contains some fine performances not just by Darin but also by Judy Garland and Sammy Davis Jr, and is worth hunting down. *New York Times* could only find one saving grace in the film, and that was its star, Cantiflas. "When you are able to find him," Bosley Crowther writes, "among all the clutter and the 'names,' [it] is like coming upon a bit of delicious confection in a huge bowl of sticky-sweet goo."[160] Despite the reviews, and the issue that the film runs for three hours (about two and three quarter hours too long), it was still nominated for seven Academy Awards.

One of the oddest recordings Bobby ever made was *She's Tanfastic*, a song Darin wrote and put down on tape to help promote Tanfastic Suntan Oil. Why? Well, *Variety* states that Bobby received $150,000 for his efforts. The song was "sold to the public only through radio, newspaper and magazines plus point of purchase displays where product is sold. Darin was offered to do the actual radio commercials but nixed that part of the deal."[161] *Cash Box* stated that portions of the song would be used in radio ads for thirteen weeks during the summer of 1960.[162] The song is hardly Darin at his best, although it's a fun, summery piece of fluff, and credit needs to be given to a guy who can write a song around the word "tanfastic" and manage to come up with the necessary rhymes. The song was one of Bobby's most obscure recordings until it

---

[157] Ken Grevatt, "R & R's Cross over the Bridge to Filmland," *Billboard*, August 31, 1959, 9.
[158] "Par Pix & Lotsa Dates for Darin," *Variety*, August 12, 1959, 55.
[159] "Bobby Darin Signs Picture Deal," *Cash Box*, August 15, 1959, 45.
[160] Bosley Crowther, "Mexican Comic Stars in *Pepe* at Criterion," *New York Times*, December 22, 1960, 18.
[161] "150G for Darin in 'Tanfastic' Tiein," *Variety*, December 16, 1959, 14.
[162] "Darin Sets Premium Disk Deal for 'Tanfastic.'" *Cash Box*, December 26, 1959, 41.

appeared on the 1991 CD compilation entitled *Splish Splash: The Best of Bobby Darin, Volume One*.

The session was completed by a pair of instrumentals, *Autumn Blues* and *Beachcomber*, that were both penned by Darin and find him pushing his piano-playing to the fore. Released as a single in August 1960, these are pleasant enough but one has to wonder exactly what market they were aimed at. The big question here is: "what is the point?" *Billboard* seemed to like them, however, saying that Bobby "plays interesting boogie work on the top against solid, string backing by Shorty Rogers. Flip is equally good in a similar vein."[163]

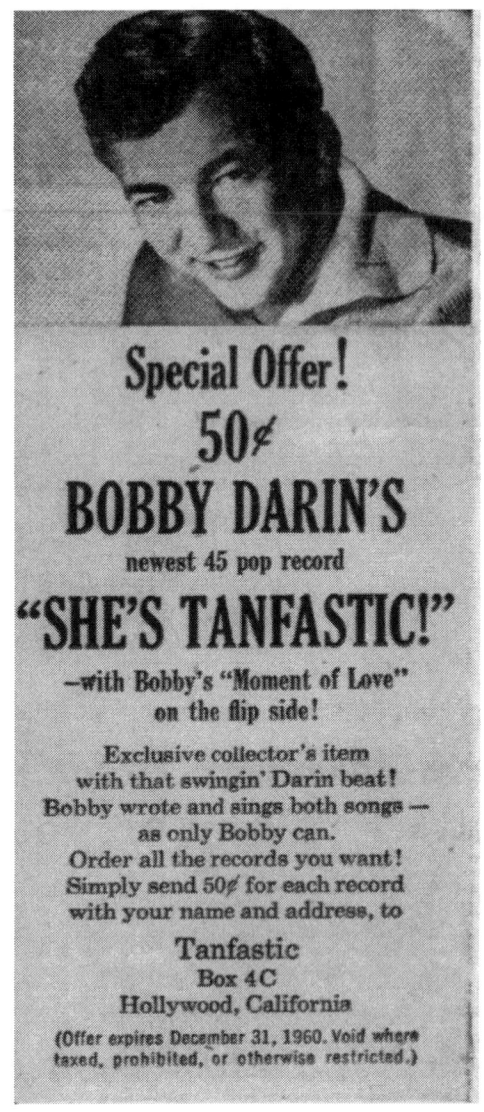

Newspaper advertisement

Since the beginning of 1960, Bobby Darin had recorded two albums and four single sides, and had a residency at the Club Casanova in Miami Beach – and all before February 5th! Meanwhile, *Cash Box* told its readers in January of a rather bizarre-sounding radio programme: "Bill Spitalsky, indy promo man was instrumental in creating a new show for airing over WNTA-Newark. Hosted by Roy Freezer, the station's librarian, the show spotlights Johnny Mathis and Bobby Darin, plus a different guest each week. It is titled (obviously) *Freezer, Mathis, Darin and Guest*."[164]

While in Pittsburgh in early January, Bobby gave an interview to local columnist George E. Pitts. In it, he takes time to praise his friend Sammy Davis Jr. "Sammy is the guy who used his influence to get me booked into some of the bigger clubs," he says.[165] "I also can say that I was definitely influenced by him. While I don't try to

---

[163] "Reviews of This Week's Singles," *Billboard*, August 15, 1960, 35.
[164] "Platter Spinner Patter," *Cash Box*, January 30, 1960, 28.
[165] George E. Pitts, "Bobby Darin Gives Credit to Sammy Davis Jr.," *Pittsburgh Courier*, January 9, 1960, 22.

copy his style, I figure he's the guy who taught me to do things I wouldn't ordinarily do." He also paid tribute to Ray Charles, saying that "he has more soul than anyone in the business. [He] is great because there is at least one outstanding quality, something that sticks with you from every record he makes." Finally, there is another indication that Bobby was becoming interested in politics and political causes, stating that "I won't play before segregated audiences. It just doesn't strike me as being right."

However, there were times when the hectic schedule took its toll.

U.S. single

Darin had withdrawn from the Playboy Jazz Festival the year before and, in February, he withdrew from a rock 'n' roll package tour of Australia organised by Lee Gordon. According to *Cash Box*, it resulted in the entire series of shows being cancelled.[166] Neil Sedaka, The Diamonds, and Bill Haley and the Comets were also due to appear. There were also plans for Bobby to have presented an awards ceremony for the Australian record industry while he was there.

Bobby was back performing before the end of the month – and in what might have been his most unusual concerts. Dave Dushoff had hired Darin the previous year to perform at his newly-built Latin Casino in Cheltenham, Philadelphia. The problem was that, by the time of the proposed shows, the Casino still wasn't finished due to a steel strike. So, Dushoff persuaded Darin to perform in his house instead, in front of his fifteen-year-old daughter and one hundred of her classmates. Bobby then did the same thing in two other homes, and for his services got the full salary he would have got at the Casino.[167]

His next venture was to perform in the UK as part of a rock 'n' roll package tour. Darin's arrival in Great Britain was much anticipated. "The fans are rarin' for Darin," wrote *Melody Maker* on February 13, before noting that "five weeks have still to go before the American big-beat package headed by Bobby Darin hits Britain."[168] The package of Darin with Clyde McPhatter and Duane Eddy was described as the "biggest

---

[166] "Australia," *Cash Box*, February 27, 1960, 47.
[167] Harry Belinger, "Bobby Darin Fufills Rare Engagement," *Mansfield News-Journal*, March 2, 1960, 22.
[168] "They're Rarin' for Darin," *Melody Maker*, February 13, 1960, 1.

capture since Bill Haley."[169] But the frenzy didn't stop there. The *Daily Mirror* ran a competition to win a "Date with Darin" in which a lucky reader (plus friend) would have tea with Bobby before watching him perform live at the London Palladium on April 10.[170] On April 16, the newspaper printed a picture of the winners, Sandra Simpson and Valerie Hutchings, both eighteen and shorthand typists, kissing Bobby following his performance at the Palladium.[171]

Not all the newspapers in the UK were treating Bobby's tour in quite such a frivolous fashion. The *Daily Express* carried an interview with a headline stating "They Call Him the Next Sinatra." It was as original an article as the headline suggests, with the interview carried out in a car as Darin was driven around London. Still, he managed to deliver some zingers: "I've been called an angry young man. Guess I got angry with some guy once."[172] However, the article also gives an indication that Bobby's time in Britain was not going as smoothly as one hoped. "That cockahoop confidence, that knack of giving the lyric a special twist that Sinatra has – they were both there," wrote Robin Douglas-Home. "But not the vocal control, the sheer musicianship, the bittersweet tones."[173] *Variety* reviewed one of the Glasgow performances, and noted that too many stars were featured in a single evening when "Darin himself, alone, would have been useful enough a marquee name for the kids."[174] Bobby's songs included *Splish Splash*, *Dream Lover*, *Clementine*, *Beyond the Sea*, and *Mack the Knife*.

Bobby had not ingratiated himself to the British audiences. David Evanier writes that "he became embroiled in controversy on opening night in Lewisham when he segued from his rock hits to a quiet rendition of *My Funny Valentine*. The rock audience jeered him, and he baited them, saying 'I thought you people lived on the other side of town.'"[175] The news of the opening night also reached America, with *Billboard* writing that "Darin had a rough passage for his first house but adapted his act, bringing his hits in earlier, for later shows to win high audience acclaim."[176] A few days into the tour, Bobby gave an interview to *Melody Maker*, saying that "I have found the British audiences the noisiest I have played to anywhere in the world – though they are the most demonstrative if they like you. That barracking at Lewisham on my first show was the most shattering thing that has happened to me as a performer. [...] When I come back to Britain next time I will insist on a concert tour for adult audiences – or

---

[169] Ibid.
[170] "A Date with Darin!" *Daily Mirror*, March 18, 1960, 13.
[171] "A Prize Date," *Daily Mirror*, April 16, 1960, 11.
[172] Robin Douglas-Home, "They Call Him the Next Sinatra," *Daily Express*, April 1, 1960, 6.
[173] Ibid.
[174] Gord, "Unit Reviews," *Variety*, March 30, 1960, 68.
[175] Evanier, *Roman Candle*, 106.
[176] "London Bow Big for Darin, Eddy, McPhatter," *Billboard*, March 28, 1960, 12.

I won't be back."[177]

Bobby's relationship with Britain didn't fully recover during the tour. When he appeared as a guest on the popular television programme *Sunday Night at the London Palladium*, Clifford Davis wrote in the *Daily Mirror*: "Between ourselves I don't go for this Mr. Darin. He has some of Johnnie Ray's qualities, but not enough. In terms of an act for television, young Mr. D. is a dead loss."[178] To be fair to the writer of that article, Bobby does seem a little reigned-in compared to some other TV guest spots of the same period, but his performance was hardly a "dead loss" and was yet another demonstration of how he could captivate an audience.

Perhaps the most significant element of Darin's time in the UK was *This is Bobby Darin*, Bobby's first one-hour TV special, with guests including Duane Eddy, Clyde McPhatter and Dorothy Squires. For this show, Darin made no concessions within his own solo numbers to the rock 'n' roll audience, mining his two albums of standards for his songs. However, he wasn't in the best of form in some sections, most notably during a surprisingly lacklustre (and sometimes off-key) rendition of *The Gal that Got Away* which, presumably, betrayed signs of wear and tear to his voice after a tiring series of concerts.[179] The musical highlight was *I'm Just a Country Boy*, a quiet folk song sung by Darin accompanied by Duane Eddy on guitar. It is a charming and sincere performance that looks forward to some of his later folk recordings. The duet with Clyde McPhatter, where Darin plays piano, is also worthy of note.

Despite the various musical highlights, however, what becomes most noticeable is that Darin wasn't quite as comfortable as the host of a show such as this as he perhaps should have been. For a man who excelled so much in front of a live audience, it appears that he never quite managed to translate this to his own television appearances when he had hosting as well singing duties. This isn't the case just for this special, but for those that

Singing "I'm Just a Country Boy" with Duane Eddy on the "This is Bobby Darin" TV special

---

[177] "Darin Slams Back at British Rock Fans," *Melody Maker*, April 2, 1960, 1 & 20.

[178] Clifford Davis, "It's a Fight Not Worth Winning," *Daily Mirror*, April 11, 1960, 26.

[179] Darin misses a number of the "big" notes during the song, but had also missed the high note at the end of *Some of these Days* on the *Sunday Night at the London Palladium* appearance as well. It could simply be that after months of near non-stop work, he and his vocal chords needed a rest.

followed in the subsequent years as well. As a guest on someone else's show, Darin blossomed and, more often than not, stole the show, but not very often when he was fronting his own. This continued right through to his own, often lacklustre, TV series during the last year of his life. There were exceptions, such as the *Sounds of the Sixties* special aired in 1969, and, most notably, his BBC TV special aired in 1967, but that was simply the filming of his live act on stage in London. It was just Bobby on stage, doing what he did so well, without having to worry about the television element or, to be more exact, connecting with the people at home as well as the people on the stage. A similar show was filmed in Australia the following year, entitled *Bobby Darin at the Silver Spade*, but this, alas, appears to be lost. This is a shame as newspaper reports suggest that the programme was a filming of Darin working in a night club and, again, should have shown him at his very best.

That said, it appears that Bobby might temporarily have lost his on-stage magic at the time of the British tour and television shows – although he is very good during the aforementioned *Sunday Night at the London Palladium* performance. On his return to America, he opened at The Cloister and, even there, the reviews were less than stellar. "Whether it was the bombastic beforehand publicity that mushroomed to heights of outer space on Bobby Darin's return to the Cloister, or just an off-night, the 23-year-old's opener Thursday wasn't as spectacular as expected," wrote *Variety*. "The weakness of his act," they go on, "lies in repetitious delivery. It's here that he loses his impact on the payees. Darin's entire repertoire is vocalled around terrific Dick Wess arrangements. But what do you do after *Mack the Knife?*"[180]

Perhaps the most cutting review of a Darin performance came in the *New York Times* following Bobby's appearance on *The George Burns Show* on June 7, 1960. "One of the songs on the program," wrote John P. Shanley, "was Mr. Darin's interpretation of the lovely Richard Rodgers-Lorenz Hart ballad, *My Funny Valentine*. Mr. Darin is a popular and well-paid young vocalist. But his distortion of this number was a painful thing. Mr. Rodgers and the estate of the late Mr. Hart are entitled to substantial damages."[181] Around the same time that the special aired, Bobby appeared on four radio programmes aired as part of a recruitment drive for the National Guard.

Elsewhere, though, Bobby's popularity didn't seem to be waning, and newspaper and magazine articles continued to appear, both talking (or, rather, speculating) about his personal life or his career (or, rather, *that* comment about Sinatra). *Modern Screen* published a lengthy article on "the love story of Bobby Darin and Jo-Ann Campbell" in April 1960. It makes out that the story comes from an interview with Darin himself, but it seems unlikely and reads more like a work of romantic fiction. "I'm sorry it had to happen this way with [Jo-Ann]," Bobby supposedly told the magazine. "I'm sorry I had to hurt her for one single minute. But what else can happen when a bitter, unhappy

---

[180] Kafa, "Cloister," *Variety*, May 2, 1960, 6.
[181] John P. Shanley, "TV: Reliving Vaudeville," *New York Times*, June 8, 1860, 79.

guy like me meets a good, sweet gal?"[182]

A rather more realistic "interview" was published in *Screenland* the following month, in which Bobby talks at length about his childhood and how he struggled to make it in the music business. "I said I'd show them," he says, "and I did. But to accomplish it, I had to do a little growing myself. I had to learn. That's what I mean by using my streak of rebellion. By using it I've found the place where I belong."[183]

In yet another interview, this time with Erskine Johnson, Darin talked about his changing musical style and his hopes for Hollywood, saying:

> A year ago I thought I had lost the kid fans, but today they're with me. They're growing up with me. I didn't change my style of singing; they just changed their style of listening. [...] I want a Jimmy-Dean type role but I want to be a personality first who acts just a little bit better than most personalities. I can wait for the right role now. I'm no longer running. I'm just walking – fast.[184]

Bobby also gives an indication that he sometimes struggled with fame, stating that "There are two Darins – the one the public sees and Walden Robert Cassotto from the Bronx…Some night I'll probably feel like hitting some newspaper fellow who has said something I don't like…I have to struggle to make Cassotto come home and smash his fist into the wall instead of into someone's face."

Perhaps Bobby's most important appearance in print during this period was the extended interview in the May 12, 1960 edition of *Down Beat* magazine. Finding himself on the front cover of the prestigious jazz magazine must have been quite a kick for Bobby. The article by Gene Lees, *Bobby Darin and the Turn from Junk Music*, is far less snobbish about Darin's rock 'n' roll roots than the title might suggest and, while it praises the singer, it's also not afraid to criticise either, noting that Bobby goes out of tune a number of times during the *This is Darin* album. Lees also discusses how his ballad singing is not as good as his up-tempo material. By the time the interview was printed, that wasn't strictly true, but nobody had yet heard the wonderful jazz combo sessions from February 1960. However, while Lees is willing to point out the faults within Darin's singing style, he's also willing to point out the thing that his competitors didn't have: "fire."[185] He then goes on to describe Darin as one of the "most stimulating and vital acts in show business today."[186] As for Bobby himself, he says he was "gassed"

---

[182] "The Bad Boy and the Good Girl," *Modern Screen*, April 1960, 78.
[183] Amy Lewis, "The Boy Who Didn't Belong," *Screenland,* May 1960, 55.
[184] Erskine Johnson, "A Two-toned Personality: That's Bobby Darin," *Ocala Star-Banner*, May 22, 1960, 13.
[185] Gene Lees, "Bobby Darin and the Turn from Junk Music," *Down Beat,* May 12, 1960, 18.
[186] Ibid.

when Sinatra was quoted as saying "I sing in saloons. Bobby Darin does my prom dates." And then he adds, "I'm only too happy to play his prom dates […] until graduation."[187]

Graduation came the following month, with Bobby's first season at the Copa. The reviews were extremely positive. *Variety* wrote:

> He is a smart and exciting performer who knows the ins and outs of brinksmanship. He knows to stop when it seems that his brashness has reached a peak…He brings an air of freshness and excitement to his efforts. His catalogue encompasses the disclicks, which form the keystone of his library, but there are ballads delivered sensitively as well. It now seems that he'll be a regular at this spot.[188]

Meanwhile, Bob Rolontz wrote in *Billboard* that "[Darin] is not only the hottest draw the club has had all season, but his personality on the floor and his ability to put over a song is exceptional for a young performer…He moves well, talks to the audience, and all in all comes thru with a magnetism that marks him as a potent newcomer to the ranks of class clubs."[189]

It was inevitable that ATCO would endeavour to capture the magic on record.

June 15-16, 1960: Live Recordings
Darin at the Copa LP

I have made the argument, above, that Bobby Darin's prowess on the night-club stage didn't necessarily transfer well to the hosting of the TV variety show format. I would also suggest that the same is somewhat true when it comes to this audio recording of his live act. This may be part of the reason why only one in-concert album was released during Bobby Darin's lifetime, with the exception of the UK-only *Something Special* LP in 1967. Since Bobby's passing, two more live albums have been released officially, as well as a handful of tracks from other dates.

It could certainly be argued that these posthumous releases surpass *Darin at the Copa*, recorded in June 1960 and released the following month. The album was a hit, reaching #9 in the U.S. album charts, and yet it doesn't quite work. Part of this is due to the relatively poor recording acoustics, and part of it is due to the sometimes ham-fisted editing on the record. But it is also true that part of it is due to Darin's live act not completely working without the visuals to go with it. That said, there are some

---

[187] Lees, "Bobby Darin and the Turn from Junk Music," 20.
[188] Jose, "Copacabana, N. Y." *Variety*, June 8, 1960, 59.
[189] Bob Rolontz, "Darin Season's Hottest Copa Draw," *Billboard*, June 13, 1960, 40.

wonderful moments during the course of the album, most noticeably on the songs that Darin didn't record studio versions of.

The medley of *Swing Low Sweet Chariot* and *Lonesome Road* with which the album starts had been in Bobby's repertoire for at least a year, and probably longer. He had also performed it on television on *The Ed Sullivan Show* and on *Sunday Night at the London Palladium*. Here it gets a slightly truncated treatment, and some of the limitations of recording in this particular venue are clear from the beginning, with the sound dry and constricted, and Darin occasionally gets lost in the mix and sings off-mic when moving around.

Some of these Days gets a workout similar (at least in arrangement) to the studio rendition, but it is also here that problems start to filter in to the album and, in particular, translating Bobby's stage performance on to record. No doubt his mid-song impressions and asides to the band were amusing and entertaining on stage, but they simply don't work well when presented with just the audio. In a strangely ironic way, the performance is actually *less* impressive because of the high level of Bobby's showmanship on stage.

Mack the Knife is taken at a faster lick than on the studio master, but is not encumbered with the various asides of the previous number. In truth, the tempo is just a touch too fast, and he would record better live versions in 1963, 1966 and 1971, but this still works better than some of the other tracks here.

Next up is a version of Cole Porter's *Love for Sale*. Nearly half of the album's fourteen tracks are numbers that Darin didn't record in the studio, which is quite a high ratio for a live album. Interestingly, it is these numbers that often get the most

Bobby on stage

committed performances, and that is certainly the case here. The arrangement is well-written and Bobby gives a strong, committed performance of a song which, at the time, was not often sung by a man. As the title suggests, the song is about a prostitute, and normally sung from her perspective, but Darin changes the lyrics slightly so that they refer to her in the third person. It is the only number from the 1930 musical *The New Yorkers* to have become part of the standard repertoire. Most of the songs were written by Cole Porter, but a handful were composed by the show's star, Jimmy Durante, with whom Bobby had appeared on TV less than a year before *Darin at the Copa* was taped.

Clementine finds Darin back in the "make as many asides as possible" frame of mind. This is a good performance, though, with some of the phrasing rather different to the studio version which makes it more than worthwhile. As with *Mack the Knife*, the tempo is quicker here than as originally heard on the *This is Darin* album.

Bobby turns once again to the Cole Porter songbook with the Academy Award-nominated *You'd Be So Nice to Come Home To*, originally written for the film *Something to Shout About* (dir. Gregory Ratoff, 1943), which didn't live up to its title. Again, this is a wonderful arrangement, starting with just the rhythm section and the rest of the band "sneaking in" as the song progresses. What's more, Darin gives an exciting performance that is perfectly executed right down to the "let's make love" remark at the very end. It is a shame that the number isn't used in compilations of Darin's work, and it certainly could have had a place in the 4CD *The Bobby Darin Collection* released in 1995.

Dream Lover which closes the first side seems out of place here, being the only pop song on the entire album. What's more, the arrangement simply doesn't work when played by what is essentially a big band. It moves the song into no-man's-land, neither pop song nor swinger (a problem that would plague many of the songs in Bobby's 1972 and 1973 TV series) and it gets a perfunctory performance at best. Jeff Bleiel notes that the song was "curiously absent from his nightclub act for years," and this issue may well be part of the reason for that.[190] The chat with the young girl in the middle of the song doesn't help matters, and may well have seemed hokey and out of date even in 1960.

Bill Bailey gets a good rendition once it actually starts. Prior to that, Bobby toys with the audience with a number of false starts of various songs over the opening vamp. Again, this might have been fun if you were there but, on record, it is tedious, especially with repeated listens. The arrangement of the song itself sees the brass joining in during the second run-through, and they sound out of place and add nothing to the song or the arrangement. A good lesson in "less is more."

There is no *schtick* during Bobby's all-too-brief rendition of *I Have Dreamed* from

---

[190] Bleiel, *That's All*, 198.

The King and I. Most of his ballad numbers on the albums of standards thus far had been quiet and subdued affairs, but here he sings something quite different. The arrangement builds to a big climax and Bobby utilises a power in his voice that he had rarely used at this time. The arrangement isn't dissimilar to that used by Frank Sinatra a couple of years later on *The Concert Sinatra* album (actually recorded in a studio despite the title), and Sinatra's remains the definitive version, but Darin holds his own here in a fine performance that is a highlight of the LP.

I Can't Give You Anything But Love is essentially the same arrangement as that on the *This is Darin* LP, but again this is a looser rendition than the studio version. This isn't as much through interaction with the audience (although there is plenty of that) but through jazzier phrasing which is reminiscent of the jazz combo recordings from earlier in the year.

There then follows a prolonged interaction with the audience which becomes very tiresome, before Darin finally launches into a rendition of *Alright, O.K., You Win* on vibraphone, switching to vocals, and then a dance routine. Considering at least three songs were cut from the LP (*Birth of the Blues*, *Splish Splash* and *My Funny Valentine*) one has to wonder why (or, rather, how) this number made the grade. No doubt it was entertaining if you were in the Copa at the time, but it makes no sense on an album. Sure, it shows off Darin's versatility, but when a significant part of the number is a dance it pretty much renders it useless on record. Any of the three cut songs would no doubt have been a better choice here.

The album gets back on track with a medley of *By Myself* and *When Your Lover Has Gone*, another number unrecorded in the studio but that had been in Bobby's nightclub act for some time. It had also been performed during an Ed Sullivan performance as well as in the UK TV special. This is a nice pairing of two standards that are given a gently swinging performance to start with before building to a great climax with the reprise of *By Myself*. Once again, Bobby seems far more committed to the material that he had not recorded elsewhere.

As the album heads towards its conclusion, Darin sits down at the piano for a rollicking rendition of *I Got a Woman*, a song that had been recorded in February but ultimately was never released. Eighteen months later, *I Got a Woman* would also be the last song of Bobby's final session for ATCO, recorded for his album-length tribute to Ray Charles. This live version is arguably better than that, and certainly less self-indulgent being some three minutes shorter than its studio counterpart. Darin appears to be more genuinely relaxed here than during the rest of the LP, and puts in a superlative, authentic performance which manages to straddle multiple genres and audience demographics in a way that the earlier version of *Dream Lover* failed to do.

The album finishes with *That's All,* which is basically used as a kind of theme tune before the orchestra plays *Mack the Knife* as Darin makes his exit.

The album performed well and the reviews were positive, but the usually enthusiastic *Billboard* noted that "some of his fans may wish he'd omitted some of the corny patter and W. C. Fields impressions" despite saying that "the sock personal magnetism and in-person drive of the young star has been fully captured in this exciting package."[191] *Cash Box* told readers that Bobby performed with "complete assurance and overdose of hipness" and that the record "will no doubt be grabbed up quickly."[192] *Variety* stated that "Darin's drive and exciting projection are heard on a potent repertory."[193] *Music Vendor* said that the album "proves [Darin] not only is a singing star but a night club showman as well."[194]

Heard today, the album doesn't totally live up to those rave reviews. As with many live albums from the period (compare it to *Sammy Davis Jr. at Town Hall*, for example), the sound quality is sometimes problematic, and the editing of the performance is obvious and sometimes amateurish. Darin himself is great for much of the album, but seems to try too hard to be something or someone he is not in other parts. The subsequent live albums that we now have available to us, recorded in 1963, 1966, and 1971, ultimately see him dispense with many of the disposable asides and a greater concentration on the music itself.

For anyone picking up *Darin at the Copa* today, the mono LP is probably the go-to version if you can find it. The stereo mix only amplifies the problems with recording live at the Copa. However, the version included in the *Original Album Series* 5CD release from 2011 may well be the best that the stereo edition has yet sounded.[195]

June 20, 1960: Studio Session

Only one song appears to have been recorded at this studio session in New York, but it is a Darin classic, albeit one that is not particularly well-known. A year earlier, Bobby had appeared on *The Ed Sullivan Show* on the same bill as Edith Piaf, and here he takes one of her signature songs and turns it into a *tour-de-force*.

Milord is one of Bobby's most infectious recordings, and there are few moments within the Darin legacy where his enjoyment of singing a particular song jumps out of every groove as much as it does here. He sings the entire number in the original French, although he changes a few words to account for the song being sung by a man

---

[191] "Reviews of this Week's LP's *(sic),*" *Billboard*, August 8, 1960, 23.
[192] "Album Reviews," *Cash Box*, August 13, 1960, 38.
[193] "Album Reviews," *Variety*, August 3, 1960, 46.
[194] "Music Vendor LP Picks of the Week," *Music Vendor*, August 8, 1960, 30.
[195] This set also includes *For Teenagers Only*, *Two of a Kind*, *Love Swings*, and *Twist with Bobby Darin*. Another set in the same series features Bobby's first album from 1958, *That's All*, *This is Darin*, *Things and Other Things*, and *Bobby Darin Sings Ray Charles*. All albums come in card sleeves recreating the original album artwork (front and back), and fit inside a slim slipcase. If you can find them (and one is out of print at the time of writing), they are a good way of getting much of Bobby's ATCO output.

1964 French EP containing "Milord" and songs from the "Winners" LP.

instead of a woman. There is a Gallic element to the orchestration thanks to the use of the accordion, but the arrangement gains momentum with each verse in typical Darin fashion, until he lets loose completely during the instrumental, singing along and clearly having a ball. The only fault, perhaps, is that it is all over in two minutes – but what a great two minutes!

Despite the wonderful singing and arrangement, ATCO clearly didn't quite know what to do with a song sung completely in French, and it languished in their vaults for four years before they released it as a single, reaching #45 in the U.S. charts during a period when Darin was having something of a lull when it came to chart success. The *Daily Mirror* in the U.K. called the release "interesting, but I can't see it tearing the charts apart."[196] Likewise, the Australian press weren't too excited either, saying "as great an entertainer as Darin is, he doesn't inject into the number the mood and feeling that Piaf did."[197]

It is hard to tell what the critics were listening to, but it certainly didn't seem to be Bobby's version of *Milord*. Find yourself a copy if you don't already have one…and play it loud!

---

[196] Patrick Doncaster, "Don't Look Now – But Here Come the Fairies," *Daily Mirror*, July 23, 1964, 17.
[197] "Following a Leader," *Teenager's Weekly*, June 10, 1964, 11.

*

One week after the recording of *Milord*, Bobby was back on television in an hour-long *Coke Time* special hosted by Pat Boone and also featuring Paul Anka and Frankie Avalon. Even now, nearly sixty years later, this remains a particularly fun hour of television with the four young men at the centre of the show easily charming the audience and demonstrating just how much talent the new kids on the block really had. *Billboard* said that Boone and Darin were the "standouts" and singled out the latter's swinging version of *All I Need is the Girl* from *Gypsy* and the duet between the two singers as highlights (despite the fact that Bobby goofs a number of times during it).[198] *Variety* also viewed the very same numbers as the "high mark" of the show.[199] However, all of the young men put in good performances, particularly when the four of them got together for an extended medley of songs from the 1940s. Even Paul Anka, who Joe Csida refers to as "loveably obnoxious" manages to be charming at the same time as he's being annoying.[200] It is a great hour of entertainment, and it is a shame that is has not been restored and remastered and officially released on DVD.

July 1960 saw Bobby back on stage, fulfilling a commitment to perform with George Burns for another season in Las Vegas. *Variety* wrote that "despite his youth, Darin shows vet savvy in his repartee with Burns, and is fast developing a song-tossing style of his own."[201] In his next record project, taped the following month, Bobby would engage in repartee with another veteran performer, this time songwriter and singer Johnny Mercer.

August 13, 14, 17 & 22, 1960: Studio Sessions
Two of a Kind LP

Bobby had started 1960 with six days in the recording studio, completing two albums and a handful of single sides. August of the same year would see him enter the studio on eight occasions, also producing two albums and some single sides. The dates included in this section were all for an album of duets with Johnny Mercer entitled *Two of a Kind*.

Johnny Mercer was a lyricist, composer and singer, as well as the co-founder of Capitol Records in 1942. Darin would sing a number of songs during his career to which Mercer had provided either the lyrics or the music or both, including *Come Rain or Come Shine, Skylark, The Days of Wine and Roses, I Wanna Be Around, Have You Got Any*

---

[198] "*Coke Time* Young Talent Field Day," *Billboard*, July 4, 1960, 31.
[199] Herm, "Swing Time," *Variety*, June 29, 1960, 45.
[200] Joe Csida, "Sponsor Backstage," *Sponsor*, July 11, 1960, 14.
[201] Duke, "Sahara, Las Vegas," *Variety*, July 20, 1960, 53.

Castles Baby, and *Moon River*.

It is fair to say that opinion on this album of duets, even amongst the most devoted of fans, is mixed. As Jeff Bleiel points out:

> [Johnny Mercer's] considerable catalog of classics was largely bypassed in favour of, as the liner notes mention, 'some of the long neglected corners of Tin Pan Alley.' But [...] the amount of humorous banter Darin and Mercer exchange calls attention to their rapport - not the songs - as the album's centrepiece.[202]

It certainly is a unique album in the Darin canon, not just because it is an LP of duets, but also in that virtually all of the songs are of a novelty nature. It is also true to say that the aforementioned banter between the two performers can either put a big smile on the face of the listener or become rather frustrating, depending on mood.

The only new song on the album is the title number which both opens and closes it. Credited to Darin and Mercer, the number is a classic, and by far the best track on the LP – not least because the full version heard at the end of the record is the only song that doesn't suffer from endless spoken banter between the two performers. The number is close in style to the better-known *Me and My Shadow* as recorded by Sinatra and Sammy Davis Jr, but it is worth remembering that *Two of a Kind* was recorded and released *prior* to that classic recording, and certainly seems to have influenced it. According to Gene Lees, *Two of a Kind* was "a song [Mercer] had written years earlier, but when Darin contributed extra lyrics, John gave him full cowriter credit."[203]

The opening version of the song is stopped in its tracks before less than a verse has been sung, giving an indication that this is an album more about personality than singing. "Humorous" spoken dialogue then leads us into a rendition of *Indiana*, with Mercer taking the first run-through and Darin taking the second. What is most remarkable here are the swinging arrangements of Billy May that go a long way to reinvigorating these old semi-worn-out musical antiquities. This is particularly true of *Indiana*, a song that had been featured prominently in the 1946 Hollywood biopic *The Jolson Story* (Alfred E. Green). The first half of the number is fun and swings like hell, but the second half is weighed down by the two singers scat-singing despite the fact they are both rather inept at the style (at least on this occasion).

Bob White, co-written by Mercer, is taken at a somewhat more relaxed tempo and vibe, although May's arrangement again becomes the star once the instrumental arrives. The number is pleasant enough, but goes on for too long and, at nearly four minutes, far outstays its welcome considering the slight material. The constant asides

---

[202] Bleiel, *That's All*, 61.
[203] Gene Lees, *Portrait of Johnny: The Life of John Herndon Mercer*, (New York: Pantheon Books, 2006), 231.

might give a sense of spontaneity in the performances, but the fact that alternate take seventeen was included on a 2017 reissue of the album would suggest that this wasn't really the case. In truth, there isn't a huge difference between the alternate and the master, other than that the asides are somewhat slicker in the master, with both men stumbling over their comments in the alternate.

Ace in the Hole, a song that dates back to around 1909, gives us the dubious pleasure of Bobby providing us with his impressions of W. C. Fields and Groucho Marx. Here the banter gets too much, and the back-and-forth between the two men becomes tiresome, especially during the second half of the number. The song was featured prominently in the 1954 film *The Naked Alibi* (dir. Jerry Hopper) where it was performed by Gloria Grahame's character — and the same scene would also be seen in *Film Stars Don't Die in Liverpool* (dir. Paul McGuigan), the 2017 movie about Grahame's final years. Darin would record a better live version of the song in 1963 in Las Vegas, although why he invested so much time in the number is something of a mystery.

East of the Rockies has none of this interaction and is better because of it being sung straight, but Darin doesn't utter a sound until nearly two minutes into the number, and one has to wonder whether those who bought the record in 1961 were really spending their cash to hear Johnny Mercer. That's not to say that I have anything against Mercer, one of the greatest of all American songwriters and an agreeable singer, but all too often the emphasis is on the wrong member of the partnership during the album. As much as Darin would have graciously denied it, his popularity was carrying Mercer here, and not the other way around.

If I Had My Druthers is another song co-written by Johnny Mercer, and had originally appeared in the musical *Li'l Abner*. Again, there is less interplay here and the

Bobby with Johnny Mercer

Billy May orchestra is once again proven to be a remarkably tight unit. What is overlooked when listening to this set of songs, though, is Darin's singing, which is probably better than it had ever been. His vocal tone is clear and crisp, and there are none of the problems with intonation that Gene Lees mentioned in the *Down Beat* article from a couple of months before.

The second side of the album opens with *I Ain't Gonna Give Nobody None of My Jellyroll*, another number where the banter gets in the way. Darin and Mercer sing this as a novelty number, but it started off its life as a double-entendre-laden song most often sung by female blues singers, and one listen to "Sweet" Emma Barnett's version, for example, tells us quite clearly that she isn't talking about cake – or anything else kept in the pantry. There is perhaps a brief acknowledgment of the songs's origins in the present recording when Darin refers to Mercer as a "dirty boy," but with the bright and breezy Billy May arrangement, and the faster tempo, the original meaning is all but lost, for better or for worse.

Lonesome Polecat is one of the more recent numbers, and another co-written by Mercer, coming from the musical *Seven Brides for Seven Brothers* (dir. Stanley Donen). Once again, though, this slight song goes on for too long, and there are some decidedly dodgy notes emerging from both singers.

My Cutey's Due at Two-to-Two Today benefits once again from Billy May's great arrangement, but suffers from there being as much talking as there is singing. By this point, the banter routine has become less tiresome and more repetitive. The alternate take on the 2017 reissue again shows that this was less improvised than the listener is led to believe.

One of the better arrangements is the medley of *Paddlin' Madelin' Home* and *Row, Row, Row* with one song providing counterpoint for the other. However, the issue here is that Bobby again feels the need to sing almost all of his part as an impersonation of other singers or film personalities. This would have worked well on stage or television, but on record it is, frankly, a bit of a bore. The number worked better a dozen years later when Bobby performed it with Flip Wilson on *The Bobby Darin Show* – with visuals it is considerably more fun.

Who Takes Care of the Caretaker's Daughter is another strange choice of material. There's nothing wrong with digging back into the early days of popular song, but some of the song choices here just seem silly, and the whole thing isn't exactly helped by Mercer wailing in a falsetto while Bobby Darin does an Elvis Presley impersonation. And there are five full verses to wade through!

The final song before the complete rendition of *Two of a Kind* is *Mississippi Mud*, one of the better tracks. There is less banter, the song is better known, and the arrangement is again one of Billy May's best.

The 2017 edition of *Two of a Kind* didn't just provide five alternate takes of the songs that made the LP, but also included two extra songs recorded for the album but not included. The first of these is *Cecilia*, about the closest the session got to a ballad. Taken at a soft-shoe tempo, it is a shame this wasn't included on the LP, as it provides a nice contrast to the other songs. Once again, though, it all falls down somewhat in the middle section as Darin and Mercer tell bad jokes to each other.

The other new song on the reissue is a rather sanatised version of *Lily of Laguna*, a song written at the end of the nineteenth century and most associated with blackface performers of the time. As with *I Ain't Gonna Give Nobody None of My Jellyroll*, Darin and Mercer manage to pull the song away completely from its original intentions. The tempo is roughly the same as *Cecilia*, but the number doesn't work as well and it is easy to see why it was cut from the original album release in 1961. *Back in Your Own Back Yard* was also recorded during these sessions but remains unreleased.

It is difficult to understand quite what audience the album was aiming at. While the presence of Johnny Mercer might well have got the more mature audience buying a Bobby Darin album for the first time, the lack of a lead-off single or almost any recognisable song titles would have put off the younger buyers – and they may well have been rather unhappy with their purchase if they did end up buying it. It is a strange concoction – a love or hate album really – which demonstrates the showmanship of the two singers, finds Darin in excellent voice, and contains some wonderful arrangements. At the same time, though, it can be extremely frustrating that Darin and Mercer simply don't let each other *sing* more. Meanwhile, the songs are less to do with the "neglected corners of Tin Pan Alley" and more to do with the Vaudeville tradition.

The liner notes state that the "performers were having a ball when they cut this one." That may be true, but whether the listener has a ball is another thing altogether. That said, the reviews at the time of release were generally positive with Mike Gross writing in *Variety*:

> Johnny Mercer, who is 27 years older than Bobby Darin, has got a vocal verve that excellently complements the youngster's piping pyrotechnics. Together they bring an unusual bounce and delightful casual flavour to a snappy disc production. The mood is jovial and bright and the sock standard repertoire has appeal for adults as well as juves.[204]

Cash Box commented that there were "shades of the two-a-day vaudeville circuit! Darin and Mercer team up for a jolly songfest in this tradition…Billy May is more than a help with his zingy arrangements, while the ad lib lines flow like water."[205]

---

[204] Mike Gross, "Album Reviews," *Variety*, March 1, 1961, 74.
[205] "Album Reviews," *Cash Box*, February 25, 1961, 30.

1960

August 18, 1960: Studio Session

This date during Bobby's mammoth series of recording sessions in August 1960 was set aside to record the A-sides of three singles, two of which would become top twenty hits in the U.S.

Artificial Flowers is the morose tale of a young girl who dies of hypothermia while trying to earn some money from making the artificial flowers of the title following the death of her parents. The song was plucked (excuse the pun) from the Broadway musical *Tenderloin* in which the song is sung as a faux-morality tale. Darin, however, takes the sombre little number and gives it a swinging, big band makeover. Once again, this is a song about death and Bobby is, basically, laughing at it by giving the song such a light-hearted, almost flippant feel. He also returns to a far less refined sound than that heard on his other swing numbers from 1960, giving it something of the energy and rawness of *Mack the Knife* and other songs from the *That's All* period. It shouldn't work – the downbeat lyrics, the upbeat arrangement, and the aggressive vocal should be completely at odds with each other. And yet it *does* work, and has become one of the songs most associated with Darin.

The single received a considerable amount of coverage in the trade magazines. *Billboard* gave the single one of their customary ambiguous good reviews, calling it a "sock reading" of an "effective nostalgic item."[206] *Cash Box* said that "the tale of the orphan girl in the up-coming musical *Tenderloin* is knocked out in sensational swing style."[207] *Variety* referred to it simply as a "snappy delivery that gives it a big appeal."[208]

Bobby's version of the song was released on ATCO, while the original soundtrack recording of the musical was released on Capitol, with a host of that label's roster of talent releasing singles of songs from the show. The producers of *Tenderloin* and Capitol took out a full-page advertisement in *Billboard* in October 1960 to advertise both the stage musical and the recordings. In a most unusual step, Capitol added a note to the bottom of their advertisement, reading: "PS. Capitol offers its heartiest congratulations to young Bobby Darin, one of the finest new stars in the entertainment world, and to the Atco label for their smash hit record of the great *Tenderloin* ballad *Artificial Flowers*."[209]

Lazy River sees Bobby once again revisiting a vintage song and giving it a swinging makeover to ensure a hit single. The formula had already worked with *Mack the Knife, Beyond the Sea, Clementine* and *Bill Bailey* and, once more, Bobby chose his material well, turning this Hoagy Carmichael chestnut into an absolute showstopper. The arrangement is top-notch, starting with a light and uptempo run-through of the song

---

[206] "Reviews of the Week's Singles," *Billboard*, September 12, 1960, 39.
[207] "Record Reviews," *Cash Box*, September 17, 1960, 8.
[208] Mike Gross, "Jocks, Jukes and Disks," *Variety*, September 21, 1960, 54.
[209] "Tenderloin, A New Musical Comedy," *Billboard*, October 24, 1960, 35.

UK sheet music

before dropping to half speed for the final chorus and a half. The resulting recording is a great piece of showmanship, and if Bobby was trying to placate a supposedly annoyed Sinatra over his misquote from the year before then he certainly didn't help his cause with the coda tagged on the end of *Lazy River*. Here, he paraphrases from Sinatra's recent single *River Stay Away From My Door*, seemingly telling Frank directly "I ain't goin' your way/ Get out of my way!" No doubt it was meant with a wink and a nudge, but it was still a gutsy move when Bobby was hardly getting the best press of his life at the time.

Lazy River reached #14 in the U.S. charts, but soared to the #2 spot in the UK, where the *Daily Express* called it "an example of how to smoulder vitality through a slow song."[210] Over in America, *Cash Box* said that the "fabulous talent pulls another one out of the evergreen dept. and injects fresh new life into it. This time it's *Lazy River* that Darin updates in this great swing style. Sensational Richard Behrke ork support rounds out a chart-topping effort."[211]

The final song recorded made little impact in the charts but is a fine recording in its own right. The next section of this chapter discusses the three remaining days of recordings in August 1960, when Darin turned his attention to one of the most unusual Christmas albums ever made by a mainstream singer. However, *Christmas Auld Lang Syne*, recorded on the same day as *Lazy River* and *Artificial Flowers* was intended solely for single release and was not included on the album (although it is included as a bonus track on some CD reissues). The song uses the melody of *Auld Lang Syne* but the words are in the mould of *The Christmas Song* with a religious nod in the final verse. Even the orchestral introduction is not unlike that used by Nat King Cole for his rendition of the Mel Tormé classic. Darin's track is warmly sung and deserved to become a seasonal evergreen, but it wasn't to be, and has instead become one of Bobby's most obscure recordings, and one that doesn't even often appear on various artist Christmas compilations despite the fact it sits nicely alongside similar tracks by Andy Williams, Perry Como, Dean Martin and Nat King Cole. *Cash Box* praised Bobby's "warm, sincere crooning mannerisms on what could become a Holiday standard."[212]

---

[210] James Thomas, "Presley Goes Square," *Daily Express*, March 25, 1961, 6.
[211] "Record Reviews," *Cash Box*, February 4, 1961, 6.
[212] "Record Reviews," *Cash Box*, November 5, 1960, 8.

August 19-21, 1960: Studio Sessions
The 25th Day of December **LP**

These remaining three days of sessions from August 1960 were dedicated to the recording of Bobby Darin's one and only Christmas album, *The 25th Day of December*. Once again, Bobby didn't decide to take the easy route and record a traditional yuletide LP. Instead, he mixes well-known carols with spirituals and even includes *Ave Maria*. The arrangements were by Bobby Scott, who had arranged the jazz combo recordings and half of the *It's You or No One* album earlier in the year. Darin isn't only accompanied by an orchestra and rhythm section, but also by a large choir. The result is a strange but ultimately compelling album which switches from track to track from the reverent singing of carols to Ray Charles-styled arrangements of gospel numbers.

The album starts with a stately version of *Oh Come All Ye Faithful*. Opening with a traditional orchestral introduction, Darin is then heard singing with the choir. He isn't positioned as the star here for the first half of the verse, but the recording is mixed in order for him to be a part of the choir. He takes more of a pivotal role in the second half of the verse, leading the choir to the climax of the chorus. He doesn't appear at all in the first lines of the next verse, with the choir taking over completely. As James Ritz in the liner notes for the latest CD release from 2013 points out, the "sing, choirs of angels" verse is completely missing here with a rarely heard verse taking its place.[213]

The year after the release of the Christmas album, *Oh Come All Ye Faithful* was released as a single backed with *Ave Maria*. This is the Bach/Gounod setting and, instead of trying to compete with the well-known classical recordings, Darin instead sings in a subdued voice, often barely rising above a whisper. This vocal quality would be used again a couple of years later during the Capitol folk albums. This is a good performance, but hardly classic Darin, mostly because he struggles during the louder, more powerful sections. Considering the quality of some of the other tracks on the album, it makes for a slightly strange B-side.

The single made no impact in the charts, but did receive some good reviews. For example, Roger Matz writes:

> Too often today's big names bring out traditional carols with dramatic arrangements that destroy or subdue much of their original meanings. But on both sides of this disc, Darin's subjugation to the music is obvious. By resisting the urge to modify either piece, Darin has preserved their original beauty. He has also given the general public a chance to evaluate his singing talents by offering standard versions of a well-known pair of songs. The general public won't be

---

[213] James Ritz, Liner notes to *The 25th Day of December*, Bobby Darin, Real Gone Music RGM-0199, 2013, CD.

disappointed."[214]

Returning to the album, Bobby is absent during the opening of *Poor Little Jesus*, with an unnamed soprano singing during the introduction. This spiritual has a kind of bluesy feel as Darin gives a somewhat aggressive vocal, entering into a back and forth dialogue between himself and the choir. There is also the influence here of Ray Charles, one of Bobby's idols.

Child of God sees Bobby leading the choir once again, but this time within an arrangement not totally dissimilar from the jazz combo sessions from February 1960. There is a similar looseness here and also a mix of styles, with the jazz group backing an entire choir on a gospel song. Oddly, it works, and, despite the melding of styles, it still seems one of the less ambitious songs on the album – which says more about the album itself than it does about this track.

There is another mix of styles on *Baby Born Today*, on which a spiritual is given a semi-rock 'n' roll rhythm alongside a kind of revivalist atmosphere. Once again, the choir is as much the lead in the song as Bobby himself. It may be over and done with in less than ninety seconds, but this is great music.

Holy Holy Holy is, like most of the ballads here, less successful. Part of this is to do with the less interesting arrangement (although the orchestral interlude between verses is gorgeous), but also Bobby is less convincing, giving quite a square, straightforward reading of the number. Again, though, his performance is totally selfless, handing over much of the limelight to the choir, who certainly have the showier role here.

Go Tell it on the Mountain brings us back into the same territory as *Baby Born Today*, with a kind of rock(ish) rhythm underpinning this traditional Christmas number. Darin himself treats it as a rocker, too. His voice has a raw quality, and he sings

Spanish EP, 1960

---

[214] Roger Matz, "Darin Makes Contribution to the Christmas Season," *Waterloo Daily Courier*, December 8, 1961, 8.

with a rasp and overtones just as he had on a song such as *Splish Splash* two years earlier.

While Shepherds Watched Their Flocks is another slow number that brings the momentum of the album almost to a halt. The mix of reverent singing such as this and the free, joyous singing of the upbeat numbers don't sit convincingly with each other. Perhaps the album would have been better programmed as *It's You or No One* had been, with ballads on one side and upbeat numbers on the other.

Things take off again with *Jehovah Hallelujah* and *Mary Where is Your Baby* which carry on the revival style of the previous upbeat numbers. The mix of spiritual, jazz, rock and blues in one song is just as successful here, with *Mary Where is Your Baby* perhaps the best cut on the whole album, and is another look forward to the *Earthy!* LP.

Silent Night, Holy Night is one of the better slow numbers here, with Bobby leading the choir with a vocal that is slightly less "pleading" than in some of the other carols. Once again, Bobby Scott's arrangement deserves special mention, particularly the rich, almost impressionistic, orchestral colours he creates.

Dona Nobis Pacem is also brilliantly arranged, but is one of the less familiar numbers here and becomes repetitive even within its short running time. Finally, in another break with convention, the final track of the album, *Amen*, doesn't even feature Darin at all.

Quite what audiences would have made of this most unusual of seasonal albums back in 1960 is not completely clear, for it has very little in common with those made by the standards singers of the day, or even an LP like *Elvis' Christmas Album*. It's certainly not an easy record to become familiar with, or even like, despite the fact that it is brilliantly executed and arranged. *Billboard* gave the album a typically bland, slightly patronising, review, saying that the "combination of gospel and spiritual tunes with familiar Christmas carols turns the set into an exciting one for the lad's fans."[215] *Cash Box*, meanwhile, picked up on how the upbeat tracks worked better than the ballads, writing that:

> Darin's contribution to Christmas is a refreshing departure from the usual seasonal fare. His program is comprised of sacred hymns and Negro sprituals. The latter, which enable him to swing vigorously, are the highlights of the album. And the entertainer appears much more at home on these tracks.[216]

The most popular Christmas albums are those that provide sounds and songs that are familiar to us, and that may well explain why Darin's sold poorly on release. With the exception of a two-song session in late December, this was Bobby's last recording

---

[215] "Reviews of this Week's LP's," *Billboard*, November 14, 1960, 27.
[216] "Album reviews," *Cash Box*, November 12, 1960, 39.

Filming "Come September."

session of 1960 and, like the first, he chose the ambitious and the complex over the straightforward and the traditional. On this occasion, however, that gamble didn't get cash tills ringing, and the LP has never managed to attain the classic status of those by the likes of Nat 'King' Cole, Perry Como, Andy Williams, and Dean Martin.

"I've got to make it," Bobby Darin was quoted as saying in July 1960. "Playing to an audience and being happily married, they're the only things I want out of life. And when you want anything that bad, nothing can get in your way."[217] Sure enough, in September 1960, *Modern Screen* ran a lengthy article, supposedly written by Bobby (but almost certainly by a ghost writer), with the headline "We're Getting Married." "I'm Bobby Darin, bachelor," the article begins. "But not for long. Because there's going to be a Mrs B. D. soon. And I'd like to tell you a little about her."[218] By the end of the year, Bobby would indeed be married, but not to Jo-Ann Campbell, whom he tells us "a little about" for all five pages of the article. Instead, around the time this edition of *Modern Screen* was on the newsstands, Bobby was in Italy falling in love with Sandra Dee.

Bobby had landed his first proper film role, fourth-billed in a romantic comedy entitled *Come September* (Robert Mulligan, 1961), and spent some of the late summer and early autumn of 1960 in Italy shooting his scenes.[219] There he met co-star Sandra Dee, one of the hottest properties in Hollywood at the time, and decided he was going to marry her. The wedding took place on December 1, 1960.[220] Bobby Darin spoke

---

[217] Bill Levinson, "Bobby," *San Antonio Light,* July 24, 1960, 7.
[218] Bobby Darin, "We're Getting Married," *Modern Screen*, September 1960, 42.
[219] *Come September* will be discussed in more detail later in this chapter.
[220] For further information and a more detailed telling of the story, check out Dodd Darin's book, *Dream Lovers*.

to Earl Wilson a few days before the wedding, telling him that meeting Dee had caused him to "have a strange desire to reform…Suddenly your values change. I have now met a human being more important than I am."[221]

Aside from his work on *Come September*, Bobby's was a regular face both on television and in newspaper and magazine articles during the second half of 1960. In September, he was seen on screen both on Dick Clark's show as well as in an acting role in *Dan Raven*. In October, he appeared on *The Bob Hope Show*, singing both *Lazy River* and *Artificial Flowers* as well as a duet of *Two Different Worlds* with Patti Page, a song which, alas, Bobby never got around to recording either in the studio or in a live setting. In December he was on *American Bandstand*, singing *Christmas Auld Lang Syne* as well as co-hosting the programme.

In the autumn of 1960, ATCO released the hodgepodge album *For Teenagers Only*. The LP seemed to take its lead from the Elvis albums that RCA had released while the star was in the army in that it was a collection of leftovers in deluxe packaging – in this case a gatefold sleeve with a large detachable colour photo. This was also an attempt to placate Bobby's younger fanbase who, it is fair to say, had been sidelined somewhat over the previous year while he concentrated on the Great American Songbook. Quite what they would have made of standards such as *That Lucky Old Sun* and *Here I'll Stay* that were included, is unknown, but the likes of *I Want You With Me*, *Somebody to Love*, and *All the Way Home* managed to find a welcome home here. *Cash Box* stated that Bobby "cavorts infectiously through a host of bright, hard-beat swingers, balancing

U. S. album cover

---

[221] Earl Wilson, "Never Thought We'd See a Humble Bobby Darin," *Arizona Republic*, December 6, 1960, 33.

them nicely with a few effective ballads."[222] The 2009 CD edition, issued by Collector's Choice Music, contains the complete mono album, plus four bonus tracks featuring the stereo versions of some of the songs (and one alternate take).

Bobby's appearances in print were as varied as the ones on television. Some articles were entirely vacuous. "We have talked to a number of the girls Bobby has dated," writes John Larsen for the *Daily Review*, "and they describe him in one sigh-filled word: Terrific!"[223] The article was not the winner of the Pulitzer Prize that year.

Other pieces did at least highlight Bobby's musicianship on-stage and how he tailored his show depending on the audience. Anita Ehrman writes:

> It is a mixed act dependent on audience response and Darin's mood. When everything is going right Bobby will play the comedian, on a strictly ad lib basis, for 15 minutes before showing off his versatility by playing the vibraphone and dancing. An unresponsive audience will get the vibraphone recital without the previous lead-up…A boisterous teen-age prom crowd, screaming for *Splish Splash* will send Bobby to the piano for a rendition of pre-1960 Darin hits. He occasionally gives in to pleas for his first big song but in doing so produces almost a parody of Bobby Darin the rock 'n' roll idol.[224]

More interesting were the interviews with Darin that gave readers a little insight into what made him tick. In an article in *Family Weekly*, he says "part of education is making flubs. The first song I sold was a flop called *My First Real Love*. But that didn't stop me. The real blunder with most kids I meet is not that they make these flubs, but that they don't make them often enough. The theory is: why try for something hard? Why try to be tops when you can join the crowd of second-raters?"[225]

Elsewhere, John Larsen defended Bobby's apparent brashness in his second interview with him in the space of a month:

> Bobby Darin is one of the most articulate young men in the entertainment world. He can talk eloquently about everything and anything. It has been said that he is brash, cocky and conceited. Not so. What Bobby has is supreme confidence in himself. 'My mother often told me when I was discouraged that, if I didn't believe in

---

[222] "Album Reviews," *Cash Box*, October 8, 1960, 44.
[223] John Larsen, "Bobby Darin Among Top Recording Stars," *Daily Review*, August 6, 1960, 13.
[224] Anita Ehrman, "Will Bobby Bobble Sudden Success? – Here's His Story" *San Antonio Light*, September 18, 1960, 22A
[225] Marya Saunders and Robert Gaines, "The Most Important Thing in the World," *Family Weekly*, October 23, 1960.

myself, no one else would. And so I believe and because I do I'm accused of having a swelled head.[226]

These are interesting quotes, particularly with regards to a book such as this that attempts to evaluate Darin's recording career. As we have already seen, and will see again, Bobby was all too willing to try new things even if they didn't end up totally successful – either artistically or commercially.

This notion of pushing himself to do better and to try different things is something he *did* have in common with Sinatra. Sinatra didn't have to make an album like *Watertown*, a brand new song cycle telling the story of the break-up of a marriage, in 1969, but he wanted to try something different and push himself to the limit artistically. The record flopped at the time, but now has something of a cult following. Likewise, the final album of his *Trilogy* boxed set is a semi-classical work lasting forty minutes, written for Sinatra, chorus and large orchestra by Gordon Jenkins. Artistically, it didn't really work, but even as a sixty-four year old man, he was keen to cover new ground. The same is true with Darin and albums such as the esoteric *It's You or No One*, the non-traditional Christmas album, or later albums such as *Earthy!* or the recordings he made for the Direction label. He didn't have to try new, more "difficult" things (difficult for his audience, that is), but it was part of who he was to push himself to the limit.

Elsewhere, *Modern Screen* published an article in November 1960 which was probably the first to outline Bobby's health issues in detail.[227] It is a rather melodramatic piece, but it makes it clear to readers just how much of an ill man Darin was, and this, in turn, gave the first explanation for what had been repeatedly termed Bobby's cockiness.[228] The cumbersome title of the article said it all: "I've Got This Feeling I'm Gonna Die Young … So What I've Gotta do I've Gotta do Fast."

In November of 1960, the Variety Clubs of America voted Bobby as the "Personality of the Year," with the chairman of the awards committee saying that "at 24, Darin possesses a degree of stage presence and a flair for showmanship that some performers never achieve in a lifetime."[229] However, Bobby wasn't having everything all his own way in late 1960, with a *Variety* review of an appearance at Miami Beach emphasising his brashness and cocky attitude on stage, and criticising him for not being

---

[226] John Larsen, "Bobby Darin Interviewed," *Argus-Leader*, August 30, 1960, 5.

[227] "I've Got This Feeling I'm Gonna Die Young … So What I've Gotta Do I've Gotta Do Fast," *Modern Screen*, November 1960, 32.

[228] Eagle-eyed members of the public would already have noticed that Darin was not a well man, however. Short comments in newspapers and trade magazines often reported that he had to cancel performances due to ill health. As the years went by, there were numerous reports of him being hospitalised.

[229] "Darin Named Variety Club's Personality of the Year," *Cash Box*, November 5, 1960, 44.

on stage for long enough and for not returning to the stage for encores.[230]

December 22, 1960: Studio Session

Bobby Darin's last recording session of 1960 was a low-key affair. Two songs were recorded, one of which, *Look for My True Love*, was set aside and re-recorded a month later. The other song was a cover of an obscure Peggy Lee number, *Similau*, first recorded in 1949. Online sessionographies state that the song was overdubbed in mid-1964 before eventually being released as a single side nearly five years after it was recorded. Bearing this in mind, it is difficult to know what elements of the recording were Darin's intention and which were not. It is an odd little recording of an odd little song, but pleasant enough, and yet another example of Bobby trying his hand at almost everything that fell within the realms of popular music, no matter what the style or genre.

---

[230] Larry, "Deauville, Miami Beach," *Variety*, December 28, 1960, 45.

Bobby in Las Vegas

CHAPTER FIVE
IRRESISTIBLE YOU: 1961

In 1960, Bobby Darin had recorded five albums, and each one was a special project: *It's You or No One* was a rather ambitious concept album, *Winners* was a jazz record, *Darin at the Copa* was a live album, *Two of a Kind* saw Bobby recording an album of duets, and *The Twenty-Fifth Day of December* was a non-traditional Christmas LP. By contrast, 1961 would see the recording of only two LPs, *Love Swings* and *Bobby Darin sings Ray Charles*. Both were themed albums just as the 1960 ones had been, but this time the premise was much simpler and, ultimately less ambitious.

January 14 or 16, 1961: Studio Session

The first session of 1961 resulted in just two relatively mediocre single sides being recorded. *Look for My True Love* had already been attempted the previous month, but no satisfactory master had been completed. This Darin-composed pop song is pleasant enough, but rather unremarkable, and the vocal seems somewhat affected. From the moment it was recorded, it was destined to be nothing more than a flip-side, and it appeared on the *Nature Boy* single later in the year.

Oo-Ee-Train was also unremarkable. While it has a driving rhythm, the song (again composed by Darin) has little in the way of originality, and the arrangement itself is too cluttered. The almost-squeaking "la la la" of the female backing singers drag the track down, and the orchestra in the second half is too heavy for the material. *Oo-Ee-Train* appeared as the B-side of *Lazy River*.

January 31, 1961 saw Bobby Darin star in what was called at the time his "first TV special," *Bobby Darin and Friends*. This wasn't true, as he had already starred in his own special the year before in the U.K., but seemingly that show was never broadcast in the U.S. Just as with the U.K. programme, there were some great, and some not so great, moments, and once again there was a feeling that Bobby's stage show persona didn't translate to television when fronting a programme within the hour-long, rather strict, variety show format. Despite this, Bobby was keen to promote the special, saying "It's been a lot of fun preparing. [...] We've got Bud Yorkin and Norm Lear producing and directing, also writing. They did the Astaire special that won all the Emmys. I was really flattered when they said they wanted to work with me."[231]

Part of the problem here is that Darin doesn't seem entirely at ease when presenting his own show. The jokes, the smiles, the casual delivery, all seem just a little too exaggerated, too faked, for the more intimate medium of television. Arnold Zeitlin, of the *Pittsburgh Post-Gazette*, was mostly positive, writing that the show was "solid, as well as profitable, evidence, he is at the peak of a career which was little more than a wistful ambition five years ago."[232] Meanwhile, the *New York Times* was particularly harsh:

> In several songs, at a fast tempo, he demonstrated that he is an accomplished finger-snapper. As a singer he is considerably less accomplished – particularly when he attempts a tender ballad, such as *I Have Dreamed*. [...] Most of it was Mr. Darin's show and it offered little in the way of entertainment.[233]

A slightly more sarcastic, but no doubt serious, comment on the show appeared in the *Bedford Gazette*, which described the show as an "appalling hour" and referred to Darin himself as a "flippant overgrown teenager."[234] The review goes on:

> We sat through most of it in the spirit of higher education. It is the same spirit in which we listen to Communistic propaganda or the ravings of Castro. We disagree violently, but we like to know what the other fellow is thinking and doing…Perhaps the big-city beatniks go for a cocky kid whose chief accomplishment is insulting pretty girls; but we hopefully think that this twisted refinement has not

---

[231] Guy Maynard, "Bobby Darin, 'Young Man in Motion,' Moves to First TV 'Special'," *Reading Eagles*, January 29, 1961, 6.
[232] Arnold Zeitlin, "The Bobby Darin Story," *Pittsburgh Post-Gazette Sunday Magazine*, January 29, 1961, 7.
[233] John P. Shanley, "Bobby Darin Heads One-Hour Program," *New York Times*, February 1, 1961, 71.
[234] "Old Man on the Moment," *Bedford Gazette*, February 3, 1961, 4.

penetrated to our sector of the backwoods.

Columnist Fred Danzig was not impressed either. "Somewhere between the conception of the show and the final taping, freshness, cohesion and drive disappeared," he wrote. "Attempts to blend Bobby into sets occupied by artful dancers and impressionistic designs were foiled by Bobby's own style...He has a facility for reducing class into flash."[235]

Interestingly, *Variety* bucked the trend and praised the show, stating:

> On his own show, Darin carried the ball with a display of vocalizing, hoofing and comedy, the whole performance super-charged with his self-assured air. He used his talent to the hilt and gave this variety hour the benefit of his sharp personality edge. The show itself was an entertaining parlay of music and comedy, well-mounted and smoothly paced within a more or less standardized format for this type of presentation.[236]

Bobby himself was at least honest about where the blame would lie if the show failed: "If the show is great, it will be because of the people in it. If it bombs out, it will be MY fault."[237] Interestingly, when the programme was shown in Australia the following year, it was referred to as "one of the best hours of TV variety entertainment yet."[238]

Was the television special as bad as the U.S. press would have us believe? Of course not. While it was not spectacularly brilliant, it was certainly on par when it came to shows of this type at this point in television history. So, what was going on? Just as a year earlier, Darin was suddenly having a hard time from the mainstream press and this continued for the first six months of 1961.

When Bobby appeared on *What's My Line* and won a $50 prize which he announced he would donate to the Heart Fund, journalist Marie Torre declared "big deal!" and said that if Darin had donated his appearance fee of $500 to charity she "might have been impressed."[239]

In May 1961, *TV Radio Mirror* tried to make out that Bobby had been lying about his age. "Music publishers figure Bobby Darin is closer to 30 than 25. Remember he was kicking around Broadway eight or nine years before he made it big."[240] This, of

---

[235] Fred Danzig, "Jack Paar, Bobby Darin Shows Offered Dull, Tired and Pointless Entertainment," *Coshocton Tribune*, February 1, 1961, 15.
[236] Herm, "Bobby Darin and Friends," *Variety*, February 8, 1961, 76.
[237] Erskine Johnson, "Bobby Darin Ain't Talking," *Eureka Humboldt Times*, February 4, 1961, 2.
[238] Nan Musgrove, "Bobby Darin's Superb TV Show," *Australian Women's Weekly*, March 28, 1962, 25.
[239] Marie Torre, "TV Show $50 Prize 'Too Small': Torre," *The Capital Times*, March 4, 1961, 2.
[240] Peter Abbott, What's New on the East Coast," *TV Radio Mirror*, May 1961, 3.

Bobby and a dancer

course, was not true.

In the *Saturday Evening Post*, a bad-mannered article by Edward Linn referred to Darin as the "Little Singer with the Big Ego," and spent nearly four pages reminding the reader of just how arrogant Bobby was. Putting words into the mouth of George Burns, but conveniently not directly quoting him, Linn states that Burns was concerned that Bobby's career could be halted by a "built-in arrogance, a poise and self-assurance that seem to challenge the audience to take him not as it might like him, but as he is."[241] The writer goes on to say "Nor does Darin's arrogance come off with his make-up. When he was first coming to public notice, he gave out interviews in which he said, presumably without blushing, 'My ambition is to be a legend by the time I am twenty-five.'"[242]

It was this "quote," and the various variations on it that had been printed over the previous year, that appear to have been at the centre of the animosity by the press at the beginning of 1961. Why? Because Darin's 25th birthday was on May 14th, and it seems that every opportunity was being taken to either knock Darin or rub his nose in the fact that he hadn't made the deadline.

Some articles were more honest about their motivations, with Bob Thomas writing a piece entitled "Bobby Darin Won't Make Legend Date." The article seemingly gives Darin's part of the story too, by quoting him as saying "writers take

---

[241] Edward Linn, "Little Singer with the Big Ego," *Saturday Evening Post*, May 6, 1961, 59.
[242] Ibid.

part of what I say, but they omit certain things, or they don't convey the tone in which I said things." However, at the same time, it is not afraid to say that Will Rogers "said he never met a man he didn't like, but then he never met Bobby Darin."[243]

The venom in these pieces is quite startling, even from a distance of nearly sixty years. However, this was the conservative press of America, and Bobby Darin had attacked their values with the misquote about surpassing Sinatra and the quip about being a legend by the time of his twenty-fifth birthday. It appears that they didn't take kindly to an upstart from the Bronx trying to rise above his station, and now he had admitted he had failed in his quest to be a "legend," they were all too keen to make the most of it. This was nothing new, it should be added, for exactly the same treatment was received by Elvis Presley (another entertainer who came from a poor background but dared to set his sights high).[244]

The *New York Times* even managed to sneak some cloaked insults into a review of his night-club performance at the Copacabana: "Mr Darin defies his audience not to accept him and this, strangely enough, appears to be one of the major ingredients of his popularity. His faith in himself is so great it would seem almost lèse-majesté not to applaud him."[245] The article also manages to contain one of the worst photos of Bobby during this period that was ever printed, with him looking remarkably smug. A *Variety* review of the same shows at the Copa was less cutting:

> Darin is a performer of great instinct and few inhibitions. Highly stylistic, he gives an impression of enormous vitality along with a roistering and jazz attitude. Yet with all this equipment appealing to the modern cats, he seems anchored in traditional music, at least as far as the nitery dates are concerned.[246]

The review also tells us of a song medley that started "with the year he said he was born," that Darin used as an encore. Sadly, we are given no details as to what songs were used in the medley.

Another reason why the press were upset with Bobby at this time was because they were keen to get a scoop, or at least some gossip, on his marriage to Sandra Dee, but numerous newspapers report that he was unwilling to talk about it in interviews. He told Margaret McManus in January 1961 that "our marriage is going to be strictly

---

[243] Bob Thomas, "Bobby Darin Won't Make Legend Date," *The Lowell Sun*, April 21, 1961, 22.
[244] See Shane Brown, *Reconsider Baby. Elvis Presley: A Listener's Guide. 2nd edition.* (Createspace, 2017), chapter 1.
[245] Arthur Gelb, "Darin Storms the Copacabana," *New York Times*, March 1, 1961, 26.
[246] Jose, "Copacabana, N.Y." *Variety*, March 1, 1961, 85.

private. It has nothing to do with her career or my career."[247] A month later, he said the same thing to Erskine Johnson: "That's part of my life I want left A-lone, with a capital A."[248] He expanded upon his reasons later in the year, in an interview with Bob Thomas:

> The number of reporters I will talk to gets smaller and smaller all the time…When I see some of the personalities in this town – I won't mention names – who disrupt their homes and families for the sake of personal publicity, it makes me physically ill. I would never want to look back on my life and see that I had done that.[249]

Despite all the bad press of this period, there were still people willing to stand up for him. On the letters page of the *Saturday Evening Post*, a Mrs Pat Lewellen wrote to say "congratulations to Mr. Bobby Darin for standing up on his own two feet and pronouncing – here I am, take it or leave it!"[250] She goes on:

> Forget the arrogance and egotism. If just one of the young singing stars of today would dare whisper just one of their own opinions in public, how their public would scream at their shattered image. Mr. Darin has it made. He shatters the public and has it begging for more, so more power to you, fellow!

It is interesting how the above comment is not far removed from the *New York Times* reaction to the March 1961 Copa season (see previous page). Meanwhile, another writer on the letters page states that "when you go to a club to hear Bobby Darin, you are never cheated."[251] These were letters in response to the "Little Singer with the Big Ego" article discussed earlier.[252] However, not everyone agreed, with Michael Church of Yale University suggesting that someone should give Bobby a "teething ring and put him to bed."[253]

What is quite remarkable is that, once the twenty-fifth birthday was past, this kind of negative press almost ceased completely. Sure, Darin still had his detractors as all artists do, but it returned to relatively normal levels and lacked the sheer spite that was present for the first six months of 1961. This may also be because Bobby was coming

---

[247] Margaret McManus, "Darin Superstitious About Reaching Heights," *Syracuse Post-Standard*, January 29, 1961, 4.
[248] Erskine Johnson, "Bobby Darin Ain't Talking," *Eureka Humboldt Times*, February 4, 1961, 2.
[249] Bob Thomas, "Bobby Darin Hires Men to Say No," *Ottawa Journal*, October 31, 1961, 39.
[250] Pat Lewellen, "Ego, Schmego?," *Saturday Evening Post*, June 10, 1961, 4
[251] David Renard, "Ego, Schmego?," *Saturday Evening Post*, June 10, 1961, 4.
[252] Edward Linn, "Little Singer with the Big Ego," 59.
[253] Michael Church, "Ego, Schmego?," *Saturday Evening Post*, June 10, 1961, 4.

out on the other side of his biggest period of success and would therefore become less of a discussion point. Sure, he had hits and was very visible for the next twelve years, but he never again hit the dizzy heights of *Mack the Knife* or *Dream Lover*. He was also absent from television for the second half of 1961. The "big ego" description would never leave him, but by July 1961 he had weathered the storm of the worst press of his career.

March 21-23, 1961: Studio Sessions
Love Swings LP

The beginning of March 1961 saw Darin returning to the Copa in a series of performances which gained (mostly) rave reviews and which also saw him incorporate *Queen of the Hop* into his adult nightclub act for possibly the first time.[254]

In the middle of the month, Bobby was back in the studio. *Love Swings* was another concept album, and the last album of standards he recorded at ATCO. The "swings" of the title didn't refer to the genre of music, but how, according to the liner notes, love swings "like a pendulum. It swings two ways: back and forth, and up and down."[255] In other words, here are twelve standards programmed in such a way that they tell the story of a love affair, from the first meeting to the resignation that the affair is over and a new boyfriend or girlfriend needs to be found. The back cover lists the song

Advertisement for "Love Swings."

---
[254] Ken Grevatt, "Darin Parades R&B Hits at Copa," *Billboard*, March 13, 1961, 7.
[255] Anon, liner notes to *Love Swings*, Bobby Darin, ATCO 33-134, LP, 1961.

titles, as well as illustrating each one with a whimsical drawing that makes the album look as if it is going to be more light-hearted than it actually is. Sure, there are some fun swingers here, especially on the first side, but there are also some heavy lost love ballads, and the arrangements by Torrie Zito are remarkably varied.

Unlike some of the more esoteric albums recorded the previous year, *Love Swings* is far more accessible and requires less commitment and patience from the listener. The songs are, on the whole, more familiar than on most of Darin's previous albums of standards. Despite this, though, it performed disappointingly. This may have been perhaps because there was no single from the album to accompany its release (or a key track that DJs could home in on), or it might have been due to over-exposure.

Love Swings opens with Jerome Kern and Ira Gershwin's *Long Ago and Far Away*, written in 1944 for the film *Cover Girl* (dir. Charles Vidor). This is less of a swing number and more of an upbeat orchestral arrangement. The only element of the number that really swings is the joyous instrumental interlude. Bobby's vocal is, for the most part, a smooth rendition before he surprises us with a reprise of the final section of the song just when we think the track is about to end. It is an interesting device, and here his voice becomes grittier and he uncharacteristically uses one breath to cover a long passage (for him) from one section to the next.

I Didn't Know What Time it Was continues in the same vein. There is more of a relaxed swing here but, again, it only really comes to the fore during the instrumental. The song itself, by Rodgers and Hart, dates back to an obscure 1939 musical entitled *Too Many Girls*. Listeners of *Love Swings* when it was first released were more likely to have recognised it from the Sinatra/Rita Hayworth film musical *Pal Joey* (dir. George Sidney, 1957).

Sinatra was also associated with *How About You* introduced in the Judy Garland and Mickey Rooney film *Babes on Broadway* (dir. Busby Berkeley, 1941), which was included on his seminal *Songs for Swingin' Lovers* album. Sinatra's version is much more laid back than Bobby's, with his vocal remarkably relaxed. Darin's arrangement is faster, however, and a tad more playful, helped along by the new lyrics used for the second run-through (including a reference to the new Mrs Darin).

The More I See You, by Mack Gordon and Harry Warren, also started its life as part of the score of a Hollywood musical, this time *Diamond Horseshoe* (dir. George Seaton, 1945). It has a similar tempo and arrangement to the previous songs on the album. The melody is more wide-ranging than on some of the other numbers, and there are moments when one realises that Darin isn't in the greatest voice here. The notes at the extremities of his range don't flow as they had done at the beginning of the previous year, for example, and there is a sense of strain in the more powerful sections.

It Had to be You is more associated today with Harry Connick Jr. than any other singer, thanks to his hit version from the film *When Harry Met Sally* (dir. Rob Reiner, 1989), the soundtrack to which not only catapulted Connick to stardom but also started a revival in big band and swing music. Bobby's version is less showy than Connick's, with the beginning of the track having the sound of a jazz combo rather than the orchestral sound of the previous numbers. Indeed, the strings are not heard until near the end of the first run-through of the song. There are moments on the album where the strings are bothersome and sound somewhat intrusive, bogging down what are otherwise light and airy arrangements. They only appear for a short space of time on *It Had to Be You* and the track is better because of it.

The first side of the album finishes with a big ballad, *No Greater Love*. Several of Darin's critics over the previous year or so had commented that his ballad singing was not of the same standard as his up-tempo recordings. It appears from what we have seen so far in our examination of Darin's output that it was not the tempo that caused him the issues, but the setting. In the jazz combo recordings from early in 1960, his ballad singing is exemplary. Here, however, he is saddled with a heavy arrangement that he almost seems to be competing with. Whispering his way through *What a Difference a Day Made* is one thing, but the control just isn't quite there when he sings a ballad requiring more volume and breath control as he does here, or on *I Have Dreamed* in the TV special from two months earlier (although he managed the latter perfectly well on the *Darin at the Copa* album).

In Love in Vain is arranged and sung in a similar way, although this time the number has a light, lilting swing. Again, this isn't Darin at anywhere near his best, but the result is a little less forced than on the previous track. There are signs that he is approaching these types of songs in a different, more sophisticated way. Following the instrumental, he sings "I thought that I would be in heaven, but I'm only up a tree," all in one breath – something he wouldn't have done just a year earlier. The problem is that it was the rawness of Darin's singing of standards that brought their original appeal. If audiences wanted to hear great phrasing, they would have been listening to Sinatra, and by trying to "improve" in this area, Darin actually robs us of some of his appeal.

We're back in swinging mode for *Just Friends*. This 1931 song is another of the more familiar titles on the album, with well-known recordings also by Sinatra, Billie Holiday, Chet Baker and Ella Fitzgerald. The strings again seem slightly out of place on a swinging tune, but the change of pace is welcome at this stage of the record. Again, though, there is some strain in Bobby's rendition of the song, and there are better ones out there.

Something to Remember You By is one of two numbers on the album written by the prolific songwriting team of Howard Dietz and Arthur Schwartz. Not as familiar names today as some of the other writers of the Great American Songbook such as Cole Porter, George Gershwin and Rodgers and Hart, the pair wrote together for a period of over thirty years, with their better known songs including *By Myself* (recorded by Bobby in 1960) and *That's Entertainment*.

Something to Remember You By is given something of a wistful reading, aided and abetted by a less cluttered arrangement than some of the songs here. This space in the arrangement means that Darin doesn't need to strain in order to make himself heard, and it is the highlight of the ballad singing on the album.

Skylark, the Johnny Mercer and Hoagy Carmichael song which follows, benefits from the solo saxophone heard during the opening and closing sections of the song. Again, Darin is taking longer phrases in one breath than we are used to, but he also isn't singing as if he is in competition with the orchestra.

Spring is Here, by Rodgers and Hart, is perhaps one ballad too many for what started out as a light-hearted album. Unlike some of the others, this is rather heavy fare too, and lacks the light swing of some of the other slower numbers.

I Guess I'll Have to Change My Plan, by the same writing duo as *Something to Remember You By*, is a light, upbeat ending to the record, with a swinging instrumental section that brings the recording alive. Just as with some of the other songs here, this will have been known to consumers buying this album in 1961, having been recorded by Sinatra for his 1957 record *A Swingin' Affair* and used in the 1953 film musical *The Band Wagon* (dir. Vincente Minnelli). The song itself dates back to 1929, however.

The album was an artistic success for Darin who, once again, had provided his followers with something different – in this case, an album that told a story. Sadly, it also lacks some of the fun and exuberance of his earliest albums of standards. What the album really needs are the arrangements of Richard Wess or Billy May. Torrie Zito's efforts are often interesting and well-written, but they often don't seem to be tailored to Darin's individual strengths, and they certainly don't have the individuality of the 1958 and 1959 swing albums.

The reviews, like the album itself, were merely pleasant, rather than exuberant. *Life* magazine wrote that the record "offers Sinatra-type songs, and the Sinatra-type delivery has just enough of the Darin brashness to let him get away with vocal larceny."[256] Mike Gross in *Variety* wrote that the arrangements give "Darin plenty of room in which to move around," and that the results are "very good."[257] *Cash Box* told readers that "the songster is excellently equipped to purvey these varied emotions convincingly."[258]

Also recorded, but rejected, at this session is thought to be a title known as *Come September*. The likelihood is that this is the same composition as *Theme from Come September* which was recorded and rejected again at the next session, and finally successfully recorded in June 1961. While lyrics were added to the theme, that version was not copyrighted as a composition until 1966,[259] thus making it unlikely to

---

[256] "Life Guide," *Life*, November 24, 1961, 27.
[257] Mike Gross, "Album Reviews," *Variety*, August 2, 1961, 82.
[258] "Album Reviews, *Cash Box*, July 22, 1961, 24.
[259] See Bleiel, *That's All*, 262.

Bobby presents Percy Faith with a Grammy award, April 13, 1961

be the version from this first attempt.

March 25, 1961: Studio Session

This session, two days after the ones for *Love Swings*, saw five titles recorded. Three of the five tracks were instrumentals, of which only one was released. The two vocal sides were released as singles.

Nature Boy sees Darin attempting to reinvent the Nat King Cole hit of 1948. Quite what Bobby was trying to do here is difficult to make out. With its cha-cha opening and "sha la la la lu" backing vocals, one could be forgiven for thinking that this is some kind of send-up of the number. However, as it progresses, it becomes clear that this isn't the case due to Darin's sincere vocals and the fine big band instrumental. Somehow, it all comes together in one intriguing mish-mash of styles and genres that ultimately *does* work. When released as a single, it barely broke the top 40 in America, and reached #24 in the UK. *Life* Magazine said that Darin gave the song a "tremulous reading," a comment which makes about as much sense as the arrangement of the song itself.[260]

Those annoying "sha la la"-ing backing singers are back again in *Golden Earrings*, a Peggy Lee hit that originated in a 1947 spy drama featuring the unlikely pairing of Marlene Dietrich and Ray Milland. Bobby's version of the number was eventually released in 1964 as the B-side of *Milord*. There is a distinct swing to the arrangement here, which sits at odds with the backing vocals which, at times, are louder than Darin himself. In short, the song never really gets going.

Walk Bach to Me is a Darin instrumental with a title that is somewhat more interesting than the track itself. Bobby plays what appears to be some kind of electric harpsichord-like instrument within an orchestral setting. It is pleasant enough, and became the flip-side to the *Theme from Come September'* single (a number attempted for the second time here but rejected), and perhaps Bobby was on to something, for the composition and arrangement is very similar in style to a number of film themes from the coming years, including the British series of Miss Marple films starring Margaret Rutherford, which also utilises the harpsichord-like instrument. *Life* magazine were impressed, writing that he "shows an unexpected flair for the harpsichord when he pings out one of his own works, a slow swinging jazzy thing with a nod to Johann Sebastian Bach in the title."[261]

April 1961 saw the release of Bobby's first "greatest hits" album, entitled *The Bobby Darin Story*. The album featured twelve of Darin's single sides as well as some linking dialogue recorded specifically for the album. This dialogue, some studio chatter, and the use of an alternate take of *Clementine* make it still an essential part of any Darin collection despite the fact all of the songs are available elsewhere. *Variety* wrote that it was a "swinging package headed for strong sales action."[262] Reaching #18 in the US album charts, it was Bobby's last top twenty album.

June 8, 1961: Studio Session

Considering how often he generally appeared as a guest star on TV shows during his career, he was curiously absent from the small screen for most of 1961, not appearing at all, it seems, from April of that year until the beginning of 1962. This was, no doubt, in part due to his movie-making activities. His first major role, in *Come September*, was released in August 1961, and he would be seen in three more films within just ten months.

---

[260] "Life Guide," *Life*, June 9, 1961, 17.
[261] "Life Guide," *Life*, August 11, 1961, 12.
[262] Herm Schoenfeld, "Album Reviews," *Variety*, April 19, 1961, 56.

Bobby with Rock Hudson and Sandra Dee in "Come September."

On June 8, Darin finally recorded a satisfactory take of the film's theme, which he had also written. With the record stating that is was arranged and conducted by Robert Mersey, it's unclear just what part Darin had in the recording process despite the track being credited to "Bobby Darin and his Orchestra." Three more numbers were recorded on the same day, all of which remain unissued: *Special Someone*, *Teenage Theme*, and *Movin' On*. It is likely these pieces were incidental music for the film.

When *Come September* was released in the summer of 1961, it was received warmly by most critics. Trade magazine *Film Bulletin* gave it a "film of distinction" title due to its commercial prospects, and called it "the kind of entertainment audiences go out of their way to see and exhibitors say 'thank you' for."[263] Meanwhile, Bosley Crowther in the *New York Times* referred to the film as a "purely 'fun' comedy-romance" in the second of his two reviews.[264] In the first, he tells readers that "Sandra Dee and Bobby Darin are attractively impish, though Mr. Darin does act at time as though he has seized, with a little too much fervor, the torch that Donald O'Connor has flung."[265] Crowther's comment might not have been intended as a compliment, but given how Bobby adored O'Connor, it is unlikely that he took umbrage at the remark.

Variety said that "Darin does a workmanlike job, and gives evidence he'll have

---

[263] "*Come September* Lively Comedy with Solid B. O. Values," *Film Bulletin*, July 10, 1961, 10.
[264] Bosley Crowther, "Vistas in Italy," *New York Times*, September 17, 1961, X1.
[265] Bosley Crowther, "The Screen: Comedy-Romance in Italy," *New York Times*, September 8, 1961, 34.

more to show when the parts provide him with wider opportunity."[266] Over in the UK, *Monthly Film Bulletin* was less enthusiastic about the film as a whole, saying that "the basic weakness is the writers' inclination to underline, repeat and pile their jokes on, especially in the first half…while Robert Mulligan directs with a lethargy that suggests he is signally ill-at-ease with the big expensive marquee production."[267] Mulligan himself was complimentary of Bobby's performance: "I've never known any actor who approached his first role with as much assurance as Bobby. He handled himself as if he had been in as many pictures as Cary Grant. He moves."[268]

"It's amazing to note that this is Darin's first film," said the *Cherokee Daily Times*. "He acts like a veteran as the brash medical student. Needless to say, his song in the night-club sequence, which he wrote himself – as well as the title tunes – are bubbly and certain to be on the hit list for a long time."[269]

Watching the film now, what is striking is just how good Bobby is here. The film itself is a bit overlong and the situations are often dragged out, but Bobby himself gives one of his best performances, and one that sees him far more natural in front of the movie camera than many of his later roles. This isn't a showy role like those in *Captain Newman M.D.* and *Pressure Point*, but his acting here is arguably more nuanced. He could have played the role as a street-wise punk, but he doesn't do that. Sure, he's cocky in places, but he doesn't overdo it, and there are also moments when he is really quite charming, and there is none of the over-acting here that he sometimes verged on in the years to come.

Italian release of the theme from "Come September."

June 19, 1961: Studio Session

Eleven days after the instrumental session that might or might not have involved Bobby, he was back in the studio to record three single sides, two of which would see

---

[266] Tube, "Come September," *Variety*, June 28, 1961, 6.
[267] "Come September," *Monthly Film Bulletin*, October 1961, 142.
[268] James Bacon, "Bobby Darin, Frustrated Actor," *Baltimore Sun*, December 17, 1961, K9.
[269] "*Come September*, Sparking Comedy," *Cherokee Daily Times*, September 28, 1961, 4.

him back near the top of the charts.

With *You Must Have Been a Beautiful Baby*, record buyers saw Bobby returning to rock 'n' roll for the first time in quite a while. The song was written by Harry Warren and Johnny Mercer back in 1938, and it certainly was not unusual for Bobby to take an old standard and give it a makeover for a single release. Here, though, instead of swinging his way through the song he gives it an arrangement that tunes into the then-current "twist" craze. It is great to hear Bobby singing with some edge back in his voice, and the resulting track is a lot of fun, and soared up the charts to #5 in America and broke into the top 10 in the UK, with the *Daily Mirror* naming it the "vocal spin of the week."[270] Quite whether *Billboard* even listened to the song before reviewing it is debatable, describing it as Darin's "old swinging form!"[271]

Sorrow Tomorrow was the flip-side of the single, and has a similar vibe. The track was penned by Doc Pomus and Mort Shuman, who had also composed both *His Latest Flame* and *Little Sister*, a double A-side by Elvis Presley which *Sorrow Tomorrow* ended up competing with in the charts. It has a lively, contemporary feel and helped Darin to update his sound. A different mix of the song can be found on the *Things and other Things* album, which does not contain the overdubbed voices heard on the single version. *Variety* said that the song "is built along strong blues lines and it's given a vocal kick that makes it a pop runaway."[272] *Cash Box* called the song a "driving, steady beat thumper that Bobby pounds out with multi-track finesse."[273]

"Sorrow Tomorrow" single from Chile

The final song recorded at this session also provided Darin with a top five hit. *Things* wasn't released until nearly a year after it was recorded and yet remains one of Darin's signature songs and his first definite move into country music. This was also Bobby's last single for ATCO before he started recording for Capitol, although ATCO would continue issuing "new" Darin material for some time to come. The song quickly became a classic, with a duet version by Nancy Sinatra and Dean Martin being released

---

[270] Patrick Doncaster, "Johnny is Worth It," *Daily Mirror*, September 28, 1961, 19.
[271] "Spotlight Singles of the Week," *Billboard*, August 14, 1961, 42.
[272] Mike Gross, "Best Bets," *Variety*, August 16, 1961, 44.
[273] "Record Reviews," *Cash Box*, August 19, 1961, 6.

in 1968, as well as later covers appearing by artists ranging from Anne Murray to Robbie Williams. *Billboard* called the song a "bright ditty" and commented on the "sharp" arrangement and that the "fem chorus is hip,"[274] while *Cash Box* decided it was a "light-hearted romantic jumper" that had an "easy-on-the-ears style."[275] More important than all of that, however, was the fact that this, like *Dream Lover*, was Darin judging the music scene perfectly and creating one of the most radio-friendly songs of the period.

Late October, 1961: Studio Session

At the end of October, Darin was back in the studio to record another trio of single sides. These sessions took place somewhere between October 29th and 31st.

Baby Face appears to have been an attempt to recreate the (probably) unexpected success in the charts of *You Must Have Been a Beautiful Baby*, although, in the end, the song didn't get released for nearly a year. Again, Darin was also cashing in on the twist craze, even shouting "let's twist a while" before the instrumental break. The results are fun, but the song doesn't make the transition to the "chart sound" with the ease of its predecessor, and it all seems just a little too relaxed. The rawness in Bobby's voice is missing during the first run-through and then doesn't seem as natural when it does appear in the second half of the song. *Billboard* oddly referred to the song as a "Dixie-like treatment of the oldie…It moves right along and should score for the lad even though it's not as strong as his recent entries."[276] *Cash Box* were also enthusiastic, saying that Bobby "should be heading right back to chartsville with his latest outing on Atco. It's a fabulous twist updating of *Baby Face* that Bobby and Jimmy Haskell's instrumentalists romp over in a manner that'll please hoofers of all ages."[277]

Irresistible You also finds Darin telling us to "twist a while" prior to the instrumental section – obviously a phrase he favoured at the time! This is a solid number, but unremarkable, which makes one wonder why, when it was released in America as a single, the song was the A-side with the far more commercial *Multiplication* (recorded the following month) as the flip. The record still reached a respectable #15 in the US. In the UK, the sides were reversed, and *Multiplication* soared all the way to #5, becoming another Darin classic. Of *Irresistible You*, *Billboard* said it was a "blues oriented tune, sold in a swingin' rocker groove."[278] Likewise, *TV Radio Mirror* stated

---

[274] "Spotlight Singles of the Week," *Billboard*, June 23, 1962, 21.
[275] "Record Reviews," *Cash Box*, June 23, 1962, 6.
[276] "Singles Reviews, *Billboard*, September 15, 1962, 23.
[277] "Record Reviews," *Cash Box*, September 15, 1962, 8
[278] "Spotlight Singles of the Week," *Billboard*, December 4, 1961, 9.

that Darin was "in the groove for a two-sided hit."[279]

The final song recorded, *Jailer Bring Me Water*, finds Bobby venturing into folk material in a song that became the flip-side to *Things*. The number sounds like a traditional song, but was actually written by Darin himself. The performance is very good, and is an intriguing look into the crystal ball, giving a glimpse of what was to come in Bobby's career. What is perhaps most surprising is that the song took on something of a life of its own, being covered by many singers including Johnny Tillotson, Johnny Rivers, The Bachelors, Freddie and the Dreamers, and Trini Lopez. Some covers were rather surprising. The Beresford Ricketts released the number as a single in 1966 in a reggae/ska-like arrangement, while The Truth gave it a rather convincing makeover in the style of The Animals' *House of the Rising Sun*. Considering the popularity of the song, it seems surprising that it didn't become a regular part of Bobby's live act when he started incorporating a folk section into his shows.

November 7, 8, 10, 14: Studio Sessions
Bobby Darin Sings Ray Charles LP

Bobby Darin's final session of the year, and of his ATCO contract, was for a more personal project, an album paying tribute to his idol Ray Charles. According to the liner notes by Leonard Feather, Darin described the album as "one of the biggest kicks of my life."[280]

The album barely entered the charts, reaching just #96 in the US, and yet it was one of the most critically acclaimed LPs of Darin's career. *TV Radio Mirror* said that "Bobby is certainly to be commended on his flexibility. […] I have no doubt it'll sell like hot cakes – it's an enjoyable tribute from one growing legend to another growing legend!"[281] The author of the review does finds it "strange," however, that Darin uses virtually the same arrangements as Charles himself, and this is certainly a legitimate concern with the album. *Billboard* declared the album a "tour de force" and that Bobby was showing off "his remarkable versatility" on the album.[282] *Life* magazine said that the album was "surprisingly successful,"[283] and *Variety* declared:

> The combination of Bobby Darin's potent vocal style and Ray Charles' moving songs add up to a powerhouse platter product.

---

[279] "Top 50 Records of the Month," *TV Radio Mirror*, March 1962, 15.
[280] Leonard Feather, liner notes to *Bobby Darin sings Ray Charles*, Bobby Darin, ATCO 33-140, LP, 1962.
[281] "Your Monthly On Record Guide," *TV Radio Mirror*, July 1962, 20.
[282] "Spotlight Albums of the Week," *Billboard*, March 31, 1962, 26.
[283] "Life Guide," *Life*, May 11, 1962, 21.

> Instead of making an outright carbon of Charles' vocal techniques, Darin has wisely developed his own interpretive impressions that add much to the Charles creations.[284]

Cash Box agreed, saying that the "chanter does not attempt to imitate or emulate Charles' potent folk-jazz style but offers a melodic musical tribute to Ray's forceful approach."[285] It is interesting how the *Cash Box* and *Variety* reviews seem to be at odds with that from *TV Radio Mirror*, but the points they are making are somewhat different. *Cash Box* and *Variety* are praising Darin for not copying Charles's vocal style, whereas *TV Radio Mirror* is criticising him for keeping the same arrangements.

The poor chart showing for the album is somewhat at odds with an article that appeared in *Cash Box* concerning advance sales:

> [ATCO] last week reported advance sales at 100,000, a reception that shapes up as Darin's strongest LP stint to date, according to Len Sachs, the label's director of album sales and merchandising. Joe Beiderman of Universal Distributors, notified the label that the firm had already sold out of its entire allocation of the LP prior to receiving the merchandise. Dumont Distribution in Boston re-ordered an additional 5,000 copies of the packages based on orders solicited in its territory before getting its initial allocation.[286]

The album opens with a lengthy rendition of *What'd I Say*. It soon becomes clear that the critic who commented that the arrangements were very similar to the originals was correct. However, Darin brings something new and exciting to these songs. The whole album is one of Bobby's most exciting, and *What'd I Say* starts it off in great fashion. The number was split into the two sides of a single and also received good reviews, with *Billboard* writing that "Darin is in sock, showmanly vocal form on this exciting Ray Charles tune."[287] *Cash Box* enthused that "it's a fabulous 2-part revival of the Ray Charles classic that Bobby and the Jimmy Haskell ork-chorus belt out in ultra-commercial fashion."[288] In the UK, the song was squeezed onto one side of the single, and was backed with *Ain't that Love*. The song saw Bobby nominated for the Best Rhythm 'n' Blues Recording Grammy at the 5th annual ceremony – only for him to lose out on the award, which went to...yes, Ray Charles.

---

[284] "Darin's 'Charles,' Burns' 'Strings,' B'Way's 'All-American' Top New LPs," *Variety*, April 11, 1962, 60.
[285] "Album Reviews," *Cash Box*, March 31, 1961, 28.
[286] "Bog Advance on *Darin Sings Charles* LP," *Cash Box*, March 31, 1962, 36.
[287] "Spotlight Singles of the Week," *Billboard*, March 17, 1962, 23.
[288] "Record Reviews," *Cash Box*, March 17, 1962, 8.

The second track of the album is the most ambitious. Darin had already recorded *I Got a Woman* at the jazz combo sessions nearly two years earlier and also for the *Darin at the Copa* album. Here he tackles it again – for a whole six and a half minutes. The song starts off in normal fashion, but then Bobby keeps the "alright" ending of the song going for in excess of three minutes despite it being basically the same line repeated over and over again. This is Darin at his most self-indulgent, and yet there is still a point to it, for he finds almost every possible variation of singing that line during this extended coda which listeners are going to love or tire of quickly and simply hit the "next" button on the remote control. This is miles away from the more polished vocals of, say, *Love Swings*. During the main section, he reaches for notes and misses them, but it doesn't matter – Darin is showing us that this music is all about "feel" and not about technical perfection, and he hits that message home time and again during the course of the album.

I Got a Woman might have been an epic, but *Tell all the World About You*, which follows, clocks in at under two minutes. There is some great interplay between Darin and vocal group The Blossoms here which elevates this otherwise straightforward rendering of the song.

Tell Me How Do You Feel opens with a funky organ introduction before Darin and The Blossoms again trade phrases in this blues number. The change of instrumentation helps to add variety to the album, and the saxophone solo (by Nino Tempo or Pas Johnson) is stunning. Bobby finishes the song with a couple of choruses of the "alright" ending that was heard in the second half of *I Got a Woman*.

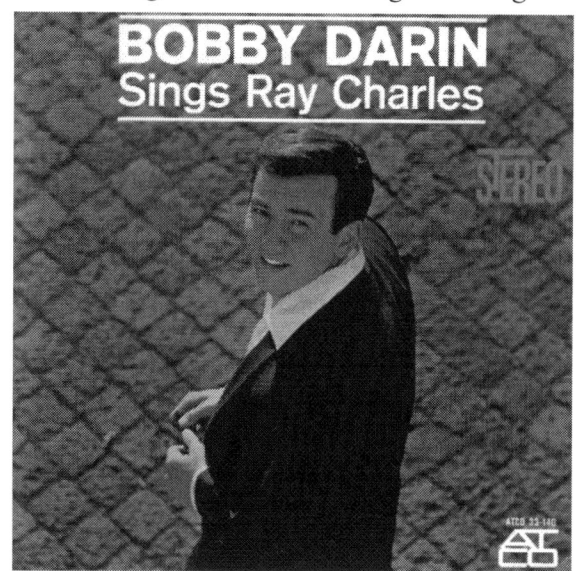

U. S. LP cover

My Bonnie, which ends the first side of the LP, continues the same high quality of singing and arranging, but suffers a little in that it is also more of the same of what has come before. The second side of the album contains two slower numbers, and perhaps moving one of these to the first side would have provided more variety to the track listing. What is noticeable here, though, is that, just as with the Christmas album, Darin is more than willing to give some of the spotlight to the backing singers (in this case The Blossoms) and/or the musicians in the band.

The second half of the album opens with one of the highlights. *The Right Time* begins with a soulful saxophone solo, and is also one of the few Darin studio recordings to be a genuine duet, with the lead being sung by Darlene Love for two whole verses. Once again, the arrangement is very similar to Charles's own, and yet Darin's vocal line is actually rather different thanks to subtle changes to phrasing.

Hallelujah I Love Her So, one of the more familiar songs here to those who are not Charles fans, is given a straightforward rendition. It would be wrong to suggest that this means it was merely album filler, but there are no risks taken here with the arrangement or the vocal delivery.

Leave My Woman Alone has a jazzier feel than some of the other numbers, thanks to the tight harmonies in the brass section. There is also a gospel tinge to the track. However, Darin sings this at the lower end of his vocal range, meaning it doesn't have as much of an intensity as some of the songs here. He also repeats the last line over and over for nearly a minute before launching into a final chorus. This device worked well with *I Got a Woman*, but this is the second time it had been repeated on the same album, and little is gained from it here.

Ain't that Love carries on the same feel as the previous couple of numbers. It is easy to forget just how well the album is recorded and mixed. Darin is undoubtedly the star here, but The Blossoms are as far forward in the mix as he is, almost making each and every track a duet.

The penultimate track, *Drown in My Own Tears*, is probably the best on the album. A slow blues, it provides contrast with much of what has come before. The arrangement is again first class, and Darin's vocal uses the "pleading" quality that sometimes was overdone, but is perfectly judged on this occasion. In the late 1960s, Darin performed the song on a television special, slowing the tempo still further and turning the number into an epic of around seven minutes.

In many ways, *Drown in My Own Tears*, is the climax of the album as there is a feeling that *That's Enough* acts more like a kind of theme song, just as *That's All* did for his sophomore album. Again, it is well sung, but seems more like a coda than the real finale of the record.

Also recorded at these sessions was the studio version of *Multiplication*, which cinema audiences had heard a number of months earlier in the film *Come September*. It seems bizarre that this catchy rock 'n' roll number wasn't recorded in advance and released at the time of the film, as it had "hit" written all over it. The studio version is certainly much better than the one in the film, which seems hesitant, bland, and, frankly, unfinished in comparison. Ultimately, this number, one of Darin's finest original rock 'n' roll songs, ended up as the flip-side to *Irresistible You* in the USA, although it was a big hit in the UK (and made the top 40 again when covered by Showaddywaddy in 1981).

According to Dorothy Kilgallen, Darin was again being headhunted for Broadway

"Too Late Blues" (Paramount).

around the time of the above sessions, this time for the musical *I Can Get it For You Wholesale* which eventually premiered in 1962 with Elliott Gould in the lead role.[289] Bobby himself purchased the screen rights to the broadway comedy *Invitation to a March* by Arthur Laurents.[290] The film was never made, although a PBS TV movie appeared in 1972, without input from Bobby.

At the same time, he was regularly seen in cinemas during 1961 and 1962. Late 1961 saw the release of *Too Late Blues* (dir. John Cassavetes), in which Darin played a struggling jazz musician. The film received much attention at the time of release, but generally mediocre reviews, although Bobby was sometimes praised for his "straight" role, with trade publication *Film Bulletin* stating that he has "moments of credibility,"[291] and UK newspaper the *Daily Mirror* saying that he gives a "sound performance."[292] The *New York Times* went further, saying the lead was "played to perfection" by Darin.[293]

It was the film itself rather than the performances that were criticised. *Monthly Film Bulletin* wrote:

> Cassavetes seems to be striving towards a warm, emotional statement about his characters, yet more often than not he is thwarted by sentimental clichés and an uncertain technical control, discernible in the flat lighting and unlived-in sets. One never fully

---

[289] Dorothy Kilgallen, "The Voice of Broadway," *Dunkirk Evening Observer*, October 14, 1961, 6.
[290] "Bobby Darin Purchases Broadway Play Rights," *Box Office*, June 19, 1961, W1.
[291] "Too Late Blues," *Film Bulletin*, January 22, 1962, 22.
[292] "After 'Shadows' – a Blues Note," *Daily Mirror*, November 24, 1961, 33.
[293] Howard Thompson, "Screen: Darin in Too Late Blues," *New York Times*, March 1, 1962, 27.

senses the combo's dedication towards their art and it is this kind of lack of personal communication which finally weakens the story's meaning.[294]

Others saw the film's failure to be due to director John Cassavetes move from independent film-making to pairing up with a major studio. Philip Oakes wrote in *Sight and Sound*:

> *Too Late Blues* is what happens when a film-maker of mingled gifts tries to match his talent for screen improvisation with the rigid demands of the front office. The result – as someone once said of Gershwin's attempt to wed classical music to jazz – is frankly a bastard, although here at least the parenthood is never in doubt. As producer, director and (with Richard Carr) co-author, John Cassavetes is triply responsible for the film's style, and its partial failure seems the consequence of a calculated compromise.[295]

The Tatler magazine summed the film up as a "decidedly dreary picture," which, to be fair, isn't far from the truth.[296] That said, *Too Late Blues* appears to have garnered more respect in recent years, even if it is still viewed as a flawed, intriguing failure.

Viewed as a whole, Bobby's film career was patchy and ultimately disappointing because it stalled within a few years, but credit needs to be given to him for taking on difficult, often unlikeable, roles in difficult, often unlikeable, films. And that doesn't mean a film needs to be likeable to be successful (and we will deal with *Pressure Point*, which proves this, in the next chapter), but as a singer turning to acting in 1960s Hollywood, you could only indulge yourself in so many serious films within a short space of time before it affected your box office potential, and one could argue that is what happened with Darin.

April 1962 saw the release of the remake of *State Fair*, a film musical by Rodgers and Hammerstein. Directed by José Ferrer and starring Darin, Ann-Margret and Pat Boone, the film got panned in reviews of the time. *TV Radio Mirror* didn't hold back when they reviewed the film and called it a "hopeless venture. It suffers terribly by comparison with the original. Pat Boone is utterly boring!"[297] At least we get told that "Darin does a bit better than his cohorts, but even he seems like he's over-deliberate." The review concludes that "certainly this is not the way to revive musicals on the screen, at least not with this kind of sound track. Lots of luck!"

---

[294] "Too Late Blues," *Monthly Film Bulletin*, December 1961, 168.
[295] Philip Oakes, "Too Late Blues and The Hustler," *Sight and Sound*, Winter 1961, 40.
[296] Elspeth Grant, "Films," *The Tatler,* December 6, 1961, 713.
[297] "Movies." *TV Radio Mirror*, July 1962, 23.

State Fair: Gaiety, Laughter and Fun!

Trade publications were, understandably, trying to sell the film to exhibitors, but even considering this, *Film Bulletin*'s description of the film as a "gay, tune-filled hunk of entertainment" seemed a little over the top.[298] *Box Office* were enthusiastic about the film as a whole, but not so much about Darin, who they described as "suitably cast."[299] In truth, *State Fair* was a rather limp remake that was too square for the youngsters who were fans of the main cast members, and an unwanted and unneeded remake in the eyes of older cinemagoers. Much can be taken from the fact that this was José Ferrer's seventh films as director, and that there was no eighth.

Bobby appeared on the soundtrack album in a couple of group numbers as well as on his solo number, *This Isn't Heaven*, a new song written for the remake by Richard Rodgers alone. Little is known about this session or when it took place, although late 1961 seems most likely. Darin does what he can with the song, but both the performance and the song itself are uninteresting and ultimately forgettable. Perhaps

---

[298] "State Fair," *Film Bulletin*, March 19, 1962, 12.
[299] Frank Leyendecker, "State Fair," *Box Office*, March, 1962, 17.

the most interesting element was that the soundtrack album nearly didn't come into being at all after a series of legal wrangles as each performer was signed to a different record label, and, later, it was unavailable for a number of years. The current digital download of it contains a demo version of one of the group numbers – but I wouldn't get excited about that either other than for its rarity value.

Bobby's movie career brought him a couple of awards in the second half of 1961. He won the Interstate circuit's award for foremost new motion picture star of the year in September, for his work in *Come September*.[300] At the other end of the spectrum, he also won the Hollywood Women's Press Club Sour Apple for being the most uncooperative actor of the year.[301] Darin took it in good spirits, appearing dressed as Santa Claus and passing out gifts to those who had voted for him. "I'm honestly flattered," he is quoted as saying. "Marlon Brando was nominated too – and he ain't doing too bad!"

December 1961 saw a compilation called *Twist with Bobby Darin* hitting the stores. Darin had gained a new lease of life in the singles charts and so this album was no doubt intended to cash in on that. Despite being filled with previously available recordings (including five that been included on *For Teenagers Only* and another that had been on *The Bobby Darin Story*, both from the year before), the LP got good reviews at the time of release. *Variety* said that the "terpsters are sure to flock around" ("terpster" was *Variety*'s slang for "dancer").[302] *Life*, meanwhile, said it was a "full-throated blast" (which we assume is a good thing).[303] Bobby also saw another "new release" in December 1961, with the birth of his son, Dodd Darin.

Bobby started appearing regularly on television again in early 1962, including an appearance on a star-filled gala called *At This Very Moment* to raise awareness of progress in cancer treatments. When more stars volunteered their services than could be fitted into the time slot, songs were cut and other stars decided to perform together rather than alone. Bearing this in mind, Bobby paired up with Jimmy Durante for a performance of *Bill Bailey*.[304] A few months earlier, he had appeared on stage (together with the cast of *State Fair*) at a benefit in Dallas for the victims of Hurricane Carla which had caused 43 fatalities and hundreds of thousands of dollars of damage the month before.[305]

Bobby's live performances continued to garner rave reviews. He performed for ten nights at the Three Rivers Inn during May and June 1962, with his setlist now

---

[300] "Interstate Circuit Award Goes to Bobby Darin," *Boxoffice*, September 25, 1961, 11.
[301] Mike Connolly, "The Best of Hollywood," *hiladelphia Inquirer*, December 30, 1961, 12.
[302] "'Nuremberg' Track, Darin's 'Twist,' Damone's 'Linger' Top New LPs," *Variety*, December 27, 1961, 26.
[303] "Life Guide," *Life*, January 12, 1962, 32.
[304] "Many Stars Join TV Cancer Show," *New York Times*, March 30, 1962, 26.
[305] "Film, Disk Stars Head Carla Victims' Benefit," *Variety*, October 4, 1961, 63.

including the Steve Allen composition *This Could Be the Start of Something Big*. It is interesting to note that *Dream Lover* was still in his repertoire at this time, although it would soon be dropped completely. At this point, *Mack the Knife* was the final song of Darin's performance.[306]

Later in June, he was also appearing in a series of concerts with Count Basie.[307] Things didn't always go according to plan, however, and the show in Boston on June 27 brought in an audience of around 2000 in an 7200-seat auditorium. "To make matters worse," *Variety* wrote, "the sound system did an off again on again Finnegan, and Darin, obviously irked, asked patrons to ask for their money back (some did), and told the audience he'd come back again 'but not here' and said 'the place should be razed.'"[308] It is worth noting that the concerts on the Basie tour were not the only Darin shows that failed to bring in large audiences around this time.

1962 would bring a big change in the recording career of Bobby Darin. After nearly four years with ATCO, he would leave the label and move to Capitol. The announcement appeared in *Billboard* on July 21, five days after Darin's first recordings for his new label. The deal was described as "the highest ever offered by Capitol to any artist."[309] The switch from the smaller label to a more prestigious one would bring Bobby mixed fortunes. He left ATCO at a time when his singles were selling considerably better than they had for some time, but he would only break the top ten twice during his three years with Capitol, and none of his albums were anywhere near as commercially successful as his best for ATCO. On the other hand, his recordings for Capitol were more consistent in quality than those he had produced for ATCO. Part of this was because he was now far more experienced (and there were no mop-up albums in the vein of *For Teenagers Only*), and, lack of commercial success notwithstanding, the Capitol years were both prolific and often artistically rewarding.

---

[306] J. W., "Darin Draws Smiles, Applause at Three Rivers," *The Post-Standard*, May 27, 1962, 18.
[307] Prescott Page, "Excellent Spring Club Business Continuing," *The Lowell Sun*, June 22, 1962.
[308] "Darin, Irked at Boston Bash, Advises Sparse Turnout Ask For Their Money Back," *Variety*, July 3, 1962, 6.
[309] "Signing of Bobby Darin Start of Capitol Beef-Up," *Billboard*, July 21, 1962, 4.

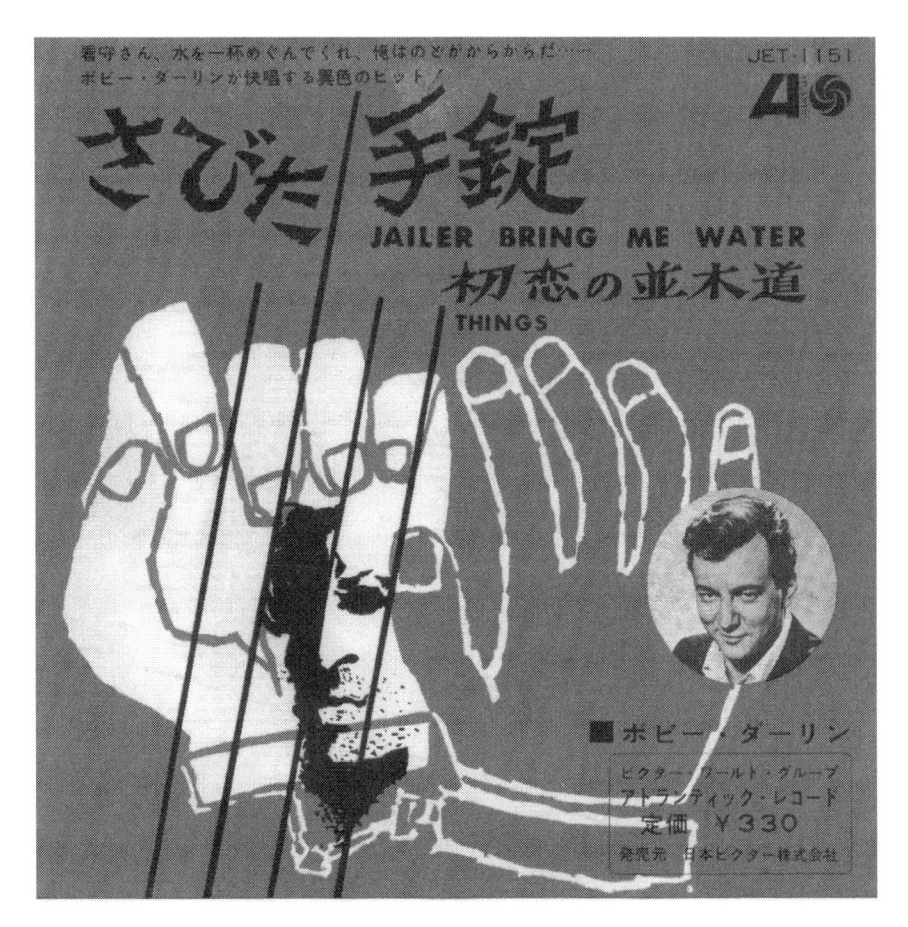

Striking Japanese picture sleeve.

CHAPTER SIX
OH! LOOK AT ME NOW: 1962

There have been a number of stories about Bobby being courted when Sinatra started his own record label, Reprise. Whether these stories are true or not are, like so many show business tales, impossible to know for certain. In all of the various accounts, certain elements don't add up, whether it be the dates, the project Sinatra was supposedly working on at the time, or something else. As an example, David Evanier's biography of Darin states the following:

> In July 1962, Frank Sinatra was on the set of the film *Sergeant's Three* when he called Steve Blauner and asked to see him. When they met, Sinatra introduced him to Moe Austin and explained that he and Moe were forming a new label, Reprise Records. Sinatra said he was planning to sign Dean Martin and Sammy Davis Jr. for Reprise, and he wanted Bobby Darin on Reprise as well.[310]

We are then told that Blauner said he would give Sinatra an answer the next day, but that he went straight away to Capitol, who agreed to sign Bobby in a better deal. Evanier goes on: "Capitol, having lost not only Sinatra but Dino and Sammy, would pull out all the stops for Bobby and Nat King Cole. Bobby signed the three-year contract with Capitol on July 12, 1962."[311]

Presumably this story was told to Evanier by Blauner himself, but much of it cannot be true. For example, *Sergeant's Three* was released in February 1962, and so Sinatra would not have rung Blauner from the set of it in July of that year. Meanwhile, Dean Martin had released his first album for Reprise in the spring of 1962, and Sammy

---

[310] David Evanier, *Roman Candle*, 141.
[311] Ibid.

Davis Jr had recorded his first LP for the label in early 1961, and so Sinatra wasn't "planning" to recruit them, but had already done so. It is also worth adding that Capitol had not lost Davis to Reprise, as he had stopped recording for the label nearly a decade earlier and had been with Decca ever since. Clearly, Blauner's account of the tale as told to Evanier plays with the truth somewhat to make his achievement of getting Bobby signed at Capitol (and snubbing Sinatra's offer) look greater. Blauner is quoted as saying "the story about that is that Bobby's deal was up with Atlantic. They made no giant overtures. Didn't come around and kiss my ass."[312] One wonders why a label that had shown great faith in Darin, supported his move in to standards, and even been willing to press ahead with his most esoteric albums should feel the need to kiss Blauner's "ass" in order to encourage Bobby to stay with them. Evanier also quotes Ahmet Ertegun of Atlantic: "Bobby also got influenced by his managers and by outside forces which were not always the best."[313] Going by the above quotes, once can sympathise with Ertegun.

The signing of Bobby to Capitol was big news within the trade papers. *Billboard* wrote that "Capitol Records gave evidence this week that is it making a concerted bid to assert a stronger foot in the pop field with the signing of Bobby Darin."[314] They went on:

> Details of the deal offered Darin were reported as being equal to the highest ever offered by Capitol to any artist. Darin's single and LP product will be independently produced by Ferrion, Inc, Darin's own firm. The singer's manager, Steve Blauner, will supervise the singer's recordings. The disks produced will be released through Capitol and the Darin firm will receive a high percentage and a high guarantee during the new long-term contact.

Several months later, Bobby denied that his contact involved a $2million guarantee for ten years, instead describing it as a "profit-sharing arrangement."[315]

No matter what the terms of the agreement, Bobby's decision to move to Capitol might not have been the best decision for him. At ATCO, Bobby had been allowed to take risks, make mistakes, and even make records that almost certainly were bound to divide opinion. Other than the *Earthy!* album, which was made within a month of signing to the label, the Capitol years saw Darin moving into generally much safer territory. The swing albums, even the one reuniting him with Richard Wess, were

---

[312] David Evanier, *Roman Candle*, 142.
[313] Ibid, 141.
[314] "Signing of Bobby Darin Start of Capitol Beef-Up," *Billboard*, July 21, 1962, 4.
[315] "Dickering Over Guarantees Killing the Disk Industry, Bobby Darin Sez," *Variety*, November 7, 1962, 45.

On stage in Las Vegas

much more predictable in their song choices and/or arrangements than those that had come before, and the sound became slick and professional rather than raw and exciting. And, while Capitol eventually released *Earthy!* a year after it was recorded, they failed to get behind Bobby's brilliant album of folk songs and sprituals from around the world and promote it in the way that ATCO would have done. Earlier, we encountered reviews of *Too Late Blues* where much of the blame for the quality of the film was aimed at John Cassavetes move from independent filmmaking to being under the control of a major studio, and the same effectively happened to Bobby when he moved to Capitol. He would have had much more creative freedom at Reprise (or staying at ATCO), and probably more encouragement to follow his own personal interests.

This does not mean that Bobby's work for Capitol is weak (far from it), and most artists would have given anything to produce albums as wonderful as *Oh! Look at Me Now* and *From Hello Dolly to Goodbye Charlie*. They feature great singing and fine arrangements – but their polish makes them sound more like Capitol albums than Darin albums, and it is difficult to know if this was because of choices made by Bobby himself, requests from the label, or poor advice from elsewhere. It seems ironic that he had given an interview a year or two earlier, bemoaning the fact that other singers of his age were not taking enough risks and making enough mistakes in their career when for the next three years he would follow his own safe path in the recording studio. During the same period, his film career faltered, success in the charts started to evade him, and his marriage to Sandra Dee ran into difficulties. His unhappiness at Capitol might not have been obvious to his fans, but the industry were made fully aware of it when he and the label abruptly parted ways in early 1964. Strangely, he signed another short-term contract with Capitol that summer, but this would only last a matter of months before he again sought a release. It may be no coincidence that his time with Motown in the early 1970s, another major label by that point, also finished through an agreed parting of the ways rather than a contract running its course.

July 16, 1962: Studio Session

One can only wonder what Capitol thought of Bobby's first recordings for the label. If they were expecting him to head into the studio and put down on tape a couple of Sinatra-like big band numbers, they were very much mistaken. Instead, he chose as his first venture to record a couple of folk songs with Jimmy Haskell arrangements, and the results sound completely unlike anything Bobby had ever recorded before.

In many respects, these performances of *Scarlet Ribbons* and *Oh Shenandoah* sound like a dress rehearsal for the *Earthy!* sessions, which would start the following week. Bobby's voice sounds unusual here, quite different to the ballad singing of the ATCO years, but it is a vocal tone he would employ often in the coming years during his folk recordings. Both songs suffer from the overuse of a choir behind Bobby (an issue that will be encountered often during the Capitol years), and *Scarlet Ribbons* seems to have a lack of focus and intention. *Oh Shenandoah* is better for the most part, although it loses its way a little during the central section when Bobby vocalises while the choir sings the tune. Both songs remained unreleased until 2016, when Capitol allowed them to escape on the unheralded download-only release *Rare Capitol Masters Deluxe Edition*, that appeared without even many devoted fans noticing.

July 23, 1962: Studio Session

The reason for this session was to record Bobby's first single for his new label. This was the title song for his new film, co-starring Bobby's wife, Sandra Dee, entitled *If a Man Answers*. The sound here follows on from that he had utilised at ATCO for his most recent hit singles, even down to the "twist" element. The song itself is a fun number, the arrangement didn't sound out of place on the charts, and Darin's performance is lively and commercial. *Cash Box* got a little over-excited, calling the song "rock-a-rock-a-rhythmic."[316] *Variety*, meanwhile, referred to the song as a "cute little number with a clever lyric which he projects with his customary savvy."[317] The single should have been a smash, and yet it stalled in the charts at #32.

Unlike *Multiplication* from *Come September*, the single was released to coincide with the film hitting cinemas. The film itself got some decent reviews, with *Film Bulletin* saying it was:

> ...generously laced with amusing situations, some of them uproarious, and plenty of sex-peppered dialogue, and handsomely beefed up with striking Eastman Color New York locations, lush interior sets and elaborate wardrobes running the gamut from sable to bikinis, *If a Man Answers* looks like a real crowd-pleaser.[318]

The film was produced by Ross Hunter, whose other credits include *Tammy and the Batchelor* (1957), *Pillow Talk* (1960) and *The Thrill of It All* (1963). Hunter had an enormously popular formula for romantic comedies at the time, but by the time *If a Man Answers* was released, it was a formula that was beginning to wear thin. *Monthly Film Bulletin* wrote:

"*If a Man Answers*" (Universal) publicity still

---

[316] "Record Reviews," *Cash Box*, September 22, 1962, 14.
[317] "Top Singles of the Week," *Variety*, September 19, 1962, 44.
[318] "If a Man Answers," *Film Bulletin*, September 3, 1962, 14.

> Yet another helping of producer Ross Hunter's romantic candyfloss, this film is an interior decorator's dream: but the 'escapist' plot is more the kind you escape from than to. The 'doggy' business, and Mum's ever-so-naughty French view of marriage, is pretty hideously coy.[319]

Time hasn't been particularly kind to the film, and it is clear that it is several grades below the best of Ross Hunter's movies, such as *Pillow Talk*. The biggest problem is perhaps that it is a romantic comedy with very few laughs. Sandra Dee shines throughout, but Bobby seems to have less to work with in his leading man role than he did as a supporting player in *Come September* and, despite his best efforts, he fails to make the viewer forget the illogical actions of his character.

The flip-side of the single, *A True, True Love*, is a rather disappointing ballad with a slight tip-of-the-hat to the country genre. Bobby's performance is sincere enough, but the whole thing is over-orchestrated and, frankly, rather dull. *TV Radio Mirror* described it simply as "maudlin."[320]

Also recorded at the same session was a revival of the old standard *I Wonder Who's Kissing Her Now*, with an arrangement that appears to have been inspired somewhat by Ray Charles's then-recent forays into country music. Darin would return to this style with *You're the Reason I'm Living*, and *I Wonder Who's Kissing Her Now* sounds like little more than a dry run for the real thing. As with the previous track, it all seems a little too heavily orchestrated, not helped by the substantial chorus that is backing Darin. Seemingly unhappy with the results, Bobby would return to the song a couple of months later for a remake, but it was this first version that was eventually released as a single side eighteen months later. On release, the song got a rather odd review from *Billboard*, who said that "this standard is given the Darin easy-wailin' treatment. The soulful reading is accented by the lonesome sound of blowing sagebrush in Nashville on a Sunday night."[321]

July 25-27 & September 4, 1962: Studio Sessions
Oh! Look at Me Now LP

Oh! Look at Me Now LP was the first album released under Bobby's new contract with Capitol. It was recorded over three days in July 1962 and a final session in

---

[319] "If a Man Answers," *Monthly Film Bulletin*, November 1962, 155.
[320] "Singles," *TV Radio Mirror*, December 1926, 20.
[321] "Singles Reviews," *Billboard*, February 15, 1964, 22.

September.[322] Sixteen songs in total were recorded, with twelve being chosen for the album, one being used as a single side, and three remaining unreleased until the 1990s.

Oh! Look at Me Now has quite a different look and feel to the albums of standards recorded for ATCO. Perhaps most noticeable is the subtitle of the album on the front cover: "moods for swingin' and lovin'," quite clearly an allusion to some of Sinatra's Capitol albums. Also rather different is the repertoire. Whereas the ATCO albums often featured obscure songs, here all of the material is well-known. There is no left-field element at all – it is a straightforward album of standards arranged and conducted by Billy May (who had also arranged and conducted the *Two of a Kind* album of duets with Johnny Mercer).

The very first thing we hear when playing the album is Darin's voice. There is no instrumental introduction to *All By Myself,* a swinging version of a 1921 song by Irving Berlin. Instead, Darin's voice is heard as a jazz combo moves in behind, with the rest of the orchestra coming in after a few lines. One of the other most noticeable differences between this album and the ATCO ones is the sound quality: the Capitol recordings are crystal clear whereas the ATCO ones often were not. Interestingly, May has chosen to use strings in his arrangement here, just as Torrie Zito had on the *Love Swings* LP, but they don't hold the song back, with there being much more of a lightness of a touch. Despite this, some elements have been carried over from one label to the other, and the sustained build up during the track is one of them. Just as with numbers such as *Mack the Knife* and *Lazy River,* there is a key-change at the end of each of the run-throughs, and the arrangement gains in intensity (as does Darin's vocal) with each of the three choruses. What starts off as a laid-back, unassuming number ends up three minutes later as a *tour-de-force,* clearly announcing to the world that Bobby Darin had now joined the big league.

Next up is the first of the ballads on the album, *My Buddy*. Often mistakenly associated with friendships between soldiers during World War I, the song actually wasn't written until 1922 when it was recorded by, among others, Al Jolson. Bobby's ballad singing here is the best it had yet been when backed by a full orchestra rather than just a jazz combo, but the effect is ruined slightly by the use of a full choir, which makes the track seem more than a little saccharine.

Darin was no stranger to *There's a Rainbow 'Round My Shoulder,* another Jolson song, which had been part of his night-club act for some years. As with the *Two of a Kind* album, the Billy May arrangements here fit Darin like a glove, with the number simmering along nicely until it comes fully to life during the swinging instrumental and a well-timed, and slightly unexpected, key change near the end of the vocal.

---

[322] Darin's *Earthy* album was started the day before and finished on July 31. As these were basically the same group of sessions but not released until a year later, I have chosen to discuss the *Oh! Look at Me Now* album and related material first, despite it slightly breaking the chronological-by-recording-date format of most of this book.

Perhaps the most obscure song on the album is *Roses of Picardy*, a song that, coincidentally, Sinatra had resurrected the month before, albeit in a ballad arrangement. Darin, on the other hand, takes this slightly worn-out number and gives it a bright, breezy and brassy makeover. What's noticeable here and throughout the album is the quality of Darin's vocal. He manages to put in a polished performance with a smoother vocal quality than before and yet does not allow this to prevent him delivering show-stopping performances laced with moments of showmanship when he waits a beat longer than expected before entering with a note, for example. What's more, his phrasing is different here too, with him taking much longer phrases with one breath than normally associated with him.

You'll Never Know follows, and is a ballad performed and arranged in a similar fashion to *My Buddy*, with the choir once again adding a syrupy effect. Interestingly, the song had been introduced two decades earlier in the film *Hello, Frisco, Hello* by Alice Faye, who went on to appear in *State Fair* with Darin, which had been released a few months prior to these sessions.

The first side of the album closes just as it had opened, with a song by Irving Berlin. With *Blue Skies*, Darin takes a leaf out of Sinatra's book by using the bridge of the song as a verse before entering into the song proper – a device that Sinatra used throughout his career, but particularly during the 1950s and 1960s. *Blue Skies* is another powerhouse performance, with Darin's voice sounding more powerful than ever before, and with the climax of the song once again showing that there was nothing wrong with Bobby's lungs as he holds a long note and then goes on to link it to the beginning of the next line. *Blue Skies* remains one of Darin's most impressive big band recordings. It is also worth mentioning that the song is yet another one with links to Al Jolson, having been performed by him in what is generally considered to be the first "talkie" feature film *The Jazz Singer* (Alan Crosland, 1927).[323]

The second side opens with yet another Irving Berlin tune, *Always*, arranged in a similar vein to the others. Once again, strings are employed in such a way as to not be intrusive. Meanwhile, Darin gives a fine performance that might not be a highlight of the album but still works well.

You Made Me Love You sees Bobby once more stuck with an arrangement that uses the choir, only this time he and the choir trade lines, meaning they are even more obtrusive. This is another of the songs on the album that was associated with Al Jolson, with him having recorded it way back in 1913.

Along with *Blue Skies*, the best recording here is Darin's classic recording of *A Nightingale Sang in Berkeley Square* which, by coincidence, Sinatra had also just recorded for the same album as *Roses of Picardy*. Here, the Billy May arrangement is a little less showy, and so all of the listener's attention is on Darin's brilliant, jazzy, mature vocal.

---

[323] Despite its reputation as the first "talkie," much of the film is, in fact, silent.

1962

Bobby enjoying a joke with George Burns and Ann-Margret.

It is difficult to remember that this is the same singer who just four years earlier had "eeked" and "yelped" his way through his first album of standards. None of those mannerisms are heard on this first Capitol album, and yet it is still unmistakably Darin.

Also very good is *I'm Beginning to See the Light*, which is possibly the best recording by Bobby of a song from the Duke Ellington songbook. It is a shame that he didn't turn to more of Duke's songs during his career. The second chorus, in which Darin slightly alters the melody on occasions, is particularly fine.

By comparison, *Oh! Look at Me Now* seems relatively subdued. With the song being in Bobby's lower register there is less chance for him to show off his vocals. What's more, while the song title was particularly apt for his first record for the new label, it isn't a standard that has dated particularly well, with some of the lyrics a little bland compared to the sophisticated efforts of, say, Cole Porter.

The final track, *The Party's Over*, is the most recent song on the package, introduced in 1956 in the musical *Bells are Ringing*. The track is particularly welcome as it gives Darin a chance to sing a ballad without having the choir to distract the listener. Now unencumbered from unwanted voices, it is possible to hear more clearly just how much his ballad singing had progressed by this point, and would continue to progress during the Capitol years.

The album was warmly received by critics, with the reviewer for *TV Radio Mirror* saying that the record featured "unquestionably the best singing, in my humble opinion, I've heard Bobby come up with" and there were "signs of his growing capabilities and sense of the dramatic."[324] The writer also draws special attention to

---

[324] "On the Record," *TV Radio Mirror*, January 1963, 12.

tracks that "build up to great shouting last choruses" with Bobby holding "back the 'Sunday punch' until it absolutely builds to it." Van Patten, writing in the Post-Standard, wrote that the album was a "sure fire winner" and "the kind of LP Darin wishes he had recorded sooner but for various reasons did not."[325] *Variety* were also enthusiastic:

> This is Bobby Darin's first album for Capitol since the shift from his Atco home and it should ring up a good sales score. Capitol doesn't yet have a Sinatra substitute in its hopper *(sic)* but until one comes along, if ever, Darin may suffice. He has a strong swinging vocal beat on the uptempo numbers and a pleasing mellow sound on the softer ballad items.[326]

Despite the good reviews, the album failed to do well in the charts. Perhaps with no single to lift from the album and carry it, it struggled to get noticed in a market flooded with similar LPs at the time. Perhaps also, for all the great singing and arranging, it lacked the edge (or sheer danger) of Bobby's previous albums of standards. Either way, the LP remains one of Darin's best and most enjoyable of his career, even if it is one of his less ambitious.

The remaining four songs could all have slotted nicely on to *Oh! Look at Me Now*. Two of them, *Alabamy Bound* and *I'm Sitting on Top of the World*, were associated with Al Jolson, making it at least half of the sixteen tracks having been recorded by him. Neither song was released until the 1990s. *Alabamy Bound* perhaps doesn't have the clout of some of the other Billy May arrangements for these sessions, and has a slightly different feel, which might be one of the reasons why the track didn't make the cut. That said, the slow, bluesy ending is superb and somewhat unexpected. *I'm Sitting on Top of the World* would have sat very snugly alongside the other swingers on the album, and ranks among the best of them. This song could also have served as the title of the album. The four rejected songs were all upbeat swingers and, in many ways, it's a shame that the ballads weren't removed and these rejected songs included instead, making it a swinging album from start to finish.

Darin had been singing *I Got Rhythm* for some time, including it in his 1961 TV special, albeit in a different arrangement. Alas, neither incarnation of the song is one of Bobby's best swingers, lacking the natural swing so associated with Darin. That said, the coda of "anyone who wants any more out of life is just plain evil" is classic Bobby.

As Long as I'm Singing was not included in the album but was released as a single

---

[325] Van Patten, "Pops – Jazz – Broadway," *Post-Standard*, October 28, 1962, 17.
[326] "Charles' 'Vol II,' Mathis 'Rapture,' Darin's 'Look,' 'Swagman' Top LPs," *Variety*, October 17, 1962, 38.

side about eighteen months later. This is the only song from the session that was written by Bobby, and is one of his more successful efforts in writing in the style of the Great American Songbook. The song itself sounds as if it was written as a show opener and, indeed, Jeff Bleiel informs us that it was used for that purpose for a while.[327] Despite the number being classic Darin, its release was actually as the flip-side to *I Wonder Who's Kissing Her Now*, recorded a few days earlier. The song was also pencilled in as the title number of a spring 1964 album that was never released. For more information on that, see the section dealing with the January 9-11, 1963 recordings

A 1967 Australian concert by British singer Matt Monro, recorded for television, finds him also using the song as the opening number. Even if the record-buying public were not interested in the song, other artists were clearly still taking notice of Darin and his songwriting capabilities. This is something that would continue (and, indeed, grow) during the Capitol period, with Darin compositions being recorded by everyone from The Osmonds to blues singer Otis Spann to surf groups such as The Rip Chords.

July 24, 28, 30 & 31, 1962: Studio Sessions
Earthy! LP

In a December 1961 interview with Hedda Hopper, Bobby Darin said that "I believe there's a field for folk songs now and will do some of them."[328] During the same set of sessions that produced the *Oh! Look at Me Now* album, Bobby was able to do just that. However, rather than simply mimicking the Peter, Paul and Mary sound that was popular at the time, he instead did something completely different, creating an album of folk songs (and songs in the folk style) ranging from prison songs to Latin American material, gospel songs, protest songs and even a song from Haiti. If *Oh! Look at Me Now* was one of Darin's less ambitious albums because of its more traditional repertoire, then *Earthy!* is at the other end of the spectrum completely.

The remark to Hedda Hopper was not the first time that Darin had referred to his admiration of folk songs. He had also done so just before singing *I'm Just a Country Boy* with Duane Eddy during the 1960 BBC TV special. On record, he had also recorded the faux work song *Timber* at his very first recording session back in 1956, the slow calypso-like love song *Lost Love* a couple of years later and, more recently, *Jailer Bring Me Water*, a Darin song that imitated the folk and prison song genres. He had also added a folk section (including *Cottonfields* and *Boil That Cabbage Down*, neither of which were tackled in the studio) into his live act by the time that this LP was recorded.

Earthy! opens with two "prison songs," with each rather different from the other.

---

[327] Bleiel, *That's All*, 110.
[328] Hedda Hopper, "Bobby Darin - He Sang 'Mack the Knife,'" *Chicago Tribune*, December 24, 1961, 17.

Long Time Man may have writer's credits given to Ian Tyson and Sylvia Fricker, but it is based on a traditional African-American prison song that went back decades. Tyson and Fricker were a Canadian folk duo who performed under the name of Ian & Sylvia, and one listen to their rendition of *Long Time Man* shows just how much Darin's version owes to theirs, with the arrangement being virtually the same. With *Earthy!* often being regarded as one of Darin's most original works, the similarities here come as quite a shock, and yet he still manages to bring things to the table that are wholly his. While *Oh! Look at Me Now* was devoid of yelps, eeks and groans, here he shrieks, whistles and shouts his way through the song as if to encourage horses or other animals to move faster, and also provides his own harmony vocals.

Perhaps the best track on the album isn't a folk song at all but a former jazz instrumental by Nat Adderley given lyrics by Oscar Brown Jr. As with the first song, *Work Song* takes the form of a prison chain gang song, but Darin's version has an arrangement not dissimilar to that of Peggy Lee's *Fever*, with just bass and percussion accompanying him. What's more, many of the words that he sings are undecipherable due to the accent he adopts for the song. In any other hands, this would be over-the-top, and the accent used might even be viewed as slightly discriminatory, but Darin judges the whole effect perfectly and the track has become viewed as a true Bobby Darin classic.

This 1963 French EP also included "Why Don't You Swing Down" and "The Sermon of Samson."

La Bamba gets a far more traditional outing here than on the more famous Ritchie Valens single from 1958. Darin sings this Mexican folk song in its original language, although he occasionally shouts to the band in English, most notably when he tells flautist Bud Shank to "play it" as the instrumental begins. Again, there are also shouts and yelps from Bobby, but somehow it doesn't all hold together in quite the way that the other songs on the album do. Perhaps the English-speaking world is just too used to hearing the number in its rock 'n' roll adaptation, but the problem seems to go beyond this. There is a great deal of effort here to make the song sound authentic, and yet it doesn't completely come off for the effort is too obvious.

I'm on My Way Great God is the first of the spiritual/gospel songs on the album, and it is quite an epic. Once again, it starts off with minimal instrumentation, with the arrangement growing subtly with each subsequent verse. The song also utilises a choir, but here they are not at all intrusive in the way that they are on the big band album recorded during the same series of sessions. It is interesting to note just how controlled Darin's vocal is, starting off at barely a whisper, and then slowly but surely getting more and more powerful over the four-and-a-half minute running time. Bobby, no doubt, was aware he had a showstopper on his hands, and included the number in the folk section of his live concerts through 1963 as well as when he appeared on *The Judy Garland Show*, filmed just days after the assassination of President Kennedy.

Two more spirituals, *The Sermon of Samson* and *Why Don't You Swing Down*, were also included on the album. Unlike *I'm on My Way Great God*, both are upbeat numbers and arranged in such a way to mix folk music and the gospel tradition. This amalgamation of genres means that the songs in question lack the authentic gospel sound of, say, Elvis Presley's recording of similar material (he also recorded *Why Don't You Swing Down* in 1960 and 1968, but under the title of *Swing Down Sweet Chariot*). Despite this, the arrangements help to make the album coherent even though the songs come from disparate sources.

The first side ends with *Strange Rain*, a then-recent song by folk singer Tom Paxton. This was the first protest song recorded by Darin and, as Jeff Bleiel points out, "recorded less than a year after Dodd's birth, the song's line 'what will become of my son?' may have made it particularly meaningful."[329] As with many of Darin's later protest songs, the number is rather ambiguous in its meaning. By the time that *Earthy!* hit record stores, Darin had already become publicly involved in politics, particularly the civil rights movement, although he rarely talked about it in public unless pressed. However, he was often seen on marches and at rallies, and spoke at the historic civil rights march on Washington.[330]

Everything's Okay, a song by legendary country singer Hank Williams, is one of the album's lighter moments – but also one of its weaker ones. Williams had recorded this song under the name "Luke the Drifter," a country preacher-type character who recites moral or religious-themed lyrics over an instrumental background. This is another example of Darin copying the original version of a song almost exactly, in this case even adopting the same accent that Williams used on his recording. He would go on to "speak" the lyrics to a number of songs during the late 1960s on his work for the Direction label, but all of those examples are better than this or *The Reverend Mr. Black*,

---

[329] Bleiel, *That's All*, 84.
[330] Dick Willis, "March Colorful and Peaceful," *Oneonta Star*, August 28, 1963, 3. Pictures of Darin speaking at the event can be found at:
http://www.bobbydarin.net/hbbdprotest.html

a similar-styled number he would record the following year.

Guantanamera is a Cuban song dating from the 1920s and, as with *La Bamba*, is sung in its original language. Darin's version has a long introduction, played on acoustic guitar and augmented by rhythmical noises and grunts that Bobby himself appears to create, and which are then overdubbed on top of his singing during the rest of the song. Unlike *La Bamba*, this is a relaxed number with the barest of backing and ultimately works better even if, with the words undecipherable to most English-speaking listeners, the aim of the song is to create a mood rather than a meaning. Once again, Bud Shank's flute comes to the fore in the latter stages of the song, but the number outstays its welcome, running to four minutes.

When Their Mama is Gone is longer still, and finds Darin singing this blues-based number about the death of a child's mother in his softest voice. The arrangement is subtle and superb, and the result is supremely moving and one of the highlights of the album.

Fay-O, the penultimate track, is another solemn effort, at least lyrically, about a mother appealing to a witch doctor to cure her sick child. Darin again almost whispers his way through the song, singing it in its original language for the first verse, and then in English. However, while the lyrics might be dark in nature, the arrangement here (again with a prominent use of flute) is actually rather light and gentle, and certainly doesn't convey the somewhat depressing nature of the story being told.

The final track sees the album ending on a somewhat lighter note. *The Er-I-Ee was a-Rising* has Darin romping his way through an old folk song about the Erie Canal. He gives the song the feeling of an old sea shanty, and it is clear that the number is, in some ways, a send-up. However, the sheer musicality that Bobby shows throughout this number is remarkable. It starts out in a straightforward way, but then things become far more complex as the number progresses. The arrival of each chorus brings an increase in tempo, but not just this, the rhythm is also varied, particularly in Darin's interactions with the backing chorus. The second half of the number is a masterpiece of precision timing, where a delay of even a millisecond would cause the entire song to break down. This can be heard through regular speakers, but is even more pronounced when listened to through headphones. It is easy to dismiss this final song as a joke, but it's actually a near masterpiece.

Earthy! was intended to be Bobby's second album at Capitol, with a scheduled release date of February 4, 1963, however that was all changed at short notice when *You're the Reason I'm Living* became a hit and it was decided that an album should be released to capitalise on it.[331] When it was finally released in mid-1963, *Earthy!* did little business, partly due to it being issued in the same month as the album built around *Eighteen Yellow Roses*. It remains one of the hardest Darin albums to find. It was briefly

---

[331] "Capitol Shelves Darin LP For Another Named After Hit," *Cash Box*, January 26, 1963, 40.

released on CD in 2002 (coupled with the follow-up, *Golden Folk Hits*), but has been out of print for over a decade, although it is now available to download. *Variety* did, at least, take note of the album's release, however, stating that "Bobby Darin's vocal versatility is spotlighted again in this all-folksong roundup. With the help of arranger-conductor Walter Raim, Darin's folk fling emerges as a standout package that's not limited to the folknik circuit alone."[332] *Cash Box* commented that "this is a new side to the Darin coin that merits plenty of attention."[333]

Over fifty years after its release, the album appears to have gained some kind of minor cult status, with many non-diehard Darin admirers often mentioning their appreciation of the album on internet forums and groups. One can only hope this continues as *Earthy!* is one of Darin's most under-appreciated works, and there is even an argument to be made that it is his finest hour.

In late 1962, Bobby Darin seemed to be everywhere. At the same time that he was recording his first two albums for Captiol, ATCO released *Things and other Things*. The album was based around Bobby's current hit, but the rest of the LP was merely a mopping up of leftover material and single sides going back years. *Billboard* said that, aside from the title track, the material was "good, but none of [the tracks] are outstanding or as exciting as Darin sides usually are."[334] *Cash Box* were cynical, but honest, in their comment that the album saw Bobby "cash in" on his single success.[335] *TV Radio Mirror* described the package as "unalterably pedestrian."[336]

July 1962 saw the release of the movie *Hell is for Heroes* (dir. Don Siegel), a war film in which Darin had a supporting role. The *New York Times* called the movie "an unusually well-made film" but said that "Bobby Darin overplays a comedy role."[337] *Film Bulletin* referred to the film as a "good, little World War II melodrama," but only mentions Bobby's name in passing, and even then fails to spell his name correctly.[338] In the UK, *Monthly Film Bulletin* criticised Steve McQueen for an "unvaried performance," before saying that "Bobby Darin is more convincing as a looting layabout at the beginning than as a good soldier at the end."[339]

Pressure Point (dir. Hubert Cornfield, 1962) saw Darin get more attention from the

---

[332] "Charles' 'Soul,' Darin's 'Earthy,' Hirt's 'Honey,' Mathis' 'Johnny,' Light's 'Themes' Top New Albums," *Variety*, August 14, 1963, 52.
[333] "Album Reviews," *Cash Box*, July 27, 1963, 22.
[334] "Album Reviews," *Billboard*, September 1, 1962, 20.
[335] "Album Reviews," *Cash Box*, September 9, 1962, 40.
[336] "Your Monthly On Record Guide," *TV Radio Mirror*, December 1962, 18.
[337] A. H. Weiler, "Screen: 'Hatari' Captures the Drama of Tanganyika Wildlife," *New York Times*, July 12, 1962, 19.
[338] "Hell is For Heroes," *Film Bulletin*, July 23, 1962, 14.
[339] "Hell is For Heroes," *Monthly Film Bulletin*, June 1962, 81.

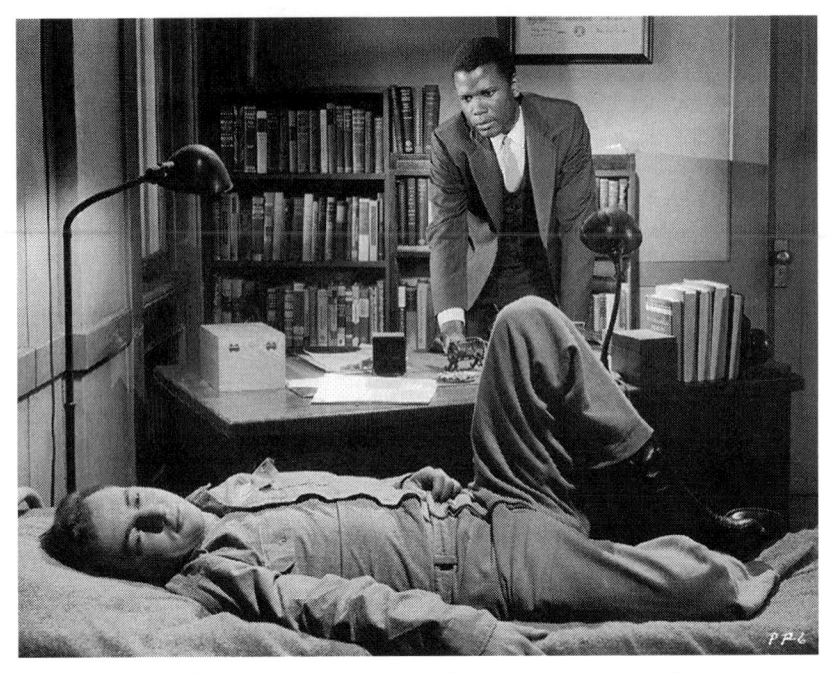

"Pressure Point" (United Artists) saw Bobby starring opposite Sidney Poitier.

press, if only for the provocative nature of his role in the film as a racist, anti-Semitic bigot. Nearly a year before the release of the film, Dorothy Kilgallen was asking readers "is the world ready for Bobby Darin as a Nazi?"[340] *Film Bulletin* stated that "Darin turns in a creditable performance" in a "generally engrossing motion picture."[341] A month or so after the release of the film, Darin penned an article about the film for *Ebony* magazine, about why he "played a film bigot:"

> I know the risk I am running in playing this kind of despicable bigot. There will be many Jews and Negroes who will walk out of the theater believing that I'm really that kind of character. But motion pictures like this must be made and somebody must portray the dangerous people in our society so that the public will recognize them and their causes for what they really are. This picture is certainly going to shatter a couple of falsehoods – or at least establish them as just that.[342]

In the UK, the film wasn't received with particularly positive reviews. *Monthly Film Bulletin* concluded that "well-intentioned as it no doubt is, this film has that contrived

---

[340] Dorothy Kilgallen, "Producer's Daring, but Bobby Darin as Nazi?" *Salt Lake Tribune*, November 19, 1961, D11.
[341] "Pressure Point," *Film Bulletin*, September 17, 1962, 17.
[342] Bobby Darin, "Why I Played a Film Bigot," *Ebony*, November 1962, 46.

air that was the undoing of another Stanley Kramer production on the colour question, *The Defiant Ones*."[343] Kenneth Eastaugh wrote in the *Daily Mirror* that "not enough emphasis is put on the struggle between the good coloured man and the bad white man. But there are some powerful scenes."[344]

Years later, Hal Erickson wrote: "Essentially a conformist psychological melodrama, *Pressure Point* truly comes to life whenever Bobby Darin is on the screen. His performance was outstanding, far better than his Oscar-nominated turn in 1963's *Captain Newman MD*."[345] I have to admit that I agree with Erickson's assessment and, while *Captain Newman, M. D.* (dir. David Miller, 1963) was not released until late in 1963, it is worth discussing it here rather than later since a comparison has already been made.

Captain Newman, M. D. is a comedy drama set in the psychiatric ward of an army hospital, and stars Gregory Peck in the title role, with Angie Dickinson as his nurse and Tony Curtis as an orderly. *Film Bulletin* stated that while the mental health narrative was:

> …a touchy, even questionable, subject for levity, it is treated so subtly and with such understanding that the humor never becomes 'sick.' […] Their patients emerge not as the grotesque caricatures of recent 'serious' films dealing with mental problems, but as troubled human beings to whom the audience can respond emotionally.[346]

Despite the film's shortcomings, most notably its episodic narrative, when viewed today this sympathetic treatment of mental health issues is rather remarkable for a film made over fifty years ago (although *Monthly Film Bulletin* thought the treatment of the subject was "dated.")[347] Indeed, the film is more "understanding" of such health conditions than many films made today, where such a problem is often likely to be seen as the motivation for a killer to go on a spree in a gory slasher movie.

Darin's character is one of a young Corporal who is bottling up his guilt after failing to save a friend from a burning plane, and has turned to alcohol to keep the memories away. The role isn't large – around fifteen minutes of screen time in the two hour movie – but, even as the film was released, Darin's performance was being highly praised, with *Film Bulletin* saying that "his performance in a small but vital role

---

[343] "Pressure Point," *Monthly Film Bulletin*, October 1963, 142.
[344] Kenneth Eastaugh, "When Love Loses Its Sting," *Daily Mirror*, October 9, 1964, 25.
[345] Hal Erickson, "Pressure Point," *New York Times* [online]. Available at: http://www.nytimes.com/movies/movie/39082/Pressure-Point/overview.
[346] "'Captain Newman, M.D.' Strong Blend of Popular Elements," *Film Bulletin*, November 11, 1963, 7.
[347] "Captain Newman, M.D." *Monthly Film Bulletin*, April 1964, 54.

places him among the top contenders for an Academy Award nomination."[348] *Box Office* states that "Darin in his terrifying and highly explosive scene when under the influence of truth serum, contributes the film's high spot."[349] Even the *New York Times* were enthusiastic about the performance, saying that "believe it or not, Bobby Darin plays the kid touchingly."[350] *Film Bulletin* were correct in their hunch about the Oscars, and Darin was indeed nominated for the supporting actor Academy Award, eventually losing to Melvyn Douglas for his appearance in the film *Hud* (Martin Ritt, 1963).

Viewed from a distance of fifty years, however, Darin's performance in *Captain Newman, M. D.* doesn't look quite so good. While there is still an argument to be made that this is a great performance, there is an equally valid one that it is completely over-the-top. When he wrote his autobiography, co-star Tony Curtis agreed: "He gave one of the worst performances I ever saw, and to my astonishment he was nominated for an Academy Award for that picture. To this day I can't understand how that happened."[351] What is clear through hindsight, however, is that Darin was more deserving of a nomination for his work in *Pressure Point* than for *Captain Newman, M. D.* Despite the latter film garnering him a nomination, it was his last important film role. Five more movies would follow over the next ten years, including two leading roles, but none of them are well-remembered today.

Returning to 1962, Darin stepped up the amount of his TV appearances once

Trade advertisement for "Captain Newman, M. D."

---

[348] "'Captain Newman, M. D" *Film Bulletin*, 7.
[349] "Feature Reviews," *Box Office*, November 4, 1963, B11.
[350] Bosley Crowther, "The Screen: 'Captain Newman, M. D'" *New York Times*, February 21, 1964, 36.
[351] Tony Curtis, *American Prince: My Autobiography* (New York: Random House, 2010), 241.

again, with seven appearances between October 3 and December 9. In October, he also filmed an episode of *The Dinah Shore Show*. Darin's portion of the show, finally shown the following April, is larger than most guest spots. He was meant to be joined on the show by Dean Martin, according to *Variety*, but he "bowed out" due to laryngitis.[352] Andre Previn was the only other guest. This is one of the finest musical hours of television that Bobby was a part of. For his part, he performed three songs: *Blue Skies*, *Work Song* and *Long Time Man*, with the inclusion of the *Earthy!* tracks showing that, at this stage, it was still planned for an earlier release. Bobby also took part in several duets and trios throughout the show. All three participants are in fine form, and it is a shame that the programme has yet to be remastered and released on DVD.

Another notable television appearance was his first visit to *The Tonight Show* in October 1962, in which Johnny Carson ended the interview early after Bobby declared that "fan magazines are for degenerates." Shortly after, he spoke (maybe loudly) to Earl Wilson about the issue. "I say they're a paper form of degeneracy," he said. "Not that they print pornography. But they present fiction to a group of minds not aware that it is fiction."[353] He then went on to cite an example where a story was made up because he wouldn't let journalists take photos of his wife and son. It was likely he was also upset at the series of articles prying into his private life and reporting his marriage was on the rocks – something he had repeatedly said was to remain private.

One of the most unusual articles was in *TV Radio Mirror* in July 1962 and entitled *The Honeymoon is Over*. The piece presents itself as a conversation with Sandra Dee, although, as always, there is no telling how accurate the quotes are. Either way, there are moments when the article seems bizarre, even slightly disturbing, and it is hardly surprising that Bobby was upset with the way his wife was being depicted in such magazines:

> 'It's funny,' Sandra Dee Darin admitted, 'but I thought the minute I saw the baby I would love him and feel like a mother. And I didn't. The first time they brought him to me, I loved the baby. But I didn't love *this* baby. I would have loved any baby they brought in, because I didn't know him yet. It was like I loved him more inside, because I carried him for so long. Then when they showed him to me, it was very hard to associate this with the baby I carried.'[354]

Bobby was also on stage. A review of his season at the Flamingo in Las Vegas in *Variety* said that he had "edited the cockiness which disturbed the stuffy; not that he has gone

---

[352] Army Archerd, "Just for Variety," *Variety*, October 1, 1962, 2.
[353] Earl Wilson, "It Happened Last Night," *Reno Gazette-Journal*, October 17, 1962, 18.
[354] Chris Alexander, "The Honeymoon is Over," *TV Radio Mirror*, July 1962, 43.

overboard on a humility jag."[355] We also learn from the review that his impressions were now part of his act, as were turns on the drums, vibraphone and piano. There was also an "effective" folk section featuring *Long Time Man*, *I'm on My Way Great God*, and *Work Song*. Such a segment must have been quite a shock to Vegas audiences in 1962.

According to *Jet* magazine, the Flamingo engagement entered a sour note when Darin went up on stage with vibraphonist Lionel Hampton, who was appearing with Della Reese. The two men had an "impromptu vibes duel" which meant that Reese was "knocked out of her time spot" on her closing night. Darin told *Jet* that he "didn't realize Della was waiting to go on. For that I am sorry."[356] They must have made up their differences as he appeared on her TV show three times in the late 1960s, and she went on to record covers of at least two Darin songs.

Bobby Scott gave his column in *TV Radio Mirror* over to a piece praising Darin in August 1962, saying:

> He always knows, firmly, what he wants in back of himself musically. He has the happy faculty of enjoying other performers – I hasten to add 'who are talented.' Make no mistake that anyone who is as critical about himself, as Bobby is, could be easy with his peers![357]

September 25, 1962: Studio Session

Three weeks after the final session for *Oh! Look at Me Now*, Darin returned to the studio to record four songs, all of which were presumably intended for single sides. He recorded versions of *You're the Reason I'm Living* and *Now You're Gone*, but both were unissued (and remain so), with Bobby redoing them about six weeks later. Also attempted was *If You Were the Only Girl in the World*, which also went unissued.

The only song from this session to have escaped from the vault thus far is a remake of *I Wonder Who's Kissing Her Now*, which Darin had already recorded a few months earlier. It was the July version which eventually ended up as a single side, and this later version didn't appear until the late 1990s. The arrangement is the same, but the vocal is rather different, with Darin appearing to literally sob his way through the song. Quite whether this was intentional, or whether Bobby was seeing a mirror of his own difficult marital situation in the lyrics of this antiquated number and was genuinely upset, is difficult to tell. If intentional, it's a case of Bobby simply "getting it wrong" and, if Bobby was genuinely upset, the song should have remained in the vaults and not

---

[355] Duke. "Nitery Review," *Variety*, August 6, 1962, 19.
[356] "Hamp, Darin Steal Show; Della Left Miffed, Tearful," *Jet*, September 6, 1962, 58.
[357] Bobby Scott, "Bobby Darin and the Double Standard," *TV Radio Mirror*, August 1962, 17.

released, even if it was thirty-seven years later. While unreleased recordings of an artist such as Darin are always welcome if they meet the high standard he set for himself, there are some things which we have no right to hear. And this may well be one of them.

December 3, 1962: Studio Session

Bobby Darin's last session of 1962, produced three songs, all of which had been attempted on September 25.

If You Were the Only Girl in the World was again not deemed suitable for release, and it was not attempted at a later session. It finally appeared in 2016 on the download/streaming release *Rare Capitol Masters*, which took the songs from *The Unreleased Capitol Sides* CD of 1999, and added in some songs released on various albums since then, two recordings made for the German market, and four previously unreleased songs. Sadly, this pulling together of these assorted rarities might well suggest that we shall never hear some of the remaining unissued Capitol tracks. *If You Were the Only Girl in the World* has very much the same feel as *I Wonder Who's Kissing Her Now*. With the bluesy piano licks and Bobby's attractive vocal, one has to wonder why it hadn't emerged previously.

The other two recordings became a single release which catapulted Bobby into the top ten once again. *You're the Reason I'm Living* finds him back in country territory, this time clearly influenced by Ray Charles's albums in the genre. The song itself is hardly original, sounding like a cross between *I Can't Stop Loving You* and *Blueberry Hill*. Meanwhile, unusually for the Capitol era, there are technical issues with distortion at various points throughout the song. Bobby himself puts in a good performance, but its popularity at the time is something of a head-scratcher for it really isn't a song or performance that is anything out of the ordinary. Bobby wrote and performed better single sides during his tenure at Capitol that were more worthy of success.

The same can be said for the flip-side, *Now You're Gone*. This is another country effort written by Bobby but the recording is marred by him

Danish release of "You're the Reason I'm Living."

adopting the fake country twang which would also be used on the later single *The Things in this House* and much of the *You're the Reason I'm Living* LP. That aside, this is, ironically, a better recording and more interesting performance than the much more familiar *You're the Reason I'm Living*. Interestingly, the reviewer in *TV Radio Mirror* agreed: "Either side could bust out," he said, "but I favour *Now You're Gone*. It's a good lyric used in an interesting way."[358] Meanwhile, *Cash Box* enthused:

> The multi-talented artist completely changes the pace on his newest for Capitol and both ends look like they're headed for paydirt. They're two country-tinged affairs, the lilting *You're the Reason I'm Living*, and the slightly up-tempo *Now You're Gone* that Darin puts across with telling effort. Strong ork-choral support from the Jimmy Haskell outfit.[359]

1962 had been a big year for Darin with his move from ATCO to Capitol, and the signs were, at least initially, that things would go well at the new label. However, changes were ahead, and, at the end of 1963, Darin would starts spending less time in the studio and give up live performances altogether.

---

[358] "On the Record," *TV Radio Mirror* April 1963, 24.
[359] "Record Reviews," *Cash Box*, January 5, 1963, 12.

"The Dinah Shore Show," recorded in 1962.

CHAPTER SEVEN
THE SWEETEST SOUNDS: 1963

1963 was another busy year for Bobby Darin, with him recording five studio albums and one live album, making over a dozen TV appearances, performing live on stage in Las Vegas and elsewhere, and setting up his own music company and producing a number of other artists. It would, however, be the last year that Bobby was that active. In November 1963, he would make his last regular appearance for over two years, and, in subsequent years, Bobby would never come close to being as productive in the recording studio again.

January 2-4, February 14, and April 13, 1963: Studio Sessions
Untitled Unreleased Album

Bobby Darin spent eight days in the recording studio in January 1963. During this time, he recorded a huge amount of work, much of which would go unreleased for decades.

From January 2-4, Bobby recorded nine songs that seemed to be built around the idea of updating songs that were mostly written *before* the Great American Songbook. He then switched his attention to other projects before returning to this ultimately aborted album in February and April. It is worth noting that the liner notes for *The Unreleased Capitol Sides* state that two of the songs recorded in April were intended to be single sides for a follow-up to the hit *18 Yellow Roses*. However, this makes little sense given the other songs recorded on that day, that they all fit in with the theme and style of this "lost album," and that *18 Yellow Roses* hadn't even been released by the time of the recording of the April 1963 sides, let alone become a hit, and so a follow-up at that stage seems unlikely.

When My Baby Smiles at Me is a number dating from 1920 and is given a treatment here that mixes genres to create a hybrid that combines both the big band genre and the current pop sounds of the charts. The instrumentation is all big band, but the female backing vocals behind Darin are much more akin to those used on the *Bobby Darin sings Ray Charles* album. The song was recorded on January 2, but was, according to sessionographies, re-recorded the next day. That second version remains unreleased. This is one of the most successful of this set of recordings, with the arrangement not sounding as forced as on some of the other tunes.

Beautiful Dreamer, written by Stephen Foster, dates back to 1864, making it one of the oldest songs that Bobby ever recorded (aside from spirituals and carols). The sound this time around is more contemporary, again with more than a hint of Ray Charles, particularly within Darin's vocal itself. The arrangement has a slight bluesy feel to it, especially within the piano solo during the instrumental break. It is more difficult to understand what Bobby was trying to achieve here, not helped by his rather affected vocal.

When You Were Sweet Sixteen is quite different, and sees Darin once again toying with the twist sound that he had employed during some of his final singles for ATCO. The big band feel of *When My Baby Smiles at Me* is almost completely abandoned here, despite the use of brass in the arrangement. The result is a strange mix of an ancient song being given an edgy, bluesy vocal over a twist rhythm. The biggest question about the recordings made for this abandoned project is that of who Darin was aiming the album at? At one minute, it's a big band record, and at another it's utilising modern sounds and rhythms. While the songs all come together nicely due to their vintage origins, there isn't a coherent sound here, which is unusual for a Bobby Darin album. That said, given the success of *You Must Have Been a Beautiful Baby* and *Baby Face* at his previous label, *When You Were Sweet Sixteen* may well have been a good choice for a single.

I Ain't Got Nobody is a song that Bobby no doubt had fond memories of, having sung it with George Burns during his first visit to Las Vegas. Here the number gets something of a subdued, if modern, interpretation. It is interesting that Bobby decides to perform his own solo during the "instrumental," on this occasion a wordless vocal that is a cross between scat singing, jugband music and a trombone impression. Unfortunately, much of the song is handed over to the female chorus (a device he employed on a number of other songs of the period). The version released in the late 1990s appears to contain a mistake. As the instrumental break starts, you can hear a member of the chorus very briefly start to sing. This might suggest that, as with some other titles released posthumously, this is an alternate take rather than one that had been approved by Bobby.

Despite the bluesy overtones, *My Melancholy Baby* is reminiscent of the ballads recorded for the *Oh! Look at Me Now*, most noticeably because it also features the substantial choir that marred those recordings. Darin can't quite make up his mind whether he's recording the song in his "standards" voice or in his "Ray Charles" sound. Strings are also employed here, although they are not obtrusive. The recording seems to have most in common with the songs recorded for what would become the *You're the Reason I'm Living* album, down to Bobby's oddly affected vocal.

In the same style, with the same orchestration, and the same back and forth between Bobby and the choir, is *You're Nobody 'til Somebody Loves You*. This is considerably less successful than Bobby's live performances of the song in a more traditional manner recorded in Las Vegas ten months later. Here, the arrangement doesn't work for the singer (it sounds more like one that could have been written for Dean Martin), and even the song is too modern to fit in with the general concept.

Whispering, recorded in April 1963, has something of a different flavour, with the song being given a contemporary feel until the instrumental break when the big band sound again takes over. Darin uses his subdued voice, giving a straight-forward vocal under which there is, once again, a bluesy piano. The song would be a hit in the 1960s for *The Bachelors* in the UK, and Nino Tempo and April Stevens in the US. Despite the slightly strange arrangement, this is very enjoyable, and it is a great shame that it stayed in the vaults for three and a half decades.

Many of these songs were first released on this 1999 CD.

For *Somebody Stole My Gal* we're back to a cross between big band, the twist, and Ray Charles. Once again, the song dates way back, this time to 1918. The general feel here is similar to *When You Were Sweet Sixteen*, recorded during the January sessions, and Darin's vocal is similar. This time, the female backing vocals give the song a much more contemporary feeling. While there are a number of missteps in these recordings, there are also numbers like this that are surprisingly successful.

The above eight tracks were released in 1999, but three more appeared more recently on a download release. *Jealous* is the most successful of these. Written by the now forgotten writing team of Dick Finch, Jack Little and Tommie Mallie, the song was originally a hit back in 1924 for Marion Harris, one of the first female white singers to record and perform jazz and blues numbers. The arrangement used by Bobby fits in with the best of the other numbers from this project, and the vocal is seductive and playful. Just as intriguing as the recording itself is how Bobby knew the song at all – as with some of the ATCO albums of standards, he demonstrates his seemingly endless knowledge of popular music of the first half of the Twentieth Century.

I Cried for You, attempted on three separate occasions, is not successful. The orchestration is almost manic with its wailing brass mixed together with a contemporary rhythm that makes it sound almost like the theme music for a TV series based on a comic strip. Bobby's vocal doesn't incorporate the sound but, instead, fights against it, and the result is a complete mess which probably had good reason to go unreleased until 2013.

Finally, *Alice Blue Gown* is more on par with the rest of the project but, again, it doesn't quite come off. The mix of new sounds with the vintage material just doesn't quite work.

The above eleven songs were almost certainly intended for an album project – probably with the intention to add either *I Wonder Who's Kissing Her Now* or *If You Were the Only Girl in the World* to make up the round dozen required for an album of that time. We don't know why it was ultimately shelved. Part of the reason is probably because other projects were seen as more commercial and, ultimately, safer propositions – Darin did, after all, record six albums-worth of material in 1963, and so something had to stay in the vaults, although, as we shall see, sometimes the choices made were questionable. Still, it is fun to put together these dozen songs to hear what the album would have been like.

January 9-11, 1963: Studio Sessions
As Long as I'm Singing LP (unreleased)

During three days in January 1963, Bobby Darin recorded twelve songs, mostly from Broadway shows, the majority of which would be compiled onto an album entitled *As Long as I'm Singing* in 1964.[360] Test pressings were made, but the album was never released, and most of the songs remained in the vaults until the 1990s. No-one really knows the reason for the withdrawal of the LP at a late stage, and Capitol released nothing in its place. The decision may well be tied up with Bobby seeking an early release from the label, but that still doesn't provide an obvious reason for the LP not being issued. No matter what the reason, the decision was a bad one for it can be argued that this batch of songs constituted the best album of standards that Bobby recorded after *That's All* and *This is Darin*. Rather than being one of his most revered releases, the songs have still not been brought together under one roof, and are instead scattered over various CDs.

---

[360] Many thanks to Kenneth Kelly Jr. for sharing his information on this proposed album.

The first side of the unreleased album opened with *As Long as I'm Singing*, which had been recorded the previous year. This was then followed by *Tall Hope*, by far the least known song here, which was from a doomed musical, *Wildcat*, by Carolyn Leigh and Cy Coleman that starred Lucille Ball in her only Broadway appearance. The opening of the show was held up by heavy snow, and when Ball repeatedly fell ill during the show's run (including collapsing on stage), it was forced to close after just a few months. The only song from the show to really have any longevity has been *Hey Look Me Over*, helped by fine recordings by both Judy Garland and Louis Armstrong. *Tall Hope* certainly isn't Leigh and Coleman at their best. Darin's performance is interesting, though, in that it mixes a big band sound with a more contemporary rhythm, rather like some of the songs at the previous session. While he tries his best, the number never reaches the showstopping quality of the best tracks here either in arrangement or vocal delivery.

The Sweetest Sounds was from *No Strings*, the only musical to which Richard Rodgers supplied both lyrics and music. As with *Tall Hope*, the arrangement has more of a contemporary feel than most of the other numbers. The rhythmic figure that causes this is dropped from the second run-through of the song, where it is replaced by a straight swing feel which works considerably better and makes for a far less cluttered sound. Darin's vocal is, as always during these sessions, very good, but he does tend to get lost in the milieu during the first half of the track.

Standing on the Corner dates back to 1956 and the musical *The Most Happy Fella*. As is perhaps befitting of the lyrical content, this gets a much lighter arrangement and a more casual vocal. There is almost a Marty Paich feel to the final section of the arrangement, and the surprise ending is a nice touch, as is the bluesy piano heard during the bridge sections. This is a fine recording that provides a nice contrast to the other songs here, but still manages to fit into the project as a whole.

Love Look Away is from the 1958 Rodgers and Hammerstein musical *Flower Drum Song*. This was their penultimate work together, and the weakest of all their stage musicals, with only two songs really having any longevity: *I Enjoy Being a Girl* and *Love Look Away*. What is interesting about Darin's performance is that there is a new timbre to his vocal, looking forward to the sound he would use on both *In a Broadway Bag* and *Bobby Darin sings Doctor Dolittle* a few years later. Even so, *Love Look Away* is probably the weakest of the ten Broadway songs recorded here, both in terms of material and performance, although its unexpected release in 1998 was certainly welcome.

Moon River, which closes the first side of the LP, remained in the vault until 1999. The opening of the song gives us a foreshadowing of Darin's second "folk phase" that would occur a few years later. Accompanied by just a guitar, Bobby almost whispers his way through the first lines of the song just as he would on the *If I Were a Carpenter* and *Inside Out* albums. However, once the orchestra moves in, the number gets a more traditional vocal, and this is something of a shame. It would have been very nice indeed

Mr. and Mrs. Darin at the "Captain Newman, M. D." premiere, 1963.

to hear Darin sing the whole song in his "quiet voice" with just the guitar accompaniment. Alas, this wasn't to be, and we are left with a pleasant but unremarkable rendition of the famous theme song from the movie *Breakfast at Tiffany's* (dir. Blake Edwards, 1961). But that isn't the entire story, as it turns out the take that was released on *The Unreleased Capitol Sides* (and all releases since) was not the master but an alternate. The intended take and mix can be found by visiting *The Bobby Darin Underground* website, which contains a link to a transfer made from one of the test pressings of the unreleased album.[361] There are a number of subtle improvements on this officially-unreleased master take, most notably the end of the song. On the released alternate, Bobby goes somewhat out of tune on the final note, but does not on the version he intended for release.

The second side opens with Bobby's version of *Fly Me to the Moon*, which was released after Darin left Capitol on *The Best of Bobby Darin* LP in 1966 – a rather strange decision given that "best of" albums normally contain only previously released material. This is a fine version of the much-recorded song, here given a ballad treatment with a sweeping orchestral arrangement that retains the waltz time of the original song (many others switched it to straight 4/4), and again shows off Bobby's

---

[361] http://thebobbydarinunderground.com/2018/06/23/bobby-darin-moon-river-unreleased-final-mix-long-im-singing-lp-acetate/

stronger, somewhat majestic, vocals.

Hello Young Lovers, from *The King and I*, became Darin's opening number for a while, and has appeared on a number of compilations since its initial belated release. Here we are in buoyant big band territory, taking a Broadway ballad and kicking it into life with a Billy May-style arrangement, even though the orchestration is actually by Bob Florence. Darin gives a loose, vibrant performance, with him in total command, playing with both the rhythm and the melody from the very beginning of his vocal – check out how he comes in just a fraction later than expected at the beginning of both of the first two lines, for example. This is classic Darin, and may well have become one of his best known recordings had it not been for the fact that it sat in a vault for over three decades before being issued.

This Nearly Was Mine is more of the same, taking this stately big ballad from *South Pacific* and turning it into fine big band material, ditching the original waltz time and switching it to 4/4. Darin's vocal is again one of his best, but the number is over too quickly, with the song simply getting sung once through with a coda on the end. It was certainly worthy of more than a simple two-minute run-through, and a repeat from the bridge section would have made sense. Bobby liked the song and arrangement enough to sing it on stage and on television.

Just in Time employs an interesting device in that the song starts with the last few lines sung as a ballad before returning to the opening in tempo. This is another great performance, this time of a song from *Bells are Ringing*. The arrangement once again provides Darin with the chance to show just how good a singer he was, not just from the point of view of showmanship but technically as well. He takes long stretches in one breath, delivering a powerful performance, but one that doesn't climax with a simple belting out of the final few lines. They are *sung*, not growled or forced. Again, Bobby was at the top of his game.

All of You gets a more laidback, jazzy vocal. Here, as with *Hello Young Lovers*, Bobby plays with the timing and melody of the song, and even the lyrics on occasion. The problem here is that this song from Cole Porter's musical *Silk Stockings* is under-developed. There is no instrumental in the middle, and the song is simply sung through twice with a short coda, and it is all over and done before two minutes are up. What we have is fine, but it pales in significance compared to the other songs here.

What Kind of Fool am I from the Leslie Bricusse and Anthony Newley musical *Stop the World, I Want to Get Off* ends the album. This is more understated than the famous Sammy Davis Jr. version, most noticeably with Darin opting to avoid a "big finish" (a slightly odd choice given that this was programmed as the final song on the album). He would take this understated ending another step further in the arrangement used later in the year for the so-called *Milk Shows*. The song and arrangement would have perhaps fitted better on the later *Venice Blue* album, but this is still a fine performance of a wonderful song.

One track recorded here was not included on the unreleased album. *Make Someone Happy*, from *Do Re Mi*, quickly became a standard after it was introduced in 1961. Though perhaps most associated with Jimmy Durante, his version wasn't actually recorded until two years after Bobby's. Darin's rendition is taken at a faster tempo that most other recordings of the song. The arrangement has a considerable kick to it, and the jazzy saxophone solo during the instrumental break only adds to this. Darin is back in showstopping mood here, singing with a vocal strength and power that proved to listeners that, even at this stage, he was still developing as a singer and that his voice was getting stronger as the years went by.

The songs here represent some of the best big band recordings Bobby Darin ever made. The arrangements were bright and brassy, and often treated a song in an unexpected way, such as the speeding up of *Make Someone Happy* or *This Nearly Was Mine*, but without losing the essence of the material itself. One can only hope that, at some point, someone at Capitol has the sense to collect all of these recordings together so that this lost album can finally be appreciated as was originally intended.

January 13-15, 1963: Studio Sessions
You're the Reason I'm Living LP

Bobby Darin had already recorded over twenty songs during January 1963 by the time he started work on the *You're the Reason I'm Living* LP. After the title song had become a hit single, the decision was made to build an album of country songs around it. While the songs all come from country origins, however, Darin's renditions of them often fall into big band territory.

This was the first time that Darin had consciously built an album around a hit single, although stablemate Nat King Cole had already done it when *Rambling Rose* and *Dear Lonely Hearts* had become hits in 1962. As the 1960s progressed, the device would be repeated more and more often, with Sinatra getting in on the act with his *Strangers in the Night*, *That's Life*, *My Way* and *Softly as I Leave You* albums.

You're the Reason I'm Living was one of the first two Darin Capitol albums to make it to CD, when it was coupled with *I Wanna Be Around* (aka. *Venice Blue*) for a UK release in 1997. It took three arrangers to provide the orchestrations for the LP. Jimmy Haskell (who had provided the musical backdrops for the *Bobby Darin sings Ray Charles* album) was the man behind the two single sides included here. Gerald Wilson then produced the arrangements for most of the ballads, with Shorty Rogers arranging most of the upbeat numbers.

The album starts with *Sally Was a Good Old Girl*, first recorded in 1962 by Hank Cochran. Darin turns the song into a big band number, and yet keeps quite close to the arrangement of the original version. There are no changes to the structure of the song, with the choir/backing singers retained each time the title of the song is sung, and the fake ending of the Cochran version is also kept, although it is a little more dramatic in Darin's recording. As with some of the performances from the previous dates, the big band sound is merged with a more contemporary rhythm, and Darin seems to be channelling Ray Charles again at times.

Be Honest With Me dates back to two decades earlier, having been written by Gene Autry and Fred Rose, included in the Autry film *Ridin' on a Rainbow* (dir. Lew Landers, 1941), and even nominated for the Best Song Academy Award, losing out to *The Last Time I Saw Paris*. As with most of the ballads on the *Oh! Look at Me Now* album from the previous year, Bobby makes the mistake of bringing in a choir to back him, and they are just as intrusive on this album as they were on the earlier one. What's more, Bobby himself gives an affected performance, and it is difficult to work out quite what he is trying to achieve. He often ends a line by taking the final note up a tone or a tone and a half, and it becomes quite tiresome by the end of the number.

Oh Lonesome Me gets us back on safer ground, with the brass playing the introduction and then taking more of a backseat as Darin sings with a more traditional country backing, although the brass still interject at not inappropriate places. This is a good enough performance, but not a highlight of the album.

(I Heard That) Lonesome Whistle is one of only two ballads here arranged by Shorty Rogers, and is the best of them. Once again, the choir appears each time the title is repeated, but this time are far less intrusive. Elsewhere, the arrangement is driven by the brass section. Darin again uses an affected voice during this prison song, but it is toned down considerably when compared to *Be Honest With Me*. *Lonesome Whistle* would memorably be reprised ten years later during the concert-style final show of Bobby's television series.

A similar arrangement, with a similarly affected vocal, can be found during *It Keeps Right on a-Hurtin'*, where he keeps adding extra syllables to words, for example "it keeps right on a-hurtin-a" or "life-a seems so empty since you went away." Again, it is difficult to work out what the intention is, and it's not a device that Darin often repeated elsewhere. The first side of the album ends with the title number, recorded the previous month.

The second side of the LP opens with *Please Help Me I'm Falling*, a song written by Don Robertson and Hal Blair. This gets much more of a straightforward country reading than most of the songs. There's no sign of the brass section, and Bobby gives a fine reading of this Hank Locklin hit, and this time the ballad is almost completely free of the fake-sounding affectations.

The Buck Owens hit *Under Your Spell Again* gets a complete makeover. Not only does the brassy arrangement breathe new life into this traditional-sounding country song, but Darin also gives it a more contemporary rhythm as well as changing some of the melody notes. It is not the very best of the upbeat numbers here, but after four straight ballads, it certainly kick-starts the album back into life.

Here I Am takes us back into ballad territory, and is again a more traditional country arrangement without the use of brass, although the string section is in evidence this time around. Once again, Bobby tones down some of the mannerisms heard on the earlier ballads, although he does alter the melody at times and seems to gain little from doing so.

Who Can I Count On is a duet with Mary Clayton (later Merry Clayton) and is an absolute blast, and the standout track on the LP. The country origins of the song are retained despite the addition of the brass section. The introduction of the female voice adds variety, and Clayton's soul-filled sound is an inspired choice on a record that mixes big band sounds with country songs – and Clayton was just 14 when this recording was made, with a *New York Times* article from a decade later stating that this duet was her first commercial recording.[362] It shouldn't work, but it does, and both singers sound as if they are having a ball.

The album ends with what is probably its weakest track. The country standard *Release Me* is taken at a slow pace, and sees Bobby trading lines with the choir again. If they are intrusive on the other tracks on which they appear,

U.S. promo single.

here they completely dominate on a number where Darin barely seems to sing at all. Add to this the fact that he has regained his mannerisms from the ballads of the first side, and it all becomes a bit of a bore. At one point, Bobby shouts out "and it hurts me" – it's not much easier listening to it.

Despite the fact that the album had the single to help promote it, it still only reached #43 in the US charts. It was warmly received at the time even if it hasn't aged as well as many of Bobby's albums. *Billboard* called it a "powerhouse package" that was "bright and soulful."[363] *TV Radio Mirror* tell us that "Bobby certainly did these tunes up right" before stating that the reviewer prefers the ballads on the album – which only

---

[362] Don Heckman, "Merry Clayton from 'Newahlins'," *New York Times*, July 16, 1972, D11
[363] "Album Reviews," *Billboard*, February 23, 1963, 63.

goes to show that no two people feel the same way about the same music.[364] The writer goes on to say that he has problems with the album not being able to make the decision "to be jazz-y or country, and thus fluctuates back and forth."[365] For many, no doubt, this was one of the most attractive things about these recordings. Finally, he/she states that there is a "nice cover shot of Bobby," and it has to be said that the front cover is one of the most stylish of Darin's career.

The January sessions had been the most productive of Darin's career. The quality was, for the most part, also very high. Bearing that in mind, it seems somewhat mind-blowing just how busy Bobby was outside of the recording studio during the first months of 1963.

In mid-January, Bobby was back at the Flamingo in Las Vegas with a show that *Variety* said was "even better than before."[366] Some of the songs from the recent sessions had been added to the act, including *This Nearly was Mine* and *Hello Young Lovers*, and *The Sermon of Samson* and *La Bamba* were also performed, with the latter (according to the reviewer) turning in to a "singalong" with Bobby conducting the orchestra. An impersonation routine was also praised in the review. Oddly, the writer seemed to get Darin confused with Sammy Davis Jr. at one point, with him referring to *What Kind of Fool Am I* as a song "which probably would bring complaints if he left [it] out" despite the fact that Bobby's version would not be released until 1999. Davis had a significant hit with the song in 1962.

The following month, Bobby was at the Cocoanut Grove in Los Angeles. On opening night, a TV special called *Darin at the Grove* aired on KCAL-TV, featuring footage of Bobby in rehearsal, interviews, and ending with a broadcast of the first few minutes of his opening night performance.

The review in *Variety* for this season was not as positive, and appears to be picking up on some of the issues of Darin's live performances which were evident in the 1960 *Darin at the Copa* album:

> He has a tendency to casually throw away the numbers the audience is waiting and clamouring for, yet, conversely, to work with great respect and discipline on less familiar material. On the one hand Darin, in the middle of a ballad, will nonchalantly advise ringsiders to go ahead and eat. Next moment, he is crooning in dead earnest, with practiced gestures that, owing to the basic irreverence of his

---

[364] "Your Monthly On Record Guide," *TV Radio Mirror*, May 1963, 10.
[365] Ibid, 11.
[366] Duke, "Flamingo, Las Vegas," *Variety*, January 23, 1963, 68,

approach, seem almost awkward and contrived.[367]

Bobby was also busy on television at the time, appearing on *What's My Line*, *Balance Teen Topics*, and *The Steve Allen Show* in January, and *The Art Linkletter Show* and *The Jerry Lester Show* in February.

Bobby also made the trade press at the beginning of 1963 because of his move into producing. He had already a made a tentative try at production a few years earlier with Addison Records, but the latest effort was a far more serious venture. *Cash Box* reported:

> Bobby Darin has formed his own disk production company, T. M. Music, Inc., for the express purpose of giving new talent a chance to be heard. Darin himself has A&R'd the company's first offering, a single by songster Wayne Newton, spotted by Darin when the artist appeared on a recent Jackie Gleason TV'er...Darin said he is presently involved in negotiations with a number of writers and disk artists.[368]

Unlike the earlier Addison records, Bobby approached T. M. Music seriously, and had the time and effort required to make it a success, especially after his retirement from live performances in November 1963.[369]

Unknown dates, 1963: Radio Recordings.
The Milk Shows

March 1963 saw the announcement that Bobby would:

> ...be featured in a Monday through Friday program series on Radio Station WIBA. The program titled *Bobby Darin* will be heard at 3.33 p.m. and will feature a talk *(sic)* and music by this young star, designed to appeal to both adults and teenagers – not rock and roll music. The *Bobby Darin* show will be sponsored by the American Dairy Association.[370]

---

[367] Tube, "Cocoanut Grove, L.A.," *Variety*, February 27, 1963, 58.
[368] "Bobby Darin Forms Indie Production Firm for New Artist Exposure," *Cash Box*, February 2, 1963, 7.
[369] The best overview of T. M. Music can be found in Bleiel, *That's All*, 99-106.
[370] "Bobby Darin Show," *Capital Times*, March 2, 1963, 3.

These five-minute radio programmes became known as *The Milk Shows*. Darin would record them at Capitol studios, and they would then be overdubbed with fake (*very* fake) applause, intending to give the impression that the songs were being performed live – although how many listeners were fooled is debatable. The tapes of these shows were found back in 2002, with a trio of songs being released on the *Aces Back to Back* CD in 2004. After this, there was an inexplicable delay of another ten years before the release of a double CD set containing more than ninety tracks.

If you're wondering how ninety tracks fit on a mere double CD set, then it's worth stating that no song featured in the series was recorded in full. Each was a bite-size version lasting, in most cases, sixty to ninety seconds. This in itself makes the release a unique listening experience, but it is also worth remembering that Darin was accompanied by just a jazz quartet featuring Richard Behrke, Ronnie Zito, Milt Norman and Billy Krist – no matter what the song. Other than the *Winners* album, this was the only other major project where Bobby would be backed by a jazz combo on multiple songs.

The material that Darin chose to record for *The Milk Shows* covered the whole range of his repertoire, from renditions of rock 'n' roll hits *Splish Splash* and *Multiplication* to a wide variety of standards and show tunes. Some of the songs had previously been recorded by Bobby for record release, and those numbers often get given a different feel here thanks to the stripped back instrumentation. Other tracks are ones that Bobby never recorded in a studio, and so these versions are the only ones we have.

The recording dates for these shows are unclear. The news article quoted earlier is from the beginning of March 1963, suggesting that the recordings began around the same time hence their place at this point in the book. Whether all tracks were recorded around the same time or over a longer period is not known, although it is worth noting that, when Darin draws upon songs he had already recorded, all of them date from studio sessions before March 1963, thus suggesting that *The Milk Shows* were recorded quickly during that early spring. For example, while *You're the Reason I'm Living* (and songs from that album) are included here, *18 Yellow Roses* and songs from that album are not. There are a couple of exceptions. *Days of Wine and Roses* would be recorded in 1964 for the *From Hello Dolly to Goodbye Charlie* album (in a very different arrangement), and *The Sheik of Araby* was recorded in late 1965, but remains unissued. However, Darin dates *The Milk Show* version of *Days of Wine and Roses* by referring to it as "this year's" Academy Award-winning song, thus dating the performance to 1963, but at some point after the ceremony that took place on April 8.

While these recordings are to be welcomed, it should be mentioned that Darin is not always in the best of voice, and certainly doesn't always give a song the care and attention he would for a commercial recording. The very first song on the double CD is a case in point. *Too Close for Comfort*, from the musical *Mr Wonderful*, hardly gets the album off to an auspicious start, with Bobby's voice sounding croaky and he hits a number of bum notes along the way. Things improve somewhat for *Pennies from Heaven*, which gets a nice run-through, but the big finish doesn't quite come off in the way it normally would on a Darin recording. Part of this is due to the low-key performances, but there is also a sense here that some of the songs simply weren't rehearsed enough. *Around the World* is an example of this. It gets an upbeat, jazzy rendition but there are points when Bobby lags behind the beat and others where he seemingly makes the melody up as he goes along.

Elsewhere, it seems to be simply a worn-out voice that is the problem. *Climb Every Mountain* starts off well, and has a better arrangement than the outing it would receive ten years later on *The Bobby Darin Show* TV series, but the second half of the song shows that Darin's voice is shot to pieces. He doesn't just sound tired, but *old*. Perhaps this was one of the numbers that should have remained in the vault. *Climb Every Mountain* isn't the only song here that wouldn't be given a studio recording but would appear years later. *Sixteen Tons* was given a brilliant (and lengthy) reworking during an appearance on *The Jerry Lewis Show* in 1968 and would emerge again on *The Bobby Darin Show* (although not included on the DVD of that series – more on that issue later).

Unsurprisingly, some of the most interesting songs here are the ones that Bobby didn't record or perform elsewhere. The choice of material is also intriguing. A number of tracks are songs associated with Bing Crosby, including *I'm an Old Cowhand* (during which Bobby can't resist throwing in some impressions), *Sweet and Lovely* and *Too-ra Loo-ra Loo-ral* which gets crooned nicely in Darin's softest voice.

Less surprising perhaps are the series of tracks associated with Al Jolson, including *April Showers*, *Rock-a-Bye Your Baby*, and *Let Me Sing and I'm Happy*. *April Showers* is particularly good, and reminds us just how good a ballad singer Bobby was during this period, particularly when not bogged down by the choir that appears to pop up at every opportunity when the tempo falls below a certain number of beats per minute on the *Oh! Look at Me Now* and *You're the Reason I'm Living* albums.

Some of Bobby's biggest hits get quite a makeover in this new setting. *Lazy River*, for example, is taken at an ultra-slow pace and is given a bluesy vocal that has little of the show-stopping nature of the studio recording. *Splish Splash*, on the other hand, seems a little bizarre when backed by a jazz quartet, although *Dream Lover* doesn't suffer in the same way – in fact it works better here than with the big band on the *Darin at the Copa* album. *You Must Have Been a Beautiful Baby* is also heard in a very different arrangement to the hit twist version. This swing version is just as credible, and makes one wish that Darin had recorded it again in this style at a later date. Not everything worked as well. *You're the Reason I'm Living* is positively painful, with Bobby not hitting the final note on the first line of each verse and sounding very weary throughout. Interestingly, *Mack the Knife* isn't sung here, but is just used as an instrumental theme tune for the radio show.

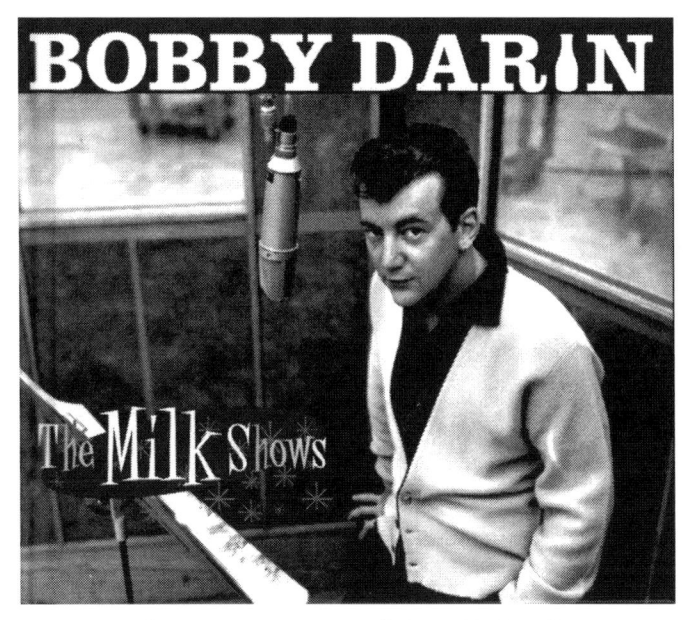

The flawed, but intriguing, "The Milk Shows" CD

It is often the ballads that get given the most care and attention by Darin in this set of performances. For example, *Autumn Leaves* is given a Latin rhythm and is beautifully sung, and a full studio recording of this lovely song would have been very nice indeed. Also given a Latin feel and a similar vocal is the song which is arguably the greatest written by Irving Berlin, *How Deep is the Ocean*, as well as *Fools Rush In*. The use of these Latin rhythms is interesting as Darin rarely employed them elsewhere, although, going by these brief outings, an album in the bossa nova style would not have been a bad move. Also of note is a sincere rendition of *La Vie en Rose*. Perhaps the most bizarre ballad performance finds Bobby reciting the lyrics of *Days of Wine and Roses* while the tune is played in the background in a style not dissimilar to Charles Boyer and Dirk Bogarde's albums in this vein.

A number of songs from the mammoth January 1963 sessions appear here. *Hello Young Lovers* and *This Nearly Was Mine* are given renditions similar to their studio counterparts, whereas the arrangements of *I Ain't Got Nobody*, *Please Help Me I'm Falling* and *Be Honest With Me* are simplified somewhat and benefit from the lack of backing vocals – although *Be Honest With Me* still sees Darin adding the same mannerisms to his voice as he does on the *You're the Reason I'm Living* LP version.

What Kind of Fool am I is given a lightly swinging version here that is arguably more effective than the more traditional performance recorded a few months earlier. What is particularly interesting is how Bobby approaches the end of the song in a completely different way. Here, he sings the final lines in his softest voice, almost a falsetto, and it is just as effective as the traditional ending.

During the Broadway album sessions, Darin had recorded *Tall Hope* from the musical *Wildcat*. Here he turns his attention to the most famous song from that show,

Hey Look Me Over. The normal march rhythm of the song is cast to one side in favour of a straight-ahead jazz approach, but it all seems a little half-hearted, and isn't helped by a rather inept and unenthusiastic attempt at scat singing.

Alongside the well-established standards are some of the novelty songs that Darin appears to have had a genuine affection for given that the album of duets with Johnny Mercer is filled with such material. Here we have *Manana*, co-written by, and a hit for, Peggy Lee, for whom Bobby often expressed his admiration. Darin puts in a great performance here, with his voice sounding stronger than on many of the other tracks. While *Manana* is fun, a number like *Mairzy Doats and Dozy Doats* is an example of a novelty song that is simply tedious. *A You're Adorable* gets a nice run-through, as does *Row, Row, Row*, which includes the verse which is not featured on the recording with Johnny Mercer on the *Two of a Kind* album.

Ironically, the best song from *The Milk Show* recordings is *All the Way*, released on *Aces Back to Back* but, oddly, not included on *The Milk Shows* set. Quite why this lovely performance wasn't included the second time around is a mystery, not least because it is the only full-length performance in the ninety or so songs. Here, Darin takes a Sinatra signature song, gives it a gentle jazz combo backing and a subdued, beautiful performance that certainly deserved to be the climax of the double CD set. Strangely, the other two songs from the shows released on the *Aces Back to Back* CD *were* reissued on *The Milk Shows* release.

There is a rather strange quality to Darin's voice in some of the selections. At times it doesn't even sound like him at all, as if he is trying to channel other singers. There are a number of occasions where he seems influenced by Bing Crosby here – and not just on the Crosby-related selections. *Blue Moon* is a key example of this, as is the rather strange-sounding *I'll Be Seeing You*, where Bobby sounds so tired that he is struggling to even form the words properly. But perhaps most surprising of all is that there are moments that seem to foreshadow the kind of performance that he would deliver during his 1973 TV series. *They Can't Take That Away From Me* and *Come Rain or Come Shine* are both in this category, and it is interesting that the climax of the latter is the same as on the 1973 TV rendition, despite there being no known performances in the interim.

The double CD release is, of course, wonderful to have, but it can also be rather frustrating. Much of this is to do with technical issues such as the fake applause and, even worse, Bobby trying to *interact* with the fake applause. It all becomes rather distracting, especially when each song only runs for a minute or so. That said, presumably the applause was already on the tapes when they were found and so couldn't be removed.

Less forgivable is where songs are joined together in such a way that Bobby is talking over his own singing, perhaps saying "thank you" to the audience that isn't there when he's already started on the next number. The same happens in reverse, where he's introducing the next song while still finishing the previous one. While one can understand why there was a desire to present each CD as one uninterrupted piece, there also seems little reason why songs couldn't have been re-ordered so that these overlaps didn't take place. If that wasn't possible, then a simple fade out and fade in would have worked better than the amateurish jarring mix of two songs together that occasionally happens. Despite this, it should be reiterated that the sound quality of these tapes that were lost for nearly forty years is very good.

Technical issues aside, the run of more than fifty songs in a space of just over an hour is almost exhausting, and with each song having the same instrumentation in its backing, they tend to run in together as if they were one long medley and thus suffer from becoming aural wallpaper. Likewise, while Bobby is on very good form in places and gives some fine, nuanced performances, there are also moments where Darin the perfectionist is, seemingly, on holiday. Back in 1960 in an article in *Down Beat* magazine, Gene Lees had commented on problems with Darin's intonation in his early albums of standards.[371] During *The Milk Shows* recordings this issue arises again, whether due to a tired voice or the sheer speed required to get everything down on tape. However, we also need to remember that these were, in all likelihood, intended for a one-off broadcast not to be repeated – and certainly not to be listened to over and over again some fifty years later.

What *The Milk Shows* undoubtedly show us is that Darin should have recorded with a jazz combo more than he did. The one album that resulted from such a set-up, *Winners*, is Bobby at his very best, and one can imagine that, with a sensible amount of studio time, a number of the songs performed here could have been recorded in full performances for a follow-up album that would have been just as good. That, sadly, didn't happen, and so *The Milk Shows* CD release is the nearest we have, and for that we should be thankful, despite the rather unfortunate, and amateurish, way they are presented on disc.

We don't know for sure just how much material was recorded for the series. However, we are aware that the show went on for at least six months thanks to a comment that Bobby makes between songs. Considering there is only just over two hours of material on the 2014 release, we can assume that much more was recorded, but whether it survives or not is unknown.

April 6, 1963: Studio Session

After what must have been the surprise hit of *You're the Reason I'm Living*, Bobby returned to the studio in April 1963 to record a follow-up in the country style.

---

[371] Lees, "Bobby Darin and the Turn from Junk Music," 16.

18 Yellow Roses managed to reach #5 in the charts in the US, just two positions lower than *You're the Reason I'm Living*, and it's fair to say that *Roses* is the better song and performance. It is a charming number which, rather like Chuck Berry's *Memphis, Tennessee*, has a twist in the lyrics of the final verse which, although a little sentimental (and unlikely, in the sense that Darin was 27 and he's singing about his teenaged daughter!), works like a dream. With Bobby double-tracking his voice it also gave the song a somewhat more contemporary feel.

18 Yellow Roses was helped along by the high quality of its flip-side. *Not for Me* could perhaps have been held back for its own separate single release. Again, the song fits in with the music scene of the time without losing sight of who Darin was. The ending is, perhaps, a little too Vegas-y and the only real downside to the recording. A simple fade-out would have worked better. Darin's friend, Sammy Davis Jr, soon picked up on the quality of the composition and featured it on his *Sammy Davis Jr Sings the Big Ones for Young Lovers* album. If anything, he improves on the original, using an arrangement that starts off quietly and builds in momentum before returning to a stripped back instrumentation during the last minute or so of the recording. Davis also adds a blues flavour through the use of a harmonica. A more recent cover of the song was recorded by Marc Almond.

"The Dinah Shore Show," broadcast in April 1963.

The single was warmly received by critics, with *Billboard* stating that *18 Yellow Roses* "is again in the c&w idiom, but more western than country. It's a ballad in the Tex-Mex groove with strong string and choral work behind the singer."[372] It's interesting that there is *no* choral work behind the singer with the exception of Darin's own double-tracked voice! *TV Radio Mirror* were a little more straightforward, if a little condescending, when they declared "the brash lad has done it again. I like 'Not' but 'Roses' will probably get the

---

[372] "Singles Reviews," *Billboard*, April 27, 1963, 24.

honors. Well-written Darin compositions, plus perfect backgrounds – add a dash of Darin and it's a hit!"[373] In the later review of the album of *18 Yellow Roses and 11 Other Hits*, *Not For Me* was referred to as "one of his best performances of the last year or so. A marching gospel-type vehicle that has in it the kind of rhythm to make you want to get up and march!"[374] *Cash Box* called *18 Yellow Roses* "a potent, big-sounding Nashville-styled affair with a surprise ending."[375] Over in the UK, Patrick Doncaster wrote in the Daily Mirror that "Mr Darin is most fetching with a cute number he wrote. […] It has leapt into the American charts, wistful as it is."[376]

May 23, 25 & 27, 1963: Studio Sessions
18 Yellow Roses and 11 Other Hits LP

18 Yellow Roses was released within a couple of weeks of it being recorded and, when it became a hit, like *You're the Reason I'm Living*, an album was built around it. This time, however, Bobby decided to record his versions of songs that had been hits for other people. The result is one of Bobby's more disappointing albums – pleasant enough, it should be said, but considering some of the material from this period that remained unreleased, it is a shame that this admittedly more commercial (but far less exciting) offering got issued instead. There are still some moments of the Darin magic, but the *18 Yellow Roses and 11 Other Hits* album is largely uninspired, and has the feeling of Bobby simply going through the motions. If the material already in the vaults was deemed to be incongruous with the single side, then he would perhaps have been better off recording an album of his own pop and country compositions, most of which he was giving away to other artists to record for T. M. Music, although other performers were recording them in significant numbers elsewhere. Hearing his version of a song such as *There Goes a Bad Girl* (recorded by Johnny Cymbal), for example, would have been more interesting than this collection of covers.

The *18 Yellow Roses* album opens with the title number, followed by *On Broadway*, the first of three songs on the LP written or co-written by Jerry Leiber and Mike Stoller, the composers of many of Elvis Presley's 1950s hits as well as songs such as *Searchin'* and *Stand by Me*. Barry Mann and Cynthia Weil were the co-writers of the song, which had been a hit for The Drifters earlier in the year. It is one of the highlights of the *18 Yellow Roses* album, aided and abetted by a fine arrangement by Jack Nitzsche that starts off with a stripped-back jazzy vibe which builds with each successive verse, and Darin letting rip as the song reaches its conclusion. While Bobby's spoken

---

[373] "On the Record," *TV Radio Mirror*, August 1963, 24.
[374] "On the Record," *TV Radio Mirror*, October 1963, 20.
[375] "Record Reviews," *Cash Box*, April 27, 1963, 8.
[376] Patrick Doncaster, "Twitching the Night Away," *Daily Mirror*, June 13, 1963, 25.

interjections only distract the listener and seem just a little forced, one could only wish that each of the other songs on the album were arranged with a jazz feel or with the same sophistication.

Ruby Baby is a cover of the Dion hit from the year before, also written by Leiber and Stoller. Here, though, we have a rather unexciting re-tread of the song that brings nothing really new to the table. The saxophone solo during the instrumental break threatens to kick start the whole thing into life, but the recording is bogged down by the intrusive female backing vocals that, at times, drown out Bobby himself. Darin's vocal itself harks back to the album of Ray Charles covers, but the arrangement isn't as good and the vocal not nearly as committed.

The Reverend Mr. Black, again by Leiber and Stoller – this time co-written with Billy Edd Wheeler - was a single for The Kingston Trio and finds Darin back in the same territory as *Everything's Okay*, which had been recorded for the *Earthy!* album.[377] Once again, the words are mostly recited over a basic backing during the verses. The choruses are sung in a very low key and contain some of the worst singing that Bobby ever put down on record. Presumably trying to mimic the type of vocal that Johnny Cash might supply (he would record the song himself for his 1981 album *The Baron*), the results are far from good. While the twist at the end of the song isn't all that different from that at the end of *18 Yellow Roses*, it doesn't rescue this rather dire effort. The problem here, and with some of the country material on the *You're the Reason I'm Living* album, is that, just as in his very early recordings, Bobby sounds as if he is trying to sing in the style of someone else. There is a fake accent here (just as there was on *Everything's Okay*) which hardly helps matters, and this only adds to the suggestion that Darin is trying for something and not achieving it. Listening to the song now, it is rather surprising that Bobby sanctioned this for release.

Australian World Record Club release of the "18 Yellow Roses" LP.

Luckily, the worst vocal on the album gives way to the best, which is Bobby's touching rendition of the Skeeter Davis hit *End of the World*. The only issue here is that the number seems to be over-produced and over-arranged, which is a shame as it takes

---

[377] The song is credited to Jed Peters and Billy Edd Wheeler. Jed Peters was a pseudonym for Leiber & Stoller.

away from the lovely vocal performance. In essence, this is another example of the arrangement being too much like the original, something which a stripped back arrangement (similar to the ones he was giving folk songs on stage) would have avoided. The first side of the LP ends with the flip-side of the *18 Yellow Roses* single, *Not For Me*.

Walk Right In, unlike the other songs on the album, dates back to the late 1920s, but was a hit for The Rooftop Singers in 1962, after which it became something of a folk-like standard and was recorded not only by folk and country singers but also by the likes of Sammy Davis Jr and Ella Fitzgerald. Darin's version has a lengthy whistled introduction. He is at home here, however, and this is a song that could just as easily have been featured on *Earthy!* or the soon-to-be-recorded *Golden Folk Hits*. Sadly, it again appears to be over-produced, with Bobby often playing second-fiddle to the prominent backing vocalists who actually sing two whole verses. At one point he interjects "I'm here," as if we have been wondering whether he has disappeared for good. However, as soon as he grabs a line, the song moves into the instrumental. While Darin's willingness to share the spotlight on some of his recordings is to be applauded, he sometimes takes it to the extreme, and forgets just why people have bought the album in the first place.

From a Jack to a King was written by Ned Miller and recorded in 1957, but didn't become a hit until five years later. It is perfectly possible that this song might have been "on the list" for the *You're the Reason I'm Living* LP but rejected before those sessions began. Either way, it fits right in with that country album concept. Here he goes for a straight-ahead country sound, although it ultimately must have sounded ten years out of date even when it was released in 1963.

I Will Follow Her had been a #1 in the USA for fifteen year old Little Peggy March, although it might well be better known to modern day listeners through the song's inclusion in the 1992 film (and subsequent stage musical) *Sister Act*. Bobby's version of the song is competent enough but, as with so many songs on this album, he fails to put his own stamp on it, partly because the arrangement is so close to the original hit, leaving him no room for manoeuvre.

Our Day Will Come gets a lovely performance from Darin, and is another highlight of the album. However, it suffers from the same problems as the previous number in that the copycat arrangement doesn't allow him to put his own identity into the song. The same can be said for *Can't Get Used to Losing You*, although Bobby's voice can be heard more upfront than in the mixes of some of the other songs here.

The final song, *Rhythm of the Rain*, sounds as if it is going to be more of the same, but then in the middle of the song there comes along a jazz-fuelled instrumental section that, at least temporarily, takes the arrangement away from the original. Alas, though, the diversion is over too quickly and the familiar arrangement returns. Again, Darin's performance is very fine indeed, and shows that he could compete in these genres just as well as anybody else, should he choose to.

In many ways, this album was a missed opportunity. It could have been a much more entertaining listen had Darin taken the ten covers and turned them into something quite different to their hit versions – perhaps recording them with a jazz combo or in swinging arrangements. However, the "easy" option appears to have been taken instead. While this makes for a pleasant listen, it also means that the album is one of the least interesting artistically within Bobby's legacy. Despite this issue, one reviewer referred to just how "inventive [Bobby] can be with his renditions of these hits," a comment that is a little perplexing.[378] He/she goes on to say that "after listening to this album, I'm happy to say I see the value of a 'hits' album. But I would caution those singers who haven't got Darin's knowledge of the popular music scene to walk softly. He has pulled off something that's not easy. A darn good album." Frank Arganbright simply said what many others must have been thinking: "we'd prefer to hear Darin singing in his usual swinging style, but this is good and will satisfy most of his young admirers."[379] Meanwhile, *Variety* stated that Darin gives the songs "a brisk treatment that should put this latest effort for Capitol into a top action orbit."[380] *Billboard* stated the "arrangements sparkle and B.D. is at his best. A set that should sell well quickly."[381] It reached just #98 in the US album charts.

June 6, 1963: Studio Session

This session was to produce German language versions of the hits *18 Yellow Roses* and *You're the Reason I'm Living*. The same arrangements were employed, although the lyrics were not a direct translation of the original, with the

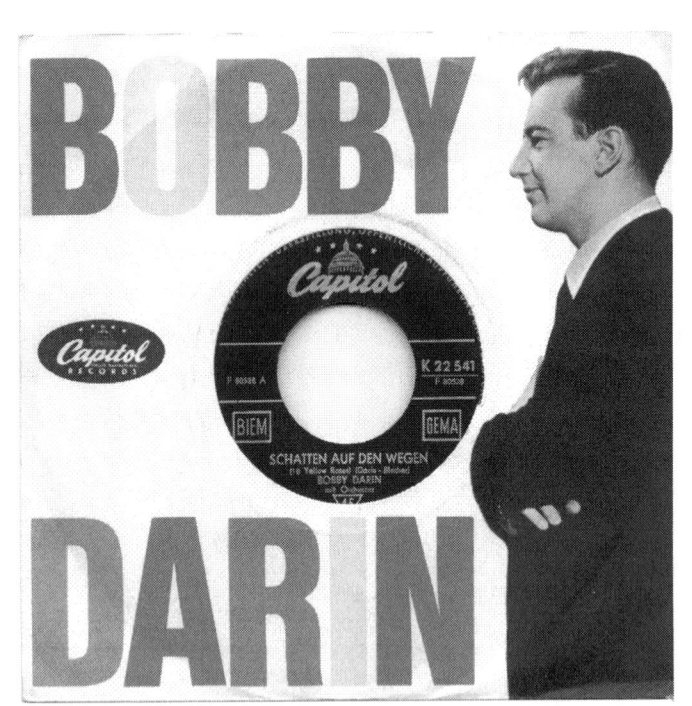

Single of the German-language recordings done on June 6, 1963.

---

[378] "On the Record," *TV Radio Mirror*, October 1963, 20.
[379] Frank Arganbright, "Listening On Records," *Lafayette Journal and Courier*, August 17, 1963, 7.
[380] "Darin's 'Roses,' '8 1/2' Track, Domino's 'Here,' Orbison's 'Dreams' Top LPs," *Variety*, July 17, 1963, 66.
[381] "Album Reviews," *Billboard*, July 27, 1963, 35.

German version of *You're the Reason I'm Living*, *Rote Rosen für Cindy*, having the literal translation of *Red Roses for Cindy*, and *18 Yellow Roses*, now *Schatten auf den Wegen*, becoming *Shadows on the Roads* or *Shadows on the Path*. These are, more than anything, curios, but it was good to see them finally get a release in English-speaking countries in 2016 on the *Rare Capitol Masters* download album.

July 2, 1963: Studio Session

The reason for this session was to produce a new single, with the hope that it would carry on the success of *18 Yellow Roses* and *You're the Reason I'm Living*.

Treat My Baby Good was one of Darin's most commercial and radio-friendly songs of the period, and showed that the quality of the previous two singles had not been a fluke. If anything, this effort, also written by Darin, was more in tune with the songs of the time and both the production and the vocal performance should have signalled another hit on the way. *Billboard* said that the number was "a dramatic piece of brokenheart material [...] sung most effectively here by Bobby Darin."[382] *Cash Box* referred to it as a "pretty, tear-compelling up tempo bouncer...that Bobby multi-tracks with telling effect."[383] However, inexplicably, the song failed to break into even the top forty.

Part of the reason for the song's lack of success may have been related to the flip-side. *Down so Long* is a bluesy number that opens with inexplicably out-of-tune backing vocalists groaning away at the bottom end of their register before Darin himself enters. The song itself is OK, but Bobby has returned here to ornamenting the melody line in the same way that he did during the ballads for the *You're the Reason I'm Living* album, and it doesn't work within the blues genre where simpler is better. It is hard to see how the take in question got released in the first place considering the appalling opening moments.

Questionable decisions were also made when it comes to the other A-side recorded here, *Be Mad Little Girl*. If anything, this was, on the face of it, even more commercial than *Treat My Baby Good*, with Darin's double-tracked voice being particularly appealing, the overall production very good, and the song being another example of Bobby effectively tuning into the sounds of the time. However, the recording is marred by the backing vocals once again – this time, someone had the bright idea of having them sing "you chicken, you chicken" at the end of each line of the verse. Suddenly, what was a potential hit became simply absurd, and reached just #63.

It is also worth noting here that the lyrics may well have put off listeners, as they

---

[382] "Singles Reviews," *Billboard*, August 17, 1963, 32.
[383] "Record Reviews," *Cash Box*, August 17, 1963, 8.

suggest that the "narrator" of the song is having a relationship with a minor. The bridge of the song states "I'm not the guy who made the laws/Telling us what to do/And telling us what not to do." This then means that when Bobby is singing "be mad little girl, but not at me," he is seemingly telling the girl to direct her anger on the lawmakers. If this reading was what Darin intended when he wrote the song (and it is hard to hear the lyrics in any other way), then it was quite a risky, not to mention absurd, theme for a mainstream entertainer. This could, of course, be one of his first attempts at making a political statement in song, but that makes the ludicrous "you chicken" backing vocals even more incongruous. Quite clearly, some reviewers were taking little notice of the lyrics, with *Cash Box* noting it was "a captivating, self-penned cha cha romancer neatly arranged and conducted by Jimmie Haskell."[384] Ultimately, this is one of Bobby's most frustrating recordings – potentially highly commercial but ruined by the backing vocals and the strange theme of the lyrics.

Swedish release of "Since You've Been Gone" and "Be Mad Little Girl."

August 28, September 3 & 6, 1963: Studio Sessions
Golden Folk Hits LP

These sessions produced the last studio album that Bobby would record for over a year. Generally seen as a follow-up to the *Earthy!* LP, it could also legitimately be viewed as a sequel to the *18 Yellow Roses and 11 Other Hits* album as well. After all, it is another example of Bobby recording his own versions of recent hits, mostly in less than adventurous arrangements. As Bobby's second folk album, it has to be said that this is nowhere near as interesting or ambitious as *Earthy!*, and yet is still a worthy effort and certainly a pleasurable listen.

Mary Don't You Weep seems to have been loosely based on the 1961 recording by The Kingston Trio, although Bobby ups the tempo and varies the melody with each successive verse. As with many of the songs on the previous folk effort, he sings as

---

[384] "Record Reviews," *Cash Box*, November 16, 1963, 10.

part of the ensemble as often as he does as a soloist. It is hardly a new approach to the song, but it's still successful and an effective opening to the album. A better version would be taped a few months later during Bobby's Las Vegas season at the Flamingo.

By the time Bobby got to *Where Have all the Flowers Gone*, it had been recorded or performed by everyone from Peter, Paul and Mary to Marlene Dietrich (with the latter keeping her devastating performance in her cabaret act for over a decade). This finds Darin in overtly political territory for perhaps the first time in his career, with the futility of war being a theme he would return to when he started writing his own protest songs. Again, the song gets a relatively predictable treatment, although there is some nice shading between verses, with some using just Darin's solo voice and others featuring the backing vocalists first and foremost.

Another political song is *If I Had a Hammer* which is, perhaps, somewhat less obvious in its meaning than *Where Have all the Flowers Gone*, and yet its talk of a "hammer of justice" and the "bell of freedom" clearly aligns itself with the civil rights movement of the period, which Bobby was a big supporter of, and he had attended the August 1963 march on Washington. In the liner notes of the now out-of-print 2002 CD reissue of the album, Bobby's producer Nik Venet is quoted as saying "Darin thought the civil rights movement was the great revolution of the twentieth century. The man was civil rights conscious long before it became radical chic. It was a passion of his."[385] The number is given a more energetic arrangement on the album than the previous two songs, with Darin giving a strong, committed vocal that showed that, even if this record was an acknowledgment that commercial concerns also had to be catered for, he was still going to make it a personal endeavour.

Bobby's take on Bob Dylan's *Don't Think Twice, it's all Right* is next, and is the only song which he recorded twice in the studio on two distinct occasions. While it wasn't unusual for him to try songs on two or three dates over the period of a few months until he got the result he was looking for, in this instance he recorded the song in 1963 and then in a completely different arrangement, in the early 1970s. Despite his admiration for Dylan, neither arrangement really does the song justice. The folk setting of the 1963 recording is just that bit too safe, and adds little to other versions of the period, and the number veers into pop territory thanks to the backing vocals.

Greenback Dollar had been previously recorded by The Kingston Trio but, as Bleiel points out, "Darin chickens out of the 'damn' that got the Trio censored."[386] One can almost hear the backing vocals from *Be Mad Little Girl* singing "you chicken!" in the background! In the place of the offending word is simply a rest for the vocalists, in the same way as one replaces an offending word when a song with "explicit" lyrics is played on family-friendly radio stations or performed on a family TV show today. As with *If I Had a Hammer*, this number is given a more rigorous workout here than some of the

---

[385] James Rose, liner notes to *Earthy* & *Golden Folk Hits*, Bobby Darin, Exemplar 2001, CD, 2002.
[386] Bleiel, *That's All*, 86.

other songs, and Darin seems to relish singing in this kind of setting.

Why, Daddy, Why is the only song on the album that hadn't been recorded elsewhere. In an interview to promote the LP, Darin explains:

> It's actually a contemporary attempt at a folk song written by a couple of friends of mine, as if to ask the cute little question of where a [...] little boy's mother has gone, and the father is having difficulty in explaining to him that she has gone away and, at the end, of course... Well, I won't tell you about that.[387]

While it's a cute song, the ending that Darin refuses to give away makes it just a little *too* cute, although it is sung beautifully with Bobby double-tracking his voice to great effect here.

Michael Row the Boat Ashore gets a faster than normal outing, but the quicker tempo also means there is more repetition, with the chorus being sung three times before a move is made to the first verse. While the song *does* build up in intensity as it progresses, it still doesn't seem to go anywhere. In a performance on *The Judy Garland Show*, recorded in November of the same year, Bobby would use basically the same arrangement, but this time with less use of backing vocals, with them not appearing until the midway point, thus allowing for the sound to grow in a much more natural way than simply increasing the volume as happens on the recorded version.

Abilene had been a hit for George Hamilton IV earlier in 1963. While originally performed more in the country genre than folk, Bobby gives it a nice, if subtle, makeover here to fit it in with the rest of the album, this time slowing down the tempo rather than speeding it up. For once, the backing vocals are used to great effect, with their rendition of the opening chorus giving way to Bobby's softly sung first verse. Also of note is the instrumental break in the centre of the song, which only goes to remind us of the quality of the instrumentalists here, which include Roger McGuinn (who would go on to be in The Byrds), James Burton (who recorded with Ricky Nelson before joining Elvis Presley's band in 1969), and Glen Campbell.

Green, Green is clearly based on the version by The New Christy Minstrels, although Bobby's vocal is considerably less edgy than the lead on that version. While it picks up the pace of the album, it adds little to it, with better, more energetic performances of similar material elsewhere.

Settle Down takes the Peter, Paul and Mary tune and makes minor adjustments to make it somewhat more commercial. Bobby changes the melody slightly, quickens the tempo and this time around uses the backing vocals to good effect. Also of note is James Burton's stunning guitar solo.

---

[387] Bobby Darin, "Golden Folk Hits Interview," www.Bobbydarin.net [online]. Available at: http://www.bobbydarin.net/bdfolkdaddy.html (accessed August 1, 2015).

The best number on the album sees Darin back in protest mode with a cover of Bob Dylan's *Blowin' in the Wind*. Here he uses his softest voice and gives a simple, uncomplicated vocal that blends well with backing vocals that are used less here than elsewhere. The song would soon become an anthem of sorts, but here it is given an honest, tender reading that is as worthy as any of the many covers of the track by other artists being recorded around the same time.

The album ends with the rousing *Train to the Sky*, an upbeat number with another fine solo by James Burton that blends gospel and folk together. However, the number runs for barely a minute and a half, and is over before it really gets going, acting more as a coda to the album than a climax.

U. S. album cover

Golden Folk Hits is not of the same stunning quality as *Earthy!*, not because it is not as well sung or as well performed, but simply because it is far less ambitious. Darin, no doubt, did what he set out to do in creating an album of his own versions of folk hits, but one feels that something more than just straightforward covers was possible here. The album is still relatively important, however, in that Bobby is firmly putting his hat into the ring with explicitly political material for the first time – and this is something he would return to time and time again. However, without adding his own arrangements to these songs, he was viewed as simply having "climbed aboard the folk train" as *Variety* put it.[388] *Billboard* said it was "packed with potential," that it was a "powerful line-up of contemporary folk hits," and even commented on the use of stereo.[389] Despite this, though, the album did not sell well, not helped by the bland cover art that didn't even feature a picture of Bobby at all on the front.

Aside from the reviews of Bobby's record releases and live shows, he was rarely mentioned in the press in 1963. There is little of the attention that he had received just a couple of years earlier, and this is despite the fact he was having a run of top ten singles. Part of the reason for this was clearly because Darin was no longer viewed as

---

[388] "B'way's '110,' Darin's 'Folk Hits,' Jones' 'Lovers,' Morgan's 'Victors,' Gore's 'Hearts' Top New Albums," *Variety*, December 4, 1963, 42.
[389] "Album Reviews," *Billboard*, December 7, 1963, 21.

the divisive or controversial figure he had been. *Variety* picked up on this in their review of his spring visit to Harrah's in Lake Tahoe: "The big obvious difference in this outing from his first time around: maturity. There's still a bit of the finger snapping noticeable, but only a fleeting trace of the youthful arrogance he displayed in his early nitery dates."[390]

In April, Darin was back at the Flamingo Hotel in Las Vegas, and was once again getting rave reviews. *Variety* wrote that he was "not only a vocalist but a comedian with flawless timing, an impressionist of top-level quality, an ad-lib expert and a performer of sensitive, remarkably effective shadings."[391] By this point, Darin had added some of the songs from the various Capitol sessions to his repertoire, including *Hello Young Lovers, Make Someone Happy, I'm On My Way Great God* and *Work Song*, as well as the unrecorded torch song *Here's That Rainy Day* and folk song *Boil That Cabbage Down*.

In the autumn of 1963, Bobby Darin announced he was retiring from night-club and concert performing, with his last engagement to be his season at The Flamingo in Las Vegas that was to end in November of that year.

Many reasons have been put forward as to why Darin took that decision. His close friend Harriet Wasser told biographer David Evanier that she thought it was "because he was warned by doctors that if he kept singing, he would be a dead man."[392] Indeed, it had not been unusual to see small news articles about Darin being admitted into hospital for short stays during his time at ATCO, but from 1962 onwards, these become even more commonplace. In July 1963 it was reported that:

> Darin collapsed Saturday night during a singing engagement at Freedomland in New York and was sent home to Hollywood to rest. Darin collapsed on stage during the engagement last Tuesday but sniffed a little oxygen and carried on. However, after Saturday night his doctor ordered him to take a complete rest.[393]

A week later, it was reported that he had spent two days in hospital for tests and ordered to rest for six to eight weeks.[394] This resulted in Darin cancelling his week-long engagement at the Steel Pier in Atlantic City that summer.[395] It also affected his film career, with him having to withdraw from *The Dubious Patriots*, a war film due to

---

[390] Long, "Harrah's, Lake Tahoe," *Variety*, March 27, 1963, 60.
[391] Duke, "Nitery Reviews," *Variety*, April 17, 1963, 9.
[392] Evanier, *Roman Candle*, 134.
[393] "Pace Too Fast for Darin?" *Detroit Free Press*, July 29, 1963, 4B
[394] "Bobby Darin Able to Leave Hospital," *Corsicana Daily Sun*, August 3, 1963, 5
[395] "A. C. Steel Pier's Names and Bands," *Variety*, May 15, 1963, 65.

be filmed in Yugoslavia starting in August 1963.[396] The film, starring Stewart Granger and Mickey Rooney, was renamed *The Secret Invasion* prior to its release.

There was also the issue of his marriage, which had been on the rocks for some time, and in March 1963, he and Sandra Dee had "officially separated. Though they reconciled a few weeks later, Darin felt that giving up live performing was a sacrifice he could make to strengthen their marriage."[397] Their brief split in 1963 had also made headlines, with *TV Radio Mirror* asking "Were they too much in love to get married?"[398] Lloyd Shearer also wrote a lengthy article centred on the Darins entitled "When Youth Rushes Into Marriage."[399] It is worth noting that, throughout the reports on Bobby's ill health during the summer of 1963, it is mentioned time and again that Sandra was staying with him and supporting him.

Years after the events, the issue of Darin's career was brought up, with manager Steve Blauner stating that there were "empty seats" at Darin gigs.[400] Darin archivist Jimmy Scalia commented that "he was really losing his career in 1963."[401] However, these comments make no sense. After all, the first half of 1963 had seen Darin enter the top 5 of the singles chart not once but twice. True, *Treat My Baby Good*, the next single, had not been a hit, but would Bobby really have thought he was "losing his career" because of one failure? Unlikely, for he'd had such flop singles before. His albums weren't charting highly, but they hadn't since 1960, so this was nothing new – but they must have been selling reasonably well for so many to have been released. As for Blauner's comment about empty seats, this is also a comment that seems incorrect. We know that the tour with Basie the previous year had resulted in half-empty venues, but Bobby was still a big draw on the nightclub circuit. *Variety* wrote of Bobby's 1963 season at the Copa that "Darin provided one of the biggest Copa openings in some time. The assembly hall was virtually filled, and come weekends, the number of students seeking matriculation privileges here should be considerable."[402]

Despite this, we *do* know that Bobby was affected by the apparent indifference to his product. In October 1964, he gave an interview on *American Bandstand* about his new album *From Hello Dolly to Goodbye Charlie*, saying that he and arranger Richard Wess had teamed up again after a few years because his (Bobby's) records had not been selling so well, and he was hoping to return to a winning formula. However, part of the problem was that, despite Bobby appearing on television numerous times each

---

[396] "Darin Out of Patriots," *Boxoffice*, August 10, 1963, NC-4.
[397] Bleiel, *That's All*, 97.
[398] Hamilton James, "Were They Too Much in Love to Get Married?," *TV Radio Mirror*, June 1963, 4-5.
[399] Lloyd Shearer, "When Youth Rushes Into Marriage," *Parade*, September 29, 1963, 6-7.
[400] Evanier, *Roman Candle*, 134.
[401] Ibid.
[402] Jose, "Copacabana, N.Y.," *Variety*, May 15, 1963, 64.

year, he rarely took those opportunities to promote his latest singles unless they were big band numbers. In fact, *I'll Be There* was the last time he had promoted a non-swinging single side on national television, meaning he was never seen singing numbers such as *Nature Boy, Things, Multiplication, You Must Have Been a Beautiful Baby, If a Man Answers, You're the Reason I'm Living, Eighteen Yellow Roses, Be Mad Little Girl* or *Treat My Baby Good*. If he wasn't willing to promote his new record it was hardly surprising that they didn't always sell well. This pattern didn't change until the release of *If I Were a Carpenter* in 1966, with Bobby plugging this and a number of later singles on TV in the coming years.

Perhaps Darin simply thought that he had his fingers in too many pies, especially now that he was in charge of T.M. Music. That he was "widening his scope" in the music business was certainly the official reason given when *Variety* reported that Bobby was to stop performing.[403] In other words, he could give more time to his new business venture, writing songs for others, and producing records for the likes of Wayne Newton. On occasion, Bobby would take part in the recordings, such as playing drums and adding vocals as part of the short-lived City Surfers group, who released two singles in 1963/4. A May 1964 article in *Billboard* states that T.M. music had "picked up around 300 songs" during the previous year, including the hit *The Shoop Shoop Song*, recorded by Betty Everett.[404]

Ultimately, his decision regarding live performances probably involved taking all of the above into account in one way or another. However, the extent of his health problems in July and August 1963 must have been something of a wakeup call to Darin that he had to slow down, and the timing of that cannot be dismissed.

October 15, 1963: Studio Session

This studio session produced just one recording, which would be issued as the flip-side of *Be Mad Little Girl*. *Since You've Been Gone* was written and arranged by Rudy Clark, one of the songwriters who had become part of T. M. Music, and with whom Bobby often collaborated on songs. It is typical 60s fair, and may well have been a better choice for the A-side of the single given the theme of the lyrics of *Be Mad Little Girl*. Here, Darin appears to be in Ray Charles mode in a song that had genuine commercial appeal but which, sadly, most people never got to hear.

---

[403] "Darin Exits Nitery Field to 'Widen His Music Biz Scope,"*Variety*, October 23, 1963, 47.
[404] "Darin Wears Many Hats; Now Busy as Executive," *Billboard*, May 16, 1964, 37. For a more in depth look at Darin's work for T.M. Music, see Bleiel, *That's All*, 99-106.

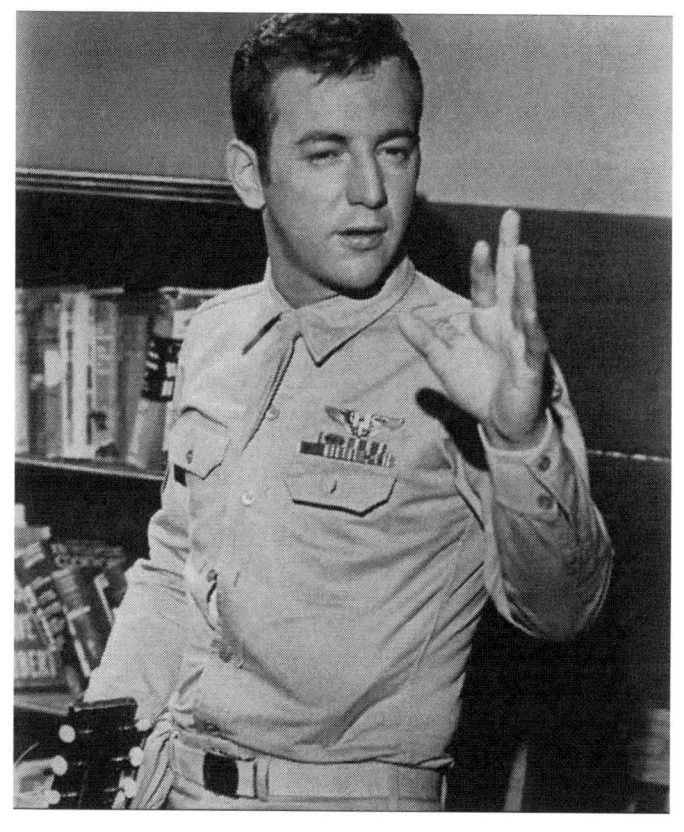

"Captain Newman, M.D." (Universal) premiered in late 1963.

November 9, 1963: Live Recordings
The Curtain Falls: Live at the Flamingo CD

It was only natural for Bobby and Capitol to want to capture on tape what was intended to be his last series of night-club performances with the view to making a live album from the results. Oddly, the resulting album wasn't released at the time – in fact, Capitol released no albums at all by Darin between November 1963 and November 1964. Songs from the engagement began to trickle out in 1995 with Rhino's career-spanning boxed set, and have continued to appear since. In 2000, Collector's Choice Music released a CD entitled *The Curtain Falls: Live at the Flamingo*, and it is this CD that is reviewed here. The recordings that have appeared elsewhere are of different performances of the same songs, but, unless noted, there is relatively little in the way of variation. All recordings on *The Curtain Falls* are dated as November 9, although some of the variants on other releases were recorded on different days.

When listening to these performances and comparing them to the *Darin at the Copa* album from little over three years earlier, it is noticeable that Darin's act had become much slicker and was concentrated much more on singing rather than entertaining and comic asides. While there *are* asides during some of the songs, and the inevitable impressions, there are far less here than on the earlier recording. There is also less banter between songs as well. In the three years since the Copa album, Bobby had fine-tuned his show considerably, and it was now more about singing rather than trying to emulate all of his showbiz heroes within a one-hour running time. *Variety* wrote of his performances that "if Darin goes through with his threat [to retire], it will be a great loss to Las Vegas, because his act has hit a peak; he has definitely joined the few powerhouse performers who appear on the Strip."[405]

The show opens with the same arrangement of *Hello Young Lovers* that had been recorded ten months earlier for the abandoned Broadway album. Here, however, it is taken at a faster pace. As with the earlier recording, he plays around with the timing and melody of the song. It is a more bombastic version, but it works well as an opening number. An even faster version recorded on a different night was issued on a bootleg disc.

Rather surprisingly, he resurrects *Ace in the Hole* from the *Two of a Kind* album, but here the song is sung, for the most part, "straight." The impressions and the banter of the studio duet are gone, and the song is turned into a mid-tempo swing number once the verse has been dispensed with. It is a strange choice of material given the amount of songs at his disposal, but it turns out to be a pleasant one, especially as it gives the listener the chance to hear the song given a more serious rendition, and the climax is genuinely thrilling.

Ace in the Hole segues into a rendition of *You're Nobody 'til Somebody Loves You* that is very different from the country-influenced studio recording from earlier in the year. The opening of the song is accompanied just by a piano before the orchestra enters halfway into the first run-through of the song. By the end of that first verse, the song has gained a gutsy, bluesy swing feel that is increased when Darin returns to the midway point in the song. Again, the climax is genuinely impressive, with Darin's voice sounding strong and powerful despite the health scare from a few months earlier.

Bobby then introduces a "medley of ballads" that turns out to be a hits medley comprising of *Splish Splash*, *Beyond the Sea*, *Artificial Flowers* and *Clementine*. Oddly, the brief snatch of *Splish Splash* works better with the big band accompaniment than one might expect. Other than that, however, the medley uses greatly shortened versions of the original arrangements, and the whole thing is over in a mere three minutes. While a medley of Darin's rock 'n' roll hits might have worked, this distillation of big band numbers does not, especially when two of them are songs that tells stories. They make no sense in this kind of setting, and one feels that Darin would have been better simply singing one of the songs in full rather than trying to do a hits medley of this nature.

My Funny Valentine follows, a song that had been in Bobby's repertoire since at

---

[405] Duke, "Flamingo, Las Vegas, *Variety*, October 30, 1963, 52.

least the beginning of 1960, and probably before. The song was recorded for the *Darin at the Copa* album, but not released. This 1963 version is certainly more polished than the version from the UK TV special of 1960, with Darin's voice noticeably suppler as he moves from the lower end of his range to the upper, and switches from a more powerful voice to a near-falsetto. This is a fine performance, and another example of Bobby's maturity.

A comedy routine built around a parody of *I Walk the Line* follows and, again, shows how Bobby has learned to refine his stage act. The impersonations and interaction with the crowd are present in this section, but separate from the music, so that they don't interfere with the serious part of the act – which was much of the problem with the *Darin at the Copa* release, as the comedy often appeared mid-song.

Next up is a charming rendition of *18 Yellow Roses*, here given a slightly Latin rhythm. The instrumentation is stripped back in comparison to the studio recording and, while this live arrangement isn't as commercial, it is, arguably, better. The folksy, acoustic, unadorned performance is refreshing, especially when it sits alongside the orchestral arrangement of some of the other songs. It might be a simple performance, but it is also one of the highlights of the album because of that.

Mack the Knife follows, with a little comedy over the opening vamp and during the first verse before it settles down into a relatively straightforward performance which, again, is better than the live version from three years earlier, which was performed at a slightly faster tempo. Another version from the same set of recordings, released on the *A&E Biography* CD finds Darin messing up the lyrics, which he amusingly equates to Moses forgetting the Ten Commandments. Unlike the songs in the hit medley, this is no throwaway performance, but a loose and yet committed performance of his signature song.

Mack the Knife forms the halfway point of the show, at which point Bobby performs a series of impersonations while singing *One for my Baby*. Again, it is good to hear him put all his impersonations into one part of the show rather than having them interfere with the singing. Bobby would repeat this routine on his 1967 BBC TV special. While it's fun to watch, it becomes a tad tedious when found in the middle of a CD that is likely to be heard regularly. This isn't to take anything away from the quality of the comedy routine here, it simply doesn't bear repeated listens.

The next section of the show is in stark contrast to the big band sounds of the first half, and sees Darin removing his "showbiz" hat and performing a sequence of four songs from his folk albums. First up is *Work Song*, from the *Earthy!* album. The arrangement is basically the same as the studio version (except for the added addition of piano), and the sequencing here is rather clever – Darin is performing what was originally written as a jazz number, but is doing so in an arrangement that mixes jazz with folk, thus providing a link, a kind of pivot, between the two parts of the show and easing his audience into the (probably unexpected) folk section.

See all 4 Bobby Darins

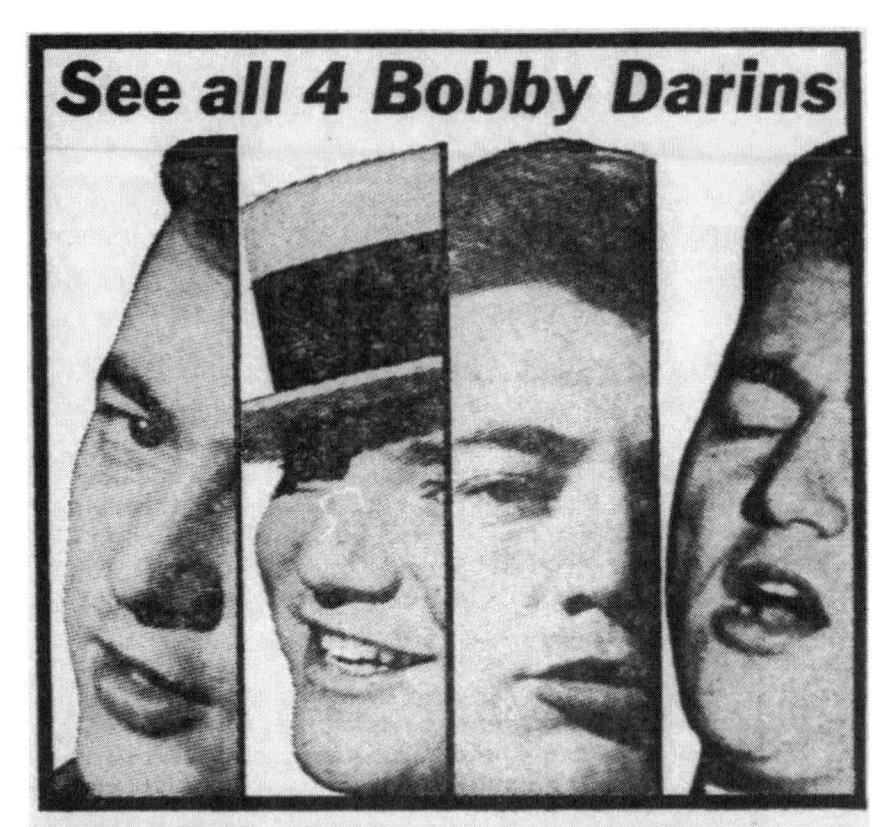

Actor, singer, writer, swinger! Oct. 24 to Nov. 20. At the Flamingo in Las Vegas.

If you want to be entertained from dusk to dawn by the titans of show biz, have a fling at the Flamingo.

If you want a Japanese houseboy to attend to your slightest whim at a pushbutton's notice, have a fling at the Flamingo.

If you want to indulge your gourmet's palate in the glories of the Candlelight Room, have a fling at the Flamingo.

If you want to swim in your own private pool underneath the desert stars, have a fling at the Flamingo.

If you want each day to yield a full 24 hours of vibrant pleasure, have a fling at the Flamingo.

If you want to have a fling, call your favorite travel agent or **CE 6-1330** (in Chicago)

The Flamingo isn't just a hotel in Las Vegas. The fabulous

FLAMINGO is Las Vegas

Newspaper advertisement for Bobby's engagement at the Flamingo.

Michael Row the Boat Ashore works better without the backing vocalists, and Darin even manages to get the audience singing along with him. The "ladies only/men only" schtick we first heard in the 1959 live version of *Plain Jane* is back here, with Bobby cleverly adding enough "showbiz" to make the folk songs palatable to a Las Vegas audience.

Mary Don't You Weep finds Bobby on acoustic guitar, and giving a much gentler performance of the song than that found on *Golden Folk Hits*. Here the song is taken at a much slower pace than in the studio and, once again, the effect is much greater than when Darin is surrounded by backing vocals. Once again, he gets the audience singing with him and, remarkably, they don't appear to resist. By the end of the song, there is almost a round-the-campfire feeling to the performance, which is quite remarkable given the Las Vegas setting, and it is strangely moving. Not only is Bobby singing songs that for the most part hadn't been sung in Vegas before, but he also has the audience eating out of his hand.

The finale of the show is *I'm on My Way Great God*, which is given an epic performance very similar to the studio recording. It is a stunning rendition, and one that he would repeat on television later in the month when he recorded an episode of *The Judy Garland Show*.

Darin returns to the stage for one more song. Here he tells the audience that the show is being recorded, and that the title of the final song will also be the title of the album of the performance (as it was – eventually). He introduces *The Curtain Falls* as a special piece of material that had been written around eighteen months before that he had liked and wanted to record, and, with it being his final Vegas season, it fitted on this occasion. *The Curtain Falls* is, indeed, a stunning piece of material. It is a brilliantly written love letter to an audience that manages to be sentimental without being remotely mawkish and Darin sings the beautiful song with absolute sincerity and without overplaying it. It is hard to fathom how this, one of his truly great recordings, remained in the vaults for over three decades.

This album of live recordings was a genuinely revelatory release when it appeared in 2000, filling in the gap most effectively between the three previously released concert albums. While the mix of the CD arguably finds Darin set too far back during the big band section of the show, this is a minor point, particularly given the quality of Bobby's performance. As with the 1971 live recordings, *Live at the Desert Inn*, Darin is shown to be the consummate performer, who manages to not only balance what his audience wants with what *he* wants to do, but also does so in such a way that they are happy to go along with him even when he strays from the expected path.

At the end of November, Bobby recorded his appearance on *The Judy Garland Show* just days after the death of President John F. Kennedy. Garland was devastated, and wanted to cancel the taping entirely, and then decided that the whole hour could be used to pay homage to JFK:

> She did not intend to mention Kennedy or indeed to speak at all: the songs would carry the message. [...] However, [CBS President] James Aubrey issued a decree that there would be no further tributes to the President when normal broadcasting resumed and, as far as he was concerned, this included Garland's planned hour of Americana.[406]

Garland eventually got much of her own way, albeit at a later date. A few weeks later she ended the show with a soaring *Battle Hymn of the Republic* that was so popular that she repeated it in a later episode. She also had an Americana medley running around a quarter of an hour put together for one of the later concert-format shows with which the doomed series ended. Ironically, it was guest Bobby Darin who managed to instil the first post-Kennedy episode with something of what Garland was aiming for, with him singing two spirituals in his solo spot, *Michael Row the Boat Ashore* and *I'm on My Way Great God*.

The Garland show went through a number of format changes during its one season run, although the series can be effectively split into two – those weeks with the variety show format, and those with a concert format. Darin's episode was in the variety show mould but, by the time of his appearance, this had been refined considerably and much of the silliness that had been present in the early episodes had been dispensed with. At this point, the show was simply Garland and her guests. Bob Newhart was also on the show, performing one of his famous monologues as well as a short sketch with Garland herself. Darin had a solo spot and a lengthy duet with Garland.

The duet stands out as one of the best in the series. It is ambitious in scope, and is loosely built around the idea of trains and travelling and includes everything from *Chattanooga Choo Choo* to *Lonesome Road*. Bobby and Judy, perhaps rather surprisingly, had great chemistry together and seemed at ease with each other both during the short comedy dialogue before the medley and within the medley itself, often sparring off each other and throwing in ad-libs as the piece went along. Garland was at her most focussed, despite the difficult circumstances, and Bobby seemed to relish the challenge of the lengthy medley which had probably been put together by Mel Tormé.

A number of Bobby's numbers as a guest on TV shows have appeared on CD over the years, but most of these have been grey market releases or public domain issues that are in poor quality. Luckily, the Darin/Garland duet was released on an official CD in very good sound on the album *Judy Duets*, which also features Garland's

---

[406] David Shipman, *Judy Garland*, (London: HarperCollins, 1993), 513.

performances with the likes of Barbra Streisand, Liza Minnelli, Count Basie, Mel Tormé, Vic Damone, and Peggy Lee. While some of the magic is lost without the visuals, this is still a worthwhile edition to any Darin (or Garland) collection. Other than a brief appearance on *Hollywood Backstage*, this was Bobby's last TV appearance of the year.

Publicity still from "That Funny Feeling" (Universal)

CHAPTER EIGHT
LONELY ROAD: 1964-1965

The remaining ten years of Bobby Darin's life would be unsettled ones personally and artistically. He would seek a release from his Capitol contract in early 1964 – only to return to the label less than six months later, and then seek another early release shortly after that. He then moved back to Atlantic, on to Direction (his own label), and then joined Motown before seeking an early release from them also. Musically, he would return to the big band sound that had given him his biggest successes, before once again recording folk albums, and then socially-conscious music, before trying to embrace the Motown sound. With the notable exception of *If I Were a Carpenter* at Atlantic, commercial success would mostly evade him during this second half of his career. In the movies, Darin also seemed restless, trying his luck with two rather run-of-the-mill mainstream films before sporadic attempts at more interesting supporting roles as well as directing his own, still unreleased movie.

January 13, 1964: Studio Session

Bobby's first session of the new year was used to produce some recordings for possible single release.

The Things in this House was released as a single in August 1964. It is a strange song and record in that is a parody of cry-in-your-beer country songs – hardly a winning formula for success in the pop charts at the same time that Beatlemania was sweeping America. Once again, Bobby puts on his country twang accent, although this time around it fits the recording and doesn't seem out of place since this appears to be a send-up in the first place. It is an amusing and entertaining recording, but would have been better served released on an LP rather than as a single.

Much more commercial was the fine flip-side, *Wait by the Water*. Loosely inspired

Trade advertisement

by the spiritual *Wade in the Water*, this was another contemporary-sounding recording that, for some inexplicable reason, simply didn't get much attention at the time. The song is also yet another recording in which Bobby approaches the subject of death, with the lyrics being considerably darker than the production might suggest. Bobby himself gives a fine, rocking, slightly bluesy performance and the result was one of his best recordings for Capitol that was not in the swinging/big band mould. This should certainly have been included on the 4CD Rhino boxed set in 1995. An alternate take appeared on CD in the early 1990s on the *Capitol Collectors Series* album.

The single was released in August 1964, just after Bobby had re-signed with Capitol. *Cash Box* said that *Wait by the Water* "is a hard-driving, shufflin', chorus-backed hope for romance with a fine gospel-style backing," and that *The Things in this House* "is a twangy...country-styled affair."[407]

Two Tickets is less successful, and remained unreleased until 1999. The recording seems to be trying to replicate the success of *18 Yellow Roses*, particularly with regards to the song telling a story. However, it doesn't have the same twist in the final verse as the earlier hit, and Bobby's vocal is rather overdone. It is an interesting experiment at taking the *18 Yellow Roses* formula and applying a more contemporary sound, but it simply doesn't come off.

One final song, *Maybe Today*, is documented as being recorded at this session, but remains unissued.

Bobby and Edie Adams on "Here's Edie." Publicity photo.

---

[407] "Record Reviews," *Cash Box*, September 5, 1964, 14.

Darin raised eyebrows when he sought an end to his contract with Capitol in early 1964, less than two years after joining the label. *Music Business* wrote:

> Bobby Darin and Capitol have split. In a startling ending to what has seemed a happy union, Darin suddenly requested and received his release last week, even though his contract is understood to have a few months to go…Indications are that the end came so abruptly that Darin has no firm future plans in mind as yet.[408]

During the summer, an article in the same magazine hinted that Bobby might be making a move to Colpix.[409] However, his return to Capitol was announced a few weeks later. *Variety* wrote that the deal was financially the same as the one he had ended a few months earlier, was for "four singles and four albums per year – minimum," and that it would run for five years instead of two.[410] It didn't last a year.

Bobby would never again be as prolific as he had been previously in the studio. Between 1958 and 1963, he had released eighteen albums, with the equivalent of four more in the can. Between 1964 and his death in 1973, he would release just twelve albums.

Bobby gave a candid interview to *Music Business* in the autumn of 1964 in which he talked about the state of his recording career:

> I know I can't be as consistent with records as some. That's partly because I'm an experimenter. You try to do something new and sometimes you fall flat on your face…But I think I do have some talent and when I left Capitol, my idea was to put all the Darin talents into one hat under one roof. I talked to a lot of people, Decca, Warner Brothers, Screen Gems, but they all just wanted the recording artist part of me. So I finally reversed myself completely, went back to Capitol and decided to get my own businesses started separately.[411]

At the same time as he was breaking up with Capitol in March 1964, he was giving a series of interviews about his hopes of winning the Academy Award for *Captain Newman, M. D.* "I'll tell you what this nomination means," he told Joseph Finnigan. "When you come from another medium, the struggle for acceptance is three times as hard. Because if you had success in another medium, which I had, you're supposed to

---

[408] "Darin Quits Capitol Pact," *Music Business*, March 21, 1964, 1.
[409] "Bobby Darin's Explosive Scene," *Music Business*, June 20, 1964, 13.
[410] Joe X. Price, "On the Beat," *Variety*, August 17, 1964, 10.
[411] Ren Grevatt, "Bobby Darin – a Happy Publisher," *Music Business*, October 31, 1964, 14.

be content."[412]

Bobby was also asked about his retirement from live performing:

> Night clubs? I'd just as soon forget them. They take me away from my home. I love my baby and my wife. I have to be in Chicago one week, and another in Miami and I'd like to let it go at that. I have a lovely home in Toluca Lake and I want to see it. Most people think we have a glamourous life on the road. They should see some of the holes they call dressing rooms.[413]

While Bobby wasn't planning to return to nightclubs, he did decide for his first album under the new Capitol contract to return to arranger Richard Wess, who had provided the charts for the *That's All* and *This is Darin* albums. The renewal of their union didn't quite provide the fireworks that it had before, but the resulting album was a return to form for Bobby.

September 17-19, 1964: Studio Sessions
From Hello Dolly to Goodbye Charlie LP

In early 1965, when talking about the *From Hello Dolly to Goodbye Charlie* LP, his first under the new Capitol contract, Darin said:

> I'm back in a new direction, which is the old direction. It was a matter of looking a gift formula in the mouth. Now I've decided to remain in this bag. This will be the formula from now on. [...] I feel now at the ripe old age of 27 I have experimented. I don't feel I can appeal as well any more to the real young record buyers. So it's time to take hold of the reins on a more consistent basis. It's very hard to give people something besides what they want. With me, it was not listen for awhile. Now the comments have been 'it's about time.'[414]

The comments that Bobby mentions may well have been the positive reviews for the

---

[412] Joseph Finnigan, "Bobby Darin Has Spot Picked for 'Oscar' He Hopes to Win," *Democrat and Chronicle*, March 22, 1964, 3E.
[413] Sheila Graham, "Darin Shakes Off Chip on Shoulder," *Orlando Evening Star*, April 1, 1964, section 8, 10.
[414] Mary Campbell, "Singer Bobby Darin Reports He Is 'One Album and One Single Old'," *The Derrick*, February 16, 1965, 10.

album, with *Variety* stating that "there isn't a weak track on the 10 sides *(sic)*. Richard Wess, who arranges-batons has done a remarkable job in bringing back the old sound which vaulted (*Mack the Knife*) Darin. This one can't miss at cash registers."[415] Likewise, *Cash Box* told readers that "chart status seems assured."[416]

Certainly, considering the quality of the album and the much-heralded reunion of Darin and arranger Richard Wess, you wouldn't have thought it could miss out with regards to sales – and yet it didn't even reach the top 100 in the album charts. This was the case despite an interview on *American Bandstand*, which was basically a promotional exercise, and a performance of one of the songs, *Once in a Lifetime*, on *The Andy Williams Show*. Despite what Bobby said about sticking with the current formula, this turned out to be the last straight-ahead all-swinging album that Bobby Darin released.

The album is comprised, for the most part, of songs from recent films and stage shows, and opens with the title number from *Hello Dolly*. The reunion with arranger Richard Wess is well and truly cemented with the opening vamp to the song replicating that from *Mack the Knife*, and that is the point here. Darin and Wess are there to convince us that this is classic Darin – and, for the most part, it is, right down to the "look out old Dolly is back" ending. Where *Hello Dolly* falls down slightly is that it doesn't have multiple verses as *Mack the Knife* has, and so each key modulation simply leads to yet another repeat of the same lyrics. In fact, we get the entire chorus three and a half times. Quite easily, one of those could have been cut and the number would have had the same effect. Is this nit-picking? Possibly, but it might explain why the song didn't have much chart success when it was lifted from the album and released as a single – although this occurring *after* the LP was issued probably didn't help matters, and neither did the fact that Louis Armstrong had had a massive hit with the song just a few months earlier, with his single reaching #1.

Italian single of "Hello Dolly."

Despite the poor chart performance, the single was well-received by critics. *Variety* suggested that the song "could repeat this singer's successful takeoff on Louis

---

[415] Joe X. Price, "On the Beat," *Variety*, December 11, 1964, 7.
[416] "Album Reviews," *Cash Box*, December 5, 1964, 32.

Armstrong's *Mack the Knife* several years ago."[417] *Billboard* declared that the song was "Darin at his swingingest"[418] while *Cash Box* stated that the performance was "sensational."[419]

The irony here is that a better *Mack the Knife II* had been recorded at the very same session. Darin's own composition *Gyp the Cat* is a clever pastiche of the earlier song, this time about a thief, and using a similar melody to the Kurt Weill song. As with *Mack the Knife*, the song tells a story, and the arrangement works in the same way, with it gaining in intensity with each successive verse. It is a lighter affair lyrically, with a nice twist in the final verse, and would have been a better choice of single. Despite the British Invasion, there was clearly still a place in the singles charts for this type of material, as Armstrong's *Hello Dolly* and the Darin-produced Wayne Newton hit *Danke Schoen* had shown. The 1964 version of *Gyp the Cat* remained unissued until thirty years later, while a 1965 re-recording of the same song was issued as a B-side. It was something of a waste of a fun Darin original in his signature style, and showed that he could poke fun at himself through a pastiche of his earlier hit.

Returning to the album, *Call Me Irresponsible* is the first of two songs from the writing team of Sammy Cahn and Jimmy van Heusen. The number was written for the film *Papa's Delicate Condition* (dir. George Marshall, 1963), and went on to win the Academy Award for Best Song. Frank Sinatra had recorded an acclaimed version for his album *Sinatra's Sinatra*, but Darin turns the song into a more upbeat swing number and manages to trump Sinatra's rendition. The arrangement is big and brassy, but not over the top in the way that some of Wess's arrangements had been several years before. Darin, meanwhile, is in fine voice and seems to be enjoying his return to the studio after a relatively lengthy break.

Both *Call Me Irresponsible* and the other Cahn/Van Heusen composition on the album, *Where Love Has Gone*, were featured prominently on the soundtrack to the 1999 film *American Beauty* (dir. Sam Mendes). *Where Love Has Gone*, from the 1964 Bette Davis film of the same name, is one of the few ballads on the album, and finds Darin proving that he was just as capable with a ballad as a swing number when he put his mind to it and didn't try to add affectations to his voice. His voice seemed to be gaining more and more strength with each passing year, as can be proven by the climax of this number which, despite its wide vocal range, is made to sound effortless.

Another writing duo represented twice on the album was Henri Mancini and Johnny Mercer. *The Days of Wine and Roses* benefits from a remarkably lush orchestral arrangement that sounds more like it was penned by Gordon Jenkins than by Richard Wess. The number is treated as a ballad here, and thankfully isn't recited as a poem in the way it had been on *The Milk Shows*. However, this doesn't seem quite as effortless

---

[417] "Top Singles of the Week," *Variety*, January 20, 1965, 48.
[418] "Singles Review," *Billboard*, January 16, 1965, 40.
[419] "Record Reviews," *Cash Box*, January 16, 1965, 35.

as the other recordings, particularly as Darin is unwilling (or unable) to take the long phrases in one breath, with the exception of the last two lines. It's a somewhat strange recording with a lengthy introduction and outro, but just a basic once-through performance of the song itself, and is more than just a little reminiscent of Sinatra's infamous 1961 recording of *Stardust*, where he sings just the verse and leaves out the actual chorus.

The other Mercer/Mancini number is the theme tune to the wonderful comedy thriller *Charade* (dir. Stanley Donen) from 1963, which starred Cary Grant and Audrey Hepburn. Most recordings of the song treat it as a lush ballad, but Darin does quite the opposite, with the track given an upbeat, jazzy makeover that is a stunning *tour-de-force*. When Bobby returned to live performances in 1966, he quickly incorporated this into his act, and also revived it again in 1973 for his TV series.

Once in a Lifetime, written by Leslie Bricusse and Anthony Newley for the musical *Stop the World, I Want to Get Off*, gets a similar transformation in an arrangement that throws in almost everything but the kitchen sink. Also normally performed as a ballad, here it is taken at a manic pace, with a bombastic orchestration that almost threatens to drown Darin under a sea of drums.

Darin himself was co-writer of two of the songs here. *The End of Never*, co-written with Francine Forest, has a wide-ranging melody that is negotiated well by Bobby, with the arrangement similar in style to the earlier *Where Love Has Gone*. Perhaps more interesting is the upbeat *Look at Me*, written for the 1964 movie *The Lively Set* (dir. Jack Arnold) and co-authored with Randy Newman. While the number gets a showy arrangement, it doesn't swing with the same relaxed vibe as the other upbeat songs here. The song was performed by Wink Martindale on the soundtrack LP that accompanied the film.

More, the theme from the 1963 documentary *Mondo Cane* (dir. Gualtiero Jacopetti, Paolo Cavara and Franco Prosperi), is given the classic Darin treatment, and has become a much-compiled performance from the album. Here the swing feels much more natural, and there are some lovely touches, such as Bobby holding on to the last note of the first run-through and linking it into the first of the repeated section. The repeated modulations are typical Wess, making this one of their best collaborations.

Sunday in New York is another recording that has found its way on to multiple compilations in recent years. Once again, the swing here is completely natural, and the lyrics themselves must have been close to Darin's heart, being a love song to his home city. He rides the arrangement with ease, just giving the required amount of effort and volume, and judging it perfectly so that he never overdoes it.

The final song, *Goodbye Charlie*, from the film of the same name, is given a jazzy feel similar to *Charade*, but this time the song is in waltz time, thus adding variety to the album. Once again, Bobby is dealing with death in a humourous way, this time murder, but he doesn't make the song a send-up in any way.

In interviews from the period, Bobby Darin seemed especially proud of the *From Hello Dolly to Goodbye Charlie* album, and it is hardly surprising. The LP was brilliantly conceived as a collection of recent Hollywood and Broadway songs, even down to the opening "hello" and the closing "goodbye." What's more, he finally got rid of the choir accompaniment during the ballad numbers, which, in itself, sets this apart from his other Capitol albums of standards. The quality of singing and arranging here was superb on the whole and, when the album flopped, Bobby must have sat wondering what he had to do to get himself back in the charts again. In the end, he did nothing, not entering the studio for another six months.

At the same sessions, Darin also recorded the theme song for *That Funny Feeling* an enjoyable but completely unremarkable and unimportant romantic comedy. The film was perhaps most notable for being the penultimate movie of prolific director Richard Thorpe, whose career had started back in the silent era and had included, among others, the 1937 version of the thriller *Night Must Fall*, the 1952 swashbucklers *Ivanhoe* and *The Prisoner of Zenda* and the Elvis Presley films *Jailhouse Rock* and *Fun in Acapulco*.

Despite filming taking place during 1964, the film wasn't released until August of the following year. This was the third film that Bobby made with his wife, Sandra Dee. However, that was not the original intention as he only took the part after negotiations with Warren Beatty broke down. Bobby told Joseph Finnigan:

"That Funny Feeling." Universal publicity photo.

> Warren was offered a very large salary, six figures. He was offered a large share of the profits. My wife is a contract player and gets paid a straight salary, no percentage. Warren wanted star billing over her. She agreed to it. However, the agency stepped in and said split the billing. He would get top billing on screen, she in the newspapers. Warren turned that down. At a certain point, the sublime becomes the ridiculous and the studio felt it had gone as far as it could.[420]

Reviewers were able to contain their excitement when the film was finally released. *Variety* said that "this is a glossy, contrived, romantic comedy mixup which is running as a dualler in Britain and that's about its strength, despite some cheery performances by the stars."[421] *Monthly Film Bulletin*, however, were less charitable:

> This sorry, run-down affair is rather like *Sunday in New York* gone wrong. Working around a similar setting and situation, it somehow contrives to lack all of the embellishments that such an essentially slight comedy must have if it's going to work. Instead, we get a tediously prolonged demonstration of what happens to this kind of movie when nothing about the script, direction or performances is sufficiently imaginative, charming or good…The most intelligent performance actually does come from a Labrador.[422]

The title song itself is very much in the style of the *Hello Dolly* album, and one can only wonder why this Darin composition didn't also make it on to the LP (which had only eleven tracks when released). The theme song is a little derivative of any number of standards, but it is still well-written, and arranged and performed with zest. *Cash Box* said that the "smooth voice, easy moving ork work and a light swing number are the elements that could grab plenty of pop and good music exposure for this offering."[423] *Variety* was enthusiastic in its review, saying that "[Darin] belts self-cleffed title tune to the Universal pic with a verve and bounce that reminds of early-day Darin – e.g. his 1959 smash *Mack the Knife*. Top tune, given wow big-beat, stringy arrangement, will stand on its own legs as an entity separate from pic. Disk can't miss."[424] It did.

*

---

[420] Joseph Finnigan, "Bobby Darin Grows Up," *Pittsburgh Press*, October 25, 1964, section 5, 11.
[421] Rich, "That Funny Feeling," *Variety*, June 23, 1965, 26.
[422] "That Funny Feeling, U.S.A., 1965," *Monthly Film Bulletin*, July 1965, 113.
[423] "Record Reviews," *Cash Box*, August 21, 1965, 22.
[424] Joe X. Price, "On the Beat," *Variety*, August 11, 1965, 11.

1964-1965

1964 had been a strange year in Bobby's career. Other than the belated release by ATCO of *Winners*, recorded in 1960, only one Darin album was issued – compared to four LPs released by Capitol the year before. Also, television appearances were less than in previous years. In fact, Bobby wasn't seen in a singing capacity on television at all between February and December, and, despite two appearance on *The Andy Williams Show* in December 1964 and January 1965, wouldn't start appearing *regularly* on variety shows again until September of the following year.

It is unknown whether Bobby had been approached to head his own variety series at this point, but he was making clear in interviews that he had no interest in doing them. He told James Devane that "a weekly variety show has to be ground out like chopped meat…T-bone steak is impossible. Talents far better than I can ever hope to be have found they can't be a week-after-week success. How could I?"[425]

Meanwhile, the roster of talent at T. M. Music continued to grow and now included football star Roosevelt Grier, Merry Clayton, Wayne Newton, and Jesse Colin Young. While the business was growing, Darin wasn't about to downplay how difficult it was. "We have one artist who is a hit," he said. "We're batting 1000."[426]

"The Andy Williams Show" publicity photo.

The beginning of 1965 saw Darin appearing on television in a number of roles. His January appearance on *The Andy Williams Show*, singing *Once in a Lifetime* as his solo number, and performing a lengthy medley with Williams and Vic Damone, is a joy. He was also to be found on two game shows, *What's My Line* and *The Match Game*, as well as a cameo acting role in *Burke's Law*.

In a newspaper interview with Doris Klein, Bobby stated that he was absent from

---
[425] James Devane, "Bobby Discusses Career, Brashness and His Marriage to Sandra Dee," *Cincinnati Enquirer*, January 23, 1964, 12.
[426] "More Mature Bobby Darin Writes and Records Music," *Troy Record*, February 13, 1965, 37.

the recording studio due to "tax complications."[427] He also says that the decision to stop doing live performances had nothing to do with his marriage difficulties. He does his best in the interview to give off an air of contentment: "Now I work five days a week and have nights and weekends off. On Sundays, I can read the *New York Times* – all the way through – and a lot of other papers."

However, just over a year later, in January 1966, that contentment had clearly worn off as Bobby was back performing again. Perhaps the roar of the crowd started to get Bobby restless after he agreed to sing at the inaugural gala for President Johnson in January 1965, where he performed *Mack the Knife*, *Once in a Lifetime*, and a new song entitled *Great Society*.[428]

The following month, he was campaigning for the American Heart Association, as he did every year. "I contribute February to whatever they want me to do," he told reporters. "TV, radio, pictures in papers with people who went through a serious heart operation." His appearance on *What's My Line* on January 31st 1965 and his week-long stint on *I've Got a Secret* in February were to promote the cause, as had been his appearances on *What's My Line* in 1961 and 1964.[429] Bobby was crowned "King of Hearts" by the association four times in a row before they awarded him the title of "Ambassador."

March 9, 15 & 16, 1965: Studio Sessions
Venice Blue (aka: I Wanna Be Around) LP

Bobby Darin's final LP for Capitol was an album of easy listening tracks that is well-performed but lacks the coherence and ambition of many of his recordings for the label. There is no obvious theme here other than the easy listening sound, with the songs coming from a disparate set of sources. The liner notes by Whit Bond try to tie them altogether by saying they are examples of the great songs still being written "today," but that theme is a decidedly loose one.

In America, the album was titled *Venice Blue* after the LP's opening song, which had been released as a single in April 1965 (a month or so before the LP). This was a French song that Bobby had fallen in love with and thought would be a big hit.[430] Darin's enthusiasm might well have been justified – the original song was written by the great Charles Aznavour, after all. Gene Lees provided the English lyrics but, despite his previous fine work in this area providing translations for songs by the likes

---

[427] Doris Klein, "Humble? Just a Little," *Tucson Daily Citizen*, November 21, 1964, 26.
[428] "Top Disk Names Appear at Inaugural Gala," *Cash Box*, January 30, 1965, 46.
[429] His flurry of chat show appearances in February 1963 may well have also been for the same reason, but tapes of these are not in circulation.
[430] See Bleiel, *That's All*, 132-133.

of Antonio Carlos Jobim, it is the English lyrics that let the song down. The new words don't sound natural enough, and are often downright clumsy. For example, there is a random line about "two pigeons in the square" that hardly fits in a song that otherwise almost drowns in its romanticism. It appears that Aznavour wasn't completely happy with the new lyrics either. He recorded *Venice Blue* with the Gene Lees lyrics in 1964 for an album on the Reprise label, but then in the early 1970s used different English lyrics, recording the song under the new title of *How Sad Venice Can Be*. It has to be said that the later lyrics are superior.

Oddly, Bobby Darin himself gets a writing credit on the single and album of his version, but he had no hand in the writing of the song at all. Aznavour's original co-author of the song in French was Françoise *Dorin*, and that was the name that should have appeared on the LP and CD releases of the album. Capitol even issued a short statement about the issue:

> Capitol Records and vocalist Bobby Darin would like to clear up an error on the credits of the artist's new outing, *Venice Blue*. The record carries the name "Darin" as one of the writers, when actually the song was penned by French lyricist Francoise Dorin. Apologies are offered to Dorin for the faux pas, which was caused by the very similar spelling and pronunciation of the two names.[431]

Despite the apology being issued following the single release, and more than a month before the release of the LP, the same mistake still appeared on the album and on the 1997 CD release. The credit was corrected to Dorin on the *Capitol Collectors Series* CD, only for Gene Lees to be misspelt *Lecs*!

Clunky lyrics aside, Darin gives a fine, committed performance, and it is evident just from listening to it that he was revelling in singing a song he loved, but the orchestral arrangement doesn't really help things. Ernie Freeman was the man responsible, and the number has his trademark triplet figure underpinning it, but the whole thing is hardly subtle. While Freeman had commercial success with Sinatra (arranging both *Strangers in the Night* and *That's Life*) and Dean Martin, his arrangements were often bombastic, not to mention repetitive, and that, together with the lyric issue, was the death knell for Darin's hopes of conquering the pop charts with *Venice Blue*. Despite this, the song was in the shops within a week or so of recording, and *Billboard* reported that the single was a "well done production" that "builds powerfully."[432] *Cash Box* were also positive, saying that Bobby "dishes-up the heart-throbbing romantic ballad in an especially emotion-packed soulful style."[433]

---

[431] "Dorin not Darin," *Cash Box*, April 3, 1965,
[432] "Singles Reviews, *Billboard*, March 20, 1965, 12.
[433] "Record Reviews," *Cash Box*, March 27, 1965, 18.

With Sandra Dee

Things improve considerably for *I Wanna Be Around*, which is arranged by Richard Wess, the arranger who probably understood Darin's brand of swing better than anyone. While Bobby doesn't really add anything new to this much-recorded song, the result sounds far more natural than *Venice Blue*, and has a swaggering, yet easy, swing to it. The song became the title of the album in the UK and possibly in some other overseas territories.

Somewhere, from the musical *West Side Story*, is sadly saddled with another slightly over-the-top Ernie Freeman arrangement, which robs the song of some of its poignancy. The orchestration is overblown, and the choir that marred so many Darin ballad performances is back, although not quite so obtrusive this time around. Bobby's performance is very good indeed, but even this powerful vocal gets a little bit lost amongst all the noise around him.

The Good Life is better, with Richard Wess back at the helm, and the song features a bluesy piano throughout. This is, in part, why this is an album that has a split personality – the Wess arrangements have a jazzy, bluesy feel underpinning them, whereas the Freeman ones are mostly lacking that feel and are pure pop. As with the best Wess orchestrations, this one racks up the tension as the song progresses, leading to an exciting climax.

Not so successful is Wess's arrangement of the rather dull *Dear Heart*, a song from the film of the same name that appears to have been recorded by most singers who veered into easy listening during the 1960s. Quite what they found so appealing about this rather sappy song is something of a mystery as the number has not aged well. There's a kind of country feel running through the arrangement, and Darin sings well, but here the choir is more obtrusive and makes the whole thing rather sickly sweet.

Ernie Freeman had already arranged *Softly as I Leave You* for Frank Sinatra in 1964, but his orchestration for Bobby is a far busier affair, with cascading strings, that favourite triplet beat of his, and a choir appearing at every opportunity. Darin gives a full-blooded performance (he doesn't have much choice considering the volume of the backing behind him) but adds little to what had already been done with the song by others. This is part of the problem with the album – despite Bobby's very good vocals throughout, much of the material is not just familiar, but had been recorded by multiple artists before him, and so it is very difficult for him to add his own stamp to the material.

That problem doesn't arise on *You Just Don't Know*, a new song composed by Darin himself. This is a country-influenced number with an arrangement similar to the ballads on *You're the Reason I'm Living* LP. However, here Bobby's voice doesn't have the same mannerisms as on that album, and is all the better for it. On hearing this fine number, one could be forgiven for asking just why Darin wasn't recording an album of his own songs in the country music or easy listening genres instead of relying on those that had been recorded so many times by others.

There is a certain irony that the liner notes of the album tell us that the LP is filled with great songs from the early 1960s, when it actually turns out that the one song that is from the 1920s is the highlight. *There Ain't No Sweet Gal That's Worth the Salt of My Tears* is given a great jazzy arrangement that is aided by the piano playing of Ray Johnston. It is also a playful number: just when you think the song is about to fade out, we are launched into another chorus which is then followed by a lengthy instrumental that eventually leads to the fade out that was expected a minute earlier. It is showstopping stuff that deserves to be much better known, and would have been great performed in a TV guest spot or live on stage.

Who Can I Turn To, from the musical *The Roar of the Greasepaint, the Smell of the Crowd*, finds Darin in show-stopping mode, but once again the whole thing becomes bogged down in the Ernie Freeman arrangement. This would work much better with a quiet, sparse opening in terms of arrangement, that builds up in sound and colour to a big finish – instead, all of the cards are laid on the table at the beginning, and so the feeling is one of bombast (from an arrangement point of view) rather than the sense of theatre that such a song really needs.

A Taste of Honey gets a much more interesting treatment, switching back and forth from a contemporary sound to a swing arrangement. Again, though, the material is too familiar and, despite a fine vocal and a good arrangement, the result comes across as merely pleasant.

The album ends with *A World Without You*, another country(ish) Darin original performed in an arrangement similar to *You Just Don't Know*. It is rather ironic that the inferior composition *You're the Reason I'm Living* is relatively well-known and yet this better song and performance is barely known at all. Bobby's performance once again is judged to perfection, and it is such a shame he didn't sing in this way for the earlier country-themed album.

Viewed from a distance of more than fifty years, *Venice Blue* stands as one of Bobby's best albums if we are simply looking at vocal performances. *Billboard* tells us that Darin "sings his heart out," and that is indeed true, but there is too much familiarity here when it comes to the material, and many of the arrangements are simply not good enough to make these renditions stand out from the many others being recorded at roughly the same time.[434]

When the album was released in Australia, it received one of the worst reviews of any Darin album. "Darin is still developing as an artist," the article says, "and *Venice Blue* is one of his bad ones." The title song was described as "the messiest translation of an Italian song I have ever heard." It was French, but let's forget that for a second. *A Taste of Honey* also gets attacked, saying that it "eschews the orginal feeling of the song and relegates it to the limbo of bouncy show tunes." The review ends by saying "let us hope that this is not an indication of a new direction being taken by Darin. If this is the case, he is wasting a very real and unusual talent."[435]

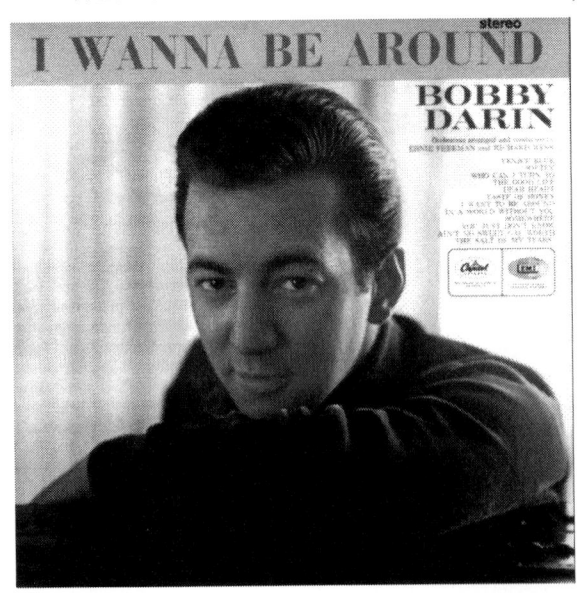

"Venice Blue" was renamed when released in the UK.

Two more songs were recorded at these sessions, and fit in with the style of the other numbers. *Just Bummin' Around* gets a rendition that very much fits in with the country/big band crossovers of the *You're the Reason I'm Living* LP. However, the sound and performance here is lighter than many of the songs on the *Venice Blue* album, and perhaps should have been used in order to add a variety of styles to the LP. Not released until 1999, this is a neglected gem.

In contrast, *Love Letters* is bogged down in a heavy orchestral arrangement with a

---

[434] "Album Reviews, *Billboard*, June 5, 1965, 25.

[435] Garry Raffaele, "Fine Jazz from a Cocktail Pianist," *The Canberra Times*, January 8, 1966, 12.

triplet beat, which suggests to us that this must have been another Ernie Freeman effort. Ketty Lester had a hit with this 1940s song a few years earlier in an arrangement that was notable for its sparseness, and slightly bluesy, slightly gospel-like piano work as well as its unornamented vocal. Elvis Presley would follow that format for his own version (itself a minor hit) in 1966. Darin and Freeman, however, completely misjudge things by going to the other extreme and making the whole thing too "pop" in its sound. While there were some errors of judgement on the *Venice Blue* album, this is probably the worst recording from the session, and remained in the vault for thirty years with good reason.

March 22 & 24, 1965: Studio Sessions.

While the songs recorded here are often referred to as coming from the *Venice Blue* sessions, that isn't quite the case. *Venice Blue* was completed almost a week earlier, and the ten tracks recorded over these two days appear to be for a different project entirely, not least because none of them were chosen for the album.

Two songs were released at the time. *Gyp the Cat* was re-recorded here and released as the flip-side to *That Funny Feeling*, taped several months earlier. Quite why *Gyp the Cat* was attempted for a second time when there is little difference in Darin's approach to the song is something that is not obvious. It was wasted as a flip-side, however, and is a clever parody of *Mack the Knife* that deserves to be better known.

Lonely Road also found itself as a B-side, but this is hardly surprising. It is a fairly decent, but completely unremarkable, swing number that is performed well but ultimately rather forgettable.

The remaining songs can be split into two camps: numbers from musicals, and recent country and easy listening hits. Two songs from *My Fair Lady* were recorded. *On the Street Where You Live* gets taken at a much faster pace than usual. However, there are moments when Darin appears to sing off-mic, and where the orchestra drowns him out, which appears to be a problem at the mixing stage. If Darin was indeed singing off-mic it is not clear why, as this was the 18th take (according to *The Unreleased Capitol Sides* CD) and not a simple run-through. What's more, one would assume that a cleaner ending from an earlier take could have been spliced on to make a more finished recording when the number was eventually released in 1999. Clearly, something was unfinished here, and this is most noticeable through Bobby's rather painfully out-of-tune lengthy final note.

Get Me to the Church on Time remained in the vaults for even longer, not escaping until 2016. This is a fine recording with much of the energy and excitement that was present in the recordings made in 1963 for the unissued *As Long as I'm Singing* LP. Perhaps these two songs from *My Fair Lady* were prompted by the release of the movie the previous year, but, if so, it's fair to say that Bobby was a few months too late in getting the most mileage from the recordings, even if they had been released at the time.

If I Ruled the World, from *Pickwick*, is really quite stunning, with the orchestration underpinned by a wonderful, bluesy piano. Bobby sounds in much better voice than on *On The Street Where You Live*. The number has a nice lilting swing to it, and while this might not have been recorded with *Venice Blue* in mind, one can only wonder why it wasn't used to replace a sappy track such as *Dear Heart*, for example, and give the LP more substance. It certainly shouldn't have been tucked away in a vault for three decades. One other song from a musical was also recorded here, *The Joker*, but is still unreleased.

Red Roses for a Blue Lady was released as a single in 1965 by Darin's protégé, Wayne Newton. Bobby's own version once again benefits from the prominent piano part, and he puts in a powerful performance that ratchets up the tension with the more dynamic second run-through. Once again, though, this seems to not be a finished recording, with Darin fluffing a line and then singing off-mic once again (or thoroughly drowned out by the band) during the final stages. It is a pity the brief liner notes on the CD release didn't give us more information on quite what was going on here.

The final song to be released from these sessions is *I Left My Heart in San Francisco*, another number which would have fitted well on the *Venice Blue* release, and is superior to a number of the tracks that were included. Darin adds nothing really new to the Tony Bennett version, although he belts out the ending with great style, while a powerful, short trumpet solo plays out under the long final note.

Two more songs from these rather mysterious sessions remain unheard: *King of the Road* and *My Kind of Town*. Both were resurrected in different guises for Darin's 1973 TV series.

May 5, 1965: Studio Session

This session produced just one song, Bobby's final recording for Capitol, and one of his best.

When I Get Home is a fine contemporary pop song that deserved to give Darin his first hit in a couple of years. There are influences here of the British Invasion, but it isn't a straight copy of that sound either. There are segments where Bobby's voice is double-tracked, and the song is propelled along by pounding drums and an edgy vocal. However, it didn't even enter the charts. In the UK, a version by The Searchers reached #35, suggesting that Bobby's songwriting was becoming relevant once more, even if it wasn't top ten material.

Part of the reason for Bobby's lack of success with the song might have been his own name. He had spent much of his time at Capitol divorcing himself from contemporary-sounding material, even when he had been releasing it as singles (and writing it for other artists), in that he didn't perform it on TV to promote it. Just the previous year, he had told Dick Clark on *American Bandstand* that he was now firmly back within the swing genre and was going to stay there. A few months later that had changed, and he had a new single out that was a fine contemporary sounding track, and nobody wanted to know - including critics and reviewers, who largely ignored the release, and those who didn't seemed even more perplexed than usual by the pairing of a contemporary sounding side such as this with the swing of *Lonely Road*. *Cash Box* called it a "rhythmic, bluesy dual-track ode,"[436] and *Variety* referred to it as a "toe-tapping rhythm number."[437] Neither could bring themselves to call it a highly commercial piece of contemporary pop music (which it was), and one has to wonder how much of that had to do with Darin's image at the time which was far from either commercial or contemporary. No-one could or should criticise Bobby's switch from genre to genre, but, at the same time, there must have been some head-scratching at the time when it came to working out exactly who he was and which part of him should be taken seriously. Three months earlier, he had been crooning *Venice Blue* and now he was taking on the British Invasion at their own game.

In the end, the title of *When I Get Home* was prophetic. It was Bobby's last recording for Capitol, and his next move would be to go back "home" to Atlantic records, of whom ATCO had been a subsidiary.

Bobby's time at Capitol had been artistically rewarding on many levels, but must have been frustrating for him and his fans on others. Albums such as *Oh! Look at Me Now* and *From Hello Dolly to Goodbye Charlie* were excellent efforts, even if both contained one or two weaker tracks. *Earthy!* was arguably the most ambitious record that Bobby had yet put out, but nobody took any notice, including his own label. On the other hand, his ballad work on his albums of standards were often dated thanks to the use of a choir that only served to get in the way. At the same time, with the exception of *18 Yellow Roses* and *You're the Reason I'm Living*, success in the singles charts eluded Bobby during these three years. He would once again reach the top ten with *If I Were a Carpenter* after his move to Atlantic, but it would be the last substantial hit of his career.

Sometimes, bizarre decisions had been made about what was released and what was left in the vaults. While the eleven tracks from the 1963 sessions that were to make up an album of contemporary versions of vintage songs had relatively little commercial potential, the same is not true for either the *As Long As I'm Singin'* album

---

[436] "Record Reviews," *Cash Box*, June 12, 1965, 8.
[437] "Top Singles of the Week," *Variety*, June 6, 1965, 50.

or the recording of Darin's live act from what was intended to be his final Vegas season. Still, it took over thirty years for them to be released, with Capitol oddly choosing not to capitalise on the success of *If I Were a Carpenter* in 1966 or the news of Bobby's passing in 1973 by releasing some of this material.

At some point in 1965, Bobby recorded the theme song for *That Darn Cat* (Robert Stevenson), a Disney movie. Sadly, his fine version of the song didn't appear on the soundtrack album, and remains unreleased, other than on the actual film itself, due to contractual reasons, and yet it's a really fine performance with a smoky night-club feel to it, and a relatively rare occasion where Darin sings a swing number in a quiet, subdued manner. It is a song well worth seeking out if you can find it.

Bobby with George and Olive Osmond, Vic Damone, and Andy Williams.

CHAPTER NINE
FEELING GOOD: 1965-1966

It is difficult to understand how Bobby Darin might have been perceived by the public as the 1960s reached their midway point. He had said publicly that he didn't want to make any more films with his wife, and then the pair had starred in *That Funny Feeling*. He then said that he was sticking with the swing/big band formula for good, but within a few months released the first of two singles that were clear efforts at competing with the British Invasion. He decided to leave Capitol, and then returned to them within a matter of months with a new five-year contract, and then left them again less than a year later. And, to cap it all, he had retired from live performances in November 1963, stressing in the months afterwards that he would not return, but, in September 1965, it was announced he would start doing live performances again after all, including a run at the Copa in New York before starring in a Broadway show about George M. Cohan – a show that never happened.[438]

When Bobby left Capitol for the second (and last) time, he had already made arrangements to return to the Atlantic fold, where he had recorded all of his biggest hits, from *Splish Splash* through to *Things*. The return to Atlantic wasn't, perhaps, a surprise considering his lack of commercial success at Capitol. It may have been that he felt he had more room to experiment and attempt other styles at Atlantic, something which Capitol never really got behind or tried to promote, despite the release of the two folk albums. *Variety* reported that Darin's "return to Atlantic was cued by his longtime friendship with Atlantic prexy Ahmet Ertegun."[439] *Billboard* quoted Ertegun as saying "the prospect of having this great recording artist back on our label is a source of tremendous pride and excitement to myself and my partners,

---

[438] "Darin back on N. Y. Café Scene Via Copa Stand," *Variety*, September 15, 1965, 71.
[439] "Bobby Darin Back in Atlantic Fold," *Variety*, July 14, 1965, 41.

Nesuhi Ertegun and Jerry Wexler."[440]

Over the next two years or so, Bobby would release five studio albums, and leave around three dozen songs in the vault – most of which are now lost due to a fire.

August 14 and 20, 1965: Studio Sessions

The first thing that Bobby needed to do at his new home was cut a single. Five tracks were recorded over these two dates, but only two were released.

We Didn't Ask to be Brought Here was a fine, adult, contemporary pop song with a clear message and, as such, was Darin's first overtly political single. While there were no specifics mentioned within the song, it would have been clear to listeners at the time that the song was referring to events such as the Vietnam War and the Cold War when Bobby sings "the world's gone mad." *Billboard* called the single "his greatest chance for the charts since *Mack the Knife*. In the current commercial protest vein, he excels with his own composition backed by a hard driving dance beat."[441] *Cash Box* were equally enthusiastic, saying:

> Darin evidently wants to get his re-association off on the right foot, for he does a terrific, strictly teen-oriented job on *We Didn't Ask to Be Brought Here,* his own gift to the 'protest' song field. Overall sound is touched by a colourful English influence.[442]

Sadly, very few got to hear the song, and the single sank almost with trace – again, one has to wonder if both Darin and the advertisements for the song had something to do with it. A press advert for the single tells the reader that the song has a "great message" but then has a picture of Darin in a suit and tie – hardly the image associated with someone singing a protest song in 1965. The image and the content were simply an anachronism.

The flip-side was just as interesting, with Darin releasing his first song that fit firmly in the blues genre, *Funny What Love Can Do*. The arrangement is superb, with a wailing harmonica setting the scene in the introduction, and Bobby is surprisingly comfortable in the gritty blues idiom. Despite the song's release in September 1965, there are listings for a re-recording during the *If I Were a Carpenter* LP sessions the following year, but, like several songs from those sessions, it has never been released. The song also made it into Bobby's live act, being performed on a BBC TV special in 1966 (shown in 1967).

---

[440] "Darin Signs with Atl'tic," *Billboard*, July 17, 1965, 4.
[441] "Spotlight Singles," *Billboard*, September 25, 1965, 18.
[442] "Record Reviews," *Cash Box*, September 25, 1965, 10.

Together, the two sides made for a classic single, but sales were poor, forcing Bobby to at least temporarily return to the big band sound for his next releases. The other three songs believed to have been recorded at this session are *Sweet Memories*, which had been a hit for country singer Webb Pierce, *Ain't that a Bunch of Nonsense* and *Baby I Miss You So*.

The end of 1965 and the beginning of 1966 was a busy time for Darin. In a candid interview with Harvey Pack in October to promote his appearance on *The Steve Lawrence Show*, he said of his television performances that "when I do a show there are two things that must happen. I've got to have fun or forget it. And, secondly, I want people to stop me in the street the next day and tell me either I was great or I was lousy. Without reaction the show is a complete waste."[443] Once again, he was asked the question of whether he would front his own variety show, and he repeated his previous answer: "I perform at too high a pitch to survive for a full season in most of the acceptable formats. I'd have to come down for television, not in attitude…but in style. […] I just don't think I could do it." When Darin did eventually get his own TV series seven years later, he proved himself right.

The day after *The Steve Lawrence Show* aired, Bobby was back in hospital, this time "as a result of a virus infection of the chest and was expected to be confined there for at three to four days on the advice of his personal physician."[444]

The Steve Lawrence Show wasn't the only TV variety show that Bobby appeared on during this period, with him returning to *The Andy Williams Show* twice and appearing on *The Merv Griffin Show*. The sketch he took part in during his appearance on *The Red Skelton Show* was referred to as a "pun-loaded comedic treat" by *Variety*.[445] Songs performed during these TV outings included *That Funny Feeling*, *Gyp the Cat*, *Get Me to the Church on Time*, and an instrumental version of *What'd I Say*. Once again, he didn't sing either side of his new single for Atlantic.

December 13-15, 1965, February 4 and March 23, 1966: Studio Sessions
Bobby Darin sings The Shadow of your Smile **LP**

Bobby Darin's first album for Atlantic wasn't released until April or May 1966, a year since his last for Capitol. The first half of *Bobby Darin sings The Shadow of your Smile* consisted of all five songs nominated for an Academy Award in 1966. The second side of the album was made up of five standards plus a Darin original in the standard style.

---

[443] Harvey Pack, "Bobby Darin Guest Stars," *Waterloo Daily Courier*, October 11, 1965, 15.
[444] "Bobby Darin Hospitalised," *Boxoffice*, October 18, 1965, W5.
[445] Mar, "Red Skelton Hour," *Variety*, September 29, 1965, 30.

Bobby with Red Skelton and Joan Swift on "The Red Skelton Show," 1965.

If you are thinking that this sounds like two projects cobbled together to make one, then you would be correct, as the standards that made up side two of the LP were clearly recorded as part of an album made up entirely of songs from the Great American Songbook, which was put on tape in December 1965. The Academy Award-nominated songs, on the other hand, were recorded in March 1966. So, while the public got to hear Bobby's versions of *The Ballad of Cat Ballou* and *What's New Pussycat*, it never got to hear the December 1965 songs that were to make up the rest of the original album of standards: *The Best is Yet to Come, The Sheik of Araby, This Could Be the Start of Something Big, I Got Plenty of Nothin', Baby Won't You Please Come Home*, and yet another version of *Ace in the Hole*. These all remain unreleased, and have probably been lost. Whatever the reason for the shelving of the original album recorded in late 1965, it is highly likely it would have been of better quality than the split personality affair that was issued instead. To make matters worse, the stereo mix on the CD release of this album is awful when it comes to the material that made up the second side of the LP, and so the best way to hear the album is by tracking down a mono vinyl copy.

Things get off to a good start, with a lilting rendition of the title song. Bobby had, for the most part, avoided Latin American rhythms over the years, with the most notable exception being some of the ballads on *The Milk Shows*. Here, however, he embraces that sound, and performs, almost caresses, *The Shadow of Your Smile* as a rhumba. Sadly, when he performed the song in concert, he ditched this lovely arrangement and replaced it with a medium-tempo swing rendition probably orchestrated by Roger Kellaway, which, sadly, loses the delicacy of the studio version.

At this point, things begin to fall apart with the sickly sweet *The Sweetheart Tree*, which somehow managed to be penned by Johnny Mercer and Henry Mancini — but even songwriting legends clearly have off days. There is a folk-like vibe to the composition itself, which first appeared in the comedy *The Great Race* (dir. Blake Edwards). The arrangement is decent enough, with the novelty value of the harpsichord (or harpsichord-like instrument) effectively distracting the listener from the saccharine nonsense of the lyrics that Darin is saddled with singing. The rather perverse thing here is that Bobby seems completely at home with the song, giving a committed, nuanced, performance which displays an added warmth to his voice which is often heard during his short time with Atlantic in the mid-1960s.

Darin is back with a Latin American rhythm for the lovely, heartbreaking *I Will Wait for You* from the French film *The Umbrellas of Cherbourg* (dir. Jacques Demy). Once again, this new extra warmth to Bobby's voice is put to good use, and thankfully the material is worthy of such a performance. The big ending is perhaps misjudged for such a tender song, something he would avoid when this number was performed in concert in a medley with the Antonio Carlos Jobim song *Meditation*.

There is relatively little to say about *The Ballad of Cat Ballou* and *What's New Pussycat* except to ask the question: *why?* Throughout the entire musical legacy of Bobby Darin, there are probably no songs less suited to him than these. *The Ballad of Cat Ballou* comes off better out of the two, and is also somewhat better than the duet version from the film featuring Stubby Kaye and Nat King Cole. Unlike Cole, however, Darin didn't have the problem of singing with Kaye, and his version is cleaner, crisper and sung somewhat more seriously.

What's New Pussycat, however, is unforgiveable. This time around, even the harpsichord last heard on *The Sweetheart Tree* can't save the day. Darin sounds completely at a loss as to what to do with the song and it is one of the rare occasions where there is nothing redeemable in his recording. In the hands of Tom Jones, the number became a classic, and the song and singer fit each other absolutely perfectly. In Darin's hands, the reverse is true — the song and singer couldn't be a more unlikely combination.

Interestingly, when performing at the Cocoanut Grove in March 1966, the overture for Darin's performance was a medley of all five of the movie songs in an arrangement by Dick Stabile. *Variety* states that it is a clever idea, "considering the current suspense. It is not Stabile's fault that some of the tunes don't register as memorable melodies."[446] Perhaps the Oscar-nominated songs seemed like a good idea at the time - and let's just be thankful that *The Shadow of Your Smile* won the award or we could be discussing an album entitled *Bobby Darin sings What's New Pussycat* at this point.

Also recorded at the March sessions was Bobby's take on *Strangers in the Night*.

---

[446] Murf, "Nitery Reviews," 10.

This recording has yet to be released.

The second side of the album opens with the charming *Rainin'*, recorded in February 1966. This is a Darin original, and for the session he pulled together a group of aging musicians who, over the years, had played for and with some of the most important men in jazz. For example, drummer Nick Fatool had played for Harry James and Tommy Dorsey, and violinist Joe Venuti had worked with Bix Beiderbecke and Benny Goodman and, in the 1970s, would record a series of albums with saxophonist Zoot Sims which may well be what he is best remembered for today. *Rainin'* was hardly a demanding chart for such a group of musicians, but the recording that resulted is one of Darin's best, and once again shows how his voice was improving as he got older. The rough edges were now almost entirely smoothed out (although this was clearly a conscious decision, as they returned with a vengeance a couple of years later) and his voice was a suppler instrument than before, with no effort or force required to move from the lower to higher register.

Also recorded at the same session as *Rainin'* was a number entitled *Weeping Willow*. At the time of the writing of the first edition of this book, back in 2015, the Darin Estate had announced that *Weeping Willow* would be released on a forthcoming album. It is now 2019, and it still hasn't appeared – although this state of affairs will be hardly surprising to the most ardent Darin fans, who are used to such projects being announced and then not happening. Luckily, *Weeping Willow* has escaped unofficially, and can easily be found online with a little bit of Googling. In many respects, the recording looks forward to the sound of Bobby's hit version of *Mame* that would be taped a few months later. *Weeping Willow* is a great recording, full of vitality and with Bobby in full showstopping mode. Why it wasn't released at the time is a mystery; that it still remains in the vaults is a travesty.

The songs from the December sessions follow. Darin had already recorded *Softly as in a Morning Sunrise* from *The New Moon* back in 1959, and here he tackles the other great song from that operetta, *Lover Come Back to Me*. This one had been a jazz standard for some time, and Bobby takes the song at a fast tempo with a big band, and some wild drumming during the instrumental break. It is hardly the most subtle of recordings, but is still probably the best of the songs that have been released from these sessions.

Less successful is *Cute*, which started off as a Neal Hefti instrumental for the Count Basie band before words were added to it later. The lyrics were never top-notch, and the piece never felt natural as a song rather than an instrumental, and this comes through in Bobby's version. The arrangement by Richard Wess is also not up to his usual standards (it doesn't even sound like a Wess arrangement), and Darin doesn't ever really sound comfortable.

After You've Gone gets a slow, bluesy treatment which is hard to appreciate due to the poor sound on CD releases of the album. Here, though, the Wess arrangement is more typical of his work, with a slow build-up during the first run-through before the number kicks into gear at the mid-way point. Darin clearly relishes the challenge of the big climax, and it is also nice that he uses the rarely-used alternate lyrics for the second run-through rather than just repeating the first set.

It's Only a Paper Moon receives a relatively straight-forward swing rendition that is pleasant enough, but doesn't add anything to this often-recorded standard. Perhaps this is something that was a problem at the December session and persuaded Bobby not to release the entire album of standards as it was originally conceived. Of the five songs we have, only a couple really hit the mark when it comes to performance, and the choice of material is also more predictable than in many of Bobby's albums of standards, which often mined the lesser-known works of American songwriters but here used more well-known numbers.

The album ends with a rather mundane version of *Liza* which, again, is perfectly pleasant but totally unremarkable. It is a description that sums up the LP in general. There is something missing from *Bobby Darin sings the Shadow of your Smile*, something which is very difficult to pinpoint. The split personality of the album certainly doesn't help matters, and it feels as if it was released purely because something *needed* to be released, as if it were a stop-gap – and with his next Atlantic album being released just a matter of weeks later, that may well have been the case. Oddly, the *Variety* review of the album gave a run-down of the contents of the album, but failed to really comment on its quality.[447] *Billboard*, on the other hand, mustered up enough enthusiasm to state that Darin recorded the movie songs with "excitement, understanding and respect."[448] *Cash Box* didn't bother, saying merely that Bobby handles the songs "in his own well known fashion."[449]

Two other songs from the December 1965 sessions appeared as a single in January 1966. Relatively little seems to be known about *The Breaking Point*, other than it was written by the songwriting team of Pete King and Paul Francis Webster. It is a fine upbeat swing number that is better than much of the album that was recorded at the same time, but it is hard to see why anyone thought it had potential as a single.

Silver Dollar, the flip-side, is another swing number, but the arrangement is far less cluttered than on *The Breaking Point*. This is, once again, a classic Richard Wess orchestration, and Darin attacks it, chews it up, and spits it out during the final half minute or so. However, it is all over too quickly. There was room here for this to be one of the epic Darin/Wess collaborations, but it needed another run-through of the song for that to happen, and so the listener comes away feeling short-changed. The single created very little interest from either buyers or critics. *Variety* said that "*Silver*

---

[447] "Wayne Newton, Johnny Mathis, Kostelanetz, Darin, Mamie Lee, Yarbrough, Syne, Hines Top LPs," *Variety*, May 4, 1966, 192.
[448] "Album Reviews, *Billboard*, May 28, 1966, 68.
[449] "Album Reviews," *Cash Box*, May 7, 1966, 46.

Dollar hits as a sharp performance that could give this oldie a big round of plays. *The Breaking Point* is another snappy slice of a classy piece of material."[450]

In September 1965, an article appeared in which Bobby announced that he was going to play some live dates again: "I'm going to play New York for a few weeks this June, but only because I think it'll be fun. [...] No, I'm not going back after June...It's just a one shot."

But the June 1966 dates in New York were not just a "one shot," and were probably never intended to be. He returned to the Flamingo in Las Vegas for a season of shows in January 1966, some five months before the announced New York dates. Prior to that, Princess Margaret and Lord Snowden persuaded him to sing at a charity fundraising party on Christmas Eve, 1965.[451] A highlight of the Flamingo shows was his *a cappella* version of *Brother Can You Spare a Dime* which, a *Variety* review informs us, segued into *King of the Road*. *Cash Box* said:

> *Gotta Travel On* builds to a devastating vocal crescendo and is followed immediately in a hushed spotlight with an appealing, plaintive and altogether touching treatment of the depression standard *Brother, Can You Spare a Dime?* It's offered without the aid of background music, a theatrical deceit reminiscent of the days when the Glen *(sic)* Miller brass section would light up the dark at the Paramount. But under Darin's consummate guise it's effective and almost shattering.[452]

From what information we have, Bobby's show had been reinvented, and contained very little of his regular live act prior to his "retirement" from the stage. *Variety* stated that the new offering "is even better than the one he had here when he established the showroom's all-time attendance and crowd turn-away record – an honor he still holds."[453] To top off Bobby's successful return to live performing, down the strip, Frank Sinatra, no less, was recommending his audiences check out Bobby's show while they were in town.

Darin's return to live performing wasn't totally without hitches, though. In Miami in February, *Variety* reported that it was a "less than full opening show" and that "singer and orchestra wandered away from each other during *King of the Road*, but Darin took a couple of reprises on [the] tune until he had it the way he wanted it."[454]

---

[450] "Top Singles of the Week," *Variety*, January 19, 1966, 62.
[451] Mike Connolly, "Mike Connolly in Hollywood," *Pittsburgh Gazette*, December 21, 1965, 15
[452] "Darin's Back Live With Dynamic Talent," *Cash Box*, February 5, 1966, 43.
[453] Duke, "Flamingo, Las Vegas," *Variety*, January 26, 1966, 58.
[454] Meyr, "Deauville, M. B.," *Variety*, February 23, 1966, 58.

Newspaper advertisement

By March 1966, Darin was back at the Cocoanut Grove, with his rendition of *Brother, Can You Spare a Dime* again singled out for praise, this time by *Variety* in their review.[455] *Billboard* noted that "on some numbers he stretches his vocal equipment to the limits but even this doesn't detract from the over-all ease and the generally loose, but still pointed, performance."[456] By this point, Bobby had added *I Left My Heart in San Francisco* to his live repertoire.[457] The return to the Cocoanut Grove was watched by Andy Williams, Eddy Fisher, Jack Benny, George Burns, Sandra Dee, Vince Edwards, Johnny Mercer, Mia Farrow, Ben Gazzara, Henry Mancini, Juliet Prowse, Edward G. Robinson, and Michael Caine.[458]

In April, Bobby was at the Copa, a couple of months earlier than the June date announced six months earlier. The reviews were unanimous in their praise, with *Variety* writing that "Darin has something for almost any person appreciating a well-turned act and a thoroughly pro warbler. He is much improved over his last appearance at the Copa back in May, 1963."[459]

Audio excerpts of a radio broadcast from the Copa shows have circulated amongst fans for years, albeit in dubious sound quality. It is clear from what limited evidence that we have that Bobby's show at this time was even more ambitious than the one recorded at The Flamingo in 1963. There are left-field choices within the material, such as the conjoining of *I've Got the World on a String* and *Yesterday* in an unlikely medley. There is also a jazzy, somewhat bluesy, rendition of Paul Clayton's folk/country song *Gotta Travel On*, an acoustic version of *Trouble in Mind*, and a show-

---

[455] Murf, "Nitery Reviews," *Variety*, March 10, 1966, 10.
[456] Mike Gross, "Darin Touches All Bases in Home Run," *Billboard*, April 16, 1966, 52.
[457] Eliot Tiegel, "Darin Marks Return to Clubs with a Solid Bit," *Billboard*, March 19, 1966, 54.
[458] John L. Scott, "New Bobby Darin Retains Old Flair," *Los Angeles Times*, March 10, 1966, part V, 15.
[459] Wear, "Copacobana, N. Y.," *Variety*, April 6, 1966, 60.

stopping *I Got Plenty of Nothin'*. Reviews tell us that the set-list also included *After You're Gone, I Left My Heart in San Francisco*, and his new single, *Mame*, which would become the lead-off track of one of his most acclaimed albums, *In a Broadway Bag*.

March 22 and May 2, 4 and 6, 1966: Studio Sessions
In a Broadway Bag LP

The day before Bobby recorded the movie songs for the *Shadow of your Smile* LP, he went into the studio in order to record the title song from a new musical, *Mame*. The resulting single would reach just #53 in the pop charts, but it would climb to #3 in the Easy Listening charts, resulting in Bobby's biggest chart success in around three years. Perhaps more importantly, it prompted the recording of an entire album of songs from recent Broadway musicals, which was not only one of Darin's best LPs, but also his last album of standards, although no-one (including Darin) could have known that at the time.

It is rather hard to work out why *Mame* clicked with a certain group of listeners more than other recent Bobby Darin singles had. That's not to say that it isn't very good, but so were a number of previous efforts that had gone unnoticed. The Dixieland arrangement in many ways follows on from the sound achieved on *Rainin'* and *Weeping Willow* just the month before, and perhaps that jazzy, razzamatazz vibe was enough to separate it from the straightforward swing of, say, *Hello Dolly*. It had virtually nothing to do with what was in the pop charts at the time, but perhaps that only made it stand out. What is also key is that Darin promoted it on television, singing it on *Mickie*

Advertisement for Bobby's single and the Broadway show

Finn's and *The Andy Williams Show*, although the latter wouldn't air until October 1966. There may well have been other performances on other now-lost and undocumented television guest spots. Whatever it was that caused *Mame* to take off (if only to a relatively low altitude), it is not as if it wasn't deserved. The arrangement is bright and brassy, and Darin sounds more at ease on this record than he had done since the *Hello Dolly* album. *Cash Box* said that "Bobby Darin has come up with a delightful vocal cover of the Al Hirt instrumental, *Mame*. The title tune from the forthcoming Broadway musical, this one is a happy Dixieland side with a wide-ranged appeal."[460] *Variety* said the recording was a "snappy workout" of the song.[461]

Also recorded at the same session was the flip-side, a so-so country number called *Walkin' in the Shadow of Love*. The song had been written by the writing team of Giant, Baum and Kaye that had been responsible for a considerable number of the increasingly-mediocre songs that appeared in the increasingly-mediocre films that Elvis Presley made during the 1960s. *Walkin' in the Shadow of Love* shows that they were certainly more capable songwriters than a listen to *Wolf Call* or *Spring Fever* might suggest. Even so, it had very little to make it stand out from hundreds of other country songs, although Darin's performance shows just how good he could be in this genre when he sang "straight" rather than adding the affectations that were present on the *You're the Reason I'm Living* album, for example. The song was even deemed good enough to be included in the 4CD career retrospective issued by Rhino in 1995.

In early May 1966, Bobby returned to the studio to record an album built around the single, an album that Jeff Bleiel refers to as "arguably the best album of standard material he ever recorded."[462] The album kicks off with *Mame* (the album is still often referred to as *Mame* rather than *In a Broadway Bag*) before moving on to *I Believe in You* from the 1961 musical *How to Succeed in Show Business Without Really Trying*. The number, which had already been recorded by the likes of Sinatra and Sarah Vaughan before Darin got around to it, is taken at a stately pace but with a pounding swing that is more than a little reminiscent of the Count Basie sound. What is key is that Bobby sounds more engaged with the material than he did on either the *Venice Blue* or *The Shadow of your Smile* albums.

A Basie-like swing is also present in *It's Today*, also taken from *Mame*. The material here isn't quite as memorable, but the brass section is as tight as a drum and given room to shine during the lengthy instrumental. It is probably the least memorable of all the songs on the album (and Bobby doesn't sound too convinced about throwing confetti) – but that's not a reflection of the quality of his performance on this particular song, but just on how good the rest of the album is.

Everybody has the Right to be Wrong is the first of two songs from the Jimmy van

---

[460] "Record Reviews," *Cash Box*, April 9, 1966, 20.
[461] "Top Singles of the Week," *Variety*, April 6, 1966, 50.
[462] Bleiel, *That's All*, 119.

Heusen and Sammy Cahn musical *Skyscraper*. The faux-Basie band is back in fine fettle, and Darin is in full show-stopping mode here, totally confident and in great voice.

The other song from the same show, *I'll Only Miss Her When I Think of Her*, appears later in the album, and is totally different in style. The warmer Darin voice, heard on the previous album, is to the fore in this ballad with heartbreaking lyrics. There is no attempt to compete with the beauty of the delicate Sinatra version, recorded a year or so earlier that slipped out on an LP that few people bought. Instead, Darin gives a vulnerable and yet defiant vocal, which is quite an unusual (if not unique) take on the song, and works just as well in its own way.

Bobby had already recorded *Who Can I Turn To* from *The Roar of the Greasepaint, the Smell of the Crowd* for the *Venice Blue* LP. Here he turns his attention to *Feeling Good* from the same show, with the awkward situation of trying to avoid comparisons with the ultimate recording of the song by Nina Simone a couple of years earlier. Bearing that in mind, instead of going into competition with Simone, Darin gives the song a faster tempo, a bluesy feel, and a funky organ to underpin it all. While he doesn't steal the song out from under Nina Simone (who could?), he still manages to stamp his own mark on it in a memorable, ballsy performance that all too often gets overlooked in compilations of Darin's best work.

The second side of the album opens with what is probably the best track here: *Don't Rain on My Parade* from *Funny Girl*, a song that Bobby would use as the opening number of his live act for a while. Again, he is faced with making someone else's signature song his own, and he not only achieves this but also comes up with a better arrangement (by Shorty Rogers) and vocal than Barbra Streisand's own. This is classic, top-drawer Darin. It is a perfectly judged vocal, mixing power with confidence, determination and a little bit of cockiness, and the half-speed section at the end is brilliantly executed.

The Other Half of Me from *I Had a Ball* is the first in a sequence of fine ballad performances, and probably the best of them. With Darin's marriage effectively at an end, one can't help thinking that he completely internalises the lyrics as he wonders whether he will ever meet his "other half." It is a beautiful, heart-felt rendition that shows a completely different side to the singer than a song such as *Don't Rain on My Parade*. The song itself also deserves to be much better known than it is.

Once Upon a Time is a more familiar song, and comes from the flop musical *All American* — one that was thought of so highly around the time of its opening that both Clark Terry and Duke Ellington recorded full albums of instrumental versions of the key songs. *Once Upon a Time* is the only number that has had any life outside the show itself, and much of that is to do with Sinatra including it in his *September of My Years* LP in 1965. Bobby's version is good, and thought of highly by most Darin fans (including this one), but there were always going to be comparisons with Sinatra's rendition, and this time the vocal comes up lacking, with much of it sung forcefully rather than wistfully. This is, in part, due to the big orchestration – this is stripped back in the live version recorded in November 1966, and the performance there is superior to the studio outing.

Try to Remember from *The Fantasticks* is up next, and this time Bobby is in a more wistful mood, and it is a shame that he didn't approach *Once Upon a Time* in the same way. This folk-like melody is given a full orchestration again, but this time it manages to not overpower the song.

The final track, after *I'll Only Miss Her When I Think of Her* (discussed above), is *Night Song* from *Golden Boy*, the boxing-themed musical that had starred Sammy Davis Jr. While still a ballad, this is more upbeat, and Darin negotiates the wide-ranging melody with ease, and the result is a fine climax to a brilliant collection of songs.

Considering the quality of this set of songs, *Variety*'s review is rather subdued, saying simply that "he belts with a theatrical style that suits this material very neatly."[463] *Billboard* said that Darin was in "top form."[464] *Cash Box* seemed most enthusiastic, stating that "the electric stylings of Bobby Darin are applied to a series of superb tunes from both on and off Broadway productions, on this set that is a must item for both the chanter's fans and devotees of the show tunes packed in here."[465]

Despite the quality of the performances, nobody seemed to care a great deal, with the album not even charting, notwithstanding the fact it is now viewed as one of Darin's best. Within a few months, Bobby would abandon albums of standards for good, not releasing one during the last seven years of his life.

April 21 and May 9, 1966: Studio Session

These two unrelated sessions are brought together here under one heading for the simple reason that no tracks have been released from either. Sessionographies tell us that *True Love's a Blessing*, a cover of a Sonny James recording, was cut on April 21, 1966. Listening to the original version of the song, it is hard to see how it would have been a good fit for Darin, and perhaps that is why it remained unreleased.

May 9 saw Darin record three more songs. The first was *L. A. Breakdown*, a song that would be recorded by a multitude of singers in the coming years from Jack Jones to its composer, Larry Marks. Marks' own version, released in 1968, has a feel not dissimilar to the folk-based albums that Darin would record in late 1966/early 1967, and it may be that Bobby's own version was an early attempt in that style. Also recorded on the same day was *I Can Live on Love* and *Manhattan in my Heart*, with the

---

[463] "Rolling Stones, Belafonte's 'Room,' Dusty Springfield, New Christys, Mindbenders, Darin, F&T Top LPs," *Variety*, June 29, 1966, 42.
[464] "Album Reviews," *Billboard*, July 9, 1966, 66.
[465] "Album Reviews," *Cash Box*, July 9, 1966, 40.

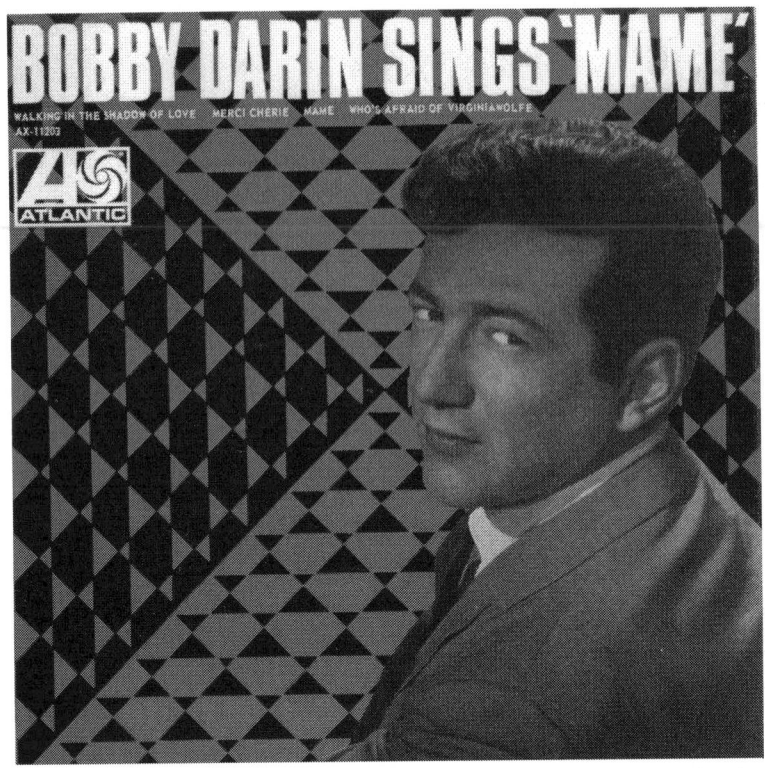

This Australian EP combined both side of the "Mame" single with both sides of the "Who's Afraid of Virginia Wolf" single (note misspelling on the EP).

latter being the only number known to have survived. The recording was played to fans at the unveiling of Bobby's star on the Las Vegas Walk of Stars in 2007. A release of the song on an album entitled *From Bronx to Broadway* was announced by Darin archivist Jimmy Scalia on January 26, 2015. The CD was never issued.[466]

May 27, 1966: Studio Session

This session was clearly to provide more material for singles. *Merry-Go-Round in the Rain* (a song co-written by Johnny Mercer) and a number only known as *Seventeen* both remain unreleased.

The remaining two songs, *Who's Afraid of Virginia Woolf* and *Merci Cherie*, were issued as Bobby's first single after the relatively successful *Mame*, and one has to wonder if he actually *wanted* to get a foothold in the charts again. *Mame* had taken Darin back to the showbiz, razzamatazz sound and had, at least, been a hit on the Easy Listening charts. So why follow it up with a single consisting of two relatively forgettable

---

[466] See the interview with Jimmy Scalia at https://youtu.be/EF9YjRTGgGE (viewed 16 October 2018).

ballads? *Who's Afraid of Virginia Woolf* is by the far the best of the two, and is a very attractive number and performance, but quite why anyone thought it was single material is a complete mystery. *Merci Cherie* is even less commercial, not helped by the choir that opens the number and then pops up throughout. There's no doubting that Bobby sings both songs well, and with commitment, but if he was getting any kind of momentum in the charts with *Mame*, this release only stopped that momentum in its tracks. Presumably *Cash Box* were being sarcastic when they said that the pairing would make "sales sparks fly."[467]

June 28-30, 1966: Studio Sessions

Late June saw Darin back in the studio to record nine standards that, presumably, would have been paired with some of the leftover tracks from December 1965 to make a complete album, had it ever been released. As it was, this session remains completely unheard, although some of the known titles such as *Lulu's Back in Town*, *Mountain Greenery*, *What Now My Love*, and *It's Magic* are mouth-watering propositions. As with most unreleased material from the Atlantic period, these recordings are thought to have been destroyed.

Darin's first year back at Atlantic had seen him release two albums made up largely of standards and show tunes, with more than another LP's worth of material left in the vaults. *The Shadow of Your Smile* had been a largely disappointing release, but *In a Broadway Bag* had found Bobby on top form, and yet, despite some success for the *Mame* single, the album did not sell well. Bobby's next move would be to return to the folk genre, and this time it would produce one of his signature songs.

---

[467] "Record Reviews," *Cash Box*, June 25, 1966, 18.

Bobby with Roger Miller on "The Roger Miller Show." Publicity photo.

CHAPTER TEN
BEAUTIFUL THINGS: 1966-1967

It was probably inevitable that the newspapers wouldn't let Bobby's thirtieth birthday pass without a series of snide remarks about him being five years late on his aim of becoming a legend by the time he was twenty-five. Perhaps most notable was a rather bitter and vindictive article by Bob Ellison, which ends:

> For Bobby, success came fast and early, and when he announced 'I want to establish myself as a legend by the time I'm 25" a lot of people feared the ID with the style that has been described as '20th century Benzedrine' just might make it. But that was a long time ago. And now Bobby is 30. May 14 was his birthday. It was not a national holiday.[468]

Two months after Bob Ellison essentially dismissed him as a has-been, Bobby went in to the studio to record a song that would become his biggest hit in years: *If I Were a Carpenter*.

August 11, October 18-20 and 31, 1966: Studio Sessions
If I Were a Carpenter LP

Bobby Darin told a humorous story many times in concert of how a couple of agents came to see him in 1965 or 1966 and offered him songs by the likes of John Sebastian

---

[468] Bob Ellison, "He's Five Years Late," *Akron Beacon Journal*, May 20, 1966, 21.

and Tim Hardin that he rejected and that went on to become hits for other people. Quite how much of the story is true is debatable, although it was no doubt at least partly based in fact, even if it had been somewhat embellished. "When they came to me the next time, I was lying in wait for them," he told an audience in 1973, and the song he ended up recording was *If I Were a Carpenter*, a number which would introduce yet another phase in his career.

Despite the fact that Bobby spent time trying to ease the rumours that Tim Hardin was annoyed at him for "stealing his song," the original stories still make for good copy. Fred Dellar, in the liner notes for the CD release of the *If I Were a Carpenter* album, repeats the story that Hardin was "incensed" that Darin had "copied Hardin's own vocal approach." He even quotes Hardin as saying "he played my version through his headphones, so that he could copy my phrasing."[469] While Darin was clearly inspired and influenced by the original Tim Hardin demo, he certainly wasn't listening to it through headphones when he recorded the song as he makes a number of small, but not unimportant, changes to both the melody and the timing. The bridge section, for example, is sung faster in Hardin's version, but in tempo in Bobby's. Meanwhile, a number of changes are made in the melody in Darin's rendition, particularly in the second verse where this happens on multiple lines. Finally, Bobby's vocal is far more intimate, more delicate, than Hardin's. Somehow, from somewhere, he had found yet another new voice that had only ever been hinted at over the previous decade.[470]

The other side recorded on the same day, presumably with the expectation it would be the flip-side, was *Misty Roses*, another Hardin composition. Here, Bobby sings so quietly that he is almost whispering the song. He doesn't even add more force during the bridge section, where the arrangement becomes just a little bit more intense. *Misty Roses* was eventually held back for the album, with the earlier *Rainin'* released as the flip-side to the single.

The single got Darin into the top ten of the charts in both America and the UK for the first time in three years and, during his time in Britain during the autumn of 1966, he sang the song on all three of his TV appearances – quite a turnaround from rarely singing his latest singles on television at all for the previous four or five years. Despite the quality of the recording, and the fact it turned into a sizeable hit forever associated with Darin, the trade publications paid little attention to the song. Only *Cash Box* got enthusiastic, and they, forever lovers of adjectives, called the song "a haunting, fascinatingly orchestrated, folk based emotion-filled love story."[471]

---

[469] Fred Dellar, liner notes to *Bobby Darin sings If I Were a Carpenter & Inside Out*, Bobby Darin, Diablo DIAB 864, CD, 1998.

[470] From a purely practical point of view, Hardin's version runs over twenty seconds longer than Bobby's, once and for all disproving Hardin's claim that Bobby was singing along to it via headphones for his own recording.

[471] "Record Reviews," *Cash Box*, September 10, 1966, 16.

The next step was an album built around the hit single, and Bobby didn't attempt to change the formula, selecting songs in the same style by Hardin, John Sebastian (of the Lovin' Spoonful) and Henry John Deutschendorf (or a young John Denver to you and me). Everything was stripped back for the album even down to the running times of each song: not one was longer that 2:40.

Reason to Believe was the second track on the album. Hardin had included the song on his first album, and this time Darin *does* follow the arrangement and vocal very closely indeed, and with little variation. Once again, though, there is almost no volume to the vocal and, even then, the voice is set far back in the mix.

(Sittin' here) Lovin' You is a clever change of pace that gives the album variety without breaking the overall feel. Here, Darin takes the Lovin' Spoonful number, adds a dash of showmanship through the scat-singing during the instrumental break, gives the arrangement a slightly jazzier jug-band feel, and still manages to keep the whole thing true to the original and in keeping with the sound of the album. When released as a single, *Billboard* said it had an "old-timey" feel to it and had the "earmarks of a no. 1 item."[472] The main thing that prevented the song from hitting the top ten was that it was the third single from the album, and by this point anyone who wanted the songs had probably bought the LP anyway.

Anyone who is familiar with *Until it's Time for You to Go* through the better-known Elvis Presley version, recorded in 1971, will probably have quite a shock on hearing

Trade advertisement.

---

[472] "Spotlight Singles," *Billboard*, January 7, 1967, 18.

the quiet, delicate version here. Whereas Elvis turns the song into a rather lumbering big ballad, Darin does quite the opposite, stripping the sound right back. He doesn't use the almost-whisper sound of some of the earlier tracks in his vocal but, instead, this is a vulnerable, resigned vocal that, this time around, is higher in the mix. It is a beautiful rendition of this fragile song and a highlight of the album.

The fuller orchestration of *For Baby*, a song written by John Denver, sits a little bit at odds with the quiet reflection of the previous number, and the resulting track sounds more country than folk. The material itself also isn't as strong, although it's interesting how Bobby was again championing an up-and-coming songwriter, with Denver still three years away from releasing his first commercial LP.

The second side of the album opens with *The Girl Who Stood Beside Me*. Darin's voice, back to its whispering style, is set way back in the mix, with the production on the song being far more complex than anything elsewhere on the album. There is a bagpipe-type sound throughout the song which, presumably, was provided by some tape manipulation. There is also a strong beat here, something else that is not prevalent on most of the LP. The results are striking, but when released as the second single from the album, it flopped. *Cash Box* said that "the throbbing, sweeping ork that backs Darin's plaintive chant makes for an irresistible combination,"[473] while *Variety* believed it was an "excellent folk-rock follow-up" to *If I Were a Carpenter*.[474]

Red Balloon is another song by Tim Hardin and, like *The Girl Who Stood Beside Me*, also has a prominent beat and a fuller orchestration. This time around, though, the song itself is less memorable, and the track doesn't seem to really lead anywhere.

Amy, written by Darin himself for the film *Gunfight in Abilene* (William Hale, 1967) in which he also starred, crosses the boundaries between folk and country, but still fits neatly on to the album. The song shows the skill that Darin the songwriter had to switch genres and styles at the drop of a hat. The arrangement is tasteful, the melody memorable, and the vocal suggests that Bobby thought more highly of the song (and the rest of his film score) than he did of the film itself which he reportedly referred to as "Gunfight at Shit Creek."[475]

The album's penultimate song, *Don't Make Promises*, was another by Tim Hardin and has a similar production to *Red Balloon* and *The Girl Who Stood Beside Me*. It is pleasant enough, but adds nothing new to the album.

The LP closes with the song that would have been most familiar to listeners in 1966, *Day Dream*, which had been a hit for The Lovin' Spoonful, and had probably been one of the songs originally offered to Darin by the agents mentioned at the beginning of this section. Bobby slows the song down a little, and strips back the arrangement, giving it an older feel. His vocal is also more laid-back than on the original recording,

---

[473] "Record Reviews," *Cash Box*, November 26, 1966, 26.
[474] "Top Singles of the Week," *Variety*, November 23, 1966, 52.
[475] Al DiOrio, *Bobby Darin*, 144.

and as it fades out, one feels, even today, that they have just listened to a rather special album.

Reviews for the album were positive. *Variety* said that the Tim Hardin numbers were "delivered with sensitivity," but the rest of its review simply listed the songs and their songwriters, making it an unusually pedestrian review for such a fine album.[476] *Billboard* were more enthusiastic, calling *If I Were a Carpenter* an "exceptional package."[477] *Cash Box* believed it was "destined for a smashing trip to the top of the pile."[478] Despite the quality of the album and the hit lead-off single, it still didn't sell in large numbers, not even making the top 100. In the UK, *The Observer* wrote: "Around for a few weeks now, but still far and away the best pop album of the year so far. It has Darin in a Bob Dylan mood with strings contributing chamber-musicish accompaniments. The result is intelligent, immediately engaging – and lasting."[479]

A number of other recordings were made for this LP, all of which have remained unreleased. Two re-recordings of *Funny What Love Can Do*, a song that had already been released on a single, were made. The Beatles song *Good Day Sunshine* and The Lovin' Spoonful's *Younger Girl* are also listed, as well as an earlier version of *Day Dream*. All of these recordings are thought to be lost.

By this point, Bobby's marriage was over, and Sandra Dee had filed for divorce. Darin's response was to increase the amount of live performances and television appearances, as well as becoming more involved in politics once again.

In August, Bobby was back at the Flamingo, this time with Roger Kellaway conducting instead of Richard Wess – it is thought that Bobby didn't work again with Wess from this point on. *Variety* said that "Darin's current turn is as electric, exciting and strong as ever; he's an outstanding showman, a fact which embellishes his tone versatility."[480]

The comedian on Bobby's bill during this season was a young man who had started to make a name for himself through a series of memorable appearances on the TV chat and variety show circuit. His name was Richard Pryor. At the end of August, Bobby threw a party for Pryor at his Belaire home. The guests included The Supremes, Quincy Jones, Henry Mancini and Groucho Marx. It was a conversation between Marx and Pryor at the party that ultimately persuaded the latter to leave behind the mainstream style he was pursuing at the time in favour of the often profanity-riddled

---

[476] "Tijuana Brass, The Lovin Spoonful, 'Walking Happy,' Darin, Pat Boone, Arnold, Joe Sherman Top New LPs,", December 7, 1966, 50.
[477] "Album Reviews," *Billboard*, December 17, 1966, 72.
[478] "Album Reviews," *Cash Box*, December 17, 1966, 36.
[479] "Briefing," *The Observer*, April 23, 1967, 26.
[480] Duke, "Flamingo, Las Vegas," *Variety*, August 24, 1966, 60.

adult material that made him a star.

The following month, Bobby opened at Harrah's in Reno. For this season, he changed up his show considerably, now including *I Wish I Were in Love Again*, *Michael Row the Boat Ashore*, *I'm On My Way Great God*, and a full performance of *Artificial Flowers* for the first time in at least four years.[481] *Don't Rain on My Parade* was now the opening number.

In November 1966, he flew to the UK where he appeared on television, singing *If I Were a Carpenter* on both *Top of the Pops* and *Ready, Steady, Go!* before filming a special for the BBC at the Shepherd's Bush Empire. He then flew to France to appear in a gala for the United Nations, which was also shown in the UK (and possibly in other countries too).

Bobby with Richard Harris

November, 1966: Live Recordings
Something Special LP

The BBC TV special was recorded in mid-November 1966, and was finally shown the following May, at which time the soundtrack from the show was released on a UK-only LP, *Something Special*, which has now become very hard to find. Various tracks from it have appeared over the years on grey market CDs, but always in less than stellar quality. All songs from the show (included one that was edited out of the broadcast) were released on the *From Sea to Sea* bootleg CD, but in a slightly different order to the album and the special. Hopefully, an official release of this forgotten album will appear at some point in the future, for it deserves to be heard.

The show and the album both start with *Don't Rain on My Parade*, with the opening line sung in the special as Bobby enters the theatre from outside. It is not the best start to a show or live album, as the end of that first line is out of tune, but that is soon

---

[481] "Harrah's Reno Billing Headed By Bobby Darin," *Reno Gazette-Journal*, September 24, 19665, 13.

forgotten once Darin reaches the stage and gives a fun, vibrant performance of what was, at this point, his usual opening number. Bobby spoke at various points during his career about how he was never quite comfortable on television, but this special shows no sign of that, mostly because it is simply a videotaped live performance on stage and not in a studio. The pacing of the show is up to Darin, and there are no guests to introduce to interrupt his momentum. This is therefore, the television programme in which we get the nearest thing possible to what a Bobby Darin concert would have looked like and how it would have been paced.

As if to prove that, he moves into *A Quarter to Nine* taking barely a second to catch his breath. The song had been recorded in the studio earlier in the year for an album that was never released. This live arrangement is likely to be roughly the same, giving us a glimpse of what that album might have sounded like. Darin is totally at ease on this Jolson classic, playing with the timing at various points, and giving a full-throttled climax to the number.

He asks the orchestra to give him a few extra seconds to catch his breath before he moves into a rendition of *Once Upon a Time*, a song that had been released on the *In a Broadway Bag* LP. Here, though, the arrangement is slightly different, with just a piano rather than the full orchestra at the opening. This allows for a more nuanced vocal than the studio version, despite the fact that Bobby is audibly running out of breath in places. Still, it is this arrangement which is better, and which has more shape, allowing the song and the vocal to build to its heartbreaking conclusion.

I Wish I Were in Love Again was not, as far as we know, ever recorded in the studio by Darin, and so this live version is rather special. This sees Bobby back in show-stopping mode again. The subtleties of *Once Upon a Time* are thrown out of the window and, instead, this is a jazzy, powerful vocal that is pure razzamatazz.

The inevitable *Mack the Knife* is up next, and quite similar in performance to the one recorded in November 1963 at the Flamingo in Las Vegas. As with that version, Bobby plays with the song a little, with a few comedic interjections, but otherwise this is a standard *Mack*, and signals an end to both the first half of the LP and the first section of the TV special.

The next song recorded for the show was *If I Were a Carpenter*, with Darin having lost his jacket and tie ready for the folk and blues songs that are to follow. However, the unedited television footage shows him losing his way after the instrumental section. The album version contains a splice to cover up the mistake.

The second side of the album opens with the impressions routine previously heard on the Flamingo recordings, again using *One for my Baby* as a hook. As with that earlier version, this is fun, but it doesn't bear repeated listens.

The Girl Who Stood Beside Me gets a live outing next, with Darin introducing it as his next single. What's interesting here is that we get to hear the song without the big production of the studio version, together with its bagpipe effects. It has to be said that the live version works better. Without the extraneous noise, the vocal can be heard more clearly and the song and recording ultimately become more commercial.

Also interesting is the rendition of *Funny What Love Can Do* which is completely unlike the studio version released on single. Perhaps the live version, which is slower and with a stripped back instrumentation, is a reflection of the later studio

The UK-only "Something Special" LP.

recordings made for the *If I Were a Carpenter* album that were never released. Either way, this is stellar stuff, and the gutsy guitar solo by Jim Sullivan is superb. It is a shame this version isn't better known.

The unedited videotape of the show then sees Bobby introducing a solo sequence in which he plays (in mime) a young boy hoping to be taken home by a couple visiting an orphanage. It is certainly an example of Darin trying new things once again, but is also rather mawkish and doesn't really fit in the middle of a concert, and it is understandable why it was cut.

Bobby takes to the piano for a great performance of *What'd I Say* that is as much a demonstration of Darin the pianist as of Darin the singer. The song segues into the final number, *That's All*, and it is interesting that this song he first recorded in 1959 is back as his closing number.

The album and the television special managed to incorporate swing numbers, show tunes, folk, blues and rhythm 'n' blues and a set of impressions within a fast-moving forty minutes. This was Darin at his best, and the second of the two live albums released during his lifetime, with the result being considerably better than *Darin at the Copa*, and the act more focussed without the constant asides etc. There is also more range of material here, and it is clear that Bobby is still enjoying his return to live performing.

*

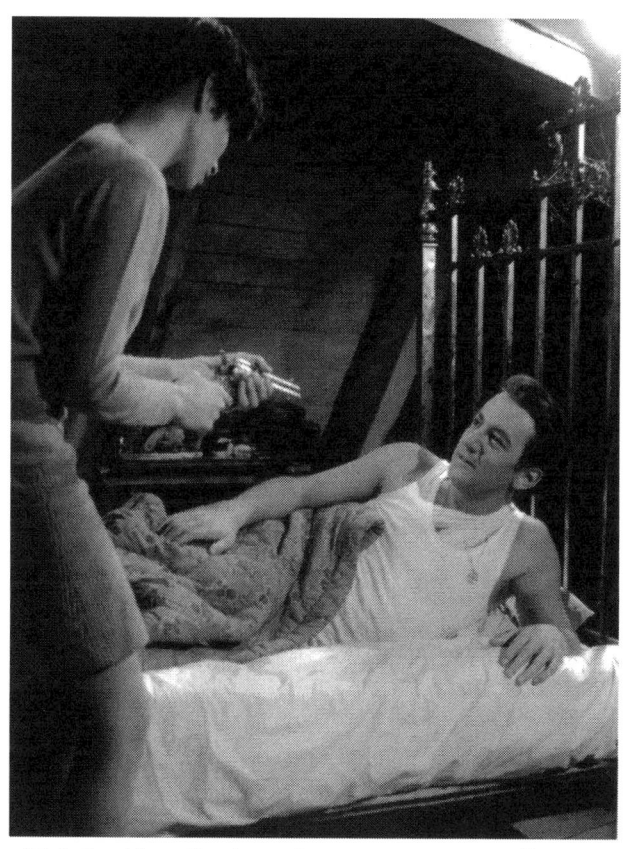

With Geraldine Chaplin in "Stranger in the House" (ABC).

Whilst in the UK, Bobby also took time to pursue other activities. It was reported that he turned his hand to film directing for the first time when he made a promotional video for his new single *The Girl Who Stood Beside Me*. It is unknown if the video still exists.

Bobby also filmed his scenes for the film *Stranger in the House* (Pierre Rouve, 1967), released as *Cop-Out* in the USA. The movie was based on a novel by George Simenon, creator of Maigret. It had already been filmed in France in 1942, but the 1967 version attempted to bring the story up to date, with the aim clearly to get down and get with it with the hip, happening youth of the swinging sixties. Bobby had high hopes for the film, despite his relatively small role. Just before filming, he said "I'm to play a rather evil sort of fellow in a flashback – they tell me it is type-casting! Geraldine Chaplin and James Mason are in the movie – so I hope it will do my film image a power of good."[482]

When the film was released six months later, *Monthly Film Bulletin* told readers that the novel had been "preposterously updated," and that the film was "absurd enough to be riotously funny" – but that was hardly the intention.[483] *Variety* were oddly enthusiastic about the movie, highlighting "Mason's firstrate performance [which] holds the pic together and is a fine study of disillusionment."[484] But the disillusionment came for Bobby himself in that the film did absolutely nothing for his film career, or the studio, for whom the film is said to have lost close to $800,000.

According to *Variety*, Darin was "asked to direct a film in London following his thesping." Whether this was simply rumour or had some truth to it is unknown.[485] Either way, *Stranger in the House* (or *Cop-Out* if you prefer) is a complete and utter mess

---

[482] "Darin Has Learnt Humility," *London Life*, November 11, 1966, 8.
[483] "Stranger in the House," *Monthly Film Bulletin*, July 1967, 110.
[484] Rich, "Stranger in the House," *Variety*, May 31, 1967, 6.
[485] Army Archerd, "Just for Variety," *Variety*, January 5, 1967, 2.

of a movie, best viewed today as a curious time-capsule of how the middle-aged adults of 1967 were viewing the youth of the time – but even seen in this way it is still a struggle to make it through nearly two hours of this nonsense.

Gunfight in Abilene had been released two months earlier. This is a modest, unambitious film, for which the term "routine western" could have been invented, but it works well as a time-filler on a wet afternoon, providing exactly the kind of entertainment it set out to. *Boxoffice* called the movie a "modest, but well-made western from Universal starring Bobby Darin. There is enough action and vivid characterisations to make the general market keep coming back for more of the same."[486] *Monthly Film Bulletin* agreed for the most part, saying that "despite a conventional and rather rambling plot, this is an above-average cowboys versus sodbusters Western, with a refreshingly unglamorous heroine, competent acting by all concerned, and a nicely subdued theme tune."[487] The film was Bobby's last starring role in a movie.

Meanwhile, the beginning of 1967 saw Bobby front the first of a number of television specials. This one, part of the *ABC Stage '67* series, was *Rodgers and Hart Today*, an attempt to bring the songs of the great songwriting partnership up to date. Darin, in a newspaper interview, was enthusiastic about the special, which also starred Count Basie, The Supremes, Petula Clark and The Mamas and the Papas. He's quoted as saying:

> Many of these great songs were written in the Dixieland era, yet a song like *Falling in Love with Love*, which The Supremes and I sing together, comes off, I think, as if it were written yesterday. That's the definition of a standard. Musical styles change with the generations – sometimes even faster – but a great song adapts itself to these changes.[488]

Despite Darin's enthusiasm, the critics, on the whole, hated the programme. Jack Gould's review in the *New York Times* was typical:

> It is quite a trick to make the fabulous virtuosity of Rodgers and Hart all sound the same, but that was the achievement of last night's performers. […] Mr. Darin and Miss Clark radiated blank stares regardless of what their lips were saying. Mr. Hart […] might have been the first to put his finger squarely on the missing element of so much modern song-making: a superficial style without the

---

[486] "Gunfight in Abilene," *Boxoffice*, March 27, 1967, 4007.
[487] "Gunfight in Abilene," *Monthly Film Bulletin*, March 1967, 45.
[488] "A Tribute to Rodgers & Hart," *Independent Star News*, February 26, 1967, 19.

foundation of intelligence.[489]

Not all reviews were negative, though, with *Variety* commenting that the show "was the best musical of the year in execution."[490]

March 7-10, 1967: Studio Sessions
Inside Out LP

Luckily for Bobby, when Jack Gould's cutting review of the *Rodgers and Hart Today* TV show was hitting the news-stands, he was preparing to enter the studio to record *Inside Out*, a follow-up to the *If I Were a Carpenter* album. This time around, however, the album had a little more variation, with Darin looking further afield than just the writing of Tim Hardin to fill up the majority of the album. True, there are two Hardin songs here, along with two by John Sebastian, but also three by Gary Bonner and Alan Gordon (who wrote a number of hits for The Turtles), one by Randy Newman, one by Mick Jagger and Keith Richards of The Rolling Stones, and two by Darin himself. There was also a variety in how the songs were structured and arranged. The previous album had all songs between 2:00 and 2:40 in length, but here there is a much wider range from the brief but fun *Bes' Friends* to the near four-minute *Back Street Girl*.

The album opens, however, in the safe hands of a Tim Hardin song, *The Lady Came from Baltimore*. Darin gets to tell a story within the song – something he had done multiple times in the past with hits such as *Mack the Knife*, *Clementine*, *Artificial Flowers*, and *18 Yellow Roses*. Here, though, he is faced with a song that bears little resemblance to those, and he narrates his tale in a quiet and restrained way, but perhaps this time around there is a lack of emotion present too, which is unfortunate. There is a very thin line between nearly whispering a song, and keeping it so restrained that it lacks feeling. *Variety* said that the song "gives this performer another neo-folk number which should sustain his pace in the pop market."[491] *Cash Box* believed it was a "sure chart topper" and that "the side is a slow, bluesy ballad for the romance minded and has a strong folk quality."[492] The song failed to follow in the footsteps of *If I Were a Carpenter*, and reached just #62 in the charts.

The flip-side of the single was another song from the album, this time written by Darin himself. *I Am* is, as might be guessed from the title, almost a stream-of-consciousness statement by Bobby, and certainly his most personal song thus far and a look ahead to both the sound and content of what would come a year or so later when

---

[489] Jack Gould, "TV: Rodgers and Hart Remembered," *New York Times*, March 3, 1967, 71.
[490] Bill, "Rodgers & Hart Today," *Variety*, March 8, 1967, 38.
[491] "Top Singles of the Week," *Variety*, March 22, 1967, 60.
[492] "Record Reviews," *Cash Box*, March 25, 1967, 14.

he started work on the first album for his own Direction label.

Darling be Home Soon, written by John Sebastian and recorded by The Lovin' Spoonful, has a beautiful production that reflects the lyrics of one of the most poignant love songs ever written. Written originally for the film *You're a Big Boy Now* (Francis Ford Coppola, 1966), this lovely performance only just broke the top 100 when it was released as a single, no doubt because it had already been a top twenty hit for The Lovin' Spoonful earlier in the year. *Billboard* called it a "smooth and very well done version."[493]

Hello Sunshine, the flip-side written by Bobby, is considerably less serious than his other song on the album, *I Am*. This has a little bit of the jug band sound and is clearly modelled on the songs of The Lovin' Spoonful. Despite being derivative, it shows that Bobby could seemingly write in almost any style he wanted and, while the results wouldn't necessarily be masterpieces, they would be more than competent and blend into an album featuring the best songwriters of the style.

The other John Sebastian song is a fun-filled romp entitled *Bes' Friends* that runs just ninety seconds but is in contrast to most of the album thanks to its heavy beat and the good-natured lyrics and vocal. There is also a hint of jazz here, helped along by the instrumentation which includes clarinet and trumpet.

Me About You is written by Gary Bonner and Alan Gordon. The song had been recorded by The Turtles, and released on the LP *Happy Together* a month after Bobby's recording was made. This puts Darin back into near-whispering mode, but perhaps once again the approach is just a little too subdued for its own good.

Bobby had co-written a song with Randy Newman a few years earlier, and here he tackles Newman's *I Think it's Gonna Rain Today*. This is one of the songs that adds variety to the album, thanks to the changes in tempo within the song as it moves from one section to the next. The arrangement here is superb, with great use of a small string section, and Darin makes the most of it, using his subdued voice throughout, but with variation coming from the switch from the chamber orchestra to the piano-led middle sections. By the end of the 1960s, this would be one of the

U. S. album cover

---

[493] "Spotlight Singles," *Billboard*, July 8, 1967, 18.

most-recorded songs in this genre, with fine versions in particular from Ricky Nelson, Peggy Lee and Nina Simone. However, Darin got to the song before it became so well-known and so often covered.

Whatever Happened to Happy is the second song written by Bonner and Gordon, and is one of the most attractive recordings on the album. The bigger production and beat once again adds variety, helped along by the double-tracking of Darin's voice during the choruses.

Black Sheep Boy, written by Tim Hardin, is, perhaps ironically, one of the least impressive songs here, with the sound, song and performance really just repeating territory covered in the previous album, whereas most of the other numbers are a variation on that earlier sound.

The third and final song by Bonner and Gordon, *Lady Fingers*, is perhaps most typical of their output. Although the instrumentation is slightly different, Darin's vocal pretty much follows that by The Magicians, who released the song as a single in early 1967. The string arrangement is once again superb, but Bobby's voice becomes slightly buried, particularly on the stereo issue of the album.

The final song of the album may well be the best. Darin's take on The Rolling Stones' song *Back Street Girl* starts off sounding as if it is going to be a straightforward version in the same style as the original. However, Bobby's vocal shows just how great an interpreter of popular song he was. The vocal on The Stones' version is often harsh (although refined for them), whereas Bobby's is subdued, and while he was never the genius of phrasing that Sinatra was, here he takes great care to take lines in one breath in order to help tell the story – something that doesn't occur in the original. Bobby also knows to take the tempo down just a little bit, making the song more fragile, and the vocal more vulnerable.

Inside Out wasn't a better album than *If I Were a Carpenter*, but it wasn't a case of simply "more of the same" either. Darin was slowly but surely developing in this style, trying new things, and drawing on songs from different sources. *Billboard* told readers that the album should be another "hot seller,"[494] and *Variety* said that Darin revealed his "usual savvy."[495] *Cash Box* said that "the artist is in his soft, lyrical band on the album, which figures to be a large smash."[496] However, the album didn't sell well, and neither of the singles were high charters, and so Darin decided to leave the folk scene behind him (at least temporarily), and his next album was reportedly one that nobody except he wanted to make.

---

[494] "Album Reviews," *Billboard*, May 27, 1967, 86.
[495] "Dean Martin, Laine, Mancini, 'Charlie Brown,' Darin, Miller, Easybeats, Chandler Top LPs," *Variety*, May 17, 1967, 46.
[496] "Album Reviews," *Cash Box*, May 20, 1967, 46.

April, 1967: Live Recordings

A semi-professional recording made in Lake Tahoe during 1967 appeared on a bootleg CD called *Rare Performances* in 1990. The sound quality is a little muffled on Darin's voice, and the orchestra is barely audible at times. However, it is an interesting item for the simple reason that it gives us a good look at the type of repertoire that constituted Bobby's nightclub performances at this time.

Don't Rain on My Parade is the standard opener, and it is basically the same as the version recorded for the BBC TV special and released on *Something Special*. This leads into a Motown-influenced version of *I've Got You Under My Skin*. It is interesting that when approaching one of Sinatra's signature songs, Darin avoids the most likely route of using a big band arrangement and goes for something else entirely, an arrangement by Roger Kellaway that makes the number sound considerably more contemporary. Darin himself is in fine voice, but the track can't be wholly enjoyed due to the mix, although a later version of the same arrangement was performed during *The Bobby Darin Show* TV series in 1973.

The Shadow of Your Smile has a lightly swinging arrangement instead of the Latin American version recorded for the album of the same name. Quite why Darin felt it necessary to have a different orchestration made for live performances is unclear, not least because the Latin sounds added variety to his repertoire. This new version works well enough, but some of the delicacy of the song is lost, with Darin rather inappropriately telling the orchestra to "kick it" at one point, and the number ending in a big brassy climax.

Next up is a rather strange medley of the Antonio Carlos Jobim song *Meditation* and *I Will Wait for You*. Sadly, the sound quality is a problem, with the arrangement and Darin's vocals so soft that they get swamped in the tape hiss. Even here, faced with a song originally written as a bossa nova, Darin avoids a Latin arrangement. The melding of the two songs together is slightly odd, despite the fact that *Meditation* contains the line "I will wait for you," which was presumably the pivot that Bobby wanted to use between the two songs. That said, it is unusual to hear him sing in this restrained manner in a live performance.

Charade is up next, with Bobby using the 1964 arrangement from the *From Hello Dolly to Goodbye Charlie* album. The live version adds nothing to the studio version, but it is nice to hear it getting an outing on the concert stage and Bobby reaching back to less obvious numbers from his back catalogue.

Mack the Knife and *If I Were a Carpenter* both get standard concert outings before Bobby moves into a fun version of *(Sittin' here) Lovin' You*. Here the arrangement has a jazzier 1920s feel than the studio rendition, partly due to the use of brass this time around. Arguably this is a better performance than the studio version, although this arrangement would obviously not have fitted on the *If I Were a Carpenter* album, being more jazz than folk.

18 Yellow Roses makes a welcome return to the live repertoire, although this time the sound is a little fuller than on the 1963 concert recordings, with trumpets included during the introduction and from the bridge section onwards. Some of the beauty of the fragile melody is lost with what sounds like the Tijuana Brass playing in the background, but it is pleasant enough.

As with the November 1966 London live recordings, the set ends with *What'd I Say* followed by *That's All*. At just over thirty minutes, this is clearly not a full Bobby Darin set, and is missing the impressions routine at least, but it is a nice little curio to have been released and gives us an insight into how quickly the set list could change over a period of just a few months.

Bobby was extremely busy as a live performer in 1967. In New York, Bobby opened at the Copa on March 23, with *Billboard* telling its readers that the show was "triumphant," and that "as a singer, mimic and purveyor of light banter, Darin goes to the head of the class."[497] *Record World* agreed. "Sinatra, look out," it said. "Bobby Darin is polishing his art, not to mention his personality, and is headed for the kind of long-range, wide public acceptance of the older entertainer."[498] *Up Tight* and *The Lady Came From Baltimore* were now part of the repertoire.

On April 8, Bobby opened at Lake Tahoe, and again the positive reviews poured in. "[Bobby's show] remains a class endeavour," *Variety* wrote, "with promanship all the way. Musical arrangements are superb and singer has the

Newspaper advertisement.

---

[497] Aaron Sternfield, "Singer, Showman, Mimic – It's Darin All the Way," *Billboard*, April 8, 1967, 26.
[498] "Darin Delights," *Record World*, April 8, 1967, 11.

know-how to sell each tune for ultimate effect."[499] Less than three weeks later he was back at the Flamingo in Las Vegas, adding *Summer Wind* to his repertoire, and opening with an uptempo cover of Matt Monro's hit *Born Free*.[500]

When Bobby performed at the Melodyland Theater in Orange County two months later, the new songs remained in the act, and *Bill Bailey* had made a welcome return to the repertoire as well.[501] It is interesting that most reviews of Bobby's shows during this period singled out his impressions routine as the highlight.

The *Santa Cruz Sentinel* criticised Bobby for some of his comments on stage at the Circle Star Theater, stating that they "were definitely not apropos for his audience, many of which were youngsters."[502] However, it went on to say:

> Enjoyed most by everyone, it seems, was Darin's portrayal of a citizen of Green Bay who came to Hollywood to see the stars. At the Stars Bar, in a drunken stupor, he went to sleep and 'saw' such personalities as JFK, Cary Grant, W. C. Fields, Clark Gable, Bob Mitchum, Dean Martin and many others, all ably impersonated by Darin.

At the end of August, "Bobby Darin had Europe's high society clapping their hands and clicking their fingers over their champagne when he starred August 25 at Monte Carlo's Red Cross gala, a $100-a-head audience at the Sporting Club."[503]

July 19, 1967: Studio Recordings

Bobby had already recorded three songs by Gary Bonner and Alan Gordon for the *Inside Out* album, and here he tackles another of their compositions, *She Knows*. This is another forgotten Darin classic that was wasted as the flip-side of a single. This is certainly in the style of The Turtles, for whom the duo had written a number of songs, but the production is superb, from the ethereal soprano voice to the heavy beat, and the chorus is reminiscent of *Happy Together*. The sound is totally unlike any other Bobby Darin recording, and may well have been the direction that his next album would have taken had personal and political issues not changed the course of his career in late 1967 and early 1968. *Billboard* got somewhat confused in their review, stating that "this driving, infectious and clever rhythm item" was from the score of *Dr*

---

[499] Hawk, "Harrah's Lake Tahoe," *Variety*, April 19, 1967, 100.
[500] Duke, "Flamingo, Las Vegas," *Variety*, May 3, 1967, 67.
[501] Robert Beckman, "Celebrity Special Opened by Darin," *Long Beach Independent*, July 6, 1967, 16.
[502] Jean Baker, "Darin's a Versatile Showman," *Santa Cruz Sentinel*, July 12, 1967, 11.
[503] "Darin's Monte Carlo Gala a Click 1-Nite Stand," *Variety*, August 30, 1967, 2.

Dolittle.[504] Cash *Box* wrote:

> Cool understatement on the part of Bobby Darin accents the build in *She Knows* and lends a softness to this throbbing rock side in mid-speed splendour. The deck is an unusual work out that will delight Darin fans and should grab the ear loves of many Turtle admirers. Bright sound with outstanding prospects.[505]

Also recorded at the same date, but unreleased, was a Randy Newman song entitled *The Biggest Night of Her Life*.

July 1967: Studio Recordings
Bobby Darin sings Doctor Dolittle LP

In July 1967, Bobby Darin and Sammy Davis Jr, two of the best live performers in the world, entered the studio to record their separate albums of songs from the film *Doctor Dolittle* (Richard Fleischer, 1967). Davis had long been a champion of the work of composer Leslie Bricusse, and so perhaps the album was less of a surprise. Bobby had already recorded such numbers co-written by Bricusse as *Once in a Lifetime*, *Feeling Good*, and *If I Ruled the World*, and was seemingly drawn to the new film score due to the message of peace and understanding wrapped up in the narrative itself, which tied into his political beliefs. Ahmet Ertegun has been quoted as saying "it wasn't a very good idea. Bobby would get an idea, and it would be hard to get him off it."[506] The album didn't sell well, and would be his last for Atlantic, and yet, decades after the event, Al DiOrio referred to the LP as a "classic."[507] It might not be quite of that status, and it may not be quite as good as Sammy Davis Jr's effort (which was,

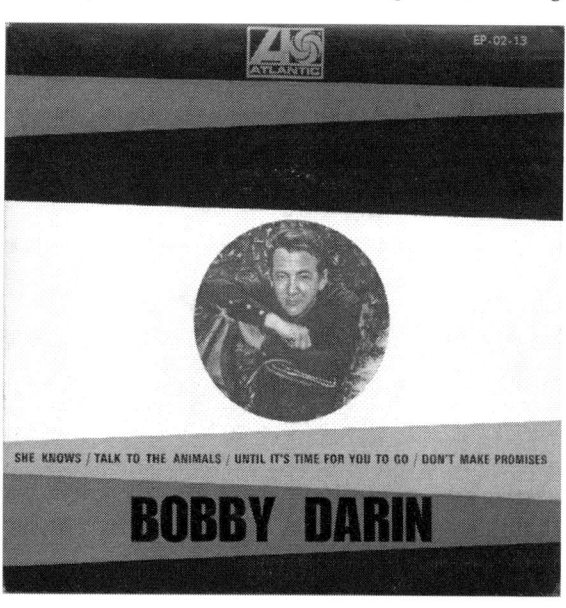

Portuguese EP

---

[504] "Spotlight Singles," *Billboard*, August 26, 1967, 18.
[505] "Record Reviews," *Cash Box*, August 26, 1967, 28.
[506] Bleiel, *That's All*, 137.
[507] DiOrio, *Bobby Darin*, 170.

arguably, his last great album), but *Bobby Darin sings Doctor Dolittle* is a thoroughly enjoyable affair that is far better than the concept or its reputation might suggest.

If there is a problem with the album at all, it is to do with the fact that it is split into a ballad side and a more upbeat side. This means there is a lack of variation in the first half of the LP but, more importantly, that the album opens with a rather downbeat version of *At the Crossroads*. Roger Kellaway's arrangement really only comes into its own during the choruses, where the sweeping strings try to breathe some life into the number. Darin's vocal is rather subdued for the most part, as if he is still partly in *If I Were a Carpenter* mode rather than the show-stopping style more required for this type of effort.

When I Look in Your Eyes is much better, with a lovely arrangement utilising a string quartet and what sounds like a harpsichord during the verses. In the film, the song is sung to a seal, but Darin turns this into a straightforward love song, and he had rarely sounded better, particularly on the final two lines where he sings softly and delicately in his high register.

I Think I Like You gets a more traditional arrangement with a lilting soft swing and more of those lush strings heard in the first song. The issue, as mentioned before, is that all the ballads are heard one after the other and the similar orchestrations on a number of them means that they are less memorable than they should be because of this. Had the album mixed up the ballads and upbeat numbers, this would not have been a problem.

Where are the Words is certainly a better song than *I Think I Like You*, and it's interesting to hear just how much commitment Darin has invested in the album. The bolder final section of the song adds some much-needed variety to the proceedings.

Something in Your Smile sees Bobby taking a rare excursion into Latin American rhythms. Roger Kellaway has cleverly turned the song into a slow bossa nova, but here Bobby doesn't take the easy option of just singing in his softest voice throughout. The middle section is beautifully, but more powerfully, sung – and, again, with long phrases within one breath. The bossa nova rhythm adds a different element to the rest of the ballads, and so it is a shame that this song wasn't programmed in the middle of the first side of the album to split them up and add variety.

When one begins the second side of the LP, it is clear that a number such as *Fabulous Places* would have made a fine opener for the album as a whole, and would have launched the listener into the LP in a way that the subdued *At the Crossroads* did not. In this second side, we hear a very different Bobby Darin. This time around we have the show-stopping Bobby in our presence, and he is remarkably welcome – especially as this is the first time he has appeared on record since the *In a Broadway Bag* album. Roger Kellaway's arrangement throws anything and everything into the mix to help conjure up the sounds of the various fabulous places of the song's title, rather like Billy May's arrangements for Sinatra's versions of *On the Road to Mandalay* and

Italian single.

Moonlight on the Ganges.

This sense of fun and frivolity carries over into the next number: *My Friend the Doctor*. Darin had tackled many show tunes before, but they were nearly always the big ballads from a production, but here he shows a different side as he takes on one of the more fun numbers from a show (or, in this case, a film with a soundtrack that sounded like it was written for a show). His Irish accent is a little dubious, but that's hardly of the greatest importance. The song is pure nonsense, of course, but it finds Bobby in stellar form, and there's nothing else quite like it within his recorded legacy. It certainly makes one wish that he had tackled other light-hearted material in this style, particularly during his movie and Broadway albums, with a song such as *Flash, Bang, Wallop!* from *Half a Sixpence* being a good example.

Probably the best performance and arrangement on the album is *Beautiful Things*, which is turned into a fine, finger-snapping swing number that rightfully made the cut for the 4CD Rhino set back in 1995. This is, for much of the time, Roger Kellaway doing his best Richard Wess impression. Darin is in great form for what would be the final upbeat swing number he would record in the studio, although it is unlikely anyone at the time would have thought this would be the case.

After Today returns us to ballad material, although this time the arrangement has a late-night jazz feel to it thanks to the prominent bluesy piano that underpins the song. This bluesy element is expanded upon during the second half when the number turns into a grinding, mid-tempo swing that Darin sings with power and yet restraint.

Talk to the Animals ends the album with Bobby singing an arrangement not dissimilar to that for *Fabulous Places*, but this time there are attempts to replicate animal noises rather than sounds associated with certain countries. Darin is in his best show-stopping form, and this most famous song from the film was the obvious choice for a single to be taken from the album. However, despite Bobby performing the song on at least two prominent television appearances, the single flopped, just as the album did. *Billboard* stated that Darin had brought his "special touch" to the material and that the album was a "strong chart contender."[508] *Variety* were not quite so excited, although they did say that Darin was "displaying an ability for many musical angles," as if this was something new for him.[509] *Cash Box* commented that "the artist gives the music and lyrics a fresh, original interpretation…The album should become a favorite with fans of the movie and with Darin's followers."[510]

November 1967: Studio Recordings

The recordings that Bobby made in November 1967 are generally referred to as "demos," suggesting that they were not made with a release in mind. This may also suggest that he was already breaking away from the Atlantic label, although this was not reported in the trade press at the time, and so may not have been the case. Either way, Bobby didn't make any commercial recordings for nearly a year.

The November 1967 demos straddle a mix of contemporary pop, folk and blues. *Easy Rider* and *Everywhere I Go* were a pair of blues numbers that built upon the style and sound of the released studio recording of *Funny What Love Can Do*. *Easy Rider*, clearly based on *C. C. Rider* (or *See See Rider*), appears to have been influenced by groups such as *The Animals*, who had taken traditional songs and added rock rhythms to them. Darin's performance here is stunning, as is the production which uses double-tracking on Bobby's voice during the chorus. What's more, Bobby himself is probably responsible for the blistering harmonica solo.

Everywhere I Go isn't quite on the same level. This is a slower blues, with a less complicated backing and some great piano playing that compliments Bobby's edgy vocal. The acetate source of the recording is apparent here, with some surface noise. Bobby is again attempting something different both from the point of genre and vocal, with his voice sounding coarser and harsher than it had since the late 1950s.

The two folk/country songs, both composed by Darin, are charming pieces that deserve to be better known. *Long Time Movin'* already sees him moving towards a more

---

[508] "Album Reviews," *Billboard*, September 16, 1967, 70.
[509] "'Dolittle' Soundtrack, John Gary, Procul Harum, Bil Evans *(sic)*, Darin, Spanky & Gang, 'Flowers,' Top LPs," *Variety*, September 6, 1967, 46.
[510] "Album Reviews," *Cash Box*, September 16, 1967, 46.

personal style of songwriting. Here we get something of a preview of the sounds he would utilise in his work for Direction, particularly during a song such as *Water Color Canvas* on the *Commitment* LP. A few months after the recording, he performed the song on television in a duet with Bobbie Gentry which, sadly, is not in circulation.

I'm Going to Love You is even better, and is a slow folk-styled song with a slight blues overtone in the vocal. It is a simple song musically, but the laid-back vocal and stripped-back arrangement make this one of the most attractive works from Bobby's later years. There is no attempt to try anything ambitious, and that is exactly why the number works so well.

All four of the above were issued on CD in 1995. *My Baby Needs Me*, which escaped from the vaults unannounced a few years later, is not nearly as interesting. This finds Bobby in a more contemporary mood and veering towards the Motown sound, but the production and the vocal are simply not convincing, and Darin sounds as if he is trying to be something he isn't, or reaching for a sound that he has yet to master.

A number of other songs are rumoured to have been recorded around this time, also as demos. These include *All Strung Out*, which was a minor hit for Nino Tempo and April Stevens in 1966; the Jerry Reed song *Tupelo Mississippi Flash*; *Natural Soul-Loving Big City Countrified Man*; *When I'm Gone*; *Prison of Your Love*, a Bobby Darin composition; and the medley of *Meditation* and *I Will Wait for You* that can be heard on the Lake Tahoe concert discussed earlier.

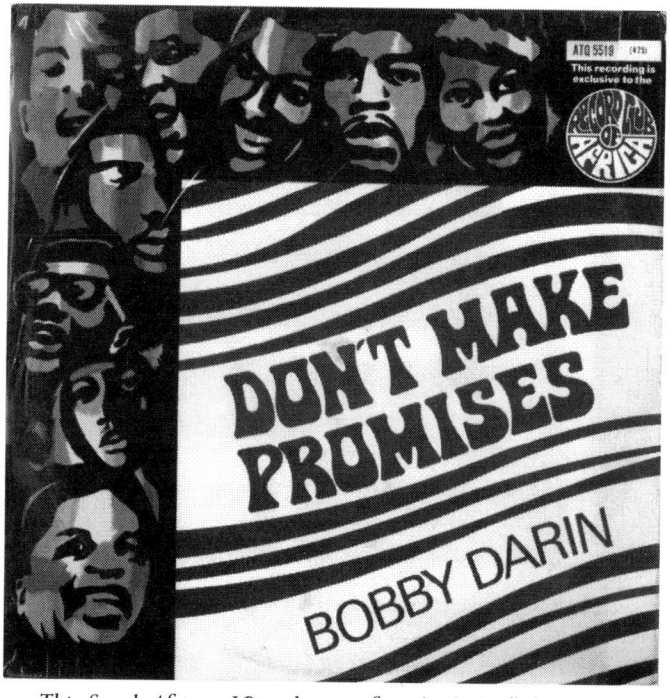

This South African LP took songs from both the "If I Were a Carpenter" and "Dr. Dolittle" albums.

*

Bobby recorded very little during the second half of 1967, although he continued to perform both on stage and on television. He paid tribute to George M. Cohan when he starred in a television variety show called *Give My Regards to Broadway* in October 1967, and he returned to *The Tonight Show* in both August and November — his first appearances on the show since 1962, when his tirade about fan magazines caused his section of the programme to be cut short.

Outside of TV, the autumn of 1967 started with yet another award for Bobby, this time being crowned "Hat Man of the Year" by the Hat Council. Bobby was somewhat modest about the achievement, telling a journalist, "I started late in learning it takes a hat to really top off your wardrobe in style."[511]

Meanwhile, the live performances continued. Around the same time as Bobby received the accolade for his sense of style, he was wowing the patrons at the Roostertail in Detroit. "Bobby Darin is a potent double-barreled attraction," wrote *Variety*. "He draws capacity audiences and then mesmerizes them with the many facets of his talent. His two-week engagement at Tom and Jerry Schoenith's riverside swankery adds up to full houses and heavy mitting."[512]

At this point, Bobby had started including a new showstopper in his live shows: an epic, slow version of *Drown in My Own Tears* lasting over seven minutes, and very different from his earlier recording for the *Bobby Darin Sings Ray Charles* album. Bobby would also perform it on a January 1968 TV special, the audio of which can be found on YouTube. It is a staggering rendition, one of his greatest performances, in fact, and it is a great shame that no professional studio or live recording was made. Also included in his live shows of the period were his versions of *Sixteen Tons*, *Work Song*, *Talk to the Animals* and a reinvention of *Splish Splash* which must have delighted audiences.

After a season at the Flamingo in Las Vegas in September, Bobby performed at the Carousel Theater in West Covina. David Otis wrote:

> Bobby Darin is a pleasant blend of confidence and warm humor. He is best when he stands before an audience, and his participation with ringsiders ('All you have to do is sing six "whoops," four "just a little bits," and as many "sock it to me's" as you can get in) alone is worth the price of admission.[513]

---

[511] "Late Starter Make Grade," *Baltimore Sun*, September 12, 1967, 21.
[512] Tew, "Roostertail, Detroit," *Variety*, September 20, 1967, 59.
[513] David Otis, "Bobby Darin Comes On Strong In Show," *San Bernadino County Sun*, October 19, 1967, D-8.

Variety were also enthusiastic about what they called Bobby's "Whoop" number.[514] Perhaps you had to be there to appreciate it.

With Bobby wowing the crowds on stage and audiences on TV, there was little outward sign that everything was about to change. And yet, in interviews, there were indications that Bobby was becoming more interested in politics and the state of the world around him. In September 1967, he told Louise Alterman:

> I like to think that people under 25 are tomorrow's leaders and giants. I'm sure happy they feel about beauty as the people of past generations should have felt…We're surrounded by a bunch of clowns. I'm not sure what they want to hang on to…When it's time for change, you better change. The old statement that "youth is wasted on the young" is diluted for the first time in history. People are forever fondling yesterday. I don't even feel like fondling today. Embracing today is groovy, but yesterday is long gone.[515]

Later in the autumn of 1967, Bobby spent several days in a state prison filming his role in *The Cage*, a TV drama screened as part of *The Danny Thomas Show*. Bobby told a newspaper:

> I was affected far more by that experience than I ever want to get into…Society is diseased – not incurably but terribly…I saw 18-year-old faces and older, hardened faces. We are criminals by not insisting that psychiatrists run prisons rather than just being consulted once in a while.[516]

As Bobby's interest in politics again began to grow, particularly his involvement in Robert Kennedy's election campaign, his family feared that the truth about his parentage would emerge as a way of discrediting him. It was therefore decided that he had to be told the truth: that the woman he had always believed to be his mother was actually his grandmother, and that his "sister" was his real mother. Bobby was shaken by the news, and it has been said that he never totally came to terms with it at any point during the remaining five years of his life.

He remained on the campaign trail for Kennedy, and in June 1968 was performing at a new night club in San Francisco when he heard the news that Robert Kennedy had been assassinated. He was reportedly the last mourner to leave the graveside at the

---

[514] Duke, "Flamingo, Las Vegas," *Variety*, September 27, 1967, 58.
[515] Louise Alterman, "Bobby Darin: Hate to Ruin His Image, But He's Nice," *Detroit Free Press*, September 13, 1967, 4B
[516] "Bobby Darin…On What Freedom Is All About," *Austin American*, December 24, 1967, 43.

funeral.[517] He later told Earl Wilson that his experience at and after the funeral were spiritual:

> It was as though all my hostilities, anxieties and conflicts were in one ball that has been flying away into space farther from me all the time, leaving me finally content with myself. [...] I've already reshaped me and I'd like to take a part in reshaping the universe. I want to give up night clubs. I want to get into college concerts. I don't want business or politics. You can't tell the truth.[518]

Publicity photo from "The Cage," one of Bobby's most acclaimed acting performances.

Bobby Darin's life was falling apart. His response was to sell his publishing company and to announce the formation of his own label, where he would release a series of protest songs and numbers that contained social commentary. Darin called the label "Direction" and the first single was the true story of murders in an Arkansas prison. It was released almost exactly a year on from the time Bobby had spent at a prison filming his role in *The Cage*. It is unlikely the theme of the single's lyrics was a coincidence.

---

[517] These events are described in detail within the biographies by Al DiOrio, David Evanier, and Dodd Darin.
[518] Earl Wilson, "New Bobby Darin Molded by Graveside 'Revelation,'" *The Lima News*, January 13, 1969, 6.

Bobby as George M. Cohan for the Kraft Music Hall "Give My Regards to Broadway" TV special

CHAPTER ELEVEN
QUESTIONS: 1968-1970

There are a number of misconceptions about Bobby's work during the late 1960s when he was making records for his own label, Direction. Many refer to this as his "protest phase," and yet the truth is that not everything he was recording was protest material. Instead, the two Direction albums, and the single sides not included on them, are more like a musical journal. They are the thoughts and feelings of Bobby Darin on a multitude of issues. Sure, some of those issues manifest themselves through protest songs, most notably about the Vietnam War or the environment. But other songs from this period are not protesting against anything, such as the comical reflections of *Distractions (Part 1)* or Darin's view of his own career, *Song for a Dollar*. There are also songs of hope such as *Simple Song of Freedom* and *Maybe We Can Get it Together*. All of these are like hearing pages from Darin's personal diary rather than a man actively protesting in each and every song. There is also the notion that he was somehow trying to be, or trying to emulate, Bob Dylan in both his style and his lyrics. Again, there is often little here in common with Dylan musically or lyrically.

It has also been said that Bobby effectively stopped working during this period, but that isn't true either. In 1969, for example, he recorded and released the *Commitment* album; performed seasons at the Copa and The Troubadour (in Los Angeles), performed at the Bonanza and Sahara hotels in Las Vegas; and made at least a dozen appearances on national television (including mainstream variety shows).

To be fair, Bobby himself encouraged the idea that he stopped working during this period, even saying that he did during a lengthy conversation about his time living in Big Sur on *The Mike Douglas Show* in 1970. The interview is fascinating, with Bobby saying:

> In June 1968, after Senator Bobby Kennedy was assassinated, a whole slew of things happened inside me that I felt needed some correcting. Suffice to say that the changes I felt were necessary could only come from me, from within. I had to do something, too, about the way I was living, about my approach to things, about my values in general. [...] I took an eighteen foot trailer [...] and I lived in it for a little less than a year in Big Sur. [...] For me, it was a question of I need that kind of existence but I also need to perform. Until I did that, until I went away, I did not know that I needed to perform.

However, Bobby's outlook on life and his career were changing prior to the death of Bobby Kennedy, and he talked about this openly in a number of interviews at the time. In December 1967, he explained how he thought that the "spirit of revolt" was a healthy one:

> We've been preparing the individual for dishonesty in the past. This is the first generation that's had it on the old man and is challenging him. We are all in part Diogenese committed to truth and honesty when we first start out in life. We protest the lack of true morality but then we quit at 22. This generation may keep going till it's forty.[519]

Bobby's defence and support here for the young in society was not anything new for him, as he had been speaking in such a way for the previous decade. What *was* new, though, was *how much* he was talking about such social issues. The above quote comes from an interview intended to promote the television drama *The Cage*, and yet finds Bobby discussing social issues for the entire article.

In a March 1968 interview, he is quoted as saying "the goals have changed and what I aspire to now is a more meaningful contribution. To be called the greatest entertainer may mean being paid more than anybody or having four limousines. These are not essentials to me any more. Being accepted universally as an entertainer and a human being are."[520]

The article also talks about Darin's interest in politics and in Kennedy in particular, but not all of the public were interested in hearing what Bobby had to say. In a letter to the editor in *Life* magazine in May 1968, a reader writes "Bobby Darin's statement, 'Kennedy has a spiritual understanding of what it means to be poor,' is reason enough for Mr. Darin to retire from political activity."[521]

---

[519] "Bobby Darin...On What Freedom Is All About," *Austin American*, December 24, 1967, 43.
[520] Earl Wilson, "Years Have Changed Bobby Darin," *The Lowell Sun*, March 25, 1968, 22.
[521] C. E. Pickett, "Letters to the Editor," *Life*, May 31, 1968, 19.

By this point, Bobby was on the campaign trail for Kennedy. In April, he made numerous appearances at campaign events, including one in Hammond, Indiana. A local newspaper reported that "Darin broke into three songs, his first was a piece written by himself – *Will and Testament*[522]...But it was the third and final song which was most significant and drew the greatest response. Darin led the crowd in the singing of *This Land is Your Land*."[523] Bobby went on to say to the crowd "I don't get paid for this in terms of dollars...but I do get paid with a sense of belonging."

Aside from all of this, Bobby was still performing regularly both on stage and on television. TV audiences got to see Bobby in one of his most acclaimed acting performances when *The Cage* aired in January 1968. Harold Schindler wrote in the *Salt Lake Tribune* that "his portrayal...was strong and convincing; much more so than other singers who have tried their hands at dramatic acting...Look for more of Bobby Darin in straight performances; with experience, he'll be one of the good ones."[524]

Other TV appearances included *A Grand Night for Swinging*, where he appeared alongside Bobbie Gentry and Bobby Van, with Darin singing *Talk to the Animals*, *Mack the Knife*, and the seven-minute arrangement of *Drown in My Own Tears*. He also sang *Long Time Movin'* with Gentry. Elsewhere, he could be seen on *The Jerry Lewis Show*, *The Merv Griffin Show*, *The Mike Douglas Show* (where he was guest host for a week), and a one-off variety show entitled *And Debbie Makes Six*. This starred Debbie Reynolds, and was originally scheduled for broadcast in November 1967, but was postponed until February 1968 due to a technical strike.

On stage, Bobby received a rare semi-negative review when he took to the stage at the Frontier in Las

Bobby was performing at Mr. D's on the night Bobby Kennedy was shot.

---

[522] Nothing is known about this song. There is no indication that Bobby copyrighted any song with this title.
[523] Marilynn Hehr, "2 Bobbys Get Young Support," *Munster Times*, April 24, 1968, 1B
[524] Harold Schindler, "Bobby Darin Carving Heroic Stature," *Salt Lake Tribune*, January 17, 1968, B3.

Vegas in February. *Mack the Knife* was referred to as a "parody," and "closing gambit, a try at audience participation on *Just a Little Bit* was more than a little bit of milking with odd blue and purple goings-on ringside at show caught. It should at least be halved in time consumed."[525] The review was much more complimentary about the comic on the bill: Flip Wilson.

It seems odd that Bobby was continuing with the audience participation routine which, in various reviews, was called the *Whoop* song, *Just a Little Bit*, and *Sock It to Me*. From what can we gather from these reports, all three titles referred to the same item, but none of the reviewers were exactly ecstatic about the inclusion of the routine, and when Bobby returned to the Copa in March 1968, a reviewer noted that Bobby "could forget" it completely.[526] Aside from this, though, Bobby's show was once again evolving, this time including *Let the Good Times Roll* and the rather inane *Pass Me By*. One element of the show that *Variety* weren't afraid to be enthusiastic about were the arrangements of the songs, which they referred to as "blueribbon, brill building brand."

At the end of May, 1968, Bobby was the first performer at a new supper club in San Francisco. This time, *Variety* were more positive of his efforts, referring to him as "the complete entertainer. He sings extremely well out of every pop bag from ballads to a hard rocking *Splish Splash*, his own composition, and at his best, as in *If I Were a Carpenter*.[527]

A few days later, Bobby Kennedy was shot dead, and everything changed.

Summer, 1968: Studio Sessions
Bobby Darin born Walden Robert Cassotto **LP**

Bobby recorded relatively little during the Direction years. Previously, he had released up to five albums per year. Between 1968 and 1973, he released just three in total. However, the two dozen or so tracks he recorded for Direction are among some of Darin's most interesting and rewarding work.

Recorded over a number of sessions in 1968, the nine songs that make up Darin's first Direction album, *Bobby Darin born Walden Robert Cassotto*, are a mixed bunch, both in message and quality. The album was released a month after the formation of the new label was announced in *Billboard*, accompanied by a picture of Bobby mixing the forthcoming album in a Las Vegas studio with engineer Brent Maher. "His first LP is controversial in the sense that it establishes a new image," the article stated.[528] "The songs are built on Darin's feeling for people and his concern for a troubled society."

---

[525] Will, "Frontier, Las Vegas," *Variety*, February 28, 1968, 54
[526] Abel, "Copacabana, N.Y.," *Variety*, March 20, 1968, 65.
[527] Rick, "Mr. D's San Francisco," *Variety*, June 12, 1968.
[528] "'New' Darin Forms Label to 'Speak Out' Via Songs," *Billboard*, August 31, 1968, 10.

One of the most surprising things about the album is the simplicity, even naivety, of the musical elements of these songs. Darin was a sophisticated musician and an intellectual to boot, and yet everything is taken back to basics musically. Virtually none of the songs have what might be called a "chorus," and most don't have a bridge section either – just a series of verses, in some cases nearly a dozen. There is inspiration here from groups such as The Beatles and The Lovin' Spoonful in the production of these songs, which ranges from the basic to the complex including the use of sounds which appear to be tapes played backwards.

Questions opens the album, and is a song about environmental damage. Like most of the album, it doesn't fit any particular genre or style. It is a mix between folk and rock, without being folk-rock itself. Recently, two songs from the *Commitment* album were included on compilation albums dedicated to "country funk," which suggests the waters are even more muddied from the point of view of genre. The truth is that the songs on *Bobby Darin born Walden Robert Cassotto* really don't sound like anything else in the charts at the time or since. On *Questions,* Darin certainly isn't shy about what he has to say, with some of the lyrics almost visceral:

> How do you kill the ocean? How do you make it dry?
> Well, you first dilute, then pollute,
> Cut the fruit, at the root.
> And the ocean's floor
> Will be like a whore
> Who will lie no more, 'cause she's dead;
> Use your head.

Jingle Jangle Jungle follows, with Darin this time turning his attention to capitalism and the power that goes with it. This is one of the more Beatlesque sounding numbers, and the sound is harsher and more rock-oriented than some of the other tracks. Anyone used to hearing the showman-like sound of Darin's swing material wouldn't recognise the singer here. There is no razzamatazz, often not even as much as a vibrato. But this is where we start to encounter songs that aren't really protest songs (as *Questions* is) but are more a kind of social commentary instead. This is Darin telling us his views on something, not actively protesting about it.

The album is cleverly sequenced. The final verse of *Jingle Jangle Jungle* refers to the Vietnam war, which is the subject of *The Proper Gander*, an allegorical tale about a group of mice encouraged by their leader to go to war to fight a Siamese Cat that doesn't actually exist, with the leader being found out as the song comes to the end of its seven verses. Once again, everything here is tied up in the lyrics. Out of each verse's 28 bars, 22 of them are simply the chord of G. The lyrics more than make up for the harmonic simplicity, however, with Darin writing them in such a way that they can not only relate to the Vietnam war but any propaganda produced by a government on any issue in order to win votes and confidence. Despite the musical simplicity, there is a remarkable confidence in the writing of the song, with Darin having complete trust in his work as a lyricist, and his use of wordplay is both intelligent and fun and shows a different side to his songwriting.

Bullfrog is an 11-verse opus in which Darin doesn't sing a note. The whole thing is spoken with a rhythm background, and finds Bobby telling a frog about the history of money. It is all rather strange, something which is reflected in the lyrics themselves: "Now, I thought I was stoned, so I started walkin'/I mean, whoever heard of a bullfrog talkin'?" Darin had tried the talking blues approach before with songs such as *Everything's Okay* and *The Reverend Mr. Black*. In both cases, he had adopted a not very convincing accent, but with *Bullfrog* that isn't the case. Here he doesn't hide behind a "character" at all, but talks his way through the song as himself.

Long Line Rider became the single taken from the album, but it made little impression in the charts. It is certainly the most commercial number of the nine songs here, not least because it actually has a chorus. It tells the true story of some killings by those in charge of an Arkansas prison farm. Darin went on TV and promoted the single, dressed in denim and without his toupee. On one occasion he was told he would have to censor the line "this kind of thing can't happen here, especially not in an election year," and Darin refused to perform at all. But it is interesting that he even performed this at all on television, as it had not been his usual practice to promote his non-swing singles in that way. Once again, it is musically simplistic, built around the basic I, IV, V chord progressions (with the exception of one bar), but the lyrics are so well-written, the production so good, and Darin's performance so committed that no-one notices. *Cash Box* wrote:

Japanese single of "Long Line Rider."

> Completely different from anything Bobby Darin has done, this side pulled from his progressive-showing LP casts a new figure from the B. D. mold. Cooking blues backup envigorates a fascinating lyric centred on a chain-gang worker. Effort should see both underground

and top forty exposure to open a solid sales spree.[529]
Billboard said that "it should hit hard and fast and take him to the top," and one can only wonder why the single didn't do better than it did.[530]

The second side of the album is decidedly more relaxed and laid-back. *Change* sounds like it could have been written by Dylan for *Nashville Skyline*. This time the musical element is somewhat more sophisticated (the song even has a bridge), but the lyrics are less biting than on the first side of the LP. This is simply a call to people not to resist change, and reflects some of the things Bobby had been saying in interviews earlier in the year and discussed at the beginning of this chapter.

The lyrics of *I Can See the Wind* are something of a mystery, and the song is ultimately the low point of the album, although it is hardly objectionable. A first listen would suggest that this was Darin somehow aligning himself to the drug culture, but there is no evidence that he ever took drugs, despite various references within a number of the songs on these albums.

Sunday, on the other hand, is far more obvious in its meaning. It is a dark, cutting, attack on organised religion, the death and misery it has caused through the years, and the hypocrisy that Bobby saw in the church itself. "Sunday," Darin sings, "bow down to the blood you've shed/Sunday, Bodies piled so steep/You say keep the faith, but there's no faith to keep." This is one of the tracks that utilises recordings played backwards (in the organ introduction to the song), and the song is well-constructed. It lures you in with relatively bland verses at the start, but each one gets more hard-hitting in its lyrical content, until a world-weary Darin sighs in the final verse "Sunday, let the people sleep." This is a brilliantly-executed song with a view of religion that is a far cry from the youthful Darin telling us to *Hear Them Bells* or about the story of *The Greatest Builder* twelve years earlier.

The final song on the album strips everything back to just Darin and an acoustic guitar. Bobby was a big supporter of Robert Kennedy, and he fell apart when he was assassinated. This final subdued song, entitled simply *In Memoriam*, never sung above a whisper, sees Darin confronting his pain at the events, and the funeral that followed. Each verse ends simply with the words "they never understood him, so they put him in the ground."

This nine-track album was Bobby's opening statement in his new role as social commentator and, while the album is uneven, it is still mightily impressive. The LP was distributed by Bell Records, and Larry Uttal, President of the label stated:

> It reveals a side of Bobby Darin's personality that has never been heard by the public before. And it will no doubt surprise some listeners, because the total effect of the album poignantly passes on

---

[529] "Record Reviews," *Cash Box*, November 30, 1968, 36.
[530] "Spotlight Singles," *Billboard*, November 30, 1968, 92.

to them Darin's sense of personal involvement in the world today. Darin's material and performance runs much deeper than the type of music that, up to now, has been his signature. The album expresses the personality of a mature artist in a perfectly realized creative whole.[531]

Few publications reviewed the album, and few people bought it. *Billboard* wrote: "Now on his own Direction label distributed by Bell, Bobby Darin deservedly steals all the credits, the cover and, of course, the music in which Darin sounds like a cross between The Lovin' Spoonful and Jerry Jeff (Mr. Bojangles) Walker."[532] *Cash Box* said that "the album is different from anything Darin has done before. He has composed a flock of message songs, full of philosophical, social, and in one case, religious musings. These songs show Darin to be a talented writer; given the right promotion, this album could be the biggest thing he's ever done."[533] In the UK, the album at least got noticed by *The Observer* newspaper, who wrote that the album "has more beauty and sensitivity than a score of others."[534]

The idea of one of the best entertainers in the business singing protest and social commentary songs probably sounded phoney to many, and Darin was once again accused of simply jumping on a bandwagon. That wasn't the case though, for this LP made no effort whatsoever to be commercial. Despite it being a financial flop, Bobby wasn't deterred, and took his new songs to the night club stage and, initially, his transition to social commentator was well received.

In July, Bobby could be seen at The Frontier in Las Vegas, but at this point the new songs and new style had not found their way into his set. In fact, the act he was presenting at this point received much praise from reviewers. *Variety* noted that "he has revised the routining since his previous stand in February. It is now taut and exciting, without long stretches of ennui where Darin was rambling along in meaningless gab or expendable tunes."[535] The performances opened with *Splish Splash* and still included an impressions routine, but this was now built around *Talk to the Animals* instead of *One For My Baby*. Reviewers commented that *Mack the Knife* "has been restored to shape again and not parodied as in his previous fluff-off."[536]

However, Bobby was unhappy at The Frontier, which was owned by Howard

---

[531] "Darin's New Direction Label Distributed by Bell," *Record World*, September 7, 1968, 43.
[532] "Album Reviews," *Billboard*, October 26, 1968, 84.
[533] "Album Reviews," *Cash Box*, October 19, 1968, 52.
[534] "Ego Briefing," *The Observer*, February 23, 1969, 32.
[535] Will, "Frontier, Las Vegas," *Variety*, July 24, 1968, 52.
[536] Ibid.

Hughes. He told audiences one night "I really saw Howard Hughes the other afternoon while I was boating on Lake Mead. He was walking across the lake."[537] Bobby had been trying to contact Hughes about the sound system at The Frontier, complaining that it was so bad that his audiences could not enjoy the shows they had paid to see.[538] Eventually, Bobby abandoned the engagement (some reports suggest he did this mid-show) and took out a full page ad in *Variety* in an effort to get his message to Hughes that way. It was the first time that Bobby had walked out of such a contractual commitment.

By the time of Bobby's appearance at the Cocoanut Grove in October 1968, he was including some of the new material. He opened the show with a set of songs that included *Let the Good Times Roll*, *Mack the Knife*, *What'd I Say*, *Try a Little Tenderness* and *Talk to the Animals*: "The mood was initially traditional Darin: rhythmic, full of fun and humor and with just the right amount of sincere soulfulness."[539] While *Long Line Rider* was featured, so too were *If I Were a Carpenter*, *I'll Be Your Baby Tonight* and a medley of *What'd I Say* and *Respect*. One reviewer wrote "those who had not dug Darin before had better look again; those who have, should appreciate the refinement of his talent."[540] *Cash Box* stated that his singing of the *Long Line Rider* lyrics "this kind of thing can't happen here/'specially not in an election year" were "synchronal *(sic)*, sardonic, and shattering."[541]

In November 1968, Bobby made a rare trip to Australia, in part to film a TV special entitled *Bobby Darin at the Silver Spade*, which was "a video of the singer at work in Sydney's Chevron Hotel."[542] It appears that, as with the BBC special from a couple of years earlier, this allowed Darin to perform his act and have it recorded without worrying about the normal restraints of television, a format that suited Bobby more than any other. Songs included *Mack the Knife*, *Let the Good Times Roll*, and *If I Were a Rich Man*. Sadly, the special is believed to be lost. Harry Robinson of the *Sydney Morning Herald* may well have believed that was a good thing. "The Bobby Darin program on ATN last night was one of those things to put in the best-forgotten pile," he wrote.[543] He went on:

> Darin sang in dull tones. Closing my eyes, I could only hear evidence that he was bored – a feeling that he successfully transmitted. At times his legs went into such spasms that he seemed to be playing an

---

[537] Ralph Pearl, "Vegas Daze and Nights," *Las Vegas Sun*, October 11, 1968, 17.
[538] See "Hughes' Isolation Foils Complaints," *Palm Beach Post*, November 13, 1968, 31.
[539] Eliot Tiegel, "Darin Shows Social Pop Sides in Varied Program," *Variety*, November 16, 1968, 14.
[540] Murf, "Cocoanut Grove, L. A.," *Variety*, November 6, 1968, 61,
[541] "Bobby Darin," *Cash Box*, November 16, 1968, 38.
[542] "Bobby Darin in Singing Show," *Sydney Morning Herald*, November 25, 1968, TV Guide 1.
[543] Harry Robinson, "Ashes to Cashbox?" *Sydney Morning Herald*, November 27, 1968, 6.

arthritic teenager, an impression accentuated by his stoop over the microphone…Some visitors [to Australia] are performers who depend on quality performances. Others are products of publicity and promotion machines. Performers are to be preferred.

In January 1969, Bobby spoke to Earl Wilson about the events of the previous year, and, in particular, the funeral of Bobby Kennedy.

> Everybody'd left except guards to lower the coffin…I'd felt compelled to stay until 4 o'clock in the afternoon. My experience was spiritual. It was as though all my hostilities, anxieties and conflicts were in one ball that has been flying away into space farther from me all the time, leaving me finally content with myself.[544]

Wilson's article coincided with Bobby's season at the Copa, where his nightclub act was still transitioning from the old Bobby to the new one. *Cash Box* reported that he opened the show with a segment that included *Mack the Knife* and *Talk to the Animals*.[545] The reviewer goes on to tell us that "carefully easing his audience into a frame of mind and receptivity, Darin comes into his own only after he has established an empathy with the viewers. He follows a stage-show first half with a gently progressive segment that includes his own protest in *Long Line Rider*."

Bobby with Sandra Dee

On television, it was *Long Line Rider* that caused Bobby to refuse to appear on Jackie Gleason's show, after the network instructed him to cut a verse from the song which it found objectionable. Darin stated that "failure on the part of CBS to define the 'objectionable material' puts me in a very precarious position. I am accused of doing something but refused an explanation as to what it is. Both NBC and ABC have cleared and, indeed, run performances of the

---

[544] Earl Wilson "Bobby Darin: A Changed Man," *Florida Today*, January 11, 1969, 4D
[545] "Bobby Darin," *Cash Box*, January 11, 1969, 32.

selection without any objection being raised."[546] CBS commented that they felt a family-oriented variety hour was not the place for "protest and anti-Establishment material." Bobby went on to file a suit claiming damages.

By this point, the general population were no doubt aware of the changes that Bobby had made to his looks and his sound. A few days after the reports of the Jackie Gleason show debacle hit news-stands, Bobby appeared on *The Dean Martin Show* wearing denim, and sporting a moustache and sideburns singing *Long Line Rider*. And yet, he was still happy to flip back into traditional showbiz mode, singing a medley of Al Jolson songs with Dean Martin during the same appearance.

A month earlier, in January 1969, he had also fronted another TV special, this one entitled *Sounds of the Sixties*. Darin's songs included his 1958 song *Splish Splash* and a decades old ditty about drugs entitled *Take a Whiff on Me* – hardly "sounds of the sixties!" Despite this, Darin's three song mini-concert segment at the end of the show, which included these songs as well as *Long Line Rider*, was one of the most exciting TV appearances out of the two hundred or so he made during his career, and that is without mentioning his duets with Stevie Wonder and Judy Collins.

Early 1969: Studio Sessions
Commitment **LP**

As with all of the studio recordings made during this period, relatively little is known about these sessions with regards to dates, etc. While the *Commitment* LP didn't appear until June or July 1969, the first single from the album, *Me and Mr. Hohner*, was reviewed as early as mid-April, and some of the other songs were sung live at around the same time, suggesting that at least parts of the album were recorded by the end of March, with the rest being cut during the next couple of months. This was the only album released under the name "Bob Darin" instead of "Bobby Darin."

The album opens with *Me and Mr. Hohner*, and it's clear from the outset that the material here is more complex, and yet more traditional, musically than in the first Direction album. Harmonically, the songs are more diverse and more complicated, and most songs have choruses and/or bridges, as one would expect from popular music. *Me and Mr. Hohner*, however, finds Darin talking, almost rapping, the lyrics, producing a sound that was considerably ahead of its time for a mainstream performer. At face value, this is a song about police harassment in general, but the references to "South Philly" at the end of each verse make it clear that this is Darin's view of Frank Rizzo, who was Police Commissioner in Philadelphia at the time. Rizzo's obituary in the *New York Times* states that he was often viewed as a "barely educated former police

---

[546] Richard Robinson, "The Changing Bobby Darin," *Detroit Free Press*, February 14, 1969, 4D.

French single of "Me and Mr. Hohner."

officer who used a hard line and tactics bordering on dictatorial to suppress opposition and keep blacks out of middle-class neighborhoods."[547] The 1991 article goes on to say that "Mr. Rizzo personally led Saturday-night round-ups of homosexuals and staged a series of raids on coffee houses and cafes — saying they were drug dens." This, together with the multiple charges against Rizzo (all of which were dropped) regarding the beating of suspects, fits in with the picture the song paints of a young man and his harmonica ("not doing nothing to no-one/When a squad car stops and out jumps cops/'You're one of them if I ever saw one'") and the fear at the end of each verse of getting a beating.

The track is brilliantly executed, with a fine production, and Darin's vocal sounds completely natural despite the nature of it. *Billboard* called it "another strong message lyric set to an infectious beat [with a] top arrangement and vocal workout."[548] *Cash Box* stated that "Darin goes Dylan in this saga of police brutality which, aside from a few up-to-date touches, could have been based on the *Subterranean Homesick Blues*."[549] Later in the year, *Variety* stated that Bobby was told he couldn't sing the song during his appearance on *This is Tom Jones*, although, if this were true, one has to wonder why Bobby didn't walk away from the show in the way he had with Jackie Gleason's show a few months earlier.[550]

The meaning of *Sugar Man* is somewhat more difficult to pin down. On the surface, it appears to be a song about drug-taking, or reliance on drugs, but, with no evidence that Darin took "sweets," it is difficult to ascertain whether this is indeed the intended meaning, and this is the case for a number of the songs here. It works reasonably well, however, as a bluesy folk-rock number, but is less memorable than most of the songs.

Sausalito, like *Me and Mr. Hohner*, makes references to events that are not

---

[547] Dennis Hevesi, "Frank Rizzo of Philadelphia Dies at 70," *New York Times* [online]. Available at: http://www.nytimes.com/1991/07/17/obituaries/frank-rizzo-of-philadelphia-dies-at-70-a-hero-and-villain.html
[548] "Spotlight Singles," *Billboard*, April 19, 1969, 77.
[549] "Record Reviews," *Cashbox*, April 19, 1969, 22.
[550] Duke, "Nitery Reviews," *Variety*, December 4, 1969, 6.

necessarily remembered today outside of the USA. While somewhat coded, the song is an attack on California Governor Ronald Reagan, and may well be referencing the People's Park protests at the University of California in which one person was killed and several hundred injured after police fired into the crowds, with tear gas used over almost the whole city just a few days later. Whether these are the events that prompted the song or not is debatable, however, as it is unknown exactly when the recording was made (before or after). Either way, it is arguably the most melodic song that Darin recorded during the entirety of his time with Direction. He sings it beautifully, almost as if it is a love song, and this mismatch of performance, melody and lyrical content was no doubt intended.

Song for a Dollar had been the flip-side of *Me and Mr. Hohner*, and is a brilliant two-minute encapsulation of what Bobby thought of his career up until that point. He tells his listeners that he has "churned out any old thing to sing" for the simple reason that he needed (or wanted) money, but that his thoughts and motives had now changed. "How many suits can you wear, boy?" he asks, "and how many homes can you own?" The song is basically the manifesto for his latest incarnation as social commentator, and not only is the song well produced and sung, but he also shows off yet again his knack for coming up with interesting, often unexpected, lyrics and rhymes.

The Harvest, which ends the first side, is another song so coded in its message that it is rather difficult to ascertain exactly what message is being conveyed. Bobby sings it well, and once again the production and arrangement is interesting, but the lyrics are just a little too cryptic.

The second side of the album is, for the most part, lighter in tone, particularly the first three songs. *Distractions (Part 1)* (part 2 never emerged) finds Bobby telling us about the things that, literally, distract him when he's working or relaxing. It is a light-hearted comical number, with the tone set by the opening lines: "Well, I'm sitting by the window, trying to write a song/ Gotta do another album before too long/ When the girl across the alley shows up with no clothes on." It is a country-folk number with light acoustic backing that helps to lighten the mood of the album, and which also worked well during television and concert appearances. When it was released as a single, *Billboard* referred to the song as a "left field winner" that should "take him to a high spot on the top 100."[551] An alternate take of the song can be heard on the *Songs from Big Sur* CD.

Water Color Canvas is one of the most attractive songs here. Once again, the lyrics appear to be coded or simply are not intended to make complete sense, although there is more than one reference to drugs again. Here, though, it doesn't matter, for the result is charming, from the unusual lyrics through to the production and the laid-back vocal.

---

[551] "Spotlight Singles," *Billboard*, August 9, 1969, 105.

Jive finds Darin telling us that he's been "stoned since half past one" in a song that clearly draws inspiration from songs like *(Sittin' here) Lovin' You* and *Day Dream* by The Lovin' Spoonful that Bobby had recorded a couple of years earlier. Here, he seems at peace with the world and his surroundings, and we get the notion of a man simply relaxing and taking one day at a time (as he probably was when this was written).

Hey, Magic Man takes us back into more serious territory with another coded lyric, although the song suffers somewhat from a rather slow pace and a melody that isn't really interesting enough to hold the listener's attention. However, critic Lew Harris of the *Chicago Tribune*, one of the few publications to note that *Commitment* had even been released, refers to this as "the most effective song" on the album.[552] Harris unravels the coding of the lyrics, and makes a case that this is Darin talking to God:

> He asks God to speak, to give 'one little sign' that will help direct man. And then he begins to question: 'So if you exist/how have you missed, making a list, of corrections?' It isn't very complicated. Nothing on the album is. These songs are not the ones that took 30 minutes to write and sound like the composer struggled for days. They are the songs that sound like they took 30 minutes to write, but the ones which you believe that the composer has been struggling with for a lifetime.[553]

The final song, *Light Blue*, is another cryptic effort, with a good production, including an interesting, rather funky, use of organ. However, Darin is set far back in the mix. Rather like *The Harvest*, the cryptic lyrics and the repetitive nature of the song doesn't make this one of the most interesting numbers here, and the album ends on a slightly down-beat note.

Few people bought the album, but at least a few more publications bothered to review it this time around, although they seemed to have more interest in the artist changing his name from "Bobby" to "Bob" in many cases. *Variety* said:

> His singing style has changed from slick to sincere and he now plays simple but effective organ and harmonica. There are 10 originals on the disc which, like the previous LP, show deep social involvement and a desire to express inner feelings. Darin has made the transition truthfully and effectively.[554]

---

[552] Lew Harris, "Now He's Bob Darin – Not 'Bobby,'" *Chicago Tribune*, September 14, 1969, Section 10, 2.
[553] Ibid.
[554] "Ray Charles, Bob Darin, Cher, Ike & Tina, Cat Mother, Spence, Velvet, Max Morath Top LPs," *Variety*, July 2, 1969, 50.

Other commentators simply took an opportunity to repeat their apparent hatred of bobby, even if they also rather begrudgingly added that they liked the new record. The review by Jon Wolf is a typical example:

> Little Bobby Darin has finally grown up. He calls himself Bob Darin now, and he has come out with an album pretentiously called *Commitment*. Both the photograph on the cover and the music inside seem more like Bobby Dylan than Bobby Darin…If someone else did this album you could almost like it. The songs, all by Darin, have possibilities…That one can say anything good at all about this album is totally unexpected….*Commitment* (God, what an awful name) really isn't too bad. For little Bobby Darin, that's a compliment.[555]

May 13-18 and July 16, 1969: Live Recordings

The earliest live recordings we have of Bobby performing his new act are from May 1969, during his stint at the Troubadour club in Los Angeles, a venue far more sympathetic to folk music and singer-songwriters than any night-club that he had played before. The four songs that have emerged from this engagement show Darin to be relaxed, enjoying himself, and having good interaction with, and response from, the audience.

U. S. album cover.

---

[555] Jon Wolf, "Donovan: A Little Less Help From His Friends," *Columbia Daily Spectator*, September 29, 1969, 4.

His spoken introduction to *Distractions (Part 1)* shows that even his speaking voice appears to be slightly different. There is none of the showbiz patter of before here. Instead, it is almost as if Bobby is chatting to a few guests at a small party. What's more, the song works even better here than it does in its studio incarnation. The humour of the number gets a good reaction from the audience, and Bobby is experienced enough to work with that reaction and play on it.

Long Line Rider is given a faster rendition than on record, which only adds to the intensity of the song. Sadly, there is no spoken introduction, although one feels that there probably was one originally in order to explain the lyrics for those that didn't already know the story behind them.

Simple Song of Freedom gets what is possibly its first performance here. A month or two earlier, Bobby had taped a basic demo of the song which was eventually released in 1995. The live recording from May 1969 is rather different from the later performances that are better known. There is no build-up from verse to verse here, just Bobby's own acoustic guitar accompanying his soft, sincere rendition of the number. Within a year, that would change and the song would gain an anthem-like status within live performances, with a big arrangement that would act as the climax to the main part of the show.

Before *Questions*, Bobby tells the story of why he set up his own label. Again, he does this with humour, laughing with the crowd, often at his own expense. But this isn't the forced humour of the past, but a relaxed, informal, seemingly unrehearsed, chat about his past and present situations. *Questions* itself doesn't quite make the transfer to live performance as well as the other selections. There is something awkward here within the rhythm of the number. Darin still puts across the message effectively, however, but it doesn't work as well as on the album. One can only hope that a complete show from this set of performances finally gets released, as they are intriguing and, it appears from what we have heard so far, of very good quality.

The reviews from the engagement at the Troubadour were generally very good, even if there was something of a dig at Bobby's previous work in *Variety*. "Darin has made his name as a suave, sophisticated supper club type, but unfortunately a carbon copy of several others in the business," the reviewer writes.[556] He then goes on to state that *Me & Mr Hohner* "displayed all his talents quite well," that *Distractions (Part 1)* is a "good number," and that he does a "nice job" on *I'll Be Your Baby Tonight* and *Gabriel*. Other songs included covers of Lennon and McCartney, Taj Mahal and Hank Williams. *Cash Box* gives an intriguing description of Bobby's version of *Lady Madonna*, saying that "he began in the folk tradition and midway through the offering switched into high-voltage rock putting the crowd in foot-stomping mood."[557] One reviewer said she missed the great entertainer of old, but reiterated that she admired "his intentions, and

---

[556] Brad, "Nitery News," *Variety*, May 15, 1969, 19.
[557] "Talent on Stage," *Cash Box*, May 24, 1969, 38.

I do not believe his motives are strictly commercial. He is committed to his beliefs at a time when we all feel the need for commitment to something."[558]

The only other live performance released from this period is a single song from a one-night stand at the Bonanza in Las Vegas in July 1969. This finds Bobby giving an intimate performance of *I'll Be Your Baby Tonight*, which had been in his act for a few months by this point, and which he had sung on television in a duet with Judy Collins as part of the January 1969 TV special.

The Bonanza show was the first time that a review of a Darin show from this period commented on any audience dissatisfaction. *Variety* wrote that "one brief locking of horns occurred during first show when someone yelled for an old Darin fave. 'That was yesterday,' Darin said simply and went on with his prearranged program."[559]

It has been reported over the years that audiences walked out of Bobby's shows during the time he was performing socially-relevant material. It should be stressed that this author has found no evidence within trade journals, magazines or newspapers to suggest that was the case, although fans were given "an icy stare" when shouting requests during Bobby's two-week season at The Sahara in Las Vegas in December 1969, and there is little doubt that some were unhappy with what Bobby was singing on stage.[560]

1969 saw Bobby return to the big screen with a supporting role in *The Happy Ending*, which starred Jean Simmons. This was the only time when he was billed as "Robert Darin," and his performance (and the film) drew little attention from either the public or the critics. *Variety* commented that "the dialogue begins to sound like a three-part *Cosmopolitan* magazine for housewives on angst, adultery and alcoholism,"[561] which can hardly be viewed as a recommendation for the film. Perhaps the movie was doomed from the start with a tagline like "We're not in love. We just make love. And damned little of that!"

In the summer of 1969, Bobby taped one of the most unusual TV appearances of his career. This was a special for NBC entitled *Burlesque is Alive and Living in Beautiful Downtown Burbank*, and the story behind it is as nearly as wacky as the title.

The special was put together by those behind *Rowan and Martin's Laugh-in*, with Carl Reiner as the host and Bobby and Goldie Hawn among the performers in this tribute to the world of burlesque. There was considerable publicity during or just after the taping of the programme with the belief that it would "catapult Miss Hawn into the forefront of television, [and] that she could become the hottest attraction in the

---

[558] Kathy Orloff, "Darin is Daring to Change Style," *Akron Beacon Journal*, June 1, 1969, B13.
[559] Will, "Bob Darin," *Variety*, July 23, 1969, 56.
[560] Duke, "Sahara," *Variety*, December 4, 1969, 6.
[561] Rick, "The Happy Ending," *Variety*, November 19, 1969, 22.

medium."[562] *Life* Magazine told readers that this was an "upcoming special" and that Hawn "does a strip, imitates Harpo Marx, sings and dances."[563] However, the *Life* article was published nearly a year after the show had been filmed.

The special was due to have been shown in November 1969, and had appeared in the various TV guides. However, it was pulled just a few days before broadcast, and was rescheduled for the following month, at which point it was pulled for the second time. Some websites state the programme was eventually broadcast in March 1970, but this didn't happen either.[564] Unsurprisingly, the problem was not to do with Bobby's role in the show which was, for the most part, as comedian, but with Goldie Hawn's striptease. NBC got cold feet about the sequence which was, it seems, at the climax of the show and so difficult to edit out. In October 1970, Hawn told an interviewer that she "loved" the special and that "I don't know what's the hangup."[565] In the end, the show was completely pulled and never aired on American television, although several newspapers in America ran a story in February 1980 saying that it was a forthcoming special. The only known broadcast of the show took place in Australia on August 9, 1971.

Bobby was no stranger to TV screens in the second half of 1969. Quite what television audiences made of the balding, moustachioed Darin on their screens is unknown. He appeared on *Della!*, hosted by Della Reese (the cover image of this book comes from one of his appearances on that show), as well as on *The Barbara McNair Show* (singing *Hey Jude*) and *This is Tom Jones*. Bobby told reporters that "after the Jones show, I am through with all my singing commitments…I want to get away to write. I'm doing a dramatic screenplay that I hope to direct later this year on location in Nashville."[566] The film in question was entitled *The Vendors*. Bobby would indeed film it the following year, but it has never been released. As for Bobby's comment about his singing commitments being over, he was back on *Della!* the following month.

Bobby, however, seemed contented at this point. He had now moved into a trailer in Big Sur. In September 1969, he wrote to his family:

> Dear Nina, Vee, Vana, and Gary, Don't faint. Yes it is a letter from B.D. former W.R.C. Anyway. I am now a turtle. Virtually everything I own is on my back and suffice to say I am one ton lighter and therefore 2,000 pounds happier. Brought the trailer up 2 weeks ago and moved in yesterday. Slept like the proverbial infant last night

---

[562] Don Page, "Burlesque Revived in Beautiful Burbank," *Sandusky Register*, August 20, 1969, 46.
[563] "How Golden to be Goldie," *Life*, June 26, 1970, 76.
[564] This date may refer to a non-U.S. broadcast of the programme, but I have found no evidence of that – although I'm happy to be proven wrong!
[565] Cecil Smith, "Goldie Hawn Likes her Husband and Home," *Troy Times Record*, October 3 1970, B5.
[566] "Last Chance to Hear Bob," *The Tennessean*, September 28, 1969, 26-S.

1968-1970

Letter from Bobby to his family.

and spent the day by sorting things out. Storing my books in closets and generally trying to get organized. All houses are gone, all extraneous (everything except LPs, tapes, books and personal doodads) items have been sold and I am out from [undecipherable]. I wish all of you the serenity of this area and the peace of these mountains. Love, Robert.[567]

---

[567] Sourced from the collection of Susan Johnson Côté.

Unknown dates, 1969 and 1970: Studio Sessions

Two singles were issued during 1969 and 1970, consisting of material not included on any Direction album. The first featured the song *Baby May*, which was inspired by the suicide of Diane Linkletter, daughter of Art Linkletter, a TV personality in America at the time. Darin had appeared on *The Linkletter Show* himself twice in 1963. Here, Bobby presents a song that basically criticises the parenting by the Linkletters. It is an odd song from the point of view of the lyrics, and something of a misjudgement on the part of Darin himself. It was one thing commenting on the tactics of Frank Rizzo or Ronald Reagan, but another thing altogether to start accusing people of causing the suicide of their daughter. While the song is well-produced and sung, there is a bitter aftertaste here.

The flip-side, *Sweet Reasons*, is one of the most attractive songs to come from the Direction years. This is a folky ballad, backed only with the barest of instrumentation, and which sees Darin once again confronting his mortality with the repeated line "sweet reason please be kind, I haven't much time, and I just want to be."

Maybe We Can Get It Together is also very good indeed. Like *Simple Song of Freedom*, the structure of the

UK single of "Maybe We Can Get it Together."

song harmonically is simple, but this time things are taken at a much slower pace and it has one of the biggest productions of any of the Direction recordings, utilising a female backing group who even get a chorus of their own – another example of Darin being willing to share the spotlight. The song is basically asking everyone to join together against prejudices and for peace. There is a gospel feel here, and it suits Darin extremely well but, alas, this wasn't a style that he recorded in again.

The flip-side was a song called *Rx-Pyro (Prescription: Fire)* which is a fun rock number that seemingly makes no sense at all. It tells us of a world that is topsy-turvy and nonsensical: the baker is trying to "fry some bread," while "peanut butter taken any other way is sure to keep the reaper busy every day." Quite what Bobby is trying to get at is impossible to tell, and the lyrics have perplexed listeners for nearly five decades.

Neither of these two singles entered the charts. Two more Direction studio recordings were unearthed several decades later and issued for the first time on the

Songs from Big Sur CD. Both *City Life* and *Route 58* are rock numbers with a contemporary sound. *City Life* sees Bobby reflecting on his early years living in poverty in New York. During his week as co-host of *The Mike Douglas Show* in 1970, he would sing the song in an arrangement that seems to work better than that on record. What is strange, though, is watching him sing this type of material and still using some of the more showbiz elements of his night-club act, such as dropping the microphone from one hand to another, for example. It is an odd mis-match of style and content.

Route 58 is also reflective but finds Darin in a different mood, this time seemingly looking back at his decision to leave rock music behind in 1959, although once again the lyrics seem to be coded in such a way that we can't quite work out what he feels about the road he took. It is a fine rock song, although it's hard to imagine that either this or *City Life* would have done any better as a single than those that were released at the time.

The general view is that the music from the Direction years was very good, but that no-one was really taking any notice. This may well have been the case when it came to critics and the general public, but a little bit of delving into the past shows that other musicians from the period were often savvy enough to pick up on what Bobby was doing, and, perhaps surprisingly considering what we have been led to believe over the years, record their own versions of some of his songs. Perhaps being told that there were numerous covers of *Simple Song of Freedom* is not such a surprise, but Magic Bubble recorded *Me and Mr. Hohner*, for example, and Eddie Floyd included a fine version of *Long Line Rider* on an LP. *Maybe We Can Get it Together*, *Sugar Man*, *Sweet Reasons*, and *The Harvest* also got picked up by other artists in the late 1960s and the first years of the 1970s.

There is no doubting Bobby's sincerity during his time on the Direction label, but by the end of 1969 it also seemed that this latest creative spurt was running out of steam. There was no sign of a third album, and none of the singles were entering the charts. Even so, Robert

Bobby at a celebrity baseball game with son Dodd, 1970.

Hilburn wrote that "there are some fine songs on his two direction albums and he has written the moving *Simple Song of Freedom*. [...] Maybe the real Bobby Darin is beginning to stand. I hope so."[568]

By the spring of 1970, Bobby was looking for ways to somehow reach a compromise between the new Bobby and the old one. However, they were clearly still at odds with each other. In May 1970, he took out a full-page advertisement in *Variety* condemning the American invasion of Cambodia. It read:

> Mr President, whatever happened to 'of the people, by the people, for the people' or does it now read 'of the Pentagon, by the Pentagon, for the Pentagon?' It is totally inconceivable that you would ignore the plea for peace for the march of massacre. As a man with the power of the pen I ask you the man with the power of the sword to stop and lay that sword down. Peace.[569]

The advertisement ends with Bobby asking people to join him for a march on Washington in June 13. However, Bobby ended up cancelling his proposed march and, instead, he was in the UK appearing on the hugely successful game show, *The Golden Shot*, and preparing for a show at the Royal Albert Hall in London – a show that now included *Mack the Knife*, a song that he had turned down requests to sing at the Sahara in Las Vegas in December 1969. It had been back in the live shows for at least a month or so, and John L. Scott, in his review of Bobby's shows at the Landmark Hotel in Las Vegas in May 1970, noted that Darin was now "Bobby" once again, although he was still including *Simple Song of Freedom*, *Long Line Rider*, and *City Life* in his act. Other songs featured included *Sweet Caroline*, *Spinning Wheel*, *Lonesome Whistle*, *Bridge Over Troubled Water*, *Everybody's Talkin*, a Beatles medley, and a tribute to Aretha Franklin consisting of *Chain of Fools*, *Respect*, and *Spirit in the Dark*.[570] These types of songs would form the core of Bobby's live shows for the next three years, with only *Mack the Knife* and the occasional rendition of a past hit such as *Lazy River* or *Beyond the Sea* the only nod to the albums of standards he was perhaps most famous for.

Bobby was finding a compromise, and it was one that had to work. His commitment to social issues was serious, but, at the same time, he was realising that what he had to say was pointless unless people were listening. Now, he was giving audiences some of what they wanted, but still attacking the establishment through numbers like *Hi-De-Ho* and *Simple Song of Freedom*. But Bobby had another shock in store for his public: during the summer of 1970 he signed to Motown records.

---

[568] Robert Hilburn, "Will the Real Bobby Darin Stand Up?" *Tuscaloosa News*, July 26, 1969, 3.
[569] Bobby Darin, "Advertisement," *Variety*, May 7, 1970, 9.
[570] John L. Scott, "Bobby Darin Back on Train," *Los Angeles Times*, May 29, 1970, Part IV, 10.

Bobby with Andrea Yeager in 1970.

CHAPTER TWELVE
I USED TO THINK IT WAS EASY: 1970-1973

In the summer of 1970, it was announced that Bobby had joined the Motown label. Over the next three years, he would release just one album and a handful of singles. In 1974, after Bobby's death, a second album emerged featuring eight more recordings, two of which had been taped for an abandoned live album recorded in 1971 and eventually released in 1987.

Bobby's time at Motown has always been shrouded in mystery. Rumours that there were other numbers left in the vaults persisted through the decades. Eventually, in 2016, a double CD emerged entitled *Another Song On My Mind*, containing all of the studio recordings and single sides that had previously been issued, with a number of them in various mixes and edits. A number of these tracks had never been on CD before. This was followed in 2018 by *Go Ahead and Back Up: The Lost Motown Masters*, which saw two dozen previously unheard studio recordings from the period. Not only that, but the liner notes for these CDs provided fans with recording dates and other information about Bobby's final years for the first time.

Most of the recording dates given in this chapter are sourced from the liner notes and information contained in these CD releases. The dates provided in the section headings refer to the dates that Bobby recorded his vocals. Other elements, such as the backing tracks and vocal and instrumental overdubs, were often done on other dates, often with many months separating them. Recording in this way was not something that was natural for Bobby, and no doubt this was partly responsible for the sometimes-underwhelming results of his studio work for Motown.

August & October 12, 1970: Studio Sessions

The omens for Bobby's association with Motown were not good from the start. These two dates saw Bobby entering the studio to add his lead vocal to two tracks. One would be released as the A-side for Bobby's first single with the label, and the other would remain unreleased until 2018.

Bobby was able to sing almost any genre of music, and so it is quite an achievement that some of the songs at Motown are in a style that didn't suit him at all. The production on *Melodie* is over-the-top, and the key is clearly too high for the singer, who strains to reach the high notes – and actually sounds as if he is straining throughout the entire song. It is hardly surprising. The liner notes for the *Go Ahead and Back Up* CD gives us information on how Bobby recorded at Motown. In the case of *Melodie*, the backing track was recorded on August 7, 1970. Bass and piano were added on August 18. Bobby's vocal was recorded on August 18 and October 20, and backing vocals and strings were added on August 19. For a man used to recording an album in three nights, the method at Motown must have seemed remarkably alien. There were even occasions when a backing track was cut for another singer and then passed over to Bobby at a later date – a situation which most likely led to the straining that can be heard on some of these songs. A key used for one singer is rarely the same as that used for another. In the case of *Melodie*, we are even told that the backing track was recorded *before* the lyrics were written.

Of course, recording a song a segment at a time is normal practice now, but Bobby was, more than anything, a singer who relied on instinct and being in the moment. There were times in the past when a song wasn't working for him in the studio and he would put it to one side and come back to it a few days, or even a few months, later, but he would invariably start the track again from scratch each time, not just add a few lines here and there, and most certainly his arrangements would have been tailored to suit him. That wasn't the case at Motown as songs got moved from one singer's to-do list to another.

On October 12, Bobby added his vocal to a ballad entitled *Child of Tears*. This was by the writing team of Mel Larson and Jerry Marcellino who had also penned *Melodie*. In a number of ways, this number looks forward to the 1972 album of ballads which was Bobby's only Motown LP release during his lifetime. The styling and arrangement is similar to the later recordings, and there is even a rather clumsy spoken section just as there would be on *Let It Be Me*. Despite the talking, this is a surprisingly commercial ballad that would probably have been a better choice of single than *Melodie*.

Bobby relaxing, late 1960s or early 1970s.

November 12, 1970: Studio Session

This session was used to create a flip side for the forthcoming single. Despite the ridiculous backing vocals, *Someday We'll Be Together*, was a little better than *Melodie*, although that isn't saying a great deal.

The single was basically a mess, and it even sounds on the fade-out of *Someday We'll Be Together* that Bobby can be heard saying "sorry" as if he has made a mistake. That mistake may well have been signing to Motown in the first place. Jeff Bleiel summed up the single release most effectively in his (highly recommended) book on Bobby:

> [Darin] was no soul shouter, and the production of *Melodie* was tailored for a singer more along the lines of the Four Tops' Levi Stubbs. Its flip side, a cover of the Supremes' swan song hit *Someday We'll Be Together*, ranks as perhaps the worst track Darin ever recorded. From background vocalists warbling "Sing It Bobby" to Darin's strained vocal which never stays on the melody, this Motown debut was quite a disappointment.[571]

Reviews were oddly positive, though, with *Cash Box* referring to the single as a

---

[571] Jeff Bleiel, *That's All*, 169-171.

"triumphant return,"[572] and *Billboard* thinking that *Melodie* was a "potent commercial rocker."[573] The 2018 *Go Ahead and Back Up* CD contains an alternate vocal take of *Melodie* coupled with a new "symphonic" mix. It doesn't save the song, but it is a distinct improvement over the version released in May 1971.

While recording his first sides for Motown, Bobby was doing his best to get himself back into the entertainment mainstream, particularly through the medium of television. In July 1970, he spent a week co-hosting *The Mike Douglas Show*. At this point he was still with moustache, sideburns, and lace shirts(!), but the lunch time ninety-minute show helped introduce Bobby back into the homes of middle America. Darin talked openly on the show about the previous two years, argued fiercely (but politely) with film censors, and sang solo songs ranging from *Mack the Knife* (with just his four-piece band, our only opportunity to hear this arrangement) and *Splish Splash* through to songs he never recorded such as *And When I Die* and *Everybody's Talkin'*. There were also memorable versions of *Got My Mojo Working* with Little Richard and *Put a Little Love in Your Heart* with Mahalia Jackson. Bobby seemed happy and content straddling new songs and old, and switching from politics to small talk.

Six weeks later he was back on *The Andy Williams Show* for the first time in years and sang *Mack the Knife* as his featured number – a performance that ranks among his best of the song. By this point, the tux and bowtie were back, even if the receding hairline was still on show. He then became a semi-regular guest on *The Flip Wilson Show*, with the two men working extremely well together and clearly having much fun at the same time. These programmes saw Bobby in prime form, singing a mix of classic hits and contemporary songs, and enjoying performing once again.

Bobby was also performing on stage regularly. He was at the King's Castle in Lake Tahoe in August 1970, an engagement that hit the newspapers not because of Bobby's performances but because he saved a boy from drowning. *Variety* described the incident:

> Darin, who just closed at Kings Castle, had been motorboating with friends. Two boys, 9 and 5, were floating within Darin's sight in a raft and a small plastic tub. The younger boy paddled to shore in the raft, but when the older began paddling back in the tub, [it] filled with water and sank. Darin, hearing the boy's screams, jumped into the lake and pulled the boy from its bottom.[574]

---

[572] "Singles Reviews," *Cash Box*, May 8, 1971, 20.
[573] "Spotlight Singles," *Billboard*, May 8, 1971, 66.
[574] "Lake Tahoe Accident, Darin to the Rescue," *Variety*, August 19, 1970, 53.

At the end of August, Bobby hosted a show celebrating Motown's 10th anniversary before returning to the Landmark in Las Vegas, where his performances of *Sweet Caroline*, *Midnight Special*, and *Hi-De-Ho* were singled out for praise by the *Variety* reviewer.[575] Bobby's opening number for this engagement was *Gabriel*.

At the end of the year, Bobby performed at The Sahara in Lake Tahoe, another engagement that was reported in the trade press for non-musical reasons. On January 20, 1971, *Variety* reported that "The Secrets, three black femmes Bobby Darin had on contract…played two shows opening night and left, not to be seen for the remainder of the two-week engagement. 'It's the most unprofessional thing I've ever seen in my life,' entertainment manager Stuart Allen said."[576] The following week, a letter from Bobby appeared in *Variety* in which he explained the situation:

> The girls somehow were not informed by their organization of the potential cold weather in the Lake Tahoe area, as well as the altitude being in excess of 6,000 ft. This resulted in one of the girls coming down with a very bad case of laryngitis…I received a call in which the girls explained to me that the laryngitis had now been complicated by a temperature of better than 100 degrees and that they were very sorry but felt it incumbent upon themselves to return to L.A…The fact that they called and were quite apologetic about having to return to L.A. clearly does not indicate a lack of professionalism as stated in your story…I would have no compunctions about using them again at some future time.[577]

Back in October 1970, Bobby had gone to Canada to film a TV special called *The Darin Invasion*, which aired in May 1971 in Canada and October 1971 in America. For the special, Bobby would avoid big band numbers, instead concentrating on lengthy showstopping covers of *Higher and Higher* and *Hi-De-Ho*, and a dramatic performance of *Reviewing the Situation* from *Oliver*, with Bobby in full costume as Fagin. The show also saw him reprise his soft shoe routine with George Burns, and perform a comedy sketch with Pat Carroll.[578] The reviews were cutting, with one newspaper in Canada reporting that Bobby looked "middle-aged…Some of the old style was there. Bobby Darin isn't untalented. But the invasion was actually a minor incursion."[579] *Variety* went further, stating that "the cocksure performer attempted a couple of tunes that

---

[575] Will, "Landmark, Las Vegas," *Variety*, September 16, 1970, 84.
[576] "Secrets, Femme Combo, In Disappearing Act," *Variety*, January 20, 1971, 52.
[577] Bobby Darin, "Bobby Darin Clarifies Secrets' Tahoe Walkout," *Variety*, January 27, 1971, 50.
[578] For reasons unknown, this sketch is edited out of the retail DVD of the show.
[579] Bob Shiels, "Bob Shiels on TV," *Calgary Herald*, May 13, 1971, 69.

seemed beyond the present-day limits of his vocal range."[580]

Oddly, despite what the critics had to say, the show holds up rather well after a period of nearly fifty years. Still, the reviewers were no doubt unaware that Bobby was running on empty at the time he made the show. His heart condition had worsened considerably. He begged doctors to help him get through his forthcoming season of shows at the Desert Inn in Las Vegas, where he was to make a live album, and promised that, straight after, he would have the open-heart surgery that he needed.

February 6, 1971: Live Recordings
Live at the Desert Inn LP

Bobby Darin's next recordings for Motown were for a live album that was intended to be issued under the title *Finally*. It was taped at the Desert Inn on February 6, 1971. For unknown reasons, the album wasn't released until some sixteen years later, when it appeared under the title *Live at the Desert Inn*. Recordings of *I'll Be Your Baby Tonight* and *Simple Song of Freedom* were, however, released as the two sides of a single in late 1971, and recordings of *Mack the Knife* and *If I Were a Carpenter* appeared in 1974 on the album *Bobby Darin 1936-1973*. Most, if not all of these, are alternate versions to those heard on the live album released in 1987 and re-released in 2005.

What is clear from the opening number, *Save the Country*, is that Bobby might have re-entered the mainstream, but he hadn't given up on singing politically-motivated material and putting his views across. We also learn here that he was listening to new, young artists and songwriters, with singer-songwriter Laura Nyro having been just twenty-one when she recorded the original version of the song in 1969. This is the weakest song on the entire album, which is not a dig at the material or the performance, but a demonstration of the quality of the rest of the live set. *Save the Country* simply doesn't sound right as an opening number, although the arrangement is very good indeed, with a lovely quiet section in the centre that foreshadows some of what

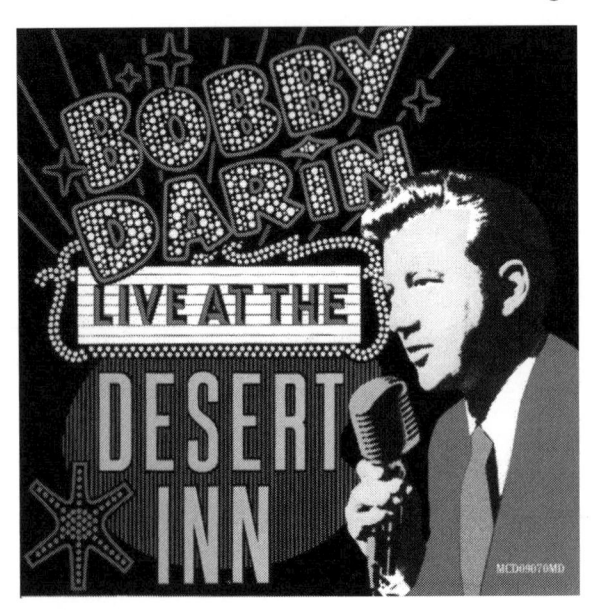

1987 CD release.

---

[580] Bok, "The Darin Invasion," October 18, 1971, 38.

is to follow.

Mack the Knife is up next, and gets a more serious rendition than on previous live albums – which is rather ironic considering Darin had refused to sing it at all just a year earlier. The arrangement is, by and large, the same as previously, but it has also been updated, with a cool, funky organ noticeable during the first half of the song. Darin's voice is full and strong, and shows no sign of the fact that he would enter the hospital just a few days later for a major heart operation. David Evanier talks of how Bobby didn't think he was going to come through the forthcoming operation, and one can only wonder if that was part of the motivation for not only the recording of this concert but its remarkable intensity, with show-stopper following show-stopper.[581]

Next, Darin takes James Taylor's recent single *Fire and Rain* and turns it into a six-minute epic. However, there is no big production here. Instead, the song is slowed down considerably in comparison to the original, and performed in a folk style. Darin sings the number with a vocal tone not dissimilar to the 1966/7 folk albums, and the sandwiching of the song between two bigger, louder numbers only demonstrates further his range of material.

Bobby had already performed *Hi-De-Ho (That Old Sweet Roll)* by Blood, Sweat and Tears on his *The Darin Invasion* TV show the previous year. Here, however, he completely usurps the earlier version. In contrast to the previous song, the whole band is in play, and the result is a fiery mix of rock and gospel that is totally captivating. Once again, Darin injects some political commentary, aligning Spiro Agnew with the devil in one verse. Darin wails on the harmonica, adding a touch of blues to the proceedings during the instrumental break. This is brilliant stuff, completely different to anything Bobby had recorded before, mixing politics with gospel, rock and pure showmanship. One has to wonder why this type of material was not pursued in the studio.

The previous two numbers had both run for six minutes each, and the next, a medley of Beatles songs, clocks in at seven. Darin didn't take the easy option of simply stringing together some big hits, but, instead, crafted a complex medley built around *Hey Jude*, which is sung in the first instance accompanied just by a piano, at a slow pace and in his folk voice. After a snatch of *Something* and *A Day in the Life*, he launches into an up-tempo rendition of *Eleanor Rigby* before a sedate, semi-gospel version of *Blackbird*, and then a big, beefy reprise of *Hey Jude* to end. Again, this is quite unlike anything Bobby had done before. While he had pulled together unlikely songs for medleys in the past, such as the pairing of *Don't Worry About Me* and *Toot, Toot Tootsie Goodbye*, here he's not aiming just for polite applause after three minutes of ballad singing. Instead, he is totally intent on bringing the house down, and manages to instil this one medley with elements of rock, pop, blues, gospel and big band music.

---

[581] David Evanier, *Roman Candle*, 222.

The remarkable run of big numbers finally reaches its climax with Darin's version of the Jackie Wilson hit *Higher and Higher*. As with *Hi-De-Ho*, this is superior to the version he had performed just a few months earlier on his TV special. Not only is the vocal energetic, but the arrangement is also superb, extending the song to nearly four and a half minutes, with the intensity rising with key change following key change. Sadly, when Bobby recorded the song in the studio later in the year, he used a very different arrangement.

There then follows a complete change of pace with Bobby giving a quiet, relaxed version of Bob Dylan's *I'll Be Your Baby Tonight*, one of the songs that had been introduced into his performances during the Direction years. This would continue to be a favourite of Darin during his final years, with him also performing it during his 1973 TV series. In the context of the *Live at the Desert Inn* album, one can see how Bobby had put all of his experience on the concert stage into structuring his latest show, piling big number on top of big number so that the final folk section becomes even more effective thanks to the contrast.

A straightforward rendition of *If I Were a Carpenter* follows, beautifully sung as always, and, again, the structure of the show here allows Darin to tell people the story of him recording Tim Hardin's song and having a hit with it, and people thinking he "stole" it, only for Hardin to repay the compliment by recording and having a hit with *Simple Song of Freedom*. It is a brilliantly worked out move, and allows the performance to flow effectively from one song to the next, something which didn't always happen back on the *Darin at the Copa* album.

Simple Song of Freedom gets its best performance here, starting with just Darin and guitar and then building up in intensity with each successive verse. Whereas the live version from 1969 is pure folk, here the song becomes a semi-gospel number, and a fitting end to the main part of the show. There is now a coda to the song, with the word "freedom" repeated over and over as Darin takes his bows, goes off stage, and then returns for a perfectly judged encore.

Without a break, Bobby introduces the members of his core group, with each providing a short solo. This ends with a return to the "freedom" coda before the start of a medley consisting of *Chain of Fools*, *Respect*, *Splish Splash*, *I Hear You Knocking* and *Johnny B. Goode*. Darin was no soul singer (as the previous recording session had shown), but here he works through a song such as *Respect* and manages to make it sound as if it was written for him. Darin takes to the piano for *Splish Splash* and transforms it from a novelty hit into a genuine rock number here. The daft words are completely forgotten by the listener, and the sound of the 1958 song brought up to date.

By the end of the medley, Darin has little voice left as he yells out the words to *Johnny B. Goode*, but it's hardly surprising. Few, if any, other stars on the strip were giving shows of this intensity. Eight years earlier, at the shows recorded at The

Bobby on stage, early 1970s.

Flamingo in 1963, Darin had a throwaway hits medley and used the impressions routine to turn the temperature down a bit and get his breath back. He had neither in his show in 1971 if the audio evidence and reviews are anything to go by – and there were two shows on the night this performance was recorded! This was Bobby Darin at his very best, giving some of the best shows of his life, perfectly mixing crowd-pleasers with songs of social commentary.

The album, released in 1987, is one of Bobby's best, even if some might bemoan the relative lack of Darin hits on display. The recordings are also poignant as they are, in essence, the last great recordings Bobby made. There would be moments of the Darin genius in his studio recordings over the next couple of years, but they would be relatively few and far between.

Live at the Desert Inn was re-released in 2005 on the Concord label. There are both good and bad elements to the reissue. On the plus side, there are two extra songs, *Work Song* and *Beyond the Sea*. However, both are simply tagged on the end of the show rather than sequenced within the main running order. This results in the rather strange listening experience of hearing Bobby saying good night to the audience and then randomly singing two more songs – and in one of them welcoming the audience to the show!

Work Song is a little more soulful than when we last heard it at the Flamingo in November 1963, but otherwise the rendition has changed little. *Beyond the Sea* doesn't appear to be sung with the same enthusiasm as the rest of the show. It has now turned into easy listening rather than swing, and doesn't survive the transition particularly well. There is also an extended coda here where Darin improvises over the line "no more sailing." This is all very well, but at over two minutes, this "comedy" outstays its welcome – but not as much as the version recorded two years later for his TV series where the song runs for nine minutes in total.

The reissue also remixes and remasters the sound. This results in considerably more reverb than on the original issue, which will be to some tastes and not to others. It is also worth noting that the new liner notes are rather short and vapid and give us no background as to why these shows were recorded, the strange history of their release, or why this engagement at the Desert Inn was important for Darin with his impending operation coming just a couple of days later. The reissue is worth getting for the bonus tracks, but it is also a missed opportunity to try and raise the profile of one of Bobby's most overlooked albums.

Bobby's heart operation was a success, and over the coming months he recuperated and built up his strength once again.

Even while he was recovering, Bobby didn't appear to lose his spark. In January 1971, Marilyn Beck had written a series of newspaper articles about the changing face of Hollywood, including one in which she discussed how many stars were now involved in politics. She refers to Darin, and quotes actor Efrem Zimbalist, who said to her, "generically speaking, the Lord in his infinite wisdom, to the extent that He endowed actors with talent, took it away from their brains. I wish to God all actors would remove themselves from politics."[582] Two months later, in a conversation with Beck, Bobby replied to the comment from Zimbalist, saying "it would seem to me Mr. Zimbalist's memory is very short, as I distinctly recall his being quite active in the 1964 presidential campaign…Please tell him that this actor will remove himself from politics the moment all politicians remove themselves from acting."[583]

March 15, 1971: Studio Session

Some previous accounts of this period have stated that Bobby remained in hospital for six weeks after his operation, but we now know that this could not have been the case. Remarkably, just a month after having heart surgery, he was back in the recording studio. Perhaps less surprisingly, the song that had lured him there was about eradicating hatred and war. *We're Getting There* was written and produced by The Corporation, a collective at Motown comprised of Berry Gordy, Alphonso Mizell, Freddie Perren, and Deke Richards. It is that the number was neither written nor

---

[582] Marilyn Beck, "Wisdom of Stumping Actors Questionable," *Orlando Evening Star*, January 12, 1971, 8-A.
[583] Marilyn Beck, "Bobby Darin Recuperating," *Binghampton Press and Sun-Bulletin*, March 16, 1971, 2B.

produced by Bobby that perhaps resulted in it being a very different recording to those with similar lyrical content that he had cut for his own Direction label.

Bobby's songs for his previous two albums had benefitted greatly from the wonderful wordplay within his lyrics. There was the allegorical nature of *Bullfrog*; the bitterness of *Long Line Rider*; the honesty of *In Memoriam*; and the hard-hitting, yet clever, rap-like lyric of *Me and Mr. Hohner*. In comparison, *We're Getting There* has all the subtlety of a brick. Bobby might have believed in the "down with hate" message, but he must have known that he (and his cause) was better than songs like this, and the recording remained in the vaults for forty-seven years.

His songs for Direction had never been preachy in their approach, but now he was trying to work with a song which preached from beginning to end:

> The world's gotta understand, the future's in our hands.
> The only way to win is making hate give in.
> Sweep inside your home until all the hate is gone.
> When it's clean you'll see that love's your destiny.

The number is the antithesis of some of the songs on *Commitment*, where Bobby's intended message was lost due to the complex lyrics. There is nothing complex here, and the words are almost hammered into the head of the listener due to the chant-like back and forth between Bobby and the backing singers.

Beyond the failings of the material, Bobby sounds in surprisingly good voice considering the operation he had only recently undergone. In fact, he sounds stronger here than on the recordings made at the end of the previous year. There are moments when he seems to struggle during the choruses, but again this may well have been due to the song being a semitone or two too high for him.

No doubt, he must have been glad to be taking small steps to returning to work, but complete fitness was still some time off, and photos from the period show him to be almost unrecognisable due to the weight gained through the steroids taken in the weeks after the operation.

June 10 and 15, 1971: Studio Session

In the summer of 1971, Bobby returned to work. He went into the studio in June to cut some numbers that, in all likelihood, were intended for single release. None of them were issued until 2018.

Stray Dog, the first song tackled was another number written and produced by The Corporation. One can't help but feel that this could have been a worthwhile track in, perhaps, a different key and with a second attempt at the vocal from Bobby. The song itself is decent enough, but Bobby seems to still be feeling his way around it, and he doesn't seem confident in this vocal.

The other two numbers from these dates were written and produced by Nickolas Ashford and Valerie Simpson, a pair who wrote, among other things, *Ain't No Mountain High Enough* and *Reach Out And Touch (Somebody's Hand)*. No-one could suggest that Bobby wasn't being paired with the best in the business.

I'm Glad About It starts off promisingly, but then runs into the recurring issue of it being sung in too high a key. According to the liner notes of the CD release, the backing track was cut with Sammy Davis Jr. in mind (he was struggling during his association with Motown as well) and then later assigned to Bobby. In the chorus, Bobby can barely reach the notes of the first line at all, let alone sing them with confidence and power. From a distance of fifty years, the situation seems ridiculous.

Oh Lord, Where Is My Baby is a more memorable song, and parts of it give hints of what Bobby was really capable of. He growls and yells his way through much of the song, with his voice adopting a rawer tone than usually associated with him, but which fits the style of the song. However, there are other moments within the number which are disastrous – most notably Bobby's attempts at a falsetto that are wincingly out of tune.

Bobby, still recovering from his heart operation, with Andrea Yeager.

It seems almost impossible that Bobby would have regarded these as finished masters, and perhaps that is why the *Go Ahead and Back Up* CD can be disappointing, with some songs presented as finished masters when it is highly likely they were not thought of as such (and hence why they remained in the vaults). The Corporation and Ashford and Simpson tracks discussed thus far seem more like experiments, as if Bobby is trying to find a new musical direction for himself and trying things out. That does not mean that they shouldn't be released, but that calling them a master is perhaps wrong.

Bobby's next move was obvious – he would take control of his own recording sessions.

July, August and December 1971: Studio Session
Go Ahead LP (unreleased)

The recent revelation that Bobby had recorded an entire studio album in 1971 that, for some reason, was never released, came as something of a surprise to most enthusiasts and followers of his career. There had always been rumours that more Motown tracks were in the vaults, but very few thought that there would be a complete, coherent album waiting to see the light of day.

The unreleased album was to have been called *Go Ahead*, with the title coming from an original song Bobby had written and recorded for the project entitled *Go Ahead and Back Up*. The rest of the album was made up of Bobby's versions of other people's hits. In many way, this seems like a natural successor to the *18 Yellow Roses* and *You're the Reason I'm Living* LPs, where a Darin composition had served as the opening track and was followed by a collection of covers.

While the 1971 ten-track album is no masterwork, there is little doubt that it contains much of Bobby's best studio work during his time at Motown. This is most likely due to the fact that this was a case of Bobby producing himself rather than being produced by others at a label that didn't necessarily understand how he worked or what he wanted to achieve. What's more, unlike many of the other tracks discussed so far in this chapter, the arrangements were written with Bobby in mind (by Art Freeman and Bill Holman), and therefore we encounter little of the vocal straining that had been apparent elsewhere. In short, this was a Bobby Darin album rather than a Motown album, and was all the better for it. The tracks will be discussed in the order in which they would have appeared on the planned LP.

Go Ahead and Back Up may be the best song Bobby recorded in the studio during his time with Motown. In many ways, the song looks back to some of his work on the Direction label, both musically and within the lyrics. The number is not dissimilar in feel to *Route 58*, *City Life*, or even *Rx-Pyro: Prescription: Fire* – although, unlike the latter, the lyrics are not so cryptic as to make them unfathomable. Like *Song for a Dollar*, *Go Ahead and Back Up* sees Bobby reflecting on his life, his career, and his current position. He sings about meeting Andrea Yeager, who was his partner for several years before they married in 1973, only to divorce shortly after. He also sings once again about his mortality, telling listeners: "Five and thirty years is hardly in the middle of a life that may be forty-odd." Presumably the recent heart operation had given Bobby hope that he might live for another decade, although that sadly did not happen. The sound created here was commercial, helped by the use of double-tracking on Bobby's voice, and could easily have been a hit for him, especially with the clout of Motown's publicity machine to help it. Even when the album was shelved, this should have been released as a single. In the 1990s, the song started to circulate amongst fans in a version that lasted close to five minutes. The version released in 2018 sadly lasts just under three minutes, and loses something because of that. Despite this, the number is a wonderful addition to the official Darin catalogue.

Higher and Higher is a number that had been in Bobby's live shows for around a year at the time this studio version was made. Sadly, he doesn't adapt the live arrangement, but uses one that is more Motown in sound. That doesn't mean that this version is bad, but it doesn't have the same energy as the live recordings, and presumably Bobby wasn't totally happy with it as he doesn't appear to have used this arrangement on stage. Bobby has fun with the production, through adding effects to his own backing vocals. Rather like the previous number, though, the song seems a little short, and a repeat of one of the verses would have righted this.

The Letter, a cover of the The Boxtops hit is up next. This is a relatively straightforward rendition that adds little to the song, although it is effective enough. Here, the key seems to be a little too high, even though it doesn't result in the straining heard on the recordings from earlier in the year. The version of the song released in 1974 (and intended for the *Go Ahead* album) always seemed too short, and in 2018 a longer edit was released which is considerably more satisfying.

Blue Monday sees Bobby doing his version of the Fats Domino classic. What is interesting here is that Bobby is known to have sung this song way back in the early days of his career before *Splish Splash* was even a hit. Here it gets a decent workout, still somewhat over-arranged, but a huge improvement on the earlier Motown tracks. What is more noticeable is that he has managed to update this 1950s number with a credible 1970s sound.

Don't Think Twice, It's all Right finds Bobby revisiting the Bob Dylan tune that he first recorded back in 1963. Again, the number is given a 1970s makeover and turned into a mid-tempo ballad. Interestingly, Bobby's voice sounds rather similar to the 1966/7 folk albums, although that doesn't necessarily work as well with the bigger arrangement. Still, the key thing here is that he was once again trying new things and approaching songs in an interesting way. *Blue Monday* and *Don't Think Twice, It's All Right* are available in two different mixes, both of which are included on the *Another Song on My Mind* CD.

The second side of the album would have opened with *Help Me Make It Through the Night*. Unlike *Higher and Higher*, this arrangement closely follows Bobby's live version of the song. It is difficult to see what Bobby was trying to achieve in his renditions of the song, as the arrangement and overall feel seems at odd with the lyrics. Still, Bobby liked it enough to keep it in his live shows for the final three years of his life, and to perform it twice on *The Bobby Darin Show* in 1973.

Watch the River Flow sees him returning to Bob Dylan, and one of the highlights of Bobby's Motown years. The song had only been released by Dylan a month earlier, but Bobby gives it a makeover, and a listener could be forgiven for thinking it had been a Fats Domino tune rather than one by Dylan.

A review of a concert from a year or so earlier had praised Bobby's version of *Lady Madonna*, stating that it started off in a folk arrangement before kicking in to a rock number for the second half. Unfortunately, we don't get to hear that version on Bobby's studio recording. Instead, the song gets quite a funky production, which is fine in itself, but it is over and done with in just a couple of minutes, and so the song doesn't have a chance to get going.

Bobby was always someone to try new ideas in his work, and he certainly seems to have been doing that in his version of Johnny Cash's *I Walk the Line*. Bobby had an association with the song going back to at least 1963, when he was performing a short parody of it in concert. For the studio recording, Bobby attempts to reinvent the song, giving it a strange, swampy feeling that simply doesn't work, and the song plods along for what seems like a very lengthy three minutes.

The *Go Ahead* album ends with Bobby's take on *You've Lost That Loving Feeling*. Here the arrangement is surprisingly buoyant compared to other versions of the song. The problem is that this is a big, somewhat beefy, ballad, and Bobby, sadly, was not at his best when singing this kind of material. It does at least provide something of a climax to the album, but the attempts to replicate the stylings of, say, Elvis in the 1970s or Tom Jones were always going to be futile.

The album was finished, and the track-listing finalised, by the end of 1971, but, for reasons unknown, just like the Desert Inn album, it was shelved. It was not unusual for Bobby to shelve completed albums, but this had nearly always been due to the amount of material in the vaults. That was not the case here. The irony is that the album that *was* released the following year was not as good as either of the shelved projects. *The Letter*, *Blue Monday*, and *Don't Think Twice, It's All Right* appeared in 1974 on the tribute album that Motown released shortly after Bobby passed away. The remaining tracks, including the wonderful title song, stayed unreleased until 2018.

Three other songs were recorded during these sessions, and at least three of the numbers were likely to have been candidates for inclusion in the LP. The best of these is *Proud Mary*. The lengthy introduction tells the listener we are back in *Blue Monday* territory, with the number taken much slower, and the horns using some of the same figures that we are familiar with from the Fats Domino cover. Darin repeats the chorus over and over for the last couple of minutes, with the horns and arrangements getting louder and louder as he does so, and this perhaps harks back to the studio recording of *I Got a Woman* from the *Bobby Darin Sings Ray Charles* album. It seems strange that Darin overlooked this number on his planned *Go Ahead* LP (it was recorded at the same time), instead including something as bland as *I Walk the Line*. A second version of *Proud Mary* has also been released, but this is a rather predictable affair, with little of the fire displayed in the longer take.

Bobby's unique version of *I Don't Know How to Love Him* from *Jesus Christ Superstar* was first heard on a 2014 BBC radio programme. Bobby changed the lyrics to *I Don't*

Know How to Love Her for obvious reasons, and it is debatable whether the song works with a man singing it. It is an interesting take on the song, but it is easy to see why this wasn't released at the time, although it may have got some attention due to the popularity of the musical in the early 1970s.

Finally from these sessions, we have Bobby's version of Donovan's hit *Catch the Wind*. One could be forgiven for thinking that Bobby might have approached this in a similar way to the *If I Were a Carpenter* and *Inside Out* albums from the mid-1960s. Unfortunately, that isn't the case, and this is a much bigger arrangement, underpinned by a rather awkward rhythmic figure, and, together with the vocal, the whole thing is just a bit too heavy-handed.

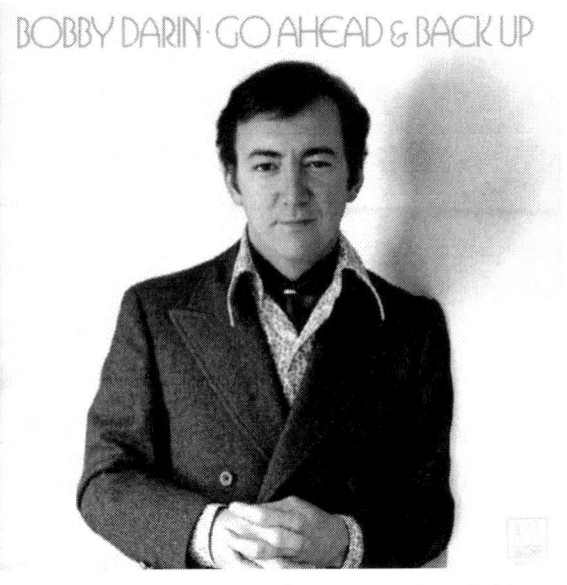

"Go Ahead and Back Up" CD, released in 2018.

October 20, 1971: Studio Sessions

Before the *Go Ahead* album was finished, Bobby started on a new project – one that appears to have been aborted after just one session. The premise was promising, with Bobby recording standards arranged by old friend Richard Behrke. The results should have been astounding, but something went wrong.

Despite the band including such musicians as Harry "Sweets" Edison and Bud Shank, it fails to create any excitement on these three numbers. In fact, they sound remarkably like the backing band used on Bobby's TV series in 1972 and 1973, in that the swing sound is essentially watered down. But, beyond that, Behrke wrote arrangements here that sound remarkably pedestrian and bland. In trying to bring Bobby's brand of swing in to the 1970s, a sound was created that is more dated than anything else he ever recorded. What is heart-breaking is that Bobby's vocals sound so good. He sounds totally at ease for probably the only time during the Motown studio recordings. His voice is strong and powerful, but it all goes to waste.

Bobby tackled *Rags to Riches*, *Smile*, and *Mona Lisa* at this session, and it has to be said that *Smile* is probably the best of the bunch. There are at least moments when the band threatens to kick the song into life, and the key changes do at least vaguely remind us of a number such as *Mack the Knife* where they were also a key feature. Bobby is crooning rather than swinging with abandon as he had in the past, though, and the long instrumental outro seems redundant. *Mona Lisa* is competent enough but utterly dull, while *Rags to Riches* is saddled with an awful arrangement that doesn't allow the performance to hold a candle either to Tony Bennett's original or the 1970 cover by Elvis Presley where he attacks the song as if he is a tiger that has just escaped his cage. In its own way, Darin's arrangement is no more subtle than Presley's, plodding along as it does with a prominent, and rather irritating, organ high in the mix that makes Bobby sound as if he is in a cheap hotel in Blackpool rather than at a luxury hotel in Las Vegas.

While this author is generally against manipulating old recordings to create artificial duets, or overdubbing a symphony orchestra on to the original vocals (at least the Bobby Darin Estate hasn't gone down that route), one has to wonder if something more worthwhile *could* be achieved here by isolating Bobby's voice and adding a more exciting big band arrangement. The Basie orchestra (long without the Count, of course) still sounds remarkably fine, and it would be interesting to hear what a good arranger could achieve with such a band and using Bobby's vocals from this session, and perhaps a handful of otherwise-unrecorded songs from the later TV series such as *Born Free*, *Climb Every Mountain*, *Some People*, and *I Get a Kick Out of You*.

November 3 and 22, 1971: Studio Recordings

Bobby entered the studio twice more in 1971, but this time he wasn't producing and handed the reigns over to others.

On November 3, Bobby set to work on two songs. The first was *Wonderin' Where it's Gonna End,* a mid-tempo ballad that finds him relaxed and sounding in good voice. Sadly, there is no "hook" here through a memorable chorus, resulting in the track being somewhat undistinguished, and yet considerably better than most of the tracks at the Motown sessions. The song was released in 1974.[584]

Young Joe Caldwell, meanwhile, went unreleased, despite being one of the better Motown tracks. The production is not all that dissimilar to the title song of the *Go Ahead* album, and Bobby's vocal grooves along nicely in a style that owes something to both rock and Motown. Unfortunately, his diction here is particularly poor, and at times it is difficult to work out exactly what the lyrics are, especially in the second half

---

[584] There is conflicting information in the only real source we have for the Motown session dates, the liner notes for *Go Ahead and Back Up*. There it is stated that *Wonderin' Where It's Gonna End* was recorded at the sessions for the *Go Ahead* album, but also that it was recorded at a different session on November 3, 1971. An assumption has been made that the November 3rd date is correct due to Bobby not being the producer of this recording.

of the song. Even so, this is still an appealing number.

Two weeks later, Bobby recorded two more songs, this time written and produced by Smokey Robinson. *I Think the Devil Must Be Beating His Wife* has, like *Young Joe Caldwell*, problems with diction, which is a shame as this is an attractive number for the most part. This still doesn't sound like what Bobby should have been singing at this point, but at least it is well executed.

The final song, *Cindy*, features the voice of Smokey Robinson, but the results are not as attractive as the previous number, not least because the song seems to be stretched out beyond its natural running time, particularly during the meandering middle section which seems to go nowhere. Bobby's voice seems thinner here than on the other numbers at this session and, despite the input of Robinson, the recording is unremarkable.

Slowly, Bobby eased himself back into work beyond the studio. His first post-operation television appearance was an uncredited (and almost unrecognisable) cameo on the Jackson 5 TV special *Goin' Back to Indiana*, in which he appears briefly in a comedy sketch. He then appeared on television in acting roles in *Cade's County*, *Ironside* and *Night Gallery*, and as a guest on *The Merv Griffin Show*.

Bobby's return to live performances in the autumn of 1971 surprisingly garnered little attention from the trade press, but, at the beginning of 1972, the number of concerts was increased. In February 1972, Bobby was back at the Desert Inn, this time with a larger band than had been the norm for some time. *Cash Box* wrote that during the performance, Bobby "shuffles, bugaloos, jokes, assays masterful impressions of Hollywood stars and celebs (even Howard Hughes), plays drums, piano, guitar, puffs out a few blues harmonica solos, and generally unleashes a torrent of versatility."[585] *Variety* reported that *For Once in My Life*, *Help Me Make it Through the Night*, *Can't Take My Eyes Off You*, *You've Lost That Lovin' Feelin'*, *Lazy River*, and *Midnight Special* were now all part of the act. The review also stated that "audience gives yocks to oldtime film clips (chases, crashes) sandwiched in before his turn at the drums – a good demo."[586]

At the end of February, Bobby was back at the Copa. Don Heckman in *The New York Times* wrote that, "elusive though his style may be – folky-humble at some points, Vegas-flashy at others – Darin is still a first-class performer."[587] *Cash Box* stated that "he has his usual confidence, of course, but it's no longer cockiness. He's matured to the point where he can kid himself (and he does about his height, his hair) and in doing so he completely wins over the audience."[588]

---

[585] *Cash Box*, "Bobby Darin," February 5, 1972, 35.
[586] Duke, "Night Club Reviews," *Variety*, February 16, 1972, 61.
[587] Don Heckman, "Bobby Darin Back in Song Program," *New York Times*, February 27, 1962, 61.
[588] M.O. "Bobby Darin," *Cash Box*, March 4, 1972, 21.

Bobby in Las Vegas, 1971 or 1972.

Bobby returned to Las Vegas in the spring, this time opening his performances with *That's All*, his former show closer. Other than that, though, it is interesting to notice that Bobby's repertoire went through relatively little change in the final couple of years of his life – quite unlike, for example, the year or two following his return to the stage in 1966. He was also busy on TV in 1972, returning to *The Tonight Show* and *The Flip Wilson Show*, as well as paying a visit to *The Dick Cavett Show* and *The Easter Seals Telethon*. March 1972 saw Bobby appearing on *The David Frost Show*, giving a lengthy interview as well as performing a number of songs. Complete with new hairpiece, Bobby looked younger than he had done for years, almost boy-like. During the interview he was thoroughly engaging, and often self-deprecating, and during the musical numbers he was on top form, particularly during a medley that saw him sing as well as play harmonica and piano before giving a fine solo on drums.

May-July, 1972: Studio Sessions
Bobby Darin LP

In what was no doubt an unintended piece of symmetry, the final album to be released in Bobby's lifetime was simply titled *Bobby Darin*, just as the first had been.

The problem with the 1972 album is that it is, for the most part, unadventurous and bland – two adjectives that would hardly ever have been used to describe Darin records prior to this point. The appearance on *The David Frost Show* had demonstrated that Bobby's abilities had not diminished, and so one can only sit and wonder just why the decision was chosen to record an MOR album of often mediocre songs with big, equally mediocre, orchestrations. The middle-of-the-road genre is not the problem here, and Bobby could have been just as successful at the genre (which was thriving at the time) as any other he tried. However, it is *how* this move was carried out that is the issue. Everything seems to be too big, too overblown, and Bobby himself spends most of his energy fighting against this, rather than giving a nuanced, intelligent performance.

The LP at least starts well with Bobby's version of Randy Newman's *Sail Away*. Darin takes the song and gives it a gospel-tinged feel, making the most out of the big chorus, but Newman didn't approve. When asked in a 2008 interview to name the worst cover of one of his songs, he cited Bobby's *Sail Away*, saying that "Bobby Darin could sing, but he did *Sail Away* and I don't think he understood it. He did it like it was a happy song about coming to America."[589] He goes on to say that Bobby didn't understand the references to slavery within the song. However, it could be that Darin fully understood the lyrics and subverted them even more by making the number *sound* as if it is about the glories of coming to America, with the real message hidden deeper in the lyrics. Whether he missed the point or not, this is undoubtedly the highlight of the album from a musical point of view. When released as a single, *Cash Box* said that "Randy Newman's sweet and pungent lyrics are a feast and Darin's at the head of the table. Could be his first big single for the label."[590]

I've Already Stayed too Long is a run-of-the-mill country song which is sadly over-arranged, with the brass in particular moving the genre from country to muzak – and this is often the issue with these recordings and the sessions that followed over the next year. Unlike virtually every other Darin album, the music here is dated rather than timeless. Even on below-par albums such as *18 Yellow Roses* and *Venice Blue*, the music hasn't dated, but here the orchestration is very much of its time. The song itself isn't particularly strong, although it is one of the few numbers on the album that is not a ballad and thus adds a little variety, but it is certainly not memorable. Bobby's voice also sounds rather thin, something which was not the case on *The David Frost Show* and so it is difficult to make a case that this is a result of the heart operation the year before.

Something in Her Love is the only song on the album which sees Bobby getting a writing credit, having written it with Tommy Amato. It is interesting that this also fits into the MOR genre, suggesting that the move into this style of music wasn't just a result of pressure or encouragement from the label, but something Bobby was seemingly invested in. Here, though, the arrangement is again overblown, and the vocal often gets lost or sounds as if it is fighting against the backing.

One of the better numbers is *Who Turned the World Around*. While Darin strains somewhat during the bridge section, at least the number has a memorable chorus that

---

[589] Tim Williams, "Interview: Randy Newman," *A Site Called Fred* [online], Available at: http://asitecalledfred.com/2008/09/11/interview-randy-newman/
[590] "Choice Programming," *Cash Box*, June 24, 1972, 20.

lingers in the mind after the record has ended – something that is all too often lacking on these songs. Because of the stronger melody, the big orchestral arrangement works better and, while this is hardly classic Darin, it is nice to hear him genuinely connecting with a song and giving it all he has.

Shipmates in Cheyenne sees Darin reaching once again into the songbook of John Denver, with a song he wrote with Joe Henry, although Denver's own recording wasn't released until 1975. The song's real name is actually *Shipmates and Cheyenne*, although this is not what Bobby appears to sing in his version. Despite the writing pedigree, this is hardly a highlight of the album, mostly because Bobby's vocal sounds so thin and has a sense of strain through most of it, something that could have been avoided with a lower key.

Let It Be Me finds Bobby saddled once again with an overblown, dated arrangement, although he hardly helps matters with his nasally vocal. The problem here and elsewhere on the album is that Bobby was, for the most part, not a singer who used volume in order to get his message across. His ballads were generally subdued affairs rather than having vocals that were bellowed in the way a Tom Jones or late-period Elvis Presley vocal might be. Here he is asked to produce that kind of vocal, and it doesn't work. Things get even worse during the final section of the track as Bobby recites the lyrics while the orchestra wails behind him, and the whole thing becomes almost laughable. This was not who Bobby Darin was.

U.S. album cover for the 1972 Motown LP.

Hard Headed Woman is considerably better, and this Cat Stevens cover was chosen as the flip-side of *Sail Away*. As with *Sail Away*, the backing vocals adds a slight gospel tinge to the proceedings, and the arrangement is relatively restrained in comparison to much of the album.

Average People is also an improvement on much of what has come before, not least because, like *Who Turned the World Around*, there is a memorable chorus. This still clearly isn't Bobby's "bag," but it comes off better than many of the numbers. Sadly, the song would also be somewhat prophetic with regards to Darin's personal life. Bobby had been in a relationship with Andrea Yeager since 1970, and the pair eventually got married in June 1973. However, as the lyrics of *Average People* state, "life was so much fun when we were living together/but as soon as we put on the rings everything changed," and the couple were divorced just five months later.

The next number, *I Used to Think it was Easy*, is a much better match of material and singer than some of the songs here. The bluesy piano at the opening of the number helps give the song a different feel from the outset, and the arrangement is also less overblown, allowing Bobby to put in a more relaxed performance. Oddly, though, the track is over and done with in just over two minutes, and if feels as if somehow something is missing or that it has been edited as it hasn't been given room to reach its potential.

The album ends with *My First Night Alone Without You*, which had been issued a few months previously on an album by David Cassidy and was later covered by Dionne Warwick in the same year. A comparison between Darin and Cassidy's versions highlights just how far the bar had dropped. Cassidy puts in a powerful vocal, whereas Bobby's is again in a key that is too high which sees him fighting against the orchestra, and he strains vocally even more than elsewhere.

The album was released in August 1972, and people didn't seem to care. This includes Bobby himself who, despite having a weekly TV series at this point, only sang *Sail Away* from the album on the show. *Variety* went through the motions of calling it a "wow" of an album, but the rest of the review is basically a list of songs.[591] One can also see just how unimportant the album was when it was released just by looking at the title of the *Variety* column of reviews for the week. Whereas Bobby's name used to be at the top of the list, now it is down at seventh. *Billboard* continued to prove that their psychic abilities were lacking by once again saying that the album would "bring him back to the charts with impact."[592] *Record World* were most enthusiastic: "Bespectacled for all photos on the album. Bobby Darin means business. He sings like blazes and the songs are combustible as well."[593] Indeed, one of the most positive things about the album was the cover, showing a picture of Bobby at work in the studio, seemingly photographed through the glass of the control booth, and using a palette of reds and oranges which is most effective.

The album was released in full on CD in 2016 as part of the double-disc set *Another Song on My Mind*, and, despite the LP's shortcomings, it is wonderful to finally have it on compact disc and in perfect sound. Alternate single mixes are also included.

---

[591] "R. Stewart, Airplane, Temptations, J.Cash, Ike & Tina, Paxton, Darin, S.Neely, Gore, Rebop Top LPs," *Variety*, August 23, 1972, 48.
[592] "Album Reviews," *Billboard*, August 19, 1972, 31.
[593] "Album Picks," *Record World*, August 19, 1972, 10.

"The Bobby Darin Amusement Company." *Bobbie Gentry was a guest on the first episode to be aired.*

BOBBY DARIN: DIRECTIONS

At a time when the momentum of Bobby Darin's career was at its lowest ebb, he was offered his own prime time variety show as the summer replacement for *The Dean Martin Show* on NBC. If the initial series, *The Bobby Darin Amusement Company*, was a success, then it was always going to be likely that a second series would follow, and that happened in January 1973 when the re-named *The Bobby Darin Show* first aired.

The series was a standard variety show for the period, neither better or worse than its competition. The seven shows managed to provide relatively big names as guest stars, such as Burt Reynolds, Bobbie Gentry, Debbie Reynolds, Dusty Springfield, Joan Rivers, Dionne Warwick and Donald O'Connor. All of these, however, appeared in the first four episodes. By the end of the series, Darin was playing host to The Smothers Brothers and Claudine Longet, who were hardly in the same league.

Perhaps the two most original elements were regular comedy sketches. The first was basically the equivalent of a five-minute sitcom featuring Bobby and Richard Bakalyan as Carmine and Angie in a sequence called *The Neighborhood*. This was a gentle comedy, always set on the steps of a tenement building, in which the two middle-aged characters talked about their lives and problems. At face value, there was nothing to it, but the sequence (which continued throughout both series) was particularly warm-hearted and very difficult to not like – and there was nothing quite like it on other variety shows of the period.

There was also nothing quite like Darin in drag as "The Godmother," which was completely unlike *The Neighborhood* in style. Darin's skits and interviews as The Godmother certainly lacked any subtlety at all, but were somewhat amusing, if only for the unscripted giggles and laughter that took place when either Darin or Geoff Edwards cracked an adlib or forgot, or messed up, lines. Edwards' part was to interview The Godmother as she enacted an agony aunt role, answering "questions from the public." Some of The Godmother sketches worked better than others, with some certainly not holding up in today's politically correct society!

Reviews of the programme were not ecstatic, but viewing figures were high enough to warrant the second series. Of *Amusement Company*, one reviewer wrote that "Darin isn't a strong enough, original enough, personality to survive in a fall TV slot, [but] it is fun to guess what he will copy next, or where the next spoof will come from." However, while "he did sing too much […] many sections were engagingly handled, and designed to bring out the best in the star. Or the best that Darin, in this borrowing mood of his, can presently show."[594]

Other reviews varied in how much they liked the series, and some were slightly bizarre. Steve Hoffman wrote that the first in the series was a "well-assembled hour" but made the comment that "an unnecessary bit in this premier was Bobby's habit of

---

[594] Dominique Paul North, "Bobby Darin Show Talent for Mimicry," *Milwaukee Journal*, July 28, 1972, 8.

kissing [George] Burns on the cheek, twice yet. It may be a sincere reflection of friendship between the two but nowadays, it causes people raise eyebrows."[595] *Variety* were more interested in the content of the show than giving questionable opinions on social mores. "Bobby Darin's summer replacement series got off to a sprightly debut," they wrote, "in an hour that was billed as 'comedy with music.' Actually, the musical portions were generally standout, with the comedic endeavours a trifle spotty – but still promising."[596]

At the time of writing, we have very little footage of *Amusement Company* available to us with which to judge it. A few songs (including a sizzling duet with Bobbie Gentry) turned up on the *Seeing is Believing* DVD, and a complete episode is available on YouTube thanks to a collector, but it is in poor quality for the first thirty minutes. That single episode, though, suggests that it was a better series than *The Bobby Darin Show* which followed in 1973. However, Bobby wasn't a natural host, and the show suffered from a lack of budget and a lack of vision. Perhaps James Nathan of the *Chicago Tribune* summed up both the 1972 and 1973 TV series best when he wrote that "what this first Darin show said to me was this: Bobby Darin is a fairly talented fellow, but the people in charge of putting his show together have all the theatrical ability of my left-hand desk drawer."[597]

Bobby's TV show got renewed, and would return the following year with a few changes (not necessarily for the better) and with the title changed to *The Bobby Darin Show*. However, *Variety* suggested that the renewal perhaps wasn't due to the quality of the programme or even audience figures. When discussing its chances of renewal, they wrote: "The skein's rating numbers have been gratifying – good news in itself – but its survival chances are enhanced by a realisation by NBC programmers that its September sked is a little topheavy with drama, and better balance would be established with more sitcom comedy or comedy-variety."[598]

During the second half of 1972, Bobby continued to perform on stage. At the Cocoanut Grove in Los Angeles, he received a rave review from the *Variety* critic, who wrote:

> Bobby Darin sings, jokes, does impersonations, plays harmonica,

---

[595] Steve Hoffman, "Darin's Series Is Well-Assembled Hour," *Cincinnati Enquirer* (Kentucky edition), July 28, 1972, 8.
[596] Bok, "Television Reviews," *Variety*, August 2, 1972, 34.
[597] James Nathan, "Bobby Darin Show Starts with a Fizzle," *Chicago Tribune*, July 28, 1972, section 2, 3.
[598] Bob Knight, "Summer TV Littered with Losers Re Prospects for Midseason, But Jury's Still Out For Darin Stanza," *Variety*, August 30, 1972, 31.

> guitar and piano, dances in places, imitates a trombone – and generally sparkles. He's brash, loud, uninhibited, engaging and thoroughly professional. Musically, he's a sort of solo rock 'n' roll revival. His appearance and approach are of the '50s and '60s – just right for the Grove crowd.[599]

The same publication was not so positive about his return to Las Vegas, however. With Shirley Bassey, no less, as his opening act, there was criticism that Bobby's act was too long: "It is his incessant '20 more times' of riffing the same old phrase that multiplies the time span needlessly. He also indulges in protracted patter, some of it amusing, but the majority only time-consuming ego stuff and nonsense. The folk period at the near-end should also be shortened."[600] *Billboard* disagreed, writing that "Bobby Darin will be the next performer to join the select rank of what is termed a Las Vegas Superstar. His Hilton outing is probably the best of his career."[601] When he played the Copa in October and November, *Variety* conceded that "Darin impresses as a performer who has gone beyond the singing medium. He delivers in all departments skilfully, even when he flings language not of the drawing room variety."[602]

More than a decade after some misjudged comments, and some misquotes, some members of the press still appeared to hold a grudge against Bobby. Following a performance in Chicago in December 1972, Will Leonard praised Bobby's talent but referred to him as brash, arrogant, hard-boiled and cold-blooded.[603] Twelve months later, when Bobby passed away, those same sentiments were present in many obituaries.

Early November, 1972

In November 1972, Bobby entered the studio to record a new song, *Happy*. Released as a single, it would be the final record release of his career, and reached #67 in the charts. That may not sound much, but it was his highest charting single since *The Lady Came from Baltimore* in 1966, and his first to chart at all since 1969.

Happy took an instrumental theme from the film *The Lady Sings the Blues*, which starred Diana Ross as Billie Holiday, and added words by Smokey Robinson. Darin

---

[599] Luc, "Grove, L. A.," *Variety*, July 26, 1972, 53.
[600] Will, "Hilton, Las Vegas," *Variety*, September 13, 1972, 87.
[601] Laura Deni, "Bobby Darin, Shirley Bassey," *Billboard*, September 30, 1972, 14.
[602] Jose, "Copacabana, N.Y.," *Variety*, November 1, 1972, 63.
[603] Will Leonard, "Bobby Turns Up the Burners Without a Care for Warmth," *Chicago Tribune*, December 1, 1972, section 2, 4.

turns the number into an epic. The song has a huge orchestral arrangement but, for once, this works out in Darin's favour, as it is more restrained than the earlier efforts. Even when the full force of the band is heard during the bridge section, Bobby shows that he can compete, and he belts out this section before turning on a dime to a much softer voice for the end of the vocal. The single clocks in at just under four minutes, but the version released posthumously on LP is two minutes longer, although Darin doesn't sing a single note extra. Instead, the extra two minutes are an extended orchestral outro, with backing vocals at the very end adding a gospel feel once again to the proceedings. The number and production were atypical Darin, but show that he could still deliver even this late in the game. His enthusiasm for the song carried over into the new year, with him singing it twice on his TV show. *Billboard* called the single "one of Darin's finest performances on record."[604]

Japanese single release of "Happy" — with Bobby's name misspelt "Bobby Darlin," and a picture of Diana Ross.

January – March 1973: TV Performances
The Bobby Darin Show

> "*The Bobby Darin Show*, [...] is as imaginative in concept as its title: Star sings, guest sings or does whatever it is that guest does, star and guest do production number, star sings, credit rolls. What lifts the Darin show a notch above its category is the genuine talent of its star."[605]

This was the verdict of the *New York Times* when the second incarnation of Bobby's TV series started airing in January 1973.

The programme was no longer called *The Bobby Darin Amusement Company*, and, instead, resorted to the more predictable *The Bobby Darin Show*. The emphasis this time around was more on music, although it did keep both *The Neighborhood* and *The*

---

[604] Don Ovens, "Radio Action and Pick Singles," *Billboard*, November 25, 1972, 57.
[605] "Keep Smiling and Pass the Dip," *New York Times*, February 4, 1973, 121.

Godmother comedy sections of the previous series. *Amusement Company* had hardly been a show to help revive the then-flagging variety format on television, but it was at least easygoing, good quality entertainment. *The Bobby Darin Show* was a decided step down in quality.

One of the writers, Howard Albrecht, wrote that "a strange thing happened at the beginning of the fall season; we lost our 'fun.' [...] The light, casual, fun-loving atmosphere that permeated the earlier edition of our little entertainment just wasn't happening in this new series."[606] Albrecht also states that it was Bobby himself who wanted to change the format for the second series and lose much of the comedy.

Certainly, there is little spark on the screen, and often even little enthusiasm from Bobby himself for the series. In an interview with Johnny Carson on *The Tonight Show* in February 1973, he said:

> I'm really excited when I'm performing. I must say that television is not my idea of a happy land in which to work, only for the simple reason that it is difficult for my kind of person to compromise as heavily and as fully as television insists upon. And I don't mean to take away from any of the executives or producers or writers, it's just the kind of medium where all of a sudden they say "we really can't do it again, the budget doesn't allow it, and we have to get it out because next Friday we're on." And I'm used to a little more control. You walk out to a night-club audience or to a theatre audience and something goes a little awry, they can relate to it because it happens right there, and there's a humanness about it. The tube seems to want to break up the rhythm between us, well between me at least, and the person at home. And I wish I could feel totally comfortable. [...] Perhaps I am too aware of it. Perhaps I am too self-conscious about the fact that there is an interrupting device called the camera.

While this may well have been how Bobby genuinely felt about television, it was hardly the sensible thing to say when trying to encourage people to watch his show.

While there were still some big names appearing as guest stars on the series, many were either past their best or simply suffered from overexposure on television. While the first episode of *The Dean Martin Show* in 1973 featured Gene Kelly as a guest star, the first of *The Bobby Darin Show* only managed Burl Ives. Ives was an amiable enough guest, but hardly a big name. Variety wrote in their review of the first episode that the guests "failed to measure up to [the] Darin powerhouse."[607]

---

[606] Howard Albrecht, *See You in Nairobi: How Work Became Fun – the Second Time Around. Adventures in the Laugh Trade* (Bloomington: AuthorHouse, 2005), 153.
[607] Tone, "The Bobby Darin Show," *Variety*, January 22, 1973, 12.

Meanwhile, the comedy skit from the end of each show in the 1972 series was excised in favour of a half-hearted, and seemingly low budget, tribute to an American city in comedy and song, with Darin acting as a roving reporter. Sadly, the comedy element of this section was often an embarrassment, and the musical part seemingly thrown together with little effort. Elsewhere, audiences were treated to Bobby playing chess against a computer for a number of weeks – an example of him completely misjudging his audience as well as being extremely self-indulgent. "I wasn't too crazy about Darin's ego trip (it's still there, all right) on the chess segment," one critic wrote, "because its presentation did not lend itself to the even flow of the rest of the program."[608]

Musically the shows were sound, but unadventurous. Most of the songs that Bobby sang as his solo numbers came from his albums of standards (including the occasional one from albums recorded but not released). There were also covers of recent hits taken from his live repertoire, such as *Song Sung Blue*, *Alone Again Naturally*, *If*, *Can't Take My Eyes Off You*, and *Sweet Caroline*. However, everything seemed very safe. There were few numbers where Bobby really shined, and he chose not to sing some of the more interesting numbers from his live act of recent years such as *Lady Madonna*, *And When I Die*, *Hi-De-Ho*, or the Beatles medley. Also missing were many of Bobby's hits, such as *Dream Lover*, *Things*, *You're the Reason I'm Living* and *18 Yellow Roses*. Interestingly, some of the songs in the first series made use of a kind of split screen format, with Bobby shown from different angles within boxes on a black background. This at least set the presentation of the songs apart from other variety shows of the period, but this idea was dropped for *The Bobby Darin Show*.

Much of the problem with the musical element was the band employed to back Darin. This wasn't as big as the one he used during live performances, nor was it the four-piece that he can be seen using during his run on *The Mike Douglas Show* back in 1970. Instead, it is a halfway house that doesn't work either for contemporary songs *or* standards. It is too brassy for one, and too small for the other. It simply sounds thin, no matter what style of music is being played. Occasionally, everything came together and Bobby showed exactly how good a vocalist he was, such as on his performance of *Dreidel* or his stunning rendition of *Come Rain or Come Shine* that starts off as Sinatra and ends as Ray Charles. However, for the most part, Bobby came over as bland, partly to do with his performance, partly to do with the watered-down arrangements for the watered down band, and partly because of the material.

Some of the material was *very* questionable. For example, one has to wonder who came up with the idea of Bobby and Carol Lawrence duetting on *There's a Hole in my Bucket*. The number might have worked with semi-regular guest Charlene Wong, but she was just eight years old, and there would have been a cuteness about it, as there

---

[608] Dan Lewis, "Can Ego and Maturity Both Be Bobby Darin?" *Lakeland Ledger*, April 1, 1973, 38.

was with all of Bobby's songs with her. However, Carol Lawrence was over forty at the time she and Bobby joined forces on the song, sung on a bare stage, and for no apparent reason. With these kinds of decisions, it was inevitable that the show would not be renewed for another season.

There was one final element that brought down *The Bobby Darin Show*, and that was Bobby's own health, which was getting steadily worse once again. There are a couple of episodes towards the end of the series where he barely smiles at all, and is clearly struggling just to get through the show.

Despite Bobby's worsening health, the series did at least go out on a high note. For the final episode, the normal format was thrown out of the window while Bobby went on stage and performed what was basically his night-club act for a full seventy minutes. The performance was edited for broadcast, and bookended a guest appearance by Peggy Lee. Lee and Darin sat together on a bench and sang a medley of songs that had appeared on the *Love Swings* album over a decade earlier, but that duet is not a highlight of the series — or even the episode. It is the unedited concert section that is very special. This was (as far we know) Darin's last television performance, and his swan song showed just how great he was when he forgot about (or, rather, ignored) all the things he disliked about television. The oxygen cylinder was beside the stage throughout the filming, and Darin is seen leaving the stage during the DVD release of the show, but no-one would know that he had health problems at this time. Highlights included a fine version of *Bridge Over Troubled Water* (another song he could and should have recorded in the studio for Motown), an epic rendition of *Midnight Special* and a final medley reminiscent of the one that ended the *Live at the Desert Inn* album.

Bobby as the Godmother.

Four songs from that final show have been released on CD. The first of these, *Beyond the Sea*, has been issued in two forms. The first is the full nine minute version, on a package called *A&E Biography: A [Musical] Anthology*, and the second, on *Aces Back to Back*, sees the number fade out after three minutes or so. The extended running time is due, as with the 1971 live version, to Darin's comedy routine based around the last line. This works fine when accompanied by visuals, but becomes tiresome when only the audio is available. Musically, the performance is sound, although the thin sound of the band is hardly a suitable replacement for the full orchestra heard on other versions.

Also on the *A&E Biography* disc is *Higher and Higher*. Again, this gets a good performance, vibrant and full of energy from a singer who clearly felt neither of those things due to his health. Strangely, the CD issue includes dialogue from the Flamingo concerts in 1963 where Darin introduces Sammy Davis Jr to the audience attached to the beginning of the 1973 performance, to make it look as if both dialogue and music are from the same show.

The last song from this show on the disc is *If I Were a Carpenter*. As with *Higher and Higher*, one has to wonder if Bobby ever gave a poor performance of this song. The two songs require such different styles of singing that it is difficult to comprehend how this is even possible, especially when Bobby was far from healthy at the time.

The final song from the final episode can be found on *Aces Back to Back*, a rather strange compilation of live cuts, rarities and regular recordings with no specific theme and, annoyingly, no recording information in the booklet. *Can't Take My Eyes Off You* sees Bobby taking on a song that had already been a hit for both Frankie Valli and Andy Williams. This is one of the highlights of the final show, with Bobby using an arrangement that doesn't change the recognised format of the song and yet allows him to put his own stamp on it.

Other songs from the series that have appeared on audio CD include covers of two recent hits for other singers, *Song Sung Blue* and *Alone Again Naturally*. The first is an amiable version of a Neil Diamond song that hasn't aged well through the years. While Diamond's *Sweet Caroline* has become a somewhat kitsch classic that is beloved by karaoke singers everywhere, *Song Sung Blue* failed to reach that kind of status, and one looks back now and wonders why so many singers wanted to cover it.

Bobby's version of *Alone Again Naturally* finds him treating the song with care and injecting genuine emotion into it. However, it still remains a remarkably morose number in anybody's hands, which is hardly surprising considering the song starts off by letting us know that the singer is thinking about committing suicide. On the plus side, Bobby gives a fine performance, and clearly loves the song and the challenges that it brings. The arrangement also helps, using the less-is-more theory when it comes to instrumentation, despite the fact it runs for nearly five minutes.

This Could Be the Start of Something Big and *A Quarter to Nine* are songs that Bobby recorded in the studio in 1965 and 1966 respectively, but remain unissued. The live versions here show Bobby in good form, although the house band just isn't beefy enough to do justice to these big band charts. Darin shouts asides to them during an instrumental, as if to try to prove to us that he is "into" it, but there is a spark missing, and he probably knew as well as everybody else that the connection between singer and band just wasn't there despite his fine vocals.

One song on *Aces Back to Back* that appears to be a bit of a mystery is *Lazy River*. The sound of both Darin and the band would suggest that this is from the 1972 or 1973 TV series, but there is no listing of *Lazy River* having been performed on either show. With the liner notes not helping us out on the origins of the performance, we will make the assumption that it is from one of the *Amusement Company* shows that we have little information on. No matter where it is from, this is a great performance of his hit, with Bobby's voice sounding more powerful here than in the 1973 shows which, again, would hint at it coming from the earlier series.

Finally on CD is the duet of *All I Have to do is Dream* with Petula Clark. This is a delight, with the song being arranged with care and the voices blending beautifully. There were certainly some duds during the series when it came to the duet numbers, but this is one of the best, and was even released as a single back in 2004 to help promote the *Aces Back to Back* release.

February 4, 1973: Studio Session

For many years, it was assumed that *Happy* was recorded at Bobby's last visit to a recording studio. We now know that this was not the case, and that a further session occurred on February 4, 1973, producing two songs.

I Won't Last a Day Without You, written by Paul Williams and Roger Nichols, is the first of the songs to stem from this date. What is most noticeable here is that Bobby's voice is clearer, stronger and higher in the mix than in the June 1972 recordings. While this is still in MOR territory (it was a hit for The Carpenters, and you can't get more MOR than that), the arrangement hasn't dated as badly as some of the earlier ones. There is no sign of strain here, and the whole thing, while hardly cutting-edge music, seems far more convincing than most of the 1972 Motown LP.

Another Song on My Mind is a song written by Darin with Tommy Amato and, as with *Something in Her Love*, shows Bobby writing with success in this genre, and producing melody and lyrics that are considerably more memorable than some of the tracks he recorded during this period. Here, again, the orchestra is present, but not overwhelming, with more emphasis on Bobby's core band. Given the success of artists such as The Carpenters during this period, this could have worked well as a single, particularly with some promotion through television appearances.

Shortly after recording these songs, Bobby gained a release from his Motown contract. *Another Song on My Mind* is the last known completed song that Bobby recorded in the studio. It was, perhaps, a fitting title with which to end a career on.

1970-1973

*

Outside of his own TV series, Bobby's last television appearance was on the *Midnight Special* show, broadcast in March 1973. His is a performance of two halves. He walks on to the stage to sing *If I Were a Carpenter* to start, and looks unwell. He even holds on to the piano during the song, as if to steady himself. However, when he sits down to play a medley of *Dream Lover*, *Splish Splash* and *Roll Over Beethoven*, he puts on a performance that still astounds. It is like watching a different performer entirely. He rocks this medley in a way that goes beyond any of the other versions of it that we have, including that in the last episode of *The Bobby Darin Show*. He doesn't just play the piano, he *pounds* it, bouncing up and down on the stool. When he pulls out his harmonica, he gives a blistering solo, and there is a feeling here that he just doesn't want the moment to end. He is thoroughly caught up in what he is doing, and the memory of the almost frail nature of *If I Were a Carpenter* from a few moments earlier is obliterated. It is a wonderful, timeless, performance, and it's great to see him being appreciated by the young crowd. A few days after the *Midnight Special* appearance, Bobby cancelled a schedule appearance at the Waldorf-Astoria in New York, presumably due to health reasons.

In June 1973, Bobby married his long-term girlfriend Andrea Yeager, but they were divorced just five months later. In July and August 1973, Bobby gave his last live performances. The shows at the Hilton in Las Vegas got good reviews, although Bobby again had barely changed his set-list, except that he was now opening with *Get Me to the Church On Time*. His last live performance was on August 26.

Also in August, the film *Happy Mother's Day, Love George* opened in cinemas. This mystery thriller starred Ron Howard and Patricia Neal, and featured Bobby in a supporting role. *Variety* had mixed feelings about the film, saying it was a "generally entertaining suspense item" but bemoaning the fact that it appeared to have been heavily edited prior to release.[609] The trade journal also commented that the film gave Bobby "his first good role since *Captain Newman M. D.*" In the *New York Times*, Roger Greenspun gave the film a mauling. He noted that the film featured several distinguished performers: "Chloris Leachman was seen to better advantage in *Last Picture Show*. Ron Howard is currently seen to better advantage in *American Graffiti*. And Patricia Neal may be seen to better advantage any time in Maxim Coffee television commercials."[610] Bobby wasn't mentioned at all in the review, for which he may have been thankful given the comments made about his fellow actors.

In truth, the film did not see Bobby ending his career on a high note. His performance was solid, but the film is a barely-watchable mess, with the script switching back and forth between pretentious twaddle and trashy horror. At one

---

[609] Robe, "Happy Mother's Day…Love George," *Variety*. August 22, 1973, 12.

[610] Roger Greenspun, "*Happy Mothers' Day* Arrives," *New York Times*, August 18, 1973, 26.

moment it has shades of *Whatever Happened to Baby Jane*, and at others it seems to take its lead from a film such as *Twisted Nerve*. Sadly, it is not successful in emulating either, and only Bobby, Simon Oakland and Ron Howard come out of the movie with any dignity, despite the starry cast.

Bobby's health got steadily worse over the next few months, and he retreated from public life. He was admitted to hospital in December 1973 for an operation to repair the artificial heart valves he had received in February 1971. He didn't recover from the procedure, and he passed away on December 20, 1973 at the age of 37.

There was no funeral; Bobby Darin left his body to medical science.

At the piano. c.1959.

CODA
HERE I'LL STAY: 1974-2019

When Bobby Darin passed away on 20th December 1973, it made little impact, and many newspapers that covered the story did so with little sympathy. The *New York Times* at least gave Bobby the dignity of a reasonable amount of column inches, and had some relatively kind things to say about his career. "He let it be known that he would become a legend by the time he was 25," they misquoted, "and he came near to achieving that goal."[611] Like other coverage of Bobby's death, the article was littered with unnecessary inaccuracies, but at least it wasn't seemingly written with the venom of some other commentators.

The *Variety* obituary was part fact, part fiction. According to the article, Bobby had composed *That's All*, which he most definitely did not, and had supposedly written the music for films that didn't even exist.[612] As was usual with *Variety* obituaries of the period, it consisted of nothing but a series of "facts" about Bobby's life, with no attempt at any real tribute. The article announcing the death in the *Chicago Tribune* was equally lacking in emotion, but at least gave a better portrait of who Bobby was and why, telling readers how he had fought, despite his health, to escape the poverty of his childhood to become a star.[613]

In the UK, *The Times* referred to *Beyond the Sea* as an "old ballad hit," and managed to muster enough enthusiasm to refer to Bobby as a "polished showman."[614] The *Daily Mirror* was particularly unkind, referring to Darin as "the son of a small-time gangster" and, in reference to the legend-at-25 quote, said he "never achieved his life's

---

[611] "Bobby Darin, Pop Singer, Dies at 37," *New York Times*, December 21, 1973, 38.
[612] "Obituaries," *Variety*, December 26, 1973, 47.
[613] "Bobby Darin Dies: Teen Rock Idol," *Chicago Tribune*, December 21, 1973, section 1A, 14.
[614] "Bobby Darin Singer and Actor," *The Times*, December 21, 1973, 17.

ambition."[615]

In early 1974, Motown pulled together a mish-mash of leftovers from the vaults for a tribute album simply called *Darin 1936-1973*, which *Variety* called an "admirable tribute,"[616] and *Billboard* were slightly more honest and said that it "represents the searching, unsteady pattern of Darin's last musical years."[617] All but two of the performances were unreleased, and one of those previously available, *Happy*, was seen here in a version two minutes longer than the single release. Two of the songs were cuts from the 1971 live album that was still unreleased at that time, and one has to wonder why that superior concert wasn't issued instead of this LP of mostly studio recordings, especially as the planned original title was *Finally*, which would have been particularly fitting given the circumstances. Three of the songs on the tribute album were picked from the unreleased studio album *Go Ahead*, which had been recorded, mixed, and shelved in 1971. At least Motown did something to commemorate the passing of Bobby Darin, his other labels didn't even put together a greatest hits package, let alone raid their vaults for unissued material.

Australian World Record Club LP

With the exception of the emergence in 1976 of a single unissued track, it would be over a dozen years before any more unreleased Darin appeared in music stores. Again, this came from Motown, who had eventually got around to issuing the wonderful 1971 live album in 1987.

It seems remarkable now to think that almost all of Bobby's albums were out of print at this time and had been for years. As the CD era progressed, slowly but surely some Darin material was issued on the new medium. In 1989, Capitol released the *Collectors Series* CD which brought together a number of his single sides for the label, most of which had been unavailable for a couple of decades. Also included, by necessity as the master was lost at the time, was an alternate take of *Wait by the Water*. A couple of years later, Atlantic issued two "best of" CDs, with one concentrating on rock 'n' roll, country and folk, and the other made up of standards. Again, these were

---

[615] Sydney Young, "Bobby Darin Dies at 37 in Heart Op," *Daily Mirror,* December 21, 1973, 11.
[616] "Morrison, Peebles, Mountain Jacks, Ingredient Kendricks, Darin, Davidson Top New LPs," *Variety*, March 6, 1974, 54.
[617] "Billboard's Recommended LP's *(sic),*" *Billboard*, March 9, 1974, 58.

welcome, but very few songs from the 1965-1967 stay at Atlantic were included, and nothing at all from *In a Broadway Bag* despite the success of *Mame*. However, at this point something was better than nothing – but the representation of Bobby Darin's legacy on CD remained pitiful.

Eventually a few of the ATCO albums started to be reissued on CD, and in 1994 things seemed to be slowly changing in Bobby's favour, not least with the release of *Spotlight on Bobby Darin*, a release from Capitol that combined a number of standards with a handful of previously unreleased recordings. This was the start of a succession of releases from Capitol which would contain unreleased performances.

1995 was a big turning point, with Rhino issuing a 4CD retrospective of Bobby Darin's career, including a number of unreleased performances. These included a handful of cuts from the shelved 1963 live album recorded at the Flamingo in Las Vegas, demo recordings of *Dream Lover* and *Simple Song of Freedom*, and material recorded just before Bobby set up the Direction label. The boxed set was most welcome, however, for presenting the consumer with a one-stop overview of Bobby's career that was desperately needed at that time. With the exception of Decca, recordings from all labels were included, and tracks that had been out of print for over thirty years were finally available to be heard once again.

The Rhino set effectively opened the floodgates when it came to issuing Bobby on CD, and over the next dozen years all but one of Bobby's domestic lifetime albums saw a re-release. What's more, the flow of unreleased material continued unabated. The *A&E Biography* CD was a slightly strange mix of old and new material that was put together for no obvious reason, but still included a new studio master in *Love Look Away*, more material from the 1963 Flamingo concerts, and a number of songs from the final episode of the 1973 TV series.

Even more interesting was *The Unreleased Capitol Sides,* a collection of more than twenty unreleased studio masters together with a couple of songs that had already been released a few years earlier. Here, Darin fans got their first taste of the unreleased albums that had been languishing in the Capitol vaults for more than thirty years. While not all the tracks were Bobby at his very best, the album also introduced us to a number of new Darin classics such as *What Kind of Fool Am I*, *This Nearly Was Mine*, and *If I Ruled the World*. After being out of print for a number of years, the album is now once again available, this time as a download with the title *Rare Capitol Masters* and including yet more previously unreleased songs.

2000 saw the eventual release of the 1963 live album recorded at the Flamingo. Again, this was a revelation for fans, not least because it allowed them to see just how much Bobby's live act had changed in the three years after the *Darin at the Copa* LP. For years, people had read about Bobby's folk set within his Las Vegas shows, and now, at long last, they were able to hear it for themselves and realise just how effective it was.

While the mid-2000s saw a slowing down in the amount of unreleased material, this was also the period when the Collector's Choice label brought a cavalcade of Bobby's lesser known ATCO albums to CD for the first time, including *Winners*, *Love Swings*, *It's You or No One*, and *Bobby Darin sings Ray Charles*. In truth, the fact that these key albums had not been reissued five or ten years earlier was something approaching criminal, but at least the wrong had eventually been righted. A couple of years later, the UK label Edsel brought the Direction albums to CD as well, complete with the non-album singles from the period, meaning that the only original album without a CD release at this time was the *Bobby Darin* Motown release from 1972.

Part of this flurry of reissues was no doubt down to the publicity created by the release of the biopic of Bobby Darin, *Beyond the Sea*, from 2004, which starred, and was directed by, Kevin Spacey.

A biopic had been planned as early as 1975, when ABC planned to make a TV movie, co-produced by Bobby's friend Don Kirshner, but it was dropped after the network was notified that "the Darin estate claims all rights to the Darin story for motion picture and all media."[618] The project then got taken to NBC, who were told by Gerald Lipsky, executor of the Darin Estate, "that if it doesn't drop its plans to telefilm a Darin special, he will file immediate proceedings to restrain" the network from doing so.[619] NBC decided that the world didn't a Bobby Darin biography after all.

In 1981, it was reported that a film was being developed based on Al DiOrio's biography *Borrowed Time*.[620] In April 1982, Variety announced that auditions had started to pick the unknown actor who would play Bobby. They had taken place at the West Side Arts Theater in New York. One of the producers of the film, Stephen Metz, told Robert B. Frederick that "our goal is to show that Bobby Darin was not just a singer or a songwriter but a major personality who touched on many people's lives."[621] Unfortunately, this film didn't get off the ground either.

The Spacey film of 2004 created publicity for Bobby and its star, but it didn't create a stampede for tickets to see it, and this author saw the film the day after release in the UK – and was the *only* person watching that particular screening. Nearly fifteen years on, the film is still a divisive issue amongst fans, and there's no doubt that it was a flawed effort. However, it also attempted to be something more than just a traditional biopic, and included fantasy sequences as well as being self-referential. In the end, the esoteric and left-field elements prevented the film from being commercial, but one has to wonder if Bobby himself would have approved of the

---

[618] "Estate Vs. NBC On a Darin Bio; Claim Prior Right," *Variety*, June 18, 1975, 35.
[619] Ibid.
[620] "Bobby Darin Story," *Variety*, September 6, 1981, 4.
[621] Robert B. Frederick, "Reno-Metz Readies Darin Biopic; Audition Looks, Voice, Chutzpah," *Variety*, April 14, 1982, 25.

chances taken with the project, and the answer is probably that he would have done. After all, Darin himself often decided not to take the tried and tested route and to push his audiences to their limits. The Christmas album was not a tradition seasonal offering; *Earthy!* wasn't a straightforward folk album; *It's You or No One* was certainly a "difficult" album of standards; and introducing a folk section into a Las Vegas act was a considerable risk, as was performing the Direction material at a venue such as the Copa. Sometimes risks and ambitious projects pay off, and sometimes they don't. In the case of *Beyond the Sea*, it was probably a case of the latter, but Bobby may well have liked the idea that something slightly left-field was being attempted, and there is little doubting that the film had its heart in the right place.

Around the same time the film was being released, an important CD appeared entitled *Songs from Big Sur* which brought together for the first time a compilation of the material Bobby recorded at Direction, as well as two new studio masters and four live cuts from his shows at the Troubadour. The CD is one of the best of the posthumous releases, especially considering the original Direction albums had yet to be re-released at this point. The new live cuts were a delight, although one has to wonder why more of them have not appeared since. A complete "live at the Troubadour" disc would be especially welcome, not least because Bobby was performing some songs at that time that he never recorded. *Songs from Big Sur* also allowed fans to hear a number of the single sides from the Direction period that never made it to an album, most notably the glorious *Maybe We Can Get it Together*.

Around the same time, a CD/DVD package entitled *Aces Back to Back* was also released, this time with substantial fanfare. The album even had a CD single taken from it, featuring Bobby in a duet with Petula Clark singing *All I Have to Do is Dream*. However, the album failed to live up to its rather boastful title. The DVD contained, amongst other things, video footage of the first seven tracks of the CD, all of which were taken from Bobby's 1972-3 TV series. However, given the amount of material from the series that was available, it seemed strange that two songs from the already-released final show of the series were repeated here, meaning fans were actually only getting five new songs and not seven. Perhaps even more bizarre was the inclusion of *Long Time Movin'* and *Jive* when both had recently appeared on the *Songs from Big Sur* album. Did both of these songs need to appear on CD twice within a few months of each other? The highlight here was undoubtedly the three tracks taken from the *Milk Shows*, the five-minute daily radio programme from 1963, and featuring Bobby accompanied by just a jazz combo.

Perhaps the most annoying thing about *Aces Back to Back* is that it was clearly made with the fan and collector in mind, and yet contained absolutely no information in the booklet as to when songs were recorded, or what they were recorded for. One could easily work out from what information *is* given that the 1972-3 TV series was the source for some of the songs, but we are told nothing about where the live *Lazy River* (mistitled *Up a Lazy River*) comes from or where *Mack the Knife* or *Simple Song of Freedom* originate. While any new Bobby Darin material was (and still is) most welcome, it doesn't take much to include basic recording information within the accompanying booklet. However, the release was, in many ways, a sign of things to come.

2006 saw the DVD release of *Seeing is Believing*, containing an hour of Bobby's television performances, mostly from the 1972-3 TV series. Once again, there are some strange decisions here, not least including *Beyond the Sea* with the ending chopped off during the main programme and picked up again during the credits section available by navigating through the main menu. *Higher and Higher* was repeated from the *Mack is Back* DVD of the complete concert segment of the final show. On two occasions, the programme switches from the 1972-3 series to appearances on *The Ed Sullivan Show* from 1959, with no explanation or logic. Surely it would have been more sensible to excise these from the main running order and to have included them as a bonus feature. As with *Aces Back to Back*, there is no information on what songs were recorded on what dates, or even who Bobby's duet partners (Bobbie Gentry and Connie Francis) are. Again, the release of new Bobby Darin material was great for fans, and this DVD managed to collect together many of Bobby's best performances from the TV series, but that doesn't excuse the slightly slap-dash approach with regards to editing or lack of information.

However, even worse was to come: nothing. 2007 brought fans a CD release of the Direction albums but, after that, Bobby Darin releases almost dried up completely. A few European releases included an alternate take or two, or a rare single side, but other than that there was virtually nothing new forthcoming for the Bobby Darin fan until 2013, when the DVD release of all episodes from the 1973 TV series was announced. Suspicions arose when Amazon first listed the product, as the running time was shown as 420 minutes, an average of just 32 minutes per show when they should have been around 47.

The Bobby Darin Show was not the greatest variety show to hit television screens to start with, but one of the main things it had going for it was

DVD release

Bobby's singing, especially songs that he hadn't recorded elsewhere, or fan favourites that he rarely performed on TV. Alas, many of these songs are missing, most notably tracks such as *Something*, *A Nightingale Sang in Berkeley Square*, *Sixteen Tons*, *Lonesome Road* and *Once Upon a Time*. This results in bringing down the standard of the episodes as a whole. With the best bits literally taken out, many episodes flounder as they move from one comedy section to the next or to Bobby playing chess against a computer (yes, folks, at least *that* section was retained for us to enjoy!).

The Bobby Darin Estate issued a disclaimer-cum-apology which, it has to be said, was an unusual and welcome move, but the chances of these shows getting a fuller release in the future seems unlikely. The reasons for the edits remain something of a mystery. Copyright issues have caused edits to occur on DVD releases of variety shows before, but the situation appears to go deeper than that. *Caravan* was cut, but had already appeared on *Seeing is Believing*, and *Happy* was included on the second of the two episodes it was performed on, but not the first. If permission can be obtained for one performance of a song to be included, logic suggests that it can be obtained for another performance of the same number in the same set of DVDs.

The May 2014 statement by the Bobby Darin Estate said that they were working on improving the quality of the concert-style final show in preparation for a new release (it last appeared in 2000). At the time of writing, nearly five years later, no announcement has been made on whether this will ever see the light of day. In January 2015, Jimmy Scalia, the Darin archivist, announced a forthcoming CD and DVD set was in the works, entitled *From Bronx to Broadway*, and that it would include at least two unreleased songs. As of January 2019, that has also not materialised.

2014 saw a release that was more successful: *The Milk Shows*. This 2CD set included ninety tracks from the 1963 radio series, all in remarkably good sound. The packaging was also attractive and the CDs put together well on the whole, despite the strange issue of Bobby talking and singing at the same time due to the amateurish crossfade between songs. For the first time in too long, though, here was a new product containing new material that was truly worthy of the Bobby Darin name (indeed, it took twelve years from the finding of this material to it being released).

2016 saw Real Gone Music release a double disc of Bobby's Motown albums and singles called *Another Song on My Mind*. This included the 1972 studio album, the tribute album from 1974, as well as all sides of Bobby's Motown singles, some in various mixes. There was no unreleased music, but this was the first time the 1972 album had been in print in four decades. Two years later, the same label surprised fans everywhere by releasing a further CD, this time containing two dozen unreleased studio tracks covering 1970-1971. *Go Ahead and Back Up* was subtitled *The Lost Motown Masters*, but one could certainly question whether some of these recordings would have

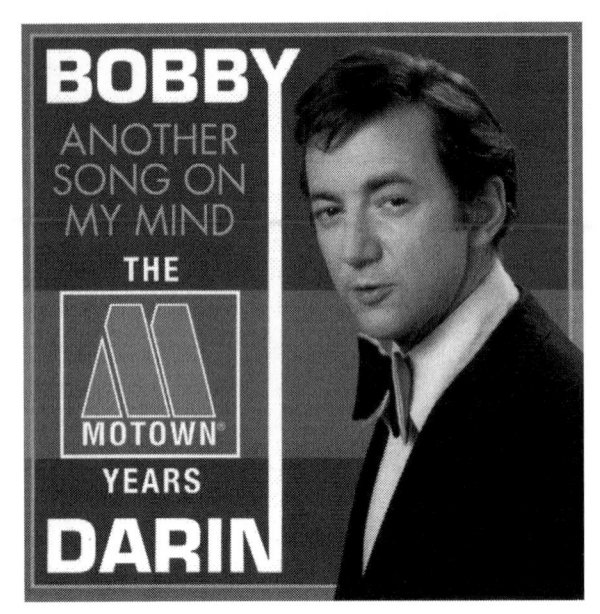

"Another Song On My Mind" CD

been viewed as masters rather than outtakes. Still, the release was something of a milestone, not just because of the music, but also because of the amount of new information supplied in the booklet about this period in Bobby's career.

Meanwhile, 2017 saw the release of an expanded version of the *Two of a Kind* album, including a handful of alternate takes and two previously unreleased songs. It is unknown why the final unreleased song from those sessions was not included.

While all of Bobby's lifetime albums have now been issued at one point or another during the CD era, the current situation isn't quite as buoyant. In 2008, all but three albums were still in print on CD. In 2018, most albums are no longer available on compact disc, with even absolute classics such as *This is Darin* and *That's All* out of print on CD in America. In Europe, Warner re-released ten of Bobby's ATCO albums over two budget five-disc sets, but only one of these is still in print, meaning some of Bobby's most iconic albums are not available anywhere in editions released by official labels.

It is an appalling state of affairs considering how good things were looking just ten years ago. It is almost as if we are going back in time to the awful situation that I talked about at the very beginning of this book where I entered a shop in the mid-1990s and was faced with just a couple of discs to choose from. Of course, the situation is a little different now, in that we can go online and find used copies of practically any compact disc that we want, but that hardly seems to be the point. Many of Bobby's contemporaries are getting expanded releases of their albums on CD, with remastered sound, bonus tracks and new informative liner notes – so why not Bobby?

The two Warner European five-disc sets at least kept ten of the ATCO albums in print, but these are albums worthy of deluxe treatment, not just a bare bones reissue in cardboard sleeves in a slipcase. Surely, nearly sixty years after they were recorded, it is time for the jazz combo performances from January 1960 to finally be released in one place resulting in a deluxe issue of *Winners* that would also include the single sides *Bill Bailey*, *Minnie the Moocher* and the unavailable-since-1965 *Swing Low Sweet Chariot*. Or what about an issue of *This is Darin* that also includes *A Sunday Kind of Love*? And it is hard to believe that the Capitol folk albums are deemed not worthy of release, particularly as their last issue was only available for what seemed like just a few months.

It would be nice to reveal that the situation with regards to streaming was better. In the UK it is, with most albums available via Amazon Music. However, the situation worldwide with Spotify is shockingly bad. The only songs available from Bobby's period with Atlantic, covering music from 1965 to 1967, are those that oddly found their way on to the *Songs from Big Sur* album (I say "oddly" as they weren't recorded at Big Sur). This means that classics such as the studio recording of *If I Were a Carpenter* are not available for streaming on Spotify. Out of more than sixty studio recordings from these three years, only six are available. On Amazon Music in the US, only eighteen of the sixty songs are available (and nothing from the big band albums). The Direction years tell a similar story. Out of two dozen studio recordings, less than half are available through streaming outlets. What is most shocking here is that the copyright for the Atlantic and Direction material is seemingly owned by the Darin Estate.

Perhaps Bobby Darin's popularity is simply going through a lull that is not recognised by fans and enthusiasts of the singer, but it truly doesn't seem that way. True, Bobby seemed to go through an extraordinary wave of renewed popularity and rediscovery from the mid-1990s through to the mid-2000s, and that was always going to come to an end, or at least subside, at some point. But we now seem to be at a point that is at the other end of the scale, and little is being done to try to change that. Projects announced several years ago have never appeared, and there is no indication that there is anything on the horizon. Recent years have seen some wonderful documentaries on Elvis Presley, Frank Sinatra, Nina Simone, and others, and one can only wonder why Bobby's story is not being told in a similarly intelligent way to a new audience. Meanwhile, the official Bobby Darin website looks antiquated, and the official Facebook and Twitter presence is underwhelming (the Bobby Darin Fan Club group and Bobby Darin Appreciation Group on Facebook are much more engaging). On YouTube there are only a handful of performances uploaded officially, and the quality of some of them is subpar. There is no Bobby Darin Vevo account.

Depite this, however, Bobby Darin will never be forgotten – not his music or his remarkable story. Even if much of his work remains out of print (and let's hope that isn't the case), his most famous recordings such as *Mack the Knife*, *Beyond the Sea* and *Dream Lover* will continue to be part of the soundtracks of our lives, forever played on the radio, used on advertisements, and appearing in film soundtracks. Each time that happens, there will be somebody somewhere asking "who *is* that?" and then they will go shopping for their first Bobby Darin CD and begin a lifelong love of some of the greatest popular music ever recorded, just as this author did back in the mid-1990s.

Shane Brown
December, 2018.

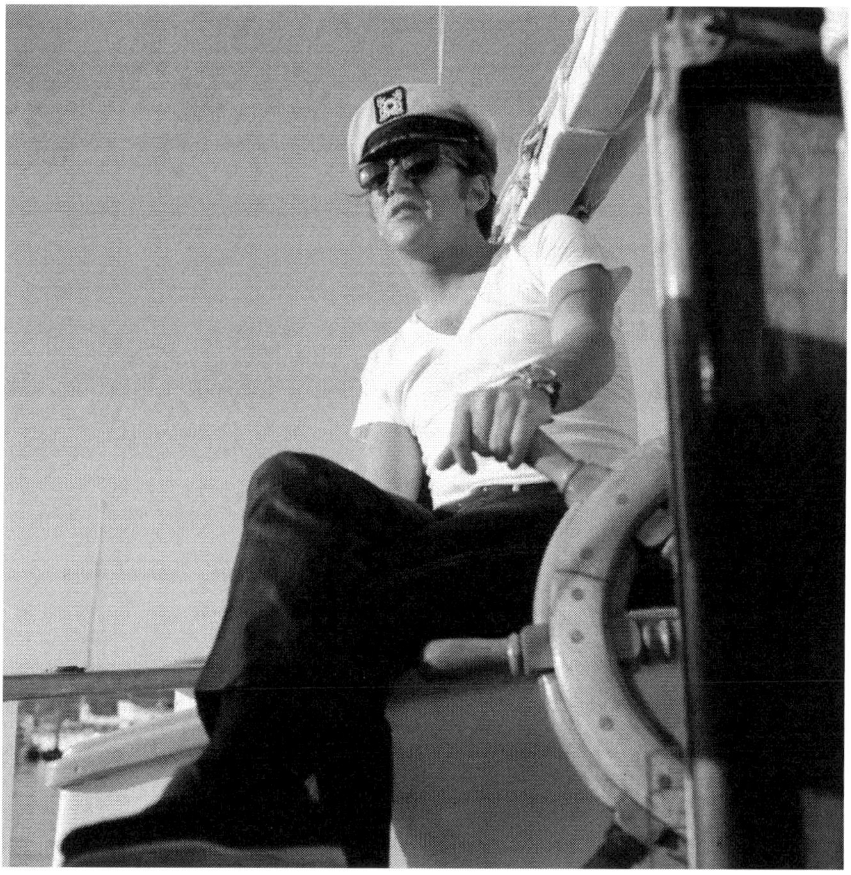

APPENDIX A
FIFTY KEY ALBUMS

The following pages provide short reviews on all of the regular Bobby Darin albums released domestically during his lifetime, and highlights some of the best and most important posthumous releases, up to and including 2018's *Go Ahead and Back Up: The Lost Motown Masters*. Bobby's albums were often put together with much care and attention, and the best way to hear the majority of them is as they were originally released.

1. Bobby Darin (1958)

As with many artists of the period, Bobby Darin's first album was self-titled and little more than a compilation of previously-released single sides and tracks that had been left in the vaults. The main selling point for most buyers was the inclusion of both sides of the *Splish Splash* single, but this remains a good summation of Bobby's first year with ATCO, and other standouts include *Talk To Me Something*, *Actions Speak Louder Than Words*, and the under-rated *Brand New House*, which is as good as anything on the album. 6/10.

2. That's All (1959)

Darin's sophomore album is also arguably his best. It catapulted Bobby to a whole new level of stardom, and brought with it the respect of many of those in the business that he looked up to. The album will forever be remembered for *Mack the Knife* and *Beyond the Sea*, but Bobby was canny in mostly choosing standards that had not been over-recorded during the previous decades. This saw him reaching back to the 1910s for the Sophie Tucker signature song *Some of These Days*, and the 1920s for *Softly as in a Morning Sunrise* from the operetta *The New Moon*, as well as digging up a moving obscure ballad like *Through a Long and Sleepless Night*. This remains a raw and exciting album and, despite everything that came after it, it is probably still the best representation of what Darin could bring to the table in an album of standards. 10/10.

3. This is Darin (1960)

It was inevitable that *That's All* would be followed by more of the same, with Darin recording another dozen standards (mostly) under the baton of arranger Richard Wess. The opening *Clementine* was very much modelled as *Mack the Knife part 2*, even if the lyrics haven't aged too well in the near-sixty years since it was recorded. Elsewhere, the formula was the same, even if the results seemed that little bit more polished this time around. Well-known standards sat alongside jazz classics, with a couple of obscurities thrown in for good measure. As a whole, it might not quite have hit the dizzy heights of its predecessor, but *Caravan* and *All Nite Long* easily rank among the best things that Darin ever recorded. 9/10.

4. Darin at the Copa (1960)

Considering how much praise Bobby was getting for his on-stage performances, it was perhaps inevitable that a live album would soon follow. However, there are a number of problems here. Firstly, the sound quality is not good in general. The mono edition of the album is better in this respect (although still not great), but has not been reissued on CD. Secondly, the editing together of various songs from various shows is not done particularly well, with the joins all too apparent in many cases. The other main issue here is Bobby himself. While his asides and jokes during and between songs might have been hilarious to the audience, they often make little sense on record, especially nearly sixty years after the event. There are some decent performances scattered through the album, mostly of the songs that Bobby didn't record at any point in the studio, but there is a feeling that this could have been a whole lot better, and one can only wish that the master tapes are one day found, remixed, remastered, and a CD put together with more skill than the original LP. 6/10

5. For Teenagers Only (1960)

Just in case Bobby's rock 'n' roll fans were feeling left out after three "adult" albums on the bounce, ATCO reached back into the archives to pull out a dozen tracks that were supposedly aimed at the teen audience. Sadly, most of these were leftovers, and the album has the same cobbled-together feel of Darin's first, although no better or worse other than the fact it didn't have a stand-out track like *Splish Splash*. Darin tries hard with *I Want You With Me*, but Elvis Presley would show him how to *really* rock it when he recorded it in 1961. Elsewhere, *That Lucky Old Sun*, *All the Way Home*, and *Somebody to Love* are the best of the rest. 5/10

6. The 25th Day of December (1960)

Bobby's fourth album of the year remains one of the most unusual Christmas albums ever recorded by a mainstream pop artist. Here are a mix of carols, gospel songs, folk songs and even a version of *Ave Maria*. It was an early sign that Darin had more in his sights than simply doing his own versions of the types of albums that other people had done. *The 25th Day of December* is certainly not the lightest of Christmas albums, and one has to wish that he had recorded a more traditional one further down the line, but you have to admire his ambition and willingness to stray from the well-trodden path of others. 7/10.

7. Two of a Kind (1961)

Darin's first album of 1961 was an LP of duets with the great Johnny Mercer. Rather than concentrating on Mercer's wonderful catalogue of compositions, the pair worked their way through a series of mostly Tin Pan Alley songs from the early part of the 20th Century. The success of the album depends on how much you enjoy the banter between the two performers, who obviously had great chemistry together, but sometimes the talk somewhat side-lines the music itself. Both men are in great form, though, although the real star is arguably Billy May's sparkling arrangements. An extended version of the album has been released on CD, including a batch of alternate takes as well as two songs not included on the original LP, and this is the recommended version for anyone looking to add this to their collections. 7/10.

8. The Bobby Darin Story (1961)

Just three years after his first hit with *Splish Splash*, Bobby Darin released his first greatest hits album. Superseded by any number of compilations released over the years, this one still has interest as a place to find an alternate take of *Clementine* and for Bobby's spoken commentary between some of the tracks. In hindsight, perhaps ATCO should have held back on this kind of disc until Darin left the label the following year, but one can't blame them for striking while the iron was hot. 8/10.

9. Love Swings (1961)

This album saw Bobby returning to the standard repertoire that had made up the bulk of the *That's All* and *This is Darin* LPs. This time around, however, he chose to put together a dozen songs that told the story of a love affair from the beginning through to the break-up. It's an ambitious project, and the arrangements aren't as dynamic as on the earlier albums, but it still works well enough, even if it isn't quite as memorable as some of Bobby's other LPs. Highlights include *It Had to Be You* and a stellar version of *How About You* which also features some fun newly-written lyrics in which Bobby gets to sing about "Mrs Darin's looks" giving him a thrill. 7/10.

10. Twist with Bobby Darin (1961)

Bobby's final album of the year was another reminder to the teenaged audience that neither Darin or the record label had forgotten about them. This is a more enjoyable collection than *For Teenagers Only*, but a number of the songs had already been released on album, some of them only seven months earlier, meaning that there wasn't much of interest here for Bobby's most hardcore fans. Still, it's good to see the wonderful *Bullmoose* kicking off an LP, and many fans were no doubt pleased to get the likes of *Multiplication*, *Irresistable You*, and *You Must Have Been a Beautiful Baby* on a long-player. Conversely, some must have been annoyed at finding *Somebody to Love* on an album for the third time in just over a year. 6/10.

11. Bobby Darin Sings Ray Charles (1962)

"He may not have lived it, but he sure has loved it" say the liner notes on the back of the album, and there is no denying that. Darin's tribute to Ray Charles is a wonderfully entertaining album, but the disappointment is that he sticks so closely to the original arrangements. It would have been more interesting if this was less an attempt of recreating the original records, and more of an effort to create something new from these wonderful songs. And yet, even here, Bobby takes chances. *I Got a Woman*, for example, runs over six minutes. Does it need to? That's up for debate, but no-one can deny that, once again, there is a pushing of boundaries here. *Drown in My Own Tears* would be resurrected in live shows in 1967, with the tempo slowed down, and Bobby giving a powerhouse performance. Sadly, that arrangement never made it to record. 7/10.

12. Things and Other Things (1962)

The title makes no attempt to hide the fact that this is a collection of single sides and whatever was kicking around in the vaults. On the plus side, the album provides a home for such fine tracks as *Things*, *Lost Love*, and *I'll Be There*, but Bobby should have been recording a new album built around the latest hit single – and probably would have done had he not been moving to a new label. Enjoyable enough, but a collection with little substance. 5/10.

13. Oh! Look at Me Now (1962)

Bobby's first album for Capitol paired him once again with arranger Billy May. This is the closest Darin came to attempting a Sinatra album. All of the songs are well-known standards. What should have been a classic, though, only works in part. The upbeat numbers are great, but the ballads are held back by the rather saccharine-sounding choir heard behind Bobby, that tends to dominate the arrangements. One can only hope for a deluxe edition of this album, with the original version on one disc, complete with the other tracks recorded at the sessions, and a remixed version on the second where the choir is erased entirely. 7/10.

14. You're the Reason I'm Living (1963)

This time when Bobby had a hit single, he *did* record an entire album around it – now moving into country music. The album suffers the same fate as the previous one, however: the choir/chorus is too dominant. Also a problem here is that Bobby seems to have gained some vocal mannerisms that do him no favours. Combine the two, and you get an occasional complete clunker like *Release Me*. Again, though, the good tracks here are really good, most notably *Sally Was a Good Old Girl* and *Who Can I Count On*. 6/10.

15. It's You Or No One (1963)

This may have been released in 1963, but it was recorded in 1960. This was one of Bobby's real misfires, as he plays around with the instrumentation on this set of standards, with half of the album not even having a rhythm section. It's a valiant effort at trying something new, but it doesn't really work, especially when the album is heard as a whole (individually, the tracks work better). Darin singing *Don't Get Around Much Anymore* should be a classic, but unfortunately this is more likely to send people to sleep. 4/10.

16. 18 Yellow Roses and 11 Other Hits (1963)

Those 11 Other Hits aren't Bobby's though. Here, he takes his latest hit and surrounds it by his covers of other singer's recent successes. It is a relatively unambitious effort that doesn't tax Bobby much, although the droning vocal of *The Reverend Mr. Black* might tax the listener. *End of the World* is quite beautiful, and tracks such as *Walk Right In*, *Not For Me*, and *Rhythm of the Rain* come off well. However, this was released at a time when a far superior album of standards was still in the vaults (and was shelved for good), and that is a shame. 6/10.

17. Earthy! (1963)

Earthy! has begun to get something of a cult status – one of those Darin albums that even non-fans seem to like a great deal (rather like Sinatra's *Watertown*). *Earthy!* wasn't just a folk album from Bobby, but one which brings together songs from around the world rather than just a collection of songs by Dylan and his contemporaries. Everything works here, and this may well be Bobby's best album. The musicianship is superb, and the choice of songs themselves complement each other wonderfully. Essential. 10/10

18. Golden Folk Hits (1963)

This follow-up to *Earthy!* is a much more conservative affair, this time a collection of covers of Peter, Paul and Mary, Bob Dylan, and the Kingston Trio. The performances are all good, but it just pales into comparison when heard alongside its predecessor. 7/10.

19. Winners (1964)

Another album from 1960 that was held back from release. This time, this is quite a classic, pulling together a recent single as well a collection of performances utilising a jazz combo. This is the nearest Bobby got to straight-ahead jazz, and much of the album is wonderful, most notably *I've Found a New Baby*, *What a Difference a Day Made*, and *Easy Living*. A couple of tracks, such as *Anything Goes*, don't quite work, but this LP really does deserve a wider audience, and a reissue including the other tracks from these sessions (*Minnie the Moocher*, *Bill Bailey*, *Swing Low Sweet Chariot*) would be most welcome. 8/10.

20. From Hello Dolly to Goodbye Charlie (1964)

After a hiatus from recording for various reasons, Bobby's "comeback" album saw him paired again with Richard Wess. Here, the album is made up of songs from recent shows and films (mostly films), and the result is his best swing album for Capitol. But that extra bit of fun and rawness, so evident on his earlier pairing with Wess, just isn't here, and despite the fine singing, this is often professional rather than exciting. Bobby's popularity was not what it had been a couple of years earlier, and while his version of *Hello Dolly* was cleverly, and knowingly, modelled on his own *Mack the Knife*, it had also been recorded by Louis Armstrong, Ella Fitzgerald, and Frank Sinatra at the same time, and the single therefore got lost in the milieu, failing to give Darin the career lift he was looking for. 8/10.

21. Venice Blue (aka: I Wanna Be Around) (1965)

Venice Blue tends to position Bobby firmly in easy listening/MOR territory. He is said to have thought that the title song would be a big hit for him, but it wasn't, dragged down mostly by the awful translation from the French (composer Charles Aznavour had a new set of lyrics written a few years later for when he re-recorded the song in English). Elsewhere, the song choices are predictable (*Somewhere*, *The Good Life*), with the occasional curveball thrown in (*There Ain't No Sweet Gal Worth the Salt of My Tears*). It's the curveball that comes off best here, otherwise this is a pleasant album, but far too safe. 6/10

22. Bobby Darin Sings the Shadow of Your Smile (1966)

This is very much an album of two halves. The first side finds Bobby trying his hand at each of the songs short-listed for the Academy Award for Best Song in 1966. Another year, it might have worked. But here we have Bobby trying to make something out of

What's New Pussycat, *The Ballad of Cat Ballou*, and *The Sweetheart Tree*, none of which are songs that fit Darin's style of singing, and *Pussycat* is particularly painful. On the second side, we have a group of standards, pulled together from a complete album recorded months earlier that would remain unreleased, with the leftover tracks eventually lost in a fire. Bobby sings well enough, but the sound quality on the stereo release is appalling, with the singer sounding as if he is in a separate room to the musicians. Perhaps they had tried to get as far away as possible during *Pussycat* and *Cat Ballou*. Overall, very disappointing. 4/10

23. In a Broadway Bag (aka: Mame) (1966)

Here, Bobby comes up with a concept that seems influenced by Sammy Davis Jr, in that this is an album of songs from recent Broadway shows. If the last couple of albums had demonstrated Darin having an artistic slump, here he reverses that completely, and this LP heralded a new golden period for him. *Mame* became a minor hit, and it is hard to find a better version of *Don't Rain On My Parade*. Darin manages to pull *Feeling Good* away from Nina Simone, and here gives it a funky, blues-tinged reading, but perhaps the biggest surprise is the beautiful rendering of *The Other Half of Me*, a rarely heard song that is beautifully performed. 9/10.

24. The Best of Bobby Darin. (1966)

Bobby Darin was back in the charts, and so Capitol released this to try to capitalise on that now that the singer was recording for Atlantic. It is a weird concoction, bringing together some genuine hits, but also leaving out the likes of *If a Man Answers*. Meanwhile a couple of album tracks make the grade, as does the previously-unreleased *Fly Me to the Moon*. With literally dozens of unreleased performances in the vaults, it is odd that Capitol didn't utilise them to make a new Darin album. As it is, this is a bizarre mish-mash of songs that was never going to make an impression. It remains the only US lifetime LP which has not been reissued on CD in its original form. 6/10.

25. If I Were a Carpenter (1966)

In a Broadway Bag might have been a return to form for Bobby Darin, but it was this album of folk songs, written by the likes of Tim Hardin, John Sebastian, and John Denver, that ultimately brought him back as a major force in popular music. The quiet reflection of the title number saw Darin have an unexpected, if fleeting, return to the charts, and also saw him host a number of TV specials in the coming years – his first since 1961. Musically speaking, this is miles away from the brash sound of *That's All*, but there is no doubt that Darin was serious with regards to the music he was offering, developing the sound further when he set up his own record company a couple of years later. 9/10

26. Inside Out (1967)

A rather straightforward follow-up to *If I Were a Carpenter*, the music is just as good as before, but the album didn't resonate with audiences as the previous one had done. That said, *Darling Be Home Soon* is a beautiful rendition of one of the best love songs ever written, and *Bes' Friends* really is great fun. There is also a more sombre mood represented here with Randy Newman's *I Think It's Gonna Rain Today* and *Whatever Happened to Happy*. But perhaps most key is Darin's own *I Am*, a song that again foreshadows not only the musical style of the Direction recordings, but the nature of the lyrics as well. 7/10

27. Something Special (1967)

This live recording, made in London, was released only in the UK, in conjunction with the TV special of the same name. The album has yet to appear officially on CD. Here, Darin, demonstrates his entire musical range, from the swing of *Don't Rain On My Parade*, through to the folk of *The Girl Who Stood Beside Me*, and on to the blues of *Funny What Love Can Do*, in a superior arrangement to that which had appeared on single. A really fine album and performance that deserves a proper reissue. 8/10

28. Bobby Darin Sings Doctor Dolittle (1967)

Darin's album of songs from the film *Doctor Dolittle* isn't quite the anomaly that some suggest. After all, this is a film about love, acceptance and peace, and therefore lyrically the songs aren't miles away from the themes that Bobby would explore for his own label the following year. Sadly, the album suffers from being split up into a ballad side and an upbeat side, but *Beautiful Things* and *Talk to the Animals* are classic Darin. Unfortunately, the release seemed to get lost amongst the official soundtrack album and the superior album of songs from the film by Sammy Davis Jr – someone who understood the songs of Leslie Bricusse better than anyone. But Darin's *Dolittle* is much better than many biographies suggest. 7/10.

29. Bobby Darin Born Walden Robert Cassotto (1968)

Bobby Darin had released twenty-eight albums in a nine-year period. In his final five years, he would release just three. This album was his first for his own Direction label. Gone are any signs of gloss and glamour, and instead we find a group of self-written songs that are simple musically, but demonstrate how great a poet Darin the lyricist could be as he tackles subjects such as the environment, capitalism, murder, organised religion, and mourning. This was an intensely personal project, and very few heard it at the time, but for anyone trying to understand the Bobby Darin story, this is essential listening. 8/10

30. Commitment (1969)

Darin's second album for Direction is a less raw affair. He's still protesting, but he's also delving into the counter-culture for inspiration, and taking part in some self-reflection with the caustic *Song for a Dollar*. This is a more complicated album, and from a distance of fifty years, few will know who or what Bobby is referring to in songs like *Me and Mr. Hohner* or *Sausalito*, but that also demonstrates just how current and on the ball he could be. But this is an album full of surprises, from the near-rap of the opening number to the beautifully trippy *Water Color Canvas*. 9/10.

31. Bobby Darin (1972)

In late 1970, Darin re-entered the mainstream, joining the Motown label. Over the next three years he recorded a live album and around forty studio masters. Other than a handful of single sides, this dismal ten-track album from 1972 is all that he released during his lifetime. A few more tracks appeared on a tribute album in 1974, the live album (which is wonderful) appeared in 1987, and 2018 saw nearly two dozen of the remaining studio tracks finally released. But this 1972 album is a major disappointment, as Bobby sings a series of big ballads, with an even bigger orchestra, and the whole album comes across as one thing Bobby Darin's music rarely was: dull and predictable. *Sail Away* is the only real saving grace here, although *Who Turned the World Around* and *Average People* threaten to kick the album into life, but give up just before they manage it. 4/10.

32. The Original Bobby Darin (1976)

This 3LP set was a compilation of Bobby's ATCO years, featuring mostly standards alongside a smattering of his rock 'n' roll hits. The reason why it is included here is that this release is the only place to find *A Sunday Kind of Love*, recorded for *This is Darin* but not used on the LP. *A Sunday Kind of Love* has never been reissued on another official release, or even on public domain CDs in recent years. 8/10

33. As Long As I'm Singin': Rare 'n' Darin (RND label, 1986)

This unofficial CD was important at the time of release as it featured a significant number of songs not available elsewhere, mostly from television appearances, but also some studio recordings that had yet to make their official release. The studio recordings have been released officially in the decades since, but this is still a useful compilation, featuring the audio from a number of Bobby's early TV appearances. A rather hard to find disc, though, and the sound varies from track to track. 6/10

34. Live at the Desert Inn (1987)

This wonderful disc contains Darin live in Las Vegas just prior to his 1971 heart operation. The CD is a tour de force, and a very different show to the other live discs that have appeared over the years. Here, Bobby concentrates on the songs of other singers, covering The Beatles (a stunning medley), James Taylor, Bob Dylan, and others. The version of *Hi-De-Ho* is one of this author's favourite Darin performances, and it is such a shame this album wasn't released in the early 1970s. The album was re-issued in 2005, with two extra songs included, but it was also remixed, and the overall sound of the reissue tends to have less punch than the 1987 version. Highly recommended. 10/10

35. Capitol Collectors Series (1989)
This is a really nice collection of the Capitol single sides, featuring a number of tracks that are more difficult to find, and a couple of alternate takes as well. Darin's Capitol singles were a mixed bunch, but it's great to have them all together, and the compilation flows really well, too. 1998 saw the release of *The Capitol Years*, a 3CD collection, with the last disc having roughly the same track listing as this 1989 compilation – but there you don't get the alternate versions. If you can't find songs such as *Be Mad Little Girl*, *Things in This House*, and *That Funny Feeling*, then this is the disc for you. 7/10.

36. Rare Performances (TYE label, 1990)
This is another unofficial release, this time presenting an almost-complete nightclub performance from around 1967 (probably Lake Tahoe). The sound quality is only fair, possibly from a soundboard recording, but it does provide us with a rare chance to hear Bobby sing *I've Got You Under My Skin* and *Meditation*, as well a different arrangement of *The Shadow of Your Smile*. The disc is rounded out with some songs from the 1963 Las Vegas engagement. 6/10 (due to sound issues).

37. From Sea to Sea (Live Gold Label, 1992)
Yet another unofficial disc, but an important one. This contains Bobby's short set as part of a rock 'n' roll package tour of Australia in 1959 – the only recording of this kind that we have. The rest of the disc contains the complete *Something Special* album from 1967, which otherwise has not seen a CD release. Not brilliant sound, but generally very good for an issue of this type. 8/10.

38. Spotlight on Bobby Darin (1994)
This release from Capitol signalled the starting point of a golden era for Darin fans, as unreleased recordings started being released, and the original albums made their way slowly but surely on to CD. This disc mines Bobby's Capitol swing albums for the most part, but also includes a handful of previously unreleased tracks. There are some nice liner notes, the sound is bright and clear, and the disc can be picked up very cheaply.

39. As Long As I'm Singing: The Bobby Darin Collection (1995)

This 4CD set from Rhino was released over twenty years ago, and yet still holds a special place in most fan's hearts. Not only did it provide a chance to hear dozens of songs that had been out of print for years, but also gave fans some "new" music such as demo versions of *Dream Lover* and *Simple Song of Freedom*, some blues numbers from the mid-1960s, and a couple of songs from Vegas in 1963. This is a beautiful set, with a very nice booklet with notes on each song based on Jeff Bleiel's groundbreaking research. You can't be without this. 10/10.

40. Roberto Cassotto: Rare, Rockin' & Unreleased (Ring of Stars label, 1997)

This unofficial release is wonderful for any Darin fan that can find it, for it includes numerous outtakes from 1950s recordings sessions, such as *Splish Splash* and *Queen of the Hop*. This is also the only place to find the incomplete recording of *Didn't It Feel Good*, which Darin gives up on with a resounding "oh, balls!" For more of the same, the Bear Family release *Bobby Rocks* from 2008 also includes a few alternate takes. 7/10.

41. A&E Biography: A [Musical] Biography (1998)

The clunky title is unfortunate, as this is an interesting compilation of previously-released and unreleased material. Some of the editing is a little odd, such as adding a 1963 introduction of Sammy Davis Jr on to the beginning of a 1973 performance of *Higher and Higher*. However, fans get some nice outtakes from the 1963 Vegas recordings, some highlights from the 1973 TV show, and the first release of the studio master of *Love, Look Away*. 7/10.

42. The Unreleased Capitol Sides (1999)

Bobby's tenure at Capitol has provided fans with a great deal of new music in recent decades, and here we have a collection containing around twenty unreleased tracks. This isn't all classic Darin, and there is a good reason why some of it remained in the vaults, but it helps us start to get a feel for some of the albums that never got finished and/or released. Some of the performances of standards here are outstanding. In 2016, Capitol renamed this as *The Rare Capitol Masters*, making it a download-only release, but adding an extra group of tracks to the original 25 songs, including German-language versions of two hits, and more unreleased tracks such as *Get Me to the Church on Time*, *Jealous* and *Oh Shenandoah*. Sadly, they didn't think to include *I Left My Heart in San Francisco*, first released on *Wild, Cool & Swinging* in 2000. 8/10.

43. Wild, Cool & Swinging (2000)

This CD, part of a multi-artist series with the same title, is a fun compilation of some of Bobby's swing numbers from the Capitol years. Highly entertaining, this also includes previously unreleased versions of *Gyp the Cat* and *I Left My Heart in San Francisco*. 8/10.

44. The Curtain Falls: Live at the Flamingo (2000)

Finally, the world got to hear this live album recorded in 1963 but, strangely, not released at the time. This is an improvement on *Darin at the Copa*, with Bobby keeping his banter quota down in comparison to that release. The hits medley is a pitiful effort that even Darin himself must have known was a travesty, but the real gems here are the folk songs towards the end of the disc. Here is an audience used to glamour and spectacle in Vegas, willingly joining in with Bobby during *Mary, Don't You Weep*, and suddenly the showroom becomes a campfire singalong. It is an oddly moving moment, and a demonstration of just how Darin could hold the audience in the palm of his hand. 8/10.

45. Aces Back to Back (2004)

This is a thoroughly weird release, pulling together recordings from all kinds of sources, and giving virtually no information on them in the liner notes. From that respect, this is a shambles (and, sadly, not the last such shambles). Musically, however, there is some interesting material here, including a group of songs from the 1973 TV series, and a TV performance of *Lazy River* which is outstanding. Also featured are three songs from Bobby's *Milk Shows*, a five-minute daily radio series from 1963. *All the Way* is worth the price of admission by itself. The disc comes with a bonus DVD, featuring eight songs from the 1973 TV series and some documentary footage. 6/10.

46. Songs from Big Sur (2004)

Theoretically, this is a collection of songs recorded during Darin's time living in a trailer in Big Sur, when he was recording for his own record label. In reality, this also includes songs from the Atlantic years which have no place here. One of those songs, *My Baby Needs Me*, was only previously available on a CD reissue of *If I Were a Carpenter/Inside Out*. Key with this release, however, is that two "new" studio recordings are featured – *City Life* and *Route 58*, both of which are superb. And we also get four recordings from Bobby's 1969 season at The Troubadour (but where is the rest of them??). It is also worth noting that the studio version of *Distractions* on this disc is not the same take as on the *Commitment* LP. 8/10.

47. The Milk Shows (2014)

As mentioned earlier, *The Milk Shows* were a five-minute radio series that Bobby had during 1963 and 1964. Virtually every song recorded for it was done with a small combo as instrumentation, and each song lasted just a minute or so. This double album contains 96 tracks. Because of how it is compiled (basically as a one-hour long medley on each disc), this is an exhausting experience, although we do get to hear Bobby sing songs he hadn't recorded elsewhere. Sadly, Bobby isn't always in good voice, sounding very tired in places, and also the editing is appalling. There are moments when crossfades result in Bobby singing AND talking simultaneously. The package looks great, but from an audio point of view, it is a complete disaster, and a 12-year-old using Goldwave could probably have done a better job. In one sense, this is essential because they are "new" recordings of songs not cut elsewhere, but on the other hand, you'll rarely listen to it. There was a much better way to present this material. 4/10.

48. Another Song on My Mind: The Motown Years (2016)

In 1974, Motown released a tribute album to Bobby Darin, featuring eight unreleased tracks, an extended version of a single side, and *Sail Away* from the 1972 Motown album. That album isn't listed under the 1974 date because all tracks are included on this release. *Another Song on My Mind* pulls together all of the 1972 album, and all of the 1974 album. It also includes all remixes and alternate versions that have previously been released (when the 1974 album was first released on CD, it included overdubs etc not on the vinyl). Also, here are the Motown single sides that have previously been hard to find. Real Gone Music have done a superb job here – this music could not be presented any better. BUT, that doesn't mean that the music itself is anything like Darin's best. The arrangements are overblown, the song choices often bland, and the singing sometimes strained. And yet every fan will want and need this material in their collection. This is Bobby's final chapter, after all, and there is no doubt, that this release is the way to own it. 6/10 for the music. 9/10 for the presentation.

49. Bobby Darin: The 1956-1962 Singles (Jackpot label, 2017)

Most music fans will tell you the public domain law in Europe are a blessing and a curse. On the one hand, it results in endless cheap copies of music available on Amazon. On the other, it means that "forgotten" music can be made available once again. Here Darin benefits from the latter. There are a number of collections of Darin's singles on public domain discs, but I believe this is the best and most complete. It includes various hard to find gems such as all the Decca sides, the Tanfastic promo record, *That's How It Went All Right* (from *Pepe*), *Tall Story* and oddities like *Walk Bach to Me*. Many fans will find these hard to find outside of PD releases, and so this effort is recommended. 64 tracks in total. 8/10.

50. Go Ahead and Back Up: The Lost Motown Masters (2018)

This 2018 release promised to be one of the most exciting Bobby Darin releases since 2000, presenting two dozen previously unheard studio recordings. The research that went into the disc and the booklet is remarkable, shining new light on the Motown years. Unfortunately, that doesn't make some of the music any more distinguished. The Darin-produced recordings that occupy the first half of the disc are welcome additions to the Darin catalogue, but some of the other material, where Bobby is curtailed by the methods of Motown, is decidedly sub-par. 7/10 for the music. 10/10 for the effort put into presenting us with it.

APPENDIX B
LIFETIME DISCOGRAPHY

The following discography includes single and album releases issued during Darin's lifetime. All items are U.S. releases unless otherwise stated.

Rock Island Line/Timber (Decca 29883, 3/56)
Silly Willy/Blue Eyed Mermaid (Decca 29922, 5/56)
Hear Them Bells/The Greatest Builder (Decca 30031, 8/56)
Dealer in Dreams/Help Me (Decca 30225, 2/57)
I Found a Million Dollar Baby/Talk to Me Something (Atco 6092, 6/57)
Don't Call My Name/Pretty Betty (Atco 6103, 10/57)
Just in Case You Change Your Mind/So Mean (Atco 6109, 1/58)
Splish Splash/Judy, Don't Be Moody (Atco 6117, 5/58)
Early in the Morning/Now We're One (Brunswick 55073, 6/58, credited to The Ding Dongs)
Early in the Morning/Now We're One (Atco 6121, 7/58 credited to The Rinky-Dinks)

Bobby Darin LP (Atco 33-102, 7/58)
Splish Splash; Just in Case You Change Your Mind; Pretty Betty; Talk to Me Something; Judy, Don't Be Moody; (Since You're Gone) I Can't Go On; I Found a Million Dollar Baby; Wear My Ring; So Mean; Don't Call My Name; Brand New House; Actions Speak Louder than Words

Queen of the Hop/Lost Love (Atco 6127, 9/58)
Mighty Mighty Man/You're Mine (Atco 6128, 9/58)
Plain Jane/While I'm Gone (Atco 6133, 1/59)

BOBBY DARIN: DIRECTIONS

Dream Lover/Bullmoose (Atco 6140, 3/59)

That's All LP (Atco 33-104, 3/59)
Mack the Knife; Beyond the Sea; Through a Long and Sleepless Night; Softly as in a Morning Sunrise; She Needs Me; It Ain't Necessarily So; I'll Remember April; That's the Way Love Is; Was There a Call For Me; Some of these Days; Where is the One; That's All

Mack the Knife/Was There a Call For Me (Atco 6147, 8/59)
Hear Them Bells/The Greatest Builder (Decca 30031, 12/59 reissue)
Beyond the Sea/That's the Way Love Is (Atco 6158, 1/60)

This is Darin LP (Atco 33-115, 1/60)
Clementine; Have You Got Any Castles Baby; Don't Dream of Anybody but Me; My Gal Sal; Black Coffee; Caravan; Guys and Dolls; Down with Love; Pete Kelly's Blues; All Nite Long; The Gal that Got Away; I Can't Give You Anything But Love

Clementine/Tall Story (Atco 6161, 3/60)
Won't You Come Home Bill Bailey/I'll Be There (Atco 6167, 6/60)
She's Tanfastic/Moment of Love (Atco n/a, summer 1960)

Darin at the Copa LP (Atco 33-122, 7/60)
Swing Low Sweet Chariot/Lonesome Road; Some of these Days; Mack the Knife; Love for Sale; Clementine; You'd Be So Nice to Come Home To; Dream Lover; Bill Bailey; I Have Dreamed; I Can't Give You Anything But Love; Alright, O.K., You Win; By Myself/When Your Lover Has Gone; I Got a Woman; That's All

Beachcomber/Autumn Blues (Atco 6173, 8/60)
Artificial Flowers/Somebody to Love (Atco 6179, 9/60)

For Teenagers Only LP (Atco 1001, 9/60)
I Want You With Me; Keep a Walkin'; You Know How; Somebody to Love; I Ain't Sharin' Sharon; Pity Miss Kitty; That Lucky Old Sun; All the Way Home; You Never Called; A Picture No Artist Could Paint; Hush, Somebody's Calling My Name; Here I'll Stay

Christmas Auld Lang Syne/Child of God (Atco 6183, 10/60)

The 25th Day of December LP (Atco 33-125, 10/60)
Oh Come All Ye Faithful; Poor Little Jesus; Child of God; Baby Born Today; Holy

Holy Holy; Ave Maria; Go Tell it on the Mountain; While Shepherds Watched Their Flocks; Jehovah Hallelujah; Mary, Where is Your Baby; Silent Night; Dona Nobis Pacem; Amen

That's How It Went All Right/What Happened on Stage 5 (George Sidney, narrator) (Colpix PC1, 11/60?)

Lazy River/Oo-Ee-Train (Atco 6188, 2/61)

Nature Boy/Look For My True Love (Atco 6196, 4/61)

Two of a Kind LP (with Johnny Mercer) (Atco 33-126, 4/61)

Two of a Kind; Indiana; Ace in the Hole; East of the Rockies; If I Had My Druthers; I Ain't Gonna Give Nobody None of My Jellyroll; Lonesome Polecat; My Cutey's Due at Two-to-Two Today; Paddlin' Madelin' Home/Row, Row, Row; Who Takes Care of the Caretaker's Daughter; Mississippi Mud; Two of a Kind

The Bobby Darin Story LP (Atco 33-131, 5/61)

Splish Splash; Early in the Morning; Queen of the Hop; Plain Jane; Dream Lover; Mack the Knife; Beyond the Sea; Clementine (alternate take); Bill Bailey; Artificial Flowers; Somebody to Love; Lazy River

Theme from *Come September*/Walk Bach to Me (Atco 6200, 6/61)

Love Swings LP (Atco 33-134, 7/61)

Long Ago and Far Away; I Didn't Know What Time it Was; How About You; The More I See You; It Had to be You; No Greater Love; In Love in Vain; Just Friends; Something to Remember You By; Skylark; Spring is Here; I Guess I'll Have to Change My Plan

You Must Have Been a Beautiful Baby/Sorrow Tomorrow (Atco 6206, 8/61)

Ave Maria/Oh Come All Ye Faithful (Atco 6211, 11/61)

Irresistible You/Multiplication (Atco 6214, 12/61)

Twist with Bobby Darin LP (Atco 33-138, 12/61)

Bullmoose; Early in the Morning; Mighty Mighty Man; You Know How; Somebody to Love; Multiplication; Irresistible You; Queen of the Hop; You Must Have Been a Beautiful Baby; Keep a Walkin'; Pity Miss Kitty; I Ain't Sharin' Sharon

What'd I Say (Part I)/What'd I Say (Part II) (Atco 6221, 3/62)

Bobby Darin sings Ray Charles LP (Atco 33-140, 3/62)

What'd I Say; I Got a Woman; Tell all the World about You; Tell Me How Do You Feel; My Bonnie; The Right Time; Hallelujah I Love Her So; Leave My Woman Alone;

Ain't that Love; Drown in My Own Tears; That's Enough
Things/Jailer Bring Me Water (Atco 6229, 6/62)
Baby Face/You Know How (Atco 6236, 7/62)

Things and other Things LP (Atco 33-146, 7/62)
Things; I'll Be There; Lost Love; Look For My True Love; Beachcomber; Now We're One; You're Mine; Oo-Ee-Train; Jailer Bring Me Water; Nature Boy; Theme From *Come September*; Sorrow Tomorrow

If a Man Answers/A True, True Love (Capitol 4837, 9/62)

Oh! Look at Me Now LP (Capitol 1791, 10/62)
All By Myself; My Buddy; There's a Rainbow 'Round My Shoulder; Roses of Picardy; You'll Never Know; Blue Skies; Always; You Made Me Love You; A Nightingale Sang in Berkeley Square; I'm Beginning to See the Light; Oh! Look at Me Now; The Party's Over

I've Found a New Baby/Keep a Walkin' (Atco 6244, 11/62)
You're the Reason I'm Living/Now You're Gone (Capitol 4897, 12//62)

You're the Reason I'm Living LP (Capitol 1866, 2/63)
Sally Was a Good Old Girl; Be Honest With Me; Oh Lonesome Me; (I Heard That) Lonesome Whistle; It Keeps Right on a-Hurtin'; You're the Reason I'm Living; Please Help Me I'm Falling; Under Your Spell Again; Here I Am; Who Can I Count On; Now You're Gone; Release Me

18 Yellow Roses/Not for Me (Capitol 4970, 5/63)

It's You or No One LP (Atco 33-124, 6/63)
It's You or No One; I Hadn't Anyone Till You; Not Mine; I Can't Believe that You're in Love with Me; I've Never Been in Love Before; All or Nothing at All; Only One Little Item; Don't Get Around Much Anymore; How About Me; I'll Be Around; All I Do is Cry; I Guess I'm Good for Nothing but the Blues

18 Yellow Roses and 11 Other Hits LP (Capitol 1942, 7/63)
18 Yellow Roses; On Broadway; Ruby Baby; Reverend Mr. Black; End of the World; Not For Me; Walk Right In; From a Jack to a King; I Will Follow Her; Our Day Will Come; Can't Get Used to Losing You; Rhythm of the Rain

LIFETIME DISCOGRAPHY

Earthy! LP (Capitol 1826, 7/63)
Long Time Man; Work Song; La Bamba; I'm on My Way Great God; The Sermon of Samson; Strange Rain; Why Don't You Swing Down; Everything's Okay; Guantanamera; When Their Mama is Gone; Fay-O; The Er-I-Ee was a-Rising

Treat My Baby Good/Down So Long (Capitol 5019, 8/63)
Be Mad Little Girl/Since You've Been Gone (Capitol 5079, 11/63)

Golden Folk Hits LP (Capitol 2007, 11/63)
Mary Don't You Weep; Where Have all the Flowers Gone?; If I Had a Hammer; Don't Think Twice, it's all Right; Greenback Dollar; Why, Daddy, Why; Michael Row the Boat Ashore; Abilene; Green, Green; Settle Down; Blowin' in the Wind; Train to the Sky

Schatten auf den Wegen/Rote Rosen für Cindy (Capitol K22451. Germany only, ?/63)
I Wonder Who's Kissing Her Now/As Long as I'm Singing (Capitol 5126, 2/64)
Milord/Golden Earrings (Atco 6297, 4/64)

Winners LP (6/64)
Milord; Between the Devil and the Deep Blue Sea; Anything Goes; Do Nothin' Till You Hear from Me; Golden Earrings; When Day is Done; I've Found a New Baby; What a Difference a Day Made; What Can I Say After I Say I'm Sorry; Hard Hearted Hannah; Easy Living; They All Laughed

The Things in this House/Wait by the Water (Capitol 5257, 8/64)
Swing Low Sweet Chariot/Similau (Atco 6316, 8/64)

From Hello Dolly to Goodbye Charlie LP (Capitol 2194, 11/64)
Hello Dolly!; Call Me Irresponsible; Days of Wine and Roses; More; The End of Never; Charade; Once in a Lifetime; Sunday in New York; Where Love Has Gone; Look at Me; Goodbye Charlie

Hello Dolly/Goodbye Charlie (Capitol 5359, 1/65)
Minnie the Moocher/Hard Hearted Hannah (Atco 6334, 2/65)
Venice Blue/In a World Without You (Capitol 5399, 4/65)

Venice Blue LP (aka: I Wanna Be Around) (Capitol 2322, 5/65)
Venice Blue; I Wanna Be Around; Somewhere; The Good Life; Dear Heart; Softly as I Leave You; You Just Don't Know; There Ain't No Sweet Gal That's Worth the Salt of My Tears; Who Can I Turn To; A Taste of Honey; In a World Without You

When I Get Home/Lonely Road (Capitol 5443, 6/65)
That Funny Feeling/Gyp the Cat (Capitol 5481, 8/65)
We Didn't Ask to be Brought Here /Funny What Love Can Do (Atlantic 2305, 9/65)
The Breaking Point/Silver Dollar (Atlantic 2317, 1/66)
Mame/Walkin' in the Shadow of Love (Atlantic 2329, 3/66)

Bobby Darin sings The Shadow of Your Smile LP (Atlantic 8121, 4/66)
The Shadow Of Your Smile; The Sweetheart Tree; I Will Wait for You; The Ballad of Cat Ballou; What's New Pussycat?; Rainin'; Lover Come Back to Me; Cute; After You've Gone; It's Only a Paper Moon; Liza

Who's Afraid of Virginia Wolf/Merci Cherie (Atlantic 2341, 6/66)

In a Broadway Bag LP (aka: Mame) (Atlantic 8126, 6/66)
Mame; I Believe in You; It's Today; Everybody has the Right to be Wrong; Feeling Good; Don't Rain on My Parade; The Other Half of Me; Once Upon a Time; Try to Remember; I'll Only Miss Her When I Think of Her; Night Song

If I Were a Carpenter/Rainin' (Atlantic 2350, 8/66)

The Best of Bobby Darin LP (Capitol 2571, 8/66)
The Good Life; Charade; Gyp the Cat; Days of Wine and Roses; Treat My Baby Good; That Funny Feeling; 18 Yellow Roses; Fly Me to the Moon; Venice Blue; You're the Reason I'm Living; Goodbye Charlie

The Girl Who Stood Beside Me/Reason to Believe (Atlantic 2367, 11/66)
Lovin' You/Amy (Atlantic 2376, 12/66)

If I Were a Carpenter LP (Atlantic 8135, 12/66)
If I Were a Carpenter; Reason to Believe; (Sittin' here) Lovin' You; Misty Roses; Until it's Time for You to Go; For Baby; The Girl Who Stood Beside Me; Red Balloon; Amy; Don't Make Promises; Day Dream

The Lady Came from Baltimore/I Am (Atlantic 2395, 3/67)

Inside Out LP (Atlantic 8142, 5/67)
The Lady Came from Baltimore; Darling be home Soon; Bes' Friends; I Am; About You; I Think it's Gonna Rain Today; Whatever Happened to Happy; Black Sheep Boy; Hello Sunshine; Lady Fingers; Back Street Girl

Something Special LP (Atlantic 587073, UK only, 5/67)
Don't Rain on My Parade; About A Quarter to Nine; Once Upon a Time; I Wish I Were in Love Again; Mack the Knife; Impressions; The Girl Who Stood Beside Me; Funny What Love Can Do; What'd I Say; That's All

Talk to the Animals/She Knows (Atlantic 2433, 8/67)
Talk to the Animals/After Today (Atlantic 2433, 12/67)

Bobby Darin sings Doctor Dolittle LP (Atlantic 8154, 8/67)
At the Crossroads; When I Look in Your Eyes; I Think I Like You; Where are the Words; Something in Your Smile; Fabulous Places; My Friend the Doctor; Beautiful Things; After Today; Talk to the Animals

Bobby Darin born Walden Robert Cassotto LP (Direction, 1936, 9/68)
Questions; Jingle Jangle Jungle; The Proper Gander; Bullfrog; Long Line Rider; Change; I Can See the Wind; Sunday; In Memoriam

Long Line Rider/Change (Direction 350, 1/69)
Me & Mr. Hohner/Song for a Dollar (Direction 351 4/69)

Commitment LP (as "Bob Darin) (Direction 1937, 7/69)
Me and Mr. Hohner; Sugar Man; Sausalito (The Governors Song); Song for a Dollar; Harvest; Distractions (Part 1); Water Color Canvas; Jive; Hey Magic Man; Light Blue

Distractions (Part 1)/Jive (Direction 352, 8/69)
(9 to 5) Jive's Alive/Sugar Man (Direction 4000, ?/69)
Baby May/Sweet Reasons (Direction 4001, ?/69)
Maybe We Can Get it Together/Rx-Pyro (Prescription: Fire) (Direction 4002, ?/70)
Melodie/Someday We'll Be Together (Motown 1183, 4/71)
I'll Be Your Baby Tonight/Simple Song of Freedom (Motown 1193, 11/71)
Sail Away/Hard Headed Woman (Motown 1203, 5/72)

Bobby Darin LP (Motown 753, 8/72)
Sail Away; I've Already Stayed too Long; Something in Her Love; Who Turned the World Around; Shipmates in Cheyenne; Let It Be Me; Hard Headed Woman; Average People; I Used to Think it was Easy; My First Night Alone Without You

Average People/Something in Her Love (Motown 1212, 12/72)
Happy/Something in Her Love (Motown 1217, 12/72)

APPENDIX C
SELECTED POSTHUMOUS DISCOGRAPHY

The following is a list of selected posthumous releases. Only those that contain previously unreleased material are included. Because of geographical variations, this is not a complete list. Only the previously unreleased tracks on each release are listed. All songs are studio masters, unless otherwise stated.

Darin 1936-1973 LP (Motown M931-V1, 1974)
I Won't Last a Day Without You; Wonderin' Where it's Gonna End; Another Song on my Mind; Happy (Love Theme from *Lady Sings The Blues*); Blue Monday; Don't Think Twice, it's all Right; The Letter; If I Were a Carpenter (live, 1971); Moritat (Mack the Knife) (live, 1971).
NB. The CD release of this album contains a number of differences to the LP, with longer introductions and fade-outs, and alternate mixes. All the variants can be found on the Another Song on My Mind *CD*

The Original Bobby Darin 3LP set (Warner SP-3501, 1976)
Sunday Kind of Love.

As Long as I'm Singin': Rare 'n' Darin number 1 CD (RND, 1986)
Swing Low Sweet Chariot/When the Saints Go Marchin' In/Lonesome Road; This Could Be the Start of Something Big/Just in Time; Clementine; Toot Toot Tootsie Goodbye/Don't Worry About Me; By Myself/When Your Lover Has Gone; Just in Time; I Got a Woman/What'd I Say/When the Saints Go Marchin' In (all from television guest appearances)
NB. This is an unauthorised "bootleg" release. This disc was unavailable for perusal, and may contain more unreleased performances than listed above. This CD also contains the first release

of a number of studio masters. These have since been released in perfect quality elsewhere and so are not listed here.

Live at the Desert Inn CD (Motown MS-738, 1987)
Save the Country; Moritat (Mack the Knife); Fire and Rain; Beatles Medley: Hey Jude/Something/A Day in the Life/Eleanor Rigby/ Blackbird; Higher and Higher; I'll Be Your Baby Tonight; If I Were a Carpenter; Simple Song of Freedom; Encore Medley: Chain of Fools/Respect/Splish Splash/ Johnny B. Goode (Live, 1971)
NB. *The 2005 reissue on the Concord label adds unreleased live versions of Work Song and Beyond the Sea from the same date.*

Capitol Collectors Series CD (Capitol CDP 7 91625, 1989)
Wait by the Water (alternate take).

Rare Performances CD (TYE Records, TCD 101, 1990)
Don't Rain on My Parade; I've Got You Under My Skin; The Shadow of Your Smile; Meditation/I Will Wait for You; Charade; Mack the Knife; If I Were a Carpenter; (Sittin' here) Lovin' You; 18 Yellow Roses; What'd I Say; That's All (all live, 1967)
NB. *This is an unauthorised "bootleg" release. This CD also contains songs from the November 1963 Las Vegas season that were unreleased at the time, but have since been made available in perfect sound quality, and so are not listed here.*

From Sea to Sea CD (Live Gold LG 130013, 1992)
Splish Splash; Early in the Morning; Queen of the Hop; Plain Jane (all live, 1959)
NB. *This is an unauthorised "bootleg" release.*

Spotlight on Bobby Darin CD (CDP 828512-2, 1994)
Alabamy Bound; Standing on the Corner; Just in Time; All of You; I Got Rhythm; I'm Sitting on Top of the World

As Long as I'm Singing: The Bobby Darin Collection 4CD set (Rhino R2 72206, 1995)
Dream Lover (demo version); Easy Rider; Everywhere I Go; My Funny Valentine (live, 1963); You're Nobody 'til Somebody Loves You (live, 1963); The Curtain Falls (live, 1963); I'm on My Way Great God (live, 1963); I'm Going to Love You; Long Time Movin'; I'll Be Your Baby Tonight (Live, 1969); Simple Song of Freedom (demo version);

Roberto Cassotto: Rare, Rockin' & Unreleased (Ring of Stars R-O-S 1001, 1997)

Splish Splash (takes 1, 2, 6, 7); Queen of the Hop (takes 5-9); Mack the Knife (takes 3, 7); Didn't it Feel Good (takes 1-4); Pretty Betty (take 5); Plain Jane (takes 4, 5, 12); That Lucky Old Sun (take 11); Judy, Don't Be Moody (take 2); Don't Call My Name (take 3)

NB. *This is an unauthorised "bootleg" release.*

A&E Biography: A [Musical] Anthology CD (Capitol, 72434-94752-0-5, 1998)

Beyond the Sea (Live, 1973); Mack the Knife (Live, 1963); 18 Yellow Roses (Live, 1963); Love Look Away; If I Were a Carpenter (Live, 1973); Higher and Higher (Live, 1973).

Bobby Darin sings If I Were a Carpenter/Inside Out CD (Diablo, DIAB 864, 1998)

My Baby Needs Me

Wild, Cool & Swingin' CD (Capitol 7244-8-20333-2, 2000)

I Left My Heart in San Francisco; Gyp the Cat (alternate take)

The Unreleased Capitol Sides CD (Collector's Choice Music CCM-079-2, 1999)

I Wonder Who's Kissing Her Now (Alternate master); When My Baby Smiles at Me; Beautiful Dreamer; When You Were Sweet Sixteen; I Ain't Got Nobody; My Melancholy Baby; You're Nobody 'Til Somebody Loves You; What Kind of Fool am I?; Moon River; This Nearly Was Mine; Tall Hope; The Sweetest Sounds; Standing on the Corner; Stop the World (and Let Me Off); Whispering; Somebody Stole My Gal; Two Tickets; Love Letters; Gyp the Cat (Alternate master); Just Bummin' Around; On the Street Where You Live; Red Roses for a Blue Lady; If I Ruled the World.

The Curtain Falls: Live at the Flamingo CD (Collector's Choice Music CCM 171-2, 2000)

Hello Young Lovers; Ace in the Hole; You're Nobody 'til Somebody Loves You; Hits Medley: Splish Splash/Beyond the Sea/Artificial Flowers/Clementine; My Funny Valentine; I Walk the Line (parody); 18 Yellow Roses; Mack the Knife; One for my Baby (impressions); Work Song; Michael Row the Boat Ashore; Mary Don't You Weep; I'm on My Way Great God; The Curtain Falls (all live, 1963)

Aces Back to Back CD/DVD (Hyena TMF 9324, 2004)

This Could Be the Start of Something Big; Can't Take My Eyes Off You; Song Sung Blue; All I Have to do is Dream (with Petula Clark); A Quarter to Nine; Alone Again

Naturally; Lazy River; Mack the Knife (all live, 1972/1973); Blue Skies; Moon River; All the Way (studio recordings made for radio)

Songs from Big Sur CD (Varese Sarabande 302 066566-2, 2004)
City Life; Route 58; Distractions (Part 1) (alternate take, possibly 7" version); Distractions (Part 1) (live, 1969); Long Line Rider (live, 1969); Simple Song of Freedom (live, 1969); Questions (live, 1969)

The Swinging Side of Bobby Darin CD (Capitol, 7243 8 63883 2 2, 2005)
Make Someone Happy

The Milk Shows CD (Edsel EDSK 7068, 2014)
Mack the Knife Theme & Intro; Too Close for Comfort; Pennies from Heaven; Just in Time; Change Partners; Buttons and Bows; I'm an Old Cowhand; Around the World; Lazy River; Come On-a My House; Learnin' the Blues; Cheek to Cheek; Something's Gotta Give; Between the Devil and the Deep Blue Sea; Autumn Leaves; Sweet and Lovely; Hello Young Lovers; All of Me; Sixteen Tons; Please; I'll Be Seeing You; This Nearly Was Mine; What is this Thing Called Love; Guys and Dolls; Come Rain or Come Shine; I Have Dreamed; I Didn't Know What Time it Was; April Showers; Climb Every Mountain; Blue Moon; I Can't Give You Anything But Love; Tea for Two; By Myself; On the Sunny Side of the Street; Standing on the Corner; My Melancholy Baby; It Ain't Necessarily So; Say it With Music; A Pretty Girl is Like a Melody; Marie; Easter Parade; I've Got My Love to Keep Me Warm; Always; All by Myself; How Deep is the Ocean; Commercial; Band Introduction; Dream Lover; Splish Splash; Multiplication; You're the Reason I'm Living; End Titles; Introduction; Fools Rush In; La Vie en Rose; Some of these Days; Beyond the Sea; Bill Bailey Won't You Please Come Home; They Can't Take That Away From Me; Mandy; Be Honest With Me; You Made Me Love You; Ac-cent-tchu-ate the Positive; I Ain't Got Nobody; Manana; Too-ra Loo-ra Loo-ral; How About You; Rock-a-Bye Your Baby; Mairzy Doats and Dozy Doats; My Gal Sal; A You're Adorable; Row, Row, Row; In a Little Spanish Town; The Whiffenpoof Song; Please Help Me I'm Falling; Put on a Happy Face; Thou Swell; What Kind of Fool am I; Clementine; Band Intro; The Second Time Around; Let Me Sing and I'm Happy; The Sweetest Sounds; That's All; Hey Look Me Over; The Sheik of Araby; You Must Have Been a Beautiful Baby; Who Can I Count On; Days of Wine and Roses; Day in Day Out; Commercial; Make Someone Happy; End Titles (all studio recordings made for radio).

The Rare Capitol Masters (Deluxe edition, download)
Get Me To the Church on Time; I Cried For You; Scarlet Ribbons; If You Were the Only Girl in the World; Jealous; Alice Blue Gown; Oh Shenandoah.

SELECTED POSTHUMOUS DISCOGRAPHY

Another Song on My Mind: The Motown Years (Real Gone Music, RGM-0440)
This 2CD set contains all previously-released studio recordings from the Motown years. It contains all variants of each song, including single mixes and edits, and the alternate mixes first released on the *Bobby Darin, 1936-1973* LP. While it contains no unreleased material, there is much here than has not been available since the 1970s, and some here never released other than on singles. The best way to buy the 1972 and 1974 Motown albums.

Two of a Kind: Special Edition (Omnivore Recordings, OVCD-216)
Cecilia (take 4); Lily of Laguna (take 7); Bob White (take 17); East of the Rockies (take 6); I Ain't Gonna Give Nobody None of My Jellyroll (take 5A); My Cutie's Due at Two-to-Two Today (take 10); Mississippi Mud (Alternate take).

Go Ahead and Back Up: The Lost Motown Masters (Real Gone Music, RGM-0714)
Go Ahead and Back Up; Higher and Higher; Help Me Make It Through the Night; Watch the River Flow; Lady Madonna; I Walk the Line; You've Lost That Lovin' Feeling; I Don't Know How To Love Her; Catch the Wind; We're Getting There; Stray Dog (Oh Let Her Be); Child of Tears; I Think the Devil Must Be Beating His Wife; Cindy; I'm Glad About It; Oh Lord, Where Is My Baby; Young Joe Caldwell; The Letter (extended version); Proud Mary; Proud Mary (2nd version); Rags to Riches; Mona Lisa; Smile; Melodie (symphonic mix).

APPENDIX D
TELEVISION APPEARANCES

This list of television appearances by Bobby Darin does not pretend to be complete. It is compiled via reference to internet databases; archives; websites; the books of Jeff Bleiel and Al DiOrio; and new research of newspapers and magazines from the period. Thanks are also due to the members of the Bobby Darin Fan Club and Bobby Darin Appreciation groups on Facebook for providing extra information.

Song lists are not always complete. When no note follows the title of a programme, this indicates that the nature of Bobby's participation in the show is not known or song titles are unavailable. Despite these issues, this is by far the most complete and accurate list of Bobby Darin TV appearances yet compiled. Broadcast dates may have varied in different parts of the U.S. Where appropriate (and possible), local TV stations are listed when the shows in question were regional broadcasts.

Stage Show. March 10, 1956.
Rock Island Line

The Big Beat. July 19, 1957. WNEW-TV.
Talk to Me Something

American Bandstand. December 17, 1957.

The Dick Clark Saturday Night Beechnut Show. May 31, 1958.
Splish Splash

The Dick Clark Saturday Night Beechnut Show. July 19, 1958.
Early in the Morning; Splish Splash

The Bob Crosby Show. August 23, 1958.
Splish Splash

The Dick Clark Saturday Night Beechnut Show. November 1, 1958.
Queen of the Hop

The Dick Clark Saturday Night Beechnut Show. November 29, 1958.
Queen of the Hop

The Dick Clark Saturday Night Beechnut Show. January 10, 1959.
Queen of the Hop

Buddy Bregman's Music Shop. January 11, 1959
NB. There is a possibility that the date of broadcast was actually January 18.

Phil McLean's Saturday Afternoon Bandstand. February 7, 1959
Plain Jane

Record Hop. March 21, 1959. KMSP-TV.

The Perry Como Show. April 18, 1959.
Dream Lover; I Got a Rose Between My Toes/What's a Matter Wit' Me (part of a medley with Perry Como and Lou Carter)

Juke Box Jury. May 1, 1959. WNTA-TV

The Dick Clark Saturday Night Beechnut Show. May 2, 1959.
Dream Lover

The Ed Sullivan Show. May 31, 1959.
Dream Lover; Mack the Knife

The Big Beat July 9, 1959. WNEW-TV
Host.

Dance Party. July 17, 1959. KPIX-TV

The Big Beat. July 19, 1959. WNEW-TV

The Jerry Lester Show. July 31, 1959, KTTV.

TELEVISION APPEARANCES

The Buddy Deane Show. July, 1959.
NB. Unknown date.

Jukebox Jury. August 7, 1959.

Dance Party. August 8, 1959. KPIX-TV

The Dick Clark Saturday Night Beechnut Show. Aug 22, 1959.
Dream Lover; Mack the Knife

Record Hop at Steel Pier. August 29 & 30, 1959.
NB. Live TV broadcast of Bobby's on-stage performances.

The Ed Sullivan Show. September 6, 1959.
Swing Low Sweet Chariot/Lonesome Road/When the Saints Go Marchin' In; By Myself/When Your Lover Has Gone

The Peter Potter Show. September 16, 1959.
Guest host.

An Evening with Jimmy Durante. September 25, 1959.
Mack the Knife; That's All; Bill Bailey Won't You Please Come Home (with Jimmy Durante); *Personality* (with Jimmy Durante)

Hennessey. October 5, 1959.
"Hennessey meets Honeyboy Jones." Acting role.

The Louis Jourdan Timex Special. November 11, 1959.
Mack the Knife; Never Set Your Laundry Out in Tuscaloosa/Ida, Sweet as Apple Cider (with Louis Jourdan); *Time Will Never Change* (with Louis Jourdan, Jane Morgan, and Abbe Lane); *Unidentified/Bye Bye Love/Witch Doctor/Unidentified* (with Louis Jourdan, Jane Morgan and Abbe Lane)

George Burns in the Big Time. November 17, 1959.
Clementine; I Ain't Got Nobody (with George Burns)

NBC Sunday Showcase. November 29, 1959.
Taped broadcast of the Grammy Awards ceremony, at which Bobby was a winner.

BOBBY DARIN: DIRECTIONS

This is Your Life. December 2, 1959.
Subject.

The Big Party. December 3, 1959.

The Ed Sullivan Show. January 3, 1960.
That's the Way Love Is; Beyond the Sea; You Make Me Feel So Young/You're the Top (with Connie Francis)

March of Dimes. January 16, 1960.

The Ed Sullivan Show. February 28, 1960.
Clementine, By Myself/When Your Lover Has Gone; Mack the Knife (parody in French); *International Show* (with rest of the cast)

The Arthur Murray Party. March 8, 1960.

The Dick Clark Saturday Night Beechnut Show. March 19, 1960.
Mack the Knife; Clementine

Sunday Night at the London Palladium. April 10, 1960. (UK)
Some of these Days; Swing Low Sweet Chariot/Lonesome Road

Cool for Cats. April 22, 1960. (UK)
Clementine

This is Bobby Darin. April 23, 1960. (UK)
Mack the Knife; Guys and Dolls; The Gal that Got Away; My Funny Valentine; Beyond the Sea; Clementine; By Myself/When Your Lover Has Gone; I'm Just a Country Boy (with Duane Eddy); *Have Mercy Baby* (with Clyde McPhatter)

What's My Line. June 5, 1960.
Mystery guest.

The George Burns Show. June 7, 1960.
My Funny Valentine.

The Dick Clark Saturday Night Beechnut Show. June 11, 1960.
Bill Bailey, Won't You Please Come Home; I'll Be There

TELEVISION APPEARANCES

Coke Time. June 27, 1960.
All I Need is the Girl; Chattanooga Choo Choo/Goody Goody/Amapola/Oh! Look at Me Now/Flying Home/I'll Never Smile Again/Marie/I've Heard That Song Before (with Pat Boone, Paul Anka, Frankie Avalon)

The Dick Clark Saturday Night Beechnut Show. September 10, 1960.
Splish Splash; Mack the Knife (highlights from previous shows)

Dan Raven. September 23, 1960.
"The High Cost of Fame." Acting role.

The Bob Hope Show. October 3, 1960.
Artificial Flowers; Two Different Worlds (with Patti Page); *Thanks for the Memory/Mack the Knife/Two Sleepy People* (with Bob Hope); *Bill Bailey/Splish Splash/Alice Blue Gown* (with Bob Hope)

American Bandstand. December 13, 1960.
Artificial Flowers; Christmas Auld Lang Syne (Bobby co-hosts).

This is Your Life: Connie Francis. January 9, 1961.
Guest.

Phillies Jackpot Bowling. January 30, 1961.
Celebrity Contestant

Bobby Darin and Friends. January 31, 1961.
I Got Rhythm/I Got Plenty of Nothin'; I Have Dreamed; Some People; Lucky Pierre (with Bob Hope); *I Wish I Were in Love Again* (with Joanie Summers); *Bill Bailey Won't You Please Come Home* (with Bob Hope and Joanie Summers)

What's My Line. February 26, 1961.
Mystery guest.

The Jackie Gleason Show. March 17, 1961.
Lazy River; When Irish Eyes are Smiling; Rock Island Line (archive footage)

The 33rd Annual Academy Awards. April 17, 1961.
Presenting role.

Here's Hollywood. February 5, 1962.
Interview

At This Very Moment. April 1, 1962.
Bill Bailey Won't You Please Come Home (with Jimmy Durante)

The Ed Sullivan Show. May 6, 1962.
This Could Be the Start of Something Big; Toot Toot Tootsie Goodbye / Don't Worry About Me; I Got a Woman / What'd I Say / When the Saints Go Marchin' In

President Kennedy's Birthday Salute. May 16, 1962
Mack the Knife

The Tonight Show. October 3, 1962.

The Merv Griffin Show. October 4 or 18, 1962.

The Mike Douglas Show. October 17, 1962.

Weekend. October 27, 1962.

Jerry Lewis Show: From This Moment On. November 17, 1962
Bobby plays piano and drums with Henry Mancini's orchestra

Here's Hollywood. November 22, 1962.

The Bob Hope Show. November 29, 1962.
All of Me

What's My Line. December 9, 1962.
Mystery guest.

Password. January 6, 1963.
Celebrity contestant role.

Ballance Teen Topics. Unknown date, January 1963.

The Steve Allen Show. January 29, 1963.

The Jerry Lester Show. February 3, 1963.

TELEVISION APPEARANCES

The Steve Allen Show. February 9, 1963.
NB. This may be a repeat of the January 29, 1963 show, and it may simply be a mistake in a TV guide. However, it is listed here in case it is neither of the above.

Hollywood '63. February 17, 1963.

The Art Linkletter Show. February 18th, 1963.

Darin at the Grove. February 22, 1963.
Hour long TV special featuring Bobby in rehearsal, interviews, and ending with a live broadcast of the start of Bobby's show on opening night.

The Linkletter Show. March 12, 1963.

The Dinah Shore Chevy Show. April 14, 1963.
Blue Skies; Long Time Man; Work Song; When You're Smiling (with Dinah Shore and Andre Previn); *Everybody's Doing It/Let's Do It; Let's Fall in Love;* (with Dinah Shore and Andre Previn); *Bidin' My Time/Lazy Afternoon/If I Had My Druthers* (with Dinah Shore and Andre Previn); *Empty Pockets Filled with Love* (with Dinah Show and Andre Previn)

Clay Cole at the Moonbeam. July 20, 1963.
Interview

The Jerry Lewis Show. October 19, 1963.
Hello Young Lovers; Some of these Days; One for my Baby (impersonations).

The Ralph Pearl Show. November 3, 1963.
Interview.

The Jerry Lewis Show. November 9, 1963.
Audience member.

The Judy Garland Show. December 29, 1963.
Michael Row the Boat Ashore; I'm on My Way Great God; Sentimental Journey/Blues in the Night/Goin' Home/Chattanooga Choo Choo/Some of these Days/Toot Toot Tootsie Goodbye/I Know That You Know/I've Been Working on the Railroad/Lonesome Road (with Judy Garland)

Hollywood Backstage. Late 1963.
Interview.

The Jack Benny Show. January 28, 1964.
As Long as I'm Singing

Here's Edie. February 6, 1964.
This Nearly Was Mine; Mack the Knife/Moon Faced and Starry Eyed/Surghaya Johnny/Here I'll Stay/Bilbao Song/Alabama Song (with Edie Adams)

What's My Line. February 9, 1964.
Guest panellist.

The Object Is. February 10, 1964.
Contestant or panellist

I've Got a Secret. February 17, 1964.
Celebrity contestant

The 36th Annual Academy Awards. April 13, 1964.
Nominee.

Wagon Train. October 4, 1964.
"The John Gillman Story." Acting role.

Bob Hope Presents the Chrysler Theater. October 9, 1964.
"Murder in the First." Acting role.

American Bandstand. October 17, 1964.
Interview.

The Andy Williams Show. December 7, 1964.
Hard Hearted Hannah; You're Nobody 'til Somebody Loves You/Real Live Girl/When You're Smiling/Style/Three of a Kind (with Andy Williams and Robert Goulet)

The Andy Williams Show. January 11, 1965.
Once in a Lifetime; There's No Business Like Show Business/A Lot o' Livin' to Do/Put on a Happy Face/I Believe in You/She Loves Me/Together/The Sweetest Sounds/Get Me to the Church on Time/You are Woman/Hello Dolly (with Andy Williams and Vic Damone); *To Be a Performer* (with Andy Williams and Vic Damone); *Leader of the Pack* (with Vic Damone and the Osmonds).

TELEVISION APPEARANCES

What's My Line. January 31, 1965.
Guest panellist.

The Match Game. February 1-5, 1965.
Team captain.

Burke's Law. April 7, 1965.
"Who Killed Hamlet?" Acting role.

The Ed Sullivan Show. June 20, 1965.
Bobby appears briefly with other stars presenting an "anniversary cake" and singing *Happy Birthday*.

The Andy Williams Show. September 13, 1965.
That Funny Feeling; Pleasure Doing Business (with Andy Williams and Robert Goulet); *Little Girl/The Most Beautiful Girl in the World/When I'm Not Near the Girl That I Love/A Fellow Needs a Girl/Thank Heaven for Little Girls/The Girl That I Marry/The Girl That Married Dear Old Dad/There is Nothing Like a Dame* (with Andy Williams and Robert Goulet); *An Honest Man* (with Andy Williams and Robert Goulet)

The Red Skelton Show (aka: The Red Skelton Comedy Hour). September 21, 1965.
That Funny Feeling; Sunday in New York (with Jackie & Gayle).

The Steve Lawrence Show. October 11, 1965.

The Danny Kaye Show. Planned airdate: November 3, 1965.
Get Me to the Church on Time; Gyp the Cat; Fascinatin' Rhythm (with Danny Kaye)
NB. The above songs are what was planned for Bobby's involvement. For reasons unknown, he withdrew from the show at a late stage, and was replaced by Pat Boone. Publicity photos of Bobby, Danny Kaye and fellow guest Carolyn Jones had already been taken and distributed.

The Merv Griffin Show. Unknown date, 1965.
What'd I Say (instrumental)

The Andy Williams Show. January 10, 1966.
Gyp the Cat; This is the Life (with Andy Williams and Eddie Fisher); *Do-Re-Mi* (with Andy Williams and Eddie Fisher); *On a Wonderful Day Like Today* (with Eddie Fisher)

Jackie Gleason and his American Scene Magazine. February 26, 1966.
Mack the Knife.

Run For Your Life. March 7, 1966.
"Who's Watching the Fleshpot?" Acting role.

The Best on Record. May 16, 1966.

Wayne and Shuster Take an Affectionate Look at George Burns. July 15, 1966. (Canada)
Guest.

Mickie Finn's. July 28, 1966.
Mame
NB. The planned airdate of this show was July 21, but it was postponed for a week for reasons unknown.

The Andy Williams Show. October 9, 1966.
Mame; I Taught Him Everything He Knows; Girl Medley (with Andy Williams and Anthony Newley)

Ready, Steady, Go! November 4, 1966. (UK)
If I Were a Carpenter

Top of the Pops. November 10, 1966. (UK)
If I Were a Carpenter

The Roger Miller Show. November 14, 1966.
Hits medley; Clementine (with Roger Miller)

United Nations All-Star Gala. November 25, 1966. (UK)
NB. This was a concert in Paris, with an edited version screened on UK TV later that evening. Other versions were screened in other countries under different names.

Hollywood Backstage. 2 episodes. Unknown dates, 1966.

The Kraft Music Hall: Rodgers and Hart Today. March 2, 1967.
The Lady is a Tramp; I Wish I Were in Love Again (with Count Basie); *Any Old Place* (with Petula Clark); *Falling in Love with Love* (with Diana Ross and the Supremes); *Mountain Greenery* (with full cast)

TELEVISION APPEARANCES

The Joey Bishop Show. April 25, 1967.

Bobby Darin in London (aka: Something Special). 20 May, 1967
Don't Rain on My Parade; A Quarter to Nine; Once Upon a Time; I Wish I Were in Love Again; Mack the Knife; If I Were a Carpenter; One for my Baby (impersonations); The Girl Who Stood Beside Me; Funny What Love Can Do; What'd I Say; That's All

Dateline: Hollywood. July 3, 1967.
Interview

Dream Girl of 1967. August 14-18, 1967.
Guest judge.

The Tonight Show. August 31, 1967.

Spotlight (UK). August 1967.
NB. This UK show has been listed online within an itinerary of Bobby's live performances in 1967, which also states that Bobby gave live shows in Britain around the same time. This author has found no evidence that this visit to the UK happened. See: http://www.jussta.com/bobby-darin-world-tour-1967.html.

The Kraft Music Hall: Give My Regards to Broadway. October 4, 1967.
Yankee Doodle Dandy; Always Leave 'em Laughing; Give My Regards to Broadway (probably ensemble number); *You're a Wonderful Girl* (with Liza Minnelli).

The Tonight Show. November 13, 1967.

First Annual All-star Celebrity Baseball Game. November 28, 1967.
Player.

The Kraft Music Hall: A Grand Night for Swinging. January 10, 1968.
Talk to the Animals; Mack the Knife; Drown in My Own Tears; Long Time Movin' (with Bobbie Gentry*); Nothin' Can Stop Us Now* (with Bobbie Gentry and Bobby Van)

The Danny Thomas Show. January 15, 1968.
"The Cage." Acting role

The Mike Douglas Show. January 29 – February 2, 1968.

The Tonight Show. February 15, 1968.

397

The Jerry Lewis Show. February 27, 1968.
Talk to the Animals; Sixteen Tons; Epicurian Delight (with Jerry Lewis and Jane Powell)

And Debbie Makes Six. March 7, 1968.
Medley; Sylvia's Mother (with Debbie Reynolds)
NB. Originally scheduled to be shown on November 19, 1967, but postponed due to a technical strike.

The Merv Griffin Show. March 27, 1968.

Rowan and Martin's Laugh-in. October 14, 1968.
Mack the Knife (parody) (duet with Artie Johnson)

The Jerry Lewis Show. October 29, 1968.
Long Line Rider; Change

Sydney Tonight. November 20, 1968. (Australia)

Bobby Darin at the Silver Spade. November 26, 1968. (Australia)
Mack the Knife; Let the Good Times Roll; If I Were a Rich Man; Talk to the Animals

Leonetti and Friends. December 19, 1968 (Australia)
NB. Archive footage from the previous month.

Sydney Tonight. December 25, 1968 (Australia)

The Joey Bishop Show. December 28, 1968.

Upbeat. January 18, 1969
Long Line Rider

The Kraft Music Hall: The Sounds of the Sixties. January 22, 1969.
Let the Good Times Roll; Splish Splash; Take a Whiff on Me; Long Line Rider; If I Were a Carpenter (with Stevie Wonder); *I'll Be Your Baby Tonight* (with Judy Collins)

The Dean Martin Show. February 20, 1969.
Long Line Rider; I'm Sitting on Top of the World / There's a Rainbow 'Round My Shoulder / Toot Toot Tootsie Goodbye (with Dean Martin)

TELEVISION APPEARANCES

Upbeat. February 22, 1969.
Long Line Rider

The Joey Bishop Show. May 13, 1969.

Della! August 11, 1969.

The Tonight Show. August 21, 1969

The Barbara McNair Show. September 28, 1969.
Hey Jude

This is Tom Jones. October 2, 1969.
Distractions (Part 1) (part 1); Aquarius/Let the Sunshine In (with Tom Jones)

The Tonight Show. November 5, 1969.

Della! November 13, 1969.

Burlesque is Alive and Living in Beautiful Downtown Burbank. Planned airdate: November 24, 1969.
Burbank Burly-Q (with Carl Reiner and Goldie Hawn); *Mack the Knife* (incomplete); *I Love Lance* (probably with Carl Reiner and Goldie Hawn); *Beautiful Ladies* (with full cast)
NB. This special was due for broadcast on the above date, but was cancelled a few days before. It has never been broadcast within the USA. It was shown in Australia on August 17, 1971.

Della! January 28, 1970.

Philbin's People. May 29, 1970.

Disco 2. June 13 or 14, 1970. (UK)

The Golden Shot. June 14, 1970. (UK)

Late Night Line-up. June 16, 1970 (UK)
This was primarily a discussion programme

The Roy Castle Show. June 20, 1970 (UK)

At Maggie's Place. June 1970 (UK)
NB. Exact date unknown.

The Mike Douglas Show. July 27 – July 31, 1970.
If I Were a Carpenter; And When I Die; Long Line Rider; Bridge Over Troubled Water; Everybody's Talkin'; Splish Splash; City Life; Mack the Knife; My Funny Valentine; Put a Little Love in Your Heart (with Mahalia Jackson); *You Smiling Now/Bill Bailey Won't You Please Come Home* (with Mike Douglas); *Got My Mojo Working* (with Little Richard)

The Jerry Lewis MDA Telethon. September 6, 1970

The Andy Williams Show. September 19, 1970.
Mack the Knife

The Flip Wilson Show. September 24, 1970.
Melodie; Who Takes Care of the Caretaker's Daughter (with Flip Wilson and Roy Clark)

The Darin Invasion. October 1970. (Canada)
Higher and Higher; Hi-De-Ho; If I Were a Carpenter; Simple Song of Freedom; Pick a Pocket or Two/Reviewing the Situation; I Ain't Got Nobody (with George Burns); *A Long Long Time* (accompanying Linda Ronstadt)

The Flip Wilson Show. November 20, 1970.
Higher and Higher; Country and Western Medley (with Flip Wilson and Charlie Pride)

The Flip Wilson Show. December 17, 1970.
Gabriel; Paddlin' Madelin' Home/Row, Row, Row (with Flip Wilson); *Noises in the Street* (with Flip Wilson and Sid Caesar)

Celebrity Bowling. January 16, 1971.
Contestant

The Flip Wilson Show. January 21, 1971.
Lazy River; If I Were a Carpenter; Toot Toot Tootsie, Goodbye (with Flip Wilson

Goin' Back to Indiana. September 19, 1971.
Comedy role

Ironside. October 5, 1971.
"The Gambling Game." Acting role.

TELEVISION APPEARANCES

Cade's County. November 28, 1971.
"A Gun for Billy." Acting role.

The Merv Griffin Show. December 27, 1971.

The Flip Wilson Show. January 13, 1972.
Mack the Knife; Simple Song of Freedom; One of Those Songs (with Flip Wilson)

Night Gallery. February 9, 1972.
"Dead Weight." Acting role

The Dick Cavett Show. February 28, 1972.

The Tonight Show. March 6, 1972.

The 14th Annual Grammy Awards. March 14, 1972
Presenter of award

The David Frost Show. March 16, 1972.
For Once in my Life; Mack the Knife; If I Were a Carpenter; Worried Man/Splish Splash/unknown jazz number (on drums)

Engelbert with the Young Generation. March 19, 1972.
Mack the Knife; If I Were a Carpenter; Blowin' in the Wind (with Nancy Wilson and Engelbert Humperdinck)

Easter Seals Telethon. April 1972.
NB. Unknown Date.

Tumwater Caravan. May 24, 1972.

The Tonight Show. July 24 and July 25, 1972
Guest host.

The Bobby Darin Amusement Company. July 27, 1972.
Can't Take My Eyes Off You; What Now My Love; You Are My Sunshine/Got My Mojo Working; Niki Hoeky/Proud Mary/Polk Salad Annie/Never Ending Song of Love (with Bobbie Gentry); *I Ain't Go Nobody* (with George Burns).
NB. While this was the first show broadcast, it wasn't the first one recorded. In the show broadcast on August 17, 1972, Bobby clearly states that it is the first show. Mack

the Knife is sung as Bobby exits at the end of each show.

The Bobby Darin Amusement Company. August 3, 1972.
Charade; Beyond the Sea; Sail Away; You and Me Babe (with Debbie Reynolds)

The Bobby Darin Amusement Company. August 10, 1972.
I'll Be Your Baby Tonight; For Once in My Life; You've Got a Friend (with Dusty Springfield)

The Bobby Darin Amusement Company. August 17, 1972.
Spinning Wheel; If I Were a Carpenter; Mack the Knife; I'll Never Fall in Love Again (with Donald O'Connor); *Bridge Over Troubled Water* (with Dionne Warwick)
NB. Mack the Knife is sung to completion on this occasion but not on other episodes.

The Bobby Darin Amusement Company. August 24, 1972.
Higher and Higher; Strangers in the Night; Simple Song of Freedom; Let It Be Me (with Claudine Longet)

The Bobby Darin Amusement Company. August 31, 1972.
That's All; Artificial Flowers; Work Song; Happy Together (with Florence Henderson)

The Bobby Darin Amusement Company. September 7, 1972.
Brother, Can You Spare a Dime?; Talk to the Animals; Side by Side by Side (with The Smothers Brothers)

The Irish Rovers. November 13, 1972. (Canada)
Beyond the Sea; Simple Song of Freedom; If I Were a Carpenter
NB. Video evidence suggests that Bobby appeared on two episodes of the series, but that both segments were recorded at the same time.

The Sonny & Cher Comedy Hour. November 19, 1972.
Sail Away; Whiffenpoof Song (parody as part of a skit)

A Matter of Time. December 1972.
Host

The Bobby Darin Show. January 19, 1973.
Once in a Lifetime; Sweet Caroline; A Quarter to Nine; Happy; Hey Lolly Lolly Low (with Burl Ives); *Something* (with Dyan Cannon) *San Francisco* (with cast)
NB. Mack the Knife is sung as Bobby exits at the end of each show.

TELEVISION APPEARANCES

The Bobby Darin Show. January 26, 1973.
Born Free; Caravan; I'll Be Your Baby Tonight; Bridge Over Troubled Water; St Louis Blues (partial); If Not For You (with Helen Reddy); *The Trolley Song* (with cast)

The Tonight Show. January 29, 1973.

The Bobby Darin Show. February 2, 1973.
Hello Young Lovers; Artificial Flowers; Happy; Fire and Rain; Give My Regards to Broadway; Paddlin' Madelin' Home/Row, Row, Row (with Flip Wilson); *All I Have to do is Dream* (with Petula Clark)

The Tonight Show. February 6, 1973.
You Are My Sunshine/Got My Mojo Working/Splish Splash

The Bobby Darin Show. February 9, 1973.
Lover Come Back to Me; King of the Road; If; Lonesome Road; Light My Fire (with Nancy Sinatra); *Bill Bailey, Won't You Please Come Home* (with Red Foxx); *My Kind of Town* (with full cast)

The Bobby Darin Show. February 16, 1973.
This Could Be the Start of Something Big; Dreidel; Sixteen Tons; Swinging on a Star (with Charlene Wong); *Ain't No Mountain High Enough* (with Freda Payne); *unknown duet* (with Taj Mahal).

The Bobby Darin Show. February 23, 1973.
Don't Rain on My Parade; Song Sung Blue; Higher and Higher; Alone Again Naturally; Basin Street Blues (partial); *Never My Love* (with Cloris Leachman); *Muskrat Ramble* (with cast)

The Bobby Darin Show. March 2, 1973.
It's Today; Mame; Once Upon a Time; Two of a Kind (with Donald O'Connor); *Let's Do It* (with Elke Sommer); *Give a Little Whistle* (with Charlene Wong)

Midnight Special. March 16, 1973.
If I Were a Carpenter; Dream Lover/Splish Splash/Roll Over Beethoven

The Bobby Darin Show. March 23, 1973.
Some People; Climb Every Mountain; Help Me Make it Through the Night; I Get a Kick Out Of You; I Know an Old Lady Who Swallowed a Fly (with Charlene Wong); *Baby I Need Your Lovin'* (with Dusty Springfield)

The Bobby Darin Show. March 30, 1973.
As Long As I'm Singin; Brooklyn Roads; I've Got You Under My Skin; If I Were a Carpenter; You've Got a Friend (with Connie Stevens)

The Bobby Darin Show. April 6, 1973.
Charade; I'll Remember April; Here's That Rainy Day; I'll Be Seeing You; Beyond the Sea; Happy Together (with Leslie Uggams)
NB. Beyond the Sea was taken from the taping of the final episode in the series, edited, and inserted into this episode.

The Bobby Darin Show. April 13, 1973.
There's a Rainbow 'Round My Shoulder'; Cry Me a River; Let the Good Times Roll; And the Band Played On (partial); *After the Ball* (with full cast)

Bobby Darin Show. April 20, 1973.
Get Me to the Church on Time; Shilo; Come Rain or Come Shine; Guys and Dolls; There's a Hole in my Bucket (with Carol Lawrence); *Words* (with Carol Lawrence); *High Hopes* (with Charlene Wong); *Let Me Call You Sweetheart/Volare/Just an Old Fashioned Song/It's DeLovely* (with Carol Lawrence)

The Bobby Darin Show. April 27, 1973.
For Once in My Life/Once in a Lifetime; Help Me Make it Through the Night; Can't Take My Eyes Off You; Bridge Over Troubled Water; Midnight Special; Lonesome Whistle; You Are My Sunshine/Bo Diddley/Splish Splash/Roll Over Beethoven; Just Friends/Something to Remember You By/Skylark/Spring is Here/Long Ago and Far Away (with Peggy Lee)

American Bandstand 20th Anniversary Show. June 23, 1973
Unknown (probably archive footage)

APPENDIX E
DARIN COMPOSITIONS RECORDED BY OTHERS

The following is a lengthy, but partial, list of songs and compositions written by Bobby Darin that have been recorded by other artists. Many of these songs were never recorded or performed by Bobby himself. This list does not pretend to be complete, but is intended to show just how wide-ranging Bobby's vast amount of compositions were around the world and how they have attracted artists from all genres of popular music. Many of these are easily available to hear via the likes of YouTube, and checking some of them out is recommended.

After School Rock 'n' Roll	The Capri Sisters
Amy	Rudy Bennett; The Motions; Tam White
As Long as I'm Singing	Freddy Cole; Matt Monro; Wayne Newton; Richard Olson; Andy Prior; Brian Setzer; Kevin Spacey; Aaron Weinstein & John Pizzarelli; Gary Williams.
Barb'ry Ann	Bobby Edge
Be Mad Little Girl	Keld Heick; Paul Wayne
Beachcomber	? and the Mysterians; The Johnny Gibson Trio; Johnny Griffin; The Semi-colons; The Soulblenders
Bi-Aza-Ku-Saza	The Mogambos
Boss Barracuda	The Barracudas; The Catalinas; The Surfaris
Brand New House	Ann Cole; Otis Spann & Muddy Waters
Bullmoose	Mike Berry & The Crickets; The Fireballs; The Firing Squad; The Keil Isles; The Wild Angels
By My Side	Otto Brandenburg; Davy Hill; Glen Mason
Casey Wake Up	Joanie Sommers

BOBBY DARIN: DIRECTIONS

Change	Andre Heller; Kevin Spacey
Come September (theme)	The Andrews Sisters; Chet Atkins; Chuck Atkins; Stirling Brandy; The Carmets; Radmila Karaklajic; Franco Leo; José Manuel Del Moral; The Ray Mills Group; Das Paul-Nero-Bar-Sextet; Fausto Papetti; Eila Pellinen; Santo & Johnny; Gesy Sebena; John Severson; Peter Steffen; Tom and Jerry; Billy Vaughan; The Ventures; Helmut Zacharius
Coming Down (with a Heartache)	Louis Jordan; Lou Rawls; Jackie Shayne; Les Vicomtes
Day Dreamer	Jimmy Boyd
Delia	Bobby Short
Distractions (Part 1)	Dean & Britta
Do the Monkey	King Curtis; James Ray; The Swinging Jaguars
Down so Long	Roosevelt (aka: Rosey) Grier
Dream Baby	Daniel Fabrice; Wayne Newton
Dream Lover	Marc Almond; Horace Andy; Richard Anthony; The Astronauts; Los Boppers; Johnny Burnette; Glen Campbell & Tanya Tucker; Howard Carpendale; Michel Chevalier; Roberto Clarence; Father Michael Cleary; Billy Crash Craddock; Dalida; Dana; Danny; Dion; The Dollyrots; Jason Donovan; Craig Douglas; Brenda Duff; Allison Durban; Duane Eddy; Debbie Elam; Tommy Elfs; The Embassy Six; Emile Ford & The Checkmates; Jorge Foster; Franks and Deans; Joe Gordon Folk Four; Max Greger; Owen Grey; Greyhound; Ronnie Hawkins; Herman's Hermits; Mary Hopkin; Johnny & The New Dodgers; Ben E. King; Lord Knud; Santi Latora; Gene Latter; The Lettermen; Gary Lewis and the Playboys; Lúdó Og Stefán; Lulu; Peter McCann; Don McLean; The Mad-Ladds; Ina Merton & the Ping Pongs; McKinley Mitchell; Derrick Morgan & Yebo; Mud; Hal Munro; Anne Murray; Johnny Nash; Ricky Nelson; Daniel O'Donnell; Tony Orlando; The Packabeats; The Paris Sisters; Sandy Posey; Duffy Power; Cliff Richard; Bobby Rydell; Frankie Sardo; Santo & Johnny; Satu; Pierre Sellin and his Orchestra; Rocky Sharpe & The Replays; Showaddywaddy; Svenne & Lotta; That Girl; The

DARIN COMPOSITIONS RECORDED BY OTHERS

	Trey Tones; Trumpet Boy; Spyder Turner; The Undivided; The Vanguards; Leslie West; Marty Wilde
Early in the Morning	Mac Curtis; Skeeter Davis; The Four Kings; Freddie and the Dreamers; Buddy Holly; Bob Horan; Johnny O' Keefe; Del Reeves; Cliff Richard; Tommy Roe; Marcel Romain; Tony and the Initials; Bobby Vee
18 Yellow Roses	Tommy Adderly; Ollie Austin; The Black Devils; Clive Bruce; Frankie Davidson; Sydney Devine; Georg Dolivo; Mack Dumis; Bobby Evans; Boris Gardiner; The Gaylords; The Hawking Brothers; Carl Mann; Midday Sun; Miki; Bobbie Prins; Johnny Reimar Marty Robbins; The Texas Tornados; Lawrence Welk; Gustav Winkler; Marty Wood
Fourteen Pairs of Shoes	Tommy Roe
Freedom to Love	Little Wayne Anthony; Claudie Dorel
Funny What Love Can Do	Della Reese
The Harvest	Juicy Lucy
Hello Sunshine	Gary Lewis and the Playboys
Hot Rod U.S.A.	The Barracudas; The Catalinas; The Fantastic Baggys; The Knights; The Rip Chords; The T-Bones
I Can't Believe a Word You Say	Lou Rawls
I Got My Own Thing Goin' On	Little Charles & the Sidewinders; The Jay Walkers
I Want to Spend Christmas with Elvis	Debbie Dabney; Little Lambsie Penn; Marlene Paula
I'll Be There	Les Carle; Cesar Et Set Romains; Frank Chacksfield; Floyd Cramer; Cass Elliott; Ethel; The Fleetwoods; Gerry & The Pacemakers; Cissy Houston; George Martin; Tony Orlando; Elvis Presley; The Uptones
I've Got it Made	Jimmy Boyd
If a Man Answers	Richard Anthony; Arch Hall Jr & The Archers; Rob de Nijs met The Lords
If You Love Him	Joanie Sommers
It's Him I Wanna Go With Mama	Debbie Stanley
It's What's Happening Baby	Billy Storm
Jailer Bring Me Water	The Bachelors; The Bells; The Beresford Ricketts; Burt Blanca and the King Creoles; Jackie DeShannon; Freddie & The Dreamers; The Hawaiian Surfers; Timo Jämsen & The Esquires; Fasia Jansen; Penny Lang; Lou & Simon; Trini Lopez; The Ravers;

	Johnny Rivers; Johnny Thunder; Johnny Tillotson; The Truth
The Lively Set	James Darren; Del Noah & The Mt Ararat Finks
Long Line Rider	Eddie Floyd
Look at Me	Wink Martindale
Look for My True Love	Al Styne
Lost Love	John Holt
Love Me Right in the Morning	LaVern Baker
Made in the Shade	Jimmy Boyd
Maybe We Can Get it Together	Teddie Palmer & the Rumble Band
Me and Mr. Hohner	Gianfranco; Magic Bubble
Multiplication	Russ Abbott; Bert Bennys; Los Clippers; Fabricio; George Freedman; Harmony Cats; Mike Kennedy; Cy Manifold; Manolo Munoz; Rauni Pekkala; The Ravers; Reynaldo Rayol; Johnny Rivers; The Rocking Boys; Los Salvages; Showaddywaddy; Victor Silvester; Petr Spaleny; Bobby Stevens
My Dog Got a Tag on Her	Jack Eden
My First Real Love	Jenna Esposito; Connie Francis
My Mom	Indiana; The Osmond Brothers
Not For Me	Marc Almond; George Chakiris; The Crescendoes; Sammy Davis Jr.; Miriam; Eddy Mitchell;
Now We're One	Buddy Holly
O.K. Girl	Tom Burt
Oo-Ee-Train	Mick Harvey; The Honeycombs
Peck-a-Cheek	Eddy Arnold
Queen of the Hop	Mike Berry & The Crickets; The Buckaroos; Danny & The Juniors; Dion & The Belmonts; Dave Edmunds; Don Lang; Hank Locklin; Robert Plant & The Honeydrippers; Sha Na Na; Shakin' Stevens
Rainin'	Val Doonican; Matt Forbes; Rita Pavone
Real Love	The Jaye Sisters; Ruby Murray
Run Little Rabbit	The Catalinas; The Five-Hundreds
Sausalito	The Shepherds
School's Out	The Jaye Sisters
Shirl Girl	Lucia Altieri; Mike Clifford; Wayne Newton
Simple Song of Freedom	Ossi Ahlapuro; Nicola di Bari; The Bells; Lars Berghagen; Sten Bramsen; Buckwheat; Petra Cernocka; I Combos; Katja Ebstein; Ulf Elfving; Bruno Glenmarks Kor Och Orkester; Tim Hardin;

DARIN COMPOSITIONS RECORDED BY OTHERS

	Lecia and Lucienne; The Mystic Moods Orchestra; Della Reese; Gro Anita Schonn; Eddie Skoller; P. F. Sloan; Kevin Spacey; Spirit of Us; United Singers; Voices of East Harlem
Since You're Gone	Dave Berry; Lee Hazlewood; Judy Jacques
So Mean	Johnny October
Somebody to Love	Richard Anthony; Heinz; The Jets; Wayne Newton; Sammy Rodgers; Johnny Waard
Song for a Dollar	Black Faith
Soul City	Roosevelt (aka: Rosey) Grier
Splish Splash	Frankie Avalon; Marc Benno; The Bob Cats; Bocephus; Roberto Carlos; Cesar et la Romains; Charlie & The Twisters; Jacques Desrosiers; Deke Devilson; Charlie Drake; Fiskomania; Michael Holm; George Hudson; The Keil Isles; Roger Kellaway Trio; Little Joe; Joe Loco and his Pachanga Band; Los Locos del Ritmo; Loggins & Messina; Mina and the Solitaires; Montezuma's Revenge; Sandy Nelson; Rita Pavone; Tommy Sands; Sha Na Na; Dee Dee Sharp; Bro Smith; The Starlite Singers; The Strato-tones; Barbra Streisand; The Three Degrees; Conway Twitty; Marty Wilde; Wizex; Frank Zander
Sugar Man	Daisy Door; Jimmy Powell
Summertime Symphony	Jamie Coe; Little Gerhard
Sweet Reasons	Judy Mayhan
That Funny Feeling	Wayne Newton; Billy Storm
There Goes a Bad Girl	Johnny Cymbal; Jonica
Things	Schlomo Artzi; Barry Biggs; Lucky Blondo; Blooblo; The Coldside Trio; Constantin Draghici; The Drivers; Jerry Dyke; Adam Faith; Remo Germani; The Glass Bottle; Winston Groovy; Katri Helena; Hayati Kafe; Paula Koivuniemi; Jerry Lee Lewis; Lúdó Og Stefán; Birgit Lystager; Dean Martin (solo); Dean Martin & Nancy Sinatra; Moustache; Anne Murray; I Nobili; Rita Pavone; Brian Poole & The Tremeloes; Alan Price; Mike Redway; Ivica Serfezi; Showaddywaddy; Vilan Subota; Johnny Tillotson; Bobby Vee; Walter Raim; Wilburn Brothers; Robbie Williams & Jane Horrocks; Francis Yip

BOBBY DARIN: DIRECTIONS

The Things in this House	Claude François; George Jouvin Y Su Trompeta De Oro; The Streaplers
This Little Girl's Gone Rockin'	Steve Alaimo; Ruth Brown; Alma Cogan; Glenda Collins; Conny; Gitte; Col Joye & the Joy Boys; ; Little Tina & Flight '56; Janice Peters & The Frank Barber Band; Bill Wyman's Rhythm Kings (under the name "Bootleg Kings"); Zebra Stripes
Two Tickets	Jimmie Rodgers
Wa'tch You Mean	The Mogambos
Wait a Minute	The Coasters
Wait by the Water	Tony Barber; Burton Cummings
We Didn't Ask to be Brought Here	Marty Kristian
Wear My Ring	Pete Boy & The Virginia Gang; Gene Vincent
When I Get Home	The Searchers
Why Oh You	Lindsey Crosby
A World Without You	Carol Fran
You Just Don't Know	Mary K. Miller; Wayne Newton
You're the Reason I'm Living	Brook Benton; Maxine Brown; Archie Campbell and Lorene Mann; Ace Cannon; Don Cherry; Ronnie Dove; Rett Hardin; Wanda Jackson; Sonny James; Brenda Lee; Harry Middlebrooks; Ronnie Milsap; Price Mitchell; Lamar Morris; The Peddlars; Elvis Presley; Lawrence Welk
Your Cute Little Ways	Vinnie Monte & The Jay Birds
Zoom-a-Roo	The Bermuda Keynotes

APPENDIX F
FILMOGRAPHY

Actor

Pepe (George Sidney, 1960)
Come September (Robert Mulligan, 1961)
Too Late Blues (John Cassavetes, 1961)
State Fair (José Ferrer, 1962)
Hell is for Heroes (Don Siegel, 1962)
Pressure Point (Hubert Cornfield, 1962)
If a Man Answers (Henry Levin, 1962)
Captain Newman, M.D. (David Miller, 1963)
That Funny Feeling (Richard Thorpe, 1965)
Gunfight in Abilene (William Hale, 1967)
Stranger in the House (aka: *Cop-Out*) (Pierre Rouve, 1967)
The Happy Ending (Richard Brooks, 1969)
Happy Mother's Day, Love George (aka: *Run Stranger Run*) (Darren McGavin, 1973)

Director
The Vendors (1969, unfinished, never screened publicly)

APPENDIX G
UNRELEASED RECORDINGS

These pages list recordings made by (or of) Bobby that, as yet, have not been released. Songs tried on multiple dates in the studio before a satisfactory take was achieved are generally not included, but a song such as *Some of These Days*, recorded in a different arrangement for a different project to the well-known version on *That's All*, is included. Dates given are in DD/MM/YY format. Survival status for most entries on this list are unknown, although most unreleased songs from 1965-1967 are thought to have been destroyed in a fire. Songs known to still exist are indicated by an asterisk (*). Please see footnotes for more information.

Please note: The decision to include this material was made at the eleventh hour, and after the index had been completed and finalised. Regrettably, this means that titles in this section are not referenced in the index.

Date	Title	Notes
??/03/56	*Rock Pile*	Studio recording
30/10/58	*Some of These Days*	Studio recording
5/12/58	*Didn't It Feel Good*	Studio recording
19/5/59	*The Breeze and I*	Studio recording for *This is Darin*
20/5/59	*Since My Love Was Gone*	Studio recording for *This is Darin*
21/5/59	*The Lamp is Low*	Studio recording for *This is Darin*
6/9/59	*I Feel a Song Coming On*	Live recording, Hollywood Bowl[622]
6/9/59	*On the Sunny Side of the Street*	Live recording, Hollywood Bowl
6/9/59	*Exactly Like You*	Live recording, Hollywood Bowl

---

[622] These recordings from September 6, 1959, were made at a concert paying tribute to songwriter Jimmy McHugh. Only Bobby's solos are listed here. A year after the concert, conductor and arranger Buddy Bregman acquired the rights to the recordings, but they have never been released. Their survival status is uncertain.

BOBBY DARIN: DIRECTIONS

Date	Title	Notes
6/9/59	Let's Get Lost	Live recording, Hollywood Bowl
6/9/59	I Can't Give You Anything But Love	Live recording, Hollywood Bowl
6/9/59	I Couldn't Sleep a Wink Last Night	Live recording, Hollywood Bowl
6/9/59	Can't Get Out of This Mood	Live recording, Hollywood Bowl
1/2/60	A Game of Poker	Studio recording for *Winners*
2/2/60	I Got a Woman	Studio recording for *Winners*
15-16/6/60	My Funny Valentine	Live recording for *Darin at the Copa*
15-16/6/60	Splish Splash	Live recording for *Darin at the Copa*
15-16/6/60	The Birth of the Blues	Live recording for *Darin at the Copa*
21/6/60	Won't You Come Home Bill Bailey*	*Let's Go to Town* radio programme[623]
21/6/60	That's the Way Love Is*	*Let's Go to Town* radio programme
21/6/60	Beyond the Sea*	*Let's Go to Town* radio programme
21/6/60	When Your Lover Has Gone*	*Let's Go to Town* radio programme
21/6/60	That's All*	*Let's Go to Town* radio programme
21/6/60	I Can't Give You Anything But Love*	*Let's Go to Town* radio programme
21/6/60	Mack the Knife*	*Let's Go to Town* radio programme
21/6/60	She Needs Me*	*Let's Go to Town* radio programme
17/8/60	Back in Your Own Backyard	Studio recording for *Two of a Kind*
25/3/61	Bobby's Blues	Studio recording, instrumental
8/6/61	Special Someone	Studio recording for *Come September*[624]
8/6/61	Teenage Theme	Studio recording for *Come September*
8/6/61	Movin' On	Studio recording for *Come September*
??/11/63	Unknown titles*	Live recording, Las Vegas[625]
13/1/64	Maybe Today	Studio recording
24/3/65	King of the Road	Studio recording
24/3/65	The Joker	Studio recording
24/3/65	My Kind of Town	Studio recording

---

[623] The *Let's Go To Town* radio programme was part of a recruitment drive for the National Guard. All of Bobby's songs were recorded especially for the shows and featured him singing with Ray Bloch and his Orchestra. The eight songs were split over four episodes, but an assumption has been made that they were all recorded on the same day. These radio shows exist within the collection of the Paley Center for Media.

[624] The June 8th 1961 recordings are likely to be instrumentals for the soundtrack of the film *Come September*.

[625] As multiple versions of some songs recorded in Las Vegas in November 1963 have been released, it stands to reason that more than one show was recorded. This means there are alternate versions of some songs still in the vaults.

UNRELEASED RECORDINGS

Date	Title	Type
14/8/65	Sweet Memories of You	Studio recording
14/8/65	Ain't That a Bunch of Nonsense	Studio recording
13/12/65	Ace in the Hole	Studio recording
13/12/65	The Best is Yet to Come	Studio recording
14/12/65	The Sheik of Araby	Studio recording
14/12/65	This Could Be the Star of Something Big	Studio recording
15/12/65	I Got Plenty of Nothin'	Studio recording
15/12/65	Baby Won't You Please Come Home	Studio recording
4/2/66	Weeping Willow*	Studio recording[626]
23/3/66	Strangers in the Night	Studio recording
31/3/66	As Long as I'm Singin'*	Live recording, Copa[627]
31/3/66	Some of These Days*	Live recording, Copa
31/3/66	After You've Gone*	Live recording, Copa
31/3/66	Mame*	Live recording, Copa
31/3/66	I've Got the World on a String/Yesterday*	Live recording, Copa
31/3/66	Mack the Knife*	Live recording, Copa
31/3/66	One for My Baby (impressions)*	Live recording, Copa
31/3/66	One of Those Songs (medley)*	Live recording, Copa
31/3/66	Gotta Travel On *	Live recording, Copa
31/3/66	Brother Can You Spare a Dime*	Live recording, Copa
31/3/66	King of the Road*	Live recording, Copa
31/3/66	Trouble in Mind*	Live recording, Copa
31/3/66	I Got Plenty of Nothin'*	Live recording, Copa
21/4/66	True Love's a Blessing	Studio recording
9/5/66	L. A. Breakdown	Studio recording
9/5/66	I Can Live on Love	Studio recording
9/5/66	Manhattan in My Heart*	Studio recording[628]
27/5/66	Merry-Go-Round in the Rain	Studio recording
27/5/66	Seventeen	Studio recording[629]
28/6/66	Lulu's Back in Town	Studio recording

---

[626] This song has circulated amongst fans for years. An official release was announced in 2015 but never materialised.

[627] These songs are from a radio broadcast of Bobby's performance at the Copa on March 31, 1966. Some titles can be found in low quality on YouTube. A full tape of the show exists at the Paley Center for Media. Thanks to Matt Forbes for confirming these titles.

[628] A release of this song was announced in 2015 but did not materialise.

[629] It is not known if this is the correct title of the song. Could it actually be The Beatles' *I Saw Her Standing There*, with the opening line "she was just seventeen?"

BOBBY DARIN: DIRECTIONS

Date	Title	Notes
28/6/66	*For You*	Studio recording
28/6/66	*What Now My Love*	Studio recording
28/6/66	*Mountain Greenery*	Studio recording
30/6/66	*It's Magic*	Studio recording
30/6/66	*Danke Schoen*	Studio recording
30/6/66	*My Own True Love*	Studio recording
30/6/66	*On a Clear Day*	Studio recording
30/6/66	*A Quarter to Nine*	Studio recording
20/10/66	*Funny What Love Can Do*	Studio recording for *If I Were a Carpenter*
20/10/66	*Good Day Sunshine*	Studio recording for *If I Were a Carpenter*
20/10/66	*Young Girl*	Studio recording for *If I Were a Carpenter*
20/10/66	*Daydreamer*	Studio recording for *If I Were a Carpenter*
2/2/67	*Saginaw, Michigan*	Studio recording for *Inside Out*
26/6/67	*Biggest Night of Her Life*	Studio recording
4/11/67	*All Strung Out*	Studio recording
18/11/67	*Tupelo Mississippi Flash*	Studio recording
19/11/67	*Natural Soul Lovin' Big City Countrified Man*	Studio recording
19/11/67	*While I'm Gone*	Studio recording
??/11/67	*Meditation/I Will Wait For You*	Demo
??/11/67	*Prison of Your Love*	Demo
??/05/69	Unknown titles	Live recordings, The Troubador[630]
16/7/69	Unknown titles	Live recordings, Las Vegas[631]

---

[630] Four tracks from this set of recordings were issued in 2004. It seems inconceivable that these were the only songs recorded

[631] One track recorded at The Bonanza in Las Vegas was issued in 1995. Presumably, more tracks were recorded at the time.

BIBLIOGRAPHY

Abbott, Peter. "What's New on the East Coast." *TV Radio Mirror*. May 1961, 2-3.
Abel. "Copacabana, N. Y." *Variety*. March 20, 1968, 65.
Ackerman, Paul. "Darin Packs Rep Savvy on Floor." *Billboard*. December 1, 1958, 10.
Albrecht, Howard. *See You in Nairobi: How Work Became Fun — the Second Time Around. Adventures in the Laugh Trade*. Bloomington: AuthorHouse, 2005.
Alexander, Chris. "The Honeymoon is Over." *TV Radio Mirror*, July 1962, 42-43 & 85-86.
Alexander, Shana. "I Want To Be a Legend by 25." *Life*. January 11, 1960, 48-52.
Alterman, Loraine. "Bobby Darin: Hate to Ruin His Image, but He's Nice." *Detroit Free Press*. September 13, 1967, 4B
Anderson, Nancy. "Tribute Planned to Bobby Darin." *Camden Courier-Post*. June 14, 1975, 18.
Anon. Liner notes to *Love Swings*. Bobby Darin. ATCO 33-134. LP. 1961.
Archerd, Army. "Just for Variety." *Variety*. February 6, 1961, 2.
---. "Just for Variety," *Variety*. October 1, 1962, 2.
---. "Just for Variety." *Variety*. January 5, 1967, 2.
Arganbright, Frank. "Listening On Records." *Lafayette Journal and Courier*. August 17, 1963, 7.
Austin American. "Bobby Darin…On What Freedom Is All About." December 24, 1967, T17.
Australian Women's Weekly. "Bob's a Boomer." January 20, 1959, 44.
Bacon, James. "Bobby Darin, Frustrated Actor." *Baltimore Sun*. December 17, 1961, K9.
Baker, Jean. "Darin's a Versatile Showman." *Santa Cruz Sentinel*. July 12, 1967, 11.
Bakersfield Californian. "Bobby Darin at Campus Deb Jamboree." October 1, 1959,

31.

Baltimore Sun. "Late Starter Makes Grade." September 12, 1967, 21.

Beck, Marilyn. "Bobby Darin Recuperating." *Binghampton Press and Sun-Bulletin.* March 16, 1971, 2B.

---. "Wisdom of Stumping Actors Questionable." Orlando Evening Star. January 12, 1971, 8-A.

Beckman, Robert. "Celebrity Special Opened by Darin." *Long Beach Independent.* July 6, 1967, 18.

Bedford Gazette. "Old Man on the Moment." February 3, 1961, 4.

Belinger, Harry. "Bobby Darin Fulfills Rare Engagement." *Mansfield News-Journal.* March 2, 1960, 22.

Bernstein. "Reviewed in Brief." *Billboard.* June 9, 1958, 7.

Bernstein, Stan. "Bobby Darin at Carousel Theater." *Los Angeles Times.* October 19, 1967, part V, 15.

Bill. "Rodgers & Hart Today." *Variety.* March 8, 1967, 38.

Billboard. "ABC-Par Gets Darin Label." June 22, 1959, 3.

---. "Album Reviews." September 1, 1962, 20.

---. "Album Reviews." February 23, 1963, 31.

---. "Album Reviews." July 27, 1963, 35.

---. "Album Reviews." December 7, 1963, 21.

---. "Album Reviews." July 25, 1964, 50.

---. "Album Reviews." June 5, 1965, 52.

---. "Album Reviews." May 28, 1966, 68.

---. "Album Reviews." July 9, 1966, 66.

---. "Album Reviews." December 17, 1966, 72.

---. "Album Reviews." May 27, 1967, 86.

---. "Album Reviews." September 16, 1967, 70.

---. "Album Reviews." October 26, 1968, 84.

---. "Album Reviews." August 19, 1972, 31.

---. "Arranger Wess Arranging Own Production Firm." April 26, 1969, 3.

---. "At ATCO a Whole Lotta Shakin' Goin On." February 10, 1958, 43.

---. "Billboard's Recommended LP's." March 8, 1974, 58.

---. "The Billboard Spotlight Winners of the Week." October 6, 1958, 51.

---. "The Billboard Spotlight Winners of the Week." January 12, 1959, 52.

---. "The Billboard Spotlight Winners of the Week." March 19, 1959, 31.

---. "The Billboard Spotlight Winners of the Week." April 6, 1959, 78.

---. "The Cash Box Sleeper of the Week." July 1, 1957, 53.

---. "*Coke Time* Young Talent Field Day." July 4, 1960, 31.

---. "Darin Back with Capitol." August 15, 1964, 1.

---. "Darin Signs with Atl'tic." July 17, 1965, 4.

BIBLIOGRAPHY

---. "Darin Wears Many Hats; Now Busy as Executive." May 16, 1964, 37.
---. "Darin's Dynamite!" July 1, 1957, 53.
---. "London Bow Big for Darin, Eddy, McPhatter." March 28, 1960, 12.
---. "New Darin Forms Label to Speak Out Via Songs." August 31, 1968, 10.
---. "Real Highspots Mark Grammy Awards." December 7, 1959, 14.
---. "Review Spotlight On…" July 1, 1957, 53.
---. "Review Spotlight On…" June 2, 1958, 42.
---. "Reviews and Ratings of New Jazz Albums." April 6, 1957, 27.
---. "Reviews of New Pop Records." March 31, 1956, 56.
---. "Reviews of New Pop Records." May 26, 1956, 50.
---. "Reviews of New Pop Records." September 29, 1956, 64.
---. "Reviews of New Pop Records." February 23, 1957, 64.
---. "Reviews of New Pop Records." November 18, 1957, 52.
---. "Reviews of New Pop Records." December 28, 1959, 27.
---. "Reviews of This Week's Singles." August 15, 1960, 35.
---. "Reviews of This Week's Singles." September 12, 1960, 39.
---. "Reviews of This Week's LP's *(sic)*." August 8, 1960, 23.
---. "Reviews of This Week's LP's *(sic)*." November 14, 1961, 27.
---. "Signing of Bobby Darin Start of Capitol Beef-Up." July 21, 1962, 4.
---. "Singles Reviews." September 15, 1962, 23.
---. "Singles Reviews." April 27, 1963, 24.
---. "Singles Reviews." August 17, 1963, 32.
---. "Singles Reviews." February 15, 1964, 22.
---. "Singles Reviews." March 20, 1965, 12.
---. "Singles Reviews." January 16, 1965, 40.
---. "Spotlight Albums of the Week." March 31, 1962, 26.
---. "Spotlight Singles." September 25, 1965, 18.
---. "Spotlight Singles." January 7, 1967, 18.
---. "Spotlight Singles." July 8, 1967, 18.
---. "Spotlight Singles." August 26, 1967, 18.
---. "Spotlight Singles." November 30, 1968, 92.
---. "Spotlight Singles." April 19, 1969, 77.
---. "Spotlight Singles." August 9, 1969, 105.
---. "Spotlight Singles." May 8, 1971, 66.
---. "Spotlight Singles of the Week." March 14, 1960, 37.
---. "Spotlight Singles of the Week." August 14, 1961, 41.
---. "Spotlight Singles of the Week." December 4, 1961, 9.
---. "Spotlight Singles of the Week." March 17, 1962, 23.

---. "Spotlight Singles of the Week." June 23, 1962. 21.

---. "Spotlight Winners of the Week." February 1, 1960, 35.

---. "Spotlight Winners of the Week." August 10, 1959, 41.

---. "Spotlight Winners of the Week." May 16, 1960, 41.

---. "Tenderloin. A New Musical Comedy." October 24, 1960, 35.

---. "Top Album Picks." March 9, 1974, 58

Bleiel, Jeff. *That's All: Bobby Darin on Record, Stage & Screen.* Ann Arbor: Popular Culture, Ink, 1993.

Bok. "The Bobby Darin Amusement Company." *Variety.* August 2, 1972, 34.

---. "The Darin Invasion." *Variety.* October 13, 1971, 38.

Boxoffice. "Bobby Darin Hospitalized." October 18, 1965, W-5.

---. "Bobby Darin Purchases Broadway Play Rights." June 19, 1961, W1.

---. "Darin Out of Patriots." August 19, 1963, NC-4.

---. "Feature Reviews." November 4, 1963, B11

---. "Gunfight in Abilene." March 27, 1967, 4007,

---. "Interstate Circuit Award Goes to Bobby Darin." September 25, 1961, 11.

Brad. "Nitery News." *Variety.* May 15, 1969, 19.

Bridgeport Post. "Rock 'n' Roll Acts are signed for Festival Ballyhoo Show." June 20, 1958, 12.

Bundy, June. "Bregman Needs Poise and Polish." *Billboard.* January 19, 1958, 22.

---. "Darin Packs Real Nitery Punch." *Billboard.* October 12, 1959, 11.

---. "Sinatra Topper on Billboard D.J. Poll." *Billboard.* December 14, 1959, 1.

Campbell, Mary. "Singer Bobby Darin Reports He Is 'One Album and One Single Old.'" *The Derrick.* February 16, 1965, 10.

Capital Times. "Bobby Darin Show." March 2, 1963, 3.

Cash Box. "Album Reviews." August 9, 1958, 34.

---. "Album Reviews." March 21, 1959, 50.

---. "Album Reviews." February 6, 1960, 38.

---. "Album Reviews." July 13, 1960, 22.

---. "Album Reviews." August 13, 1960, 38.

---. "Album Reviews." October 8, 1860, 44.

---. "Album Reviews." November 12, 1960. 39.

---. "Album Reviews." February 25, 1961, 30.

---. "Album Reviews." March 31, 1962, 28.

---. "Album Reviews." September 8, 1962, 40

---. "Album Reviews." July 27, 1963, 22.

---. "Album Reviews." July 25, 1964, 22.

---. "Album Reviews." December 5, 1964, 32.

---. "Album Reviews." May 7, 1966, 46.

---. "Album Reviews." July 9, 1966, 40.

- ---. "Album Reviews." December 17, 1966, 36.
- ---. "Album Reviews." May 20, 1967, 46.
- ---. "Album Reviews." September 16, 1967, 46.
- ---. "Album Reviews." October 19, 1968, 52.
- ---. "Atco Stereo Singles." February 28, 1959, 46.
- ---. "Australia." February 27, 1960, 47.
- ---. "Big Advance on 'Darin Sings Charles' LP." March 31, 1962, 36.
- ---. "Bobby Darin." November 16, 1968, 39.
- ---. "Bobby Darin." January 11, 1969, 32.
- ---. "Bobby Darin Forms Indie Production Firm for New Artist Exposure." February 2, 1963, 7.
- ---. "Bobby Darin Signs Picture Deal." August 15, 1959, 45.
- ---. "Bobby Darin: That's All." March 21, 1959, 43.
- ---. "Capitol Shelves Darin LP For Another Named After Hit." January 26, 1963, 40.
- ---. "Choice Programming." June 24, 1972, 20.
- ---. "Darin Gets Billing On Rinky Dinks' Record." July 26, 1958, 49.
- ---. "Darin Named Variety Club's Personality of the Year." November 5, 1960, 44.
- ---. "Darin Opens at Cloister; Atco Fetes Trade." August 15, 1959, 35.
- ---. "Darin Sets Premium Disc Deal for Tanfastic." December 26, 1959, 41.
- ---. "Darin Sets Sciolla Record." December 12, 1959, 63.
- ---. "Darin's Back Live with Dynamic Talent." February 5, 1966, 43.
- ---. "Decca Debut." April 7, 1956, 26.
- ---. "Decca Releases First Roberta Sherwood Disk." March 24, 1956, 18.
- ---. "Dorin not Darin." April 3, 1965.
- ---. "Platter Spinner Patter." January 30, 1960, 28.
- ---. "R & B Ramblings." November 2, 1957, 42.
- ---. "R & B Reviews." May 31, 1958, 48.
- ---. "Ramblings." September 20, 1958, 50.
- ---. "Record Reviews." March 31, 1956, 8.
- ---. "Record Reviews." September 29, 1956, 10.
- ---. "Record Reviews." June 22, 1957, 10.
- ---. "Record Reviews." February 15, 1958, 10.
- ---. "Record Reviews." June 14, 1958, 12.
- ---. "Record Reviews." September 20, 1958, 16.
- ---. "Record Reviews." October 11, 1958, 10.
- ---. "Record Reviews." April 11, 1959, 10.
- ---. "Record Reviews." August 22, 1959, 8.
- ---. "Record Reviews." January 2, 1960, 20.
- ---. "Record Reviews." May 21, 1960, 12.
- ---. "Record Reviews." September 17, 1960, 8.

---. "Record Reviews." November 5. 1960, 8.
---. "Record Reviews." February 4, 1961, 6.
---. "Record Reviews." August 19, 1961, 6.
---. "Record Reviews." March 17, 1962, 8.
---. "Record Reviews." June 22, 1962, 6.
---. "Record Reviews." September 15, 1962, 8.
---. "Record Reviews." September 22, 1962, 14.
---. "Record Reviews." January 5, 1963, 12.
---. "Record Reviews." April 27, 1963, 8.
---. "Record Reviews." August 17, 1963, 8.
---. "Record Reviews." November 16, 1963, 10.
---. "Record Reviews." September 5, 1964, 14.
---. "Record Reviews." January 16, 1965, 35.
---. "Record Reviews." March 27, 1965, 18.
---. "Record Reviews." June 12, 1965, 8.
---. "Record Reviews." August 21, 1965, 22
---. "Record Reviews." April 9, 1966, 20.
---. "Record Reviews." June 25, 1966, 18.
---. "Record Reviews." September 10, 1966, 16.
---. "Record Reviews." November 26, 1966, 26.
---. "Record Reviews." March 25, 1967, 14.
---. "Record Reviews." August 26, 1967, 28.
---. "Record Reviews." November 30, 1968, 36.
---. "Record Reviews." March 19, 1969, 8.
---. "Record Reviews." April 19, 1969, 22.
---. "Richard Wess Dies at 43." March 31, 1973, 128.
---. "Singles Reviews." May 8, 1971, 20.
---. "Talent on Stage." May 24, 1969, 38.
---. "Talent on Stage." February 6, 1972, 35.
---. "Top Disk Names Appear at Inaugural Gala." January 30, 1965, 46.
---. "Tourmates." August 27, 1966, 50.
---. "Wess Arrangements Bring Trade Laudits." October 10, 1959, 52.

Cherokee Daily Times. "*Come September*, Sparkling Comedy." September 28, 1961, 4.

Chicago Tribune. "Bobby Darin Dies; Teen Rock Idol." December 21, 1973, section 1A, 14.

Christy, George. "So You Want to be a Singer!" *Modern Screen.* August 1959, 25 and 53-54.

Church, Michael. "Ego, Schmego?" *Saturday Evening Post.* June 10, 1961, 4.

Connolly, Mike. "The Best of Hollywood." *Philadelphia Inquirer.* December 30, 1961, 12.

BIBLIOGRAPHY

---. "Mike Connolly in Hollywood." *Pittsburgh Post-Gazette*. December 21. 1965, 15.

Corsicana Daily Sun. "Bobby Darin Able Leave Hospital." August 3, 1963, 5.

Crowther, Bosley. "Mexican Comic Stars in *Pepe* at Criterion." *New York Times*. December 22, 1960, 18.

---. "The Screen: 'Captain Newman, M. D.'" *New York Times*. February 21, 1964, 36.

---. "The Screen: Comedy-Romance in Italy." *New York Times*. September 8, 1961, 34.

---. "Vistas in Italy." *New York Times*. September 17, 1961, X1.

Csida, Joe. "Sponsor Backstage." *Sponsor*. September 5, 1959, 13-14.

---. "Sponsor Backstage." *Sponsor*. July 11, 1960, 14.

Cullum Democrat. "Your's Very Musically *(sic)*." April 12, 1957, 5.

Culpepper, Stuart. "2 Local Youngsters, Bobby Darin Cheered By 1,800 At City's Biggest *Teen-Time* Show." *Montgomery Advertiser*. September 8, 1957, B4.

Curtis, Jack. "Winter Makes Disk Debut." *Arizona Republic*. June 8, 1958, section 1, 11.

Curtis, Tony. *American Prince: My Autobiography*. New York: Random House, 2010.

Daily Mirror. "After 'Shadows' – a Blues Note." November 24, 1961, 33.

---. "A Date with Darin!" March 18, 1960, 13.

---. "A Prize Date!" April 16, 1960, 11.

Danzig, Fred. "Jack Paar, Bobby Darin Shows Offered Dull, Tired and Pointless Entertainment." *Coshocton Tribune*. February 1, 1961, 15.

Darin, Bobby. "Advertisement." *Variety*. May 7, 1970, 9.

---. "Bobby Darin Clarifies Secrets' Tahoe Walkout." *Variety*. January 27, 1971, 50.

---. "Golden Folk Hits Interview." *www.Bobbydarin.net* [online]. Available at: http://www.bobbydarin.net/bdfolkdaddy.html (accessed August 1, 2015).

---. "We're Getting Married." *Modern Screen*. September 1960, 42 & 77-80.

---. "Why I Played a Film Bigot." *Ebony*. November 1962, 45-50.

Darin, Dodd. *Dream Lovers: The Magnificent Shattered Lives of Bobby Darin and Sandra Dee*. New York, Warner: 1994.

Davis, Clifford. "It's a Fight Not Worth Winning." *Daily Mirror*. April 11, 1960, 26.

Dellar, Fred. Liner notes to *Bobby Darin sings If I Were a Carpenter & Inside Out*. Bobby Darin. Diablo DIAB 864. CD. 1998.

Deni, Laura. "Bobby Darin." *Billboard*. September 30, 1972, 14.

Denis, Paul. "A Boy's Dream…A Man's Nightmare." *Modern Screen*. March 1959, 46.

Detroit Free Press. "Pace Too Fast For Darin?" July 29, 1963, 4B.

Devane, James. "Bobby Discusses Career, Brashness and His Marriage to Sandra Dee." *Cincinnati Enquirer* (Kentucky Edition). January 23, 1964, 12.

DiOrio, Al. *Bobby Darin. The Incredible Story of an Amazing Life*. Philadephia: Running Press, 2004.

Doncaster, Patrick. "Don't Look Now – But Here Come the Fairies!" *Daily Mirror*. July 23, 1964, 17.

---. "Johnny is Worth It!" *Daily Mirror*. September 28, 1961, 19.

---. "Twitching the Night Away." *Daily Mirror*. June 13, 1963, 25.

Douglas-Home, Robin. "They Call Him the Next Sinatra." *Daily Express*. April 1, 1960, 6.

Duke. "Flamingo, Las Vegas." *Variety*. January 23, 1963, 68.

---. "Flamingo, Las Vegas." *Variety*. January 26, 1966, 58

---. "Flamingo, Las Vegas." *Variety* August 24, 1966, 60.

---. "Flamingo, Las Vegas." *Variety*. May 3, 1967, 67.

---. "Flamingo, Las Vegas." *Variety*. September 27, 1967, 58.

---. "Night Club Reviews." *Variety*. February 16, 1972, 61,

---. "Nitery Review." *Variety*. August 6, 1962, 19.

---. "Nitery Reviews." *Variety*. April 17, 1963, 9.

---. "Nitery Reviews." *Variety*. December 4, 1969, 6.

---. "Sahara." *Variety*. December 4, 1969, 6.

---. "Sahara, Las Vegas." *Variety*. July 20, 1960, 53.

Dumont, Lee. "Bobby Darin's Escape from Poverty." *Screenland*. January 1960, 46-49 & 59.

Eastaugh, Kenneth. "When Love Loses Its Sting." *Daily Mirror*. October 9, 1964, 25.

Ehrman, Anita. "Will Bobby Bobble Sudden Success? – Here's His Story." *San Antonio Light*. September 18, 1960, 22A.

Ellison, Bob. "He's Five Years Late." *Akron Beacon Journal*. May 29, 1966, 21.

Erickson, Hal. "Pressure Point." *New York Times* [online]. Available at: http://www.nytimes.com/movies/movie/39082/Pressure-Point/overview [Accessed July 14, 2015].

Evanier, David. *Roman Candle: The Life of Bobby Darin*. Emmaus: Rodale Publishing, 2004.

Evans, Peter. "Disc Verdicts." *Daily Express*. September 18, 1959, 16.

Feather, Leonard. Liner notes to *Bobby Darin sings Ray Charles*. Bobby Darin. ATCO 33-140. LP. 1962.

Film Bulletin. "'Captain Newman, M. D.' Strong Blend of Popular Elements." November 11, 1963, 7.

---. "*Come September* Lively Comedy with Solid B. O. Values." July 10, 1961, 10.

---. "Hell is for Heroes." July 23, 1962, 14.

---. "If a Man Answers." September 3, 1962, 14.

---. "Pressure Point." September 17, 1962, 17.

Finnigan, Joseph. "Bobby Darin Grows Up." *Pittsburgh Press*. October 25, 1964, section 5, 11.

---. "Bobby Darin Has Spot Picked for 'Oscar' He Hopes to Win." *Democrat and*

BIBLIOGRAPHY

Chronicle. March 22, 1964, 3E.

Frederick, Robert B. "Reno-Metz Readies Darin Biopic; Audition Looks, Voice, Chutzpah." *Variety*. April 24, 1982, 25

Galveston Daily News. "Sullivan Gave Bobby Darin Chance to 'Reach Adults.'" August 30, 1959, 9C.

Gelb, Arthur. "Darin Storms the Copacabana." *New York Times*. March 1, 1961, 26.

Gord. "Unit Reviews." *Variety*. March 30, 1960, 68.

Gould, Jack. "TV: Hour with Durante." *New York Times*. September 26, 1959, 47.

---. "TV: Rodgers and Hart Remembered." *New York Times*. March 3, 1967, 71.

Graham, Sheila. "Darin Shakes Off Chip On Shoulder." *Orlando Evening Star*, April 1, 1964, section 8, page 10.

Grant, Elspeth. "Films." *The Tatler*. December 6, 1961, 712-713.

Green, Ted. "Main Street." *Radio-Television Daily*. October 19, 1964, 4.

Greenspun, Roger. "*Happy Mothers' Day* Arrives." *New York Times*, August 18, 1973, 26.

Grevatt, Ken. "Darin Parades R.&B. Hits at Copa." *Billboard*. March 13, 1961, 7.

---. "R & R's Cross over the Bridge to Filmland." *Billboard*. August 31, 1959, 4 & 9.

Gross, Mike. "Album Reviews." *Variety*. March 1, 1961, 74.

---. "Album Reviews." *Variety*. August 2, 1961, 82.

---. "Best Bets." *Variety*. August 16, 1961, 44.

---. "Darin Touches All Bases in Home Run." *Billboard*. April 16, 1966, 52.

---. "Jocks, Jukes and Disks." *Variety*. June 12, 1957, 60.

---. "Jocks, Jukes and Disks." *Variety*. October 8, 1958, 52.

---. "Jocks, Jukes and Disks." *Variety*. March 16, 1960, 54.

---. "Jocks, Jukes and Disks." *Variety*. September 21, 1960, 54.

Harris, Lew. "Now He's Bob Darin – Not 'Bobby.'" *Chicago Tribune*. September 14, 1969, section 10, 2.

Heckman, Don. "Bobby Darin Back in Song Program." *New York Times*. February 27, 1972, 61.

---. "Merry Clayton from 'Newahlins.'" *New York Times*. July 16, 1972, D11.

Hehr, Marilynn. "2 Bobby's Get Young Support." *Munster Times*. April 24, 1968, 13.

Herm. "Bobby Darin & Friends." *Variety*. February 8, 1961, 76.

---. "Swing Time." *Variety*. June 29, 1960, 43.

Hevesi, Dennis. "Frank Rizzo of Philadelphia Dies at 70." *New York Times* [online]. Available at http://www.nytimes.com/1991/07/17/obituaries/frank-rizzo-of-philadelphia-dies-at-70-a-hero-and-villain.html (accessed August 20, 2015).

Hiburn, Robert. "Will the Real Bobby Darin Stand Up?" *Tuscaloosa News*. July 26, 1969, 3.

Hoffman, Steve. "Darin's Series Is Well-Assembled Hour." *Cincinnati Enquirer*. July

28, 1972, 8.

Hopper, Hedda. "Bobby Darin – He Sang 'Mack the Knife.'" *Chicago Tribune.* December 24, 1961, 17.

Humphrey, Hal. "Bobby Darin Takes It On His Braided Cuff." *Minneapolis Star Tribune.* December 14, 1959, 43.

Independent Star News. "A Tribute to Rodgers & Hart." February 26, 1967, 19.

J.W. "Darin Draws Smiles, Applause at Three Rivers." *The Post-Standard.* May 27, 1962, 18.

James, Hamilton. "Were They Too Much in Love to Get Married?" *TV Radio Mirror.* June 1963, 4-5.

Jet. "Hamp, Darin Steal Show; Della Left Miffed, Tearful." September 6, 1962, 58.

Johnson, Erskine. *Eureka Humboldt Times.* "Bobby Darin Ain't Talking." February 4, 1961, 2.

---. "A Two-toned Personality: That's singer Bobby Darin." *Ocala Star-Banner.* May 22, 1960, 13.

Jose. "Copacabana, N.Y." *Variety.* June 8, 1960, 59.

---. "Copacabana, N. Y." *Variety.* March 1, 1961, 85.

---. "Copacabana, N. Y." *Variety.* May 15, 1963, 64.

---. "Copacabana, N. Y." *Variety.* November 1, 1972, 63.

---. "New Acts." *Variety.* December 19, 1958, 67.

Kafa. "Cloister." *Variety.* May 2, 1960, 6.

---. "The Cloisters." *Variety.* August 3, 1959, 6.

Killgallen, Dorothy. "The Voice of Broadway." *Dunkirk Evening Observer.* July 18, 1959, 6.

---. "The Voice of Broadway." *Dunkirk Evening Observer.* October 14, 1961, 6.

---. "Wess is Riled." *Ottawa Journal.* May 21, 1961, 55.

Klein, Doris. "Humble? Just a Little." *Tucson Daily Citizen.* November 21, 1964, 26.

Knight, Bob. "Summer TV Littered With Losers Re Prospects For Midseason, But Jury's Still Out For Darin Stanza." *Variety.* August 30, 1972, 31 & 41.

Laine, George. "Wax Museum." *Pasadena Independent.* April 20, 1960, 12.

Landy, Ilene. "Darin Sets Off Musical Rockets in July 4 Date." *Billboard.* July 22, 1967, 26-28.

Larry. "Deauville, Miami Beach." *Variety.* December 28, 1960, 45.

Larsen, John. "Bobby Darin Among Top Recording Stars." *Daily Review.* August 6, 1960, 13.

---. "Bobby Darin Interviewed." *Argus-Leader.* August 30, 1960, 5.

Lees, Gene. "Bobby Darin and the Turn from Junk Music." *Down Beat.* May 12, 1960, 16-20.

---. *Portrait of Johnny: The Life of John Herndon Mercer.* New York: Pantheon Books, 2006.

BIBLIOGRAPHY

Leonard, Will. "Bobby Turns Up the Burners Without a Care for Warmth." *Chicago Tribune*. December 1, 1972, section 2, 4.

Lewellen, Pat. "Ego, Schmego?" *Saturday Evening Post*. June 10, 1961, 4.

Lewis, Amy. "The Boy Who Didn't Belong." *Screenland*. May 1960, 52-55 & 71.

Lewis, Dan. "Can Ego and Maturity Both Be Bobby Darin?" *Lakeland Ledger*. April 1, 1973, 38.

Levinson, Bill. "Bobby." *San Antonio Light*. July 24, 1960, 7.

Leyendecker, Frank. "State Fair." *Box Office*. March 19, 1962, 17.

Life. "How Golden to be a Goldie." June 26, 1970, 76.

---. "Life Guide." June 9, 1961, 17.

---. "Life Guide." August 11, 1961, 12.

---. "Life Guide." November 24, 1961, 27.

---. "Life Guide." January 12, 1962, 32.

---. "Life Guide." May 11, 1962, 21.

Linn, Edward. "Little Singer with the Big Ego." *Saturday Evening Post*. May 6, 1961, 26-27 & 59-63.

London Life. "Darin Has Learnt Humility." November 12, 1966, 8.

Long. "Harrah's, Lake Tahoe." *Variety*. May 13, 1959, 69.

---. "Harrah's, Lake Tahoe." *Variety*. March 27, 1963, 60.

---. "Harrah's, Lake Tahoe." *Variety*. April 19, 1967, 100.

Los Angeles Times. "Hollywood Bowl Program Tonight." September 5, 1959. Part III, 8.

Luc. "Grove, L.A." *Variety*. July 26, 1972, 53.

M.O. "Bobby Darin." *Cash Box*. March 4, 1972, 21.

Mar. "The Red Skelton Hour." *Variety*. September 29, 1965, 30.

Matz, Roger. "Darin Makes Contribution to the Christmas Season." *Waterloo Daily Courier*. December 8, 1961, 8.

McManus, Margaret. "Darin Superstitious About Reaching Heights." *Syracuse Post-Standard*. January 29, 1961, 4.

Melody Maker. "Darin Slams Back at British Rock Fans." April 2, 1960, 1 & 20.

---. "They're Rarin' for Darin." February 13, 1960, 1.

Merwin, Gregory. "The Splish Splash Boy." *TV Radio Mirror*. 22-23 & 75-76.

Meyr. "Deauville, M. B." *Variety*. February 23, 1966, 58.

Modern Screen. "The Bad Boy and the Good Girl." April 1960, 22-23 & 78-82.

---. "I've Got This Funny Feeling I'm Gonna Die Young ... So What I've Gotta Do I've Gotta Do Fast." November 1960, 32 & 81-82.

Montgomery Advertiser. "Bobby Darin Fan Club Is Formed Here." December 15, 1957, Teen Topic, 8.

---. "Teen Timers Greet Darin with Cheers." April 24, 1957, 8.

---. "Teen-Ager to Elect *Teen Time* Winners." September 1, 1957, 33.

Monthly Film Bulletin. "Captain Newman, M. D." April 1964, 54.
---. "Come September." October 1961, 142.
---. "Gunfight in Abilene." March 1967, 45.
---. "Hell Is for Heroes." June 1962, 81.
---. "If a Man Answers." November 1962, 155.
---. "Pressure Point." October 1963, 141-142.
---. "Stranger in the House." July 1967, 110.
---. "That Funny Feeling." July 1965, 113.
---. "Too Late Blues." December 1961, 168.
Murf. "Cocoanut Grove, L. A." *Variety*. November 6, 1968, 61.
---. "Nitery Reviews." *Variety*. March 10, 1966, 10.
Musgrove, Nan. "Bobby Darin's Superb TV Show." *Australian Women's Weekly*. March 28, 1962, 25.
Music Business. "Bobby Darin – a happy publisher." October 31, 1964, 14.
---. "Bobby Darin's Explosive Scene." June 20, 1964, 13.
---. "Darin Quits Capitol Pact." March 21, 1964, 1.
Music Vendor. "Music Vendor LP Picks of the Week." August 8, 1960, 30.
Nathan, James. "Bobby Darin Show Starts With a Fizzle." *Chicago Tribune*. July 28, 1972, section 2, 13.
New York Times. "Bobby Darin, Pop Singer, Dies at 37." December 21, 1973, 38.
---. "Keep Smiling, and Pass the Dip." February 4, 1973, 121.
---. "Many Stars Join TV Cancer Show." March 30, 1962, 26.
North, Dominique Paul. "Bobby Darin Show Talent for Mimicry." *Milwaukee Journal*. July 28, 1972, 8.
Oakes, Paul. "Too Late Blues and The Hustler." *Sight and Sound*. Winter, 1961, 40-41.
The Observer. "Briefing." April 23, 1967, 26.
---. "Ego Briefing." February 23, 1969, 32.
Orloff, Kathy. "Darin is Darin to Change Style." *Akron Beacon Journal*. June 1, 1969, B13.
Otis, David L. "Bobby Darin Comes on Strong in Show," *San Bernadino County Sun*. October 19, 1967, 67.
Ovens, Don. "Radio Action and Pick Singles." *Billboard*. November 25, 1972, 57.
Pack, Harvey. "Bobby Darin Guest Stars." *Waterloo Daily Courier*. October 11, 1965, 15.
Page, Don. "Burlesque Revived in Beautiful Burbank." *Sandusky Register*. August 20, 1969, 46.
Page, Prescott. "Excellent Spring Club Business Continuing." June 22, 1962, 22.
Palm Beach Post. "Hughes' Isolation Foils Complaints." November 13, 1968, 31.
Parsons, Louella. "Bobby Darin's Opening." *Modern Screen*. November, 1959, 21.

BIBLIOGRAPHY

Patten, Van. "Pops – Jazz – Broadway." *Post-Standard.* October 23, 1962, 17.

Pearl, Ralph. "Vegas Daze and Nights." *Las Vegas Sun.* October 11, 1968, 17.

Pickett, C. E. "Letters to the Editor." *Life.* May 31, 1968, 19.

Picturegoer. "Cha-Cha is Saving the Bands." November 29, 1958, 14-15.

Pit. "Chez Paree, Chi." *Variety.* December 9, 1959, 66.

Pitts, George E. "Bobby Darin Gives Credit to Sammy Davis Jr." *Pittsburgh Courier.* January 9, 1960, 22.

Price, Joe X. "On the Beat." *Variety.* August 17, 1964, 10.

---. "On the Beat." *Variety.* December 11, 1964, 7.

---. "On the Beat." *Variety.* August 11, 1965, 11.

Raffaele, Gerry. "Fine Jazz from a Cocktail Pianist." *Canberra Times.* January 8, 1966, 12.

Record World. "Album Picks." August 19, 1972, 10.

---. "Darin Delights." April 8, 1967, 11 & 17.

---. "Darin's New Direction Label Distributed By Bell." September 7, 1968, 3&43.

Renard, David. "Ego, Schmego?" *Saturday Evening Post.* June 10, 1961, 4.

Reno Gazette-Journal. "Harrah's Reno Billing Headed By Bobby Darin." September 24, 1966, 13.

Rich. "Mr. D's, San Francisco." *Variety.* June 12, 1968, 53.

---. "Stranger in the House." *Variety.* May 31, 1967, 6.

---. "That Funny Feeling." *Variety.* June 22, 1965, 26.

Rick. "The Happy Ending." *Variety.* November 19, 1969, 22.

Ritz, James. Liner notes to *The 25th Day of December*. Bobby Darin. Real Gone Music RGM-0199. CD. 2013.

Robe. "Happy Mother's Day...Love, George." *Variety.* August 22, 1973, 12

Robinson, Harry. "Ashes to Cashbox?" *Sydney Morning Herald.* November 27, 1968, 6.

Robinson, Richard. "The Changing Bobby Darin." *Detroit Free Press.* February 14, 1969, 4D.

Rolontz, Bob. "Darin Season's Hottest Copa Draw." *Billboard.* June 13, 1960, 40.

Rose. "An Evening with Jimmy Durante." *Variety.* September 30, 1959, 27.

Rose, James. Liner notes to *Earthy & Golden Folk Hits*. Bobby Darin. Exemplar 2001. CD. 2002.

San Antonio Light. "Bobby Darin – Adult Teenager." September 6, 1959, 4E.

Schindler, Harold. "Bobby Darin Carving Heroic Stature." *Salt Lake Tribune.* January 17, 1968, B3.

Schoenfeld, Herm. "Album Reviews." *Variety.* April 19, 1961, 56.

---. "1958: Look Back in Hunger." *Variety.* December 17, 1958, 53.

---. "Jocks, Jukes and Disks." *Variety.* March 14, 1956, 50.

---. "Jocks, Jukes and Disks." *Variety.* October 8, 1956, 62.

---. "Jocks, Jukes and Disks." *Variety*. May 28, 1958, 54.

---. "Jocks, Jukes and Disks." *Variety*. September 17, 1958. 66.

Schumach, Murray. "Film Work Grinds to a Halt; Industry Gloomy as Actors Ready Walkout Tomorrow -- No Contract Talks Set." *New York Times*. March 6, 1960, 79.

Scott, Bobby. "Bobby Darin and the Double Standard." *TV Radio Mirror*. August 1962, 17.

Scott, John L. "Bobby Darin Back on Trail." *Los Angeles Times*. May 29, 1970, Part IV, 10.

---. "New Bobby Darin Retains Old Flair." *Los Angeles Times*. March 10, 1966, part V, 15.

Shanley, John P. "Bobby Darin Heads One-Hour Program." *New York Times*. February 1, 1961, 71.

---. "TV: Reliving Vaudeville." *New York Times*. June 8, 1960, 79.

Shearer, Lloyd. "When Youth Rushes Into Marriage." *Parade*. September 29, 1963, 6-8.

Sheridan, Phil. "Record Review." *Philadelphia Inquirer*. June 21, 1957, 30.

Shiels, Bob. "Bob Shiels on TV." *Calgary Herald*. May 13, 1971, 69.

Shipman, David. *Judy Garland*. London: HarperCollins, 1993.

Smith, Cecil. "Goldie Hawn Likes her Husband and Home." *Troy Times Record*. October 3, 1970, B5.

Sternfield, Aaron. "Singer, Showman, Mimic – It's Darin All the Way." April 8, 1967, 26.

Sullivan, Brian. "Teen-agers Rock Into '58." *Democrat and Chronicle*. January 1, 1958, 44.

Suskin, Steve. *Broadway Yearbook, 1999-2000: A Relevant and Irreverent Record*. New York: Oxford University Press, 2001.

Sternfield, Aaron. "Singer, Showman, Mimic – It's Darin All The Way." *Billboard*. April 8, 1967, 26.

Sydney Morning Herald. "Bobby Darin in Singing Show." November 28, 1968, TV Guide 1.

Teenager's Weekly. "Following a Leader." June 10, 1964, 11.

The Tennessean. "Last Chance to Hear Bob." September 28, 1969, 26-S.

Tew. "Roostertail, Detroit." *Variety*. September 20, 1967, 59.

---. "Roostertail, Detroit." *Variety*. July 10, 1968, 43.

Thomas, Bob, "Bobby Darin Hires Men to Say No." *Ottawa Journal*. October 31, 1961, 39.

---. "Bobby Darin Won't Make Legend Date." *The Lowell Sun*. April 21, 1961, 22.

Thomas, James. "Presley Goes Square." *Daily Express*. March 25, 1961, 6.

Thompson, Howard. "Screen: Darin in Too Late Blues." *New York Times*. March 1,

BIBLIOGRAPHY

1962, 27.

Tiegel, Eliot. "Darin Marks Return to Clubs with a Solid Bit." *Billboard*. March 19, 1966, 54. "Darin Shows Social Pop Sides in Varied Program." *Variety*. November 16, 1968, 14.

The Times. "Bobby Darin Singer and Actor." December 21, 1973, 17.

Tone. "The Bobby Darin Show." *Variety*. January 22, 1973, 12.

Torre, Marie. "TV Show $50 Prize 'Too Small': Torre." *The Capital Times*. March 4, 1961, 21.

Troy Record. "More Mature Bobby Darin Writes and Records Music." February 13, 1965, 37.

Tube. "Cocoanut Grove, L.A." *Variety*. February 27, 1963, 58.

---. "Come September." *Variety*, June 28, 1961, 6.

TV Radio Mirror. "And all that Jazz." May 1959, 10.

---. "On the Record." January 1963, 12.

---. "On the Record." April 1963, 24.

---. "On the Record." August 1963, 24.

---. "On the Record." October 1963, 20.

---. "Top 50 Records of the Month." March 1962, 15.

---. "Singles." December 1962, 20.

---. "Your Monthly On Record Guide." July 1962, 20.

---. "Your Monthly On Record Guide." December 1962, 18.

---. "Your Monthly On Record Guide." May 1963, 10-11.

Variety. "150G for Darin in 'Tanfastic' Tiein." December 16, 1959, 14.

---. "A. C. Steel Pier's Names and Bands." May 15, 1963, 65.

---. "Album Reviews." August 13, 1958, 46.

---. "Album Reviews." March 25, 1959, 56.

---. "Album Reviews." August 3, 1960, 46.

---. "Album Reviews." March 1, 1961, 74.

---. "B'way's '110,' Darin's 'Folk Hits,' Jones' 'Lovers,' Morgan's 'Victors,' Gore's 'Hearts' Top New Albums." December 4, 1963, 42.

---. "Bobby Darin Back in Atlantic Fold." July 14, 1965, 41.

---. "Bobby Darin Dies at 37 After 2D Heart Op." December 21, 1973, 1 & 26.

---. "Bobby Darin Organizes Diskery But Continues To Cut For Atco Label." June 17, 1959, 39.

---. "Bobby Darin Story." September 6, 1981, 4.

---. "Charles' 'Soul,' Darin's 'Earthy,' Hirt's 'Honey,' Mathis' 'Johnny,' Light's 'Themes' Top New Albums." August 14, 1963, 52.

---. "Charles' 'Vol II,' Mathis 'Rapture,' Darin's 'Look,' 'Swagman' Top LPs." October 17, 1962, 38.

---. "Darin Back on N.Y. Café Scene Via Copa Stand." September 15, 1965, 71.

---. "Darin Exits Nitery Field to 'Widen His Music Biz Scope." October 23, 1963, 47.
---. "Darin, Irked At Boston Bash, Advises Sparse Turnout Ask For Their Money Back." July 3, 1962, 6.
---. "Darin's 'Charles,' Burns' 'Strings,' B'Way's 'All-American' Top New LPs." April 11, 19612, 60.
---. "Darin's Monte Carlo Gala A Click 1-Nite Stand." August 30, 1967, 2.
---. "Darin's 'Roses,' '81/2' Track, Domino's 'Here,' Orbison's 'Dreams' Top LPs" July 17, 1963, 66.
---. "Dean Martin, Laine, Mancini, 'Charlie Brown,' Darin, Miller, Easybeats, Chandler Top LPs." May 17, 1967, 46.
---. "Dickering Over Guarantees Killing the Disk Industry, Bobby Darin Sez." November 7, 1962, 45.
---. "'Dolittle' Soundtrack, John Gary, Procul Harum, Bil Evans *(sic)*, Darin, Spanky & Gang, 'Flowers,' Top LPs." September 6, 1967, 46.
---. "Estate Vs. NBC On a Darin Bio; Claim Prior Right." June 18, 1975, 35.
---. "Film, Disk Stars Head Carla Victims' Benefit." October 4, 1961, 65.
---. "Lake Tahoe Accident, Darin to the Rescue." August 19, 1970, 52.
---. "Morrison, Peebles, Mountain Jacks, Ingredient Kendricks, Darin, Davidson Top New LPs." March 6, 1974, 54.
---. "'Nuremberg' Track, Darin's 'Twist,' Damone's 'Linger' Top New LPs." December 27, 1961, 26.
---. "Obituaries." December 26, 1973, 47.
---. "On the Upbeat." August 17, 1960, 45.
---. "Par Pix and Lotsa Dates for Darin." August 12, 1959, 55.
---. "R&B Show 14G in Pitt." October 23, 1958, 62.
---. "R. Steward, Airplane, Temptations, J. Cash, Ike & Tina, Paxton, Darin, S. Neely, Gore, Rebop Top LPs." August 23, 1972, 48.
---. "Ray Charles, Bob Darin, Cher, Ike & Tina, Cat Mother, Spence, Velvet, Max Morath Top LPs." July 2, 1969, 50.
---. "Rolling Stones, Belafonte's 'Room,' Dusty Springfield, New Christys, Mindbenders, Darin, F&T Top LPs." June 29, 1966, 42.
---. "Secrets, Femme Combo, In Disappearing Act." January 20, 1971, 52.
---. "Tijuana Brass, The Lovin Spoonful, 'Walking Happy,' Darin, Pat Boone, Arnold, Joe Sherman Top New LPs." December 7, 1966, 50.
---. "Top Singles of the Week." September 19, 1962. 48.
---. "Top Singles of the Week." January 20, 1965, 48.
---. "Top Singles of the Week." June 6, 1965, 50.
---. "Top Singles of the Week." January 19, 1966, 62.
---. "Top Singles of the Week." April 6, 1966, 50.
---. "Top Singles of the Week." September 7, 1866, 42.

BIBLIOGRAPHY

---. "Top Singles of the Week." November 23, 1966, 52.

---. "Top Singles of the Week." March 22, 1967, 60.

---. "Wayne Newton, Johnny Mathis, Kostelanetz, Darin, Mamie Lee, Yarbrough, Syne, Hines Top LPs." May 4, 1966, 192.

Wear. "Copacabana, N. Y." *Variety*. April 6, 1966, 60.

Weiler, A. H. "Screen: 'Hatari' Captures the Drama of Tanganyika Wildlife." *New York Times*. July 12, 1962, 19.

Will. "Bob Darin." *Variety*. July 23, 1969, 56.

---. "Frontier, Las Vegas." *Variety*. February 28, 1968, 54.

---. "Frontier, Las Vegas." *Variety*, July 24, 1968, 52.

---. "Hilton, Las Vegas." *Variety*. September 13, 1972, 87.

Williams, Tim. "Interview: Randy Newman." *A Site Called Fred* [online]. Available at: http://asitecalledfred.com/2008/09/11/interview-randy-newman/ (accessed August 26, 2015).

Willis, Dick. "March Colorful but Peaceful." *Oneonta Star*. August 28, 1963, 3.

Wilson, Earl. "Bobby Darin: A Changed Man." *Florida Today*. January 11, 1969, 4D.

---. "Earl Wilson's TV People." *Des Moines Register*. August 21, 1960, 3TV.

---. "It Happened Last Night." *Reno Gazette-Journal*. October 17, 1962, 18.

---. "Never Thought We'd See a Humble Bobby Darin." *Arizona Republic*. December 6, 1960, 33.

---. "New Bobby Darin Molded by Graveside 'Revelation.'" *The Lima News*. January 13, 1969, 6.

---. "Years Have Changed Bobby Darin." *The Lowell Sun*. March 25, 1968, 22.

Wilson, John S. "Showmanship in Some Pop Singers." *New York Times*. February 21, 1960, X13.

Wolf, Jon. "Donovan: A Little Less Help From His Friends." *Columbia Daily Spectator*. September 29, 1969, 4.

Wolfe, Al. "Record Review." *Tyrone Daily Herald*. December 27, 1957, 6.

Young, Sydney. "Bobby Darin Dies at 37 in Heart Op." *Daily Mirror*. December 21, 1973, 11.

Zeitlin, Arnold. "The Bobby Darin Story." *Pittsburgh Post-Gazette Sunday Magazine*. January 29, 1961, 7-9.

INDEX

?

? and the Mysterians, 405

1

18 Yellow Roses, 181, 193, 198, 199, 200, 201, 202, 203, 204, 213, 223, 239, 271, 275, 330, 339, 376, 378, 382, 383, 407

18 Yellow Roses and 11 Other Hits (album), 20, 199-202, 204, 323, 363, 376

2

25th Day of December, The (album), 119, 147, 361, 374

A

A You're Adorable, 196, 384
A&E Biography: A [Musical] Biography (album), 213, 340, 341, 349, 369, 383
Abbott, Bud, 61
Abbott, Russ, 408
ABC Stage '67 (TV), 270
Abilene, 206, 377
About You, 378
Ac-cent-tchu-ate the Positive, 384
Ace in the Hole, 114, 212, 246, 375, 383
Aces Back to Back (album), 193, 196, 341, 342, 351, 352, 370, 383

Actions Speak Louder than Words, 45, 46, 359, 373
Adams, Edie, 394
Adderley, Nat, 168
Adderly, Tommy, 407
After School Rock 'n' Roll, 405
After the Ball, 404
After Today, 279, 379
After You've Gone, 248, 252, 378
Agnew, Spiro, 317
Ain't No Mountain High Enough, 322, 403
Ain't that a Bunch of Nonsense, 245
Ain't that Love, 146, 148, 376
Alabama Song, 394
Alabamy Bound, 166, 382
Alaimo, Steve, 410
Alberghetti, Anna Marie, 81
Albrecht, Howard, 338
Alexander, Shana, 85
Alice Blue Gown, 184, 384
All American (musical), 254
All by Myself, 384
All I Do is Cry, 92, 376
All I Have to do is Dream, 342, 351, 383, 403
All I Need is the Girl, 112, 391
All Nite Long, 76, 360, 374
All of Me, 384, 392
All of You, 187, 382
All or Nothing at All, 91, 376
All Shook Up, 44

All Strung Out, 281
All the Way, 196, 370, 384
All the Way Home, 44, 45, 46, 50, 123, 360, 374
Allen, Steve, 153, 192
Allen, Stuart, 315
Almond, Marc, 406
Alone (Judy Garland album), 92
Alone Again Naturally, 58, 339, 341, 384, 403
Alright, O.K., You Win, 109, 374
Altieri, Lucia, 408
Always, 164, 376
Always Leave 'em Laughing, 397
Amapola, 391
Amato, Tommy, 330, 342
Amen, 121, 375
American Bandstand (TV), 42, 123, 209, 226, 239, 387, 391, 394, 404
American Beauty (film), 227
American Graffiti (film), 343
Amy, 264, 378
And Debbie Makes Six (TV), 289, 398
And the Band Played On, 404
And When I Die, 314, 339, 400
Andrews Sisters, The, 406
Andy Williams Show, The (TV), 95, 226, 231, 245, 253, 314, 394, 395, 396, 400
Andy, Horace, 406
Animals, The, 145, 280
Anka, Paul, 56, 65, 112, 391
Ann-Margret, 150
Another Song on my Mind, 342, 381
Another Song on My Mind: The Motown Years (album), 311, 324, 332, 342, 371, 381, 385
Anthony, Little Wayne, 407
Anthony, Richard, 406, 407, 409
Any Old Place, 396
Anything Goes, 95, 96, 377
Anything Goes (musical), 95
Appaloosa, The (film), 63
April Showers, 194, 384
Aquarius, 399
Arganbright, Frank, 202
Arlen, Harold, 95
Armstrong, Louis, 29, 54, 57, 185, 226, 227, 364
Arnold, Eddy, 408

Around the World, 194, 384
Art Linkletter Show, The (TV), 192, 393
Arthur Murray Party, The (TV), 390
Artificial Flowers, 58, 79, 117, 118, 123, 212, 266, 271, 374, 375, 383, 391, 402, 403
Artzi, Schlomo, 409
As Long As I'm Singin' 166-167, 239, 394
As Long as I'm Singing: The Bobby Darin Collection (album), 16, 108, 166, 185, 239, 349, 369, 382 394, 405
As Long as I'm Singing (1964 unissued album), 167, 184-188, 239
As Long As I'm Singin': Rare 'n' Darin (album), 367, 381
Ashford, Nickolas, 322
Astaire, Fred, 130
Astronauts, The, 406
At Maggie's Place (TV), 400
At the Crossroads, 278, 379
At This Very Moment (TV), 152, 392
Atkins, Chet, 406
Atkins, Chuck, 406
Aubrey, James, 216
Auld Lang Syne, 118
Austin, Moe, 157
Austin, Ollie, 407
Australian's Women's Weekly (magazine), 84
Autry, Gene, 189
Autumn Blues, 100, 374
Autumn Leaves, 195, 384
Avalon, Frankie, 52, 65, 112, 391, 409
Ave Maria, 119, 361, 375
Average People, 331, 367, 379
Aznavour, Charles, 232

B

Babes on Broadway (film), 136
Baby Born Today, 120, 374
Baby Face, 80, 144, 376
Baby I Miss You So, 245
Baby I Need Your Lovin', 404
Baby May, 306, 379
Baby Won't You Please Come Home, 246
Bach, Johann Sebastian, 140
Bachelors, The, 145, 183, 407
Back in Your Own Back Yard, 116
Back Street Girl, 271, 273, 378

INDEX

Bakalyan, Richard, 334
Baker, Chet, 61, 137
Baker, LaVern, 25, 408
Balance Teen Topics (TV), 192
Ball, Lucille, 185
Ballad of Billy Blue, The (film), 65
Ballad of Cat Ballou, The, 246, 247, 365, 378
Ballance Teen Topics (TV), 392
Band Wagon, The (film), 138
Barb'ry Ann, 405
Barbara McNair Show, The (TV), 304, 399
Barber, Tony, 410
Bari, Nicola di, 408
Barnett, "Sweet" Emma, 115
Baron, The (Johnny Cash album), 200
Barone, Frank, 79
Barracudas, The, 405, 407
Basie, Count, 15, 74, 76, 153, 217, 248, 253, 270, 396
Basin Street Blues, 403
Bassey, Shirley, 336
Battle Hymn of the Republic, 216
Baum, Bernie, 253
Be Honest With Me, 189, 195, 376, 384
Be Mad Little Girl, 203, 205, 210, 368, 377, 405
Beachcomber, 100, 374, 376, 405
Beatles, The, 19, 265, 291, 308, 317, 339, 368, 382
Beatty, Warren, 229, 230
Beautiful Dreamer, 182, 383
Beautiful Ladies, 399
Beautiful Things, 279, 366, 379
Beck, Marilyn, 320
Bedford Gazette (newspaper), 130, 414
Been, Jan-Jaap, 21
Behrke, Richard, 118, 193, 326
Beiderbecke, Bix, 248
Beiderman, Joe, 146
Belafonte, Harry, 28, 34
Bells are Ringing (musical), 165, 187
Bells, The, 407, 408
Bennett, Rudy, 405
Bennett, Tony, 238, 327
Benno, Marc, 409
Benny, Bert, 408
Benny, Jack, 251, 394
Benton, Brook, 410

Beresford Ricketts, The, 145, 407
Berghagen, Lars, 408
Berle, Milton, 85
Berlin, Irving, 65, 163, 164, 195
Bermuda Keynotes, The, 410
Bernstein, Elmer, 63
Berry, Chuck, 198
Berry, Dave, 409
Berry, Mike, 405, 408
Bes' Friends, 271, 272, 366, 378
Best is Yet to Come, The, 246
Best of Bobby Darin, The (album), 186, 378
Best on Record, The (TV), 396
Between the Devil and the Deep Blue Sea, 96, 377, 384
Bewitched (TV), 63
Beyond the Sea, 59, 102, 117, 212, 308, 319, 340, 347, 351, 352, 355, 359, 374, 375, 382, 383, 384, 390, 402, 404
Beyond the Sea (film), 350
Bi-Aza-Ku-Saza, 405
Bidin' My Time, 393
Big Beat, The (TV), 42, 80, 387, 388
Big Party, The (TV), 390
Biggest Night of Her Life, The, 277
Biggs, Barry, 409
Bilbao Song, 394
Bill Wyman's Rhythm Kings, 410
Billboard (publication), 27, 28, 30, 32, 33, 34, 39, 40, 41, 46, 47, 49, 50, 55, 62, 63, 70, 71, 73, 77, 79, 82, 83, 95, 98, 99, 100, 102, 106, 110, 112, 117, 121, 143, 144, 145, 146, 153, 158, 162, 171, 190, 198, 202, 203, 207, 210, 226, 233, 236, 243, 244, 249, 251, 255, 263, 265, 272, 273, 275, 276, 280, 290, 293, 294, 298, 299, 314, 332, 336, 337, 348,
Birth of the Blues, The, 109
Black Coffee, 74, 374
Black Devils, The, 407
Black Faith, 409
Black Sheep Boy, 273, 378
Blackbird, 317, 382
Blackwell, Otis, 44
Blair, Hal, 189
Blauner, Steve, 84, 157, 158, 209
Bleiel, Jeff, 21, 52, 71, 108, 113, 167, 169, 205, 253, 313, 369, 387, 416

437

Blitzstein, Marc, 57
Blooblo, 409
Blood, Sweat and Tears, 317
Blossoms, The, 147, 148
Blowin' in the Wind, 207, 377, 401
Blue Monday, 56, 324, 325, 381
Blue Moon, 196, 384
Blue Skies, 164, 175, 376, 384, 393
Blueberry Hill, 177
Blue-Eyed Mermaid, 26, 29, 30, 32, 373
Blues in the Night, 393
Bo Diddley, 404
Bob Cats, The, 409
Bob Crosby Show, The (TV), 50, 388
Bob Hope Presents the Chrysler Theater (TV), 394
Bob Hope Show, The (TV), 123, 391, 392
Bob White, 113, 385
Bobby Darin (1958 album), 40, 41, 44, 50, 373
Bobby Darin (1972 album), 20, 329-332, 350, 367, 379
Bobby Darin (Al DiOrio book), 69
Bobby Darin (radio show). See Milk Shows, The
Bobby Darin Amusement Company, The (TV), 334-335, 337, 338, 342, 401, 402
Bobby Darin and Friends (TV), 130, 137, 166, 391
Bobby Darin and the Turn from Junk Music (article), 105-106
Bobby Darin at the Silver Spade (TV), 104, 295, 398
Bobby Darin born Walden Robert Cassotto (album), 16, 19, 290-294, 366, 379
Bobby Darin in London (TV), 244, 397
Bobby Darin Show, The, 20, 59, 115, 194, 228, 274, 324, 334, 335, 337-342, 343, 352, 402, 403, 404, 416, 424, 427
Bobby Darin sings Doctor Dolittle (album), 16, 185, 277-280, 366, 379
Bobby Darin sings Ray Charles (album), 18, 109, 145-148, 188, 282, 325, 350, 362, 375
Bobby Darin sings the Shadow of your Smile (album), 18, 64, 65, 245-249, 252, 257, 253 364, 368, 378
Bobby Darin Story, The (album), 73, 140, 152, 361, 375
Bobby Darin: The 1956-1962 Singles (album), 371
Bobby Rocks (album), 369

Bocephus, 409
Bogarde, Dirk, 195
Boil That Cabbage Down, 167, 208
Bond, Whit, 232
Bonner, Gary, 271, 272, 273, 276
Boone, Pat, 31, 65, 112, 150, 391, 395, 428
Bootleg Kings, The, 410
Born Free, 327, 403
Boss Barracuda, 405
Box Office (publication), 151, 174, 270
Boxtops, The, 324
Boy! What a Girl! (film), 40
Boy, Pete, 410
Boyd, Jimmy, 406, 407, 408
Boyer, Charles, 195
Bramsen, Sten, 408
Brand New House, 44, 45, 46, 359, 373, 405
Brandenburg, Otto, 405
Brando, Marlon, 63, 152
Brandt, Alan, 84
Brandy, Stirling, 406
Breakfast at Tiffany's (film), 186
Breaking Point, The, 249, 250, 378
Brecht, Bertolt, 57
Breeze and I, The, 73
Bregman, Buddy, 70, 76, 81, 416
Brewer, Teresa, 31
Bricusse, Leslie, 187, 228, 277, 366
Bridge Over Troubled Water, 308, 340, 400, 402, 403, 404
Brooklyn Roads, 404
Brother, Can You Spare a Dime, 250, 251, 402
Brown, Maxine, 410
Brown, Oscar Jr., 168
Brown, Ruth, 64, 410
Bruce, Clive, 407
Bubble Gum Pop, 25
Buckaroos, The, 408
Buckwheat, 408
Buddy Bregman's Music Shop (TV), 70, 388
Buddy Deane Show, The (TV), 50, 78, 389
Bullfrog, 292, 321, 379
Bullmoose, 40, 71, 72, 362, 374, 375, 405
Burbank Burly-Q, 399
Burke's Law (TV), 231, 395
Burlesque is Alive and Living in Beautiful Downtown Burbank (TV), 303-304, 399
Burnette, Johnny, 406

INDEX

Burns, George, 78, 80, 95, 104, 112, 132, 182, 251, 315, 335, 389, 400
Burt Blanca and the King Creoles, 407
Burt, Tom, 408
Burton, Ed, 79
Burton, James, 206, 207
Buttons and Bows, 384
By My Side, 25, 405
By Myself, 109, 137, 163, 374, 376, 381, 384, 389, 390
Bye Bye Love, 389

C

C. C. Rider, 280
Cade's County (TV), 328, 401
Caesar, Sid, 400
Cage, The (TV), 284, 288, 289
Cahn, Sammy, 227, 254
Caine, Michael, 251
Call Me Irresponsible, 227, 377
Calloway, Cab, 96
Campbell, Archie, 410
Campbell, Glen, 206, 406
Campbell, Jo-Ann, 104, 122
Can't Get Out of This Mood, 82
Can't Get Used to Losing You, 201, 376
Can't Take My Eyes Off You, 328, 339, 341, 383, 401, 404
Cannon, Ace, 410
Cantiflas, 99
Capitol Collectors Series (album), 223, 233, 348, 368, 382
Capitol Years, The (album), 368
Capri Sisters, The, 405
Captain Newman, M. D. (film), 142, 173-174, 224, 343, 411
Caravan, 74, 76, 353, 360, 374, 403
Carle, Les, 407
Carlos, Roberto, 409
Carmets, The, 406
Carmichael, Hoagy, 117, 138
Carpendale, Howard, 406
Carpenters, The, 342
Carroll, Pat, 315
Carson, Johnny, 175, 338, 340
Carter, Lou, 388
Casey Wake Up, 405

Cash Box (publication), 27, 28, 30, 33, 39, 40, 43, 47, 48, 49, 51, 55, 62, 63, 71, 72, 73, 77, 79, 92, 95, 98, 99, 100, 101, 110, 116, 117, 118, 121, 123, 138, 143, 144, 146, 161, 171, 178, 192, 199, 203, 204, 223, 226, 227, 230, 233, 239, 244, 249, 250, 253, 255, 257, 262, 264, 265, 271, 273, 277, 280, 292, 294, 295, 296, 298, 302, 313, 328, 330
Cash, Johnny, 16, 27, 200, 325
Cassavetes, John, 149, 150, 159, 411
Cassidy, David, 332
Cassotto, Vanina "Nina", 70, 273
Cassotto, Vivian "Polly" Walden, 69, 70
Castro, Fidel, 130
Cat Ballou (film), 247
Catalinas, The, 405, 407, 408
Catch the Wind, 326, 385
Cecilia, 116, 385
Celebrity Bowling (TV), 400
Cernocka, Petra, 408
Cesar et la Romains, 407, 409
Chacksfield, Frank, 407
Chain of Fools, 308, 318, 382
Change, 293, 379, 398, 406
Change Partners, 384
Chaplin, Geraldine, 269
Charade, 228, 274, 377, 378, 382, 402, 404
Charade (film), 228
Charles, Ray, 17, 18, 44, 47, 80, 101, 109, 119, 120, 129, 145, 146, 147, 162, 177, 182, 183, 189, 200, 210, 339, 362, 420, 428
Charlie & The Twisters, 409
Chattanooga Choo Choo, 216, 391, 393
Cheek to Cheek, 384
Cherokee Daily Times (newspaper), 142, 418
Cherry, Don, 410
Chevalier, Michel, 406
Chicago Tribune (newspaper), 300, 335, 347, 418, 421, 422, 423, 424
Child of God, 120, 374
Child of Tears, 312, 385
Christmas Auld Lang Syne, 118, 123, 374, 391
Christmas Song, The, 118
Church, Michael, 134
Cindy, 328, 385
Circulate (Neil Sedaka album), 65

439

City Life, 307, 323, 370, 384, 400
City Surfers, 210
Clarence, Roberto, 406
Clark, Dick, 48, 50, 70, 78, 123, 239
Clark, Petula, 270, 342, 351, 383, 396, 403
Clark, Roy, 400
Clark, Rudy, 210
Clay Cole at the Moonbeam (TV), 393
Clayton, Merry, 190, 231, 421
Clayton, Paul, 251
Cleary, Father Michael, 406
Clementine, 18, 58, 73, 98, 102, 108, 117, 140, 212, 271, 360, 361, 374, 375, 381, 383, 384, 389, 390, 396
Clifford, Mike, 408
Climb Every Mountain, 194, 327, 384, 403
Cloud Lucky Seven, 32
Coasters, The, 52
Coben, Cy, 33
Cochran, Hank, 188
Coe, Jamie, 79, 409
Cogan, Alma, 410
Cohan, George M., 243, 282
Cohn, Al, 64
Coke Time (TV), 112, 391, 414
Col Joye & the Joy Boys, 410
Coldside Trio, The, 409
Cole, Ann, 405
Cole, Freddy, 405
Cole, Nat 'King', 31, 38, 65, 118, 139, 157, 188, 247
Coleman, Cy, 185
Collins, Glenda, 410
Collins, Judy, 297, 303, 398
Come On-a My House, 384
Come Rain or Come Shine, 112, 196, 339, 384, 404
Come September, 138
Come September (film), 122, 123, 140, 141, 148, 152, 161, 162, 406, 411, 418, 420, 424, 427
Come to the Stable (film), 59
Coming Down (with a Heartache), 406
Commitment (album), 19, 281, 287, 291, 297-301 321, 367, 379
Como, Perry, 78, 118, 388
Concert Sinatra, The (Frank Sinatra album), 109
Connick, Harry Jr., 136

Connor, Chris, 64
Conny, 410
Cool for Cats (TV), 390
Cop-Out. See Stranger in the House (film)
Corporation, The, 320, 321, 322
Cosmopolitan (magazine), 303
Costello, Lou, 61
Cottonfields, 167
Cover Girl (film), 136
Craddock, Billy Crash, 406
Cramer, Floyd, 407
Crickets, The, 405, 408
Crosby, Bing, 77, 194
Crosby, Lindsey, 410
Crowther, Bosley, 99, 141
Cry Me a River, 404
Csida, Joe, 63, 79, 112
Cummings, Burton, 410
Curtain Falls, The, 211, 215, 382, 383
Curtain Falls: Live at the Flamingo, The (album), 211,-215, 349, 370, 382, 383
Curtis, Jack, 47
Curtis, King, 406
Curtis, Mac, 407
Curtis, Tony, 173, 174
Cute, 248, 378
Cymbal, Johnny, 199, 409

D

Dabney, Debbie, 407
Daily Express (newspaper), 63, 102, 118, 420, 426
Daily Mirror (newspaper), 102, 103, 111, 143, 149, 173, 199, 347
Daily Review (newspaper), 124
Daisy Door, 409
Dalida, 406
Damone, Vic, 81, 217, 231, 394
Dan Raven (TV), 123, 391
Dana, 406
Dance Party (TV), 388, 389
Danke Schoen, 227
Danny, 406
Danny & The Juniors, 45, 408
Danny Kaye Show, The (TV), 395
Danny Thomas Show, The (TV), 283, 397
Danzig, Fred, 131

INDEX

Darin 1936-1973 (album), 316, 348, 381, 382, 385
Darin at the Copa (album), 61, 106-110, 129, 137, 147, 191, 194, 211, 213, 268, 318, 349, 360, 370, 374
Darin at the Grove (TV), 191, 393
Darin Invasion, The (TV), 315, 317, 400
Darin, Dodd, 21, 69, 152
Darling be Home Soon, 272, 366, 378
Darren, James, 408
Dateline: Hollywood (TV), 397
David Frost Show, The (TV), 20, 30, 329, 330, 401
Davidson, Frankie, 407
Davis, Bette, 227
Davis, Clifford, 103
Davis, Sammy Jr., 6, 18, 20, 62, 63, 65, 76, 84, 98, 99, 100, 110, 113, 157, 158, 187, 191, 198, 200, 201, 255, 277, 322, 341, 365, 366, 369, 408
Davis, Skeeter, 407
Day Dream, 264, 265, 300, 378
Day Dreamer, 406
Day in Day Out, 384
Day in the Life, A, 317, 382
Day, Doris, 90
Days of Wine and Roses, The, 112, 193, 195, 227, 377, 378, 384
Dealer in Dreams, 33, 34, 37, 42, 43, 373
Dean & Britta, 406
Dean Martin Show, The (TV), 84, 297, 334, 338, 398
Dean, James, 105
Dear Heart, 234, 238, 377
Dear Lonely Hearts, 188
Dee, Sandra, 122, 133, 141, 160, 162, 175, 209, 243, 251, 265
Deep in my Heart (film), 59
Defiant Ones, The (film), 173
deHeer, Dik, 21
Del Noah & The Mt Ararat Finks, 408
Delia, 25, 406
Della! (TV), 304, 399
Dellar, Fred, 262
Denver, John, 263, 264, 331, 365
DeShannon, Jackie, 407
Desrosiers, Jacques, 409
DeSylva, Buddy, 97

Devilson, Deke, 409
Devine, Sydney, 407
Diamond Horseshoe (film), 136
Diamonds, The, 101
Dick Cavett Show, The (TV), 329, 401
Dick Clark's Saturday Night Beechnut Show (TV), 50, 78, 387, 388, 389, 390, 391
Dickinson, Angie, 173
Didn't it Feel Good, 55, 369, 383
Dietrich, Marlene, 140, 205
Dietz, Howard, 137
Dinah Shore Chevy Show, The (TV), 21, 175, 393
Ding-Dongs, The, 48
Dion/Dion & The Belmonts, 52, 200, 406, 408
DiOrio, Al, 21, 56, 69, 277, 387, 419
Disco 2 (TV), 399
Distractions (Part 1), 19, 287, 299, 302, 370, 379, 384, 399, 406
Do Nothin' Till You Hear from Me, 96, 377
Do Re Mi (musical), 188
Do the Monkey, 406
Doctor Dolittle (film), 277, 366
Dolivo, Georg, 407
Dollyrots, The, 406
Domino, Fats, 41, 324, 325
Don't Be Cruel, 44
Don't Call My Name, 41, 42, 373, 383, 387
Don't Dream of Anybody but Me, 74, 76, 374
Don't Get Around Much Anymore, 91, 363, 376
Don't Leave Me Now, 33
Don't Make Promises, 264, 378
Don't Rain on My Parade, 254, 266, 274, 365, 366, 378, 379, 382, 397, 403
Don't Think Twice, it's all Right, 205, 324, 325, 377, 381
Don't Worry About Me, 317, 381, 392
Dona Nobis Pacem, 121, 375
Doncaster, Patrick, 199
Donegan, Lonnie, 27, 30
Donovan, 326
Donovan, Jason, 406
Doonican, Val, 408
Dorel, Claudie, 407
Do-Re-Mi, 395
Dorin, Françoise, 233
Dorsey, Jimmy, 30

441

Dorsey, Tommy, 30, 248
Douglas, Craig, 406
Douglas, Melvyn, 174
Dove, Ronnie, 410
Down Beat (magazine), 58, 105, 115, 197
Down so Long, 203, 406
Down with Love, 75, 374
Draghici, Constantin, 409
Drake, Charlie, 409
Dream Baby, 406
Dream Girl of 1967 (TV), 397
Dream Lover, 71, 79, 102, 108, 109, 135, 144, 153, 194, 339, 343, 349, 355, 369, 374, 375, 382, 384, 388, 389, 403, 406
Dream Lovers (book), 69, 419
Dreidel, 339, 403
Dresser, Paul, 74
Drifters, The, 199
Drivers, The, 409
Drown in My Own Tears, 18, 148, 282, 289, 362, 376, 397
Duff, Brenda, 406
Dumis, Mack, 407
Dumont, Lee, 83
Durante, Jimmy, 108, 152, 188, 389, 392
Durban, Allison, 406
Dushoff, Dave, 101
Dyke, Jerry, 409
Dylan, Bob, 18, 19, 205, 207, 265, 287, 293, 318, 324, 364, 368

E

Early in the Morning, 48, 49, 70, 373, 375, 382, 387, 407
Earthy! (LP), 18, 19, 27, 51, 58, 97, 121, 125, 158, 159, 160, 170, 167-171, 175, 200, 201, 204, 207, 213, 239, 351, 363, 376
East of the Rockies, 114, 375, 385
Eastaugh, Kenneth, 173
Easter Parade, 384
Easter Seals Telethon (TV), 329, 401
Easy Living, 96, 364, 377
Easy Rider, 280, 382
Ebony (magazine), 172
Ebstein, Katja, 408
Ed Sullivan Show, The (TV), 78, 80, 107, 109, 110, 352, 388, 389, 390, 392, 395

Eddy, Duane, 101, 103, 167, 390, 406
Eden, Jean, 408
Edge, Bobby, 405
Edison, Harry "Sweets", 326
Edmunds, Dave, 408
Edwards, Geoff, 334
Edwards, Vince, 251
Ehrman, Anita, 124
Elam, Debbie, 406
Eleanor Rigby, 317, 382
Elfs, Tommy, 406
Elfving, Ulf, 408
Ellington, Duke, 15, 16, 74, 91, 96, 165, 254
Elliott, Cass, 407
Ellison, Bob, 261
Elvis' Christmas Album (Elvis Presley album), 38, 121
Embassy Six, The, 406
Empty Pockets Filled with Love, 393
End of Never, The, 228, 377
End of the World, The, 200, 363, 376
Engelbert with the Young Generation (TV), 401
Epicurian Delight, 398
Erickson, Hal, 173
Er-I-Ee was a-Rising, The, 170, 377
Ertegun, Ahmet, 38, 46, 158, 243, 277
Ertegun, Nesuhi, 244
Esposito, Jenna, 408
Ethel, 407
Evanier, David, 21, 69, 84, 102, 157, 208, 317, 420
Evans, Bobby, 407
Evening with Jimmy Durante, An (TV), 80, 389
Everett, Betty, 210
Everybody has the Right to be Wrong, 253, 378
Everybody's Doing It, 393
Everybody's Talkin', 308, 314, 400
Everything's Okay, 169, 200, 292, 377
Everywhere I Go, 280, 382
Exactly Like You, 81

F

Fabian, 99
Fabrice, Daniel, 406
Fabricio, 408
Fabulous Places, 278, 280, 379
Faith, Adam, 409

INDEX

Falling in Love with Love, 270, 396
Family Weekly (magazine), 124
Fantastic Baggys, The, 407
Fantasticks, The (musical), 255
Farmer's Daughter (TV), 63
Farrow, Mia, 251
Fatool, Nick, 248
Faye, Alice, 164
Fay-O, 51, 170, 377
Feather, Leonard, 145
Feeling Good, 254, 277, 365, 378
Fellow Needs a Girl, A, 395
Ferber, Edna, 95
Ferrer, José, 59, 150
Fever, 168
Fields, W. C., 110, 114
Film Bulletin (publication), 141, 149, 151, 161, 171, 172, 173, 174
Film Stars Don't Die in Liverpool (film), 114
Finally (album). *See Live at the Desert Inn* (album)
Finch, Dick, 183
Finnigan, Joseph, 229
Fire and Rain, 19, 317, 382, 403
Fireballs, The, 405
Firing Squad, The, 405
First Annual All-star Celebrity Baseball Game (TV), 397
Fisher, Eddie, 37, 43, 395
Fisher, Eddy, 251
Fiskomania, 409
Fitzgerald, Ella, 15, 64, 74, 75, 96, 137, 201, 364
Five-Hundreds, The, 408
Flash, Bang, Wallop!, 279
Fleet's In, The (film), 91
Fleetwoods, The, 407
Flip Wilson Show, The (TV), 314, 329, 400, 401
Florence, Bob, 187
Flower Drum Song (musical), 185
Floyd, Eddie, 307, 408
Fly Me to the Moon, 186, 365, 378
Flying Home, 391
Fonda, Jane, 98
Fools Rush In, 195, 384
For Baby, 264, 378
For Once in My Life, 328, 401, 402, 404

For Teenagers Only (album), 44, 52, 54, 55, 123, 152, 153, 360, 362, 374
Forbes, Matt, 408
Ford, Emile, 406
Foster, Jorge, 406
Foster, Stephen, 182
Four Aces, The, 31
Four Coins, The, 31
Four Kings, The, 407
Fourteen Pairs of Shoes, 407
Francis, Connie, 25, 352, 390, 391, 408
François, Claude, 410
Frank Barber Band, The, 410
Franklin, Aretha, 64
Franks and Deans, 406
Freddie & The Dreamers, 407
Freddie and the Dreamers, 145, 407
Frederick, Robert B., 350
Freedman, George, 408
Freedom to Love, 407
Freeman, Art, 323
Freeman, Ernie, 233, 234, 235, 236, 237
Freezer, Mathis, Darin and Guest (radio), 100
Freezer, Roy, 100
Fricker, Sylvia, 168
From a Jack to a King, 201, 376
From Bronx to Broadway (CD), 256, 353
From Hello Dolly to Goodbye Charlie (album), 18, 64, 159, 193, 209, 225-229, 230, 239, 253, 274, 364, 377
From Sea to Sea (CD), 70, 266, 368, 382
Fun in Acapulco (film), 229
Funny Girl (musical), 254
Funny What Love Can Do, 244, 265, 268, 280, 366, 378, 379, 397, 407

G

Gabler, Milt, 27
Gabriel, 302, 315, 400
Gal that Got Away, The, 76, 103, 374, 390
Game of Poker, A, 94, 95
Gardiner, Boris, 407
Garland, Hank, 38
Garland, Judy, 21, 38, 75, 76, 92, 99, 136, 169, 185, 206, 215, 216, 217, 393, 426
Gary Lewis and the Playboys, 406, 407
Gaylords, The, 407

443

Gazarra, Ben, 251
Gentry, Bobbie, 281, 289, 334, 335, 352, 397, 402
George Burns in the Big Time (TV), 389
George Burns Show, The (TV), 104, 390
Germani, Remo, 409
Gerry & The Pacemakers, 407
Gerry and the Pacemakers, 80
Gershwin, George, 95, 137, 150
Gershwin, Ira, 136
Get Me to the Church on Time, 237, 245, 343, 369, 384, 394, 395, 404
Ghost Riders in the Sky, 28, 29, 30
Gianfranco, 408
Giant, Bill, 253
Gibson, Johnny, 405
Girl That I Marry, The, 395
Girl That Married Dear Old Dad, The, 395
Girl Who Stood Beside Me, The, 264, 267, 269, 366, 378, 379, 397
Gitte, 410
Give a Little Whistle, 403
Give My Regards to Broadway, 397
Give My Regards to Broadway (TV), 282, 397, 403
Glass Bottle, The, 409
Gleason, Jackie, 30, 192, 296, 298
Glenmarks, Bruno, 408
Go Ahead (album), 311, 312, 314, 322, 323-325, 326, 327, 348
Go Ahead and Back Up, 323, 385
Go Ahead and Back Up: The Lost Motown Masters (album), 311, 312, 314, 322, 353 359, 372
Go Tell it on the Mountain, 120, 375
Goin' Back to Indiana (TV), 328, 400
Goin' Home, 393
Golden Boy (musical), 255
Golden Earrings, 94, 140, 377
Golden Earrings (film), 140
Golden Folk Hits (album), 19, 171, 201, 204-207, 215, 363, 377, 419, 425
Golden Shot, The (TV), 308, 399
Gololobov, Michal, 21
Good Day Sunshine, 265
Good Golly Miss Molly, 41
Good Life, The, 234, 364, 377, 378
Good Luck Charm, 54
Goodbye Charlie, 58, 225, 228, 377, 378

Goodbye Charlie (film), 228
Goodman, Benny, 248
Goody Goody, 391
Gordon, Alan, 271, 272, 273, 276
Gordon, Mack, 136
Gordy, Berry, 45, 320
Gordy, Berry Jr., 45
Got a Lot of Livin' to Do, 49
Got My Mojo Working, 314, 400, 401, 403
Gotta Travel On, 250, 251
Gould, Elliott, 149
Gould, Jack, 80, 270, 271
Goulet, Robert, 394, 395
Grahame, Gloria, 114
Grand Night for Swinging, A (TV), 289, 397
Grant, Cary, 142, 228
Great Race, The (film), 247
Great Society, 232
Greatest Builder, The, 31, 32, 33, 293, 373, 374
Greeenfield, Howard, 52
Green, Green, 206, 377
Greenback Dollar, 205, 377
Greenspun, Roger, 343
Greger, Max, 406
Grey, Owen, 406
Greyhound, 406
Grier, Roosevelt (aka Rosey), 231, 406, 409
Griffin, Johnny, 405
Griffith, Lee, 15
Gross, Mike, 116, 138
Guantanamera, 170, 377
Gunfight in Abilene (film), 264, 270, 411, 416, 424
Guys and Dolls, 75, 374, 384, 390, 404
Guys and Dolls (musical), 91
Gyp the Cat, 58, 227, 237, 245, 370, 378, 383, 395
Gypsy (musical), 112

H

Hairspray (film), 50
Haley, Bill, 43, 85, 101, 102
Haley, Jack Jr., 85
Half a Sixpence (musical), 279
Hall, Arch Jr., 407
Hallelujah I Love Her So, 56, 148, 375
Hamilton, George IV, 206

INDEX

Hammerstein, Oscar, 150, 185
Hampton, Lionel, 176
Happy, 336, 348, 353, 379, 381, 402, 403
Happy Birthday, 395
Happy Ending, The (film), 303, 411
Happy Mother's Day, Love George (film), 343, 411
Happy Together, 276, 404
Happy Together (The Turtles album), 272, 402
Hard Headed Woman, 331, 379
Hard Hearted Hannah, 58, 94, 95, 377, 394
Hardin, Rett, 410
Hardin, Tim, 262, 263, 264, 265, 271, 273, 318, 365, 409
Harmony Cats, 408
Harris, Lew, 300
Harris, Marion, 183
Harris, Woody, 25, 44, 48, 52, 61, 73
Hart, Lorenz, 76, 104, 136, 137, 138, 270, 271, 396, 421, 422
Harvest, The, 299, 300, 307, 379, 407
Harvey, Mick, 408
Haskell, Jimmy, 144, 146, 160, 188
Have Mercy Baby, 390
Have You Got Any Castles Baby, 74, 113, 374
Hawaiian Surfers, The, 407
Hawking Brothers, The, 407
Hawkins, Ronnie, 406
Hawkins, Screamin' Jay, 45
Hawn, Goldie, 303, 304, 399
Haymes, Bob, 84
Hayworth, Rita, 136
Hazel (TV), 63
Hazlewood, Lee, 409
Hear Them Bells, 31, 32, 293, 373, 374
Heckman, Don, 328
Hefti, Neal, 248
Heick, Keld, 405
Heinz, 409
Helena, Katri, 409
Hell is for Heroes (film), 171, 411, 420
Heller, Andre, 406
Hello Dolly, 226, 227, 252, 364, 377, 394
Hello Dolly (musical), 226
Hello Sunshine, 272, 378
Hello Young Lovers, 187, 191, 195, 208, 212, 383, 384, 393, 403
Hello, Frisco, Hello (film), 164

Help Me, 33, 34, 373
Help Me Make it Through the Night, 324, 328, 385, 403, 404
Henderson, Florence, 402
Hennessey (TV), 81, 389
Henry John Deutschendorf. *See* Denver, John
Hepburn, Audrey, 228
Here I Am, 190, 376
Here I'll Stay, 9, 53, 54, 123, 374, 394
Here's Edie (TV), 394
Here's Hollywood (TV), 392
Here's That Rainy Day, 208, 404
Herman's Hermits, 406
Heusen, Jimmy van, 227, 254
Hey Jude, 19, 304, 317, 382, 399
Hey Lolly Lolly Low, 402
Hey Look Me Over, 185, 196, 384
Hey Magic Man, 300, 379
Hi-De-Ho (That Old Sweet Roll), 308, 315, 317, 318, 339, 368, 400
Higher and Higher, 315, 318, 324, 341, 352, 369, 382, 383, 385, 400, 402, 403
Hilburn, Robert, 308
Hill, Davy, 25, 405
Hirt, Al, 253
His Latest Flame, 143
Hoffman, Steve, 334
Holden, Libby, 92
Holiday, Billie, 137, 336
Holly Twins, The, 26
Holly, Buddy, 48, 52, 407, 408
Hollywood '63 (TV), 393
Hollywood Backstage (TV), 393, 396
Holm, Celeste, 59
Holm, Michael, 409
Holman, Bill, 323
Holmes, Marty, 61
Holt, John, 408
Holy Holy Holy, 120, 375
Honest Man, An, 395
Honeycombs, The, 408
Hope, Bob, 123, 391
Hopkin, Mary, 406
Hopper, Hedda, 167
Horan, Bob, 407
Horrocks, Jane, 409
Hot Rod U.S.A., 407
House of the Rising Sun, 145

Houston, Cissy, 407
How About Me, 92, 376
How About You, 136, 361, 375, 384
How Deep is the Ocean, 195, 384
How Sad Venice Can Be, 233 (see also *Venice Blue*)
How to Succeed in Show Business Without Really Trying (musical), 253
Howard, Bart, 74
Howard, Ron, 343, 344
Hud (film), 174
Hudson, George, 409
Hughes, Howard, 294
Humperdinck, Engelbert, 401
Humphrey, Hal, 83
Hunter, Ross, 161, 162
Hush, Somebody's Calling My Name, 55, 374
Hutchings, Valerie, 102

I

I Ain't Gonna Give Nobody None of My Jellyroll, 115, 116, 375, 385
I Ain't Got Nobody, 182, 195, 383, 384, 389, 400
I Ain't Sharin' Sharon, 52, 55, 374, 375
I Am, 271, 272, 366, 378
I Believe in You, 253, 378, 394
I Can Get it For You Wholesale (musical), 149
I Can Live on Love, 255
I Can See the Wind, 293, 379
I Can't Believe a Word You Say, 407
I Can't Believe That You're in Love With Me, 91, 376
I Can't Give You Anything But Love, 76, 82, 109, 374, 384
(Since You're Gone) I Can't Go On, 42, 373
I Can't Stop Loving You, 177
I Combos, 408
I Couldn't Sleep a Wink Last Night, 82
I Cried For You, 184, 384
I Didn't Know What Time it Was, 136, 375, 384
I Don't Know How to Love Her/Him, 325, 326, 385
I Enjoy Being a Girl, 185
I Feel a Song Coming On, 81
I Found a Million Dollar Baby, 38, 39, 41, 373
I Get a Kick Out of You, 327, 404

I Go Ape, 52
I Got a Rose Between My Toes, 388
I Got a Woman, 18, 94, 109, 147, 148, 325, 362, 374, 375, 381, 392
I Got My Own Thing Goin' On, 407
I Got Plenty of Nothin', 246, 252, 391
I Got Rhythm, 166, 382, 391
I Guess I'll Have to Change My Plan, 138, 375
I Guess I'm Good for Nothing but the Blues, 92, 376
I Had a Ball (musical), 254
I Hadn't Anyone Till You, 90, 376
I Have Dreamed, 108, 130, 137, 374, 384, 391
I Hear You Knocking, 318
I Know an Old Lady Who Swallowed a Fly, 404
I Know That You Know, 393
I Left My Heart in San Francisco, 238, 251, 252, 369, 370, 383
I Love Lance, 399
I Nobili, 409
I Taught Him Everything He Knows, 396
I Think I Like You, 278, 379
I Think it's Gonna Rain Today, 272, 366, 378
I Think the Devil Must Be Beating His Wife, 328, 385
I Used to Think it was Easy, 332, 379
I Walk the Line, 213, 325, 383, 385
I Wanna Be Around, 112, 233, 377
I Wanna Be Around (album). See *Venice Blue* (LP)
I Want to Spend Christmas with Elvis, 26, 407
I Want You With Me, 51, 52, 123, 360, 374
I Will Follow Her, 201, 376
I Will Wait for You, 247, 274, 281, 378, 382
I Wish I Were in Love Again, 266, 267, 379, 391, 396, 397
I Won't Last a Day Without You, 342, 381
I Wonder Who's Kissing Her Now, 162, 167, 176, 177, 184, 377, 383
I'll Be Around, 92, 376
I'll Be Seeing You, 196, 384, 404
I'll Be There, 64, 79, 94, 210, 362, 374, 390, 407
I'll Be Your Baby Tonight, 295, 302, 303, 316, 318, 379, 382, 398, 402, 403
I'll Never Fall in Love Again, 402
I'll Never Smile Again, 391
I'll Only Miss Her When I Think of Her, 254, 255, 378

INDEX

I'll Remember April, 61, 374, 404
I'm an Old Cowhand, 194, 384
I'm Beginning to See the Light, 165, 376
I'm Glad About It, 322, 385
I'm Going to Love You, 281, 382
I'm Gonna Live Till I Die, 18
I'm Just a Country Boy, 103, 167, 390
I'm on My Way, Great God, 169, 176, 215, 216, 266, 376, 382, 383, 393
I'm Sitting on Top of the World, 166, 382, 398
I've Already Stayed too Long, 330, 379
I've Been Working on the Railroad, 393
I've Found a New Baby, 94, 96, 364, 376, 377
I've Got a Secret (TV), 232, 394
I've Got it Made, 407
I've Got the World on a String, 251
I've Got You Under My Skin, 274, 368, 382, 404
I've Gotta Be Me, 63
I've Heard That Song Before, 391
I've Never Been in Love Before, 91, 376
Ian & Sylvia, 168
Ida, Sweet as Apple Cider, 389
If, 339, 403
If a Man Answers, 160-161, 210, 365, 376, 407
If a Man Answers (film), 160-161, 411
If I Had a Hammer, 205, 377
If I Had My Druthers, 114, 375, 393
If I Ruled the World, 18, 238, 277, 349, 383
If I Were a Carpenter, 221, 240, 261, 262, 265, 266, 267, 268, 271, 273, 274, 278, 290, 295, 316, 318, 341, 343, 355, 378, 381, 382, 383, 396, 397, 398, 400, 401, 402, 403, 404, 419
If I Were a Carpenter (album), 185, 244, 261-265, 326, 365, 378
If I Were a Rich Man, 295
If Not For You, 403
If You Love Him, 407
If You Were the Only Girl in the World, 176, 177, 184, 384
I'll Be There, 376
In a Broadway Bag (album), 18, 185, 252-255, 257, 267, 278, 349, 365, 378
In a Little Spanish Town, 384
In Love In Vain, 137, 375
In Memoriam, 16, 58, 293, 321, 379
Ina Merton & the Ping Pongs, 406
Indiana, 113, 375, 408

Inside Out (LP), 185, 271-273, 276, 326, 366, 378, 419
Invitation to a March (play), 149
Irish Rovers, The (TV), 402
Ironside (TV), 328, 401
Irresistible You, 144, 148, 362, 375
It Ain't Necessarily So, 60, 74, 81, 374, 384
It Had to be You, 136, 137, 361, 375
It Keeps Right on a-Hurtin', 189, 376
It Never Entered My Mind, 76
It's Him I Wanna Go With Mama, 407
It's Magic, 257
It's Now or Never, 54
It's Only a Paper Moon, 249, 378
It's Today, 253, 378, 403
It's What's Happening Baby, 407
It's You or No One, 90, 376
It's You or No One (LP), 89-92, 94, 98, 119, 121, 125, 129, 350, 351, 363, 376
Ivanhoe (film), 229
Ives, Burt, 338, 403

J

Jack Benny Show, The (TV), 394
Jackie Gleason and his American Scene Magazine (TV), 396
Jackie Gleason Show, The (TV), 30, 391
Jackson, Bull Moose, 40
Jackson, Mahalia, 31, 38, 314, 400
Jackson, Wanda, 410
Jacques, Judy, 409
Jagger, Mick, 271
Jailer Bring Me Water, 145, 167, 376, 407
Jailhouse Rock (film), 33, 229
James, Harry, 248
James, Sonny, 255
Jämsen, Timo, 407
Jansen, Fasia, 407
Jay Birds, The, 410
Jay Walkers, The, 407
Jaye Sisters, The, 25, 50, 408
Jazz Singer, The (film), 164
Jealous, 183, 369, 384
Jehovah Hallelujah, 121, 375
Jenkins, Gordon, 65, 90, 91, 227
Jerry Lester Show, The (TV), 192, 388, 392
Jerry Lewis MDA Telethon, The (TV), 400

447

Jerry Lewis Show, The (TV), 194, 289, 393, 398
Jesus Christ Superstar (musical), 325
Jet (magazine), 176
Jets, The, 409
Jingle Jangle Jungle, 291, 379
Jive, 300, 351, 379
Jobim, Antonio Carlos, 232, 247, 274
Joe Gordon Folk Four, 406
Joey Bishop Show, The (TV), 397, 398, 399
Johnny & The New Dodgers, 406
Johnny B. Goode, 52, 318, 382
Johnson, Erskine, 105, 134
Johnson, Pas, 147
Johnston, Ray, 235
Joker, The, 238
Jolson, Al, 113, 163, 164, 166, 194, 267, 297
Jolson Story, The (film), 113
Jones, Carolyn, 395
Jones, Jack, 255
Jones, Quincy, 265
Jones, Tom, 247, 331, 399
Jonica, 409
Jordanaires, The, 38
Jourdan, Louis, 80, 389
Judy Duets (album), 216
Judy Garland Show, The (TV), 21, 169, 206, 215, 393
Judy, Don't Be Moody, 46, 47, 373, 383
Juicy Lucy, 407
Juke Box Jury (TV), 78, 388
Jukebox Jury (TV), 389
Just a Little Bit, 290
Just Bummin' Around, 236, 383
Just Friends, 137, 375, 404
Just in Case You Change Your Mind, 40, 41, 42, 373
Just in Time, 187, 381, 382, 384

K

Kafe, Hayati, 409
Karaklajic, Radmila, 406
Kaye, Danny, 395
Kaye, Florence, 253
Kaye, Stubby, 247
Keel, Howard, 95
Keep a Walkin', 52, 374, 375, 376
Keil Isles, The, 405, 409

Kellaway, Roger, 246, 265, 274, 278, 279, 409
Kelly, Gene, 338
Kennedy, John F., 215
Kennedy, Mike, 408
Kennedy, Robert, 58, 169, 216, 283, 287, 288, 290, 293, 296
Kern, Jerome, 136
Kilgallen, Dorothy, 149, 172
King and I, The (musical), 109, 187
King of the Road, 238, 250, 403
King, Ben E., 406
King, Morgana, 46
King, Pete, 249
Kingston Trio, The, 200, 204, 205, 364
Kirkham, Millie, 38
Kirshner, Don, 25, 26, 27, 30, 33, 38, 41, 42, 350
Klein, Doris, 231
Knights, The, 407
Knud, Lord, 406
Koivuniemi, Paula, 409
Kraft Music Hall, The (TV), 396, 397, 398
Kramer, Stanley, 173
Krist, Billy, 193
Kristian, Marty, 410

L

L. A. Breakdown, 255
La Bamba, 168, 170, 191, 376
Lady Came from Baltimore, The, 271, 275, 336, 378
Lady Fingers, 273, 378
Lady is a Tramp, The, 396
Lady Madonna, 325, 339, 385
Lady Sings the Blues, The (film), 336
Laine, Frankie, 27, 29, 54
Lamp is Low, The, 73
Lane, Abbe, 389
Lang Penny, 407
Lang, Don, 408
Larsen, John, 124
Larson, Mel, 312
Last Picture Show, The (film), 343
Last Time I Saw Paris, The, 189
Late Night Lineup (TV), 399
Latora, Santi, 406

INDEX

Latter, Gene, 406
Laurents, Arthur, 149
Lawrence, Carol, 95, 339, 340, 404
Lazy Afternoon, 393
Lazy River, 61, 117, 118, 123, 129, 163, 194, 308, 328, 342, 351, 370, 375, 384, 391, 400
Leachman, Chloris, 343
Leachman, Cloris, 403
Leader of the Pack, 394
Lear, Norm, 130
Learnin' the Blues, 384
Leave My Woman Alone, 148, 375
Lecia and Lucienne, 409
Lee, Brenda, 410
Lee, Peggy, 60, 74, 75, 126, 140, 168, 196, 217, 273, 340, 404
Lees, Gene, 105, 113, 115, 197, 232, 233
Leiber, Jerry, 199, 200
Leigh, Carolyn, 185
Lennon, John, 302
Lenya, Lotte, 57
Leo, Franco, 406
Leonard, Will, 336
Leonetti and Friends (TV), 398
Lerner, Alan Jay, 53
Lester, Ketty, 236
Let It Be Me, 312, 331, 379, 402
Let Me Sing and I'm Happy, 194, 384
Let the Good Times Roll, 290, 295, 398, 404
Let the Sunshine In, 399
Let's Do It, 393, 403
Let's Fall in Love, 393
Let's Get Lost, 82
Letter, The, 324, 325, 381, 385
Lettermen, The, 406
Lewellen, Pat, 134
Lewis, George, 29
Lewis, Jerry, 70, 194, 398
Lewis, Jerry Lee, 409
Li'l Abner (musical), 114
Li'l Darlin', 74
Life (magazine), 85, 138, 139, 145, 152, 288, 304
Light Blue, 300, 379
Light My Fire, 403
Lily of Laguna, 116, 385
Linkletter Show, The (TV), 306, 393

Linkletter, Art, 306
Linkletter, Diane, 306
Linn, Edward, 64, 132
Lipsky, Gerald, 350
Little Anthony and the Imperials, 52
Little Charles & the Sidewinders, 407
Little Gerhard, 409
Little Girl, 395
Little Joe, 409
Little Richard, 314, 400
Little Sister, 143
Little Tina & Flight '56, 410
Little, Jack, 183
Live at the Desert Inn (album), 367
Live at the Desert Inn (LP), 19, 215, 316-320, 340, 348, 367, 382
Lively Set, The, 408
Lively Set, The (film), 228
Liza, 249, 378
Locklin, Hank, 189, 408
Loco, Joe, 409
Logan, Joshua, 98
Loggins & Messina, 409
Lonely Road, 237, 239, 377
Lonesome Polecat, 115, 375
Lonesome Road, 80, 97, 107, 216, 353, 374, 381, 389, 390, 393, 403
Lonesome Whistle, 189, 308, 376, 404
Long Ago and Far Away, 136, 375, 404
Long Line Rider, 16, 58, 292, 295, 296, 297, 302, 307, 321, 379, 384, 398, 399, 400, 408
Long Long Time, A, 400
Long Time Man, 168, 175, 176, 376, 393
Long Time Movin', 16, 280, 351, 382, 397
Longet, Claudine, 334
Look at Me, 228, 377, 408
Look For My True Love, 126, 129, 375, 376
Lopez, Trini, 145, 408
Los Boppers, 406
Los Clippers, 408
Los Locos del Ritmo, 409
Los Salvages, 408
Lost Love, 47, 51, 167, 362, 373, 376
Lot o' Livin' to Do, A, 394
Lotta Lovin', 41
Lou & Simon, 407
Louis Jourdan Timex Special, The (TV), 389

449

Love for Sale, 107, 374
Love Letters, 236, 383
Love Life (musical), 53
Love Look Away, 185, 349, 383
Love Me Right, 25
Love Me Right in the Morning, 408
Love Swings (album), 16, 20, 89, 129, 135-138, 139, 147, 163, 340, 350, 361, 375
Love, Darlene, 148
Love, Look Away, 369
Lover Come Back to Me, 60, 248, 378, 403
Lovin' Spoonful, The, 263, 264, 265, 272, 291, 294, 300
(Sittin' here) Lovin' You, 263, 274, 300, 378, 382
Lowe, Mundell, 64
Lucille, 41
Lucky Blondo, 409
Lucky Pierre, 391
Lúdó Og Stefán, 406, 409
Lulu, 406
Lulu's Back in Town, 257
Lystager, Birgit, 409

M

Mack is Back (DVD), 352
Mack the Knife, 15, 18, 53, 56, 58, 59, 61, 63, 64, 70, 73, 77, 78, 79, 80, 81, 83, 84, 102, 104, 107, 108, 109, 117, 135, 153, 163, 194, 213, 226, 227, 230, 232, 237, 244, 267, 271, 274, 289, 294, 295, 296, 308, 314, 316, 317, 327, 352, 355, 359, 360, 364, 374, 375, 379, 381, 382, 383, 384, 388, 389, 390, 391, 392, 394, 396, 397, 398, 399, 400, 401, 402, 403
Mack the Knife and Other Big Band Hits (Richard Wess album), 64
Mad-Ladds, The, 406
Magic Bubble, 307, 408
Magicians, The, 273
Magnus, Johnny, 81
Mahal, Taj, 302
Maher, Brent, 290
Mairzy Doats and Dozy Doats, 196, 384
Make Someone Happy, 188, 208, 384
Mallie, Tommie, 183
Mamas and the Papas, The, 270

Mame, 248, 252, 253, 256, 257, 349, 365, 378, 396, 403
Mame (musical), 252
Manana, 196, 384
Mancini, Henry, 227, 228, 247, 251, 265, 428
Mandy, 384
Manhattan in my Heart, 255
Manifol, Cy, 408
Mann, Barry, 199
Mann, Carl, 407
Mann, Lorene, 410
Manne, Shelly, 98
Marcellino, Jerry, 312
March of Dimes (TV), 390
March, Little Peggy, 201
Marie, 384, 391
Marks, Larry, 255
Martin, Dean, 65, 84, 118, 122, 143, 157, 175, 183, 233, 297, 338, 398, 409, 428
Martin, George, 407
Martindale, Wink, 408
Marx, Groucho, 114, 265
Mary Don't You Weep, 204, 215, 370, 377, 383
Mary, Where is Your Baby, 121, 375
Mason, James, 269
Match Game, The (TV), 231, 395
Mathis, Johnny, 100
Matter of Time, A (TV), 402
Matz, Roger, 119
May, Billy, 64, 65, 91, 113, 115, 116, 138, 163, 164, 166, 187, 278, 361, 362
Maybe Today, 223
Maybe We Can Get it Together, 287, 306, 307, 351, 379, 408
Mayhan, Judy, 409
McCann, Peter, 406
McCartney, Paul, 302
McGuinn, Roger, 206
McHugh, Jimmy, 81
McLean, Don, 406
McManus Margaret, 133
McPhatter, Clyde, 52, 101, 103, 390, 415
McQueen, Steve, 171
Me About You, 272
Me and Mr. Hohner, 297, 298, 299, 307, 321, 367, 379, 408
Me and My Shadow, 113

INDEX

Meditation, 247, 274, 281, 368, 382
Melodie, 312, 313, 314, 379, 385, 400
Melody Maker (publication), 101, 102
Memphis, Tennessee, 198
Mercer, Johnny, 74, 89, 95, 112, 113, 114, 115, 116, 138, 143, 163, 196, 227, 228, 247, 251, 256, 361, 375
Merci Cherie, 256, 257, 378
Merry-Go-Round in the Rain, 256
Mersey, Robert, 141
Merv Griffin Show, The (TV), 245, 289, 328, 392, 395, 398, 401
Metz, Stephen, 350
Michael Row the Boat Ashore, 206, 215, 216, 266, 377, 383, 393
Mickie Finn's (TV), 253, 396
Midday Sun, 407
Middlebrooks, Harry, 410
Midnight Special, 315, 328, 340, 404
Midnight Special (TV), 20, 343, 403
Mighty Mighty Man, 49, 50, 373, 375
Mike Douglas Show, The (TV), 287, 289, 307, 314, 339, 392, 397, 400
Miki, 407
Milk Shows, The (album), 192, 193, 196, 197, 227, 246, 351, 353, 371, 384
Milland, Ray, 140
Miller, Mary K., 410
Miller, Ned, 201
Milord, 94, 98, 110, 111, 112, 140, 377
Milsap, Ronnie, 410
Mina and the Solitaires, 409
Minnelli, Liza, 138, 217, 397
Minnie the Moocher, 29, 58, 94, 96, 354, 364, 377
Mississippi Mud, 115, 375, 385
Misty Roses, 262, 378
Mitchell, Eddy, 408
Mitchell, Guy, 29, 32
Mitchell, McKinley, 406
Mitchell, Price, 410
Mizell, Alphonso, 320
Modern Screen (magazine), 20, 39, 77, 82, 104, 122, 125, 418, 419, 423, 424
Modern Sounds in Country and Western (Ray Charles album), 17
Mogambos, The, 405, 410
Moment of Love, 64, 80, 374

Mona Lisa, 326, 385
Mondo Cane (film), 228
Monro, Matt, 167, 405
Monte, Vinnie, 410
Montezuma's Revenge, 409
Montgomery Advertiser (newspaper), 37, 42, 419, 423
Monthly Film Bulletin (publication), 142, 161, 171, 172, 173, 230, 269, 270
Moon Faced and Starry Eyed, 394
Moon River, 113, 185, 383, 384
Moonlight on the Ganges, 278
More, 228, 377
More I See You, The, 136, 375
Morgan, Derrick, 406
Morgan, Jane, 389
Morris, Lamar, 410
Most Beautiful Girl in the World, The, 395
Most Happy Fella, The (musical), 185
Motions, The, 405
Mottola, Tony, 64
Mountain Greenery, 257, 396
Moustache, 409
Movin' On, 141
Mr Wonderful (musical), 193
Mud, 406
Mulligan, Robert, 142
Multiplication, 144, 148, 161, 193, 210, 362, 375, 384, 408
Munoz, Manolo, 408
Munro, Hal, 406
Murder in the First (TV), 394
Murray, Anne, 144, 406, 409
Murray, Ruby, 408
Music Business (publication), 224
Music Vendor (publication), 110
Muskrat Ramble, 403
My Baby Needs Me, 281, 370, 383
My Bonnie, 147, 375
My Buddy, 163, 164, 376
My Cutey's Due at Two-to-Two Today, 115, 375, 385
My Dog Got a Tag on Her, 408
My Fair Lady (musical), 237
My First Night Alone Without You, 332, 379
My First Real Love, 25, 124, 408
My Friend the Doctor, 279, 379

451

My Funny Valentine, 54, 102, 104, 109, 212, 382, 383, 390, 400
My Gal Sal, 74, 374, 384
My Heart Sings, 65
My Kind of Town, 238, 403
My Melancholy Baby, 182, 383, 384
My Mom, 408
My Truly Truly Fair, 32
My Way (Frank Sinatra album), 188
Mystic Moods Orchestra, The, 409

N

Naked Alibi, The (film), 114
Nash, Johnny, 406
Nashville Skyline (Bob Dylan album), 293
Nathan, James, 335
Natural Soul-Loving Big City Countrified Man, 281
Nature Boy, 129, 139, 210, 375, 376
NBC Sunday Showcase (TV), 389
Neal, Patricia, 343
Neighborhood, The (TV), 334
Nelson, Ricky, 65, 206, 273, 406
Nelson, Sandy, 409
Never Ending Song of Love, 401
Never My Love, 403
Never Set Your Laundry Out in Tuscaloosa, 389
New Christy Minstrels, The, 206
New Moon, The (operetta), 59, 60, 248, 359
New York Times, The (newspaper), 22, 77, 80, 98, 99, 104, 130, 133, 134, 141, 149, 171, 174, 190, 232, 270, 297, 328, 337, 343, 347, *New Yorkers, The* (musical), 108
Newhart, Bob, 216
Newley, Anthony, 187, 228, 396
Newman, Randy, 228, 271, 272, 277, 330, 366, 429
Newton, Wayne, 192, 210, 227, 231, 238, 405, 406, 408, 409, 410, 429
Nichols, Roger, 342
Night Gallery (TV), 328, 401
Night Must Fall (film), 229
Night Song, 255, 378
Nightingale Sang in Berkeley Square, A, 164, 353, 376
Niki Hoeky, 401
Nitzsche, Jack, 199

Nixon, Richard, 308
No Greater Love, 137, 375
No Strings (musical), 185
Noises in the Street, 400
Norman, Milt, 193
Not For Me, 198, 199, 201, 363, 376, 408
Not Mine, 91, 376
Nothin' Can Stop Us Now, 397
Now We're One, 49, 373, 376, 408
Now You're Gone, 176, 177, 178, 376
Nyro, Laura, 316

O

O.K. Girl, 408
O'Brien, Bill, 43
O'Connor, Donald, 141, 334, 402, 403
O'Keefe, Johnny, 407
O'Sullivan, Gilbert, 58
Oakland, Simon, 344
Object Is, The (TV), 394
Observer, The (newspaper), 265, 294, 422, 424
October, Johnny, 409
O'Donnell, Daniel, 406
Oh Come All Ye Faithful, 119, 374, 375
Oh Lonesome Me, 189, 376
Oh Lord, Where Is My Baby, 322, 385
Oh Shenandoah, 160, 369, 384
Oh! Look at Me Now, 165, 239, 391
Oh! Look at Me Now (album), 15, 20, 21, 92, 149, 162-166, 167, 168, 176, 182, 189, 194, 362, 376
Old MacDonald, 18
Oliver (musical), 315
Olson, Richard, 405
On a Wonderful Day Like Today, 395
On Broadway, 199, 376
On the Road to Mandalay, 278
On the Street Where You Live, 237, 383
On the Sunny Side of the Street, 81, 384
Once in a Lifetime, 226, 228, 231, 232, 277, 377, 394, 402, 404
Once Upon a Time, 254, 255, 267, 353, 378, 379, 397, 403
One for my Baby, 56, 213, 267, 383, 393, 397
One of Those Songs, 401
Only One Little Item, 91, 376
Oo-Ee-Train, 129, 375, 376

INDEX

Original Album Series (CD), 110
Original Bobby Darin, The (album), 76, 367, 381
Orlando, Tony, 406, 407
Osmond Brothers, The, 408
Osmonds, The, 167, 394
Other Half of Me, The, 254, 365, 378
Our Day Will Come, 201, 376
Owens, Buck, 189

P

Pack, Harvey, 245
Packabeats, The, 406
Paddlin' Madelin' Home, 115, 375, 400, 403
Page, Patti, 123, 391
Paich, Marty, 98, 185
Pal Joey (film), 136
Palmer, Teddie, 408
Papa's Delicate Condition (film), 227
Papetti, Fausto, 406
Paris Sisters, The, 406
Parker, Tom, 18
Parsons, Louella, 82
Party's Over, The, 165, 376
Pass Me By, 290
Password (TV), 392
Patten, Van, 166
Paula, Marlene, 26, 407
Paul-Nero-Bar-Sextett, Das, 406
Pavone, Rita, 408, 409
Paxton, Tom, 169
Payne, Freda, 403
Peck, Gregory, 173
Peck-a-Cheek, 408
Peddlars, The, 410
Peggy Sue, 41
Pekkala, Rauni, 408
Pellinen, Eila, 406
Penn, Little Lambsie, 26, 407
Pennies from Heaven, 194, 384
Pepe (film), 98, 99, 411, 419
Percussion Ltd (Richard Wess album), 65
Perkins, Anthony, 98
Perren, Freddie, 320
Perry Como Show, The, 78, 388
Pete Boy & The Virginia Gang, 410
Pete Kelly's Blues, 75, 81, 374

Pete Kelly's Blues (film), 60, 75, 96
Peter Potter Show, The (TV), 389
Peter, Paul and Mary, 18, 167, 205, 206
Peters, Janice, 410
Phil McLean's Saturday Afternoon Bandstand (TV), 388
Philadelphia Inquirer (newspaper), 39
Philbin's People (TV), 399
Phillies Jackpot Bowling (TV), 391
Piaf, Edith, 110
Pick a Pocket or Two, 400
Pickwick (musical), 238
Picture No Artist Could Paint, A, 54, 374
Picturegoer (magazine), 47, 51, 425
Pierce, Webb, 245
Pillow Talk (film), 161, 162
Pitts, George E., 100
Pittsburgh Post-Gazette (newspaper), 130, 429
Pity Miss Kitty, 52, 374, 375
Pizzarelli, John, 405
Plain Jane, 42, 48, 52, 54, 71, 215, 373, 375, 382, 383, 388
Plant, Robert, 408
Please, 384
Please Help Me I'm Falling, 189, 195, 376, 384
Pleasure Doing Business, 395
Pleis, Jack, 27
Polk Salad Annie, 401
Pomus, Doc, 42, 54, 143
Poole, Brian, 409
Poor Little Jesus, 120, 374
Porgy and Bess (opera), 61, 74
Porter, Cole, 95, 107, 108, 137, 165, 187
Posey, Sandy, 406
Post-Standard (newspaper), 166
Powell, Dick, 74
Powell, Jane, 398
Powell, Jesse, 46, 55
Powell, Jimmy, 409
Power, Duffy, 406
Praguefrank, 21
President Kennedy's Birthday Salute (TV), 392
Presley, Elvis, 1, 16, 18, 19, 20, 21, 26, 30, 33, 38, 44, 49, 51, 54, 80, 115, 121, 123, 133, 143, 169, 199, 206, 229, 237, 253, 263, 264, 327, 331, 355, 360, 407, 410
Pressure Point (film), 142, 150, 171, 173, 174, 411

453

Pretty Betty, 41, 42, 46, 50, 51, 373, 383
Pretty Girl is Like a Melody, A, 384
Previn, Andre, 98, 175, 393
Previn, Dory Langdon, 98
Price, Alan, 409
Pride, Charley, 400
Prins, Bobbie, 407
Prior, Andy, 405
Prison of Your Love, 281
Prisoner of Zenda, The (film), 229
Proper Gander, The, 19, 291, 379
Proud Mary, 325, 385, 401
Prowse, Juliet, 251
Pryor, Richard, 265
Put a Little Love in Your Heart, 314, 400
Put on a Happy Face, 384, 394

Q

Quarter to Nine, A, 267, 341, 379, 383, 397, 402
Queen of the Hop, 44, 47, 48, 51, 56, 71, 135, 369, 373, 375, 382, 383, 388, 408
Questions, 291, 302, 379

R

Rags to Riches, 326, 385
Raim, Walter, 409
Rainin', 248, 252, 262, 378, 408
Ralph Pearl Show, The (TV), 393
Rambling Rose, 188
Rare Capitol Masters Deluxe Edition (album), 160, 349, 369
Rare Performances (album), 274, 368, 382
Ravers, The, 407, 408
Rawls, Lou, 406, 407
Ray Mills Group, The, 406
Ray, James, 406
Ray, Johnnie, 34, 103
Reach Out And Touch (Somebody's Hand), 322
Ready, Steady, Go! (TV), 266, 396
Reagan, Ronald, 299, 306
Real Live Girl, 394
Real Love, 25, 408
Reason to Believe, 263, 378
Record Hop (TV), 388
Record World (magazine), 332
Red Balloon, 264, 378

Red Roses for a Blue Lady, 238, 383
Red Skelton Show, The (TV), 245, 395
Reddy, Helen, 403
Reed, Jerry, 281
Reese, Della, 176, 304, 407, 409
Reeves, Del, 407
Reeves, Jim, 38
Reimar, Johnny, 407
Reiner, Carl, 303, 399
Release Me, 190, 363, 376
Respect, 295, 308, 318, 382
Reverend Mr. Black, The, 169, 200, 292, 363, 376
Reviewing the Situation, 315, 400
Reynolds, Burt, 334
Reynolds, Debbie, 289, 334, 398, 402
Rhythm of the Rain, 201, 363, 376
Richard, Cliff, 406, 407
Richards, Deke, 320
Richards, Keith, 271
Riddle, Nelson, 65, 91
Ride 'em Cowboy (film), 61
Ridin' on a Rainbow (film), 189
Right Time, The, 148, 375
Rinky-Dinks, The, 48, 373
Rip Chords, The, 167, 407
Ritz, James, 119
River Stay Away From My Door, 118
Rivers, Joan, 334
Rivers, Johnny, 145, 408
Rizzo, Frank, 297, 306, 421
Roar of the Greasepaint, the Smell of the Crowd, The (musical), 235, 254
Rob de Nijs met The Lords, 407
Robbins, Marty, 407
Roberto Cassotto: Rare, Rockin' & Unreleased (album), 47, 369, 382
Robertson, Don, 189
Robinson, Edward G., 251
Robinson, Harry, 295
Robinson, Smokey, 328, 336
Rock Island Line, 22, 26, 27, 28, 30, 84, 373, 387, 391
Rock Pile, 30
Rock-a-Bye Your Baby, 194, 384
Rocking Boys, The, 408
Rocky Sharpe & The Replays, 406
Rodgers and Hart Today (TV), 270

INDEX

Rodgers, Jimmie, 410
Rodgers, Richard, 76, 104, 136, 137, 138, 150, 151, 185, 270, 271, 396, 421, 422
Rodgers, Sammy, 409
Roe, Tommy, 407
Roger Miller Show, The (TV), 396
Rogers Cha-Cha, The, 25
Rogers, Shorty, 100, 188, 189, 254
Rogers, Will, 133
Roll Over Beethoven, 343, 403, 404
Rolling Stones, The, 271, 273, 428
Rolontz, Bob, 106, 425
Romain, Marcel, 407
Roman Candle (book), 69, 317, 420
Romance on the High Seas (film), 90
Romberg, Sigmund, 59, 60
Ronstadt, Linda, 400
Rooftop Singers, The, 201
Rooney, Mickey, 136
Roses of Picardy, 164, 376
Ross, Diana, 336, 396
Rote Rosen für Cindy, 203, 377
Route 58, 307, 323, 370, 384
Row, Row, Row, 115, 196, 375, 384, 400, 403
Rowan and Martin's Laugh-in (TV), 303, 398
Roy Castle Show, The (TV), 400
Ruby Baby, 200, 376
Run For Your Life (TV), 396
Run Little Rabbit, 408
Ruppli, Michel, 21
Rutherford, Margaret, 140
Rx-Pyro (Prescription: Fire), 306, 323, 379
Rydell, Bobby, 406

S

Sachs, Len, 146
Sail Away, 16, 330, 331, 367, 379, 402
Sally Was a Good Old Girl, 188, 363, 376
Salt Lake Tribune (newspaper), 289
Sammy Davis Jr. at Town Hall (Sammy Davis Jr. album), 110
Sammy Davis Jr. Sings the Big Ones for Young Lovers (Sammy Davis Jr. album), 198
San Francisco, 403
Sands, Tommy, 82, 409
Sansom, Sara Ann, 42
Santa Cruz Sentinel (newspaper), 276

Santo & Johnny, 406
Saratoga (musical), 95
Saratoga Trunk (novel), 95
Sardo, Frankie, 406
Satu, 406
Saturday Evening Post (newspaper), 64, 132, 134, 418, 423, 425
Saturday Night (musical), 82
Sausalito, 19, 298, 367, 379
Save the Country, 316, 382
Say it With Music, 384
Scalia, Jimmy, 209, 256, 353
Scarlet Ribbons, 160, 384
Schatten auf den Wegen, 203, 377
Scheck, George, 25, 26, 27
Schindler, Harold, 289
School is Over, 50
School's Out, 25, 408
Schroeder, Aaron, 54
Schwartz, Arthur, 137
Scott, Bobby, 89, 94, 95, 119, 121, 176
Scott, Vernon, 84
Screenland (magazine), 83, 105, 420, 423
Searchers, The, 238, 410
Searchin', 199
Sebastian, John, 261, 263, 271, 272, 365
Sebena, Gesy, 406
Second Time Around, The, 384, 413
Secret Invasion, The (film), 209
Secrets, The, 315
Sedaka, Neil, 52, 65, 72, 101
See See Rider. See C. C. Rider
Seeger, Pete, 18
Seeing is Believing (DVD), 352, 353
Sellin, Pierre, 406
Semi-colons, The, 405
Sentimental Journey, 393
September of My Years (LP), 254
Sergeant's Three (film), 157
Sermon of Samson, The, 169, 191, 377
Settle Down, 206, 377
Setzer, Brian, 405
Seven Brides for Seven Brothers (film), 115
Seventeen, 256
Severson, John, 406
Sha Na Na, 408, 409
Shadow of Your Smile, The, 246, 247, 274, 378, 382

Shank, Bud, 168, 170, 326
Shanley, John P., 104
Sharp, Dee Dee, 409
Shaw, George M., 27, 30
Shayne, Jackie, 406
She Knows, 276, 277, 379
She Loves Me, 394
She Needs Me, 60, 75, 81, 96, 374
She Shot Me Down (Frank Sinatra album), 76
She's Tanfastic, 99, 374
Shearer, Lloyd, 209
Sheik of Araby, The, 193, 246, 384
Sherwood, Roberta, 28
Shilo, 404
Shipmates and Cheyenne, 331, 379
Shirl Girl, 408
Shoop Shoop Song, The, 210
Shore, Dinah, 21, 175, 393
Short, Bobby, 25, 96, 406
Showaddywaddy, 148, 406, 408, 409
Shuman, Mort, 42, 54, 143
Side by Side by Side, 402
Sidney, George, 98, 99, 136, 375
Sight and Sound (magazine), 150, 424
Silent Night, 121, 375
Silk Stockings (musical), 187
Silly Willy, 26, 28, 29, 30, 373
Silver Dollar, 249, 250, 378
Silvester, Victor, 408
Simenon, George, 269
Similau, 94, 126, 377
Simmons, Jean, 303
Simone, Nina, 254, 273, 355, 365
Simple Song of Freedom, 16, 287, 302, 306, 307, 308, 316, 318, 349, 352, 369, 379, 382, 384, 400, 401, 402, 408
Simpson, Sandra, 102
Simpson, Valerie, 322
Sims, Zoot, 248
Sinatra & Strings (Frank Sinatra album), 90
Sinatra, Frank, 15, 16, 17, 18, 20, 54, 58, 59, 60, 61, 62, 63, 65, 74, 75, 76, 77, 84, 85, 86, 90, 91, 94, 102, 104, 106, 109, 113, 118, 125, 133, 136, 137, 138, 143, 157, 158, 163, 164, 188, 196, 227, 228, 233, 235, 250, 253, 254, 273, 274, 278, 339, 355, 362, 363, 364, 403, 416, 420
Sinatra, Nancy, 85, 409

Sinatra, Tina, 85
Sinatra's Sinatra (Frank Sinatra album), 227
Since My Love Has Gone, 73
Since You Been Gone, 210
Sister Act (film), 201
Sixteen Tons, 194, 282, 353, 384, 398, 403
Skoller, Eddie, 409
Skylark, 112, 138, 375, 404
Skyscraper (musical), 254
Sloan, P. F., 409
Smile, 326, 385
Smith, Bro, 409
Smith, Johnny, 64
Smothers Brothers, The, 334, 402
So Mean, 42, 373
Sock It to Me, 290
Softly as I Leave You, 235, 377
Softly as I Leave You (Frank Sinatra labum), 188
Softly as in a Morning Sunrise, 18, 59, 60, 64, 248, 359, 374
Some of these Days, 18, 54, 56, 61, 78, 107, 359, 374, 384, 390, 393
Some People, 327, 391, 403
Somebody Stole My Gal, 183, 383
Somebody to Love, 79, 123, 360, 362, 374, 375, 409
Someday We'll Be Together, 313, 379
Something, 317, 353, 382
Something for Everybody (LP), 51
Something in Her Love, 330, 342, 379
Something in Your Smile, 278, 379
Something Special (album), 106, 206, 266-268, 366, 368, 379
Something Special (TV). See *Bobby Darin in London* (TV)
Something to Remember You By, 137, 138, 375, 404
Something to Shout About (film), 108
Something's Gotta Give, 384
Somewhere, 234, 364, 377
Sommer, Elke, 403
Sommers, Joanie, 405, 407
Sondheim, Stephen, 82
Song for a Dollar, 287, 299, 323, 367, 379
Song Sung Blue, 339, 341, 383, 403
Songs for Swingin' Lovers (Frank Sinatra album), 136

INDEX

Songs from Big Sur (album), 299, 307, 351, 355, 370, 384
Sonny & Cher Comedy Hour, The (TV), 402
Sorrow Tomorrow, 143, 375, 376
Soul City, 409
Soulblenders, The, 405
Sounds of the Sixties (TV), 104, 297, 398
South Pacific (musical), 187
Spacey, Kevin, 350, 405, 406, 409
Spaleny, Petr, 408
Spann, Otis, 44, 167, 405
Special Someone, 141
Spinning Wheel, 308, 402
Spirit in the Dark, 308
Spirit of Us, 409
Spitalsky, Bill, 100
Splish Splash, 15, 26, 28, 44, 45, 46, 47, 48, 50, 52, 54, 55, 66, 69, 70, 72, 78, 81, 86, 100, 102, 109, 121, 124, 193, 194, 212, 243, 282, 290, 294, 297, 314, 318, 324, 343, 359, 360, 361, 369, 373, 375, 382, 383, 384, 387, 388, 391, 398, 400, 401, 403, 404, 409, 423
Splish Splash: The Best of Bobby Darin, Volume One (album), 15, 100
Sponsor (magazine), 63
Spotlight (TV), 397
Spotlight on Bobby Darin (album), 15, 349, 368, 382
Spring Fever, 253
Spring is Here, 138, 404
Springfield, Dusty, 255, 334, 402, 404, 428
St Louis Blues, 403
St Theresa of the Roses, 32
Stabile, Dick, 247
Stage Show (TV), 30, 84, 387
Stand by Me, 199
Standing on the Corner, 185, 382, 383, 384
Standing Room Only (Frank Sinatra album), 85
Stanley, Debbie, 407
Stardust, 228
Starlite Singers, The, 409
Stars in their Eyes (TV), 15
State Fair (film), 150, 151, 152, 164, 411, 423
Steffen, Peter, 406
Steve Allen Show, The (TV), 192, 392, 393
Steve Lawrence Show, The (TV), 245, 395
Stevens, April, 183, 281

Stevens, Bobby, 408
Stevens, Cat, 331
Stevens, Connie, 404
Stevens, Shakin', 408
Stoller, Mike, 199, 200
Stop the World (and Let Me Off), 383
Stop the World, I Want to Get Off (musical), 187, 228
Stordahl, Alex, 65
Storm, Billy, 407, 409
Strange Rain, 169, 377
Stranger in the House (film), 269, 411, 424, 425
Strangers in the Night, 233, 247, 402
Strangers in the Night (Frank Sinatra album), 188
Strato-tones, The, 409
Stray Dog (Oh Let Her Be), 385
Streisand, Barbra, 75, 217, 254, 409
Style, 394
Style, Al, 408
Styne, Jule, 82
Subota, Vilan, 409
Subterranean Homesick Blues, 298
Sugar Man, 298, 307, 379, 409
Sullivan, Jim, 268
Summer Wind, 276
Summers, Joannie, 391
Summertime Symphony, 409
Sunday, 19, 32, 293, 379
Sunday in New York, 228, 377, 395
Sunday in New York (film), 230
Sunday Kind of Love, A, 73, 76, 354, 367, 381
Sunday Night at the London Palladium (TV), 103-104, 107, 390
Supremes, The, 265, 270, 396
Surfaris, The, 405
Surghaya Johnny, 394
Svenne & Lotta, 406
Sweet and Lovely, 194, 384
Sweet Caroline, 308, 315, 339, 341, 402
Sweet Memories, 245
Sweet Reasons, 306, 307, 379, 409
Sweetest Sounds, The, 185, 383, 384, 394
Sweetheart Tree, The, 246, 247, 365, 378
Swing Down Sweet Chariot, 169
Swing Low Sweet Chariot, 56, 80, 94, 97, 107, 354, 364, 374, 377, 381, 389, 390
Swingin' Affair, A (Frank Sinatra album), 138

Swingin' on a Rainbow (Frankie Avalon album), 65
Swinging Jaguars, The, 406
Swinging on a Star, 403
Swinging Side of Bobby Darin, The (album), 384
Sydney Morning Herald (newspaper), 295
Sydney Tonight (TV), 398
Sylvia's Mother, 398

T

T.M. Music, 210
Take a Whiff on Me, 297, 398
Talk to Me Something, 38, 39, 40, 41, 42, 359, 373, 387
Talk to the Animals, 279, 282, 289, 294, 295, 296, 366, 379, 397, 398, 402
Tall Hope, 185, 195, 383
Tall Story, 98, 99, 371, 374
Tall Story (film), 98
Tammy and the Batchelor (film), 161
Taste of Honey, A, 235, 236, 377
Tatler, The (magazine), 150, 421
Taylor, James, 19, 317, 368
T-Bones, The, 407
Tea for Two, 384
Teenage Theme, 141
Tell all the World about You, 147, 375
Tell Me How Do You Feel, 147, 375
Tempo, Nino, 147, 183, 281
Tender Trap, The, 61
Tenderloin (musical), 58, 117
Texas Tornados, The, 407
Thank Heaven for Little Girls, 395
Thanks for the Memory, 391
That Darn Cat, 240
That Darn Cat (film), 240
That Funny Feeling, 229, 237, 245, 368, 378, 395, 409, 424, 425
That Funny Feeling (film), 65, 229, 243, 411
That Girl, 406
That Lucky Old Sun, 54, 123, 360, 374, 383
That Old Black Magic, 62
That's All, 59, 84, 268, 275, 329, 347, 379, 382, 384, 397
That's All (album), 184, 359, 360, 361, 365
That's All (album), 17, 20, 21, 53, 54, 56-63, 65, 66, 69, 72, 73, 74, 75, 76, 77, 90, 96, 109, 117, 148, 184, 354, 359, 360, 361, 365, 374, 389, 402, 416
That's All Right, 26
That's Enough, 148
That's Entertainment, 137
That's How It Went All Right, 98, 99, 371, 375
That's Life, 233
That's Life (Frank Sinatra album), 188
That's the Way Love Is, 61, 374, 390
That's Enough, 376
Theme from Come September, 138, 140, 375, 376, 406
There Ain't No Sweet Gal That's Worth the Salt of My Tears, 235, 364, 377
There Goes a Bad Girl, 199, 409
There Is a Tavern in a Town, 18
There is Nothing Like a Dame, 395
There's a Hole in my Bucket, 339, 404
There's a Rainbow 'Round My Shoulder, 55, 163, 376, 398, 404
There's No Business Like Show Business, 394
They All Laughed, 95, 377
They Can't Take That Away From Me, 196, 384
Things, 143, 145, 243, 339, 362, 376, 409
Things and other Things (album), 16, 143, 171, 362, 376
Things in this House, The, 178, 221, 223, 368, 377, 410
This Could Be the Start of Something Big, 153, 246, 341, 381, 383, 392, 403
This is Bobby Darin (TV), 75, 103, 109, 167, 390
This is Darin (album), 184
This is Darin (LP), 9, 20, 63, 64, 72-77, 79, 91, 96, 105, 109, 147, 184, 354, 360, 361, 367, 374
This is the Life, 395
This is Tom Jones (TV), 298, 304, 399
This is Your Life (TV), 80, 390, 391
This Isn't Heaven, 151
This Land is Your Land, 289
This Nearly Was Mine, 187, 188, 191, 195, 349, 383, 384, 394
Thomas, Bob, 132
Thorpe, Richard, 33, 229
Thou Swell, 384
Three Degrees, The, 409
Three of a Kind, 394

INDEX

Threepenny Opera, The (stage play), 57
Thrill of It All, The (film), 161
Through a Long and Sleepless Night, 59, 60, 69, 360, 374
Thunder, Johnny, 408
Tillotson, Johnny, 145, 408, 409
Timber, 26, 27, 28, 29, 167, 373
Time Will Never Change, 389
Times, The (newspaper), 347
To Be a Performer, 394
Tom and Jerry, 406
Tonight Show, The (TV), 175, 282, 329, 338, 392, 397, 398, 399, 401, 403
Tony and the Initials, 407
Too Close for Comfort, 193, 384
Too Late Blues (film), 149, 150, 159, 411, 424, 426
Too Many Girls (musical), 136
Too-ra Loo-ra Loo-ral, 194, 384
Toot Toot Tootsie Goodbye, 317, 381, 392, 393, 398, 400
Top of the Pops (TV), 266, 396
Tormé, Mel, 74, 118, 216, 217
Torre, Marie, 131
Train to the Sky, 207, 377
Treat My Baby Good, 203, 209, 210, 377, 378
Tremeloes, The, 409
Trey Tones, The, 407
Trilogy (Frank Sinatra album), 125
Trolley Song, The, 403
Trouble in Mind, 251
True Love's a Blessing, 255
True, True Love, A, 162, 376
Trumpet Boy, 407
Truth, The, 145, 408
Try a Little Tenderness, 295
Try to Remember, 255, 378
Tucker, Sophie, 61, 359
Tucker, Tanya, 406
Tumwater Caravan (TV), 401
Tupelo Mississippi Flash, 281
Turner, Spyder, 407
Turtles, The, 271, 272, 276
Tutti Frutti, 42
TV Radio Mirror (magazine), 62, 69, 131, 145, 150, 162, 165, 175, 176, 178, 190, 198, 209
Twist with Bobby Darin (LP), 55, 152, 362, 375

Twisted Nerve (film), 344
Twitty, Conway, 409
Two Different Worlds, 123, 391
Two of a Kind, 113, 196
Two of a Kind (album), 115, 354, 361, 385
Two of a Kind (album), 20, 96, 112-116, 129, 163, 196, 212, 354, 361, 375, 385, 403
Two Tickets, 223, 383
Tyson, Ian, 168

U

Uggams, Leslie, 404
Umbrellas of Cherbourg, The (film), 247
Under Your Spell Again, 189, 376
Undivided, The, 407
United Nations All-Star Gala (TV), 396
United Singers, 409
Unreleased Capitol Sides, The (album), 177, 186, 369
Unreleased Capitol Sides, The (CD), 181, 237, 349, 383
Until it's Time for You to Go, 263, 378
Up Tight, 275
Upbeat (TV), 398, 399
Uttal, Larry, 293

V

Valens, Ritchie, 168
Valente, Caterina, 64
Valli, Frankie, 341
Van, Bobby, 289, 397
Vanguards, The, 407
Variety, 303
Variety (publication), 22, 28, 33, 39, 46, 49, 50, 51, 52, 55, 62, 73, 78, 79, 80, 81, 82, 99, 102, 104, 106, 110, 112, 116, 117, 125, 131, 133, 138, 140. 141, 143, 145, 146, 152, 153, 161, 166, 171, 175, 191, 202, 207, 208, 209, 210, 212, 224, 225, 226, 230, 239, 243, 245, 247, 249, 250, 251, 253, 255, 264, 265, 269, 271, 273, 275, 280. 282, 290, 294, 295, 298, 300, 302, 303, 308, 314, 315, 328, 332, 335, 336, 338, 343, 347, 348, 350
Varsity Show (film), 74
Vaughan, Billy, 406
Vaughan, Malcolm, 32

Vee, Bobby, 407, 409
Vendors, The (film), 304, 411
Venet, Nik, 205
Venice Blue, 233, 234, 236, 239, 364
Venice Blue (album), 64, 187, 188, 232-237, 238, 253, 254, 330, 377, 378
Ventures, The, 406
Venuti, Joe, 248
Vie en Rose, La, 195, 384
Vincent, Gene, 41, 410
Voices of East Harlem, 409

W

Wa'tch You Mean, 410
Waard, Johnny, 409
Wade in the Water, 223
Wagon Train (TV), 394
Wait by the Water, 221, 223, 348, 377, 382, 410
Walk Bach to Me, 140, 371, 375
Walk Right In, 201, 363, 376
Walker, Collins (Boogie), 42
Walker, Jerry Jeff, 294
Walkin' in the Shadow of Love, 253, 378
Warren, Harry, 136, 143
Warwick, Dionne, 332, 334, 402
Was There a Call For Me, 61, 374
Washington, Dinah, 97
Wasser, Harriet, 208
Watch the River Flow, 324, 385
Water Color Canvas, 19, 281, 299, 367, 379
Waters, Muddy, 44, 405
Watertown (Frnk Sinatra album), 125, 363
Watson, Deek, 40
Wayne and Shuster Take an Affectionate Look at George Burns (TV), 396
Wayne, Paul, 405
We Didn't Ask to be Brought Here, 244, 378, 410
We're Getting There, 320, 321, 385
Wear My Ring, 41, 51, 373, 410
Webster, Paul Francis, 249
Weekend (TV), 392
Weeping Willow, 248, 252
Weil, Cynthia, 199
Weill, Kurt, 53, 57, 227
Weinstein, Aaron, 405
Welk, Lawrence, 407

Wess, Richard, 57, 59, 61, 63, 64, 65, 72, 74, 77, 104, 138, 158, 209, 225, 226, 227, 228, 233, 234, 248, 249, 265, 279, 360, 364, 414, 418, 422
West Side Story (musical), 234
West, Leslie, 407
Wexler, Jerry, 244
What a Difference a Day Made, 96, 137, 364, 377
What Can I Say After I Say I'm Sorry, 96, 377
What is this Thing Called Love, 384
What Kind of Fool am I, 18, 187, 191, 195, 349, 383, 384
What Now My Love, 257, 401
What'd I Say, 146, 245, 268, 275, 295, 375, 379, 381, 382, 392, 395, 397
What's a Matter Wit' Me, 388
What's My Line (TV), 131, 192, 231, 232, 390, 391, 392, 394
What's New Pussycat, 246, 247, 365, 378
Whatever Happened to Baby Jane (film), 344
Whatever Happened to Happy, 273, 366, 378
Wheeler, Billy Edd, 200
When Day is Done, 97, 377
When Harry Met Sally (film), 136
When I Get Home, 238, 377, 410
When I Look in Your Eyes, 278, 379
When I'm Gone, 281
When I'm Not Near the Girl That I Love, 395
When Irish Eyes are Smiling, 391
When My Baby Smiles at Me, 182, 383
When the Saints Go Marchin' In, 80, 381, 389, 392
When Their Mama is Gone, 58, 170, 377
When You Were Sweet Sixteen, 182, 183, 383
When You're Smiling, 393, 394
When Your Lover Has Gone, 109, 374, 381, 389, 390
Where are the Words, 278, 379
Where Have all the Flowers Gone, 205, 377
Where is the One, 56, 61, 374
Where Love Has Gone, 227, 228, 377
Where Love Has Gone (film), 227
Whiffenpoof Song, The, 384, 402
While I'm Gone, 55, 373
While Shepherds Watched Their Flocks, 121, 375
Whispering, 137, 183, 383
White, Tam, 405

INDEX

Whiting, Richard A., 74
Who Can I Count On, 190, 363, 376, 384
Who Can I Turn To, 235, 254, 377
Who Takes Care of the Caretaker's Daughter, 115, 375, 400
Who Turned the World Around, 330, 331, 367, 379
Who's Afraid of Virginia Woolf, 256, 257
Whoop song, The, 290
Why Don't You Swing Down, 169, 377
Why Oh You, 410
Why, Daddy, Why, 206, 377
Wilburn Brothers, 409
Wilco Jingle, 25
Wild Angels, The, 405
Wild, Cool & Swinging (album), 369, 370, 383
Wildcat (musical), 185, 195
Wilde, Marty, 407, 409
Will and Testament, 289
Williams, Andy, 95, 118, 122, 226, 231, 245, 251, 253, 314, 341, 394, 395, 396
Williams, Hank, 169, 302
Williams, Joe, 76
Williams, Paul, 342
Williams, Robbie, 144, 409
Willie the Weeper, 29
Wilson, Earl, 84, 123, 175, 283, 296, 429
Wilson, Flip, 115, 290, 314, 400, 401, 403
Wilson, Gerald, 188
Wilson, Jackie, 318
Wilson, John S., 77
Wilson, Nancy, 401
Winkler, Gustav, 407
Winners (album), 20, 74, 94-98, 129, 197, 350, 354, 364, 377, 414, 416
Witch Doctor, 389
Wizex, 409
Wolf Call, 253
Wolf, Jon, 301
Wolfe, Al, 42
Woman's Weekly (magazine), 22
Won't You Come Home Bill Bailey, 79, 94, 95, 97, 108, 117, 152, 276, 364, 374, 375, 384, 389, 390, 391, 392, 400, 403
Wonder, Stevie, 297, 398
Wonderin' Where it's Gonna End, 327, 381
Wong, Charlene, 339, 403, 404
Won't You Come Home Bill Bailey, 354

Wood, Marty, 407
Words, 404
Work Song, 16, 168, 175, 176, 208, 213, 282, 319, 376, 382, 383, 393, 402
World Without You, A, 235, 377
Worried Man, 401

Y

Ya Better Stop, 60
Yaeger, Andrea, 331, 343
Yankee Doodle Dandy, 397
Yesterday, 19, 251
Yip, Francis, 409
Yorkin, Bud, 130
You and Me Babe, 402
You Are My Sunshine, 401, 403, 404
You are Woman, 394
You Just Don't Know, 235, 236, 377
You Know How, 64, 80, 374, 375, 376
You Made Me Love You, 164, 376, 384
You Must Have Been a Beautiful Baby, 143, 144, 182, 194, 210, 362, 375, 384
You Never Called, 44, 374
You Smiling Now, 400
You'd Be So Nice to Come Home To, 108, 374
You'll Never Know, 164
You're a Big Boy Now (film), 272
You're a Wonderful Girl, 397
You're Mine, 49, 50, 373
You're Nobody 'til Somebody Loves You, 183, 212, 382, 383, 394
You're Nobody 'Til Somebody Loves You, 383
You're the Reason I'm Living, 17, 162, 170, 176, 177, 178, 193, 194, 197, 198, 199, 202, 203, 210, 236, 239, 339, 376, 378, 384, 410
You're the Reason I'm Living (LP), 178, 183, 188-191, 194, 195, 200, 201, 203, 235, 236, 253, 323, 363, 376
You're the Reason I'm Living, 188, 376
You've Got a Friend, 402, 404
You've Lost That Lovin' Feelin', 325, 328, 385
You'll Never Know, 376
Young Joe Caldwell, 327, 328, 385
Young, Jesse Colin, 231
Young, Loretta, 59

461

Younger Girl, 265
Your Cute Little Ways, 410
You're Mine, 376

Z

Zacharius, Helmut, 406

Zander, Frank, 409
Zebra Stripes, The, 410
Zeitlin, Arnold, 130
Zimbalist, Efram Jr., 320
Zito, Ronnie, 193
Zito, Torrie, 89, 98, 136, 138, 163
Zoom-a-Roo, 410

Printed in Great Britain
by Amazon